AIA

Foundation Level

BUSINESS MANAGEMENT
LEARNING & PRACTICE WORKBOOK

In this 2025 edition

- A **user-friendly format** for easy navigation
- **Exam-centred topic coverage**, directly linked to AIA's syllabus
- **Exam focus points** showing you what the examiner will want you to do
- Regular **fast forward** summaries emphasising the key points in each chapter
- **Questions** and **quick quizzes** to test your understanding
- **Practice question bank** containing exam-standard questions with answers
- **Exam question bank** containing recent exam questions with answers
- 2 Mock exams
- A full index

FOR EXAMS FROM 2025

Second edition October 2024

ISBN 9781 0355 2571 3

eISBN 9781 0355 2599 7

British Library Cataloguing-in-Publication Data
A catalogue record for this book is available from the British Library

Published by

BPP Learning Media Ltd
BPP House, Aldine Place
142-144 Uxbridge Road
London W12 8AA

learningmedia.bpp.com

Printed in the United Kingdom

> Your learning materials, published by BPP Learning Media Ltd, are printed on paper obtained from traceable sustainable sources.

All rights reserved. No part of this publication may be reproduced, stored in a retrieval system or transmitted in any form or by any means, electronic, mechanical, photocopying, recording or otherwise, without the prior written permission of BPP Learning Media.

The contents of this book are intended as a guide and not professional advice. Although every effort has been made to ensure that the contents of this book are correct at the time of going to press, BPP Learning Media makes no warranty that the information in this book is accurate or complete and accept no liability for any loss or damage suffered by any person acting or refraining from acting as a result of the material in this book.

We are grateful to the Association of International Accountants for permission to reproduce past examination questions. The suggested solutions in the exam answer bank have been prepared by BPP Learning Media Ltd.

©
BPP Learning Media Ltd
2024

A note about copyright

Dear Customer

What does the little © mean and why does it matter?

Your market-leading BPP books, course materials and e-learning materials do not write and update themselves. People write them on their own behalf or as employees of an organisation that invests in this activity. Copyright law protects their livelihoods. It does so by creating rights over the use of the content.

Breach of copyright is a form of theft – as well as being a criminal offence in some jurisdictions, it is potentially a serious breach of professional ethics.

With current technology, things might seem a bit hazy but, basically, without the express permission of BPP Learning Media:

- Photocopying our materials is a breach of copyright

- Printing our digital materials in order to share them with or forward them to a third party or use them in any way other than in connection with your BPP studies is a breach of copyright.

You can, of course, sell your books, in the form in which you have bought them – once you have finished with them. (Is this fair to your fellow students? We update for a reason.) Please note the e-products are sold on a single user licence basis: we do not supply 'unlock' codes to people who have bought them secondhand.

And what about outside the UK? BPP Learning Media strives to make our materials available at prices students can afford by local printing arrangements, pricing policies and partnerships which are clearly listed on our website. A tiny minority ignore this and indulge in criminal activity by illegally photocopying our material or supporting organisations that do. If they act illegally and unethically in one area, can you really trust them?

NO AI TRAINING. Unless otherwise agreed in writing, the use of BPP material for the purpose of AI training is not permitted. Any use of this material to "train" generative artificial intelligence (AI) technologies is prohibited, as is providing archived or cached data sets containing such material to another person or entity.

Contents

Page

Introduction

The introductory pages contain lots of valuable advice and information. They include tips on studying for and passing the exam, also the content of the syllabus and what has been examined.

How the BPP Learning Media Learning & Practice Workbook can help you pass – Help yourself study for your AIA exams – Syllabus – Command words

Part A Management: Nature, evolution and approaches
1. The organisation of work and the role of management 3
2. Effective leadership 27

Part B Management planning and decision-making
3. Strategic planning and management by objectives 57
4. Internal analysis 99
5. Environmental analysis 121
6. Sustainability, CSR and ethics 149

Part C Organisational structures, cultures and systems
7. Organisation structure 197
8. Organisation culture 227

Part D Managerial control: Managing information systems and technology
9. Budget planning and control 243
10. Managerial control 259
11. Organisational information requirements 285
12. The impact of IT on work practices 323

Practice question bank 373
Practice answer bank 417
Exam question bank 453
Exam answer bank 475
Mock exam 1 491
Mock exam 2 501
Bibliography 511
Index 517

How the BPP Learning Media Learning & Practice Workbook can help you pass

> It provides you with the knowledge and understanding, skills and application techniques that you need to be successful in your exams

This Learning & Practice Workbook has been targeted at the **Business Management** syllabus.

- It is **comprehensive**. It covers the syllabus content. No more, no less.
- It is written at the **right level**. Each chapter is written with AIA's syllabus in mind.
- It is aimed at the **exam**. We have taken account of recent exams, guidance the examiner has given and the assessment methodology.

> It allows you to study in the way that best suits your learning style and the time you have available, by following your personal Study Plan (see page vii)

You may be studying at home on your own or you may be attending a course. You may like to read every word, or you may prefer to do a fast read through and learn through doing practice questions the rest of the time. However, you study, you will find the BPP Learning Media Learning & Practice Workbook meets your needs in designing and following your personal Study Plan.

# Help yourself study for your AIA exams

Exams for professional bodies such as AIA are very different from those you have taken at college or university. You will be under **greater time pressure before** the exam – as you may be combining your study with work. Here are some hints and tips.

The right approach

1 **Develop the right attitude**

Believe in yourself	Yes, there is a lot to learn. But thousands have succeeded before and you can too.
Remember why you're doing it	You are studying for a good reason: to advance your career.

2 **Focus on the exam**

Read through the Syllabus	This tells you what you are expected to know and is supplemented by **Exam focus points** in the text.
Study the Exam paper section	Past papers are likely to be good guides to what you should expect in the exam.

3 **The right method**

See the whole picture	Keeping in mind how all the detail you need to know fits into the whole picture will help you understand it better. • The **Introduction** of each chapter puts the material in context. • The **Syllabus content** and **Exam focus points** show you what you need to **grasp**.
Use your own words	To absorb the information (and to practise your written communication skills), you need to **put it into your own words**. • Take **notes**. • Answer the **questions** in each chapter. • Draw **mind maps**. • Try '**teaching**' **a subject** to a colleague or friend.
Give yourself cues to jog your memory	The Learning & Practice Workbook uses **bold** to **highlight key points**. • Try **colour coding** with a highlighter pen. • Write **key points** on cards.

4 **The right recap**

Review, review, review	Regularly reviewing a topic in summary form can **fix it in your memory**. The Learning & Practice Workbook helps you review in many ways. • **Chapter roundups** summarise the 'Fast forward' key points in each chapter. Use them to recap each study session. • The **Quick quiz** actively tests your grasp of the essentials. • Go through the **Examples** in each chapter a second or third time.

Developing your personal Study Plan

BPP recommends that you follow a study plan. Planning and sticking to the plan are key elements of learning successfully.

Step 1 **How do you learn?**

What types of intelligence do you display when learning? You might be advised to brush up on certain study skills before launching into this Learning & Practice Workbook but refer to the 'tackling your studies' section below which will help.

Step 2 **What do you prefer to do first?**

If you prefer to get to grips with a theory before seeing how it is applied, we suggest you concentrate first on the explanations we give in each chapter before looking at the examples and case studies. If you prefer to see first how things work in practice, read through the detail in each chapter, and concentrate on the examples and case studies, before supplementing your understanding by reading the detail.

Step 3 **How much time do you have?**

Work out the time you have available per week, given the following:

- The standard you have set yourself
- The other exam(s) you are sitting
- Practical matters such as work, travel, exercise, sleep and social life

Note your time available in box A. A [ ] Hours

Step 4 **Allocate your time**

- Take the time you have available per week for this Learning & Practice Workbook shown in box A, multiply it by the number of weeks available and insert the result in box B. B [ ]
- Divide the figure in box B by the number of chapters in this text and insert the result in box C. C [ ]

Remember that this is only a rough guide. Some of the chapters in this book are longer and more complicated than others, and you will find some subjects easier to understand than others.

Step 5 **Implement**

Set about studying each chapter in the time shown in box C, following the key study steps in the order suggested by your particular learning style.

This is your personal **Study Plan**. You should try to combine it with the study sequence outlined below. You may want to modify the sequence to adapt it to your **personal style**.

Tackling your studies

The best way to approach this Learning & Practice Workbook is to tackle the chapters in order. Taking into account your individual learning style, you could follow this sequence for each chapter.

Key study steps	Activity
Step 1 **Topic list**	This topic list helps you navigate each chapter; each numbered topic is a numbered section in the chapter.
Step 2 **Introduction**	This sets your objectives for study by giving you the big picture in terms of the context of the chapter. The content is referenced to the syllabus, and Exam guidance shows how the topic is likely to be examined. The Introduction tells you **why** the topics covered in the chapter need to be studied.
Step 3 **Fast forward**	Fast forward boxes give you a quick summary of the content of each of the main chapter sections. They are listed together in the roundup at the end of each chapter to help you review each chapter quickly.
Step 4 **Explanations**	Proceed methodically through each chapter, particularly focusing on areas highlighted as significant in the chapter introduction, or areas that are frequently examined.
Step 5 **Key terms and Exam focus points**	• Key terms are definitions of important concepts that you really need to know and understand before the exam. • Exam focus points highlight areas or topics that may be examined.
Step 6 **Note taking**	Take brief notes, if you wish. Don't copy out too much. Remember that being able to record something yourself is a sign of being able to understand it. Your notes can be in whatever format you find most helpful; lists, diagrams, mind maps.
Step 7 **Examples**	Work through the examples very carefully as they illustrate key knowledge and techniques.
Step 8 **Case studies**	Study each one and try to add flesh to them from your own experience. They are designed to show how the topics you are studying come alive in the real world.
Step 9 **Questions**	Attempt each one, as they will illustrate how well you've understood what you've read.
Step 10 **Answers**	Check yours against ours, and make sure you understand any discrepancies.
Step 11 **Chapter roundup**	Review it carefully, to make sure you have grasped the significance of all the important points in the chapter.
Step 12 **Quick quiz**	Use the Quick quiz to check how much you have remembered of the topics covered and to practise questions in a variety of formats.
Step 13 **Question practice**	Attempt the multiple choice questions contained in the question bank at the end of this Learning & Practice Workbook.

AIA Achieve Academy

AIA provides an interactive course of study AIA Achieve Academy, which offers students the tools, resources and learning environment to study for the exams. The study tools include a course of study e-book, marked practice questions, marked mock exam paper and feedback and technical advice via an e-Tutor. Contact the Study Support team at: Achieve@aiaworldwide.com

Moving on...

When you are ready to start revising, you should still refer back to this Learning & Practice Workbook.

- As a source of **reference** (you should find the index particularly helpful for this)
- As a way to review (the Fast forwards, Exam focus points, Chapter roundups and Quick quizzes help you here)

PQ Qualification Syllabus

The assessment requirements in the AIA exams at the Foundation, Professional 1 and 2 stages reflect a progression of cognitive levels which successful students are expected to demonstrate in satisfying each stage of the qualification. The levels progress from an emphasis on 'knowledge and comprehension' at the Foundation stage, to a predominance of 'application and analysis' at the subsequent Professional 1 and 2 stages and incorporate 'synthesis and evaluation' at the Professional 2 stage.

Indicative weightings for the cognitive levels at each stage of the qualification are defined in the following table.

Stage of qualification	Cognitive levels of learning*			Associated learning outcomes
	Knowledge and comprehension	Application and Analysis	Synthesis and evaluation	
Foundation Level	90%	10%	0%	Outcomes consistent with the International Education Standards Board (IAESB) standards
Professional 1 Level	50%	50%	0%	
Professional 2 Level	10%	70%	20%	

*The cognitive levels of learning are associated with the following:

'Knowledge and comprehension' refer to:

The acquisition of concepts, ideas, terms, facts, practices and techniques in accounting and related disciplines and understanding of how they relate to the conduct, management, reporting and assessment of the activities of business and other organisations.

'Application and analysis' refer to:

The ability to apply knowledge and comprehension to actual circumstances and situations and to identify constituent components involved (concepts, ideas, terms, facts, practices, and techniques) and the relationship between these elements.

'Synthesis and evaluation' refer to:

The ability to bring together a variety of components in order to form a coherent whole, and to form judgements about the application of and value of those components in a particular context or for a particular purpose. learning outcomes.

Foundation Level Syllabus

The Foundation level examination is intended to establish that students have attained the necessary knowledge of accounting in its economic context and relevant skills to be permitted to commence study for the first Professional stage examinations of the Association. It does so by assessing students in four foundational areas of knowledge and understanding relevant for prospective professional accountants, offered within the Foundation Unit:

In designing the syllabus and the related examination papers AIA has employed 'intended learning outcomes' as the means to communicate expectations to potential students and stakeholders and to inform the specification requirements to be tested in the assessment of students.

The use of learning outcomes:

- Is consistent with what is commonly acknowledged as good practice in the higher education sector; and
- Is consistent with the approach embodied in International Accounting Education Standards

At Foundation Level, students are expected to demonstrate that they are able to achieve the following:

Intended learning outcomes[1] – Description of expectations	
Foundation Level	At the Foundation Level students are expected to demonstrate that they: - Understand basic principles and concepts underpinning accounting and related practices in organisations - Understand the role of accounting and related practices within the financial and governance context of organisations - Know and can execute basic recording and measurement techniques relevant to accounting, management and assurance - Are able to analyse financial information and interpret it for the purpose of supporting decision making

Foundation level syllabus components

The Foundation Unit is made up of four components:

- Section A: Financial accounting
- Section B: Corporate governance and audit
- Section C: Management accounting
- Section D: Business management

---

[1] The description of the levels of proficiency supports the IAESBs use of learning outcomes in its International Education Standards (IESs) 2, 3, and 4.

Relationship to Qualification Structure

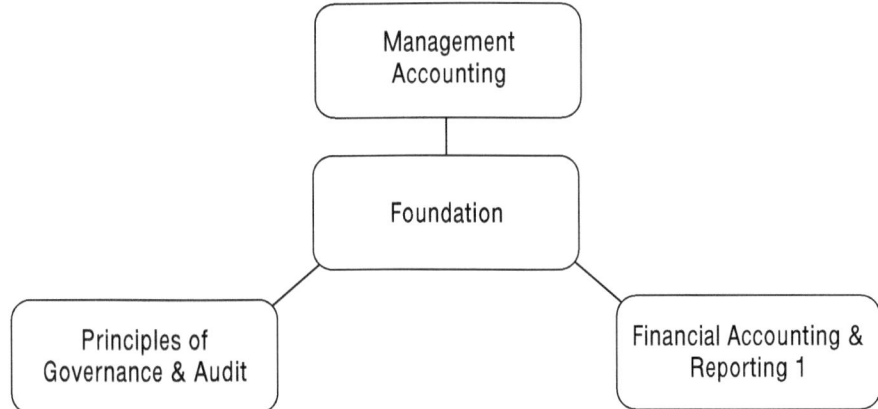

This Learning & Practice Workbook covers **Section D: Business management.**

Demonstrating that the learning outcomes associated with the Foundation syllabus have been met is a requirement for all students before they are permitted to proceed to Professional level studies.

Students able to demonstrate they have met the learning outcomes based on prior study and educational qualification can be granted exemption from the Foundation Examination. For those students unable to do so, passing the Foundation Examination is a core requirement to Professional levels studies.

Aims

The aim of Foundation Level paper is to develop and examine the candidate's knowledge and understanding of:

1. The theory of accounting and its application to the practical situations indicated in the syllabus
2. The fundamental elements of corporate governance and audit and the inter-relationship between these areas
3. The fundamentals of management and cost accounting and their application in cost ascertainment, the control of operations, and the provision of information to assist management decision-making and policy formulation
4. Business management and the role of the manager in modern business organisations

Foundation Level learning outcomes

In order to successfully complete this paper, candidates will demonstrate that they are able to:

FINANCIAL ACCOUNTING

1. Explain and identify accounting concepts and the regulatory purpose of accounting standards and sustainability standards
2. Describe, prepare and summarise basic accounting records
3. Identify accounting concepts in presenting financial statements for sole traders and limited companies
4. Describe and explain the financial position and performance of an organisation

CORPORATE GOVERNANCE AND AUDIT

1. Identify and explain the purpose of corporate governance and auditing
2. Explain the inter-relationship between corporate governance and auditing
3. Relate the contribution of corporate governance and auditing to the safeguarding of capital markets

INTRODUCTION

MANAGEMENT ACCOUNTING

1. Explain the role of management and cost accounting within an organisation
2. Describe the nature of costs and how and why they are classified in different ways for different purposes
3. Calculate material, labour, expense and overhead costs for products, processes, services and functions
4. Identify and discuss appropriate principles and techniques to advise managers on short-term and long-run decision-making

BUSINESS MANAGEMENT

1. Describe the major schools of management thought, their development and their implications
2. Explain the key aspects of organisational structure and design
3. Identify the nature and importance of managerial control, including the main elements and types of control in the business organisation and the role and importance of management information in the control process
4. Describe the use of information technology in modern business management

This Learning & Practice Workbook covers **Section D: Business management.**

Detailed learning outcomes for Section D: Business management

D1 MANAGEMENT: NATURE EVOLUTION AND APPROACHES (LEARNING OUTCOME 12)

Topic weighting 20%

The nature and process of management including what managers do, methods of management and the different roles and agendas of managers. **See Chapters 1 and 2.**

The levels and types of managers and the key management skills. **See Chapters 1 and 2.**

The evolution of management theories including classical, behavioural, and contemporary theories of management. **See Chapter 1.**

D2 MANAGEMENT PLANNING AND DECISION MAKING (LEARNING OUTCOME 14)

Topic weighting 30%

The nature and scope of managerial decision making, including the elements and levels of planning, including strategic management and sustainability and environmental factors. **See Chapters 3 and 6.**

The nature of organisational goals and plans. **See Chapter 3.**

Candidates should demonstrate an understanding of how to improve managerial decision making and some of the main inputs and aids to this process, including:

- Competitor, environmental and sustainability analysis;
- Internal analysis including portfolio analysis and value chain analysis;
- Forecasting, planning and control models;
- Management by objectives, decision trees; and
- Quantitative aids for decision making.

See Chapters 3, 4, 5 and 6.

D3 ORGANISATIONAL STRUCTURES, CULTURES AND SYSTEMS (LEARNING OUTCOME 13)

Topic weighting 20%

The nature of organisational structure and the key decisions in organisational structures and systems, including:

- The design of organisational structures
- Job design
- Procedures for vertical and horizontal co-ordination

See Chapter 7.

The meaning and implications of different organisational cultures and the relationship between strategy and structure in organisations. **See Chapter 8**.

D4 MANAGERIAL CONTROL: MANAGING INFORMATION SYSTEMS AND TECHNOLOGY (LEARNING OUTCOME 15)

Topic weighting 30%

The nature and purpose of control as a management function, including an understanding of the main elements of the control process. **See Chapter 9**.

The types of control and control systems including:

- The planning control lifecycle
- Budgetary and inventory control
- The balanced score-card
- Benchmarking and planning and control operations in services management

See Chapter 10.

The nature, role and uses of management information and information systems and technology in the modern business organisation and developing technology in this area. **See Chapters 11 and 12**.

Structure of the Foundation Level exam

Assessment is by a three-hour and 15 minutes examination (including 15 minutes reading time) consisting of 100 questions. There are 25 objective test style questions in the form of multiple-choice questions covering each component area of the syllabus. All questions are compulsory.

The assessment covers the learning outcomes for each of the four component areas of study in the foundation syllabus.

The coverage of questions will reflect the weighting of different areas of syllabus content as specified in the Foundation examination syllabus, but the format of questions associated with each area of study may vary between sittings of the examination.

Relationship to overall AIA syllabus

An accountant in practice and in business needs an understanding of the nature, importance and issues in effective business management. Not only are all accountants by definition managers, but they also have to have a wider appreciation and understanding of how their function and activities relate to other parts of the business. The implications of effective business management are important aspects of the contemporary accountant's function. A professionally qualified accountant must understand the nature of business management in a contemporary business organisation and have an awareness of how this understanding can contribute to overall efficiency and effectiveness.

Foundation Level Business Management therefore seeks to ensure that the professional accountant has this necessary understanding and can use this to increase their effectiveness in organisations as accountants.

Ethics

Candidates are advised that the standards outlined in The Code of Ethics for Professional Accountants issued by the International Ethics Standards Board for Accountants (IESBA Code) are implicit in, and examinable throughout, the AIA syllabus. The Code can be accessed via the AIA website at www.aiaworldwide.com.

Recommended reading

This reading list is recommended and not essential for your studies.

You can purchase any of the books listed quickly and easily on the AIA website www.aiaworldwide.com/books

AIA Magazine – International Accountant
ISSN   1465 5144

AIA Learning and Practice Workbooks
Foundation Unit
Publisher: BPP Learning Media

Four books – one for each component:

Financial Accounting
ISBN: 9781035525737

Management Accounting
ISBN: 9781035525744

Corporate Governance and Audit
ISBN: 9781035525720

Business Management
ISBN: 9781035525713

Financial Accounting (14th Edition 2018)
Business Accounting Volume 1
Author: Wood, F and Sangster, A
Publisher: Pearson Education Limited
ISBN: 9781292208626

Free website providing comprehensive information about IFRS: www.iasplus.com

Corporate Governance and Audit (11th Edition UK 2018)
Author: Millichamp, A and Taylor, R
Publisher: Cengage Learning EMEA
ISBN: 9781473749306

Corporate Governance: Principles Policies and Practices
Author: Bob Tricker
Publisher: Oxford University Press
ISBN: 9780198702757

Modern Auditing (3rd Edition 2009)
Author: Cosserat, G We; and Rodda, N
Publisher: Wiley
ISBN   9780470319734

The Audit Process: Principles practice and cases (7th Edition)
Author: Gray, L, Manson, S and Crawford, L
Publisher: London Thomson
ISBN: 9781473760189

Principles of External Audit (4th Edition e-book)
Author: Porter, B, Hatherley, D J, Simon, J
Publisher: John Wiley and Sons Ltd
ISBN: 9780470574452

Management Accounting and Business Management and Cost Accounting (7th Edition 2019)
Author: Bhimani A. and Horngren,
Publisher: Pearson
ISBN: 9781292232669

Management Accounting (UK Edition 2013)
Author: Burns, J., Quinn, M., Warren, L., Olivera, J
Publisher: McGraw-Hill Education/Europe, Middle East & Africa
ISBN: 9780077121617

Management and Cost Accounting (10th Edition 2017)
Author: Drury, C
Publisher: Cengage Learning EMEA
ISBN: 9781473748873

Management (1st International Edition 2016)
Author: Daft, R L and Benson, A
Publisher: Cengage Learning EMA
ISBN: 9781408063859

Essentials of Contemporary Management (8th Edition 2018)
Author: Jones, G. and George, J
Publisher: McGraw-Hill,
ISBN: 9781260141054

Management and Organisational Behaviour (11th Edition 2016)
Author: Mullins, L. J
Publisher: Pearson
ISBN: 9781292088488

Management (14th Edition 2017)
Author: Robbins, S. P. and Coulter, M
Publisher: Pearson
ISBN: 9781292215639

INTRODUCTION

PART A

Management: Nature, evolution and approaches

The organisation of work and the role of management

Topic list	Syllabus reference
1 Introduction to organisations	D1
2 Principles of organisation structures	D1
3 The purpose of management	D1
4 Classical writers on management	D1
5 Writers on management	D1
6 Management and supervision	D1
7 The manager's role in organising work	D1

Introduction

We begin our study of management by looking at the most common context within which it takes place: an organisation. The term 'organisation' is commonly used to describe corporate entities (a company, club or charity): we look at some of these in **Section 1**.

In **Section 2**, we introduce **organisation structure**, and at some of the classical and modern theories about how to 'do it' best. Organisation structure is covered further in Chapter 6.

In **Section 3** we attempt to get an overview of the manager's task. What is management? How should people be managed? What do managers actually do?

Sections 4 and 5 trace the **development of management theory** from its focus on efficiency and control (classical and scientific management), through a recognition of the importance of people factors (human relations and neo-human relations), to a more complex understanding that a variety of factors influence the managerial role.

In **Section 6**, we note the difference between a manager and a **supervisor**: the interface between managerial and non-managerial levels of the organisation.

In **Section 7**, we look at briefly at the management of resources, activities and projects.

PART A   MANAGEMENT: NATURE, EVOLUTION AND APPROACHES

1 Introduction to organisations

Here are some examples of organisations.

- A multinational car manufacturer (eg Ford)
- An accountancy firm (eg EY)
- A charity (eg Oxfam)
- A local authority
- A trade union
- An army

1.1 Why do organisations exist?

FAST FORWARD

> **Organisations** achieve results which individuals cannot achieve by themselves.

Organisations:

(a) **Overcome people's individual limitations**, whether physical or intellectual

(b) **Enable people to specialise** in what they do best

(c) **Save time**, because people can work together or do two aspects of a different task at the same time

(d) **Accumulate** and share **knowledge** (eg about how best to build cars)

(e) Enable people to **pool their expertise**

(f) Enable **synergy** – the combined output of two or more individuals working together exceeds their individual output ('None of us is as smart as all of us')

In brief, organisations enable people to be **more productive**.

1.2 What organisations have in common

FAST FORWARD

> An organisation is a **social arrangement** which pursues collective goals and controls its own performance.

The definition below states broadly what all organisations have in common.

Key term

> An **organisation** is: 'a **social arrangement** which pursues collective **goals,** which **controls** its own performance and which has a **boundary** separating it from its environment'.
> **(Buchanan & Huczynski,** *Organizational Behaviour,* 2010)

The following table shows how this definition applies to two organisational examples.

Characteristic	Car manufacturer (eg Ford)	Army
Social arrangement: individuals gathered together for a purpose	People work in different divisions, making different cars.	Soldiers are in different regiments. There is a chain of command from top to bottom.
Collective goals: the organisation has goals over and above the goals of the people within it.	Sell cars, make money	Defend the country, defeat the enemy, international peace-keeping

Characteristic	Car manufacturer (eg Ford)	Army
Controls performance: performance compared with goals and may be adjusted to ensure the goals are achieved	Costs and quality are reviewed and controlled. Standards are constantly improved.	Strict disciplinary procedures, training
Boundary: the organisation is distinct from its environment.	Physical: factory gates Social: employment status	Physical: barracks Social: different rules than for civilians

1.3 How organisations differ

FAST FORWARD

Organisations **differ** according to their: ownership, control, activity, orientation, size, legal status, funding and technology.

Organisations differ in many ways. Here are some possible differences.

Factor	Example
Ownership (public vs private)	Private sector: owned by private investors/ shareholders Public sector: owned by the government
Control	By the owners themselves, by people working on their behalf, or indirectly by government-sponsored regulators
Activity (ie what they do)	Manufacturing, healthcare, services (and so on)
Profit or non-profit **orientation**	Business exists to make a profit. An army or a charity, on the other hand, are not profit-orientated.
Size	Sole trader, small business or multinational corporation
Legal status	Limited company or partnership
Sources of **finance**	Borrowing, government funding, share issues
Technology	High use of technology (eg computer firms) vs low use (eg corner shop)

Two key differences in the list above are **what the organisation does** and whether or not it is **profit-orientated.**

1.3.1 What the organisation does

Organisations do many different types of work. Here are some examples.

Industry	Activity
Agriculture	Producing and processing food
Manufacturing	Acquiring raw materials and, by the application of labour and technology, turning them into a product (eg a car)
Extractive/raw materials	Extracting and refining raw materials (eg mining)
Energy	Converting one resource (eg coal) into another (eg electricity)

PART A MANAGEMENT: NATURE, EVOLUTION AND APPROACHES

Industry	Activity
Retailing/distribution	Delivering goods to the end consumer
Intellectual production	Producing intellectual property eg software, publishing, films, music etc
Service industries	These include retailing, distribution, transport, banking, various business services (eg accountancy, advertising) and public services such as education, medicine.

1.3.2 Profit v non-profit orientation

The basic difference in outlook is expressed in the diagram below. Note the distinction between **primary** and **secondary** goals. A primary goal is the most important: the other goals support it.

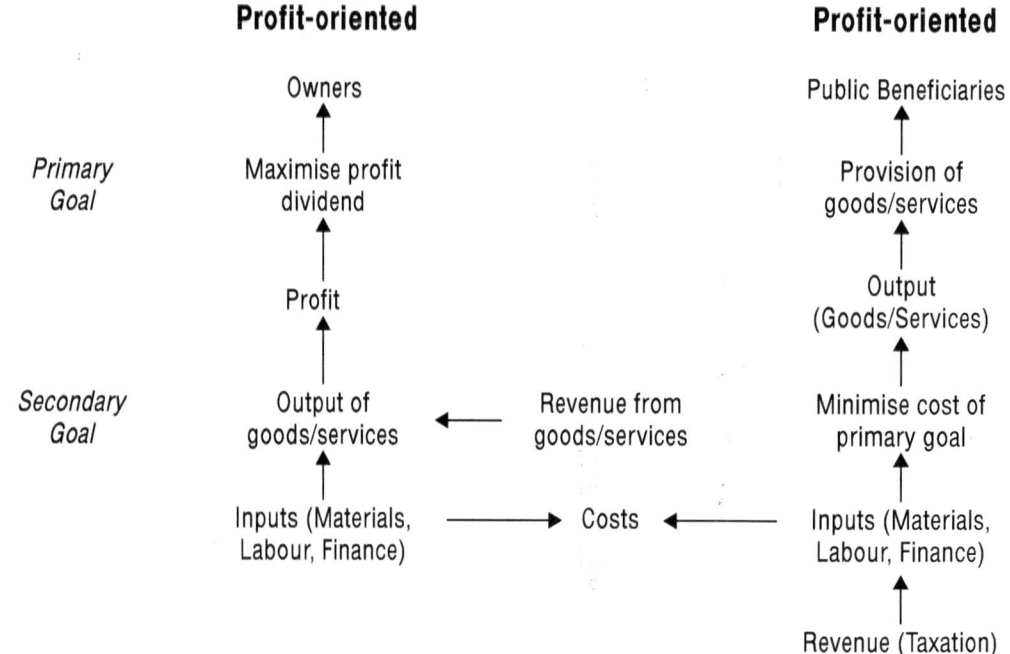

Question Organisation

Which of the following would NOT be classified as an organisation?

A   A school
B   A golf club
C   An on-line forum for AIA students
D   A charity

Answer

C   An on-line forum for AIA students

This would not be an organisation as it exists to express opinions, not pursue goals and achieve and control performance.

The others all pursue goals and can control their own performance.

2 Principles of organisation structures

2.1 What is organisation structure?

FAST FORWARD

Organisation structure is formed by the grouping of people into departments or sections and the allocation of responsibility and authority.

Organisation structure implies a framework intended to:

(a) **Link individuals** in an established network of relationships so that authority, responsibility and communications can be controlled

(b) **Allocate the tasks** required to fulfil the objective of the organisation to suitable individuals or groups

(c) Give each individual or group the **authority** required to perform the allocated tasks, while controlling their behaviour and use of resources in the interests of the organisation as a whole

(d) **Co-ordinate** the objectives and activities of separate units, so that overall aims are achieved without gaps or overlaps in the flow of work

(e) Facilitate the **flow of work**, information and other resources through the organisation

2.2 Components of organisation structure

FAST FORWARD

Mintzberg suggests that all organisation structures have **five components: strategic apex, middle line** and **operating core**, plus **technostructure** and **support staff.**

Mintzberg (*The Structuring of Organizations*, 1979) suggests that all organisations can be analysed into five components, according to how they relate to the work of the organisation.

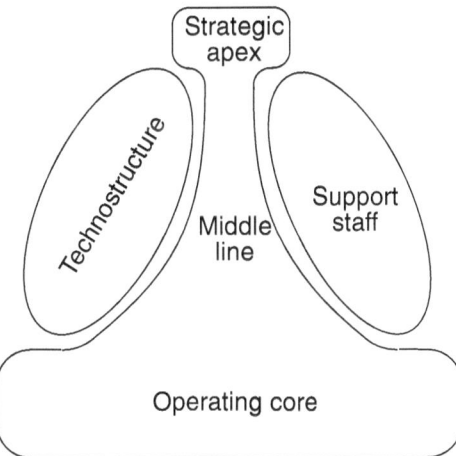

Component	Function
Strategic apex	Ensures the organisation follows its mission; manages the organisation's relationship with the environment; commonly known as executive management
Operating core	People directly involved in the process of obtaining inputs, and converting them into outputs
Middle line	Conveys the goals set by the strategic apex and controls the work of the operating core in pursuit of those goals: ie middle management

PART A MANAGEMENT: NATURE, EVOLUTION AND APPROACHES

Component	Function
Technostructure	Analysers determine and standardise work processes and techniques. Planners determine and standardise outputs (eg goods must achieve a specified level of quality). Personnel analysts standardise skills (eg through training programmes).
Support staff	Ancillary services such as PR, legal counsel, the cafeteria and security staff. Support staff do not plan or standardise production. They function independently of the operating core.

Exam focus point

Mintzberg's components are particularly useful when discussing issues of organisational structure.

2.3 Classical principles of organisation

FAST FORWARD

Classical organisations are based on the principle of **hierarchy**. There is a line of decision-making power from the top of the organisation to the bottom. This **scalar chain** is intimately connected to the concept of **span of control**, which is the number of individuals under the direct supervision of any one person.

Henri Fayol's principles of management and research were published in the book *General and Industrial Management*, 1916, suggesting that all organisations should follow the 14 guiding principles outlined in the table below, in order to function effectively and efficiently.

Principle	Comment
Division of work	Work should be divided and allocated rationally, based on **specialisation**.
Scalar chain	Authority should flow vertically down a clear **chain of command** from highest to lowest rank.
Correspondence of **authority** and **responsibility**	The holder of an office should have **enough authority** to carry out all the responsibilities assigned to him.
Appropriate **centralisation**	Decisions should be taken **at the top** of the organisation where appropriate.
Unity of **command**	For any action, a subordinate should receive orders from **one boss** only. **Fayol** saw dual command as a disease, whether it is caused by imperfect demarcation between departments, or by a superior giving orders to an employee, without going via the intermediate superior.
Unity of **direction**	There should be one head and **one plan** for each activity. Unity of direction relates to the organisation itself, whereas unity of command relates to the personnel in the organisation.
Initiative	Employees should be encouraged to use **discretion**, within the bounds of their authority.
Subordination of individual interests	The interest of one employee or group of employees should not prevail over that of the **general interest** of the organisation.

Principle	Comment
Discipline	A **fair disciplinary system** can be a strength of an organisation. Members of the organisation should behave in agreed ways.
Order	People and resources should **reliably** be where they are supposed to be.
Stability of personnel	There should be **continuity** of employment where possible.
Equity	Organisational policies should be **just**.
Remuneration	**Rewards** should be 'fair', satisfying both employer and employee alike.
Esprit de corps	**Harmony and teamwork** are essential to promote discipline and contentment.

Urwick, the leading British proponent of classical management principles, suggested a similar set of organising principles.

(a) **The scalar chain**

(b) **Specialisation**

(c) **Unity of command**

(d) **Correspondence of authority and responsibility**

(e) **Span of control**: an optimum number of subordinates reporting to each superior

(f) **Reporting by exception**: decisions to be taken as far down the chain as possible, with reference back limited to deviations from plan

(g) **Objective**: structures and processes should only exist if they contribute to the organisation's purposes

(h) **Scientific method**: decisions should be taken rationally on the basis of data

Question — Principles of organisation

Considering each of Fayol's 'classical' principles of organisation, what challenges to these principles can you identify in modern methods of working?

Answer

You may have identified the following important points.

Specialisation is challenged by modern ideas such as 'multi-skilling' and team project management: instead of specialised functions, organisations are trying to encouraged cross-functional working to aid co-ordination in a more flexible way.

Unity of command ('one person, one boss') is challenged by modern ideas such as project/product management and matrix structures where individuals report to different managers according to the task.

Scalar chain is challenged, to an extent, by organisational delayering, empowerment and teamworking. Vertical authority structures (embodied by the idea of the chain) are being replaced by collaborative, 'horizontal' structures which directly link people in multi-functional teams with shared decision-making responsibility.

2.4 Modern approaches to organisation

> **FAST FORWARD**
>
> Modern management theory stresses **flexibility** as a key value, and organisational measures such as matrix and horizontal structures, multi-skilling, empowerment and flexible labour deployment are currently being explored.

Modern management theorists have moved away from 'classical' organisational principles such as those outlined by **Fayol**. They instead emphasise values such as the following.

(a) **Multi-skilling**. Contrary to the idea of specialisation, multi-skilled teams (where individuals are trained to perform a variety of team tasks, as required) enable tasks to be performed more flexibly, using labour more efficiently.

(b) **Flexibility**. This is perhaps the major value of modern management theory. Arising from the competitive need to respond swiftly (and without organisational trauma) to rapidly-changing customer demands and technological changes, organisations and processes are being re-engineered. This has created a trend towards flexible structures such as the following.

  (i) Smaller, multi-skilled, temporary structures, such as project or task-force teams

  (ii) Multi-functional units, facilitating communication and co-ordination across departmental boundaries. This is called **matrix organisation**, and it blurs the principle of 'unity of command', since an employee may report both to his department superior and to a project or product manager whose job is to manage all areas of activity related to the product or project.

  (iii) Flexible deployment of the labour resource, for example through part-time and temporary working, contracting out tasks, flexitime, annual (rather than daily) hours contracts and so on. We look at outsourcing in Chapter 4.

(c) **Empowerment**

  (i) The purpose of empowerment is to free employees from rigorous control by instructions and supervision, and give them freedom to take responsibility for their goals and actions. This may release hidden resources (creativity, initiative, leadership, innovation), which would otherwise remain inaccessible.

  (ii) People are asked to use their own judgement in the interests of the organisation and the customer, within a disciplined context of agreed goals.

2.5 Contingency theory

> **FAST FORWARD**
>
> **Contingency theory** suggests that there is no one best way to structure (or manage) an organisation. 'It all depends [...]' on a number of variables.

Contingency theory holds that there is no universally best organisation structure, but that the best structure for a given organisation will depend on a number of contingent factors outlined below.

(a) **Age**. The older the organisation, the more formalised its behaviour. Work is repeated, so is more easily formalised.

(b) **Size**. The larger the organisation and the more elaborate and bureaucratic its structure, the larger the average size of the units within it and the more formalised its behaviour needs to be in order to maintain control.

(c) **Technology**

  (i) The stronger the technical system, the more formalised the work will be, and the more bureaucratic the structure of the operating core.

  (ii) The more sophisticated the technology, the more elaborate and professional the support staff will be.

(d) **Geographical** dispersion. An organisation on one site will be organised differently to one which has geographically separate units, perhaps with different environmental demands (customer groups, infrastructure, legal/economic constraints).

(e) **Personnel** employed. Formalised, standardised structures might be needed for a large, low-skilled work-force.

(f) The type of **activities** the organisation is involved in, which may suit different types of organisation (from assembly lines to creative teams to individual professionals).

(g) The organisation's **objectives**, which may include goals for efficiency, innovation or staff development – with implications for structure.

2.6 The systems approach

> **FAST FORWARD**
>
> An organisation can be viewed as an **open system**, interacting with its environment.

The **systems approach** sees organisations, more dynamically, in terms of a system: 'an entity which consists of interdependent parts'. Rather than focus on administrative structures, this approach views the organisation as an **open system**, which is connected to and interacts with its environment. It takes in inputs from its environment and, through various organisational processes, converts them into outputs.

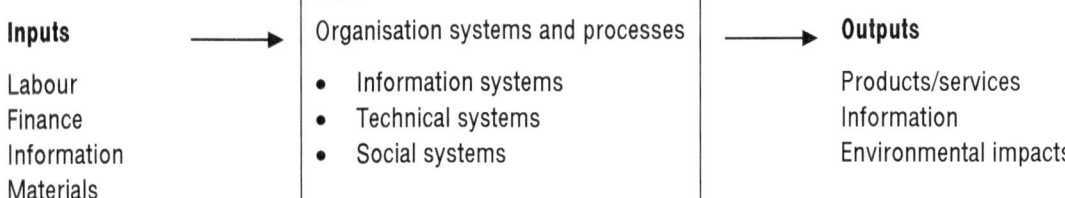

As an open system, an organisation must remain sensitive to changes in its external environment. It must also make **internal adjustments** in order to remain stable.

The systems approach is helpful in:

(a) Drawing attention to the dynamic nature of organisations

(b) Creating an awareness of subsystems which must be integrated (eg the needs of task processes may conflict with the human needs of workers)

(c) Focusing attention on the relationship of the organisation with its environment. (Outward focus is particularly important for customer satisfaction: a shortcoming of the bureaucratic approach.)

3 The purpose of management

> **FAST FORWARD**
>
> **Management** is responsible for using the organisation's resources to meet its goals. It is accountable to the owners: shareholders in a business, or government in the public sector.

Key term

> **Management** may be defined, most simply, as 'getting things done through other people'.
> (**Rosemary Stewart**, *The Reality of Management*, 1963)

Why is it that organisations have to be managed, and what is the purpose of management?

(a) **Objectives** have to be set for the organisation.

(b) Somebody has to **monitor progress and results** to ensure that objectives are met.

(c) Somebody has to communicate and sustain **corporate values**, ethics and operating principles.

(d) Somebody has to look after the interests of the **organisation's owners** and other **stakeholders**.

PART A   MANAGEMENT: NATURE, EVOLUTION AND APPROACHES

Question | Management structure

John, Paul, George and Ringo set up in business together as repairers of musical instruments. Each has contributed £5,000 as capital for the business. They are a bit uncertain as to how they should run the business, and, when they discuss this in the pub, they decide that attention needs to be paid to planning what they do, reviewing what they do and controlling what they do.

Suggest two ways in which John, Paul, George and Ringo can manage the business assuming no other personnel are recruited.

Answer

The purpose of this exercise has been to get you to separate the issues of management functions from organisational structure and hierarchy. John, Paul, George and Ringo have a number of choices. Here are some extreme examples.

(a) All the management activities are the job of one person.

   In this case, Paul, could plan direct and control the work and the other three would do the work.

(b) Division of management tasks between individuals (eg repairing drums and ensuring plans are adhered to would be Ringo's job, and so on).

(c) Management by committee. All of them could sit down and work out the plan together etc. In a small business with equal partners this is likely to be the most effective.

Different organisations have different structures for carrying out management functions. For example, some organisations have separate strategic planning departments. Others do not.

In a **private sector business**, managers act, ultimately, on behalf of shareholders. In practical terms, shareholders rarely interfere, as long as the business delivers profits year-on-year.

In a **public sector organisation**, management acts on behalf of the government. Politicians in a democracy are in turn accountable to the electorate. More of the objectives of a public sector organisation might be set by the 'owners' – ie the government – rather than by the management. The government might also tell senior management to carry out certain policies or plans, thereby restricting management's discretion.

3.1 Skills required by management

Different management models emphasise the relative importance of skills differently, but a number of basic skills can be identified:

(a) **Technical** – the underlying job-specific knowledge and techniques required to perform tasks proficiently

(b) **Communication** – the ability to work well with other people and in a group. It includes the ability to explain clearly and to persuade listeners

(c) **Cognitive** – the ability to consider and comprehend abstract and complex situations

(d) **Leadership** – the ability to inspire commitment (discussed further in Chapter 2)

4 Classical writers on management

> **FAST FORWARD**
> The classical writers on management and organisation were largely concerned with **efficiency**.

4.1 Henri Fayol: Five functions of management

> **FAST FORWARD**
> **Fayol** was an administrator and proposed universal principles of organisation.

Fayol was a French industrialist who put forward and popularised the concept of the existence of universal principles of management: in other words, the idea that all organisations could be structured and managed according to certain rational principles. **Fayol** himself recognised that applying such principles in practice was not simple.

Fayol classified five **functions of management** which apply to any organisation.

Function	Comment
Planning	This involves determining **objectives**, and strategies, policies, programmes and procedures for achieving those objectives, for the organisation and its sub-units.
Organising	Establishing a **structure of tasks** which need to be performed to achieve the goals of the organisation; grouping these tasks into jobs for individuals or teams; allocating jobs to sections and departments; **delegating** authority to carry out the jobs; and providing **systems of information** and communication, for the co-ordination of activities.
Commanding	Giving **instructions** to subordinates to carry out tasks, for which the manager has authority (to make decisions) and responsibility (for performance).
Co-ordinating	**Harmonising** the goals and activities of individuals and groups within the organisation. Management must reconcile differences in approach, effort, interest and timing, in favour of overall (or 'super-ordinate') shared goals.
Controlling	**Measuring** and **correcting** the activities of individuals and groups, to ensure that their performance is in accordance with plans. Deviations from plans are identified and corrected.

You may be struck by two key 'omissions' from **Fayol's** classification, from a more modern viewpoint.

(a) '**Motivating**' is not mentioned. It is assumed that subordinates will carry out tasks when 'commanded' or instructed to do so, regardless of whether or how far they may 'want' to.

(b) '**Communicating**' is not mentioned, although it is implied by the process of commanding (giving instructions), co-ordinating (sharing information) and controlling (giving feedback).

This reflects the classical view of the function of management as a matter of controlling resources and processes rather than people: an awareness of management as an **interpersonal** process, involving communication and influence, only developed later.

4.2 F W Taylor: Scientific management

> **FAST FORWARD**
> **Taylor** was an engineer and sought the most efficient methods.

Frederick W Taylor (1856–1915) was an engineer who pioneered the **scientific management** movement in the USA with his book *Principles of Scientific Management,* 1911.

Taylor's principles include the following.

(a) The development of a true **science of work**, whereby all knowledge contained within the organisation should be collected and recorded, as a kind of 'evidence' that could be used to improve performance

(b) The **scientific selection** and **progressive development** of workers: workers should be carefully trained and given jobs to which they are best suited

(c) The application of techniques to **plan, measure and control work** for maximum productivity

(d) The constant and intimate **co-operation between management and workers**

In practice, scientific management techniques included the following key elements.

(a) **Work study techniques** were used to analyse tasks and establish the most efficient methods to use. No variation was permitted in the way work was done, since the aim was to use the 'one best way'.

(b) **Planning and doing were separated**. It was assumed that the persons who were intellectually equipped to do a particular type of work were probably unlikely to be able to plan it to the best advantage: this was the manager's job.

(c) Jobs were **micro-designed**: divided into single, simple task components which formed a whole specialised 'job' for an individual, rather than permitting an individual to perform whole or part-task processes. (Task 'meaning' and 'significance', now considered essential to job satisfaction, had not yet emerged as important values.)

(d) Workers were **paid incentives** on the basis of acceptance of the new methods and output norms; the new methods greatly increased productivity and profits. Pay was assumed to be the only important motivating force.

Scientific management was very much about **manual work**. However, elements of scientific management are still practised today, whenever there is a concern for productivity and efficiency.

Case Study

Elements of Taylorism – maximising managerial control through the micro-design of jobs, automation and close supervision – can be seen in the management of junior staff in businesses such as:

- Large fast-food franchises (eg McDonalds)
- Call-centres, where calls are scripted, timed and monitored

4.3 Elton Mayo: Human relations

FAST FORWARD

Mayo and his colleagues investigated individual and group behaviour at work, as a factor in productivity.

In the 1920s, research began to show that managers needed to consider the complexity of **human behaviour**. It was recognised that an exclusive focus on technical competence (under scientific management) had resulted in social incompetence: managers were not taught how to manage people. At the same time, it emerged that being a 'small cog in the machine' was experienced as alienating and demoralising by workers – whatever the financial incentives offered. A more complex picture of human motivation began to emerge.

Elton Mayo (*The Human Problems of an Industrial Civilisation*, 1933) was Professor of Industrial Research at the Harvard Business School. He was involved in a series of large scale studies at the Western Electric Company's Hawthorne works in Chicago between 1924 and 1932.

An important element in these so-called 'Hawthorne Studies' was the investigation of the dynamics of work groups. The group was very effective in enforcing its behavioural norms, 'freezing out' unpopular supervisors and restricting output. It was concluded that people are motivated at work by a variety of psychological needs. This became the basis of the **human relations school** of management theory.

4.3.1 Neo-human relations

Later writers focused on a wider variety of workers' 'higher-order' needs, including the need for challenge, responsibility and personal development in the job. This became known as the **neo-human relations school**, which proposed important theories of motivation and job satisfaction.

The human relations approaches contributed an important awareness of the influence of the human factor at work (and particularly in the work group) on organisational performance. Most of its theorists attempted to offer guidelines to enable practicing managers to satisfy and motivate employees and so (theoretically) to obtain the benefits of improved productivity.

5 Writers on management

> **FAST FORWARD**
>
> Subsequent writers have taken a more flexible view of what managers do.

In the second half of the twentieth century, writing on management became more diverse.

(a) The early emphasis on the organisation of work has been continued in the field of **supervisory studies** and the development of specific management techniques such as **project management**. The search for efficiency continues in the field of **work study** and **industrial engineering**.

(b) Human relations theory has been enhanced by developments in the study of motivation, group and individual behaviour, leadership and other aspects of **industrial psychology**.

(c) There has been much new writing on the nature of the **manager's task**: what it is to be a manager and what managers do, in increasingly complex and chaotic business environments.

5.1 Peter Drucker: The management process

> **FAST FORWARD**
>
> Drucker emphasised the economic objective of managers in businesses.

Peter Drucker worked in the 1940s and 1950s as a business adviser to a number of US corporations. He was also a prolific writer on management.

Drucker argued that the manager of a business has one basic function – **economic performance**. In this respect, the business manager is different from the manager of any other type of organisation.

5.1.1 Management tasks

Drucker (*Management: Tasks, Responsibilities, Practices*, 1993) described the jobs of management within this basic function of economic performance as follows.

(a) **Managing a business**. The purposes of the business are to create a customer and innovation.

(b) **Managing managers**. The requirements here are:

    (i) Management by objectives (or performance management)
    (ii) Proper structure of managers' jobs
    (iii) Creating the right spirit (culture) in the organisation
    (iv) Making a provision for the managers of tomorrow (managerial succession)
    (v) Arriving at sound principles of organisation structure

(c) **Managing workers and work**

A manager's performance in all areas of management, including management of the business, can be enhanced by a study of the principles of management, the acquisition of 'organised knowledge' (eg management techniques) and systematic self-assessment.

5.1.2 Management processes

Later, Drucker grouped the work of the manager into five categories.

(a) **Setting objectives for the organisation**. Drucker popularised the term 'management by objectives' (MBO), the process of defining objectives within an organisation so that management and employees agree to them, and also understand what they need to do in the organisation in order to achieve them.

(b) **Organising the work**. The work to be done in the organisation must be divided into manageable activities and manageable jobs. The jobs must be integrated into a formal organisation structure, and people must be selected to do the jobs.

(c) **Motivating** employees and communicating information to them to enable them to do their work.

(d) **The job of measurement**. Management must:

   (i) **Establish objectives** or yardsticks of performance for all personnel

   (ii) **Analyse actual performance**, appraise it against the objectives or yardsticks which have been set, and analyse the comparison

   (iii) **Communicate** the findings and explain their significance both to subordinate employees and also to superiors

(e) **Developing people**

Every manager performs all five functions listed above, no matter how good or bad a manager they are. However, a bad manager performs these functions badly, whereas a good manager performs them well. Unlike Fayol, Drucker emphasised the importance of **communication** in the functions of management.

5.2 Ouchi: Theory Z

FAST FORWARD | **Ouchi** combined the American and Japanese ways of management in an ideal 'Theory Z' approach.

When the Japanese economy was performing well, it became fashionable to study Japanese management methods. Profiling American management culture as 'Theory A' and typical Japanese management as 'Theory J', **William Ouchi** sought to synthesise the two, to propose a form of Japanese-style management that could be successfully applied in Western contexts called 'Theory Z' Ouchi called these methods 'Theory Z' in *Theory Z*, 1982.

The characteristics of a Theory Z organisation offer some interesting contrasts with the Western way of doing things, notably in key Japanese values such as consensus decision-making and mutual loyalty in the employment relationship.

Ouchi described the Theory Z organisation as being characterised by:

(a) Long-term employment, with slow-progressing managerial career paths (as in the Japanese system, but with a more Western specialisation of skills)

(b) Broad concern for employee welfare, both inside and outside the work context (not just work performance, as in the Western system): commitment to the 'organisation family'

(c) Implicit informal controls (such as guiding values) alongside explicit, formal measures.

(d) Collective consensus decision-making processes (Japanese), but with individual retention of ultimate responsibility for defined areas of accountability (Western)

(e) Industrial relations characterised by trust, co-operation and mutual adjustment, rather than unionisation, demarcation and artificial status barriers

5.3 Peters and Waterman: Excellence

FAST FORWARD

Peters and Waterman set out the characteristics (supposedly) common to excellent organisations, and pioneered the concept of organisation culture.

Peters and Waterman (in their book *In Search of Excellence*, first published in 1982) designated certain companies as excellent because over a 20-year period they had given an above average return on investment and they had a reputation for innovation.

Peters and Waterman identified eight attributes of excellent or successful firms.

- **A bias for action** rather than analysis: not getting stuck in 'analysis paralysis', but doing something to keep improving
- **Closeness to customers**: listening to their needs, wants, values and feedback
- **Autonomy and entrepreneurship**: encouraging employees to take initiative, spot and seize opportunities (especially to win and please customers and enhance quality)
- **Productivity through people**: valuing employee commitment as the key resource of the business
- **Hands-on, value driven**: commitment to shared corporate values, at all levels
- **Stick to the knitting**: not diversifying the business into areas for which it lacks expertise
- **Simplicity**: avoiding the over-complication of structures and processes
- **Simultaneous loose-tight properties**: few rules and procedures (loose) but strong values guiding behaviour (tight) as a means of control

The key contribution of Peters and Waterman was perhaps their finding that the dominance and coherence of a **corporate culture** was an essential feature of the 'excellent' companies they observed. Guiding values appeared to be more powerful than manuals, rule books, norms and controls.

Excellence theories are accessible and appealing, but they have also been criticised. Key problems are:

(a) Many 'excellent' companies, such as IBM, have stumbled since the original studies.

(b) Excellence concentrates on operational issues rather than long-term strategy.

(c) Strong cultures can impede necessary change, as well as support it.

(d) Excellence appears to propose that there is 'one best way' to succeed, contrary to prevailing contingency theories which suggest that 'it all depends' on a range of internal and external factors.

5.4 Rosabeth Moss Kanter: Managers and innovation

FAST FORWARD

Kanter was concerned with innovation and its demands on managers.

Many large companies seek to retain some of the innovation and flexibility supposedly characteristic of small firms. They move towards a balance between bureaucracy (the old order) and entrepreneurial innovation (the new order) based on **synergies**, **alliances** and '**newstreams**'.

(a) A **synergy** is a combination of businesses, internal services and organisation structures which means that the whole is worth more in value than the sum of the parts. People at all levels focus on doing what they do best.

(b) Organisations are also seeking to extend their reach without increasing their size by forming closer working relationships or **strategic alliances** with other organisations. This involves partnerships, joint ventures, outsourcing functions to sub-contractors, and other forms of business networking.

(c) A **newstream** is a flow of new business possibilities within the organisation. Instead of relying on innovation just happening, official mechanisms are used to speed the flow of new ideas such as special funds, creativity centres and incentives. This implies a management approach which is sensitive, flexible, persistent and autonomous.

Rosabeth Moss Kanter has written extensively on the subject of change management and innovation. She has described some of the impossible or incompatible demands made on managers when seeking improved performance and excellence through innovation.

DEMANDS MADE ON MANAGERS

Be entrepreneurial and risk-taking	but	Don't lose money
Invest in the future	but	Keep profitable now
Do everything you're doing now but even better	but	Spend more time communicating, on teams and new projects
Lead and direct	but	Participate, listen, co-operate
Know everything about your business	but	Delegate more
Work all hours	but	Keep fit
Be single-minded in your commitment to ideas	but	Be flexible and responsive

DEMANDS MADE ON ORGANISATIONS

Be 'lean and mean'	but	Be a good employer
Be creative and innovative	but	'Stick to the knitting'
Decentralise to small, simple autonomous units	but	Centralise to be efficient and integrative
Have a sense of urgency	but	Deliberately plan for the future

5.5 Mintzberg: The manager's role

> **FAST FORWARD**
>
> **Mintzberg** described managerial roles, arguing that management is a disjointed, non-systematic activity.

Henry Mintzberg, (*Mintzberg on Management*, 1989) conducted a study of a relatively small sample of US corporations to see how senior managers actually spend their time. He suggests that in their daily working lives, managers fulfil three types of managerial role.

Role category	Role	Comment
Interpersonal Based on manager's formal authority or position	**Figurehead** (or ceremonial)	A large part of a Chief Executive's time is spent representing the company at dinners, conferences and so on.
	Leader	Hiring, firing and training staff, motivating employees, and reconciling individual goals with the objectives of the organisation.
	Liaison	Making contacts outside the vertical chain of command. Some managers spend up to half their meeting time with their peers rather than with their subordinates.
Informational Based on managers' access to: • Upward and downward channels • Many external contacts	**Monitor**	The manager monitors the environment, and receives information from subordinates, superiors and peers in other departments. Much of this information is of an informal nature, derived from the manager's network of contacts.
	Spokesperson	The manager provides information on behalf of the unit and/or organisation to interested parties.
	Disseminator	The manager disseminates relevant information to subordinates.
Decisional Based on the manager's formal authority and access to information, which allow them to take decisions relating to the work of the department as a whole.	**Entrepreneur**	A manager initiates projects to improve the department or to help it react to a changed environment.
	Disturbance handler	A manager has to respond to unexpected pressures, taking decisions when there is deviation from plan.
	Resource allocator	A manager takes decisions relating to the mobilisation and distribution of limited resources to achieve objectives.
	Negotiator	Both inside and outside the organisation, negotiation takes up a great deal of management time.

Mintzberg's research challenged the classical view of the manager as separate to, or above, the routine demands of day-to-day work.

(a) Managers are not always able to be reflective, systematic planners.

(b) Managerial work is disjointed and discontinuous.

(c) Managers do have routine duties to perform, especially of a ceremonial nature (receiving important guests) or related to authority (signing cheques as a signatory) – contrary to the myth that all routine work is done by juniors.

(d) Managers prefer verbal and informal information to the formal output of management information systems.

(e) Management cannot be reduced to a science or a profession. According to Mintzberg, managerial processes cannot be analysed scientifically or codified into an examinable body of theory.

Mintzberg states that general management is, in practice, a matter of **judgement and intuition**, gained from **experience** in **particular situations** rather than from abstract principles.

5.6 McGregor: Theory X and Theory Y

> **FAST FORWARD**
>
> **McGregor** suggested that a manager's approach is based on attitudes somewhere on a scale between two extreme sets of assumptions: Theory X (workers have to be coerced) and Theory Y (workers want to be empowered).

Douglas McGregor (*The Human Side of Enterprise*, 1987) suggested that managers (in the US) tended to behave as though they subscribed to one of two sets of assumptions about people at work: Theory X and Theory Y.

(a) **Theory X** suggests that most people dislike work and responsibility and will avoid both if possible. Because of this, most people must be coerced, controlled, directed and/or threatened with punishment to get them to make an adequate effort. Managers who operate according to these assumptions will tend to supervise closely, apply detailed rules and controls, and use 'carrot and stick' motivators.

(b) **Theory Y** suggests that physical and mental effort in work is as natural as play or rest. The ordinary person does not inherently dislike work: according to the conditions it may be a source of satisfaction or dissatisfaction. The potentialities of the average person are rarely fully used at work. People can be motivated to seek challenge and responsibility in the job, if their goals can be integrated with those of the organisation. A manager with this sort of attitude to his staff is likely to be a consultative, facilitating leader, using positive feedback, challenge and responsibility as motivators.

Both are intended to be extreme sets of assumptions – not actual types of people. However, they also tend to be self-fulfilling prophecies. Employees treated as if 'Theory X' were true will begin to behave accordingly. Employees treated as if 'Theory Y' were true – being challenged to take on more responsibility – will rise to the challenge and behave accordingly.

Theory X and Theory Y can be used to heighten managers' awareness of the assumptions underlying their motivational style.

6 Management and supervision

There are different levels of management in most organisations. A finance department in an organisation might be headed by the finance director (A) supported by a chief financial accountant (B) and chief management accountant (C). Lower down in the hierarchy assistant accountants might report to (B) and (C).

> **FAST FORWARD**
>
> **Supervision** is the interface between the operational core (non-managerial workers) and management.

6.1 The supervisor's role

The supervisor is the lowest level of management, at the **interface** between managerial and non-managerial staff. The role can also be called **first-line** or **front-line** management.

The key features of supervision are as follows.

(a) A supervisor usually deals with the levels of the organisation where the bread-and-butter work is done. (S)he will deal with matters such as staffing and health and safety at the day-to-day operational level, where a manager might deal with them at a policy-making level.

(b) A supervisor does not spend all his or her time on the managerial aspects of his job. Much of the time will be spent doing **technical/operational work**.

(c) A supervisor is a **gatekeeper** or filter for communication between managerial and non-managerial staff, both **upward** (conveying reports and suggestions) and **downward** (conveying policies, instructions and feedback).

(d) The supervisor monitors and controls work by means of **day-to-day, frequent and detailed information**: higher levels of management plan and control using longer-term, less frequent and less detailed information, which must be 'edited' or selected and reported by the supervisor.

Question — Supervising work

Bert Close has decided to delegate the task of identifying the reasons for machine 'down' time (when machines are not working) over the past three months to Brenda Cartwright. This will involve her talking to operators, foremen and supervisors and also liaising with other departments to establish the effects of this down time. What will Bert need to do to delegate this task effectively? List at least four items he will need to cover with Brenda.

Answer

- Identify task objectives
- Explain limits within which Brenda will work
- Deadlines
- Formats of reporting results
- Progress monitoring

7 The manager's role in organising work

FAST FORWARD Managers have **key roles** in work planning, resource allocation and project management.

7.1 Work planning

Work planning is the establishment of work methods and practices to ensure that predetermined objectives are efficiently met at all levels.

(a) **Task sequencing** or **prioritisation** ie considering tasks in order of importance for achieving objectives and meeting deadlines

(b) **Scheduling** or **timetabling tasks**, and allocating them to different individuals within appropriate time scales

(c) Establishing **checks and controls** to ensure that:
  (i) Priority deadlines are being met and work is not 'falling behind'
  (ii) Routine tasks are achieving their objectives

(d) **Contingency plans:** arrangements for what should be done if changes or problems occur, eg computer system failure or industrial action

(e) **Co-ordinating** the efforts of individuals: integrating plans and schedules so that data and work flows smoothly from one stage of an operation to another

Some jobs (eg assembly line work) are entirely routine, and can be performed one step at a time, but for most people, some kind of ongoing planning and adjustment will be required.

7.2 Assessing where resources are most usefully allocated

In broad terms, managers and supervisors have access to the following resources, which can be allocated or deployed to further the unit's objectives.

(a) **Human resources**: staff time and skills

(b) **Material resources**, including raw materials, equipment, machine time, office space and so on

(c) **Financial resources**, within budget guidelines

(d) **Information**

A manager or supervisor may be responsible for allocating resources between:

(a) Different ways to achieve the same objective (eg to increase total profits, sell more – or cut costs)

(b) Competing areas, where total resources are limited

A piece of work will be **high priority** in the following cases.

- If it has to be completed by a certain time (ie a deadline)
- If other tasks depend on it
- If other people depend on it
- If it has important potential consequence or impact

Routine priorities or regular peak times (eg tax returns) can be planned ahead of time, and other tasks planned around them.

Non-routine priorities occur when unexpected demands are made. Thus planning of work should cover routine scheduled peaks and contingency plans for unscheduled peaks and emergencies.

7.3 Projects

Key term

> A **project** is 'an undertaking that has a beginning and an end and is carried out to meet established goals within cost, schedule and quality objectives'. (**Haynes**, *Project Management*, 1997)

The main difference between project planning and other types of planning is that a project is not generally a repetitive activity. Projects generally:

- Have specific start and end points
- Have well-defined objectives, cost and time schedules
- Cut across organisational and functional boundaries

The relocation of offices, the introduction of a new information system or the launch of a new product may be undertaken as a project. Other examples include building/capital projects, such as factory construction or bridge building.

7.3.1 Project management

The job of **project management** is to foresee as many contingencies as possible and to plan, organise, co-ordinate and control activities.

Management task	Comment
Outline project planning	• Developing project targets such as overall costs or timescale (eg project should take 20 weeks) • Dividing the project into activities (eg analysis, programming, testing), and placing these activities into the right sequence, often a complicated task if overlapping • Developing the procedures and structures, managing the project (eg plan weekly team meetings, performance reviews etc)
Detailed planning	Identifying the tasks and resource requirements; network analysis for scheduling
Teambuilding	The project manager has to meld the various people into an effective team
Communication	The project manager must let key project stakeholders know what is going on, and ensure that members of the project team are properly briefed
Co-ordinating project activities	Between the project team and clients/users, and other external parties (eg suppliers of hardware and software)
Monitoring and control	The project manager should determine causes of any departure from the plan, and take corrective measures
Problem-resolution	Unforeseen problems may arise, and it falls upon the project manager to sort them out, or to delegate the responsibility for so doing to a subordinate

Question — Human resource practices

A human resources consultant has recently reviewed management and human resource practices at Rezillo Co and noted a number of features.

Which of the following is NOT characteristic of the scientific school of management?

A   Regular meetings between employees and managers
B   Collective planning of employees' time by employees and managers
C   Regular staff training
D   Recruitment programme targeted at the skills needed by the company

Answer

B   Collective planning of employees' time by employees and managers

The scientific school suggests a separation of managers' responsibilities (including planning) and employees' responsibilities. Collective, consensual decision-making is characteristic of Ouchi's Theory Z.

The other features are all scientific management techniques, designed to boost employee performance.

Chapter roundup

- **Organisations** achieve results which individuals cannot achieve by themselves.
- An organisation is a **social arrangement** which pursues collective goals and controls its own performance.
- Organisations **differ** according to their: ownership, control, activity, orientation, size, legal status, funding and technology.
- **Organisation structure** is formed by the grouping of people into departments or sections and the allocation of responsibility and authority.
- **Mintzberg** suggests that all organisation structures have **five components: strategic apex, middle line** and **operating core**, plus **technostructure** and **support staff**.
- Classical organisations are based on the principle of **hierarchy**. There is a line of decision-making power from the top of the organisation to the bottom. This **scalar chain** is intimately connected to the concept of **span of control**, which is the number of individuals under the direct supervision of any one person.
- Modern management theory stresses **flexibility** as a key value, and organisational measures such as matrix and horizontal structures, multi-skilling, empowerment and flexible labour deployment are currently being explored.
- **Contingency theory** suggests that there is no one best way to structure (or manage) an organisation. 'It all depends [...]' on a number of variables.
- An organisation can be viewed as an **open system**, interacting with its environment.
- **Management** is responsible for using the organisation's resources to meet its goals. It is accountable to the owners: shareholders in a business, or government in the public sector.
- The classical writers on management and organisation were largely concerned with efficiency:
    - **Fayol** was an administrator and proposed universal principles of organisation.
    - **Taylor** was an engineer and sought the most efficient methods.
    - **Mayo** and his colleagues investigated individual and group behaviour at work, as a factor in productivity.
- **Subsequent writers** have taken a more **flexible** view of what managers do:
    - **Drucker** emphasised the economic objective of managers in businesses.
    - **Ouchi** combined the American and Japanese ways of management in an ideal 'Theory Z' approach.
    - **Peters and Waterman** set out the characteristics (supposedly) common to excellent organisations and pioneered the concept of organisation culture.
    - **Kanter** was concerned with innovation and its demands on managers.
    - **Mintzberg** described managerial roles, arguing that management is a disjointed, non-systematic activity.
    - **McGregor** suggested that a manager's approach is based on attitudes somewhere on a scale between two extreme sets of assumptions: Theory X (workers have to be coerced) and Theory Y (workers want to be empowered).
- **Supervision** is the interface between the operational core (non-managerial workers) and management.
- Managers have **key roles** in work planning, resource allocation and project management.

Quick quiz

1. List **Fayol**'s principles of organisation.
2. List **Mintzberg**'s organisational components.
3. Which of the following is not one of **Fayol**'s five functions of management?

    A   Commanding
    B   Controlling
    C   Communicating
    D   Co-ordinating

4. State **Taylor**'s principles of scientific management.
5. What advance did the Hawthorne studies make in the management of people?
6. The overriding responsibility of the management of a business, according to **Drucker**, is employee development. True or False?
7. What managerial roles did **Mintzberg** describe and what categories did he group them into?
8. **Ouchi**'s synthesis of Japanese management culture for Western contexts is called:

    A   Theory X
    B   Theory Y
    C   Theory Z
    D   Theory J

9. What criticisms have been made of **Peters and Waterman**'s ideas about excellence?

PART A MANAGEMENT: NATURE, EVOLUTION AND APPROACHES

Answers to quick quiz

1. Division of work; authority and responsibility; discipline; unity of command; unity of direction; subordination of individual interests; remuneration; scalar chain

2. Strategic apex, middle line, operating core, technostructure, support staff

3. C: Communicating

4. The development of a true science of work; the scientific selection and progressive development of workers; the bringing together of the science and the workers; constant and intimate co-operation between management and workers

5. An understanding that individual attitudes and group relationships help determine the level of output

6. False: The overriding responsibility is economic performance

7.
Category	Roles
Interpersonal:	Figurehead; leader; liaison
Informational:	Monitor; spokesperson; disseminator
Decisional:	Entrepreneur; disturbance handler; resource allocator; negotiator

8. C: Theory Z

9. Many excellent companies have stumbled. Long-term strategy is ignored. Strong culture can impede change. It supports a single solution to success.

Effective leadership

Topic list	Syllabus reference
1 What is leadership?	D1
2 Trait theories of leadership	D1
3 Style theories of leadership	D1
4 Contingency approaches to leadership	D1
5 Power and authority	D1
6 Responsibility and accountability	D1
7 Delegation	D1
8 Empowerment	D1

Introduction

We covered the role of the manager in Chapter 1.

Opinions vary on how much, if at all, leadership can be distinguished from management. We look at these issues in **Section 1** of this chapter, together with core **leadership skills**.

In **Sections 2 to 4**, we work through some of the major **leadership theories**, which are examinable in detail.

In **Section 5**, we look at **power** and **authority**: the source of a manager's right to make decisions and expect them to be carried out.

In **Section 6** we look at the other side of that coin: **responsibility**, whereby the manager is liable to be held to account for the decisions (s)he has made.

In **Section 7**, we look at how authority 'flows' down from the top of the organisation, via **delegation**. This is a highly practical matter of how managers give tasks to their subordinates – and why they often don't!

Finally, we look at **empowerment**: the trend towards giving more authority and responsibility to lower levels of the organisation.

PART A MANAGEMENT: NATURE, EVOLUTION AND APPROACHES

1 What is leadership?

1.1 Management and leadership

FAST FORWARD

> The term 'leadership' and 'management' are often used in the same way, with the same meaning. However, a distinction can be made between management and leadership.
>
> There are many different definitions of **leadership**. Key themes (which are also used to distinguish leadership from management) include: interpersonal influence; securing willing commitment to shared goals; creating direction and energy; and an orientation to change.

The terms 'management' and 'leadership' are often used interchangeably in everyday use. In some cases, management skills and theories have simply been relabelled to reflect the more fashionable term. However, there have been many attempts to distinguish meaningfully between them.

(a) **Kotter** (*A force for change: How leadership differs from management*, 1990) argues that leadership and management involve two distinct sets of action. Management is about coping with **complexity**: its functions are to do with logic, structure, analysis and control, and are aimed at producing order, consistency and predictability. Leadership, by contrast, is about coping with **change**: its activities include creating a sense of direction, communicating strategy, and energising, inspiring and motivating others to translate the vision into action.

(b) **Yukl** (*Leadership in Organisations*, 1981) suggests that while management is defined by a prescribed role and position in the structure of the organisation, leaders are given their roles by the perception of others, through election, choice or influence. Leadership is an interpersonal process. In other words, managers have **subordinates**, but leaders have **followers**.

(c) **Zaleznik** (in his *Harvard Business Review* article 'Managers and Leaders: are they different?', 1977) suggests that managers are mainly concerned with order and **maintaining the status quo**, exercising their skills in diplomacy and focusing on decision-making processes within the organisation. Leaders, in contrast, direct their energies towards introducing **new approaches and ideas**. They create excitement and vision in order to arouse motivation, and focus with empathy on the meanings of events and actions for people. Leaders search out opportunities for change.

(d) **Katz and Kahn** (*The Social Psychology of Organisations*, 1978) point out that while management aims to secure compliance with stated organisational objectives, leadership aims to secure willingness, enthusiasm and commitment. Leadership is the **influential increment** over and above mechanical compliance with the routine directives of the organisation.

Management can be exercised over resources, activities, projects and other essential non-personal things. Leadership can only be exercised over **people**.

Some of the values used to distinguish between managers and leaders have also been identified by Burns in his 1978 book *Leadership*.

(a) **Transactional leaders** see the relationship with their followers in terms of a trade: they give followers the rewards they want in exchange for service, loyalty and compliance.

(b) **Transformational leaders** see their role as inspiring and motivating others to work at levels beyond mere compliance. Only transformational leadership is said to be able to change team/organisation cultures and create a new direction.

1.2 Key leadership skills

> **FAST FORWARD**
>
> **Key leadership skills** may be identified in a range of interpersonal and business areas.

Transformational leadership is achieved through what **Bass & Avolio** (*Improving organizational effectiveness through transformational leadership,* 1994) call the 'Four Is'. These represent a useful description of key leadership skills.

(a) **Idealised influence**: identified with 'charisma'. The leader acts as a role model: putting the needs of others before personal interests; taking risks; demonstrating high standards of ethical conduct – and attracting the admiration, respect, trust and imitation of followers.

(b) **Inspirational motivation**: also identified with 'charisma'. The leader articulates the challenge, significance and meaning in work; arouses team spirit; shows enthusiasm and confidence; communicates high expectations and demonstrates commitment.

(c) **Intellectual stimulation**: the leader encourages free thinking and emphasises rational problem-solving, by: questioning assumptions; reinterpreting problems and issues in new ways; encouraging innovation and creativity; and avoiding punishing or publicly criticising mistakes.

(d) **Individualised consideration**: the leader treats followers on their own merits and seeks to develop them: accepting individual differences; attending to individuals' higher-level needs for growth and challenge; acting as coach/mentor; creating learning opportunities through delegation; and avoiding close monitoring of performance.

In addition, you might identify a range of business and managerial skills as important to a good leader, including:

(a) **Entrepreneurship**: the ability to spot business opportunities and mobilise resources to capitalise on them

(b) **Interpersonal skills**: such as networking, rapport-building, influencing, negotiating, conflict resolution, listening, counselling, coaching and communicating assertively

(c) **Decision-making and problem-solving skills**: including seeing the big picture (sometimes called 'helicopter ability')

(d) **Time-management and personal organisation**: being able to manage time well, through effective planning, setting deadlines, delegation and prioritising activities according to their importance.

(e) **Self-development** skills: the ability to learn continuously from experience, to grow in self-awareness and to exploit learning opportunities.

1.3 Warren Bennis on leaders and managers

> **FAST FORWARD**
>
> Bennis suggested that a leader innovates and develops, whereas a manager administers and controls.

Warren Bennis made a useful distinction between the role of the manager and the role of the leader.

(a) The manager administers and maintains, by focusing on systems and controls and the short term.

(b) The leader innovates, focuses on people and inspires trust, and holds a long-term view.

The leader innovates and develops, whereas the manager administers and controls. The manager focuses on 'non-people' aspects of systems, whereas the focus of the leader is on providing leadership to people.

Bennis described the manager as someone who 'does things right' and the leader as someone who 'does the right thing.'

He studied leadership by examining leaders of every description in the hope of finding some common characteristics. His book *Leaders* (1985) did not conclude that there is one right way to lead, but it does set out common competencies displayed by leaders. Bennis calls them:

(a) The management of attention: A compelling cause or vision, to give focus
(b) The management of meaning: The ability to communicate
(c) The management of trust: Being consistent and honest
(d) The management of self: Being aware of personal weaknesses and strengths

Other tasks of the leader that Bennis sees as important are:

(a) Constantly reminding people why their work is important
(b) Creating an atmosphere of trust
(c) Encouraging curiosity and risk taking in the organisation culture
(d) Fostering an atmosphere of 'hope' which can be particularly helpful when things go wrong

Bennis believes that leadership in the modern age is a shared task, with power spread around rather than centralised. It could be that the most important role of modern leaders is deciding who will be in their teams.

1.4 Why develop managers as 'leaders'?

FAST FORWARD

Leadership offers key **benefits** in a competitive, turbulent environment: activating commitment, setting direction, developing people and energising and supporting change.

Attempts to define what makes leadership 'special' (such as those outlined above) have suggested some key points about the benefits effective leadership can bring and why it is valuable.

(a) Leaders energise and support **change**, which is essential for survival in highly competitive and fast-changing business environments. By setting visionary goals, and encouraging contribution from teams, leaders create environments that:

- Seek out new information and ideas
- Allow challenges to existing procedures and ways of thinking
- Invite innovation and creativity in finding better ways to achieve goals
- Support and empower people to cope with the turbulence

(b) Leaders secure **commitment**, mobilising the ideas, experience and motivation of employees – which contributes to innovation and improved quality and customer service. This is all the more essential in a competitive, customer-focused, knowledge-based business environment.

(c) Leaders set **direction**, helping teams and organisations to understand their purpose, goals and value to the organisation. This facilitates team-working and empowerment (allowing discretion and creativity about how to achieve the desired outcomes) without loss of co-ordination or direction.

(d) Leaders support, challenge and develop **people**, maximising their contribution to the organisation. Leaders use an influence-based, facilitate-empower style rather than a command-control style, and this is better suited to the expectations of empowered teams and the need for information-sharing in modern business environments.

 Question

Leadership

Reflect on your own experience of working under the direction of others. Identify the 'best' leader you have ever 'followed'. (You may need to think about non-work leaders such as a sports coach or school teacher.) Think about how this person behaved and interacted with you and others.

What qualities makes you identify this person as a 'great leader', from your point of view as a follower?

1.5 Theories of leadership

FAST FORWARD

There are three basic **schools of leadership theory**: trait theories, style theories and contingency theories.

School	Comment
Trait theories	Based on analysing the personality characteristics or preferences of successful leaders.
Style theories	Based on the view that leadership is an interpersonal process whereby different leader behaviours influence people in different ways. More or less effective patterns of behaviour (or 'styles') can therefore be adopted.
Contingency theories	Based on the belief that there is no 'one best way' of leading, but that effective leaders adapt their behaviour to the specific and changing variables in the leadership context: the nature of the task, the personalities of team members, the organisation culture and so on.

2 Trait theories of leadership

FAST FORWARD

Early theories suggested that there are certain personality characteristics common to successful leaders.

Various studies have attempted to determine exactly which traits are essential in a leader, but trait theory has been more or less discredited. The premise that certain traits are absolutely necessary for effective leadership has never been substantiated, and the lists of traits proposed for leaders have been vast, varied and contradictory.

Early theories suggested that there are certain personal qualities ('traits') that are common to successful leaders. In other words, 'leaders are born, not made'. Individuals either have the qualities to be a good leader, or they do not.

Various studies have attempted to determine exactly which qualities are essential in a leader. One US study cites the following:

- Judgement
- Drive
- Fairness
- Energy
- Initiative
- Human relations skills
- Ambition
- Emotional stability
- Integrity
- Decisiveness
- Dedication
- Co-operation
- Foresight
- Dependability
- Objectivity

Trait theory has been more or less discredited.

(a) The argument that certain traits (or qualities) are absolutely necessary for effective leadership has never been proved or successfully demonstrated.

(b) A very large number of traits that make a good leader have been suggested. There are far too many varied traits to make a convincing theory.

(c) Trait theories ignore the complexities of the leadership situation. Not everyone with the desirable 'traits' turns out to be a good leader.

3 Style theories of leadership

> **Leadership styles** are clusters of leadership behaviour that are used in different ways in different situations. While there are many different classifications of style, they mainly relate to the extent to which the leader is focused primarily on task/performance (directive behaviour) or relationships/people (supportive behaviour). Key style models include:
>
> - The **Ashridge Model**: tells, sells, consults, joins
> - **Likert**: exploitative authoritative, benevolent authoritative, consultative, participative
> - **Lewin**, **Lippitt and White**: autocratic, democratic, *laissez-faire*
> - **Blake and Mouton**'s **Managerial Grid**: concern for task, concern for people

Although the labels and definitions of leadership styles vary, style models are often talking (broadly) about the same thing: a continuum of behaviours from:

(a) Wholly task-focused, directive leadership behaviours (representing high leader control) at one extreme; and

(b) Wholly people-focused, supportive/relational leadership behaviours (representing high subordinate discretion) at the other.

3.1 A continuum of leadership styles

Tannenbaum and Schmidt ('How to Choose a Leadership Pattern', *Harvard Business Review*, 1973) proposed a continuum of behaviours (and associated styles) which reflected the balance of control exercised in a situation by the leader and the team.

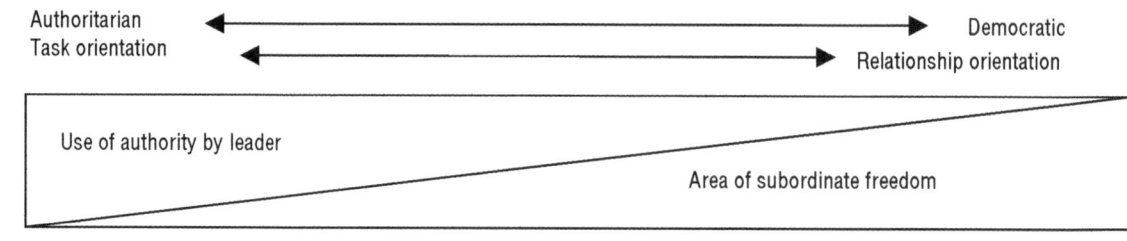

| Leader makes decision and announces it | Leader 'sells' decision | Leader presents ideas and invites questions | Leader presents intended decision, subject to amendment | Leader presents a problem, gets suggestions, and makes a decision | Leader defines limits and goals and asks the group to make the decision | Leader allows his subordinates to act as they wish, within specified limits |

3.2 The Ashridge Management College model

The Research Unit at Ashridge Management College distinguished four different management styles. (These are outlined, with their strengths and weaknesses, in the following table.) The researchers labelled their styles:

- Tells
- Sells
- Consults
- Joins

2: EFFECTIVE LEADERSHIP

The Ashridge studies found that:

(a) In an ideal world, subordinates preferred the 'consults' style of leadership.

(b) People led by a 'consults' manager had the most favourable attitude to their work.

(c) Most subordinates feel they are being led by a 'tells' or 'sells' manager.

(d) In practice, **consistency** was far more important to subordinates than any particular style. The least favourable attitudes were found amongst subordinates who were unable to perceive any consistent style of leadership in their superiors.

Style	Characteristics	Strengths	Weaknesses
Tells (autocratic)	The leader makes all the decisions, and issues instructions which must be obeyed without question.	(a) Quick decisions can be made when speed is required. (b) It is the most efficient type of leadership for highly-programmed routine work.	(a) It does not encourage subordinates to give their opinions when these might be useful. (b) Communication between leader and subordinates will be one-way and the leader will not know until afterwards whether the orders have been properly understood. (c) It does not encourage initiative and commitment from subordinates.
Sells (persuasive)	The leader still makes all the decisions, but believes that subordinates have to be motivated to accept them and carry them out properly.	(a) Employees are made aware of the reasons for decisions. (b) Selling decisions to staff might make them more committed. (c) Staff will have a better idea of what to do when unforeseen events arise in their work because the leader will have explained his intentions.	(a) Communications are still largely one-way. Subordinates might not accept the decisions. (b) It does not encourage initiative and commitment from subordinates.
Consults	The leader confers with subordinates and takes their views into account, but retains the final say.	(a) Employees are involved in decisions before they are made. This encourages motivation through greater interest and involvement. (b) An agreed consensus of opinion can be reached and, for some decisions, this can be an advantage (eg increasing ownership). (c) Employees can contribute their knowledge and experience to help solve more complex problems.	(a) It might take much longer to reach decisions. (b) Subordinates might be too inexperienced to formulate mature opinions and give practical advice. (c) Consultation can too easily turn into a façade, concealing a 'sells' style.

Style	Characteristics	Strengths	Weaknesses
Joins (democratic)	Leader and followers make the decision on the basis of consensus.	(a) It can provide high motivation and commitment from employees. (b) It shares the other advantages of the consultative style (especially where subordinates have expert power).	(a) The authority of the leader might be undermined. (b) Decision making might become a very long process, and clear decisions might become difficult to reach. (c) Subordinates might lack experience.

Question

Styles of leadership

Suggest an appropriate style of leadership for each of the following situations. Think about your reasons for choosing each style in terms of the results you are trying to achieve, the need to secure commitment from others, and potential difficulties with both.

(a) Due to outside factors, the personnel budget has been reduced for your department and 25% of your staff must be made redundant. Records of each employee's performance are available.

(b) There is a recurring administrative problem which is minor, but irritating to everyone in your department. Several solutions have been tried in the past, but without success. You think you have a remedy which will work, but unknown problems may arise, depending on the decisions made.

Answer

(a) You may have to 'tell' here: nobody is gong to like the idea and, since each person will have his or her own interests at heart, you are unlikely to reach consensus. You could attempt to 'sell', if you can see a positive side to the change in particular cases: opportunities for retraining, say.

(b) You could 'consult' here: explain your remedy to staff and see whether they can suggest potential problems. They may be in a position to offer solutions – and since the problem affects them too, they should be committed to solving it.

3.3 Rensis Likert

Likert (*New Patterns of Management*, 1961) also describes a range of four management styles or 'systems':

(a) System 1: **Exploitative authoritative**. The leader has no confidence or trust in his subordinates, imposes decisions, never delegates, motivates by threat, has little communication with subordinates and does not encourage teamwork.

(b) System 2: **Benevolent authoritative**. The leader has only superficial trust in subordinates, imposes decisions, never delegates, motivates by reward and, though sometimes involving others in problem-solving, is basically paternalistic.

(c) System 3: **Participative**. The leader has some confidence in subordinates, listens to them but controls decision-making, motivates by reward and a level of involvement, and will use the ideas and suggestions of subordinates constructively.

(d) System 4: **Democratic**. The leader has complete confidence in subordinates who are allowed to make decisions for themselves. Motivation is by reward for achieving goals set by participation, and there is a substantial amount of sharing of ideas, opinions and co-operation.

Likert's research suggested that effective managers naturally use a System 3 or System 4 style. Both are seen as viable approaches, balancing the needs of the organisation and the individual.

3.4 Lewin, Lippitt and White

In an early study using boys' clubs, **Lewin, Lippitt and White** ('Patterns of aggressive behaviour in experimentally created social climates', *Journal of Social Psychology*, 1939) identified three styles of leadership.

(a) **Autocratic**: issuing orders, overseeing work activities and giving out criticism and praise on a whim

(b) **Democratic**: showing concern for team member welfare, participating in group activities, making suggestions as to what should be done but allowing team members to make decisions

(c) *Laissez-faire*: tending to be 'stand-offish', not getting involved in team activities or welfare, and effectively letting the group run itself

In a follow-up study in 1943, **Lippitt & White** investigated the effect of leadership on productivity in different groups. They proposed the following conclusions.

(a) **Work-orientated conversation** was greatest in a democratic group, less in an autocratic group and least in a *laissez-faire* group.

(b) The amount of **work actually done** was greatest in an autocratic group and least in a *laissez-faire* group.

(c) **Motivation** was strongest in a democratic group, where members often carried on working even when the leader was absent. Even so, motivation was not sufficient to increase output above the level of the autocratic group.

(d) **Hostility and discontent** were greatest in an autocratic group: some members even left the group. In contrast, originality, group-mindedness and friendly playfulness were greatest in a democratic group.

Question — Participative leadership

In your career so far, you might have worked for a number of managers. Jot down the following features of each situation on a scale of 1–5 for comparative purposes.

(a) The degree to which you had autonomy over your own work
(b) The degree to which you were consulted on decisions which affected you
(c) The degree to which your advice was sought about decisions affecting your section

If you worked for managers who had different approaches to these issues, do you think these approaches influenced **your** effectiveness? What score to questions (a), (b) and (c) would you give your **ideal boss**? and your **current boss**?

3.5 Blake and Mouton's Managerial Grid

Robert Blake and **Jane Mouton** (*The Managerial Grid: The Key to Leadership Excellence*, 1964) carried out research (The Ohio State Leadership Studies) into managerial behaviour and observed two basic dimensions of leadership: **concern for production** (or task performance) and **concern for people**.

Along each of these two dimensions, managers could be located at any point on a continuum from very low to very high concern. Blake and Mouton observed that the two concerns did not seem to correlate, positively or negatively: a high concern in one dimension, for example, did not seem to imply a high or low concern in the other dimension. Individual managers could therefore reflect various permutations of task/people concern.

Blake and Mouton modelled these permutations as a grid. One axis represented concern for people, and the other concern for production. They then allotted nine points to each axis, from 1 (low) to 9 (high).

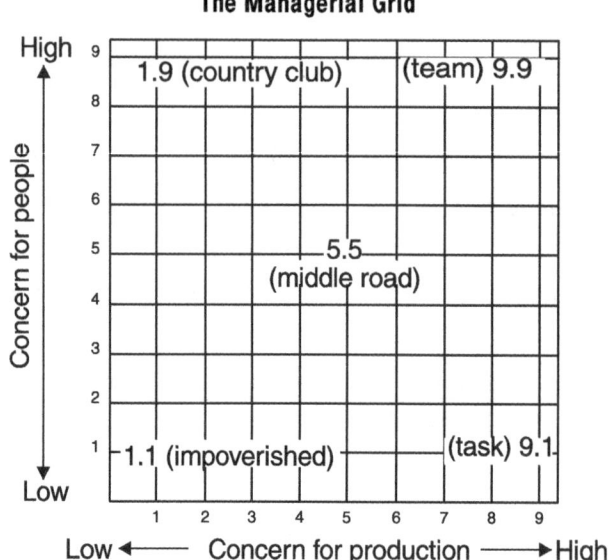

The extreme cases shown on the Grid are:

(a) 1.1 **impoverished**: the manager is lazy, showing little interest in either staff or work.

(b) 1.9 **country club**: the manager is attentive to staff needs and has developed satisfying relationships. However, there is little attention paid to achieving results.

(c) 9.1 **task management**: almost total concentration on achieving results. People's needs are virtually ignored.

(d) 5.5 **middle of the road** or the **dampened pendulum**: adequate performance through balancing (or switching between) the necessity to get out work with team morale.

(e) 9.9 **team**: high work accomplishment through 'leading' committed people who identify themselves with the organisational aims.

The Managerial Grid was intended as an appraisal and management development tool. It recognises that a balance is required between concern for task and concern for people, and that a high degree of both is possible (and highly effective) at the same time.

3.5.1 Evaluating the Managerial Grid

The Grid thus offers a number of useful insights for the identification of management **training and development** needs. It shows where the behaviour and assumptions of a manager may exhibit a lack of balance between the dimensions and/or a low degree of concern in either dimension or both. It may also be used in team member selection, so that a 1.9 team leader is balanced by a 9.1 co-leader, for example.

However, the Grid is a simplified model, and as such has practical limitations.

(a) It assumes that 9.9 is the desirable model for effective leadership. In some managerial contexts, this may not be so. Concern for people, for example, would not be necessary in a context of comprehensive automation: compliance is all that would be required.

(b) It is open to oversimplification. Scores can appear polarised, with judgements attached about individual managers' suitability or performance. The Grid is intended as a simplified 'snapshot' of a manager's preferred style, not a comprehensive description of his or her performance.

(c) Organisational context and culture, technology and other factors influence the manager's style of leadership, not just the two dimensions described by the Grid.

(d) Any managerial theory is only useful in so far as it is useable in practice by managers: if the Grid is used only to inform managers that they 'must acquire greater concern for people', it may result in stress, uncertainty and inconsistent behaviour.

Question — The Managerial Grid

Here are some statements about a manager's approach to meetings. Which position on Blake and Mouton's Grid do you think each might represent?

(a) I attend because it is expected. I either go along with the majority position or avoid expressing my views.

(b) I try to come up with good ideas and push for a decision as soon as I can get a majority behind me. I don't mind stepping on people if it helps a sound decision.

(c) I like to be able to support what my boss wants and to recognise the merits of individual effort. When conflict rises, I do a good job of restoring harmony.

Answer

(a) 1.1: Low task, low people
(b) 9.1: High task, low people
(c) 1.9: High people, low task

3.6 Limitations of style approaches

Perhaps the most important criticism of the style approach is that it does not consider all the variables that contribute to the practice of effective leadership.

(a) The manager's personality (or 'acting' ability) may simply not be **flexible** enough to utilise different styles effectively.

(b) The demands of the task, technology, organisation culture and other managers **constrain** the leader in the range of styles effectively open to them. (If their own boss practises an authoritarian style, and the team are incompetent and require close supervision, no amount of theorising on the desirability of participative management will make it possible.)

(c) **Consistency** is important to subordinates. If a manager adapts their style to changing situations, they may simply perceive them to be fickle, or may suffer insecurity and stress.

It is the consideration of this wide set of variables that has led to the development of the contingency approach to leadership.

Question — Managerial style

Nick is production director in a publishing company. He allows his authors some flexibility in meeting deadlines as he believes this will make them happier, and that they will be more likely to be motivated to do work urgently at short notice.

Which of Blake and Mouton's managerial styles is Nick demonstrating?

A   Team
B   Country club
C   Task
D   Dampened pendulum

Answer

D Dampened pendulum

This is the middle position. Nick is showing some flexibility because of concern for employees, but he is also concerned to make sure urgent tasks are done on time and that is part of the reason for treating employees the way he does.

The team approach would reconcile personal interests and task requirements, with employees always being willing to meet task requirements. The country club approach would imply personal interests are paramount, and Nick has some concern for tasks being done. However, he allows some flexibility in meeting deadlines, which indicates that his approach is not fully Task-focused, as that would mean he allows no flexibility.

4 Contingency approaches to leadership

In essence, contingency theory sees effective leadership as being dependent on a number of variable or contingent factors. There is no one right way to lead that will fit all situations.

> **FAST FORWARD**
>
> Leaders need to adapt their style to the needs of the team and situation. This is the basis of **contingency approaches** such as:
>
> - **Fiedler**'s 'psychologically close' and 'psychologically distant' styles
> - **Hersey and Blanchard**'s 'situational leadership' model
> - **John Adair**'s 'action-centred' leadership model
> - **Handy**'s 'best fit' model

4.1 F E Fiedler

Perhaps the leading advocate of contingency theory is **Fiedler**. He studied the relationship between style of leadership and the effectiveness of the work group and identified two types of leader (*A Theory of Leadership Effectiveness*, 1967).

(a) **Psychologically distant managers** (PDMs) maintain distance from their subordinates.

  (i) They formalise the roles and relationships between themselves and their superiors and subordinates.

  (ii) They choose to be withdrawn and reserved in their inter-personal relationships within the organisation (despite having good inter-personal skills).

  (iii) They prefer formal consultation methods rather than seeking the opinions of their staff informally.

  PDMs judge subordinates on the basis of performance, and are primarily task-orientated: Fiedler found that leaders of the most effective work groups tend to be PDMs.

(b) **Psychologically close managers** (PCMs) are closer to their subordinates.

  (i) They do not seek to formalise roles and relationships with superiors and subordinates.

  (ii) They are more concerned to maintain good human relationships at work than to ensure that tasks are carried out efficiently.

  (iii) They prefer informal contacts to regular formal staff meetings

Fiedler suggested that the effectiveness of a work group depended on the **situation**, made up of three key variables.

- The relationship **between the leader and the group** (trust, respect and so on)
- The extent to which the **task** is defined and structured
- The **power** of the leader in relation to the group (authority, and power to reward and punish)

A situation is **favourable** to the leader when:

- The leader is liked and trusted by the group
- The tasks of the group are clearly defined
- The power of the leader to reward and punish with organisation backing is high

Fiedler concluded:

(a) A structured (or psychologically distant) style works best when the situation is either very favourable, or very unfavourable to the leader.

(b) A supportive (or psychologically close) style works best when the situation is moderately favourable to the leader.

4.2 Charles Handy

Handy (*Understanding Organisations*, 1976) argued that the ability of a manager to lead and to influence the work group will vary according to three factors.

(a) The **leader**: their personality and preferred style of operating

(b) The **subordinates**: their individual and collective personalities, and their preference for a particular style of leadership

(c) The **task**: its structure, complexity and variety

In addition, there is the wider leadership 'context', including:

(a) The position of **power** held by the leader within the organisation and the group. A leader with power is better able to manage the other variables.

(b) The norms, structure and technology of the **organisation** as a whole. No manager can act contrary to organisational constraints.

Each of the key variables can be plotted on a spectrum from 'tight' to 'flexible'. Handy suggests that the most effective managerial approach in any situation is one that brings all three variables as close as possible to a 'best fit', where they all align on the same level in the spectrum. While there may be long-term benefits to be achieved from re-defining the task (eg job enlargement) or from developing the subordinates, in the short term the most easily changed variable is often the leader's style.

	The leader	The subordinates	The task
Tight	Preference for autocratic style, high estimation of his own capabilities and a low estimation of his subordinates. Dislikes uncertainty.	Low opinion of own abilities, do not like uncertainty in their work and like to be ordered. They regard their work as trivial; past experience in work leads to acceptance of orders, cultural factors lean them towards autocratic/dictatorial leaders.	Job requires no initiative, is routine and repetitive or has a certain outcome; short time scale for completion. Trivial tasks.
Flexible	Preference for democratic style, confidence in his subordinates, dislikes stress, accepts reasonable risk and uncertainty.	High opinion of own abilities; like challenging, important work; prepared to accept uncertainty and longer time scales for results; cultural factors favour independence.	Important tasks with a longer timescale; problem-solving or decision-making involved, complex work.

(The spectrum runs from Tight to Flexible)

4.3 Hersey and Blanchard: Situational leadership

In their influential **Situational Leadership** model, **Hersey and Blanchard** ('Life cycle theory of leadership', *Training and Development Journal*, 1969) focused on the **readiness of the team members** to perform a given task, in terms of their **task ability** (experience, knowledge and skills) and **willingness** (whether they have the confidence, commitment and motivation) to complete the task successfully.

(a) **High-readiness** (R4) teams are able and willing. They do not need directive or supportive leadership: the most appropriate leadership style may be a joins or 'delegating' (S4) style.

(b) **High-moderate readiness** (R3) teams are able, but unwilling or insecure. They are competent, but require supportive behaviour to build morale: the most appropriate leadership style may be a consults or 'participating' (S3) style.

(c) **Low-moderate readiness** (R2) teams are willing and confident, but lacking ability. They require both directive and supportive behaviour to improve their task performance without damaging morale: the most appropriate leadership style may be a 'selling' (S2) style.

(d) **Low-readiness** (R1) teams are lacking ability and motivation/confidence. They require more directive behaviours in order to secure an adequate level of task performance: the most appropriate leadership style may be a 'telling' (S1) style.

This can be summed up as follows (drawn from Hersey and Blanchard).

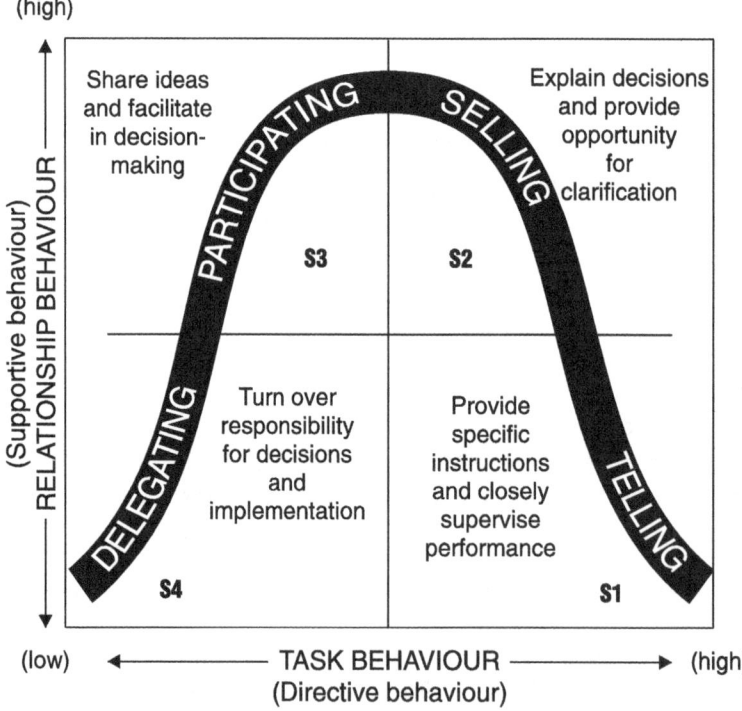

 **Question** — Hersey and Blanchard

Diagnose the 'readiness' of a work or study group of which you are a member. What sort of leadership is likely to be most effective, according to Hersey and Blanchard's model? What sort of leadership does your team leader actually exercise?

4.4 John Adair: Action-centred leadership

John Adair's model (variously called 'action-centred', 'situational' or 'functional', from his book *Action-Centred Leadership,* 1973) is part of the contingency school of thought, because it sees the leadership process in a context made up of three interrelated variables: task needs, the individual needs of group members and the needs of the group as a whole. These needs must be examined in the light of the whole situation, which dictates the relative priority that must be given to each of the three sets of needs. Effective leadership is a process of identifying and acting on that priority, exercising a relevant cluster of roles to meet the various needs.

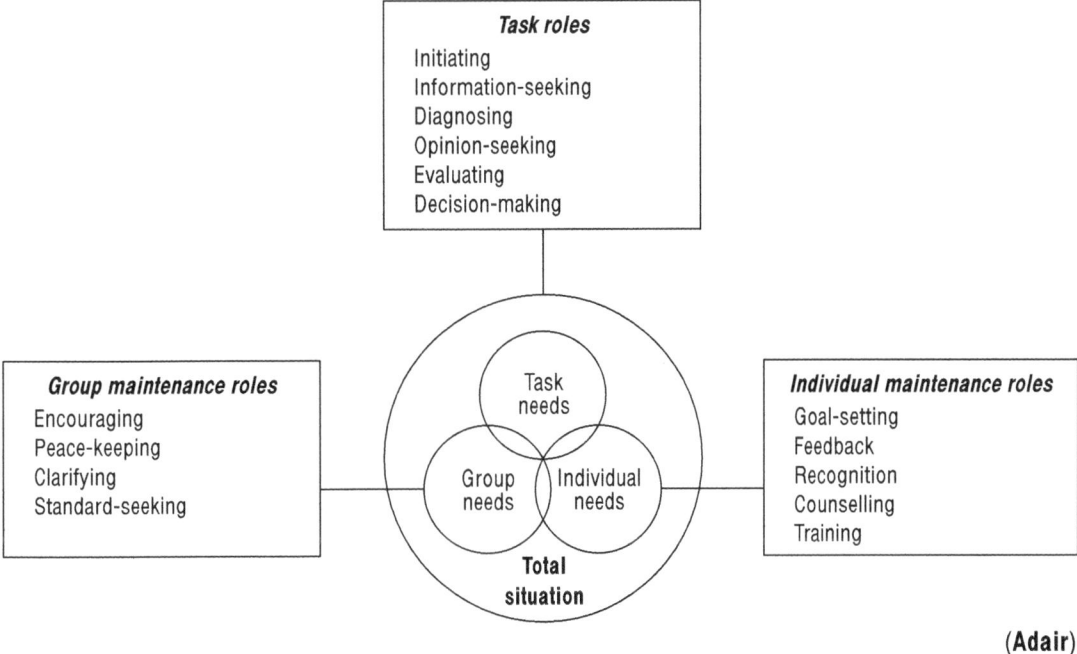

(Adair)

Adair argued that the common perception of leadership as 'decision-making' was inadequate to describe the range of action required by this complex situation.

He developed a scheme of leadership training based on eight leadership 'activities' which are applied to the task, the team and the individual: hence, the **'action-centred leadership'** model.

- Defining the task
- Planning
- Briefing
- Controlling
- Evaluating
- Motivating
- Organising
- Setting an example

4.5 An appraisal of contingency theory

Contingency theory usefully makes people aware of the factors affecting the choice of leadership style. However:

(a) Key variables such as task structure, power and relationships are difficult to measure

(b) Contingency theories do not always take into account the need for the leader to have relevant technical competence

Perhaps the major difficulty for any leader seeking to apply contingency theory, however, is actually to modify his or her behaviour as the situation changes.

5 Leadership in modern organisations

The principles of leadership suggested by early writers and theorists remain valid today, but other ideas have been developed that apply more directly to the modern business environment. Some of these ideas are described here. They are the concept of emotional intelligence in leaders, ideas about team leadership and moral leadership, and the contingency approach to leadership theory.

FAST FORWARD

Leadership ideas that apply more directly to the modern business environment include:
- **Emotional** leadership
- **Team** leadership
- **Moral** leadership

5.1 Emotional leadership

Some studies have concluded that emotional intelligence (EI) is a better indicator of an individual's leadership qualities than expertise or measures of intelligence (IQ). Without EI, a person may be exceptionally well trained and might have a highly analytical mind, a long-term vision and an endless supply of terrific ideas, but they will still not make a great leader.

Good leaders demonstrate EI by exhibiting all five of the following component elements:

(a) Self-awareness: Demonstrated by self-confidence, the ability to make realistic self-assessments and a self-deprecating sense of humour

(b) Self-management: Demonstrated by trustworthiness and integrity and willingness to accept change

(c) Self-motivation: Demonstrated by a strong drive to achieve, optimism and a high level of commitment to the organisation

(d) Empathy: Demonstrated by expertise in building and retaining talent in subordinates, a sensitivity to cross-cultural issues and providing a service to clients and customers

(e) Social skills: Demonstrated by an ability to lead efforts to make changes, skills in persuading others and expertise in building and leading teams

5.2 Team leadership

Leadership is provided within a team. Team leadership is important in organisations that have a team culture, for example organisations in which there is extensive use of project work. The role of team leaders includes coaching, facilitating, handling disciplinary problems, reviewing team/individual performance, training and communication. These roles tend to be generic for all types of leader, not just team leaders. However, team leaders focus on two priorities, namely managing the team's relationships with other people outside the team, and facilitating the 'team process.' These two priorities are further divided into four specific roles.

(a) Team leaders liaise with people outside the team, such as senior management, other teams within the organisation, customers and suppliers.

(b) Team leaders are 'trouble-shooters' who resolve problems (of a non-technical nature) faced by their team.

(c) Team leaders are conflict managers. When conflicts arise, the team leader deals with the conflict by identifying the cause or source of conflict, who is involved, and what are the options for resolving the problem.

(d) Team leaders are coaches who clarify expectations and roles of team members, teach, offer support, act as a cheer leader and do anything else that would make team members improve their work performance.

5.3 Moral leadership

Leadership is not free from moral or ethical values. Leaders may act ethically or unethically.

(a) Unethical leaders are more likely to use charisma to enhance their power over their followers, and to direct their power towards self-serving ends.

(b) Unethical business leaders might abuse their power when they give themselves large salaries and bonuses, when at the same time they seek to cut costs by laying off long-time workers.

Ethical leaders use their charisma in a socially constructive way to provide benefits to others. The effectiveness of an individual as a leader should be judged by the means the leader uses to achieve their goals and the moral content of these goals. Are the changes that the leader seeks for the organisation morally acceptable?

For example:

- Is the leader effective if they build an organisation's success by selling products that damage the health of its users?

- Is a military leader successful by winning a war that should not have been fought in the first place?

6 Power and authority

Organisations have a large number of different activities to be co-ordinated, and large numbers of people whose co-operation and support is necessary for a manager to get anything done. As you have probably noticed if you have worked for any length of time, organisations rarely run as clockwork, and all depend on the directed energy of those within them.

6.1 Power

FAST FORWARD

Power is the ability to get things done. There are many types of power in organisations: position or **legitimate power**, expert power, personal power, resource power and negative power are examples.

Key term

Power is the **ability** to get things done.

Power is not something a person 'has' in isolation: it is exercised over other individuals or groups, and – to an extent – depends on their recognising the person's power over them.

6.1.1 Types of power

French and **Raven** in their study (*The Bases of Social Power*, 1959) classified power into six types or sources.

Type of power	Description
Coercive power	The power of physical force or punishment. Physical power is rare in business organisations, but intimidation may feature, eg in workplace bullying.
Reward (or resource) power	Based on access to or control over valued resources. For example, managers have access to information, contacts and financial rewards for team members. The amount of resource power a person has depends on the scarcity of the resource, how much the resource is valued by others, and how far the resource is under the manager's control.
Legitimate (or position) power	Associated with a particular position in the organisation. For example, a manager has the power to authorise certain expenses, or issue instructions, because the authority to do so has been formally delegated to her.
Expert power	Based on experience, qualifications or expertise. For example, accountants have expert power because of their knowledge of the tax system. Expert power depends on others recognising the expertise in an area which they need or value.
Referent (or personal) power	Based on force of personality, or 'charisma', which can attract, influence or inspire other people.
Negative power	The power to disrupt operations: for example, by industrial action, refusal to communicate information, or sabotage.

Question — Power

The finance director of ABC Co has strong relationships with the company's owners, employees and customers. She generates strong feelings of loyalty and commitment among the people that currently work for her and they know that she is immensely capable.

What type of power does he have?

A   Legitimate
B   Referent
C   Coercive
D   Expert

Answer

B   Referent

The finance director has referent power because her staff are loyal and committed to her and she fosters strong relationships.

Her power goes beyond the legitimate power given by her position. Her likeability is emphasised, which suggests no coercion is involved. There is no mention of her expertise.

6.2 Authority

FAST FORWARD **Authority** is related to position power. It is the right to take certain decisions within certain boundaries.

Key term

Authority is the **right** to do something, or to ask someone else to do it and expect it to be done. Authority is thus another word for position or legitimate power.

Managerial authority is exercised in such areas as:

(a) **Making decisions within the scope of authority** given to the position. For example, a supervisor's authority is limited to his/her team and with certain limits. For items of expenditure more than a certain amount, the supervisor may have to go to someone else up the hierarchy.

(b) **Assigning tasks** to subordinates, and expecting satisfactory performance of these tasks.

Question
Types of power

What types of power are being exercised in the following case?

Aamna is an accountant supervising a team of eight technicians. She has to submit bank reconciliation statements every week to the chief accountant. However, the company runs four different bank accounts and Aamna gets a team member, Dave, to do it for her. Aamna asks Isabella to deal with the purchase ledger – the company obtains supplies from all over the world, and Isabella, having worked once for an international bank, is familiar with letters of credit and other documentation involved with overseas trade. Isabella has recently told Aamna that Maphia Ltd, a supplier, should not be paid because of problems with the import documentation, even though Aamna has promised Maphia to pay them. Aamna is getting increasingly annoyed with Sandra, who seems to be leaving her typing until last, although she says she has piles of other work to do. 'Like reading the newspaper,' thinks Aamna, who is considering pulling rank by giving her an oral warning.

Answer

Aamna exercises position power because she has the right, given to her by the chief accountant, to get staff members, such as Dave, to do bank reconciliations. Dave does not do bank recs because of Aamna's personality or expertise, but because of the simple fact that Aamna is his boss. Aamna also exercises position power by getting Isabella to do the purchase ledger.

However, Isabella exercises expert power because she knows more about import/export documentation than Aamna. She does not have the authority to stop the payment to Maphia, and Aamna can ignore what she says, but that would be a bad decision.

Sandra is exercising negative power as far as Aamna is concerned, although she is claiming, perhaps, to exercise resource power – her time is a scarce resource.

6.2.1 Line and staff authority

When analysing the types of authority which a manager or a department may have, the terms **line**, **staff** and **functional authority** are often used.

Key terms

> **Line authority** is the authority a manager has over a subordinate, down the vertical chain (or line) of command.
>
> **Staff authority** is the authority one manager or department may have in giving specialist advice to another manager or department, over which there is no line authority. Staff authority does not entail the right to make or influence decisions in the advisee department. An example might be the HR department advising the accounts manager on selection interviewing methods.
>
> **Functional authority** is a hybrid of line and staff authority, whereby the technostructure manager or department has the authority, in certain circumstances, to direct, design or control activities or procedures of another department. An example is where a finance manager has authority to require timely reports from line managers.

Question — Line and staff authority

What sort of authority is exercised:

(a) By the financial controller over the chief accountant?
(b) By the production manager over the production workforce?
(c) By the financial controller over the production manager?

Answer

(a) and (b) are both examples of line authority.
(c) is staff or perhaps functional authority.

There are inevitable tensions involved in asserting staff authority.

Problem	Possible solution
The technostructure can **undermine** the **line managers'** authority, by empire building.	Clear demarcations of line, staff and functional authority should be created.
Lack of seniority: middle line managers may be more senior in the hierarchy than technostructure advisers.	Use functional authority (via policies and procedures). Experts should be seen as a resource, not a threat.
Expert managers may **lack realism**, going for technically perfect but commercially impractical solutions.	Technostructure planners should be fully aware of operational issues and communicate regularly with the middle line.
Technostructure experts **lack responsibility** for the success of their ideas.	Technostructure experts should be involved in implementing their suggestions and share accountability for outcomes.

7 Responsibility and accountability

7.1 Responsibility

FAST FORWARD

Responsibility is the obligation a person has to fulfil a task they have been given. Responsibility can be delegated, but the person delegating responsibility still remains accountable to his or her boss for completion of the task.

Key terms

Responsibility is the **obligation** a person has to fulfil a task, which they have been given.

Accountability is a person's **liability** to be called to account for the fulfilment of tasks they have been given.

The definitions given above are useful because the term 'responsibility' is used in two ways.

(a) A person is said to be responsible **for** a piece of work when he or she is required to ensure that the work is done.

(b) The same person is said to be responsible **to** a superior when he or she is given work by that superior: in this sense, the term 'accountable' is often used.

One is thus accountable to a superior for a piece of work for which one is responsible.

The principle of **delegation** (which we discuss in the next section) is that a manager may make subordinates **responsible for** work, but remains **accountable to** his or her own superior for ensuring that the work is done. Appropriate decision-making **authority** must be delegated together with the delegated responsibility.

7.2 Responsibility/authority mismatch

FAST FORWARD

Authority/responsibility mismatch or **ambiguity** is stressful for the individual.

In practice, matters are rarely clear-cut, and in many organisations responsibility and authority are:

	Comments
Not clear	When the organisation is doing something new or in a different way, its existing rules and procedures may be out-of-date or unable to cope with the new development. Various people may try to 'empire build'. The managers may not have designed the organisation very well.
Shifting	In large organisations there may be real conflict between different departments; or the organisation may, as it adapts to its environment, need to change.

Authority without responsibility is a recipe for arbitrary and irresponsible behaviour: the person has the right to make decisions – without being held accountable for them.

Responsibility without authority places a subordinate in an impossible and stressful position: they are held accountable for results over which they have no control.

Question — Responsibility and authority

You have just joined a small accounts department. The financial controller keeps a very close eye on expenditure and, being prudent, believes that nothing should be spent that is not strictly necessary. She has recently gone on a three-week holiday to Venezuela. You have been told that you need to prepare management accounts, and for this you have to obtain information from the payroll department in two weeks' time. This is standard procedure. However, there are two problems. One of the other people in your department has gone sick, and a temporary replacement will be needed very shortly. The personnel department say: 'We need a staff requisition from the financial controller before we can get in a temp. Sorry, you'll just have to cancel your weekend'. The payroll department is happy to give you the information you need – except directors' salaries, essential for the accounts to be truly accurate.

What is the underlying cause of the problem and what, in future, should you ask the financial controller to do to put it right?

Answer

The immediate problem is that the financial controller should have considered these issues before she went to Venezuela. The underlying cause, as far as you are concerned, is that you have responsibility to do a task but without the authority – to obtain all the information you need and to hire a temp – to do the job. In future the financial controller should, when delegating the task, delegate the authority to do it.

8 Delegation

Key term

Delegation of authority is the process whereby a superior gives to a subordinate part of his or her own authority to make decisions.

Note that delegation can only occur if the superior initially possesses the authority to delegate; a subordinate cannot be given organisational authority to make decisions unless it would otherwise be the superior's right to make those decisions.

8.1 Why delegate?

FAST FORWARD

Delegation is necessary for division of labour and technical/managerial specialisation.

Managers must delegate some authority for four reasons.

(a) There are **physical and mental limitations** to the work load of any individual or group in authority.

(b) Managers need time to concentrate on **higher-level tasks** (such as planning), which only they are competent (and paid) to do.

(c) The **increasing size and complexity** of some organisations calls for specialisation, both managerial and technical.

(d) Delegated authority contributes to the **job satisfaction and development** of lower levels of employees.

However, by delegating authority to assistants, the manager takes on two extra tasks:

- **Monitoring** their performance
- **Co-ordinating** the efforts of different assistants

8.2 How to delegate

FAST FORWARD

Successful delegation requires that people have the right skills and the authority to do the job, and are given feedback.

The process of delegation can be outlined as follows.

Step 1 **Specify performance**: the goals and standards expected of the subordinate, keeping in mind his or her level of expertise.

Step 2 **Formally assign tasks** to the subordinate, who should formally agree to do them.

Step 3 **Allocate resources and authority** to the subordinate to enable him or her to carry out the delegated tasks at the expected level of performance.

Step 4 **Back off** and allow the subordinate to perform the delegated tasks.

Step 5 **Maintain contact**, to review progress made, make constructive criticism and be available to give help and advice if requested.

8.3 When to delegate

The decision of when to delegate is equally important.

(a) Is the **acceptance of staff affected** required for morale, relationships or ease of implementation of the decision? (If so, it may be worth involving them in the decision.)

(b) Is the **quality of the decision** most important? (Many technical/financial decisions may be of this type, and should be retained by the manager if he or she alone has the knowledge and experience to make them.)

(c) Is the **expertise or experience of assistants** relevant or necessary to the task, and will it enhance the quality of the decision? (If so, it may be worth involving them in the decision.)

(d) Can trust be placed in the **competence and reliability of assistants**? (If not, it will be difficult to delegate effectively.)

8.4 Upward delegation

In instances where **reference upwards** to the manager's own superior (upward delegation) may be necessary, the manager should consider:

(a) Whether the decision is **relevant** to the superior: will it have any impact on the boss's area of responsibility, such as strategy, staffing, or the departmental budget?

(b) Whether the superior has **authority or information** relevant to the decision that the manager does not possess: for example, authority over issues which affect other departments or interdepartmental relations, or information only available at senior levels.

(c) The **political climate** of the organisation: will the superior expect to be consulted, and resent any attempt to make the decision without his authority?

8.5 Problems of delegation

FAST FORWARD

> Successful delegation requires skill training, cultural support and resolution of the **'trust-control' dilemma**.

Many managers are **reluctant to delegate** and attempt to handle many routine matters themselves in addition to their higher-level tasks, because of:

(a) **Low confidence and trust** in the abilities of their staff: the suspicion that 'if you want it done well, you have to do it yourself'.

(b) The burden of **accountability for the mistakes of subordinates**, aggravated by (a) above.

(c) A **desire to 'stay in touch'** with the department or team – both in terms of workload and staff – particularly if the manager does not feel 'at home' in a new management role.

(d) **Feeling threatened**. An unwillingness to admit that assistants have developed to the extent that they could perform some of the manager's duties. The manager may feel threatened by this sense of 'redundancy'.

(e) **Poor control and communication systems** in the organisation, so that the manager feels he has to do everything himself, if he is to retain real control and responsibility for a task, and if he wants to know what is going on.

(f) An **organisational culture** that has failed to reward or recognise effective delegation, so that the manager may not realise that delegation is positively regarded (rather than being seen as shirking responsibility).

(g) **Lack of understanding** of what delegation involves – ie not giving assistants total control, or making the manager himself redundant.

(h) **Lack of training** and development of managers in delegation skills and related areas (such as assertiveness and time management).

Handy (*Understanding Organisations,* 1993) describes a **trust-control dilemma** in a superior-subordinate relationship as:

$$T + C = Y$$

where T = the trust the superior has in the subordinate, and the trust which the subordinate feels the superior has in them

C = the degree of control exercised by the superior over the subordinate

Y = a constant, unchanging value

The less the superior feels able to trust the subordinate, the more control (s)he will exercise. The more trustworthy the subordinate, the less control will be needed.

8.6 Overcoming the reluctance of managers to delegate

Encouraging managers to delegate therefore partly involves increasing trust.

(a) **Train the subordinates** so that they are capable of handling delegated authority in a responsible way.

(b) Have a system of **open communications** between the manager and subordinates. If the subordinate is given all the information needed to do the job, and if the manager is kept informed of progress or problems:

  (i) The subordinate will make better-informed decisions.
  (ii) The manager will not need to exercise constant close control.

(c) **Ensure that a system of control is established**. If responsibility and accountability are monitored at all levels of the management hierarchy, the risks of relinquishing authority and control to subordinates are significantly lessened.

In addition, managers should be trained (or coached by their own superiors) in delegation skills, and should be recognised and rewarded for positive and effective delegation.

9 Empowerment

FAST FORWARD

Empowerment takes the process of delegation further. Its advantages are not simply that it releases managers to do more important things, but that front line staff closest to customers are able to take decisions concerning them.

Empowerment and delegation are related.

Key term

Empowerment is the current term for making workers (and particularly work teams) responsible for achieving, and even setting, work targets, with the freedom to make decisions about how they are to be achieved.

9.1 The context of empowerment

Empowerment goes in hand-in-hand with:

(a) **Delayering**, or cutting the number of levels (and managers) in the chain of command, since responsibility previously held by middle managers is, in effect, being given to operational workers.

(b) **Flexibility**, since giving responsibility to the people closest to the products and customer encourages responsiveness – and cutting out layers of communication, decision-making and reporting speeds up the process.

(c) **New technology**, since there are more 'knowledge workers'. Such people need less supervision, being better able to identify and control the means to clearly understood ends. Better information systems also remove the mystique and power of managers as possessors of knowledge and information in the organisation.

9.2 The effects of empowerment

The change in organisation structure and culture as a result of empowerment can be shown in the diagram below.

Traditional hierarchical structure: fulfilling management requirements

Empowerment structure: supporting workers in serving the customer

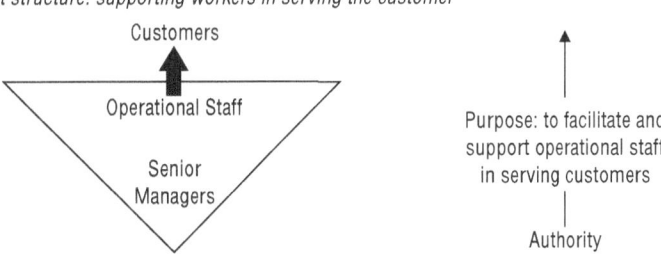

The argument for empowerment, in a nutshell, is that by empowering workers (or 'decentralising' control of business units, or devolving/delegating responsibility, or removing levels in hierarchies that restrict freedom), not only will the job be done more effectively, but the people who do the job will get more out of it.

Chapter roundup

- The terms 'leadership' and 'management' are often used in the same way, with the same meaning. However, a distinction can be made between management and leadership.
- There are many different definitions of **leadership**. Key themes (which are also used to distinguish leadership from management) include: interpersonal influence; securing willing commitment to shared goals; creating direction and energy; and an orientation to change.
- **Key leadership skills** may be identified in a range of interpersonal and business areas.
- Bennis suggested that a leader innovates and develops, whereas a manager administers and controls.
- Leadership offers key **benefits** in a competitive, turbulent environment: activating commitment, setting direction, developing people and energising and supporting change.
- There are three basic **schools of leadership theory**: trait theories, style theories and contingency theories.
- Early theories suggested that there are certain personality characteristics common to 'great men' or successful leaders. In other words, '**leaders are born, not made**'.
- **Leadership styles** are clusters of leadership behaviour that are used in different ways in different situations. While there are many different classifications of style, they mainly relate to the extent to which the leader is focused primarily on task/performance (directive behaviour) or relationships/people (supportive behaviour). Key style models include:
    - The **Ashridge Model**: tells, sells, consults, joins
    - **Likert**: exploitative authoritative, benevolent authoritative, consultative, participative
    - **Lewin, Lippitt and White**: autocratic, democratic, *laissez-faire*
    - **Blake and Mouton's Managerial Grid**: concern for task, concern for people
- Leaders need to adapt their style to the needs of the team and situation. This is the basis of **contingency approaches** such as:
    - **Fiedler**'s 'psychologically close' and 'psychologically distant' styles
    - **Hersey and Blanchard**'s 'situational leadership' model
    - **John Adair**'s 'action-centred' leadership model
    - **Handy**'s 'best fit' model
- Leadership ideas that apply more directly to the modern business environment include:
    - **Emotional** leadership
    - **Team** leadership
    - **Moral** leadership
- **Power** is the ability to get things done. There are many types of power in organisations: position or **legitimate power**, expert power, personal power, resource power and negative power are examples.
- **Authority** is related to position power. It is the right to take certain decisions within certain boundaries.
- **Responsibility** is the obligation a person has to fulfil a task they have been given. Responsibility can be delegated, but the person delegating responsibility still remains accountable to his or her boss for completion of the task.
- **Authority/responsibility mismatch** or **ambiguity** is stressful for the individual.
- **Delegation** is necessary for division of labour and technical/managerial specialisation.
- **Successful delegation** requires that people have the right skills and the authority to do the job, and are given feedback.
- Successful delegation requires skill training, cultural support and resolution of the '**trust-control**' **dilemma**.
- **Empowerment** takes the process of delegation further. Its advantages are not simply that it releases managers to do more important things, but that front line staff closest to customers are able to take decisions concerning them.

Quick quiz

1. What is the difference between a manager and a leader?

2. A 'manager' might also be identified as a transformational leader. True or False?

3. If a manager confers with subordinates, takes their views and feelings into account, but retains the right to make a final decision, this is a:

    A   Tells style
    B   Sells style
    C   Consults style
    D   Joins style

4. What is the most effective style suggested by **Blake and Mouton**'s Managerial Grid? Why is it so effective in theory, and why might it not be effective in practice?

5. **John Adair** formulated the:

    A   Best fit model of leadership
    B   Action-centred model of leadership
    C   Follower-readiness model of leadership
    D   Trait theory of leadership

6. Which of the following is likely to be beneficial in an organisation that carries out mostly project-based work?

    A   Emotional leadership
    B   Team leadership
    C   Moral leadership
    D   Management

7. Power arising from an individual's formal position in the organisation is called:

    A   Referent power
    B   Legitimate power
    C   Expert power
    D   Resource power

8. Give an example of negative power.

9. Why might functional authority be a good thing for the organisation?

10. Why can't accountability be delegated?

11. Why are there problems in determining authority and responsibility?

12. List the stages in the process of delegation.

13. List some problems in delegation.

14. 'Empowerment' is equivalent to the centralisation of authority. True or False?

PART A   MANAGEMENT: NATURE, EVOLUTION AND APPROACHES

Answers to quick quiz

1. See Section 1.1 for a full range of points.

2. False: Management is identified with 'transactional' leadership.

3. C: Make sure you can define the other styles as well.

4. 9.9. It is effective if there is sufficient time and resources to attend fully to people's needs, if the manager is good at dealing with people and if the people respond. It is ineffective when a task has to be completed in a certain way or by a certain deadline, whether or not people like it.

5. B: (You should be able to identify A as the work of **Handy**, and C as the work of **Hersey and Blanchard**.)

6. B: Team leadership is important in organisations that have a team culture, for example organisations in which there is extensive use of project work.

7. B: (Or 'position' power)

8. Going on strike; refusal to communicate; withhold information; delaying etc

9. Because it is exercised impersonally, impartially and automatically (avoiding the political problems of staff authority) while taking advantage of expertise.

10. Because the delegator has been given the task by their own boss

11. Because the boundaries are often unclear and/or shifting

12. Specify performance levels; formally assign task; allocate resources and authority; back off; give feedback

13. Low trust, low competence, fear, worry about accountability

14. False. Empowerment implies decentralised (delegated) authority.

Management planning and decision-making

Strategic planning and management by objectives

Topic list	Syllabus reference
1 Strategic management	D2
2 Organisational objectives and targets	D2
3 Corporate strategy and financial strategy	D2
4 Stakeholder groups	D2
5 Objectives of business enterprises	D2
6 Financial objectives	D2
7 Non-financial objectives	D2
8 Personal objectives and targets	D2
9 Performance management	D2

Introduction

In Chapter 1, we noted that an organisation's basic purpose is 'the **controlled performance** of **collective goals**'. In this chapter, we look at what this means in practice for the strategic management of an organisation.

We start with the basic cycle of **planning and control**: a useful framework for looking at all kinds of management activity.

In **Section 2**, we look at the different levels and types of goals an organisation might have.

It is important to grasp the variety of organisational objectives – and the potential tension between them. It's not just about maximising profit! In **Section 7**, for example, we look at **non-financial objectives.**

Another key point is the **hierarchy** of objectives flowing from the overall corporate mission right down to the detailed day-to-day plans of individuals and teams: this is what keeps all the activity heading in the same direction.

PART B MANAGEMENT PLANNING AND DECISION-MAKING

1 Strategic management

Strategic or executive management involves the formulation and implementation of the strategies chosen by a company's top management on behalf of owners, based on consideration of available resources and assessment of the internal and external environments in which the company competes.

1.1 The strategic planning model

All organisations need to plan if they are going to maintain their direction and scope over the long term. Planning ensures that the organisation has clear goals. If organisations do not plan, they are liable to drift and lose their competitive advantage in a changing environment. Other reasons for planning include reduction of uncertainty and risk, and efficiency in the use of resources.

It involves the entire cycle of **planning and control**, at a **strategic** level, in the following steps:

- Strategic analysis
- Strategic choice
- Implementation of chosen strategies
- Review and control

Key term

> **Strategic planning** is the first step in strategic management, and is the systematic process of envisioning a desired future, and translating this vision into defined goals or objectives and a sequence of steps to achieve them.

Johnson, Scholes and Whittington (*Exploring Corporate Strategy*, 2005) define strategy as follows:

'**Strategy** is **the direction and scope** of an organisation over the **long term** which **achieves advantage** in a **changing environment** through its configuration of **resources and competences** with the aim of fulfilling **stakeholder expectations**.'

Taking the highlighted phrases out of this definition, we can expand them to indicate that there is general agreement on what constitutes the key elements of strategy.

Phrase	Comments
Direction and scope	Strategy gives at least an initial deliberate direction, range of activities and future for the company to aim at, even if environmental circumstances conspire to send it off course and demand management action.
Long term	Strategy is the long-term direction of an organisation. This long-term direction can include both planned strategy, and more incremental, emergent patterns of strategy.
Achieves advantage	Strategy affects the overall wellbeing of the organisation, and its position against competitors. For commercial organisations, strategy is ultimately a means to achieve a sustainable competitive advantage against its competitors.
Changing environment	Organisations are inextricably linked with their environments, and strategy can help organisations to cope with changes and complexity in those environments. An organisation needs to match its activities to its capabilities and the environment in which it operates.
Resources and competences	Strategies require processes to guide the effective utilisation of resources and competences in order to achieve competitive advantage. Strategies also require integration across functional and operational boundaries, and need to be supported by operational decisions.
Stakeholder expectations	Stakeholders (in particular shareholders) have their own interests in the organisation. Should the pursuit of shareholder wealth be the main concern of management? What about customers' expectations and satisfying market demand? And what about the organisation's employees?

To develop a business strategy, an organisation has to decide the following:
- What it is good at
- How the market might change
- How customer satisfaction can be delivered
- What might constrain its ability to realise its plan
- What should be done to minimise risk
- What actions should be put in place
- How to compete (eg in terms of cost, or quality)
- Where to compete (which geographical markets, and which market segments to compete in)

The context of strategy is very important. For example, small businesses tend to have limited resources and face strong competition. Large multinationals will have more resources, but have to make decisions about structure, resource allocation, and which markets to compete in. Any organisation also needs to decide the level of risk that it is prepared to accept.

Public sector and not-for-profit organisations are influenced by ideology, politics and a range of stakeholders.

1.2 Approaches to strategic planning

It is important to recognise that firms can take different approaches to their strategic planning, meaning that they prioritise different elements of strategic analysis. There are three main approaches to strategic planning:

Accounting-led: An organisation adopting an accounting-led approach starts by looking at its key stakeholders and their objectives (eg to increase pre-tax profits by x% per year, and earnings per share (EPS) by y% per year). The organisation then develops plans which are designed to achieve those objectives.

However, critics argue that such an approach to strategic planning is flawed because it doesn't take sufficient account of market conditions and the external environment, and places a greater focus on the interests of shareholders as opposed to other stakeholder groups.

Position-based approach: By contrast, an organisation adopting a position-based approach analyses its environment (eg markets and competitors; using PEST analysis and Porter's five forces) before setting its objectives and strategy. In this way, the organisation can try to ensure its strategic plans provide a good 'fit' with its environment.

Importantly, the external focus of the position-based approach should help organisations be aware of changes in their environments. Moreover, if an organisation is able to predict changes in advance of them happening, this could help the organisation plan how to deal with those changes rather than simply having to react to them.

(We look in more detail at the external environment in Chapter 5.)

Resource-based approach: Critics of the position-based approach argue that the extent of the changes in the environment make it very difficult for organisations to predict the future with any certainty. Therefore, rather than trying to focus on a 'fit' with the environment, organisations should focus their strategy on their own core competences and capabilities – what they are good at.

However, the potential flaw with this approach is that it is too inward-looking. For example, it would be little use an organisation being good at something if there is no longer a market demand for it. Equally, environmental changes may mean that the organisation's core competences are no longer a source of competitive advantage (for example, due to the emergence of new technologies or substitute products).

(We discuss resources, competences and capabilities in more detail in Chapter 4.)

PART B MANAGEMENT PLANNING AND DECISION-MAKING

1.3 The structure of strategic planning

FAST FORWARD

> The **rational model of strategic planning** involves strategic analysis, strategic choice and strategy implementation. It is a comprehensive approach to strategic management, suggesting a logical sequence which involves analysing the current situation, generating choices (relating to competitors, products and markets) and implementing the chosen strategies.

The **rational model** of strategic planning divides into a number of different stages: strategic **analysis**, strategic **choice** and strategy **implementation**. This is illustrated in the diagram below.

1.3.1 Strategic analysis

Strategic analysis can be viewed as understanding the **strategic position** of any organisation.

We can break down the strategic analysis stage of strategic planning into a series of steps:

	Stage	Comment	Key tools, models, techniques
Step 1	Mission and/or vision	Mission denotes values, the business's rationale for existing; vision refers to where the organisation intends to be in a few years' time	• Mission statement
Step 2	Goals	Interpret the mission to different stakeholders	• Stakeholder analysis
Step 3	Objectives	Quantified embodiments of mission	• Measures such as profitability, time scale, deadlines
Step 4	Environmental analysis	Identify opportunities and threats	• PEST analysis • Porter's five forces analysis; 'diamond' (competitive advantage of nations) • Scenario building
Step 5	Position audit or situation analysis	Identify strengths and weaknesses Firm's current resources, products, customers, systems, structure, results, efficiency, effectiveness	• Resource audit • Distinctive competence • Value chain • Product life cycle • BCG matrix • Marketing audit
Step 6	Corporate appraisal	Combines Steps 4 and 5	• SWOT analysis
Step 7	Gap analysis	Compares outcomes of Step 6 with Step 3	• Gap analysis

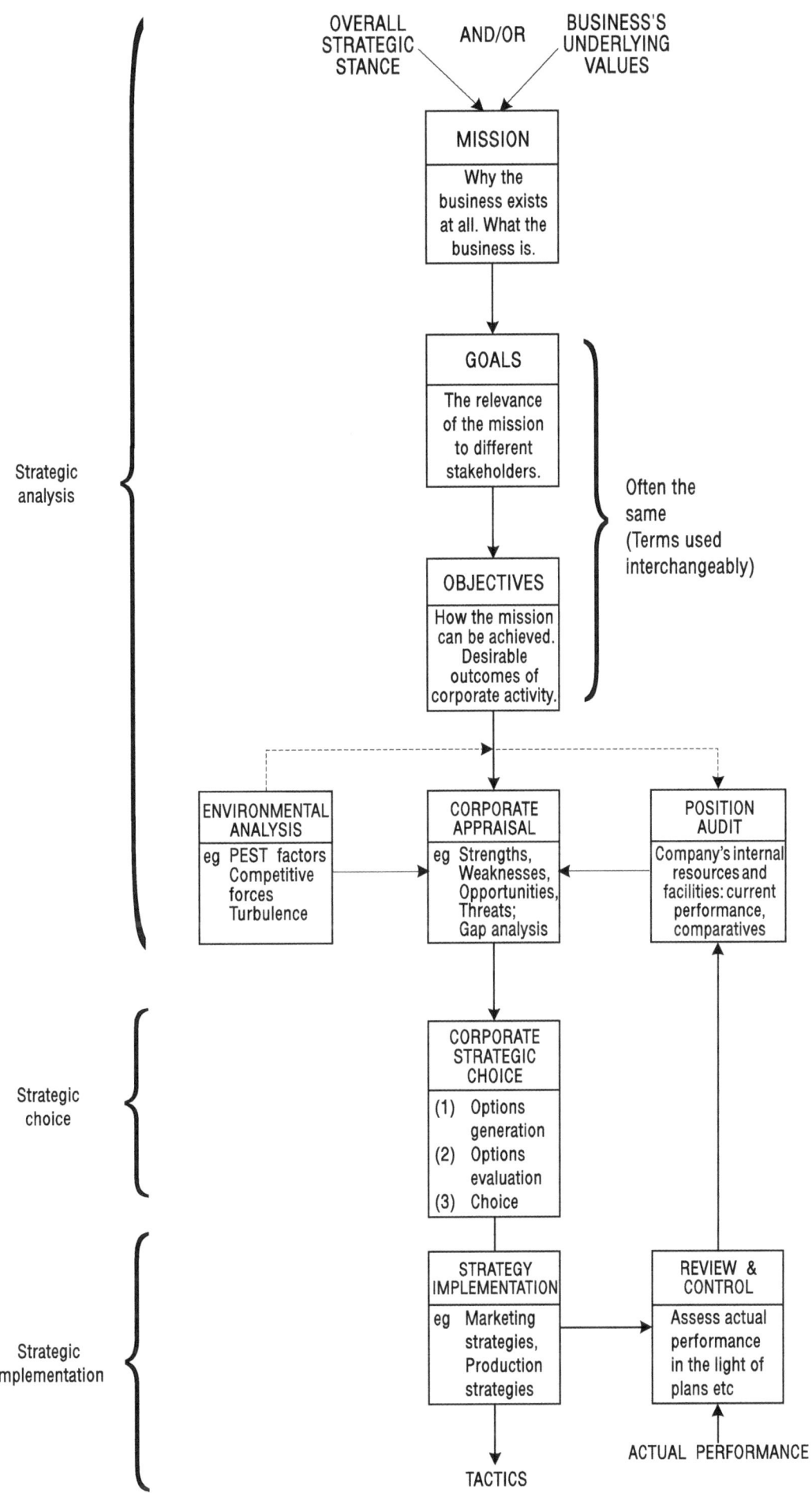

1.3.2 Strategic choice

Stage	Comment	Key tools, models, techniques
Strategic options generation	Come up with new ideas on how to compete (competitive advantage), where to compete and method of growth	• Value chain analysis • Scenario building • Acquisition vs organic growth
Strategic options evaluation	Normally, each strategy has to be evaluated on the basis of: • Acceptability • Suitability • Feasibility • Environmental fit	• Stakeholder analysis • Risk analysis • Decision-making tools such as decision trees, matrices, ranking and scoring methods • Financial measures (eg ROCE, DCF)
Strategy selection	Involves choosing between the alternative strategies. • **Competitive strategies** are the generic strategies for competitive advantage an organisation will pursue (which determine **how you compete**). • **Product-market strategies** (which markets you should enter or leave) determine **where you compete** and the direction of growth. • **Institutional strategies** (ie relationships with other organisations) determine the **method of growth**.	

1.3.3 Strategy implementation

Strategy implementation is the **conversion** of the **strategy into detailed plans or objectives** for operating units. In this respect, strategic implementation is a vital part of the strategic management process, because a strategy can only start delivering benefit to an organisation once it has been put into practice.

The **planning of implementation** has several aspects.

(a) **Resource** planning (ie finance, human resources) involves assessing the key tasks that need to be carried out and determining the timing of them.

(b) **Operations** planning looks at the systems employed to manage the organisation.

(c) **Organisation** structure and control systems may need to be changed. **Change** is often a critical component of strategy implementation, because organisations have to change in order to achieve their chosen strategies.

Johnson, Scholes and Whittington argue that the three elements of analysis, choice and implementation are interlinked and feed back on each other. For example, when an organisation starts to implement a strategy, it may discover things about its environment or capabilities that may in turn help it with future strategic analysis and choices.

1.3.4 Review and control

Ultimately, the success of any strategy comes from the results it delivers. However, it is equally important for an organisation to monitor and evaluate its progress towards its strategic objectives.

This not only highlights the need for performance measurement (eg key performance indicators (KPIs); comparing actual results to targets), but equally importantly, it also highlights the need to set budgets and targets in the first place in order to provide a benchmark to compare actual performance against.

1.4 Types of strategy

Corporate strategy is the highest level of strategy in an organisation, identifying the strategy for the organisation as a whole. For example, this might include setting the overall objectives for the organisation and identifying its corporate values, whether to enter a new industry or market, or to leave an existing industry/market.

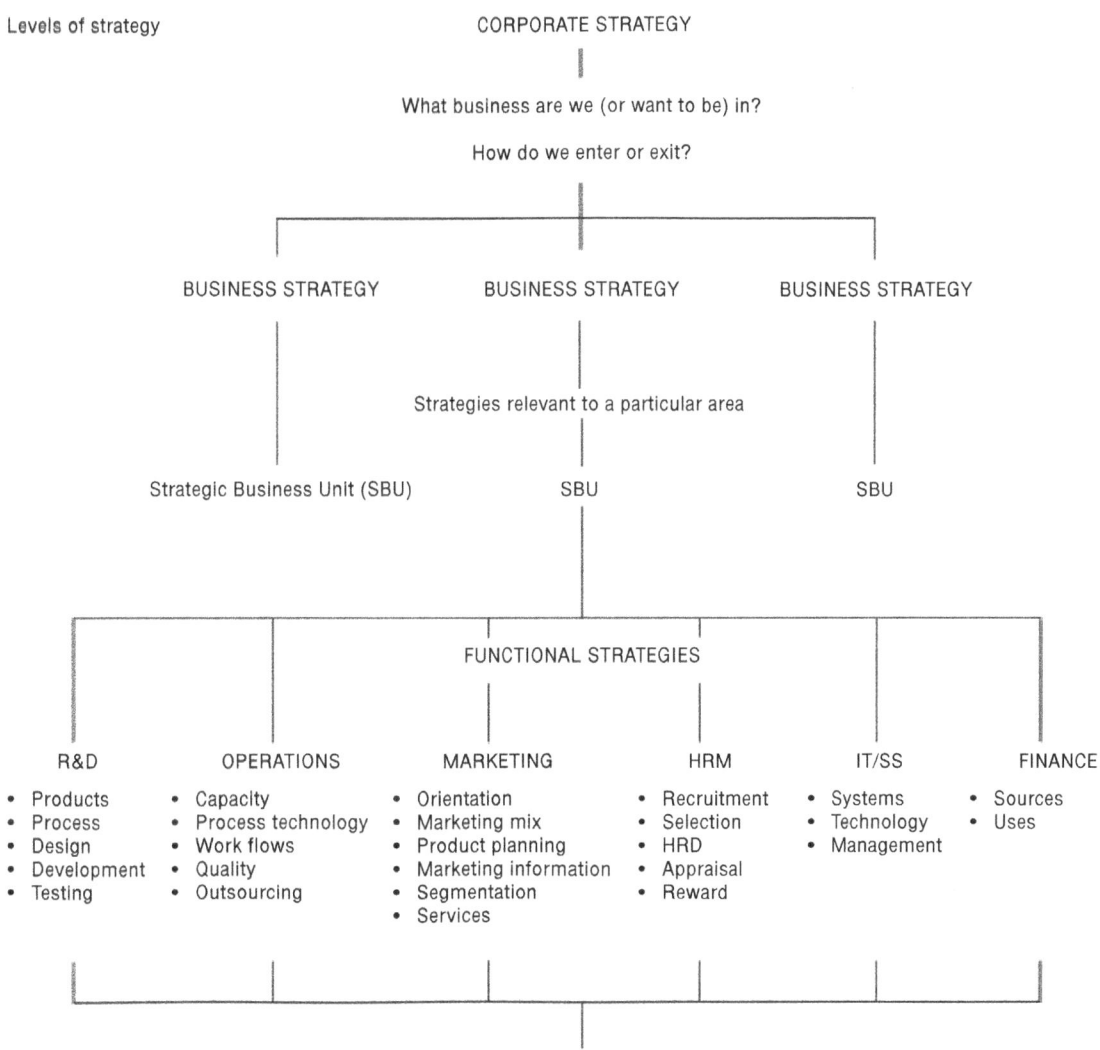

Defining aspects of corporate strategy

Characteristic	Comment
Scope of activities	Strategy and strategic management impact on the whole organisation: all parts of the business operation should support and further the strategic plan.
Environment	The organisation counters threats, and exploits opportunities, in the environment (customers, clients, competitors).
Resources	Strategy involves choices about allocating or obtaining corporate resources now and in future.
Values	The value systems of people with power in the organisation influence its strategy.
Timescale	Corporate strategy has a long-term impact.
Complexity	Corporate strategy involves uncertainty about the future, integrating the operations of the organisation and change.

Business strategy relates to how an organisation approaches a particular market, or the activity of a particular business unit. For example, this might include the way a business unit adapts to customer requirements or competitor's actions, and how it manages unique competences to compete successfully in specific markets.

While corporate strategy relates to an organisation as a whole, business strategy focuses **on strategic business units** (SBUs). Large, diversified firms usually have separate SBUs dealing with particular areas. Business strategy for such large organisations is strategy at the SBU level.

Operational and functional strategies involve decisions which are made at operational level and affect the day-to-day operation of the business. These decisions include marketing strategy, HR strategy, IT/IS strategy and so forth. The contributions of these different functions determine the success of the strategy.

Functional area	Comment
Human resources management	Secure personnel of the right skills in the right quantity at the right time, and to ensure that they have the right skills and values to promote the firm's overall goals
Marketing	Devising products and services, pricing, promoting and distributing them, in order to satisfy customer needs at a profit. Marketing and corporate strategies are interrelated
Production	Factory location, manufacturing techniques, outsourcing, and so on
Information systems	A firm's information systems are becoming increasingly important, as an item of expenditure, as administrative support and as a tool for competitive strength. Not all information technology applications are strategic, and the strategic value of IT will vary from case to case

A strategic plan is ultimately only likely to be successful if it is delivered effectively at an operational level. The strategic management process is therefore multi-layered.

1.5 The Anthony hierarchy of managerial activity

Reflecting what we have outlined above, Robert Anthony (*Planning and control systems: a framework for analysis,* 1965) classified managerial activity as follows.

(a) **Strategic management** (carried out by senior management) is concerned with direction setting, policy making and crisis handling. The time frame of decisions made at strategic management level would typically have implications for three to five years.

(b) **Tactical management** (carried out by middle management) is concerned with establishing means to the corporate ends, mobilising resources and innovating (finding new ways to achieve business goals). Decisions made at this level would have medium-term implications.

(c) **Operational management** (carried out by supervisors and operatives) is concerned with routine activities to carry out tactical plans. Decisions at this level would deal with day-to-day matters.

Question
Strategy creation

A consultant has told the board of ABC Ltd that its strategic planning process should result in determining strategy at all levels of an organisation. He has shared a document setting out how overall objectives are to be achieved, by specifying what is expected from specific functions, stores and departments.

What type of strategy has he created?

A   Corporate
B   Business
C   Functional
D   Competitive

Answer

C   Functional

Because the consultant has been specific about how functions, stores and departments' contributions will help the overall strategy, this is a functional strategy.

Corporate strategy is the setting of overall objectives; business strategy is the translation of those objectives into tasks at the business unit level. Competitive strategy considers how a company will respond to/beat its competition.

2 Organisational objectives and targets

2.1 Mission

FAST FORWARD

> The **mission** is the organisation's overall purpose and reason for existence. It has implications for the commercial strategy, the values of the organisation, and policies and actual standards of behaviour of the people within it.

Overall, the main direction of an organisation is set by its mission.

Key term

> **Mission** describes the organisation's function in society – what it exists to do, and for what reasons.

Mission has four elements:

Elements	Comments
Purpose	Why does the organisation exist and for whom (eg shareholders)?
Strategy	Mission provides the operational logic for the organisation: • What do we do? • How do we do it?
Policies and standards of behaviour	Mission should influence what people actually do and how they behave: the mission of a hospital is to save lives, and this affects how doctors and nurses interact with patients.
Values	What the organisation believes to be important: that is, its principles.

Mission statements vary enormously between organisations with respect to both their nature and scope. Some organisations have mission statements which are very general in nature and wide-ranging in their coverage, whereas other organisations have mission statements which are much more precise and include, for example, measurable objectives.

2.1.1 Purposes of a mission statement

Even though the mission can be very general, you can see it should have real implications for the policies and activities of the organisation, and how individuals go about what they do. The purposes of a mission statement include to provide:

- An overall framework for the objectives and direction of the organisation
- A framework which allows individuals and groups both within and outside of the organisation to understand what the organisation is about
- A way of differentiating a company from its major competitor
- A way of defining the business
- Inspiration and motivation to organisational members
- An overall control mechanism for the actions of the company and its major stakeholders

Overall, without mission statements, companies can lack direction.

2.1.2 Key factors affecting the development of mission statements

Because mission statements encompass the whole of an organisation and encompass both internal and external groups, they are influenced and affected by many factors, including the following:

- **Management values**: Inevitably, mission statements are affected by the values of senior management, so for example, senior managers who are more profit-orientated will reflect this in their company mission statements.
- **Stakeholder values and power**: Exactly how and to what extent these stakeholder values are reflected in mission statements will be affected by the relative power of the different stakeholder groups (shareholders, employees, suppliers and so on).
- **Legal issues**: Mission statements often need to reflect legal and regulatory requirements, for example with regard to, say, the approach to dealing with customers.
- **Ethical issues**: In addition to the regulatory issues referred to above, mission statements will tend to reflect the ethical values of the society/culture in which the organisation operates.
- **Corporate governance arrangements**: These determine to a large extent whom the organisation is there to serve and how the purposes and priorities between different and often conflicting groups should be decided. Corporate governance arrangements are closely related to the legal and regulatory factors previously described and vary according to the nature of the organisation, eg profit versus voluntary organisations.

Overall, without mission statements, companies can lack direction.

2.1.3 Vision

Vision is distinct from mission. It represents the organisation's aspiration towards achieving a future state or destination.

2.2 Goals, aims and objectives

FAST FORWARD

Goals give flesh to the mission. They can be quantified (**objectives**) or not quantified (**aims**). Most organisations use a combination of both. Quantified or specific objectives have SMART characteristics.

There are two types of goal:

- Non-operational, **qualitative** goals (**aims**)
- Operational, **quantitative** goals (**objectives**)

Characteristics	Example
Objectives are SMART • Specific • Measurable • Achievable • Relevant • Time-bounded	• Operational goal: cut costs • Objective: reduce budgeted expenditure on office stationery by 5% by 31 December 20X6

In practice, people often use the words goals, aims and objectives interchangeably.

Question — Aims and objectives

Most organisations establish closed or quantifiable objectives. Give reasons why aims (non-operational goals) might still be important.

Answer

Aims can be just as helpful. Customer satisfaction, for example, is not something which is achieved just once. Some goals are hard to measure and quantify, eg 'to retain technological leadership'. Quantified objectives are hard to change when circumstances change, as changing them looks like an admission of defeat. Aims may support greater flexibility.

2.3 The purpose of organisational objective setting

Objectives in these key areas should enable management to:

(a) **Implement** the mission, by outlining what needs to be achieved

(b) **Publicise** the direction of the organisation to managers and staff, so that they know where their efforts should be directed

(c) **Appraise** the validity of decisions about **strategies** (by assessing whether these are sufficient to achieve the stated objectives)

(d) **Assess and control actual performance**, as objectives can be used as targets for achievement

3 Corporate strategy and financial strategy

> **Strategy** is a course of action to achieve an objective. Strategies are set at the corporate, business and operational levels.
>
> To assist in the realisation of financial strategy, **financial accounting systems** ensure that the assets and liabilities of a business are **properly accounted for, and provide information about profits and so on** to shareholders and to other interested parties. **Management accounting systems** provide information specifically for the use of managers within an organisation.

3.1 Strategy

Strategy can be **short-term** or **long-term**, depending on the time horizon of the objective it is intended to achieve.

This definition also indicates that since strategy depends on objectives or targets, the obvious starting point for a study of corporate strategy and financial strategy is the **identification and formulation of objectives**.

3.2 What determines strategies?

The evolution of strategies can be seen as the result of:

(a) General and environmental influences
(b) The power and influence of stakeholder groups
(c) Economic and financial objectives
(d) Social responsibilities of the organisation

3.3 Environmental influences

General environmental influences consist of the following.

3.3.1 External influences

(a) The **values** of **society**
(b) The **influence** of **organised groups**, such as government departments, consumer groups and environmentalist groups

3.3.2 Nature of the business

(a) The **market situation** and **market conditions** it is in (eg depressed market, growth market)
(b) The **products** it makes
(c) The **technology** it uses (influencing its methods of operating, the skills of its employees and so on)

3.3.3 Organisation's culture

(a) Its **tradition** (history)
(b) Its **organisation** structure
(c) Its **management**/leadership style

3.4 Financial accounting and management accounting

Management information provides a common source from which information is drawn for two groups of people.

(a) **Financial accounts** are prepared for individuals **external** to an organisation: shareholders, customers, suppliers, tax authorities, employees.

(b) **Management accounts** are prepared for **internal** managers of an organisation.

3.5 Strategic financial management

Key term

> **Strategic financial management** can be defined as 'the identification of the possible strategies capable of maximising an organisation's net present value, the allocation of scarce capital resources among the competing opportunities and the implementation and monitoring of the chosen strategy so as to achieve stated objectives'.
> (CIMA Official Terminology, 2005)

Financial strategy depends on stated **objectives** or **targets**.

4 Stakeholder groups

FAST FORWARD

> Different groups of stakeholders have different objectives which can lead to conflicts between competing groups.
>
> - **Internal** – managers, employees
> - **Connected** – shareholders, banks, customers, suppliers
> - **External** – government, pressure groups, local communities
>
> By understanding the different stakeholders and their needs and goals, then an organisation can determine strategies to resolve stakeholder conflicts which may prevent an organisation from achieving its strategic objectives.

4.1 Objectives of stakeholder groups

When formulating and evaluating financial strategies, it is important to bear in mind the organisation's stakeholders. These are people or groups who have an interest in the organisation's activities. Depending on the precise relationship between the organisation and the stakeholder group the success of the financial strategy can be affected significantly by the stakeholder group.

The various groups of internal and external stakeholders of an organisation will have diverse goals. They will exercise different levels of influence on the organisation and, in some cases, will affect the organisation's financial strategy. For example, an organisation's lenders have significant legal rights that have to be fulfilled by an organisation. Failure on the company's part to satisfy their obligations in relation to this powerful stakeholder group could lead to the company being liquidated.

Key term

> **Stakeholders** are groups or individuals having a legitimate interest in the activities of an organisation, generally comprising customers, employees, the community, shareholders, suppliers and lenders.

A summary of typical stakeholders is provided in the following diagram:

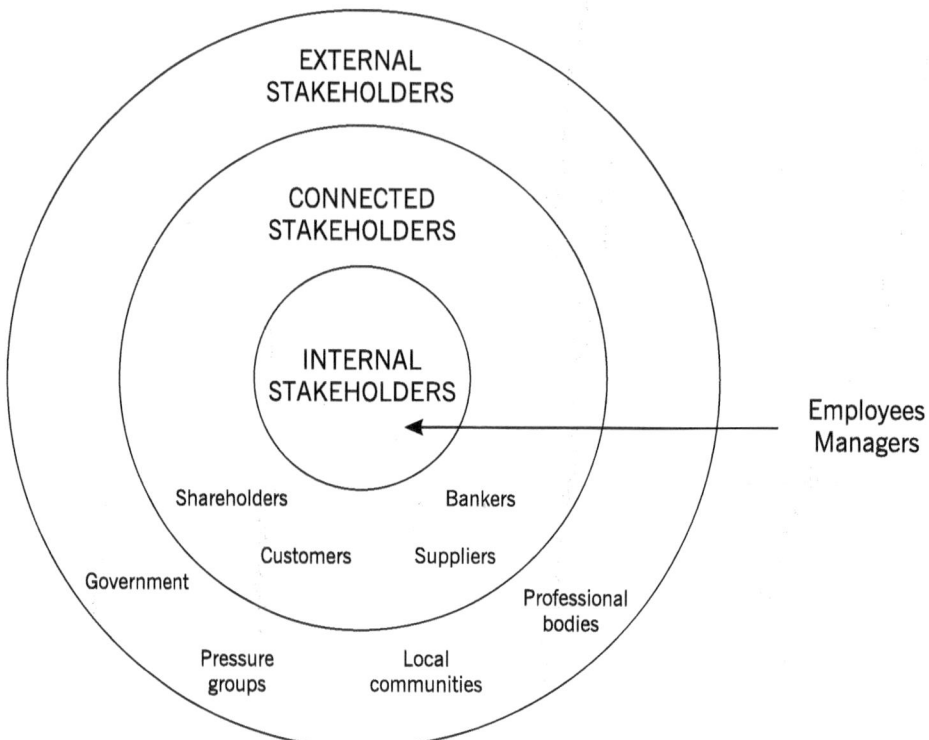

The various groups of stakeholders in a firm will have different goals which will depend in part on the situation of the organisation. The following table is a summary of wider stakeholder objectives:

Stakeholder goals	
Shareholders	Providers of risk capital aim to maximise wealth
Suppliers	Often, other businesses aim to be paid full amount by date agreed, but want to continue long-term trading relationship, and so may accept later payment.
Long-term lenders	Wish to receive payments of interest and capital on loan by due date for repayment
Employees	Maximise rewards paid to them in salaries and benefits, also prefer continuity in employment
Government	Political objectives such as sustained economic growth and high employment
Community	Wish to have a good 'corporate neighbour'. Source of stable employment and income for the local community; economic regeneration
Management	Maximising their own rewards

The actions of stakeholder groups in pursuit of their various goals can exert influence on strategy. The **greater** the **power** of the **stakeholder**, the greater their influence will be.

Many managers acknowledge that the interests of some stakeholder groups (eg themselves and employees) should be recognised and provided for, even if this means that the interests of shareholders might be adversely affected. Not all stakeholder group interests can be given specific attention in the decisions of management, but those stakeholders for whom management recognises and accepts a responsibility are referred to as **constituents** of the firm.

All organisations have a range of stakeholders or stakeholder groups. Some stakeholders may be relatively passive or lack influence. However, some organisations have stakeholders whose influence can be disruptive of the achievement of strategic goals.

4.2 Stakeholder objectives

The **stakeholder view** is particularly important in the business context, where shareholders own the business but employees, customers and government also have particularly strong claims to having their interests considered.

4.2.1 Stakeholder objectives

The following are some examples of stakeholders' objectives. These examples are not intended to be comprehensive, more to demonstrate why organisations are driven to improve business performance, adapt to external markets or innovate and diversify.

(a) **Employees and managers**

    (i)   Job security (over and above legal protection)
    (ii)   Good conditions of work (above minimum safety standards)
    (iii) Job satisfaction
    (iv) Career development and relevant training
    (v)   Personal achievement

(b) **Customers**

    (i)   Products of a certain quality at a reasonable price
    (ii)   Products that should last a certain number of years
    (iii) A product or service that specifically meets customer needs
    (iv) A product or service which is new, innovative or provides a seamless customer experience

(c) **Suppliers**: Regular orders in return for reliable delivery and good service

(d) **Shareholders**: Long-term wealth enhancement within acceptable risk levels

(e) **Providers of loan capital (stockholders):** Reliable payment of interest and capital repayments due and maintenance of the value of any security

(f) **Society as a whole**

    (i)   Control environmental pollution, reduce energy consumption and increase usage of renewable resources
    (ii)   Provide fair wages, employment rights and conditions, training and advancement opportunities
    (iii) Provide a regular source of tax from profits
    (iv) Financial assistance to charities, sports and community activities
    (v)   Co-operate with government in identifying and preventing health hazards

Organisations which communicate with the different stakeholder group will understand the specific expectations on business performance and this often helps management to pursue an optimal strategy for the organisation.

It is suggested that modern corporations are so powerful, socially, economically and politically, that unrestrained use of their power will inevitably damage other people's rights. For example, they may blight an entire community by closing a major facility, thus enforcing long-term unemployment on a large proportion of the local workforce.

However, organisations are now much more cautious about how their actions are perceived and as a response some organisations invest in corporate communications departments specifically to manage brand image and perception, media briefings, press statements and direct communications with stakeholders.

The exercise of corporate social responsibility (CSR) constrains the organisation to act at all times as a good citizen.

4.2.2 Stakeholder risks

Each group of stakeholders will react to the severity of the risk it faces, for example, employees will strike if they fear their employments rights are being threatened. Organisations can analyse the various risks to stakeholders to understand and respond to likely stakeholder reactions.

Stakeholder	Risk (Interests to defend)	Stakeholder response to risk
Internal Managers and employees (eg restructuring, relocation)	• Jobs/careers • Money • Promotion • Benefits • Satisfaction	• Pursuit of systems goals rather than shareholder interests • Industrial action • Negative power to impede implementation • Refusal to relocate • Resignation
Connected Shareholders (corporate strategy)	• Increase in shareholder wealth, measured by profitability, P/E ratios, market capitalisation, dividends and yield • Risk	• Sell shares (eg to predator) or replace management
Bankers (cash flows)	• Security of loan • Adherence to loan agreements	• Denial of credit • Higher interest charges • Receivership
Suppliers (purchase strategy)	• Profitable sales • Payment for goods • Long-term relationship	• Refusal of credit • Court action • Wind down relationships
Customers (product market strategy)	• Goods as promised • Future benefits	• Buy elsewhere • Sue
External Government	• Jobs, training, tax	• Tax increases • Regulation • Legal action
Interest/pressure groups	• Pollution • Rights • Other	• Publicity • Direct action • Sabotage • Pressure on government

How stakeholders relate to the management of the company depends very much on what type of stakeholder they are: internal, connected or external: and on the level in the management hierarchy at which they are able to apply pressure. Clearly, a company's management will respond differently to the demands of, say, its shareholders and the community at large.

The way in which the relationship between company and stakeholders is conducted is a function of the parties' relative stakeholder bargaining strength and the philosophy underlying each party's objectives.

4.3 Influence of stakeholders

The actions of stakeholder groups in pursuit of their various goals can exert influence on strategy. The **greater** the **power** of the **stakeholder**, the greater his influence will be. Johnson and Scholes (*Exploring Corporate Strategy*, 2005) separate power groups into 'internal coalitions' and 'external stakeholder groups'.

We can look in detail at the stakeholder groups that not only have an **interest** in an organisation but also **power** over it.

The external coalition	The internal coalition
• Owners (who hold legal title) • Associates (suppliers, customers, trading partners) • Employee associations (unions, professional bodies) • Public (government, media)	• The chief executive and board at the strategic apex • Line managers • Operators • The technostructure • Support staff • Ideology (ie culture)

Each of these groups has three basic choices:

(a) **Loyalty**. They can do as they are told.

(b) **Exit**. For example by selling their shares, or getting a new job.

(c) **Voice**. They can stay and try to change the system. Those who choose **voice** are those who can, to varying degrees, influence the organisation. Influence implies a degree of power and willingness to exercise it.

Existing **structures and systems** can **channel stakeholder influence**.

(a) They are the **location of power**, giving groups of people varying degrees of influence over strategic choices.

(b) They are **conduits of information**, which shape strategic decisions.

(c) They **limit choices** or give some options priority over others. These may be physical or ethical constraints over what is possible.

(d) They **embody culture**.

(e) They **determine the successful implementation** of strategy.

(f) The **firm has different degrees of dependency** on various stakeholder groups. A company with a cash flow crisis will be more beholden to its bankers than one with regular cash surpluses.

Strategic options pose varying degrees of risk to the **interests** of the different stakeholders. It is possible that they may respond in such a way as to reduce the attractiveness of the proposed strategy.

Different stakeholders will have their own views as to strategy. As some stakeholders have **negative power**, in other words power to impede or disrupt the decision, their likely response might be considered.

Many managers acknowledge that the interests of some stakeholder groups – eg themselves and employees – should be recognised and provided for, even if this means that the interests of shareholders might be adversely affected. Not all stakeholder group interests can be given specific attention in the decisions of management, but those stakeholders for whom management recognises and accepts a responsibility are referred to as **constituents** of the firm.

Stakeholders' bargaining strength can be shown by means of a spectrum as illustrated in the following diagram.

```
                              Stakeholders'
        Weak                  bargaining strength                    Strong
<------------------------------------------------------------------------->
         |  Command/  | Consultation |           | Participation |           |           |
Company's|  dictated  | and          |Negotiation| and           | Democratic| Command/  |
conduct of  by       | consideration |           | acceptance    | voting by | dictated  |
relationship company | of            |           | of            | stakeholders| by stakeholders |
         |           | stakeholders' |           | stakeholders' |           |           |
         |           | views         |           | views         |           |           |
```

Illustration of stakeholders' bargaining strength

The relative stakeholder bargaining strength exerted by each of the various stakeholder groups can shape strategic decisions made by its management as well as the overall strategic direction of an organisation as they seek to meet the various stakeholder needs.

For example. stakeholders, such as shareholders or government, impose specific targets for the organisation to achieve. For example, a 5% rise in the share price or dividend or a 2% reduction in CO_2 emissions.

Without ethical safeguards in place and under pressure to meet performance targets, organisations can make decisions and implement policies which prioritise financial performance and profitability. This can sometimes result in unethical practises which can cause harm to individuals, to the environment, to the community or other stakeholder groups.

Here, stakeholders perform an important role in regulating company behaviour by making clear the expectations in terms of adhering to ethical principles or responding when unethical practices become known.

4.4 Stakeholder roles and responsibilities

We have considered how stakeholders can influence the **strategy** of an organisation. Now we consider how stakeholders can affect the **performance** of an organisation. We use specific examples of stakeholder groups to show how these affect the performance of organisations.

4.4.1 Employees and management

Employees and management are internal stakeholders. They may exert considerable power over the performance of the organisation. Organisations should aim to align the interests of their staff with those of the organisation.

In other words, organisations should look at ways of motivating their employees and managers to perform better by agreeing to organisational objectives, such as:

- **Motivation for employees** to perform well comes in a variety of guises. Some will work harder and better for more money whereas others prefer benefits or promotion. Many employees rank the environment in which they work as important for their well-being and productivity.

- **Performance measurement** for managers is usually designed so that by attaining targets set by the organisation, they earn rewards. These targets can be negotiated or imposed depending on the culture of the organisation. The rewards are linked to the attainment of the targets using various means.

- **Simple bonuses** can be paid on the achievement of a target return or profit.
- **Share options** can be granted whereby the reward is linked to the growth in the share price of the organisation. Thus, on the exercise of the option, and receipt of the shares, any growth in the share price from the date of grant is realised by the employee if they sell the shares or earn income from dividends on shares received.

However, there is a danger of dysfunctional behaviour where individuals concentrate on attaining just the measure that leads to the reward to the exclusion of other activities. There is also a risk of the measure being manipulated so that it is achieved whatever the consequences. A good example of this manipulation is return on capital employed (ROCE) where the return can be improved by retaining older written down assets thereby keeping the capital employed figure low. This may not be the optimum replacement policy for assets but will improve the measure of ROCE.

4.4.2 Shareholders

Shareholders represent a class of connected stakeholders, who provide funds for investment. They often take a short-term view of their involvement in an organisation.

Shareholders can be influential stakeholders, encouraging management to improve performance, by their decision to hold or sell shares.

Institutional shareholders often have significant holdings in companies. They usually hold shares for capital growth or their revenue stream, so they tend to monitor performance closely and dispose of under-performing shares. They can be a strong influence on the decisions made by the organisation in which they hold their shares.

Profit-making organisations tend to focus on financial performance in general and on the interests of shareholders in particular.

The traditional argument for this is that shareholders are the legal owners, the company belongs to them and so their interests are paramount. This means:

(a) Maximising shareholder wealth is a long-term goal for an organisation, inevitably managers must decide between what funds they want to disburse now and what funds need to be maintained in the business to ensure the prospects of long-term profitability.

(b) Shareholders own the business, and so the directors of the company have a duty to safeguard their interests.

(c) What the shareholders require as a return is used to judge the validity of investment projects.

(d) Shareholders assess the quality of management by how well the business performs financially.

(e) Shareholders are the principal source of capital investment in an organisation. They provide funds on share issues or permit managers to retain profits for investment.

A company's senior management should remain aware of who its major shareholders are, and it will often help to retain shareholders' support if the chairman or the managing director meets occasionally with the major shareholders, to exchange views.

(a) The company's management might learn about shareholders' preferences for either high dividends or high retained earnings for profit growth and capital gain.

(b) For public companies, changes in shareholdings might help to explain recent share price movements.

(c) The company's management should be able to learn about shareholders' attitudes to both risk and gearing. If a company is planning a new investment, its management might have to consider the relative merits of seeking equity finance or debt finance, and shareholders' attitudes would be worth knowing about before the decision is taken.

(d) Management might need to know its shareholders in the event of an unwelcome takeover bid from another company, to identify key shareholders whose views on the takeover bid might be crucial to the final outcome.

4.4.3 Consumer groups

Consumer groups are a connected group representing consumers' interests. They exist to ensure that products give good value. They promote safeguards for consumers against unethical business practice.

Consumerism reflects the increased importance and power of consumers. It appears in organised consumer groups, and the recognition by producers that consumer satisfaction is the key to long-term profitability.

4.4.4 Suppliers

Suppliers are a connected group of stakeholders. They can influence the cost and quality of goods and services. Suppliers can directly influence the performance of an organisation through the quality of the goods and services that they supply to an organisation. Poor quality goods will affect the saleability of the product to the customer, depressing sales and revenues.

The prices that suppliers charge will also affect the profitability of the end product if margins are eroded.

Organisations have developed a number of strategies for controlling price and quality from their suppliers. The best known of these is just-in-time that commits suppliers to supply on-demand zero-defect parts. If an organisation has confidence in its supplier, a long-term relationship will be established.

4.4.5 Government

Government is an external stakeholder group. Central government sets the regulatory framework in which organisations operate. Local government has devolved powers and can raise local revenues from business.

Question — Identifying stakeholders

You work as a senior advisor to the board of a large, listed organisation that operates in the construction industry. The services offered range from homebuilding to large civil engineering projects, such as bridges and dams, and can be undertaken for central and local government bodies as well as other profit-making companies. All projects are carried out by staff who require formal accreditation by their professional body.

Draft a list of stakeholders for the board and briefly explain the nature of each stakeholder's claim.

Answer

The list of stakeholders is likely to include the following (with their claims in brackets)

- **Shareholders** who require a return on their investment – (this is a direct claim because they are in contact with the organisation already)
- **Lenders** who require their loans to be serviced in full and on time (also direct)
- **Customers** who require good quality projects to be completed (also direct)
- **Suppliers** who require being paid on time (also direct)
- **Employees** who require good working conditions and being paid on time (also direct)
- **The general public** who requires no adverse effects from the organisation and its projects (such as safe housing, reliable infrastructure)(direct/indirect)
- **The government** which requires tax to be paid on corporate profits and other expenses, plus the ideal of maximising employment levels in the economy (probably also direct)
- **Professional bodies** which require the organisation's accreditation process to be robust to maintain their reputation (also direct)

- **Flora and fauna** whose natural environment is affected by civil engineering projects being built – (they require a clean, unspoilt environment to live in, but their claims are indirect because they did not ask to be affected by the organisation's projects)
- **People living near a construction project** (whether housing or some other kind) who require a quiet, clean and safe environment in which to live but who may be adversely affected by either the construction process or the finished asset (again, likely to be indirect)

4.5 Stakeholder mapping

Different stakeholder groups will assess differently the risk a strategy poses to their interests due to their attitude and appetite to for risk. Some stakeholders are able to exercise power over management to direct strategic direction to actively manage this.

It is helpful for management to understand which stakeholders are likely to exert most influence. Stakeholder mapping may be used to analysis the influence of various stakeholder groups.

Stakeholder mapping uses Mendelow's matrix (Johnson, Scholes & Whittington, 2007) and helps an organisation establish its priorities in relation to managing stakeholder expectations. The matrix classifies stakeholders in terms of the power they can exert on the organisation, and the likelihood that they will show an interest in the organisation's activities (and therefore exert that power).

These factors (power and interest) will help define the type of relationship the organisation should seek with its stakeholders.

	Level of interest	
Power	Low	High
Low	A	B
High	C	D

(**Source:** Johnson, Scholes & Whittington, 2007: p. 156)

(a) **Minimal effort** is expended on segment A. These stakeholders have both **low power and low interest.**

(b) Stakeholders in segment B have **low** power and **high** interest. They do not have great ability to influence strategy in their own right, but their views can be important in influencing more powerful stakeholders, perhaps by lobbying. They should therefore be **kept informed**. Community representatives and charities might fall into segment B.

(c) Stakeholders in segment C have **high power** but **low interest**. They must be **treated with care**. While often passive, they are capable of becoming key players (segment D) if their level of interest increases. They should, therefore be **kept satisfied**. Large institutional shareholders could be an example of this type of stakeholder: with increasing levels of shareholder activism in recent years also demonstrating their potential to move from 'keep satisfied' to 'key players'.

(d) **Key players** are found in segment D. These stakeholders have a **high level of power and interest**: An organisation's strategy must be acceptable to them, at least, and they need to be managed carefully. An example would be a major customer.

Stakeholder mapping is used to assess the significance of stakeholder groups. This in turn has implications for the organisation.

(a) The framework of **corporate governance** should recognise stakeholders' levels of interest and power.

(b) It may be appropriate to seek to **reposition** certain stakeholders and discourage others from repositioning themselves, depending on their attitudes.

(c) Key **blockers** and **facilitators** of change must be identified.

Stakeholder mapping can also be used to establish **political priorities**. A map of the current position can be compared with a map of a desired future state. This will indicate critical shifts that must be pursued.

Stakeholder mapping, demonstrates that different stakeholders can have varying degrees of influence on management and the strategy of an organisation. Specific groups of stakeholders are motivated by different aims. In the next section, we will look at the role of the management accountant in helping management to analyse the different needs and provide management with analysis to support business performance and meet specific performance targets.

4.6 Consensus of objectives

The **stakeholder view** of company objectives is that many groups of people have a stake in what the company does. Shareholders own the business, but there are also suppliers, managers, workers and customers. Each of these groups has its own objectives so that a compromise or balance is required. Management must balance the profit objectives with the pressures from the non-shareholder groups in deciding the strategic targets of the business.

The **consensus theory** of company objectives was developed by **Cyert & March** (*A Behavioral Theory of the Firm*, 1992). Managers do not necessarily set objectives for the company, but rather they look for objectives which suit their own inclinations. However, objectives emerge as a **consensus** of the differing views of shareholders, managers, employees, suppliers, customers and society at large, but (in contrast to the stakeholder view) they are not all selected nor controlled by management.

Question — Stakeholders

The board of Cuddlydudley Co is currently discussing its relationships with the following stakeholder groups:

- An environmental pressure group, which is raising objections to the impact of Cuddlydudley Co's business on the local community and countryside

- A group of shareholders, who own less than 1% of shares each and who do not generally attend the annual general meeting

- The company's most significant shareholder, who owns 25% of share capital, sometimes attends the annual general meeting but has not raised any concerns recently

- The company's biggest customer, whose orders are for around 20% of the company's revenue, which is seeking closer integration between its systems and Cuddlydudley Co's systems due to recent delays in product delivery

According to Mendelow's stakeholder mapping, which of the stakeholders should be kept informed about Cuddlydudley's activities?

A Environmental pressure group
B Shareholders with less than 1% of shares
C Most significant shareholder
D Biggest customer

Answer

A   Environmental pressure group

Keeping the pressure group informed reflects its having high interest and low direct power, but being able to influence more powerful stakeholders.

Minimal effort is needed with the shareholders with small shareholdings, as individually they have neither interest nor power. The most significant shareholder has some power, but it seems limited interest, so can be kept satisfied. The biggest customer has high power because of the revenue it generates and high interest because of delivery problems, so its request for closer integration needs careful consideration.

4.7 Enhancing stakeholder engagement

Key terms

> **Stakeholder engagement** is the process of involving all parties affected by a company's operations in its decision-making processes.

Integrating sustainability into business practice requires a robust framework of corporate accountability and proactive stakeholder engagement.

Organisations that embrace these principles not only enhance their reputations and build trust but also drive long-term sustainable value for all stakeholders. By doing so, they contribute to a more sustainable and equitable world, addressing critical global challenges such as climate change, social inequality, and environmental degradation.

4.7.1 Donaldson and Preston's stakeholder engagement theory

According to Donaldson and Preston's stakeholder engagement theory, businesses have a duty to consider the interests of all their stakeholders, not just shareholders and argue that organisations have a responsibility to balance the needs and expectations of these diverse groups of stakeholders to achieve sustainability. (**Source:** Donaldson, T., and Preston, L. E. (1995) The Stakeholder Theory of the Corporation: Concepts, Evidence, and Implications. *Academy of Management Review*, 20(1), 65–91.)

Donaldson and Preston (1995) theory to stakeholder engagement is divided into three interrelated perspectives:

Perspectives of stakeholder engagement	Description
Normative approach	The **normative approach** asserts that considering stakeholders' interests is inherently the right thing to do. It is based on ethical principles and the intrinsic value of treating all stakeholders with respect and fairness.
Descriptive approach	The **descriptive approach** describes how companies actually operate, showing that businesses naturally interact with various stakeholders and that these interactions influence corporate behaviour.
Instrumental approach	The **instrumental approach** perspective suggests that attending to stakeholders' interests can lead to better business outcomes, such as increased loyalty, improved reputation, and long-term profitability.

4.7.2 Enhancing stakeholder engagement

Effective stakeholder engagement enhances corporate accountability by ensuring that boards of directors take stakeholder expectations and feedback seriously which means a company actions are much more likely to align with stakeholder needs and wider societal values.

Conversely, by implementing corporate accountability practices delivers the drivers for organisations to invest in meaningful stakeholder engagement.

Therefore, organisations require a methodology to achieve effective stakeholder engagement. Donaldson and Preston (1995) theory of stakeholder engagement recommends the following three stages.

(a) **Identify key stakeholders**

Organisations must recognise the diverse groups affected by their actions, including employees, customers, suppliers, local communities, and investors.

(b) **Deploy stakeholder engagement strategies**

Effective stakeholder engagement involves open communication, transparency, and responsiveness. Organisations use various methods such as surveys, public consultations, and social media platforms to engage with stakeholders.

(c) **Integrate stakeholder feedback to organisation's strategic and operational objectives**

Organisations should evaluate then incorporate feedback from stakeholders into their strategic planning and operations.

5 Managing stakeholder conflict

FAST FORWARD

> The fundamental objective of any organisation should be the maximisation of shareholders' wealth. In its purest sense, this means pursuing the maximum amount of profit from the organisation's operations. A threat to this objective is conflicting shareholder objectives.

Organisations must consider the interests of managers and owners may conflict so areas of conflict can be effectively managed. Shareholder wealth may be maximised by reducing the local workforce or changing the nature of the work done due to new technology being available. This would be perceived as a conflict with the goals of employee.

5.1 Separation of ownership from control

In most modern organisations the owners do not actually manage the company. Whilst the equity shareholders own the company, the day-to-day operations are managed on their behalf by the board of directors.

The directors and managers within the organisation have their own personal goals that may conflict with those of the shareholders. The problem that shareholders have is that they are seen as being passive stakeholders: that is, they do not (and are not expected to) contribute to business decisions that affect the company.

Whilst managers are privy to privileged information about the company, shareholders have to rely on publicly available details such as annual reports and press articles, a situation known as information asymmetry. As a result, managers are very much left to their own devices when making business decisions.

The relationship between management and shareholders is sometimes referred to as an agency relationship, in which managers act as agents for the shareholders. Here, there is separation of ownership from management is sometimes characterised as the 'agency problem' which is where shareholder conflict arises as a difference between the interests of managers and those of owners.

For example, if managers hold none or very little of the equity shares of the company they work for, what is to stop them from working inefficiently, not bothering to look for profitable new investment opportunities, or giving themselves high salaries and perks?

The goal of agency theory is to find governance structures and control mechanisms that minimise the problem caused by the separation of ownership and control. In that sense agency theory is the cornerstone of the theory of corporate governance. More specifically agency theory tries to find means for the owners to control the managers in such a way that the managers will operate in the interest of the shareholders.

Examples of conflicts of interest between managers and shareholders include:

- **Short-termism:** There is evidence that in many companies the primary driver of decision-making has been to increase share prices and hence managerial rewards in the short term. The longer-term benefits of investment in research and development may be ignored in the short-term drive to cut costs and increase profits thus jeopardising the long-term prospects of the company.

- **Sales maximisation:** This strategy is often employed by managers to increase market share and therefore the importance of the company within its sector. An increase in importance for the company will mean greater status for management but will not necessarily be in the best interests of the shareholders.

- **Overpriced acquisitions:** Takeovers is another manifestation of the non-alignment of the interests of shareholders and managers. Managers have motives other than shareholder value maximisation and may choose to acquire another business to seek growth and status.

- **Resistance to takeovers:** The management of a company may tend to resist takeovers if they feel that their position is threatened even if in doing so shareholder value is also reduced.

- **Relationships:** Many companies' pursuit of short-term cost reduction may lead to difficult relationships with their wider stakeholders. Relationships with suppliers may be disrupted by demands for major improvements in terms and in reduction of prices. Employees may be made redundant in a drive to reduce costs and customers may be able to buy fewer product lines and have to face less favourable terms. These policies may aid short-term profits, but in the long-term suppliers and employees are able to take full advantage of market conditions and move to other companies, and customers can shop elsewhere or over the internet.

- **Avoiding risk:** In order to maximise shareholder wealth in the long-term a company needs to evolve which means some risk must be taken. When managers' attitudes are conservative and risk-averse they are seeking the easiest path. Risk-averse managers seeks to avoid conflict or change because of the disruption it could cause. However, this may not be in the best interests of the shareholders.

- **Dividend policy:** Managers may decide to maintain high dividend pay-outs in order to avoid resistance from the shareholders. This is not necessarily the best thing for shareholder wealth maximisation in the long-term as it may be better to invest in new technology so that new products can be made, or existing products made more effectively and efficiently.

5.2 Conflict between stakeholders

Although we discussed the conflict between managers and owners, there are other areas of potential conflict between managers, owners and other stakeholders who provide capital, namely the debt holders. The relationship between the long-term creditors of a company, the management and the shareholders of a company encompasses the following factors:

- Management may decide to raise finance for a company by taking out long-term or medium-term loans.

- Investors who provide debt finance will rely on the company's management to generate enough net cash inflows to make interest payments on time, and eventually to repay loans. Long-term creditors will often take security for their loan, perhaps in the form of a fixed charge over an asset (such as a mortgage on a building). Debentures are also often subject to certain restrictive covenants, which restrict the company's rights to borrow more money until the debentures have been repaid.

- The money that is provided by long-term creditors will be invested to earn profits, and the profits (in excess of what is needed to pay interest on the borrowing) will provide extra dividends or retained profits for the shareholders of the company. In other words, shareholders will expect to increase their wealth using creditors' money.

Sometimes the needs of shareholders and debtholders may conflict:

- Managers may be tempted to take risky decisions using debtholders' money to finance them, knowing that the benefits of these decisions will accrue to the shareholders. If the projects go badly and the company fails, the debtholders may suffer a greater loss than the equity shareholders.
- In many jurisdictions there are rules limiting the proportion of company assets that can be paid out as dividends. However, it may still be possible to pay out lawfully considerable sums as dividends, enough to jeopardise the company's future and hence the amounts that the debtholders have advanced, should trading results turn bad in the near future.
- Shareholders and managers may wish to prolong the company's life as long as possible, whereas debtholders may wish to safeguard the amount loaned and realise their security as soon as the company appears to be getting into difficulties.
- Managers may attempt to undermine the position of debtholders by seeking further loan capital, committing the company to an increased interest burden and hence greater risk of insolvency. The additional loan capital may also have superior claims on the company's assets to the original amounts borrowed.

5.2.1 Strategies to manage stakeholder conflict

We will now show how ensuring goal congruence and enforcing corporate governance best practice can help manage conflict between different groups of stakeholders.

- **Reward systems:** Agency theory sees employees of businesses, including managers, as individuals, each with their own objectives. Within a department of a business, there are departmental objectives. Goal congruence between managers, directors and shareholders may be better dealt with by giving managers some profit-related pay, or by providing incentives which are related to profits or share price.

  Examples of such remuneration incentives are:

  - **Profit-related/economic value-added pay**

    Pay or bonuses related to the size of profits or economic value added

  - **Rewarding managers with shares**

    This might be done when a private company 'goes public' and managers are invited to subscribe for shares in the company at an attractive offer price. This means that directors and employees, as well as shareholders, have a stake in the long-term profitability of an organisation.

  - **Executive share options plans**

    In a share option scheme, selected employees are given a number of share options, each of which gives the holder the right after a certain date to subscribe for shares in the company at a fixed price. The value of an option will increase if the company is successful, and its share price goes up.

- **Separation of roles and corporate governance:** Complying with corporate governance principles ensured that not too much power accrues to a single individual within an organisation which increases the risk of disagreement between a chief executive offers and the board of directors, the company shareholders and the employees. Also, the adoption of a corporate governance framework of decision making will restrict the power of managers and increase the role of independent non-executive directors in key decisions.

3: STRATEGIC PLANNING AND MANAGEMENT BY OBJECTIVES

- **Negotiation:** Stakeholder conflict between shareholders and directors can be resolved by negotiating contracts that allow the principal to control the agent in such a way to ensure that the agent will operate in the interests of the principal. Also, a board of directors may schedule regular investors updates which allow key investors to voice their concerns and to provide feedback on strategic decisions made by a board of directors. Differences of opinion between a company and its customers or suppliers can also be resolved by negotiation of contractual terms, price or deliverables.

- **Self-regulation:** A voluntary code of conduct is a statement by an organisation of the standards by which it seeks to do business. Codes are usually developed by a trade association and individual members incorporate the code into the dealings they have with their customers. Organisations in some business sectors self-regulate their dealings by voluntary codes of conduct. Voluntary codes usually include a mechanism for resolving disputes through arbitration.

6 Objectives of business enterprises

> **FAST FORWARD**
>
> **Objectives** can be classified as:
>
> - **Mission** – all-pervasive, open-ended
> - **Corporate** – relevant for organisation as a whole, relating to key factors for business success
> - **Unit** – specific, operational objectives
>
> There will often be a trade-off between objectives.

6.1 Mission, corporate objectives and unit objectives

Objectives of organisations will be heavily influenced by the 'coalition' or stakeholder group that has the most power. This is usually an organisation's senior management. However, this group will be influenced by the expectations of other coalitions and stakeholders. Objectives come in hierarchies, with the objectives lower down in the hierarchy contributing to the objectives higher up.

Three types of objective have been identified:

- Mission
- Corporate objectives
- Unit objectives

6.1.1 Mission

We discussed mission earlier in this chapter.

6.1.2 Corporate objectives

Corporate objectives are those which are concerned with the firm as a whole. Objectives should be **explicit, quantifiable** and **capable of being achieved**. The corporate objectives outline the expectations of the firm and the strategic planning process is concerned with the means of achieving the objectives.

Objectives should relate to the **key factors for business success**, which are typically as follows.

- Profitability (return on investment)
- Market share
- Growth
- Cash flow
- Customer satisfaction
- The quality of the firm's products
- Industrial relations
- Added value

6.1.3 Unit objectives

Unit objectives are objectives that are specific to individual units of an organisation, and are often 'operational' objectives. Examples are:

(a) From the **commercial sector**:

   (i) Increasing the number of customers by x% (an objective of a sales department)

   (ii) Reducing the number of rejects by 50% (an objective of a production department)

   (iii) Producing monthly reports more quickly, within five working days of the end of each month (an objective of the management accounting department)

(b) From the **public sector**:

   (i) Providing cheap subsidised bus travel (an objective of a local authority transport department)

   (ii) Introducing more nursery education (an objective of a borough education department)

   (iii) Responding more quickly to calls (an objective of a local police station, fire department or hospital ambulance service)

6.2 Primary and secondary objectives

6.2.1 Primary objectives

Some objectives are more important than others. It could be argued that in the hierarchy of objectives, there is a **primary corporate objective** (restricted by certain constraints on corporate activity). There are also other **secondary objectives** which are strategic objectives which should combine to ensure the achievement of the overall corporate objective.

Many writers accept that **profitability** must be the primary objective for a profit-making commercial organisation, but there are different ways of measuring profitability, in one form or another.

6.2.2 Secondary objectives

Whereas the primary objective of a profit-orientated organisation is to make money, it must fulfil certain **secondary objectives** to do so. For example, the secondary objective of a motor company whose primary objective might be to make money for its shareholders must be to build the best cars for its market or market niche. Other secondary objectives include areas such as promoting environmentally friendly production processes, if that is what consumers indicate they require, or what the law stipulates.

6.3 Trade-off between objectives

When there are several key objectives, some might be achieved only at the expense of others. For example, a company's objective of achieving good profits and profit growth might have adverse consequences for the cash flow of the business, or the quality of the firm's product.

There will be a trade-off between objectives when strategies are formulated, and a choice will have to be made. For example, there might be a choice between the following two options.

Option A   15% sales growth, 10% profit growth, a £2 million negative cash flow and reduced product quality and customer satisfaction.

Option B   8% sales growth, 5% profit growth, a £500,000 surplus cash flow, and maintenance of high product quality/customer satisfaction.

If the firm chose option B in preference to option A, it would be trading-off sales growth and profit growth for better cash flow, product quality and customer satisfaction.

6.4 Profitability and profit measurement

The shorter-term financial objectives of companies include targets for profitability. The measurement of profit under historical cost accounting follows the principles of the generally accepted fundamental accounting concepts.

Although profits do matter, they are not the best measure of a company's achievements.

(a) Accounting profits are not the same as 'economic' profits. Accounting profits can be manipulated to some extent by choices of accounting policies.

(b) A company might make an accounting profit without having used its resources in the most profitable way possible.

(c) Profits on their own take no account of the **volume of investment** that it has taken to earn the profit. Hence measures of financial achievement include:

- Accounting return on capital employed
- Earnings per share
- Yields on investment, eg dividend yield as a percentage of stock market value

(d) Profits are reported every year (with half-year interim results for quoted companies). They are measures of **short**-term performance, whereas a company's performance should ideally be judged over a longer term.

Question — Manipulation of profits

Give three examples of how accounting profits might be so manipulated.

Answer

Here are some examples you might have chosen.

(i) Provisions, such as provisions for depreciation or anticipated losses
(ii) The capitalisation of various expenses, such as development costs
(iii) Adding overhead costs to stock valuations

7 Financial objectives

FAST FORWARD

In financial management of businesses, the key objective is the **maximisation of shareholders' wealth**.

7.1 The prime financial objective of a company

The theory of company finance is based on the assumption that the objective of management is to **maximise the market value of the company's shares**. Specifically, the main objective of a company should be to maximise the wealth of its ordinary shareholders.

A company is financed by ordinary shareholders, preference shareholders, loan stock-holders and other long-term and short-term creditors. All surplus funds, however, belong to the legal owners of the company, its ordinary shareholders. Any retained profits are undistributed wealth of these equity shareholders.

7.2 Measuring wealth and value

If the financial objective of a company is to maximise the value of the company, and in particular the value of its ordinary shares, we need to be able to put values on a company and its shares. How do we do it? Three possible methods of valuation might occur to us.

Methods of company valuation	
Going concern basis	Based on the company's balance sheet. Rising retained profits indication of potential dividends
Break-up basis	Only of interest if company is threatened with insolvency, or if individual assets are being sold to raise cash
Market values	Trading prices of stocks and shares, most relevant to financial objectives

The **wealth** of the shareholders in a company comes from **dividends** received and the **market value** of the shares. A shareholder's **return on investment** is obtained in the form of dividends received and capital gains from increases in the market value of his or her shares.

7.3 How is the value of a business increased?

If a company's shares are traded on a stock market, the wealth of shareholders is increased when the share price goes up. The price of a company's shares will go up when the company makes attractive profits. However, the company should achieve such profits without taking business risks and financial risks which worry shareholders.

If there is an increase in earnings and dividends, shareholders should benefit from both **higher revenue** (dividends) and also **capital gains** (higher share prices).

Earnings are the profits attributable to equity (that is, to ordinary shareholders) after tax.

7.4 Financial targets

In addition to targets for earnings, earnings per share and dividend per share, a company might set other financial targets:

Examples of other financial targets	
Restriction on gearing	Ratio of debt: equity shouldn't exceed 1:1 or finance costs shouldn't be higher than 25% of profit from operations
Profit retentions	Dividend cover (Profit for the year: Dividends) should exceed 2.5
Profit from operations	Target profit from operations: revenue ratio or minimum return on capital employed
Cash generation	As well as generating profits, businesses need to generate enough cash to ensure they remain liquid
Value added	Creation of economic value for shareholders, to be discussed later in this text

These financial targets should help a company to achieve its main financial objective without incurring excessive risks.

7.5 Short- and long-term targets

Targets are usually measured over a year rather than over the long term, and it is the **maximisation of shareholder wealth** in the **long term** that ought to be the **corporate objective**. Short-term measures of return can encourage a company to pursue short-term objectives at the expense of long-term ones, for example by deferring new capital investments, or spending only small amounts on research and development and on training.

7.6 Multiple financial targets

A major problem with setting a number of **different financial targets**, either primary targets or supporting secondary targets, is that they might not all be consistent with each other, and so might not all be achievable at the same time. When this happens, some compromises will have to be accepted.

7.7 Value for money

Value for money is emphasised particularly for non-profit making organisations and public sector bodies but it can be important for profit-seeking businesses as well.

Key terms

> **Effectiveness** is the measure of achievement and is assessed by reference to goals.
>
> **Economy** is attaining the appropriate quantity and quality of resource inputs at the lowest cost
>
> **Efficiency** is concerned with the relationships between the outputs produced and the resources used to produce them. It means producing the maximum output from a given set of resource inputs, or using the minimum inputs for any given quantity and quality of product or service provided. Efficiency is therefore a combination of effectiveness and economy.

8 Non-financial objectives

FAST FORWARD

> **Non-financial objectives** such as welfare, service provision and fulfilment of responsibilities are also important for businesses.

8.1 Examples of non-financial objectives

An enterprise may have important non-financial objectives, which could limit the achievement of financial objectives.

Question — Non-financial objectives

Before looking at what follows, write out your own list of the various non-financial objectives which an enterprise might have.

Examples of non-financial objectives are as follows.

Non-financial objectives	
Welfare of employees	Competitive wages and salaries, comfortable and safe working conditions, good training and career development
Welfare of management	High salaries, company cars, perks
Welfare of society	Concern for environment
Provision of service to minimum standard	For example regulations affecting utility (water, electricity providers)
Responsibilities to customers	Providing quality products or services, fair dealing
Responsibilities to suppliers	Not exploiting power as buyer unscrupulously
Leadership in research and development	Failure to innovate may have adverse long-term financial consequences
Maintaining competitive position and market share	Preventing rivals from becoming too large and enjoying benefits of size such as economies of scale

8.2 The relationship between financial and non-financial objectives

Non-financial objectives do not negate financial objectives, but they do mean that the simple theory of company finance, that the objective of a firm is to maximise the wealth of ordinary shareholders, is too simplistic. Financial objectives may have to be compromised in order to satisfy non-financial objectives.

8.3 Environmental concerns

There has been an increase in the use of the 'green' approach to market products. 'Dolphin friendly' tuna and paper products from 'managed forests' are examples.

8.4 The impact of green issues on business practice

Environmental impacts on business may be **direct**:

- Changes affecting costs or resource availability
- Impact on demand
- Effect on power balances between competitors in a market

They may also be **indirect**, as legislative change may affect the environment within which businesses operate. Finally, pressure may come from customers or staff as a consequence of concern over environmental problems.

8.5 Ecology and strategic planning

Physical environmental conditions are important.

(a) **Resource inputs**

Managing physical resources successfully (eg oil companies, mining companies) is a good source of profits.

The physical environment presents logistical problems or opportunities to organisations. Proximity to road and rail links can be a reason for siting a warehouse in a particular area.

(b) **Government**

The physical environment is under the control of other organisations.

(i) Local authority town planning departments can influence where a building and necessary infrastructure can be sited.

(ii) Governments can set regulations about some of the organisation's environmental interactions.

(c) **Disasters**

In some countries, the physical environment can pose a major 'threat' to organisations in the form of natural disasters such as wildfires or floods.

Issues relating to the effect of an organisation's activities on the physical environment have come to the fore in recent years, and sustainability is now an important consideration for organisations. This will be covered in depth in Chapter 6.

9 Personal objectives and targets

9.1 Behavioural theories of objective setting

> **FAST FORWARD**
>
> In order for learning and motivation to be effective, it is essential that **people** know exactly what their **objectives** are.

People are purposive: that is, they act in pursuit of particular goals or purposes. Individual objectives influence:

(a) **Perception**, since we filter out messages not relevant to our goals, and select those which are relevant

(b) **Behaviour**, since people behave in such a way as to satisfy their goals

(c) **Motivation**, since organisations can motivate people by offering them the means to fulfil their goals

(d) **Learning**, which is a process of adapting our behaviour so that our goals may be more effectively met 'next time'

In order for learning and motivation to be effective, it is essential that people know exactly what their objectives are. This enables them to:

(a) **Plan and direct their effort** towards the objectives

(b) **Monitor their performance** against objectives and adjust (or learn) if required

(c) Experience the **reward of achievement** once the objectives have been reached

(d) Feel that their tasks have **meaning and purpose**, which is an important element in job satisfaction

(e) Experience the **motivation of a challenge:** the need to expend energy and effort in a particular direction in order to achieve something

(f) Avoid the **de-motivation** of impossible or inadequately rewarded tasks. If objectives are vague, unrealistic or unattainable, there may be little incentive to pursue them: hence the importance of SMART objectives.

9.2 Individual and organisational objectives

FAST FORWARD

Individual objectives must be directed towards, or 'dovetailed with', organisational goals.

Individual objectives must be directed towards, or '**dovetailed with**', organisational goals.

(a) **Direction**. All jobs are directed towards the same organisational goals. Each managerial job must be focused on the success of the business as a whole, not just one part of it.

(b) **Targets**. Each manager's targeted performance must be derived from targets of achievement for the organisation as a whole.

(c) **Performance measurement**. A manager's results must be measured in terms of their contribution to the business as a whole.

(d) **Each manager must know** what their targets of performance are.

9.3 Types of objectives for individuals and teams

Different types of objectives include:

(a) **Work objectives**

   (i) At team level, these relate to the purpose of the team and the contribution it is expected to make to the goals of the department and the organisation.

   (ii) At individual level, these are related specifically to the job. They clarify what the individual is expected to do and they enable the performance of the individual to be measured.

(b) **Standing aims and objectives**

   (i) **Qualitative aims** cover issues such as promptness and courtesy when dealing with customer requests.

   (ii) A **quantified target** for a sales team would be to ensure that all phone calls are picked up within three rings.

(c) **Output or improvement targets**

   A sales person may be given a target of increasing the number of sales made in a particular district in a certain time. Many firms have targets which involve reducing the number of defects in goods produced, or seek to find ways of working more efficiently.

(d) **Developmental goals**

   These deal with how an individual can improve their own performance and skills. These goals are often set at the appraisal interview and are part of the performance management system.

9.4 Management by objectives (MbO)

FAST FORWARD

Techniques have been suggested to break down organisational goals into targets for departments and individuals. **Management by Objectives (MbO)** is one such technique.

Integrating objectives is not always easy to achieve. However, a method of doing so was suggested by proponents of **Management by Objectives**, including **Peter Drucker** (*The New Realities: in Government and Politics, in Economics and Business, in Society and World View,* 1989).

9.4.1 Stages in MbO

MbO is a process whereby individual goals are integrated with the corporate plan, as part of an on-going programme of goal-setting and performance review involving all levels of management. The stages in developing such a programme are as follows.

Step 1 Clarifying **organisational goals and objectives**: MbO will only be effective within the framework of a coherent strategic plan.

Step 2 Collaboratively defining each individual's major **areas of responsibility** and their purpose within the corporate plan.

Step 3 Jointly defining and agreeing the **key tasks** which are directly related to the achievement of objectives, and in which any performance shortfall would negatively impact on the organisation's effectiveness.

Step 4 Jointly defining and agreeing **key results** (which must be achieved in order for the key tasks to be successfully performed and objectives met) and methods of monitoring and measuring performance in these areas.

Step 5 Agreeing individual **performance improvement plans** for a defined planning period: selecting specific improvement objectives for each key task and formulating an action plan to achieve those objectives.

Step 6 **Monitoring, self-evaluation and review** of performance at agreed intervals, with revision of objectives, targets and action plans as required.

Step 7 **Periodic review of performance** against individual improvement objectives and key results (reflected at the organisation level in a review of performance against the corporate plan).

A fresh cycle of planning and control would then continue the process.

9.4.2 Evaluating MbO

There are a number of **advantages** to an MbO programme.

(a) Clarifying organisational and sub-unit **goals**. This is crucial in establishing direction and co-ordination. It helps to focus organisation structures according to defined responsibilities.

(b) Focusing organisational attention on **key tasks**, results and problem areas, for more efficient targeting of effort.

(c) Systematically converting strategic plans into **co-ordinated** managerial action plans and budgets. Each individual manager knows clearly what is expected of him or her, while retaining a big-picture perspective and unity of purpose.

(d) Securing the **commitment** of individuals to defined targets and areas of accountability, as well as potentially improving morale and motivation through greater involvement and discretion in performing tasks (within defined targets).

(e) **Systematic information** for managerial planning and control, individual performance appraisal, reward and development planning.

There are **disadvantages** too.

(a) Potential **rigidity**: individual objectives must be set and, once set, are not changed because the overall plan is difficult to revise.

(b) Potential requirement for a significant **change** in attitudes, the style of leadership and organisation structure. This may involve time and labour costs of change management – and may ultimately be unsuccessful if not supported (and sustained) by senior management.

(c) Potential for **conflict** and de-motivation: staff may perceive increasing accountability for defined results as a command-and-control pressure tactic, thinly disguised as involvement/empowerment.

9.5 Performance measures for individuals

FAST FORWARD

Standards of performance set for individuals should be job-related, controllable and observable.

Some principles for devising performance measures are as follows.

Principle	Comment
Job-related	They should be related to the actual job, and the key tasks outlined in the job description.
Controllable	People should not be assessed according to factors which they cannot control.
Objective and observable	This is contentious. Certain aspects of performance can be measured, such as volume sales, but matters such as friendliness which are important to some businesses are harder to measure.
Data must be available	There is no use identifying performance measures if the data cannot be collected efficiently.

Question — Performance indicators

A senior sales executive has a job which involves: 'building the firm's sales' and maintaining 'a high degree of satisfaction with the company's products and services'. The firm buys sports equipment, running machines and so on, which it sells to gyms and individuals. The firm also charges fees to service the equipment. Service contracts are the sales executive's responsibility, and he has to manage that side of the business.

Here some possible performance indicators to assess the sales executive's performance in the role. What do you think of them? Are they any good?

(a) Number of new customers gained per period
(b) Value of revenue from existing customers per period
(c) Renewal of service contracts
(d) Record of customer complaints about poor quality products
(e) Regular customer satisfaction survey

Answer

These measures do not all address the key issues of the job.

(a) **Number of new customers**. This is helpful as far as it goes but omits two crucial issues: how much the customers actually spend and what the potential is. Demand for this service might be expanding rapidly, and the firm might be increasing sales revenue but losing market share.

(b) **Revenue from existing customers** is useful – repeat business is generally cheaper than gaining new customers, and it implies customer satisfaction.

(c) **Renewal of service contracts** is very relevant to the executive's role.

(d) **Customer complaints about poor quality products.** As the company does not make its own products, this is not really under the control of the sales manager. Instead the purchasing manager should be more concerned. Complaints about the service contract are the sales executive's concern.

(e) **Customer satisfaction survey.** This is a tool for the sales manager to use as well as a performance measure, but not everything is under the sales executive's control.

10 Performance management

FAST FORWARD

> **Performance management** suggests that people must agree performance standards, that the responsibility for performance management is principally that of line management, and that it is a conscious commitment to developing and managing people in organisations. It is a continuous process.

Key term

> **Performance management** is: 'a means of getting better results…by understanding and managing performance within an agreed framework of planned goals, standards and competence requirements. It is a process to establish a shared understanding about what is to be achieved, and an approach to managing and developing people [... so that it ...] will be achieved' (**Armstrong**, *A Handbook of Human Resource Management Practice*, 1999).

10.1 Features of performance management

Armstrong expands on this definition, and describes some other features of performance management.

Aspect	Comment
Agreed framework of goals, standards and competence requirements	As in MbO, the manager and the employee agree about a standard of performance, goals and the skills needed.
Shared understanding	People need to understand the nature of high levels of performance, so they can work towards them.
Approach to managing and developing people	(a) How managers work with their teams. (b) How team members work with managers and each other. (c) Developing individuals to improve their performance.
Achievement	The aim is to enable people to realise their potential and maximise their contribution to the organisation's well-being.
Future-based	Performance management is forward-looking, based on the organisation's future needs and what the individual must do to satisfy them.

10.2 The process of performance management

The process of performance management may be outlined as follows.

Step 1 From the **business plan**, identify the requirements and competences required to carry it out.

Step 2 Draw up a **performance agreement**, defining the expectations of the individual or team, covering standards of performance, performance indicators and the skills and competences people need.

Step 3 Draw up a **performance and development plan** with the individual. These record the actions needed to improve performance, normally covering development in the current job.

Step 4 **Manage performance continually throughout the year**, not just at appraisal interviews done to satisfy the personnel department.

Step 5 **Performance review**. At a defined period each year, success against the plan is reviewed, but the whole point is to assess what is going to happen in future.

Question: Performance management

What are the advantages to employees of introducing such a system?

Answer

The key to performance management is that it is forward looking and constructive. Objective-setting gives employees the security in knowing exactly what is expected of them, and this is agreed at the outset with the manager, thus identifying unrealistic expectations. The employee at the outset can indicate the resources needed.

3: STRATEGIC PLANNING AND MANAGEMENT BY OBJECTIVES

Chapter roundup

- The **rational model of strategic planning** involves strategic analysis, strategic choice and implementation. It is a comprehensive approach to strategic management, suggesting a logical sequence which involves analysing the current situation, generating choices (relating to competitors, products and markets) and implementing the chosen strategies.
- The **mission** is the organisation's overall purpose and reason for existence. It has implications for the commercial strategy, the values of the organisation, and policies and actual standards of behaviour of the people within it.
- **Goals** give flesh to the mission. They can be quantified (**objectives**) or not quantified (**aims**). Most organisations use a combination of both. Quantified or specific objectives have SMART characteristics.
- **Strategy** is a course of action to achieve an objective. Strategies are set at the corporate, business and operational levels.
- To assist in the realisation of financial strategy, **financial accounting systems** ensure that the assets and liabilities of a business are **properly accounted for, and provide information about profits and so on** to shareholders and to other interested parties. **Management accounting systems** provide information specifically for the use of managers within an organisation.
- Different groups of stakeholders have different objectives which can lead to conflicts between competing groups.
    - **Internal** – managers, employees
    - **Connected** – shareholders, banks, customers, suppliers
    - **External** – government, pressure groups, local communities

  By understanding the different stakeholders and their needs and goals, then an organisation can determine strategies to resolve stakeholder conflicts which may prevent an organisation from achieving its strategic objectives.
- The fundamental objective of any organisation should be the maximisation of shareholders' wealth. In its purest sense, this means pursuing the maximum amount of profit from the organisation's operations. A threat to this objective is conflicting shareholder objectives.
- **Objectives** can be classified as:
    - **Mission** – all-pervasive, open-ended
    - **Corporate** – relevant for organisation as a whole, relating to key factors for business success
    - **Unit** – specific, operational objectives

  There will often be a trade-off between objectives.
- In financial management of businesses, the key objective is the **maximisation of shareholders' wealth**.
- **Non-financial objectives** such as welfare, service provision and fulfilment of responsibilities are also important for businesses.
- In order for learning and motivation to be effective, it is essential that **people** know exactly what their **objectives** are.
- **Individual objectives** must be directed towards, or 'dovetailed with', **organisational goals**.
- Techniques have been suggested to break down organisational goals into targets for departments and individuals. **Management by objectives (MbO)** is one such technique.
- **Standards of performance** set for individuals should be job-related, controllable and observable.
- **Performance management** suggests that people must agree performance standards, that the responsibility for performance management is principally that of line management, and that it is a conscious commitment to developing and managing people in organisations. It is a continuous process.

Quick quiz

1. How can organisations direct their activities?
2. The rational model of strategic planning divides into three different stages: what are they?
3. XYZ Ltd focuses its strategy upon its core competences and capabilities. What type of approach to strategic planning is this:

    A   Ad-hoc
    B   Resource-based
    C   Accounting-led
    D   Position-based

4. What are the elements of a control system?
5. What are four elements of mission?
6. What do you understand by the acronym SMART?
7. List four types of objectives for an individual.
8. How must objectives be interlocked?
9. Fill in the blanks in the following definition.

    Performance management is 'a means of getting better _____ [...] by _____ and managing performance within an agreed framework of planned _____, standards and _____ requirements. It is a process to establish a _____ understanding about what is to be achieved, and an approach to managing and _____ people [... so that it ...] will be achieved'.

    (**Armstrong**, A Handbook of Human Resource Management Practice, 1999)

10. List five steps in performance management.
11. How can managers and staff become more committed to objectives, according to supporters of MbO and performance management?

Answers to quick quiz

1. By deciding what should be done, how it should be done, reviewing outcomes, and monitoring performance

2. Strategic analysis, strategic choice and strategy implementation

3. B: Proponents of the resource-based approach to strategy argue that rather than trying to focus on a 'fit' with their environment (a position-based approach), organisations should focus their strategy on their own core competences and capabilities – in other words, what they are good at.

4. Plans and standards; sensor to detect actual performance; comparator to compare performance with plans and standards; effector to take control action where necessary. Feedback is information about performance.

5. Purpose; business strategy; policies and standards of behaviour; values

6. Specific, measurable, achievable, relevant, time-bounded

7. Work-based; standing; output or improvement; developmental

8. Vertically; horizontally (across departments); over time

9. Performance management is 'a means of getting better **results** [...] by **understanding** and managing performance within an agreed framework of planned **goals**, standards and **competence** requirements. It is a process to establish a **shared** understanding about what is to be achieved, and an approach to managing and **developing** people [... so that it ...] will be achieved'.

10.
Step 1	From the business plan, identify the requirements and competences required to carry it out
Step 2	Develop a performance agreement
Step 3	Draw up a performance and development plan with the individual
Step 4	Manage performance continually throughout the year
Step 5	Performance review

11. By participating in setting them

PART B MANAGEMENT PLANNING AND DECISION-MAKING

Internal analysis

Topic list	Syllabus reference
1 The position audit	D2
2 Resources and limiting factors	D2
3 Competences and critical success factors	D2
4 Converting resources: The value chain	D2
5 Outputs: The product portfolio	D2
6 The customer base	D2
7 Drawing the threads together	D2

Introduction

In this chapter we examine some of the key aspects of the organisation's current **position**. A **resource audit** identifies any gaps in resources and limiting factors on organisational activity. **Value chain** analysis identifies how the business adds value to the resources it obtains, and how it deploys these resources to satisfy customers. A **competence** is a skill which the organisation has which can ensure a fit between the environment and the organisation's capability. The internal appraisal should identify **strengths and weaknesses**.

We then review the organisation's current outputs, its **product portfolio**.

The purpose of all this activity is the customer, and a review of the **customer base** should identify trends and developments.

# 1 The position audit

> **FAST FORWARD**
>
> A **position audit** reviews the organisation's current position.

Key term

> **Position audit** is the part of the planning process that examines the current state of the business entity. A wide range of factors is examined. Here are some examples.
>
> - Resources of tangible and intangible **assets**
> - Products, brands and markets
> - Operating systems such as production and distribution
> - Internal organisation
> - Current results
> - Financial resources

2 Resources and limiting factors

> **FAST FORWARD**
>
> **Resource audits** identify human, financial and material resources and how they are deployed.

A **resource audit** is a review of all aspects of the resources the organisation uses.

Resource	Example
Material inputs	Source, suppliers, waste, new materials, cost, availability, future provision
Human resources	Number, skills, efficiency, industrial relations, adaptability, innovatory capacity
Management	Size, skills, loyalty, career progression, structure
Fixed assets	Age, condition, utilisation rate, value, replacement cost, technologically up-to-date?
Finance	Short-term and long-term capital, gearing levels, working capital, cash flow
Intangible assets	Patents, goodwill, brands, image
Organisation	Culture and structure
Knowledge	Ability to generate and disseminate ideas, innovation

Unique resources are particularly valuable and an important source of competitive advantage.

Key term

> A **unique resource** is one which is both better than its equivalent employed by competitors and difficult to imitate.

Resources are of no value unless they are organised into systems, and so a resource audit should go on to consider how well or how badly resources have been utilised, and whether the organisation's systems are effective and efficient.

2.1 Limiting factors

Every organisation operates under resource **constraints**.

2.1.1 Examples

- A shortage of production capacity
- A limited number of key personnel, such as salespeople with technical knowledge
- A restricted distribution network
- Too few managers with knowledge about finance, or overseas markets
- Inadequate research design resources to develop new products or services
- A poor system of strategic intelligence
- Lack of money
- A lack of adequately trained staff

Once the limiting factor has been identified, the planners should do two things.

- In the short-term, make best use of the resources available
- Try to reduce the limitation in the long-term

2.2 Resource use

Resource use is concerned with the efficiency with which resources are used (that is, the relationships between the goods and services produced and the resources used to produce them), and the effectiveness of their use in achieving the planning objectives of the business.

3 Competences and critical success factors

FAST FORWARD

Competences are crucial to strategic success. They should be difficult to imitate and give market advantage. **Critical success factors** are the types and standards of performance that allow objectives to be achieved.

Competences develop in a variety of ways:

- **Experience** in making and marketing a product or service
- The talents and potential of individuals in the organisation
- The **quality of co-ordination**

Key term

Core competences critically underpin the organisation's competitive advantage.

An organisation must achieve at least a **threshold** level of competence in **everything** it does. The organisation's **core competences** are those where it **outperforms competitors** and that are **difficult to imitate**.

Competitiveness depends on **unique resources** or core competences. The organisation's level of performance in its core competences may be judged in three ways.

- Comparison with past results
- Comparison with industry norms
- Benchmarking

Hamel and Prahalad ('The Core Competence of the Corporation', *Harvard Business Review*, 1990) suggest that an important aspect of strategic management is the determining of the competences the company will require **in the future** in order to be able to provide new benefits to customers. They say a **core competence** must have three qualities.

- It must make a **disproportionate** contribution to the **value** the customer perceives.
- It must be '**competitively unique**', which means one of three things: actually unique; superior to competitors; or capable of dramatic improvement.
- It must be **extendable**, in that it must allow for the development of an array of new products and services.

Tests for identifying a core competence:

(a) **It provides potential access to a wide variety of markets**.

(b) **It contributes significantly to the value enjoyed by the customer**.

(c) **It should be hard for a competitor to copy**.

This will be the case if it is technically complex, involves specialised processes, involves complex interrelationships between different people in the organisation or is hard to define.

In many cases, a company might choose to combine competences.

Bear in mind that **relying on a competence is no substitute for a strategy**. However, a core competence can form a basis for a strategy. A competence must be difficult to imitate if it is to confer lasting competitive advantage.

3.1 Preparing resource plans

3.1.1 Critical success factors

Competences can be related to **critical success factors**.

> **Key terms**
>
> **Critical success factors (CSFs)** 'are those product features that are particularly valued by a group of customers, and, therefore, where the organisation must excel to outperform the competition'
> (**Johnson, Scholes and Whittington**, *Exploring Corporate Strategy*, 2005, p.96).
>
> **Key tasks** are what must be done to ensure each critical success factor is satisfied.
>
> **Priorities** indicate the order in which tasks are completed.

3.1.2 Example

- Some CSFs are generic to the whole industry, others to a particular firm. The critical success factor to run a successful **mail order business** is speedy delivery.
- A CSF of a **parcel delivery service** is that it **must be quicker than the normal post**.
- Underpinning critical success factors are **key tasks**. If **customer care** is a CSF, then a key task, and hence a measure of performance, would include responding to enquires within a given time period.

Question
CSFs

Draw up a list of four critical success factors for the strategy of the organisation for which you work.

3.1.3 Relationship between competences and CSFs

- A competence is what a organisation **has or is able to do**.
- A **CSF** is what is **necessary to achieve an objective**.

Competences thus fulfil the CSF. In the example quoted above, a competence of faster delivery supports a CSF that a courier service must be faster than a competitor.

The aim is to identify a small number of performance requirements that are **fundamental to competitive success** and the skills, processes and activities that support them.

Johnson and Scholes describe six stages in the process of managing strategy using CSFs.

Step 1	Identify the **CSFs**.
Step 2	Identify the **competences** that must be displayed if the CSFs are to be achieved.
Step 3	The core competences identified must then be considered to determine whether they are adequate to provide genuine **competitive advantage**, or whether they must be improved or supplemented.
Step 4	**A key performance indicator** must be identified for each competence so that strategic control may be exercised.
Step 5	The fifth step is to ensure that core competences both **outperform competitors** and are **difficult to imitate**. If they are not, competitive advantage will not be achieved.
Step 6	**Competitors' responses** must be monitored and their effects on the CSF structure forecast.

4 Converting resources: The value chain

FAST FORWARD

The **value chain** describes those activities of the organisation that add value to purchased inputs. Primary activities are involved in the production of goods and services. Support activities provide necessary assistance. **Linkages** are the relationships between activities. Managing the value chain, which includes relationships with outside suppliers, can be a source of strategic advantage.

The **value chain** model of corporate activities offers a bird's eye view of the firm and what it does. Competitive advantage arises out of the way in which firms organise and perform **activities** to add value.

4.1 Value activities

Key term

Value activities are the means by which a firm creates value in its products.

Activities incur costs, and, in combination with other activities, provide a product or service which earns revenue.

4.2 The value chain

Porter (*Competitive Advantage*, 1985) grouped the various activities of an organisation into a **value chain**, as illustrated in the following diagram.

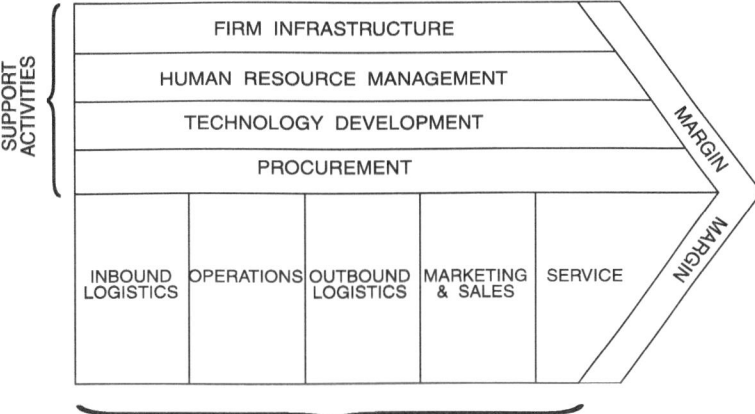

The **margin** is the excess the customer is prepared to **pay** over the **cost** to the firm of obtaining resource inputs and providing value activities. It represents the **value created** by the value activities themselves and by the **management of the linkages** between them.

Primary activities are directly related to production, sales, marketing, delivery and service.

Activity	Comment
Inbound logistics	Receiving, handling and storing inputs to the production system: warehousing, transport, stock control and so on.
Operations	Convert resource inputs into a final product. Resource inputs are not only materials. People are a resource especially in service industries.
Outbound logistics	Storing the product and its distribution to customers: packaging, testing, delivery and so on.
Marketing and sales	Informing customers about the product, persuading them to buy it, and enabling them to do so: advertising, promotion and so on.
After-sales service	Installing products, repairing them, upgrading them, providing spare parts and so forth.

Support activities provide purchased inputs, human resources, technology and infrastructural functions to support the primary activities.

Activity	Comment
Procurement	Acquire the resource inputs to the primary activities (eg purchase of materials, subcomponents equipment).
Technology development	Product design, improving processes and/or resource utilisation.
Human resource management	Recruiting, training, developing and rewarding people.
Firm infrastructure	Planning, finance, quality control: Porter believes they are crucially important to an organisation's strategic capability in all primary activities.

Linkages connect the activities of the value chain.

(a) **Activities in the value chain affect one another**. For example, more costly product design or better quality production might reduce the need for after-sales service.

(b) **Linkages require co-ordination**. For example, Just-In-Time requires smooth functioning of operations, outbound logistics and service activities such as installation.

4.3 The value chain and core competences

The purpose of value chain analysis is to understand how the company creates value. It is unlikely that any business has more than a handful of activities in which it outperforms its competitors. There is clear link here with the idea of core competences: a core competence will enable the company to create value in a way that its competitors cannot initiate. These value activities are the basis of the company's unique offering.

4.4 The value chain and core competences

There can be a strong case for outsourcing non-core activities so that management can concentrate on what the company does best.

There are also practical considerations relating to outsourcing.

- It can save on costs by making use of a suppliers' economies of scale.
- It can increase effectiveness where the supplier deploys higher levels of expertise.
- It can lead to loss of control, particularly over quality.
- It means giving up an area of threshold competence that may be difficult to require.
- It introduces the problems inherent in managing a third party relationship.

4.5 Problems with value chain management

Robbins and Coulter (in *Management*, 2017) highlighted a number of possible issues with value chain management.

(a) **Organisational barriers**. These include reluctance to change the status quo and share information, and security issues.

(b) **Cultural issues**. Lack of trust can be a particular problem, also the feeling that by co-operating with a partner the organisation is losing control of its own destiny.

(c) **Capabilities**. The business may not have the capabilities (coordination, collaboration, education, management experience) to capture and exploit the value chain.

(d) **People**. Full commitment and flexibility from staff is required and they must be highly motivated, given the time and energy needed for successful implementation.

Question

Service provision

ABC Co provides financial planning services for small businesses. Its management accountant has been tasked with a review of the company's activities in providing its services to customers.

In terms of Porter's value chain, which are NOT primary activities they should consider?

- A Inbound logistics
- B Firm infrastructure
- C Marketing and sales
- D Service

Answer

B   Firm infrastructure

Firm infrastructure is a support activity.

For a services company inbound logistics, marketing and sales and service are the most important factors. Inbound logistics usually refers to bringing goods/raw materials into a company, but can also refer to bringing people, such as getting passengers onto an aeroplane.

4.6 Value system

Activities and linkages that add value do not stop at the organisation's **boundaries**. For example, when a restaurant serves a meal, the quality of the ingredients – although they are chosen by the cook – is determined by the grower. The grower has added value, and the grower's success in growing produce of good quality is as important to the customer's ultimate satisfaction as the skills of the chef. A firm's value chain is part of a **value system**.

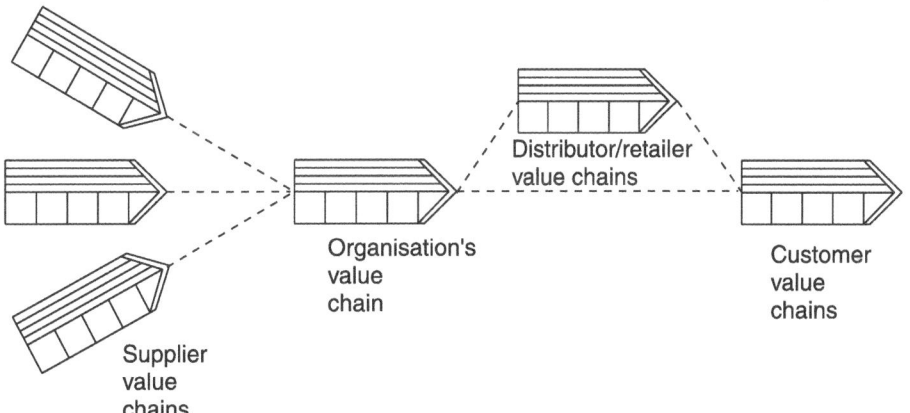

It may be possible to capture the benefit of some of the value generated both upstream and downstream in the value system. An obvious way to do this is by **vertical integration** through the acquisition of supplies and customers.

A more subtle advantage is gained by fostering good relationships that can promote **innovation** and the **creation of knowledge**.

PART B MANAGEMENT PLANNING AND DECISION-MAKING

Case Study

Toyota is well-known for close involvement with its suppliers. The company works with suppliers to improve their methods and the quality of their output; and to develop new, improved materials and components for input into its own operations. The relationship has benefits for all parties, but tends to be unequal, with Toyota dominating the operations of a large number of semi-captive suppliers.

Using the value chain. A firm can secure competitive advantage in several ways.

- Invent new or better ways to do activities
- Combine activities in new or better ways
- Manage the linkages in its own value chain
- Manage the linkages in the value system

Question   Value chain

Sana Sounds is a small record company. Representatives from Sana Sounds scour music clubs for new bands to promote. Once a band has signed a contract (with Sana Sounds) it makes a recording. The recording process is subcontracted to one of a number of recording studio firms which Sana Sounds uses regularly. (At the moment Sana Sounds is not large enough to invest in its own equipment and studios.) Sana Sounds maintains its own website for digital downloads of its recordings and subcontracts the production of CDs to a number of manufacturing companies. Sana Sounds then distributes the discs to selected stores, and engages in any promotional activities required.

What would you say were the activities in Sana Sounds' value chain?

Answer

Sana Sounds is involved in the record industry from start to finish. Although recording and CD manufacture are contracted out to external suppliers, this makes no difference to the fact that these activities are part of Sana Sounds' own value chain. Sana Sounds earns its money by managing the whole set of activities. If the company grows then perhaps it will acquire its own recording studios.

5 Outputs: The product portfolio

Many firms make a number of different products or services. Each product or service has its own financial, marketing and risk characteristics. The combination of products or services influences the attractiveness and profitability of the firm.

5.1 The product life cycle

FAST FORWARD

> The **product life cycle** concept holds that products have a life cycle, and that a product demonstrates different characteristics of profit and investment at each stage in its life cycle. The life cycle concept is a model, not a prediction. (Not all products pass through each stage of the life cycle.) It enables a firm to examine its portfolio of goods and services as a whole.

The profitability and sales of a product can be expected to change over time. The **product life cycle** is an attempt to recognise distinct stages in a product's sales history. Marketing managers distinguish between different aspects of the product.

(a) **Product class:** this is a broad category of product, such as cars, washing machines, newspapers' also referred to as the **generic product**.

(b) **Product form:** within a product class products take different forms, for example five-door hatchback cars or two-seater sports cars.

(c) **Brand:** the particular type of the product form (eg Ford Focus).

The product life cycle applies in differing degrees to each of the three cases. A product-class (eg cars) may have a long maturity stage, and a particular make or brand (eg Rolls Royce) might have an erratic life cycle or not. Product forms tend to conform to the classic life cycle pattern however.

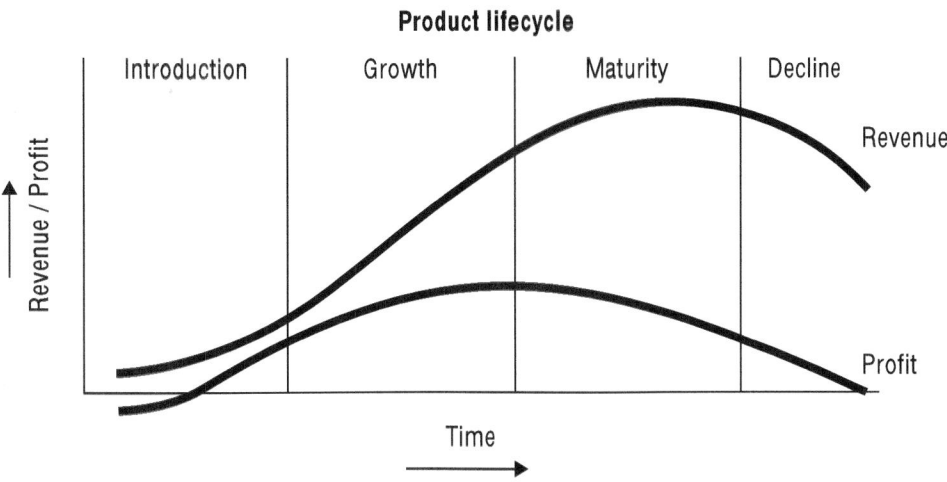

5.1.1 Introduction

- A new product takes time to be accepted. There is a slow growth in sales. Unit costs are high due to low output and costly promotions. High marketing costs in order to get product recognised by customers.
- There may be early teething troubles with production technology.
- Limited product range
- The product for the time being is a loss-maker, and has negative cash flows.
- The product is high risk because it is new and has not yet been accepted by the market.
- The product has few competitors (because they are not willing to take similar risks).

5.1.2 Growth

- If the new product gains market acceptance, sales will eventually rise more sharply and the product will start to make profits.
- Capital investments are needed to fulfil levels of demand meaning cash flow remains lower than profit. Cash flow likely to remain negative.
- Competitors are attracted with similar products, but as sales and production rise, unit costs fall.
- There is a need to add additional features to differentiate from competitors, so product complexity likely to rise. Alternatively, firm may choose to lower price and compete on price grounds.
- Continued marketing expenditure is required to differentiate the firm's product from competitors' offerings.
- Growth is sustained by attracting new types of customers.

5.1.3 Maturity

- The market is no longer growing. Purchases are now based on repeat or replacement purchases, rather than new customers.

- This is probably the longest period of a successful product's life as customers buy to replace existing products when they reach the end of their useful lives.

- Most products on the market will be at the mature stage of their life.

- Profits remain good, and levels of investment are low, meaning cash flow is also positive.

- Prices likely to start to decline, as firms compete with one another to try to increase their share of a fixed-size market.

- Firms try to capitalise on existing brand name by launching spin-off products under the same name.

- The number of firms in industry reduces again, due to consolidation in the industry in an attempt to restore profitability.

5.1.4 Decline

Eventually, the product is superseded by **technically superior substitutes**. Sales begin to decline and there is over-capacity of production in the industry. Severe competition occurs, **profits fall** and some **producers leave the market**. The remaining producers try to prolong the product life by modifying it and searching for new (niche) market segments. Although some producers are reluctant to leave the market if they haven't found alternative industries to move into, many inevitably do because of falling profits.

Case Study

Television

Over time, the design and specification of television sets has changed. Black and white screens have been superseded by colour; cathode ray tubes have been superseded by flat screen and plasma screens, and manufacturers have developed home cinema systems.

However, the switch to online distribution methods of video content is also now having significant implications for the television set industry, and there are already indications that viewer habits are changing.

Online TV, mobile phone TV and free TV catch up services offered by the major channels give viewers much greater choice and flexibility, allowing them to watch programmes at their own convenience. Figures now indicate that TV audience figures are dropping, whilst internet access is on the rise. Suggestions have even been made that television sets could become a thing of the past.

5.1.5 The relevance of the product life cycle to strategic planning

In reviewing outputs, planners should assess products in three ways in order to determine an appropriate strategy.

(a) The **stage of its life cycle** that any product has reached. For example, in the growth stage, a firm's strategy might focus on trying to differentiate its product from those of its competitors, and it might have to incur high marketing costs to achieve this. However, for a mature product, the focus will be on controlling costs.

(b) The **product's remaining life**, ie how much longer it will contribute to profits?

(c) How **urgent is the need to innovate**, to develop new and improved products?

5.1.6 The product life cycle and marketing planning

It is essential that firms plan their portfolio of products to ensure that new products are generating positive cash-flow before existing 'earners' enter the decline stage.

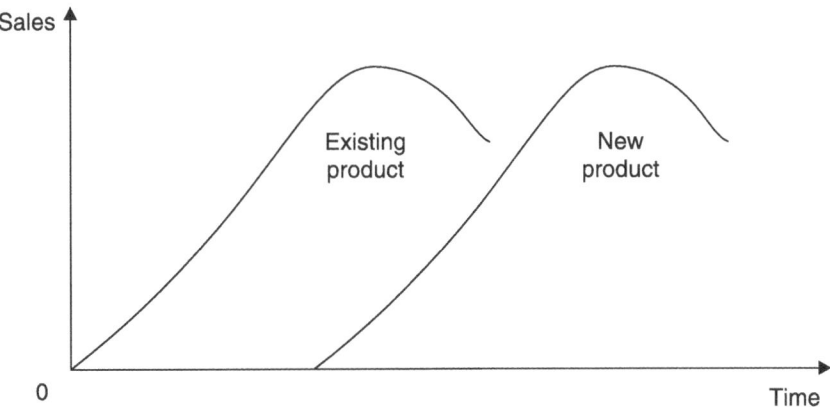

In the situation above the company is likely to experience cash-flow problems.

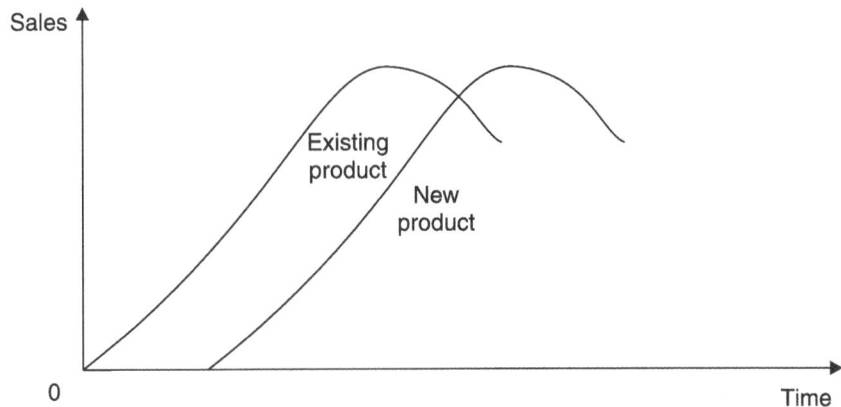

By considering the product life cycle of the existing product when planning the timing for launch of a new product cash-flow problems can be avoided.

It is perhaps easy enough to accept that products have a life cycle, but it is not so easy to sort out how far through its life a product is, and what its expected future life might be.

5.1.7 Difficulties of the product life cycle concept

(a) **Recognition**. How can managers recognise where a product is in its life cycle?

(b) **Not always true**. Some products have no maturity phase, and go straight from growth to decline. Some never decline if marketed competitively.

(c) **Descriptive not predictive**. Managers cannot use the lifecycle to predict future sales, because the model describes general trends, rather than having any value for detailed predictions.

(d) **Changeable**. Strategic decisions can change or extend a product's life cycle.

(e) **Competition varies** in different industries. The financial markets are an example of markets where there is a tendency for competitors to copy the leader very quickly, so that competition has built up well ahead of demand.

(f) **Focus on the product**. Sometimes a customer group or market is a better unit of strategic analysis than a single product. A product may be at different stages of its life cycle in different **markets**.

(g) **Lack of clarity** about 'the product'. For example, for a car manufacturer, is its 'product' a car in general terms, a type of car (eg petrol vs diesel car) or a specific brand or model of car?

(h) **Single product only**. The model only looks at a single product at a time. It does not consider the connections between that product and other products in a company's product portfolio. For example, are some products which are mature necessary in order to attract customers who will then buy products which are in their growth stage?

5.1.8 The industry life cycle concept

In the same way we can identify a product life cycle, it may also be possible to discern an **industry life cycle**, which will have wider implications for the nature of competition and competitive advantage.

An industry is a group of firms producing the same product or products that are close substitutes for one another. So, the stages of the industry life cycle do not relate just to products, but to aspects such as the number of competitors in the industry, the number of customers, and the level of profits which firms can sustain.

This cycle reflects changes in demand and the spread of technical knowledge among producers. Innovation creates the new industry, and this is normally product innovation. Later, innovation shifts to processes in order to maintain margins. The overall progress of the industry lifecycle is illustrated below.

	Inception	Growth	Maturity	Decline
Products	Basic, no standards established	Better, more sophisticated, differentiated	Superior, standardised	Varied quality but fairly undifferentiated
Competitors	None to few	Many entrants Little concentration in industry	Competition increases, weaker players leave	Few remain. Competition may be on price
Buyers	Early adopters, prosperous, curious must be induced	More customers attracted and aware	Mass market, brand switching common	Enthusiasts, traditionalists, sophisticates
Profits	Negative – high first mover advantage	Good, possibly starting to decline	Eroding under pressure of competition	Variable
Strategy	Dominate market, build quality	React to competitors with marketing spend	Cost reductions sought	Control costs

5.2 Portfolio planning

Portfolio analysis examines the current status of the organisation's products and their markets. Portfolio analysis is the first stage of **portfolio planning**, which aims to create a balance among the organisation's market offerings in order to maximise competitive advantage. The same approach is equally applicable to products, market segments and even strategic business units (SBUs).

Four **major strategies** can be pursued with respect to products, market segments and, indeed, strategic business units (SBUs).

(a) **Build**. A build strategy forgoes short-term earnings and profits in order to increase market share.

(b) **Hold**. A hold strategy seeks to maintain the current position.

(c) **Harvest**. A harvesting strategy seeks short-term earning and profits at the expense of long-term development.

(d) **Divest**. Divestment reduces negative cash flow and releases resources for use elsewhere.

5.2.1 Market share, market growth and cash generation: The Boston classification

FAST FORWARD

The **Boston classification** classifies products in terms of their capacity for growth within the market and the market's capacity for growth as a whole. A firm should have a balanced **portfolio of products**.

The **Boston Consulting Group** (BCG) developed a matrix based on empirical research that assesses a company's products in terms of potential cash generation and cash expenditure requirements. Products or SBUs are categorised in terms of market growth rate and relative market share.

(a) Assessing rate of **market growth** as high or low depends on the conditions in the market.

(b) **Relative market share** is assessed as a ratio: it is market share compared with the market share of the **largest competitor**. Thus a relative market share greater than unity indicates that the product or SBU is the market leader.

To illustrate how to evaluate a portfolio, a simulated company example will be provided. An industrial equipment company has five products with the following sales and market characteristics

Product	Sales £m	Top 3 firms £m sales			Market growth rate %	Relative share
A	0.5	0.7	0.7	0.5*	15%	0.71
B	1.6	1.6	1.6*	1.0	18%	1.0
C	1.8	1.8*	1.2	1.0	7%	1.5
D	3.2	3.2*	0.8	0.7	4%	4.0
E	0.5	2.5	1.8	1.7	4%	0.2

* Company sales within the market

This information can then be plotted on to a matrix. The circles indicate the contribution the product makes to overall turnover. The centre of circles indicates their position on the matrix:

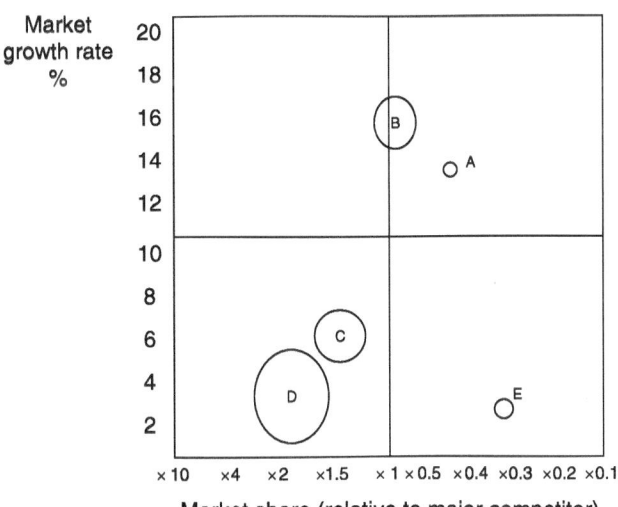

This growth/share matrix for the classification of products into cash cows, cash dogs, stars and question marks is known as the **Boston classification** (or the **Boston Matrix**).

BCG matrix

	Relative market share	
	High	Low
Market growth High	Stars	Question marks
Market growth Low	Cash cows	Dogs

(Adapted from: **Henderson**, *The Product Portfolio*, 1970)

The product portfolio should be balanced, with cash cows providing finance for stars and question marks; and a minimum of dogs.

(a) **Stars**. In the short term, these require capital expenditure in excess of the cash they generate, in order to maintain their market position, but promise high returns in the future. Strategy: **build**.

(b) In due course, stars will become **cash cows**. Cash cows need very little capital expenditure and generate high levels of cash income. However, it is important to remember that apparently mature products can be invigorated, possibly by competitors, who could thus come to dominate the market. Cash cows can be used to finance the stars. Strategy: **hold** or **harvest** if weak.

(c) **Question marks**. Do the products justify considerable capital expenditure in the hope of increasing their market share, or should they be allowed to die quietly as they are squeezed out of the expanding market by rival products? Strategy: **build** or **harvest**.

(d) **Dogs**. They may be ex-cash cows that have now fallen on hard times. Although they will show only a modest net cash outflow, or even a modest net cash inflow, they are cash traps which tie up funds and provide a poor return on investment. However, they may have a useful role, either to complete a product range or to keep competitors out. There are also many smaller niche businesses in market that are difficult to consolidate that would count as dogs but which are quite successful. Strategy: **divest** or **hold**.

Question — Juicy Drinks Ltd

The marketing manager of Juicy Drinks Ltd has invited you in for a chat. Juicy Drinks Ltd provides fruit juices to a number of supermarket chains, which sell them under their own label. 'We've got a large number of products, of course. Our freshly squeezed orange juice is doing fine – it sells in huge quantities. Although margins are low, we have sufficient economies of scale to do very nicely in this market. We've got advanced production and bottling equipment and long-term contracts with some major growers. No problems there. We also sell freshly squeezed pomegranate juice: customers loved it in the tests, but producing the stuff at the right price is a major hassle: all the seeds get in the way. We hope it will be a winner, once we get the production right and start converting customers to it. After all the market for exotic fruit juices generally is expanding fast.'

What sort of products, according to the Boston classification, are described here?

Answer

(a) Orange juice is a cash cow.
(b) Pomegranate juice is a question mark, which the company wants to turn into a star.

5.2.2 The General Electric Business Screen

The approach of the GE Business Screen (GEBS) is similar to that of the BCG matrix. The GEBS includes a broader range of company and market factors. A typical example of the GE matrix is provided below. This matrix **classifies products** (or **businesses**) according to **industry attractiveness** and **company strengths**. The approach aims to consider a variety of factors which contribute to both these variables.

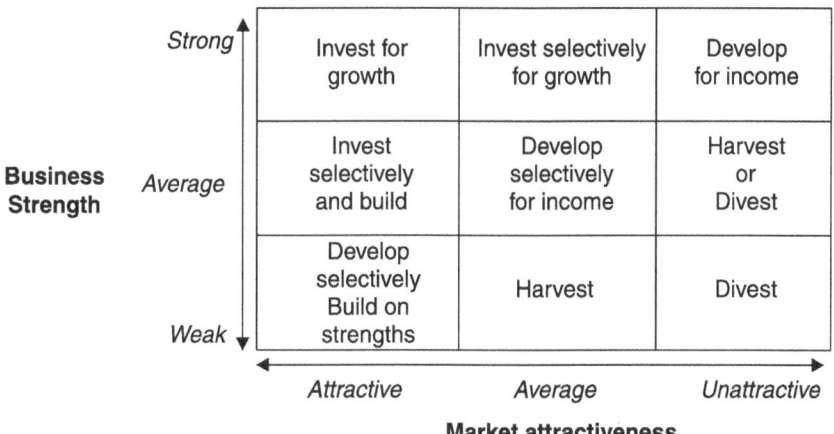

5.2.3 The Shell directional policy matrix

There have been several other matrices designed as guides to strategy. The **Shell directional policy matrix** is similar to the GEBS in that its classifications depend upon **managerial judgement** rather than simple **numerical scores**, as in the BCG matrix. Its axes are **competitive capability** and **prospects for sector profitability**. Clearly, these measures are very similar to those used in the GEBS.

		Prospects for sector profitability		
		Unattractive	Average	Attractive
	Weak	Disinvest	Phased withdrawal	Double or quit
Enterprise's competitive capabilities	Average	Phased withdrawal	Custodial Growth	Try harder
	Strong	Cash generation	Growth Leader	Leader

The Shell directional policy matrix

Question — Product strategy

Metune Co is constantly developing new brands, but currently faces a situation where it wishes to make a large investment in a new brand with excellent long-term prospects according to forecasts. Profits from one of its long-term brands have been growing slowly over a number of years and this trend is expected to continue. A competitor has just made an offer to take over this long-term brand that Metune Co's board believes to be generous.

Which of the following strategies is Metune Co likely to adopt in relation to the long-term brand?

A   Build
B   Hold
C   Harvest
D   Divest

Answer

C   Harvest

Harvest is likely to be chosen in preference to Hold as the brand has limited long-term prospects and can be sold to achieve the short-term flow of funds that Metune Co requires.

The brand is unlikely to be built (have further investment) as other brands offer better prospects. Divest is only appropriate if the brand is making losses and has negative cash flows.

6 The customer base

FAST FORWARD

> A **marketing audit** involves a review of an organisation's products and markets, the marketing environment, and its marketing system and operations. The profitability of each product and each market should be assessed, and the costs of different marketing activities established.

6.1 The marketing audit

In effect, the marketing audit is the marketing equivalent of the corporate strategic analysis.

The marketing audit provides the basis upon which a plan of action to improve marketing performance can be built. It also provides answers to the following questions in relation to a firm's marketing strategy.

- Where are we now?
- How did we get here?
- Where are we heading?

A marketing audit can be contrasted with market research activities because of its clear objectives. Market research relates to activities that gather information about target customers and markets.

6.1.1 Aspects of a marketing audit

There are five aspects to a marketing audit:

(a) **Market analysis.** This looks at:

- Market size, market growth and trends. A company cannot know whether its market share objectives are feasible unless it knows the market's overall size and the position of competitors. Forecasting areas of growth and decline is also important.

- Customer analysis and buyer behaviour. The analysis needs to identify who a company's (or a brand's) customers are, what they need, and characteristics of their buying behaviour. This kind of customer analysis could help to point out opportunities for a company.

- Companies need to monitor changing customer tastes, lifestyles, behaviours, needs and expectations so that they can continue to meet existing customer needs effectively, as well as seeking out new customer needs which have not yet been met.

- Competitor analysis – Competitor analysis helps an organisation understand its competitive advantages/disadvantages compared with its competitors. Who are the competitors? What are their strategies and objectives? What are their strengths and weaknesses? How are they likely to respond to the organisation's own strategies? What is their market share?

- Analysis of different distribution channels and their relative strengths and weaknesses. Changes in distribution channels can open up new fields of opportunity (most notably in the growth of e-commerce).
- Supplier analysis – trends in the supply chain; power of suppliers; strengths and weaknesses of key suppliers.

(b) **Strategic issues analysis**. This involves considering the suitability of the organisation's marketing objectives in relation to the marketplace and any changes in the market. Points to consider are likely to include: market segmentation; basis of competitive advantage; core competences; positioning; and product portfolio.

(c) **Review of marketing mix effectiveness** – including an analysis of product, price, promotion and distribution

(d) **Marketing structure** – including marketing organisation (does the organisation of the marketing department fit with the strategy and the market?); marketing training; and intra- and inter-departmental communication

(e) **Marketing systems**. Three different types of system are considered:
- Marketing information systems: What information do they provide about current performance? Is this information sufficient?
- Marketing planning systems: How effective are they in setting marketing objectives and formulating the plans for achieving them?
- Marketing control systems: Can the systems provide an evaluation of marketing campaigns?

6.2 Detailed market information

(a) **Size of the customer base**. Does the organisation sell to a large number of small customers or a small number of big customers?

(b) **Size of individual orders**. The organisation might sell its products in many small orders, or it might have large individual orders. Delivery costs can be compared with order sizes.

(c) **Sales revenue and profitability**. The performance of individual products can be compared.

(d) **Segments**. An analysis of sales and profitability into, for instance, export markets and domestic markets.

(e) **Market share**. Estimated share of the market obtained by each product group.

(f) **Growth**. Sales growth and contribution growth over the previous four years or so, for each product group.

(g) Whether the **demand** for certain products is **growing, stable or likely to decline**.

(h) Whether **demand is price sensitive** or not.

(i) Whether there is a growing tendency for the market to become **fragmented**, with more specialist and custom-made products.

Information about current marketing activities
- Comparative pricing
- Advertising effectiveness
- Effectiveness of distribution network
- Attitudes to the product, in comparison with competitors

6.3 Detailed customer analysis

Many firms, especially in business-to-business markets, sell to a relatively small number of customers. **Key customer analysis** calls for seven main areas of investigation.

(a) **Key customer identity** (name, location, size, product market)

(b) **Customer history**: order size and frequency, reasons for purchase, key decision-makers

(c) **Relationship of customer to product**
- Are the products purchased to be resold? If not, why are they bought?
- Do the products form part of the customer's service/product?

(d) **Relationship of customer to potential market**
- What is the size of the customer in relation to the total end-market?
- Is the customer likely to expand, or not? Diversify? Integrate?

(e) **Customer attitudes and behaviour**
- What interpersonal factors affect sales by the firm and by competitors?
- Does the customer also buy competitors' products?
- To what extent may purchases be postponed?
- What emotional factors exist in buying decisions?

(f) **The financial performance of the customer**

How successful is the customer in his own markets?

(g) **The profitability of selling to the customer**
- What profit/contribution is the organisation making on sales to the customer, after discounts and selling and delivery costs?
- What would be the financial consequences of losing the customer?
- Is the customer buying in order sizes that are unprofitable to supply?
- What is return on investment in plant used?
- What is the level of inventory required specifically to supply these customers?
- Are there any other specific costs involved in supplying this customer, such as technical and test facilities, R&D facilities, special design staff?
- What is the ratio of net contribution per customer to total investment on both a historic and replacement cost basis?

7 Drawing the threads together

Organisational performance depends on the interplay of a range of elements. This interdependence is illustrated by the **McKinsey 7S model** (**Peters & Waterman**, *In Search of Excellence,* 1982), which is a useful illustration of the way culture fits into an organisation. In particular, it shows the links between the organisation's behaviour and the behaviour of individuals within it.

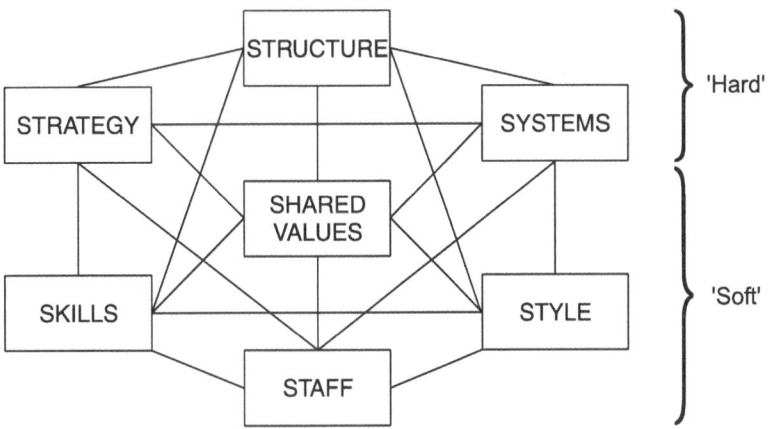

Three of the elements are considered 'hard'.

(a) **Structure**. The organisation structure determines division of tasks in the organisation and the hierarchy of authority from the most senior to junior.

(b) **Strategy**. Strategy is the way in which the organisation plans to outperform its competitors, if it is a business, or how it intends to achieve its objectives.

(c) **Systems**. Systems include the technical systems of accounting, personnel, management information and so forth.

These 'hard' elements are easily quantified or defined, and deal with **facts and rules**.

However, the McKinsey model suggests that certain 'soft' elements are equally important.

(a) **Shared values** are the guiding beliefs of people in the organisation as to why it exists.
(For example, people in a hospital seek to save lives.) It forms part of the corporate culture.

(b) **Staff** are the people in the organisation. They have their own complex concerns and priorities.

(c) **Style** is another aspect of the **corporate culture,** which includes the shared assumptions, ways of working and attitudes of management.

(d) **Skills** refer to those things that the organisation does well.

PART B   MANAGEMENT PLANNING AND DECISION-MAKING

Chapter roundup

- A **position audit** reviews the organisation's current position.
- **Resource audits** identify human, financial and material resources and how they are deployed.
- **Competences** are crucial to strategic success. They should be difficult to initiate and give market advantage. **Critical success factors** are the types and statements of performance that allow objectives to be achieved.
- The **value chain** describes those activities of the organisation that add value to purchased inputs. Primary activities are involved in the production of goods and services. Support activities provide necessary assistance. **Linkages** are the relationships between activities. Managing the value chain, which includes relationships with outside suppliers, can be a source of strategic advantage.
- The **product life cycle** concept holds that products have a life cycle, and that a product demonstrates different characteristics of profit and investment at each stage in its life cycle. The life cycle concept is a model, not a prediction. (Not all products pass through each stage of the life cycle.) It enables a firm to examine its portfolio of goods and services as a whole.
- **Portfolio analysis** examines the current status of the organisation's products and their markets. Portfolio analysis is the first stage of **portfolio planning**, which aims to create a balance among the organisation's market offerings in order to maximise competitive advantage. The same approach is equally applicable to products, market segments and even strategic business units (SBUs).
- The **Boston classification** classifies products in terms of their capacity for growth within the market and the market's capacity for growth as a whole. A firm should have a balanced **portfolio of products**.
- A **marketing audit** involves a review of an organisation's products and markets, the marketing environment, and its marketing system and operations. The profitability of each product and each market should be assessed, and the costs of different marketing activities established.

Quick quiz

1. What is a limiting factor?
2. What is a core competence?
3. What is the significance of the value chain?
4. Distinguish between product class and product form.
5. List the stages of the product life cycle.
6. What is a cash cow?
7. What is a marketing audit?
8. What is key customer analysis?

Answers to quick quiz

1. Any factor that limits activity, usually because of a shortage
2. Competences where the organisation outperforms competitors and that are difficult to imitate
3. The value chain illustrates how value is created by value activities and linkages.
4. Product class is a broad generic category, eg 'car'. Product form is a specific type within the class, eg 'executive saloon'.
5. Introduction, growth, maturity, decline
6. A product that requires little expenditure but generates plentiful revenue. Cash cows have a relatively high market share, in markets where there is little growth.
7. A comprehensive review of products and markets, the marketing environment and marketing system
8. Establishment of important data about important customers

PART B MANAGEMENT PLANNING AND DECISION-MAKING

Environmental analysis

Topic list	Syllabus reference
1 The organisation as an open system	D2
2 The general environment	D2
3 Competitive forces	D2
4 SWOT analysis	D2
5 Strategic intelligence and decision-making aids	D2

Introduction

The aim of environmental analysis is to review the environment for **opportunities** and **threats**, and to secure environmental fit. An organisation has many interchanges with its environment. It draws inputs from it and outputs goods and services to it. The environment is a major **source of uncertainty**.

An organisation is affected by **general environmental trends** usefully summarised in the **PEST** model. Issues relating specifically to its particular industry reflect the **competitive environment**, and we discuss **Porter's five forces model** as a way of analysing it.

PART B MANAGEMENT PLANNING AND DECISION-MAKING

1 The organisation as an open system

FAST FORWARD

General system theory would see the organisation as an **open system**, interacting with its environment.

1.1 Systems theory

Key term

Curtis defines a **system** as a collection of interrelated parts which taken together forms a whole such that:

(a) The collection has some purpose.
(b) A change in any of the parts leads to or results from a change in some other part or parts.

An organisation is a type of system.

1.2 Open and closed systems

General systems theory makes a distinction between open, closed and semi-closed systems.

(a) **A closed system is isolated from its environment and independent of it**, so that no environmental influences affect the behaviour of the system, nor does the system exert any influence on its environment.

(b) **An open system is connected to and interacts with its environment**. It takes in influences from its environment and also influences this environment by its behaviour. An open system is a stable system which is nevertheless continually changing or evolving.

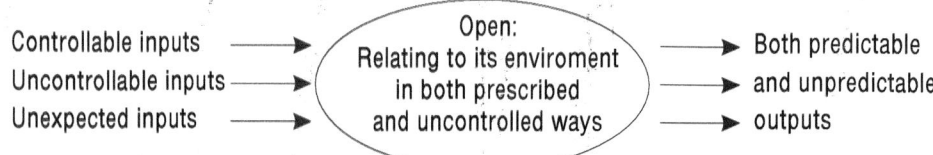

(c) **Few systems are entirely closed**. Many are **semi-closed**, in that their relationship with the environment is in some degree restricted. An example of a semi-closed system might be a pocket calculator. Its inputs are restricted to energy from its batteries and numerical information entered to it in a particular way (by the operator depressing a sequence of keys). The calculator is restricted in what it will do.

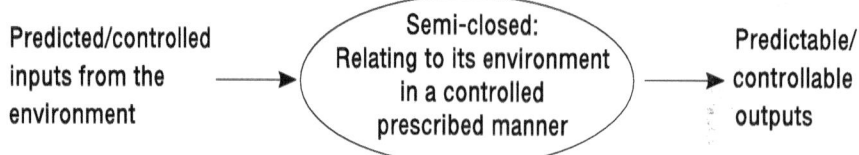

Social organisations, such as businesses and government departments, are by definition open systems.

Organisations have a variety of interchanges with the environment, obtaining inputs from it, and generating outputs to it.

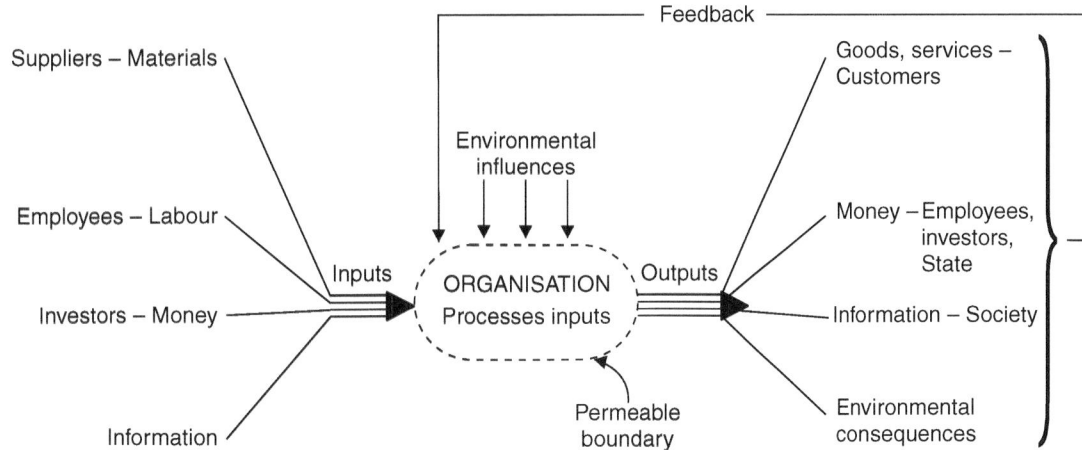

1.3 Environmental uncertainty

FAST FORWARD

Environmental uncertainty depends on the degree of **complexity** and the degree of **stability** present.

A large part of business strategy consists of making the organisation's interaction with its environment as efficient as possible. In the context of strategic management, therefore, the degree of **uncertainty** in the environment is of great importance. The greater the uncertainty, the greater the strategic challenge.

Uncertainty depends on **complexity** and **stability**: the more complex or dynamic the environment is, the more uncertain it is.

(a) An **uncomplicated**, **stable** environment can be dealt with as a matter of routine. The security and efficiency of a **mechanistic** or **bureaucratic** approach to management can be exploited. Since the future is likely to resemble the past, extrapolation from history is a satisfactory way of preparing for future events.

(b) Where the environment is **dynamic**, the management approach must emphasise response to rapid change. **Scenario planning**, **intuition** and a **learning approach** are all valid features of such a response.

(c) **Complexity** makes an environment difficult to understand. Diversity of operations and technological advance contribute to complexity. Complexity is difficult to analyse. It may be that it is best dealt with by a combination of **experience** and **extensive decentralisation**.

PART B MANAGEMENT PLANNING AND DECISION-MAKING

2 The general environment

FAST FORWARD

The **organisation's environment** is a source of **uncertainty**, depending on how **complex** or **dynamic** it is. General factors (PEST) affect all organisations.

The environment of an organisation is everything outside its boundaries.

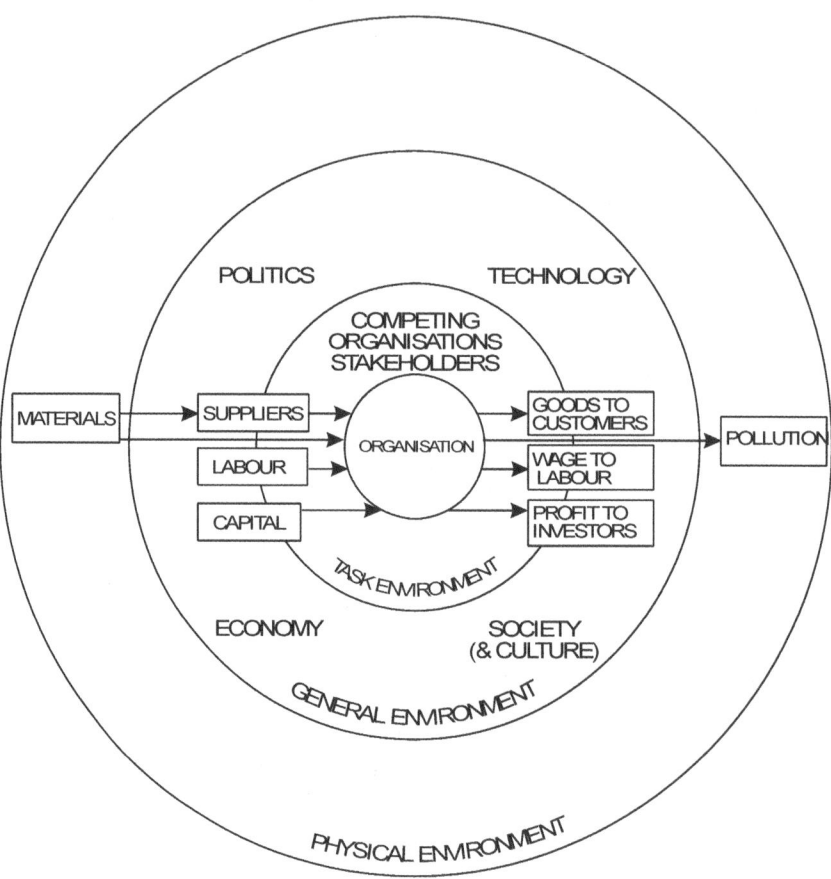

As you can see:

(a) The **task** (or micro- or near) **environment** is of immediate concern, and is uniquely configured for each organisation: no organisation has a network of suppliers, customers, competitors or stakeholders identical to another's.

(b) The **general** (or macro- or far) **environment** relates to PEST factors in the environment affecting all organisations.

- Political-legal factors
- Economic factors
- Social and cultural factors
- Technological factors

2.1 The political and legal environment

Laws come from common law, parliamentary legislation and government regulations derived from it, and obligations under international treaties.

Legal factors affecting all companies

Factor	Example
General legal framework: contract, tort, agency	Basic ways of doing business; negligence proceedings; ownership; rights and responsibilities, property
Criminal law	Theft; insider dealing; bribery; deception

5: ENVIRONMENTAL ANALYSIS

Factor	Example
Company law	Directors and their duties; reporting requirements; takeover proceedings; shareholders' rights; insolvency
Employment law	Trade Union recognition; minimum wage; unfair dismissal; redundancy; maternity; equal opportunities
Health and Safety	Fire precautions; safety procedures
Data protection	Use of information about employees and customers
Marketing and sales	Laws to protect consumers (eg refunds and replacement, 'cooling-off' period after credit agreements); what is or isn't allowed in advertising
Environment	Pollution control; waste disposal
Tax law	Corporation tax payment; Collection of income tax; sales tax
Competition law	General illegality of cartels

Some legal and regulatory factors affect **particular industries**, if the public interest is served. For example, electricity, gas, telecommunications, water and rail transport may be subject to **regulators** who have influence over market access, competition and pricing policy (can restrict price increase).

2.1.1 Public policy on competition

FAST FORWARD

Public policy on **competition** and **consumer protection** is particularly relevant to business strategy.

Monopolies may have economic disadvantages and economic advantages.

(a) A **beneficial monopoly** achieves **economies of scale** in an industry where the **minimum efficient scale** is at a level of production that would mean having to achieve a large share of the total market supply.

(b) A monopoly would be detrimental to the public interest if **cost efficiencies** are not achieved. For example, managers might instead try to maximise sales, or try to maximise their own prestige.

Consumer protection policies

(a) Control over markets can arise by firms eliminating the opposition, either by merging with or taking over rivals or stopping other firms from entering the market. When a single firm controls a big enough share of the market it can begin to behave as a monopolist even though its market share is below 100%.

(b) Several firms could behave as monopolists by agreeing with each other not to compete. Such a **collusive oligopoly** is called a cartel.

Countries have a variety of policies aiming to restrict the domination of a particular market by one firm and to prevent cartels.

2.1.2 Government policy

The political environment is not simply limited to legal factors. Government policy affects the whole **economy**, and governments are responsible for enforcing and creating a **stable framework** in which business can be done. The quality of **government policy is important in providing** three things:

- Physical infrastructure (eg transport)
- Social infrastructure (education, a welfare safety net, law enforcement, equal opportunities)
- Market infrastructure (enforceable contracts, policing corruption)

However, it is **political change** which complicates the planning activities of many firms.

Consideration	Example
Possibility of political change	Dissatisfaction with low prices at which utilities were sold to private sector
Likely nature of impact	Windfall tax
Consequences	How much will be paid
Coping strategies	Cash flow planning
Influence on decision-making	Lobbying

2.1.3 Political risk

The political risk in a decision is the risk that political factors will invalidate the strategy and perhaps severely damage the firm. Examples are wars, political chaos, corruption and nationalisation.

2.2 The economic environment

The economic environment is an important influence at local and national level.

Factor	Impact
Overall growth or fall in gross domestic product	Increased/decreased demand for goods (eg dishwashers) and services (eg holidays)
Local economic trends	Type of industry in the area, office/factory rents, wage rates, house prices
Inflation	Low in most countries; distorts business decisions; wage inflation compensates for price inflation
Interest rates	How much it costs to borrow money affects cash flow. Some businesses carry a high level of debt. How much customers can afford to spend is also affected as rises in interest rates affect people's mortgage payments.
Tax levels	Corporation tax affects how much firms can invest or return to shareholders. Income tax and sales tax affect how much consumers have to spend, hence demand.
Government spending	Suppliers to the government (eg construction firms) are affected by spending.
The business cycle	Economic activity is always punctuated by periods of growth followed by decline, simply because of the nature of trade. Government policy can cause, exacerbate or mitigate such trends, but cannot abolish the business cycle.

The **forecast state of the economy** will influence the planning process for organisations which operate within it.

2.2.1 Impact of international factors

Factor	Impact
Exchange rates	Cost of imports, selling prices and value of exports; cost of hedging against fluctuations
Characteristics of overseas markets	Desirable overseas markets (demand) or sources of supply
International capital markets	Generally, advanced economies accept that supply and demand set the value of their currencies, using interest rates only to control inflation.
Large multinational companies	MNCs have huge turnovers and significant political influence because of governments' desire to attract capital investment.

2.3 The social environment

The **social and cultural** environment features long-term social trends and people's beliefs and attitudes (eg concern with 'green' issues).

2.3.1 Demography

Key term

Demography is the study of human population and population trends.

Factors of importance to organisational planners

Factor	Comment
Growth	The rate of growth or decline in a national population and in regional populations
Age	Changes in the age distribution of the population
Geography	The concentration of population into certain geographical areas
Ethnicity	A population might contain groups with different ethnic origins from the majority.
Household and family structure	A household is the basic social unit and its size might be determined by the number of children, whether elderly parents live at home and so on..
Social structure	The population of a society can be broken down into a number of subgroups, with different attitudes and access to economic resources. Social class, however, is hard to measure (as people's subjective perceptions vary).
Employment	In part, this is related to changes in the workplace. Many people believe that there is a move to a casual flexible workforce; factories will have a group of **core employees**, supplemented by a group of insecure **peripheral employees**, on part-time or temporary contracts, working as and when required. Some research indicates a 'two-tier' society split between '**work-rich**' (with two wage-earners) and '**work-poor**'. However, despite some claims, **most employees are in permanent, full-time employment**.
Wealth	Rising standards of living lead to increased demand for certain types of consumer good. This is why developing countries are attractive as markets.

Implications of demographic change

(a) **Changes in patterns of demand**: an ageing population suggests increased demand for healthcare services: a young growing population has a growing demand for schools, housing and work.

(b) **Location of demand**: people are moving to the suburbs and small towns.

(c) **Recruitment policies**: there are relatively fewer young people so firms will have to recruit from less familiar sources of labour.

(d) **Wealth and tax**: patterns of poverty and hence need for welfare provisions may change. The tax base may alter.

2.3.2 Culture

Through contact with a particular culture, individuals learn a language, acquire values and learn habits of behaviour and thought.

(a) **Beliefs and values**: beliefs are what we feel to be the case on the basis of objective and subjective information (eg people can believe the world is round or flat). **Values** are beliefs which are relatively enduring, relatively general and fairly widely accepted as a guide to culturally appropriate behaviour.

(b) **Customs**: modes of behaviour which represent culturally accepted ways of behaving in response to given situations.

(c) **Artefacts**: all the physical tools designed by human beings for their physical and psychological well-being: works of art, technology, products.

(d) **Rituals**: a ritual is a type of activity which takes on symbolic meaning, consisting of a fixed sequence of behaviour repeated over time.

The learning and sharing of culture is made possible by **language** (both written and spoken, verbal and non-verbal).

Underlying characteristics of culture

(a) **Purposeful**. Culture offers order, direction and guidance in all phases of human problem-solving.

(b) **Learned**. Cultural values are transferred in institutions (the family, school and church) and through ongoing social interaction and mass media exposure in adulthood.

(c) **Shared**. A belief or practice must be common to a significant proportion of a society or group before it can be defined as a cultural characteristic.

(d) **Cumulative**. Culture is handed down to each new generation. There is a strong traditional/historical element to many aspects of culture (eg classical music).

(e) **Dynamic**. Cultures adapt to changes in society: eg technological breakthrough, population shifts, exposure to other cultures.

Knowledge of the culture of a society is clearly of value to businesses in a number of ways.

(a) **Marketers** can adapt their products accordingly, and be fairly sure of a sizeable market. This is particularly important in export markets.

(b) **Human resource managers** may need to tackle cultural differences in recruitment.

Culture in a society can be divided into **subcultures** reflecting social differences. Most people participate in several of them.

Subculture	Comment
Class	People from different social classes might have different values reflecting their position of society.
Ethnic background	Some ethnic groups can still be considered a distinct cultural group.
Religion	Religion and ethnicity are related.
Geography or region	Distinct regional differences might be brought about by the past effects of physical geography (socio-economic differences etc). Speech accents most noticeably differ.
Age	Age subcultures vary according to the period in which individuals were socialised to an extent ('Youth culture'; the 'generation gap').
Sex	Some products are targeted directly to women or to men.
Work	Different organisations have different corporate cultures, in that the shared values of one workplace may be different from another.

Cultural change might have to be planned for. There has been a revolution in attitudes to female employment, despite the well-publicised problems of discrimination that still remain.

Question — Club Fun

Club Fun is a UK company which sells packaged holidays. Founded in the 1960s, it offered a standard 'cheap and cheerful' package to resorts in Spain and, more recently, to some of the Greek islands. It was particularly successful at providing holidays for the 18–30 age group.

What do you think the implications are for Club Fun of the following developments?

- A fall in the number of school leavers
- The fact that young people are more likely now to go into higher education
- Programmes on television and items on social media which feature a much greater variety of locations
- Greater disposable income among the 18–30 age group

Answer

The firm's market is shrinking. There is an absolute fall in the number of school leavers. Moreover, it is possible that the increasing proportion of school leavers going to higher education will mean there will be fewer who can afford Club Fun's packages. That said, a higher disposable income in the population at large might compensate for this trend. People might be encouraged to try destinations other than Club Fun's traditional resorts if these other destinations are publicised in the various media channels.

2.3.3 Business ethics

The conduct of an organisation, its management and employees will be measured against **ethical standards** by the customers, suppliers and other members of the public with whom they deal.

We consider business ethics in detail in Chapter 6.

2.4 Technological factors

The word 'technology' is used to mean three rather different things.

(a) **Apparatus or equipment** such as a TV camera

(b) **Technique**: for instance how to use the TV camera to best effect, perhaps in conjunction with other equipment such as lights

(c) **Organisation**: for example the grouping of camera-operators into teams, to work on a particular project

Technology contributes to overall economic growth. The **production possibility curve** describes the total production in an economy. There are three ways in which technology can increase total output.

(a) Gains in productivity (more output per units of input)
(b) Reduced costs (eg transportation technology, preservatives)
(c) New types of product

Effects of technological change on organisations

(a) **The type of products or services that are made and sold**

(b) **The way in which products are made** (eg robots, new raw materials)

(c) **The way in which services are provided.** For example companies selling easily transportable goods – for instance, books and music – can offer much greater consumer choice and are enjoying considerable success over the internet (e-books and music downloads, for example).

(d) **The way in which markets are identified.** Database systems make it much easier to analyse the marketplace.

(e) **The way in which firms are managed.** IT encourages delayering of organisational hierarchies, homeworking, and better communication.

(f) **The means and extent of communications with external clients.** The financial sector is rapidly going electronic – call centres are now essential to stay in business.

The impact of recent technological change also has potentially important social consequences, which in turn have an impact on business.

(a) **Homeworking.** Whereas people were once collected together to work in factories, home working will become more important.

(b) **Analytical skills.** Certain sorts of skill, related to interpretation of data and information processes, are likely to become more valued than manual or physical skills.

(c) **Services.** Technology increases manufacturing productivity, releasing human resources for service jobs. These jobs require **greater interpersonal skills** (eg in dealing with customers).

2.5 The physical environment

FAST FORWARD

> The **physical** environment is important for logistical reasons, as a source of resources, and because of increasing regulation. The **economic** environment affects firms at national and international level, both in the general level of economic activity and in particular variables (eg exchange rates). The **law** impinges on organisations, defining what they can or cannot do. **Political change** is a source of environmental uncertainty.

The importance of physical environmental conditions

(a) **Resource inputs**. Managing physical resources successfully (eg oil companies, mining companies) is a good source of profits.

(b) **Logistics**. The physical environment presents logistical problems or opportunities to organisations. Proximity to road and rail links can be a reason for siting a warehouse in a particular area.

(c) **Government**. The physical environment is under the control of other organisations.

   (i) Local authority town planning departments can influence where a building and necessary infrastructure can be sited.

   (ii) Governments can set regulations about some of the organisation's environmental interactions.

(d) **Disasters**. In some countries, the physical environment can pose a major threat to organisations.

> **FAST FORWARD**
>
> The impact of business activity on the physical environment is now a major concern. Companies are under pressure to incorporate measure to protect the environment into their plans. This presents both challenges and opportunities, since some measures will impose costs, but others will allow significant savings. There is also a new range of markets for goods and services designed to protect or have minimum impact on the environment.

2.5.1 Environmental protection policy

Pressure on businesses for better environmental performance is coming from many quarters. It reflects the greater emphasis upon corporate social responsibility that we first looked at in Chapter 3.

(a) **Green pressure groups** have increased their membership and influence dramatically.

(b) **Employees** are increasing pressure on the businesses in which they work for a number of reasons – partly for their own safety, partly in order to improve the public image of the company.

(c) **Legislation** is increasing almost by the day. Most countries now have laws to cover land use planning, smoke emission, water pollution and the destruction of animals and natural habitats.

(d) **Environmental risk screening** has become increasingly important. Companies in the future will become responsible for the environmental impact of their activities.

2.5.2 Environmental audit

The **Valdez principles** were drafted by the Coalition for Environmentally Responsible Economics (CERES) to focus attention on environmental concerns and corporate responsibility. They include:

- Eliminate pollutants and hazardous waste
- Conserve non-renewable resources
- Market environmentally safe products and services
- Prepare for accidents and restore damaged environments
- Provide protection for employees who report environmental hazards
- Companies should appoint an environmentalist to the board of directors, name an executive for environmental affairs and develop an environmental audit of global operations.
(**Source**: www.ceres.org/about-us/our-history/ceres-principles [Accessed 7 October 2024])

2.5.3 How green issues will impinge on business

Possible issues to consider are:

- **Consumer demand** for products which appear to be environmentally friendly
- Demand for **less pollution** from industry
- Greater **regulation** by governments
- Demand that **businesses be charged** with the external cost of their activities
- Possible requirements to conduct **environmental audits**
- Opportunities to develop **products and technologies** which are environmentally friendly
- Taxes (eg landfill tax)

There are several ways in which a company's concern for the environment can impact on its performance.

(a) Savings through waste minimisation and energy efficiency schemes can be substantial.

(b) Companies with poor environmental performance may face **increased cost of capital** because investors and lenders demand a higher risk premium.

(c) There are a growing number of **energy and environmental taxes**, such as the UK's landfill tax.

(d) Accidents and long-term environmental effects can result in **large financial liabilities**.

(e) **Pressure group campaigns** can cause damage to reputation.

(f) Environmental legislation may cause the withdrawal of certain products, and opportunities for replacements.

There are many ways in which business and environmental benefits can be achieved.

(a) **Understanding and managing environmental costs**. Environmental costs are often 'hidden' in overheads and environmental and energy costs are often not allocated to the relevant budgets.

(b) **Introducing waste minimisation schemes**. An awareness of the benefits of waste minimisation and recycling would encourage the purchase of recycled materials, and the favouring of suppliers who have strong environmental principles.

(c) **Understanding and managing life cycle costs**. For many products, the greatest environmental impact occurs upstream (such as mining raw materials) or downstream from production (such as energy to operate equipment).

(d) **Measuring environmental performance**. Business is under increasing pressure to measure all aspects of environmental performance, both for statutory reasons and due to customer demands.

(e) **Involving accountants in a strategic approach to environment-related accounting and performance evaluation**. A 'green accounting team' incorporating the key functions should identify opportunities for practical initiatives.

2.5.4 Renewable and non-renewable resources

Key term

> **Sustainability** involves developing strategies so that the company only uses resources at a rate that allows them to be replenished. At the same time, emissions of waste are confined to levels that do not exceed the capacity of the environment to absorb them.

Sustainability means that resources consumed are **replaced** in some way: for every tree cut down another is planted. Some resources, however, are inherently non-renewable. For example, oil will eventually run out, even though governments and oil firms have consistently underestimated reserves.

(a) Metals can be recycled. Some car manufacturers are building cars with recyclable components.

(b) An argument is that as the price of resources rise, market forces will operate to make more efficient use of them or to develop alternatives. When oil becomes too expensive, solar power will become economic.

Sustainability is covered in depth in Chapter 6. As we will see, sustainability embraces not only environmental and economic questions, but also social and ethical dimensions.

2.6 Environmental factors and strategic planning

Issues relating to the effect of an organisation's activities on the physical environment have come to the fore in recent years, and consumer demand for products which claim environmental soundness has waxed and waned, with initial enthusiasm replaced by cynicism as to 'green' claims.

(a) **Marketing**. Companies such as The Body Shop have utilized environmental friendliness as a marketing tool.

(b) **Publicity**. Perhaps companies have more to fear from the impact of bad publicity (relating to their environmental practices) than they have to benefit from positive environmental messages as such. Public relations is a vital competitive weapon.

(c) **Lifestyles**. There may be a limit to which consumers are prepared to alter their lifestyles for the sake of environmental correctness.

(d) Consumers may be **imperfectly educated** about environmental issues, believing some products to be 'greener' than they actually are.

Question — PEST

ABC Co's management accountant is carrying out a PEST analysis. During her research she discovers a significant growth across the country in the number of female-led small businesses, which she deems to be an important strategic issue for the company.

In which section of her analysis should she record this matter?

A   Political
B   Economic
C   Social
D   Technological

Answer

C   Social

Social includes long-term cultural changes, such as greater female involvement in business leadership.

This change has no clear political or economic consequences and is not a function of technology.

PART B MANAGEMENT PLANNING AND DECISION-MAKING

3 Competitive forces

FAST FORWARD

The **competitive environment** is structured by five forces: **barriers to entry**; **substitute products**; the bargaining power of **customers**; the bargaining power of **suppliers**; **competitive rivalry**.

In discussing competition, **Porter** (*Competitive Strategy: Techniques for Analyzing Industries and Competitors*, 1980) distinguishes between factors which characterise the nature of competition.

(a) **In one industry compared with another** (eg in the chemicals industry compared with the clothing retail industry, some factors make one industry as a whole potentially more profitable than another (ie yielding a bigger return on investment).

(b) Factors **within a particular industry** lead to the competitive strategies that individual firms might select.

Porter (1980) suggested that **five competitive forces** influence the state of competition in an industry, which collectively determine the profit (ie long-run return on capital) potential of the industry as a whole.

- The threat of **new entrants** to the industry
- The threat of **substitute** products or services
- The bargaining power of **customers**
- The bargaining power of **suppliers**
- The **rivalry** amongst current competitors in the industry

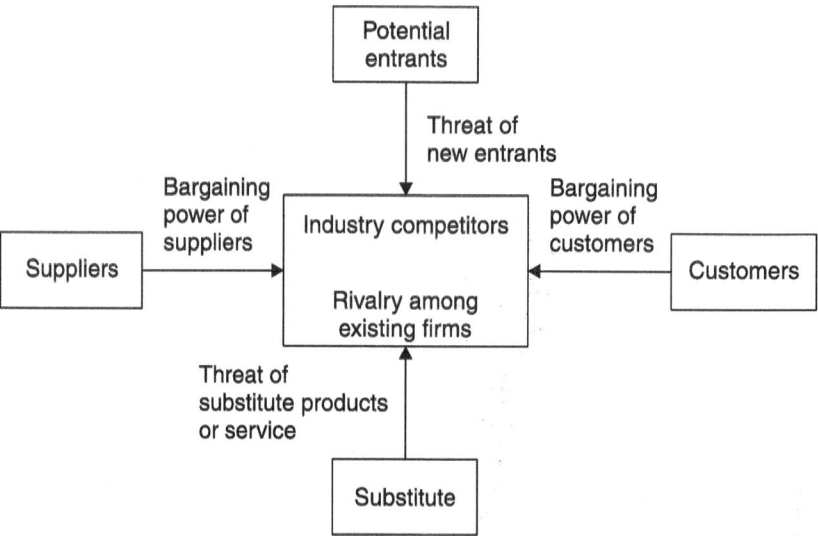

3.1 The threat of new entrants (and barriers to entry to keep them out)

A new entrant into an industry will bring extra capacity and more competition. The strength of this threat is likely to vary from industry to industry and depends on two things:

- The strength of the **barriers to entry**. Barriers to entry discourage new entrants.
- The likely **response of existing competitors** to the new entrant.

Barriers to entry

(a) **Scale economies**. High fixed costs often imply a high breakeven point, and a high breakeven point depends on a large volume of sales. If the market as a whole is not growing, the new entrant has to capture a large slice of the market from existing competitors. This is expensive.

(b) **Product differentiation**. Existing firms in an industry may have built up a good brand image and strong customer loyalty over a long period of time. A few firms may promote a large number of brands to crowd out the competition.

(c) **Capital requirements**. When capital investment requirements are high, the barrier against new entrants will be strong, particularly when the investment would possibly be high-risk.

(d) **Switching costs**. Switching costs refer to the costs (time, money, convenience) that a customer would have to incur by switching from one supplier's products to another's.

(e) **Access to distribution channels**. Distribution channels carry a manufacturer's products to the end-buyer. New distribution channels are difficult to establish, and existing distribution channels hard to gain access to.

(f) **Cost advantages of existing producers, independent of economies of scale** include:
- Patent rights
- Experience and know-how (the learning curve)
- Government subsidies and regulations
- Favoured access to raw materials

Entry barriers might be **lowered** by the impact of change.

- Changes in the environment
- Technological changes
- Novel distribution channels for products or services

3.2 The threat from substitute products

A **substitute product** is a good or service produced by **another industry** which satisfies the same customer needs.

3.3 The bargaining power of customers

Customers want better quality products and services at a lower price. Satisfying this want might force down the profitability of suppliers in the industry. Just how strong the position of customers will be depends on a number of factors.

- How much the customer buys
- How critical the product is to the customer's own business
- Switching costs (ie the cost of switching supplier)
- Whether the products are standard items (hence easily copied) or specialised
- The customer's own profitability: a customer who makes low profits will be forced to insist on low prices from suppliers
- Customer's ability to bypass the supplier (or take over the supplier)
- The skills of the customer purchasing staff, or the price-awareness of consumers
- When product quality is important to the customer, the customer is less likely to be price-sensitive, and so the industry might be more profitable as a consequence

3.4 The bargaining power of suppliers

Suppliers can exert pressure for higher prices. The ability of suppliers to get higher prices depends on:

- Whether there are just **one or two dominant suppliers** to the industry, able to charge monopoly or oligopoly prices
- The threat of **new entrants** or substitute products to the **supplier's industry**

- Whether the suppliers have **other customers** outside the industry, and do not rely on the industry for the majority of their sales
- The **importance of the supplier's product** to the customer's business
- Whether the supplier has a **differentiated product** which buyers need to obtain
- Whether **switching costs** for customers would be high

3.5 The rivalry amongst current competitors in the industry

The **intensity of competitive rivalry** within an industry will affect the profitability of the industry as a whole. Competitive actions might take the form of price competition, advertising battles, sales promotion campaigns, introducing new products for the market, improving after-sales service or providing guarantees or warranties.

Competition can stimulate demand, expanding the market, or it can leave demand unchanged, in which case individual competitors will make less money, unless they cut costs.

Competitor analysis aims to gather information about competitors that allows managers to anticipate competitor actions.

Factors determining the intensity of competition

(a) **Market growth**. Rivalry is intensified when firms are competing for a greater market share in a total market where growth is slow or stagnant.

(b) **Cost structure**. High fixed costs are a temptation to compete on price, as in the short run any contribution from sales is better than none at all. A perishable product produces the same effect.

(c) **Switching**. Suppliers will compete if buyers switch easily (eg Coke vs Pepsi).

(d) **Capacity**. A supplier might need to achieve a substantial increase in output capacity, in order to obtain reductions in unit costs.

(e) **Uncertainty**. When one firm is not sure what another is up to, there is a tendency to respond to the uncertainty by formulating a more competitive strategy.

(f) **Strategic importance**. If success is a prime strategic objective, firms will be likely to act very competitively to meet their targets.

(g) **Exit barriers** make it difficult for an existing supplier to leave the industry.

3.6 The impact of information technology on the competitive forces

 Case Study

The internet has had a variety of impacts.

Retailers are increasingly at risk of losing market share because customers can compare prices using the internet. A shopper with a credit card and computer can sit at home and order from around the world.

Barriers to entry and IT

(a) **IT can raise entry barriers** by increasing economies of scale, raising the capital cost of entry (by requiring a similar investment in IT) or effectively colonising distribution channels by tying customers and suppliers into the supply chain or distribution chain.

(b) **IT can surmount entry barriers**. Examples are the use of online banking and online retailing, which sometimes removes the need to establish a branch network.

Bargaining power of suppliers and IT

(a) **Increasing the number of** accessible **suppliers**. Supplier power in the past can derive from various factors such as geographical proximity and the fact that the organisation requires goods of a certain standard in a certain time. IT enhances supplier information available to customers.

(b) **Closer supplier relationships**. Suppliers' power can be shared. CAD can be used to design components in tandem with suppliers. Such relationships might be developed with a few key suppliers. The supplier and the organisation both benefit from performance improvement, but the relations are closer.

(c) **Switching costs**. Suppliers can be integrated with the firm's administrative operations, by a system of electronic data interchange.

Bargaining power of customers. IT can lock customers in.

(a) **IT can raise switching costs**, but it is also the case that the internet increases price transparency, which should increase the bargaining power of customers.

(b) **Customer information systems** and data analytics software can enable a thorough analysis of marketing information so that products and services can be tailored to the needs of certain segments.

Substitutes. In many respects, **IT itself is the substitute product**. Here are some examples.

(a) Video-conferencing systems (such as Skype) might substitute for air travel in providing a means by which managers can get together in a meeting.

(b) IT is the basis for new leisure activities (eg computer games) which substitute for TV or other pursuits.

(c) Email acts as a substitute for many postal deliveries.

IT and the state of competitive rivalry

(a) IT can be used in support of a firm's **competitive** strategy of cost leadership, differentiation or focus. These are discussed later in this text.

(b) New **online competitors** increases rivalry in the industry. Again, retail is the obvious example of this, with the online retailers such as Amazon competing with traditional 'bricks and mortar' retailers.

(c) IT can be used in a **collaborative** venture, perhaps to set up new communications networks.

3.7 Using the Five Forces Model: A caution

The original Five Forces model focussed on the profitability of an industry; but the profitability of different firms in an industry will also be influenced by their specific competences and capabilities.

Furthermore, Porter's model is based on the idea of firms competing with each other, so it tends to underemphasise the potential for alliances and competition.

3.8 Further considerations

3.8.1 Government

It is possible to view the influence of **government** as so great as to justify viewing it as a separate force.

3.8.2 Complexity and stability

An awareness of general industrial characteristics is necessary if a good insight is to be gained into the way an industry works. Such characteristics include **complexity** and **volatility**.

3.8.3 Industry life cycle

The extent and even the existence of the five competitive forces is likely to vary as an industry progresses through its life cycle. We looked at the industry life cycle in Chapter 4.

3.9 Strategic group analysis

Five Forces analysis deals with the competitive environment in broad **industry-wide** terms. It is possible to refine this by considering **strategic groups**. These are groups of close competitors following similar strategies. Such groups arise for a variety of reasons, such as barriers to entry or the attractiveness of particular market segments.

The identification of potential competitive advantage is the reason for analysing strategic groups. It improves knowledge of competitors and shows gaps in the organisation's current segments of operations. It may also reveal opportunities for migration to more favourable segments. Strategic problems may also be revealed.

4 SWOT analysis

FAST FORWARD

> **SWOT analysis** looks at internal strengths and weaknesses and external opportunities and threats.

4.1 SWOT analysis

Another method of environmental analysis looks at an organisation's internal **strengths** and **weaknesses** as well as external **opportunities** and **threats**. This is known as **SWOT** analysis.

4.1.1 Internal appraisal: strengths and weaknesses

An internal appraisal will identify:

(a) The areas of the organisation that have **strengths** that should be exploited by suitable strategies
(b) The areas of the organisation that have **weaknesses** which need strategies to improve them

The strengths and weaknesses analysis is intended to shape the organisation's approach to the external world. For instance, the identification of shortcomings in products could lead to a programme of product development.

4.1.2 External appraisal: opportunities and threats

The external appraisal identifies **opportunities** that can be exploited by the organisation's strengths and also to anticipate environmental **threats** against which the company must protect itself.

Opportunities

(a) What opportunities exist in the business environment?
(b) What is their inherent profit-making potential?
(c) Can the organisation exploit the worthwhile opportunities?
(d) What is the comparative capability profile of competitors?
(e) What is the company's comparative performance potential in this field of opportunity?

Threats

(a) What threats might arise to the company or its business environment?
(b) How will competitors be affected?
(c) How will the company be affected?

4.2 Using a SWOT analysis

The SWOT analysis can be used in one of two ways.

(a) The organisation can develop **resource-based strategies** which enable the organisation to extend the use of its strengths. This is common in retailing, for example, as supermarket chains extend their own brands from food to other areas.

(b) The business can develop **positioning-based strategies**. In other words identifying what opportunities are available and what the firm has to do to exploit them.

Question — SWOT analysis

Terrdicks Co has asked a consultant to carry out a review of the most important factors affecting the business. The review has highlighted the following factors. Which of the following would be classified as a weakness in the SWOT analysis?

A Need for significant investment in research and development due to changes in technology
B Worldwide shortage of raw materials used in products
C Principal competitor introducing a new customer relationship management system
D High staff turnover

Answer

D High staff turnover

This is an internal factor about which Terrdicks Co should be able to do something.

Increasing research and development relates to internal expenditure, but it is something the company has to do because of the threat of being left behind by new technology.

The worldwide shortage of raw materials and the new customer relationship management system of the competitor are external threats that Terrdicks Co cannot influence. Terrdicks Co not having a proper customer relationship management system of its own would, however, be a weakness.

5 Strategic intelligence and decision-making aids

> **FAST FORWARD**
>
> There are many sources of environmental information. Analysing this information, much of which is not quantitative, is no easy task. Forecasts and scenarios must be rooted in sound data.

Many firms' intelligence gathering procedures reflect the organisation structure. Each function of the organisation collects information relevant to its own concerns, without any wider corporate viewpoint.

(a) The data collected reflects the **restricted functional view**, not the overall corporate view.

(b) There are inevitable **gaps and blind-spots** in the information collected.

(c) Until recently (with the arrival of email and intranet applications) **sharing information** across functional departments **has been very difficult**.

Why information should be shared

(a) Not all strategic knowledge or decision-making capacity resides at the top of the firm.

(b) Sharing encourages a wide range of views. For example, the marketing department may realise the commercial significance of new technology that may have escaped R&D.

(c) As companies delayer and lose management levels, the **organisation hierarchy** which used to distribute information is **less effective** at this task.

A model of the process of creating strategic intelligence is outlined below.

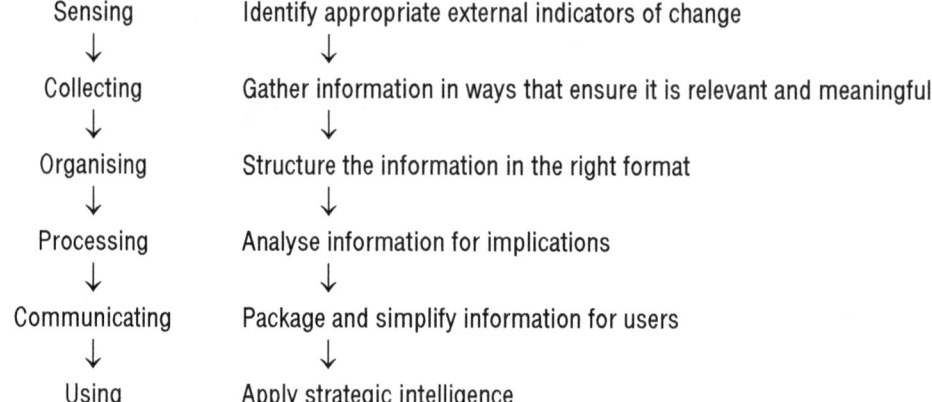

Key dimensions of strategic intelligence

Dimension	Comment
Information culture	What is the role of information in the organisation? Is it only distributed on a 'need to know basis' or do people have to give specific reasons for secrecy?
Future orientation	Is the focus on specific decisions and trade-offs, or a general attitude of enquiry?
The structure of information flows	Is communication vertical (up and down the hierarchy), or horizontal?
Processing strategic intelligence	Are 'professional' strategists delegated to this task or is it everybody's concern?
Scope	Is strategic intelligence dealt with by senior management only, or is it dispersed throughout the organisation?
Time horizon	Short-termist or orientated towards the long term?
The role of IT	Many firms are using IT to enhance communication across business functions.
Organisational memory	Do managers keep in mind the lessons of past successes or failures?

5.1 Sources of strategic intelligence

Strategic intelligence can be obtained internally (from the management information system (MIS) or personnel) or externally (via media, trade associations, government, internet, social media networks).

5.2 Forecasts

Forecasting attempts to reduce the uncertainty managers face. In **simple/static conditions the past is a relatively good guide** to the future.

(a) **Time series analysis**. Data for a number of months/years is obtained and analysed. The aim of time series analysis is to distinguish seasonal and other cyclical fluctuations from long-term underlying trends. An example of the use of this approach is the UK's monthly inflation statistics which show a headline figure and the underlying trend.

(b) **Regression analysis** is a quantitative technique to check any underlying correlations between two variables (eg sales of ice cream and the weather). Remember that the relationship between two variables may only hold between certain values. (You would expect ice cream consumption to rise as the temperature becomes hotter, but there is probably a maximum number of ice creams an individual can consume in a day, no matter how hot it is.)

Dynamic/complex conditions

- **Future developments**: the past is not a reliable guide.
- Techniques such as **scenario building** are useful as they can propose a number of possible futures.
- **Complex environments** require techniques to reduce the effects of complexity on organisational structure and decision-making.

5.2.1 Technological forecasting

Technological change is a source of uncertainty, but can be countered in two ways:

- Ensuring that employees are kept up-to-date with relevant developments
- The **Delphi model**, which is explained in detail later in this section

5.2.2 Econometric models for medium-term forecasting

Econometrics is the study of economic variables and their interrelationships.

(a) **Leading indicators** are indicators which change before market demand changes. For example, a sudden increase in the birth rate would be an indicator of future demand for children's clothes.

(b) The ability to predict the span of time between a change in the indicator and a change in market demand. Change in an indicator is especially useful for demand forecasting when they reach their highest or lowest points (when an increase turns into a decline or vice versa).

5.3 Scenario building

Because the environment is so complex, it is easy to become overwhelmed by the many factors. Firms therefore try to model the future and the technique is scenario building.

Key term

A **scenario** is 'an internally consistent view of what the future might turn out to be'.
(**Porter**, *Competitive Advantage*, 1985)

5.3.1 Macro scenarios

Macro scenarios use macro-economic or political factors, creating alternative views of the future environment (eg global economic growth, political changes, interest rates). Macro scenarios developed because the activities of oil and resource companies (which are global and at one time were heavily influenced by political factors) needed techniques to deal with uncertainties.

5.4 Building scenarios

Steps in scenario planning (Mercer, 'Simpler scenarios', *Management Decision*, 33 (4), 1995)

Step 1	Decide on the drivers for change
Step 2	Bring drivers together into a viable framework
Step 3	Produce seven to nine mini-scenarios
Step 4	Group mini-scenarios into two or three larger scenarios containing all topics
Step 5	Write the scenarios
Step 6	Identify issues arising

5.5 Industry scenarios

An **industry scenario** is an internally consistent view of an **industry**'s future structure. It is not a forecast, but a possibility. Different competitive strategies may be appropriate to different scenarios.

Using scenarios to formulate competitive strategy

(a) A strategy built in response to only one scenario is **risky**, whereas one supposed to cope with them all might be **expensive**.

(b) Choosing scenarios as a basis for decisions about competitive strategy.

Approach	Comment
Assume the most probable	This choice puts too much faith in the scenario process and guesswork. A less probable scenario may be one whose **failure** to occur would have the **worst** consequences for the firm.
Hope for the best	A firm designs a strategy based on the scenario most attractive to the firm: this is wishful thinking.
Hedge	The firm chooses the strategy that produces **satisfactory** results under **all** scenarios. **Hedging, however, is not optimal**. The **low risk** is paid for by a **low reward**.
Flexibility	A firm taking this approach plays a 'wait and see' game. It is safer, but sacrifices first-mover advantages.
Influence	A firm will try and influence the future, for example by influencing demand for related products in order that its favoured scenario will be realised in events as they unfold.

5.6 Delphi technique

FAST FORWARD

Delphi is a forecasting technique based on interactive refinement of expert judgements.

The **Delphi technique** was developed to permit the best use to be made of **judgement** in forecasting. The technique overcomes the problems of **groupthink** and dominance by one or two individuals that commonly undermine the usefulness of expert panels. The technique is used **to answer specific questions** about the future.

A co-ordinator asks a number of experts to respond to a question. Their areas of expertise must all be relevant to the subject matter of the question, but they must bring differing perspectives to it. The experts never meet and they are unaware of each other's identity. Each expert gives an answer and justifies it with reasons.

The co-ordinator collates the answers and reasons and re-distributes them to the experts, still without attribution. The experts then re-consider their original views in the light of any divergent opinions, perhaps revising them, perhaps explaining why they do not accept the need for amendment. The co-ordinator then collates and redistributes as before.

After sufficient iterations of this process of reconsideration, it is likely that a reasonably consistent overall answer will emerge.

5.7 Expected values

FAST FORWARD

The expected value is the weighted average of the possible outcomes.

Key term

Expected value is the value obtained by multiplying the financial forecast of an outcome by the probability of achieving that outcome.

In order to have a **rational** basis for decision-making it is necessary to have some estimate of the probabilities of the various outcomes and then to use them in a decision criterion. One such criterion is the **maximisation of expected value**.

The expected value $\bar{x}$ of a particular action is defined as the **sum of the values of the possible outcomes, each multiplied by their respective probabilities** (it is analogous to the arithmetic mean): $\bar{x} = \sum px$

The criterion of expected value is only valid where the decision being made is either:

(a) One that is **repeated regularly** over a period of time; or

(b) A **one-off** decision, but where its size is fairly small in relation to the total assets of the firm, and many similar decisions are faced regularly.

5.8 Decision trees

FAST FORWARD

A **decision tree** is a way of applying the expected value criterion to situations where a number of decisions are made sequentially. It is so called because the decision alternatives are represented as **branches** in a **tree** diagram.

Where a number of decisions have to be made sequentially the complexity of the decision-making process increases considerably. By using **decision trees**, however, highly complex problems can be broken down into a series of simpler ones while providing, at the same time, opportunity for the decision-maker to obtain specialist advice in relation to each stage of the problem.

PART B MANAGEMENT PLANNING AND DECISION-MAKING

5.8.1 Example

A retailer must decide whether to sell a product loose or packaged. In either case, the product may sell, or not sell.

The decision facing the retailer can be represented by a tree diagram:

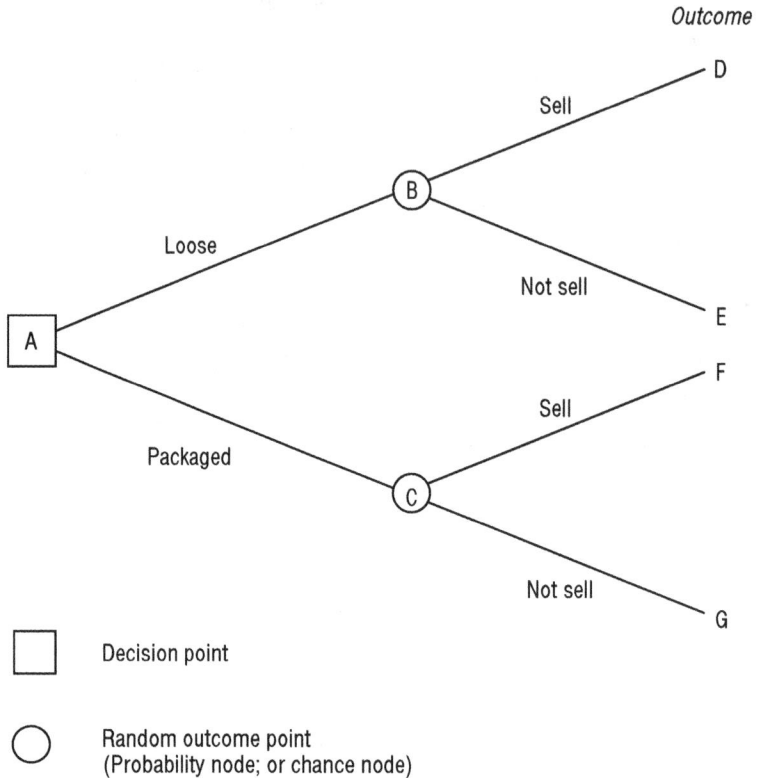

As you can see, in a decision tree there are two types of events (points where a branch occurs).

- **Decision points**, signified by a ☐ in the tree. At this point the decision or branch taken can be chosen by the decision-maker. In this example the decision point is ☐ where the decision-maker can choose whether to sell the product loose or packaged.

- **Random outcome points**, signified by a ◯. At this point the branch taken is completely outside the control of the decision-maker. In the example above, the random outcome points are at Ⓑ and Ⓒ; the retailer has no control over which branch is followed from this point, the product will either sell or it won't.

5.8.2 Expected values and the roll-back method

The profitability of selling packaged products is $10, loose products $15. The loss through not selling is $5 in either case. The probability of the product being sold is 0.7 for packaged products, 0.5 for loose products.

You are required to evaluate the expected values of each decision alternative.

Step 1 Add all the relevant information ie, probabilities and profits and losses, to the decision tree ending at the right hand side of the tree with a column for outcomes.

Step 2 Evaluate the decision tree by working back from right to left towards the first decision under consideration. In this example it is decision point (A). At each random outcome point calculate the EV of revenue, cost, profit or whatever type of pay off the question gives.

Step 3 Block off all other routes from the decision point (sometimes called a decision **fork**) with a double parallel line '//'. (This is important when trees have several decision forks.)

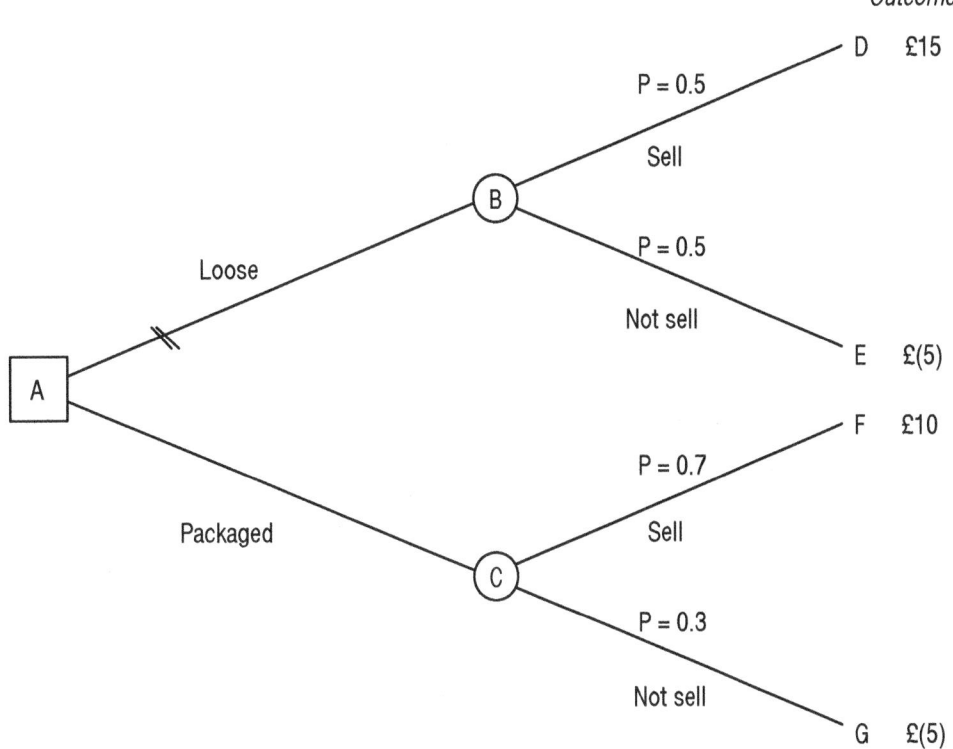

The diagram is evaluated as follows (using obvious notation):

EV_B = $(0.5 \times EV_D) + (0.5 \times EV_E)$
= $(0.5 \times \$15) + (0.5 \times (-\$5))$
= $\$5$

EV_C = $(0.7 \times EV_F) + (0.3 \times EV_G)$
= $(0.7 \times \$10) + (0.3 \times (-\$5))$
= $\$5.5$

∴ At decision point A the retailer will choose to go towards node C as this has the higher EV. The discarded routes are indicated by drawing two short parallel lines across that particular path.

Therefore, the decision to sell a packaged product has the higher expected value.

The method just described is known as the **rollback technique**.

Note. The expected values here (EV) are sometimes called expected monetary values (EMV). At point C the probability that the product will sell is 0.7, therefore the probability that it will not is 1 – 0.7 = 0.3. The total probability at any chance fork must be 1.00.

Chapter roundup

- General system theory would see the organisation as an **open system**, interacting with its environment.
- Environmental uncertainty depends on the degree of **complexity** and the degree of **stability** present.
- The **organisation's environment** is a source of **uncertainty**, depending on how **complex** or **dynamic** it is. General factors (PEST) affect all organisations.
- Public policy on **competition** and **consumer protection** is particularly relevant to business strategy.
- The **social and cultural** environment features long-term social trends and people's beliefs and attitudes (eg concern with ecological issues).
- The **physical** environment is important for logistical reasons, as a source of resources, and because of increasing regulation. The **economic** environment affects firms at national and international level, both in the general level of economic activity and in particular variables (eg exchange rates). The **law** impinges on organisations, defining what they can or cannot do. **Political change** is a source of environmental uncertainty.
- The impact of business activity on the physical environment is now a major concern. Companies are under pressure to incorporate measure to protect the environment into their plans. This presents both challenges and opportunities, since some measures will impose costs, but others will allow significant savings. There is also a new range of markets for goods and services designed to protect or have minimum impact on the environment.
- The **competitive environment** is structured by five forces: **barriers to entry; substitute products**; the bargaining power of **customers**; the bargaining power of **suppliers**; **competitive rivalry**.
- **SWOT analysis** looks at internal strengths and weaknesses and external opportunities and threats.
- There are many sources of environmental information. Analysing this information, much of which is not quantitative, is no easy task. Forecasts and scenarios must be rooted in sound data.
- Delphi is a forecasting technique based on interactive refinement of expert judgements.
- **Expected value** is the weighted average of the possible outcomes.
- A **decision tree** is a way of applying the expected value criterion to situations where a number of decisions are made sequentially. It is so called because the decision alternatives are represented as **branches** in a **tree** diagram.

Quick quiz

1. What are the features of a closed system?
2. What are the features of an open system?
3. What factors will be considered in the creation of a political risk checklist?
4. Name three ways in which green issues affect business.
5. What is meant by sustainability?
6. What are the five competitive forces outlined by Porter?
7. What is strategic intelligence?

Answers to quick quiz

1 A closed system is isolated from its environment and independent of it.

2 An open system is connected to and interacts with its environment.

3 Stability and strength of the current political system; length the government is likely to remain in power; what changes would be made on a change in government; what decisions and actions should be taken now

4 Consumer demand for environmentally friendly goods; demand for less pollution; greater regulations

5 Sustainability is the term describing developing strategies so the company only uses reserves at a rate that allows them to be replenished.

6 Barriers to entry; substitute products; the bargaining power of customers; the bargaining power of suppliers; competitive rivalry

7 What a company needs to know about its business environment to be able to anticipate change, and design strategies that will create value for customers and profitability for the business in the future.

Sustainability, CSR and ethics

Topic list	Syllabus reference
1 Introduction to sustainability	D2
2 Sustainable development	D2
3 Sustainability and environmental, social and governance (ESG)	D2
4 Sustainable organisations	D2
5 Integrated reporting	D2
6 Sustainability strategy setting and management decision making	D2
7 ESG risk management and metrics for sustainability performance monitoring and reporting	D2
8 The role of accountants and management in developing sustainability within organisations	D2
9 Ethics and social responsibility	D2

Introduction

As the adverse effects of climate change have gained global attention, so too has awareness of environmental, social, and governance (ESG) issues. This has resulted in a rising trend for global stock exchanges to impose mandatory sustainability reporting for listed companies, meaning that boards of directors must now consider the ESG impact of their products and operations when making business and strategic decisions.

This chapter starts by looking at the concept of sustainability and the development of regulations. It then investigates different aspects of sustainability and its impact on and application to areas such as strategy setting, decision making, performance measurement, monitoring and reporting requirements.

Finally we look at the role of accountants and management in developing sustainability within organisations and providing transparency of ESG and related performance to investors and other stakeholders.

PART B MANAGEMENT PLANNING AND DECISION-MAKING

1 Introduction to sustainability

1.1 Introduction to sustainability

FAST FORWARD

Sustainability is a multifaceted concept aimed at improving people's lives and safeguarding the planet for future generations.

Key term

Sustainability is defined as 'development that meets the needs of the present without compromising the ability of future generations to meet their own needs' (Brutland report, 1987).

The scope of sustainability has evolved beyond environmental concerns to encompass a wide range of issues, including increasing disparities in wealth, population growth, biodiversity loss, deteriorating air and water quality, climate change, human rights, bribery and corruption.

In recent years, heightened awareness of environmental, social, and governance (ESG) issues has prompted global stock exchanges to mandate sustainability reporting for listed companies. Consequently, board directors are now expected to integrate ESG considerations into their business strategies and decision-making processes.

Unsustainable consumption and production patterns, coupled with resource depletion and environmental degradation, pose risks to long-term economic stability.

Sustainable enterprise is therefore crucial in today's world due to its potential to drive economic growth, enhance social well-being, and protect the environment.

By adopting sustainable practices and investing in clean technologies, businesses can mitigate risks associated with resource scarcity, regulatory changes, and reputational damage, tap into new markets, spur innovation, create new job opportunities, and drive economic growth while minimising environmental impacts.

Achieving global sustainability requires collaborative efforts from diverse stakeholders, including governments, businesses, civil society organizations, and individuals.

- **Governments** play a crucial role in setting regulatory frameworks, implementing policies, and mobilising resources to support sustainability initiatives.
- **Businesses** have a responsibility to integrate sustainability into their operations, supply chains, and corporate strategies, driving innovation and promoting responsible practices.
- **Civil society organisations** and grassroots movements play a vital role in advocating for change, raising awareness, and holding stakeholders accountable for their actions.
- **Individuals** also have a role to play through their consumption choices, lifestyle habits, and active participation in community initiatives.

1.2 Challenges of creating a sustainable world

FAST FORWARD

The challenges of creating a sustainable world include addressing finite global resources, ensuring energy security, promoting water conservation, enhancing food production, and tackling poverty.

In recent years, the concept of sustainability has gained significant traction across various sectors, from business and finance to environmental conservation and social development.

The pressing challenges of climate change, resource depletion, and social inequality have underscored the urgent need for a paradigm shift towards sustainable practices on a global scale.

1.2.1 Climate change

Key term

> **Climate change** refers to the long-term alteration of global or regional climate patterns, primarily driven by human activities that disrupt the Earth's natural systems and processes.

Climate change encompasses shifts in temperature, precipitation, sea levels, and weather patterns, with profound consequences for ecosystems, societies, and economies worldwide.

The scientific evidence for action on climate change and environmental damage includes increasing global temperatures, rising sea levels, increased air pollution, loss of natural forests, melting ice caps and glaciers, ocean acidification and increased frequency and intensity of extreme weather events such as hurricanes.

World scientists and climate experts, along with many governments, concur that urgent action is needed to mitigate greenhouse gas emissions, adapt to changing climatic conditions, and build resilience in vulnerable communities to address the challenges posed by climate change.

Case Study

Current examples of the consequences of climate change

The Arctic region is experiencing accelerated warming due to elevated greenhouse gas concentrations. This has led to the rapid melting of polar ice caps and glaciers, disrupting global climate patterns. The loss of Arctic sea ice is altering ocean currents and atmospheric circulation, impacting weather systems worldwide. For instance, changes in the polar jet stream have been linked to extreme weather events, such as prolonged heatwaves and severe winter storms, in regions far beyond the Arctic.

Precipitation

The Indian subcontinent has witnessed erratic precipitation patterns in recent years, with alternating periods of drought and intense rainfall. These changes have affected agricultural productivity and water availability, leading to crop failures, water shortages, and socioeconomic disruptions. Additionally, increased rainfall intensity has resulted in devastating floods, such as the Pakistan floods and landslides in 2022, which submerged vast areas and caused widespread destruction of infrastructure and livelihoods. Over 33 million people were impacted, including the loss of over 1,700 lives, injury of almost 13,000 people, and the displacement of millions more.

Storm frequency and intensity

The Atlantic hurricane season has become increasingly active and destructive due to rising sea surface temperatures fuelled by climate change. Hurricanes like Harvey, Irma, and Maria in 2017 demonstrated unprecedented intensity and destructive power, causing widespread devastation across the Caribbean and south-eastern United States. The 2019 season was the fourth consecutive above average and damaging Atlantic hurricane season, followed by a fifth in 2020. The 2020 season was the most active on record with thirty named storms, fourteen of which developed into hurricanes, of which seven were classed as 'major' hurricanes. These extreme weather events highlight the heightened risks faced by coastal communities, including storm surges, flooding, and infrastructure damage, underscoring the urgent need for climate-resilient infrastructure and disaster preparedness measures.

Growing zones of instability and inhabitability

The Lake Chad Basin region in Africa is experiencing environmental degradation and resource depletion exacerbated by climate change, leading to conflicts over dwindling water and land resources. Competition among pastoralists, farmers, and fishing communities for access to water and grazing lands has intensified, fuelling tensions and violence. This has resulted in population displacement, food insecurity, and humanitarian crises, highlighting the interconnectedness between environmental degradation, social instability, and conflict in vulnerable regions.

These real-world examples illustrate how climate change is already impacting communities and ecosystems, underscoring the urgent need for concerted global action.

The Paris Agreement

The Paris Agreement is an international treaty on climate change that was signed by nearly 200 countries in 2015 at the United Nations Framework Convention on Climate Change's 21st Conference of Parties.

This agreement is generally regarded as the framework for international action towards mitigating climate change and its impacts through a global commitment to collective action on climate change, with the goal of achieving a sustainable and resilient future for all.

The Paris Agreement set the ambition of a maximum of 2°C global temperature increase, with the preferred goal of limiting the increase to 1.5 °C above pre-industrial levels.

Note, the term 'net Zero' refers to ta situation where the emissions of greenhouse gases due to human activities are balanced by the removal of these gases from the environment. Achieving Net Zero by 2050 is the action required to limit temperature rise to 1.5 degrees Celsius.

The Paris Agreement also includes provisions for financial assistance to developing countries and promotes transparency and accountability through regular reporting mechanisms.

1.2.2 Resource depletion

A further major challenge of creating a sustainable world is the depletion of resources, for example:

- Finite global resources, including minerals, fossil fuels, and freshwater, are being depleted at an unsustainable rate, threatening ecosystems and human well-being.

- Energy security is a pressing issue as dependence on fossil fuels contributes to climate change and geopolitical tensions.

- Water scarcity and pollution jeopardise access to clean water for drinking, sanitation, and agriculture, exacerbating social inequalities and environmental degradation.

- Food production is under pressure from population growth, land degradation, and climate change, necessitating sustainable agriculture practices to ensure food security and nutrition for all.

In a resource-constrained world, the unsustainable depletion of finite resources poses significant challenges to global sustainability. Addressing these challenges requires a shift towards resource-efficient technologies, circular economy models, and sustainable consumption patterns.

The risk of increased tension and conflicts over scarce resources further exacerbates the urgency of addressing resource constraints. Competition for access to essential resources could lead to geopolitical instability, economic disruptions, and social unrest, emphasising the need for collaborative and equitable solutions to resource management.

1.2.3 Social inequality

Poverty remains a persistent challenge, with millions of people worldwide living in extreme poverty and lacking access to basic necessities such as clean water, food, healthcare, education, and economic opportunities.

Gender inequality, discrimination, and marginalisation further exacerbate social disparities, hindering efforts to build resilient and inclusive societies. Global sustainability demands actions to eradicate poverty, promote human rights, and foster social cohesion and inclusivity.

Sustainability cannot be achieved without addressing social inequities and promoting social justice. Addressing social inequities is therefore essential for building resilient communities, fostering social cohesion, and promoting inclusive growth.

1.2.4 Potential solutions to create a more sustainable world

The challenges described above are interlinked and require comprehensive solutions at a global level that integrate economic, social, and environmental considerations. For example:

- **Transitioning to renewable energy sources** involves adopting solar, wind, and hydroelectric power to diminish reliance on fossil fuels.

- **Implementing water conservation measures** such as promoting water-efficient irrigation techniques and rainwater harvesting systems, investment in water recycling and reuse technologies, and the implementation of pricing mechanisms and regulations.

- **Greenhouse gas emission reduction initiatives** can be developed and implemented on a global scale, such as CO2 emission caps, carbon trading, and carbon capture.

- **Promoting sustainable agriculture practices** for example encouraging organic farming, supporting agroforestry, and implementing agroecological techniques. Additionally, sustainable livestock management practices and investments in agricultural extension services contribute to sustainable agriculture.

- **Addressing poverty through inclusive economic development** entails implementing social protection programs, investing in education and vocational training, and promoting microfinance initiatives. Creating job opportunities in emerging sectors like renewable energy and eco-tourism fosters economic growth and social inclusion.

Coordinated political action at local, national, and global levels is required to address these challenges. Governments, businesses, civil society organisations, and individuals must work together to implement innovative solutions and transformative policies to achieve global sustainability.

2 Sustainable development

> **FAST FORWARD**
>
> Sustainable development acknowledges the interconnectedness of economic, environmental, and social factors to address current challenges will safeguarding the well-being of future generations.

2.1 Introduction

Sustainable development encompasses the idea of balancing economic growth, environmental protection, and social equity to ensure a prosperous and harmonious future for all, across the world.

For example, initiatives promoting renewable energy sources like solar and wind power contribute to sustainable development by reducing reliance on finite fossil fuels and mitigating climate change impacts for future generations.

Sustainable development

Recognises the complexity of social, economic, and environmental systems

- Acknowledges the dependence of human societies on healthy ecosystems for essential resources and services

- Emphasises the need to conserve and restore those ecosystems to ensure the continued availability of resources for current and future generations

- Ensures equitable distribution of resources and opportunities within the current generation

- Seeks to address challenges holistically by emphasising the need for integrated solutions that consider multiple factors and stakeholders

- Advocates for the adoption of economic models that prioritise environmental sustainability, social inclusivity, and ethical business practices
- Supports the transition towards circular economies, where resources are used efficiently, waste is minimised, and social well-being is prioritised alongside economic growth

Corporate sustainability starts with a company's value system and a principles-based approach to doing business. This means operating in ways that, at a minimum, meet fundamental responsibilities in the areas of human rights, labour, environment, and anti-corruption.

Responsible businesses should consistently apply the same values and principles wherever they operate in the world to ensure their good practices in one region of the world are not offset the harm they incur in another part of the world.

In this section, we will look at various sets of principles that have been developed to encourage global sustainable development:

- Ten Principles of sustainable development,
- United Nations Sustainability Development Goals
- Global Reporting Initiative (GRI)

2.2 Ten Principles of sustainable development

FAST FORWARD

> The United Nations Global Compact is a non-binding United Nations pact of countries to persuade businesses and firms worldwide to adopt sustainable and socially responsible policies, and to report on their implementation. The Ten Principles of the United Nations Global Compact cover human rights, labour, the environment, and anti-corruption.

The United Nations Global Compact call on companies to align their strategies and operations with ten universal principles detailed below.

2.2.1 Human Rights

Principle 1: Businesses should support and respect the protection of internationally proclaimed human rights.

For example, a multinational technology company Google is committed to the protection of freedom of speech in the diverse legal environments in which it operates. It does this through initiatives such as transparency reports which publicly disclose government requests for content removal and a 'notice and take down' process which ensures local laws are complied with while minimising the impact on free expression.

Principle 2: Businesses should ensure they are not complicit in human rights abuses.

For example, a clothing manufacturer conducts thorough audits of its supply chain to ensure that none of its subcontractors engage in practices such as forced labour or human trafficking. If any instances of abuse are found, the company takes immediate action to address them and terminates contracts with offending suppliers.

2.2.2 Labour

Principle 3: Businesses should uphold the freedom of association and the effective recognition of the right to collective bargaining.

For example, a technology company allows its employees to form labour unions and actively engages in collective bargaining negotiations to ensure fair wages, benefits, and working conditions for its workforce.

Principle 4: Businesses should strive for elimination of all forms of forced and compulsory labour.

For example, a construction company prohibits the use of forced labour in all its projects and conducts regular inspections to verify compliance. It also provides training and support to workers to empower them to report any instances of coercion or exploitation.

Principle 5: Businesses should strive for the effective abolition of child labour.

For example, a global agriculture corporation implements strict policies to prevent child labour in its supply chain. It verifies the age of workers in its farms and cooperates with local authorities and NGOs to provide education and alternative livelihood opportunities for affected children.

Principle 6: Businesses should strive for the elimination of discrimination in respect of employment and occupation.

For example, an automotive manufacturer promotes diversity and inclusion in its hiring practices by actively recruiting women, minorities, and individuals from underrepresented communities. It also provides equal opportunities for career advancement and ensures a non-discriminatory work environment for all employees.

2.2.3 Environment

Principle 7: Businesses should support a precautionary approach to environmental challenges.

For example, an energy company invests in research and development to explore renewable energy sources and adopts a precautionary approach by implementing measures to mitigate environmental risks associated with its operations, such as carbon emissions and water pollution.

Principle 8: Businesses should undertake initiatives to promote greater environmental responsibility.

For example, a retail company implements recycling programs in its stores and offices, reduces packaging waste by using sustainable materials, and encourages customers to opt for reusable shopping bags. It also partners with environmental organisations to support conservation projects and raise awareness about environmental issues.

Principle 9: Businesses should encourage the development and diffusion of environmentally friendly technologies.

For example, an automobile manufacturer develops hybrid and electric vehicles to reduce carbon emissions and dependence on fossil fuels. It also licenses its environmentally friendly technologies to other companies and collaborates with suppliers to improve the sustainability of its supply chain.

2.2.4 Anti-Corruption

Principle 10: Businesses should work against corruption in all its forms, including extortion and bribery.

For example, a pharmaceutical company adopts a zero-tolerance policy towards corruption and bribery in its business dealings. It conducts regular training sessions for employees and partners on ethical business practices and implements robust internal controls and reporting mechanisms to detect and prevent corruption. Additionally, the company refuses to engage in bribery or kickback schemes to secure contracts or regulatory approvals.

(Source: https://unglobalcompact.org/what-is-gc/mission/principles [Accessed 7 October 2024])

By incorporating the Ten Principles of the UN Global Compact into strategies, policies and procedures, and establishing a culture of integrity, organisations are not only upholding their basic responsibilities to people and planet, but also setting the stage for long-term success.

PART B   MANAGEMENT PLANNING AND DECISION-MAKING

Question

Food2U is an online supermarket which allows customers to place orders for groceries online and book a delivery. The groceries are then delivered to the customer during the specified delivery slot. Food2U has recently made the following changes to its business practices.

(1) All petrol delivery vans have been replaced with fully electric vehicles.

(2) Shopping is no longer delivered in plastic carrier bags, and must be unloaded directly from the delivery crates

Which of the below Principles of sustainable development do these changes support?

Principle 8:   Businesses should undertake initiatives to promote greater environmental responsibility

Principle 9:   Businesses should encourage the development and diffusion of environmentally friendly technologies

A   Change 1 relates to Principle 8; change 2 relates to Principle 9
B   Change 1 relates to Principle 9, change 2 relates to Principle 8
C   Both changes relate to Principle 8
D   Both changes relate to Principle 9

Answer

C   Both changes relate to initiatives that have been taken by Food2U to improve the carbon footprint and ecological impact of their own operations.

Neither of these initiatives involve developing technologies nor encouraging the uptake of these technologies by others.

Therefore they both relate to Principle 8: Businesses should undertake initiatives to promote greater environmental responsibility

2.3 United Nations Sustainability Development Goals

FAST FORWARD

The United Nations Sustainable Development Goals (UN SDG's), also known as the Global Goals, are a universal call to action to end poverty, protect the planet, and ensure that all people enjoy peace and prosperity by 2030.

Key term

Sustainable Development Goals are specific, stated, objectives which aim to transform our world. SDG's are a call for action to end poverty and inequality, protect the planet, and ensure that all people, everywhere, enjoy health, justice, and prosperity.

The seventeen UN SDGs address a wide range of interconnected issues, including poverty, inequality, climate change, environmental degradation, peace, and justice. Each goal has specific targets to be achieved by 2030, with the aim of addressing the root causes of global challenges and promoting sustainable development in all its dimensions.

The UN SDGs can be broadly categorised into three dimensions:

(a) **Planet (Biosphere):** Goals related to environmental sustainability, including climate action (Goal 13), responsible consumption and production (Goal 12), and the conservation and sustainable use of terrestrial and marine ecosystems (Goals 14 and 15). These goals aim to protect and preserve the planet's natural resources, mitigate climate change, and promote sustainable management practices that ensure the well-being of current and future generations.

(b) **Society:** Goals focused on social progress and inclusion, such as ending poverty (Goal 1), achieving gender equality (Goal 5), ensuring quality education for all (Goal 4), and promoting health and well-being (Goal 3). These goals aim to eradicate poverty, reduce inequality, improve access to essential services, and promote social cohesion and inclusivity within communities and societies.

(c) **Economy:** Goals related to economic growth, employment, and sustainable development, including decent work and economic growth (Goal 8), industry, innovation, and infrastructure (Goal 9), and building sustainable cities and communities (Goal 11). These goals aim to foster inclusive and sustainable economic growth, promote innovation and infrastructure development, and create opportunities for prosperity and employment while minimising negative environmental impacts.

The 17 Sustainable Development Goals provide a shared framework and roadmap for governments, businesses, civil society organisations, and individuals to work together towards a more equitable, resilient, and sustainable future.

The 17 UN SDG's are as follows:

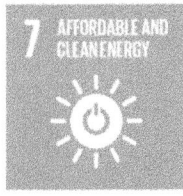     

(**Source**: https://www.un.org/sustainabledevelopment/sustainable-development-goals/ [Accessed 7 October 2024])

PART B   MANAGEMENT PLANNING AND DECISION-MAKING

United Nations Sustainable Development Goals

1. No poverty Economic growth must be inclusive to provide sustainable jobs and promote equality.	**2. Zero hunger** The food and agriculture sector offer key solutions for development and is central for hunger and poverty eradication.	**3. Good health and well-being** Ensuring healthy lives and promoting the well-being for all at all ages is essential to sustainable development.
4. Quality education Obtaining a quality education is the foundation to improving people's lives and sustainable development.	**5. Gender inequality** Gender equality is not only a fundamental human right, but a necessary foundation for a peaceful, prosperous and sustainable world.	**6. Clean water and sanitation** Clean, accessible water for all is an essential part of the world we want to live in.
7. Affordable and clean energy Energy is central to nearly every major challenge and opportunity.	**8. Decent work and economic growth** Sustainable economic growth will require societies to create the conditions that allow people to have quality jobs.	**9. Industry, innovation and infrastructure** Investments in infrastructure are crucial to achieving sustainable development.
10. Reduced inequality To reduce inequalities, policies should be universal in principle, paying attention to the needs of disadvantaged and marginalised populations.	**11. Sustainable cities and communities** There needs to be a future in where cities provide opportunities for all, with access to basic services, energy, housing, transportation and more.	**12. Responsible consumption and production** Sustainable consumption and production can contribute substantially to poverty alleviation and the transition towards low-carbon and green economies.
13. Climate action Climate change is a global challenge that affects everyone, everywhere.	**14. Life below water** Careful management of this essential global resource is a key feature of a sustainable future.	**15. Life on land** Sustainably manage forests, combat desertification, halt and reverse land degradation, halt biodiversity loss.
16. Peace and justice strong institutions Access to justice for all, and building effective, accountable institutions at all levels.	**17. Partnerships to achieve the goal** Revitalise the global partnership for sustainable development.	

(**Source:** https://www.un.org/sustainabledevelopment/sustainable-development-goals/ [Accessed 7 October 2024])

By aligning their strategies, policies, and actions with the 17 UN SDGs, companies and their stakeholders can contribute to global efforts to address pressing challenges and achieve a world where no one is left behind. Some organisations specifically align their published strategic and operating objectives to the 17 UN Sustainable Development Goals.

 **Case Study**

The following are examples of companies aligning their operations with the United Nations' 17 Sustainable Development Goals.

Unilever: Unilever operates in the consumer goods and food manufacture industry sectors.

Unilever has integrated sustainability into its business strategy, aligning with multiple SDGs such as Goal 2 (Zero Hunger) through initiatives to improve food security and nutrition, Goal 6 (Clean Water and Sanitation) by reducing water usage in its manufacturing processes, and Goal 12 (Responsible Consumption and Production) by promoting sustainable sourcing and reducing waste.

For further reading, see the Unilever's pages on sustainability.

https://www.unilever.com/news/news-search/2023/leading-and-delivering-on-sustainability-through-our-compass-commitments/

BMW Group: BMW group is a global automotive manufacturer.

BMW is contributing to Goal 9 (Industry, Innovation, and Infrastructure) by researching into, and developing, innovative technology for urban mobility, such as electromobility and hydrogen technology, Goal 12 (Responsible consumption and production) by working to improve resource efficiency through the entire lifecycle of a vehicle through principles for a circular economy, and Goal 13 (Climate Action) by advocating for the transition to sustainable transportation, such as electric vehicles, and increased use of renewable energies and effective measures to reduce CO^2 in the supply chain.

For further reading, see the 'BMW Group's pages on sustainability.

https://www.bmwgroup.com/en/sustainability.html

IKEA: IKEA operates in the furniture and homeware retail industry sector.

IKEA supports Goal 11 (Sustainable Cities and Communities) by promoting sustainable urban development through affordable and energy-efficient home furnishing solutions, Goal 12 (Responsible Consumption and Production) by implementing initiatives to reduce waste and promote recycling, and Goal 17 (Partnerships for the Goals) by collaborating with stakeholders to drive sustainability initiatives.

For further reading, see the Ikea's pages on sustainability.

https://www.ikea.com/gb/en/this-is-ikea/climate-environment/the-ikea-sustainability-strategy-pubfea4c210

Patagonia: Patagonia operates in the outdoor apparel industry sector.

Patagonia aligns with Goal 14 (Life Below Water) by advocating for marine conservation and supporting initiatives to protect oceans and coastal ecosystems, Goal 15 (Life on Land) by promoting biodiversity conservation and sustainable land management practices, and Goal 16 (Peace, Justice, and Strong Institutions) by advocating for social and environmental justice.

For further reading, see the Patagonia 's pages on sustainability.

https://www.patagonia.com/our-footprint/

Danone: Danone operates in the food and beverage manufacturing sectors.

Danone contributes to UN SDG 2 (Zero Hunger) by promoting food security and nutrition through sustainable agricultural practices and nutritious food products, UN SDG 3 (Good Health and Well-being) by producing healthy and environmentally friendly food and beverage products, and UN SDG 6 (Clean Water and Sanitation) by implementing water stewardship initiatives across its operations.

For further reading, see the Danone's pages on sustainability.

https://www.danone.com/impact/un-sustainable-developement-goals.html

2.4 Global Reporting Initiative (GRI)

FAST FORWARD

The Global Reporting Initiative (GRI) is an independent international organisation that provides guidelines for sustainability reporting, helping organisations communicate their impacts transparently.

The Global Reporting Initiative (GRI) is an independent organisation which exists to "help organisation be transparent and take responsibility for their future impact so that we can create a sustainable future".

The GRI publishes comprehensive guidelines for sustainability reporting to

- Help organisations to understand their economic, environmental, and social impacts; and
- Improve the structure and transparency of sustainability reporting.

GRI guidelines cover various aspects of sustainability performance, including governance, environmental impacts, labour practices, human rights, and community involvement.

GRI's reporting framework is based on principles of stakeholder inclusiveness, materiality, completeness, and accuracy.

Many organisations use the GRI sustainability reporting framework as a basis for their sustainability reports to their stakeholders.

Organisations following GRI guidelines are encouraged to disclose their sustainability impacts and performance metrics in a standardised format, enabling stakeholders to compare and assess their sustainability efforts consistently.

Case Study

As an example, National Grid plc sustainability report follows the GRI Standards. The 2023/24 providing comprehensive information on its environmental, social, and governance (ESG) performance.

On page 49 is the reference to the application of GRI Standards.

'Global Reporting Initiative (GRI)

This report has been prepared in accordance with the GRI Standards. We believe that all the requirements to claim alignment have been met. Further details on the requirements and our disclosures can be found in our GRI index. While we have used the GRI Standards as our primary resource in developing our Responsible Business Report, we have also prepared separate sustainability reporting disclosures described below […].'

The full Responsible Business Report can be viewed here:

https://www.nationalgrid.com/document/149761/download

6: SUSTAINABILITY, CSR AND ETHICS

Question — Global Reporting Initiative (GRI)

What is the main objective of the Global Reporting Initiative (GRI)?

- A To improve the structure and transparency of financial reporting
- B To provide guidelines for sustainability reporting
- C To regulate international trade agreements
- D To provide funding for worldwide sustainability projects

Answer

B   The main objective of the GRI is to provide guidelines for sustainability reporting. It achieves this objective by offering a framework for sustainability reporting and encourages standardised disclosure of sustainability impacts and performance metrics.

The GRI aims to improve the structure and transparency of sustainability, not financial, reporting.

The GRI does not get involved in the development of legislation or regulations, such as the regulation of international trade agreements.

The GRI and does not provide funding for worldwide sustainability projects.

3 Sustainability and environmental, social and governance (ESG)

FAST FORWARD

Environmental, social and governance (ESG) is also referred to as the three pillars of sustainability. ESG issues derive from increasing political and stakeholder concerns on the growing adverse effect of business operations on human sustainability.

3.1 Defining ESG

There are no standard definitions of ESG issues, however, the Principles of Responsible Investment (PRI) define ESG issues as follows.

Key terms

Environmental: These are issues relating to the quality and functioning of the natural environment and natural systems. These include biodiversity loss; greenhouse gas (GHG) emissions, climate change, renewable energy, energy efficiency, air, water or resource depletion or pollution, waste management, stratospheric ozone depletion, changes in land use, ocean acidification and changes to the nitrogen and phosphorus cycles.

Social: These are issues relating to the rights, well-being and interests of people and communities. These include human rights; labour standards in the supply chain; child, slave and bonded labour; workplace health and safety; freedom of association and freedom of expression; human capital management and employee relations; diversity; relations with local communities; activities in conflict sones; health and access to medicine; HIV/AIDS; consumer protection; and controversial weapons.

Governance: These are issues relating to the governance of companies and other investee entities. In the listed equity context these include, board structure, size, diversity, skills and independence, executive pay, shareholder rights, stakeholder interaction, disclosure of information, business ethics, bribery and corruption, internal controls and risk management, and, in general, issues dealing with the relationship between a company's management, its board, its shareholders and its other stakeholders. This category may also include matters of business strategy.

(**Source:** https://www.unpri.org/sustainability-issues/environmental-social-and-governance-issues [Accessed 7 October 2024])

3.2 Sustainability versus ESG

Sustainability describes a world of thriving economies and just societies based on what nature can afford. It incorporates consideration of both the impacts and dependencies of an organisation and so includes those factors that are material both to the organisation but also to society.

Environmental, social and governance (ESG) approaches this issue through a corporate lens and considers only how these risks and opportunities affect a business and its enterprise value.

Whilst sustainability includes the concept of environmental and social limits (planetary limits and a social foundation) within which there is a safe operating space, ESG does not.

ESG focusses on enterprise value and does not include consideration of planetary limits and a social foundation, together considered the 'safe operating space' within which companies, governments and individuals can sustainably operate. Therefore, ESG is separate from the overall concept of sustainability.

Note, organisations tend to consider only how ESG related risks and opportunities affect a business and its enterprise value.

3.3 Environmental management accounting (EMA)

3.3.1 Environmental accounting

In their capacity as information-providers, accountants may be required to report on a firm's environmental impact and possible consequences.

Key term

> **Environmental management accounting (EMA):** Generating and analysing financial and non-financial information to support environmental management and decision making.

EMA involves the provision of both financial and non-financial information to support the organisation's environmental management and decision making.

The purposes of EMA are to:

- Ensure sufficient resources are allocated to ESG issues;
- Avoid environmental costs, such as pollution and emission fines, legal costs, environmental taxes, loss of land value and so on; and to
- Improve the organisations reputation, for example by responding to the needs of green customers, increasing awareness of the need to protect the environment, avoid loss of sales from a damaged reputation, and developing and maintaining a competitive advantage.

It complements, rather than replaces traditional management accounting.

EMA may contribute in a variety of ways, for example applications of EMA might include budgeting, pricing of products and services, estimating environmental costs and savings from environmental initiatives, and investment appraisal.

Examples of environmental management accounting (EMA) are as follows.

(a) **Eco-balance**

   The firm identifies the raw materials it uses and outputs such as waste, noise etc, which it gives a notional value. The firm can identify these outputs as a social 'cost'.

(b) **Cleaner technology**

   This can be used in the manufacturing process to avoid waste. Simple waste-minimisation measures can increase profit on purely economic grounds.

(c) **Corporate liabilities**

Firms are being sued for environmental damage, and this might need to be recorded as a liability, with a suitable risk assessment. This might have to be factored into the project appraisal and risk.

(d) **Performance appraisal**

This can include reducing pollution.

(e) **Life cycle assessments**

The total environmental impact of a product is measured, from the resources it consumes, the energy it requires in use, and how it is disposed of, if not recycled. It may be that a product's poor ecological impact (and consequent liability or poor publicity) can be traced back to one component or material, which can be replaced.

(f) **Budgetary planning and control system**

These can be used to develop variances analysing environmental issues.

The role of the accountant will include:

- Determining environmental costs
- Identifying sustainability CSFs and appropriate KPIs through which to measure progress
- Measuring, controlling, reporting, and monitoring performance.

3.3.2 Environmental costs

The US Environmental Protection Agency identify four categories of environmental cost

- **Conventional costs:** These are the environmental costs of materials and energy which can be captured within cost systems
- **Potentially hidden costs:** These costs are difficult to identify, for example they may be captured in the costing system but lost within 'general overheads'.
- **Contingent costs:** These are environmental costs the organisation may face in the future, for example clean-up cost
- **Image and relationship costs:** These environmental costs are intangible by nature and relate to the costs associated with developing and promoting an environmental image for the company. This category also includes the costs of poor environmental activities, for example the revenue that is lost following an environmental disaster such as an oil spill.

3.3.3 Environmental reporting

More companies are now producing an external report for external stakeholders, covering:

- What the **business does** and how it impacts on the environment
- An **environmental objective** (eg use of 100% recyclable materials within x years)
- The **company's approach** to achieving and monitoring these objectives
- An **assessment of its success** towards achieving the objectives
- An **independent verification** of **claims made**

PART B   MANAGEMENT PLANNING AND DECISION-MAKING

4 Sustainable organisations

FAST FORWARD

> A **sustainable organistion** is one that builds ESG factors into its decision making in such a way that it can ensure its own long-term survival without damaging the environment, communities, or society as a whole.

4.1 Sustainable organisations

Key term

> A **sustainable organistion** is one that builds ESG factors into its decision making in such a way that it can ensure its own long-term survival without damaging the environment, communities, or society as a whole.

In today's business environment, sustainability is a critical factor for long-term success.

4.2 Sustainable business practices

> **Sustainable value creation** is where organisation engage with stakeholders helps organisations identify opportunities for creating sustainable value.

By considering the needs and interests of all stakeholders, companies can create long-term value and achieve sustainable growth. This approach not only benefits the company but also contributes positively to society and the environment.

Donaldson and Preston (1995) suggest that when organisations engage with their stakeholders and uphold corporate accountability then sustainable business practices follow and an organisation's sustainability performance improves.

Examples of sustainable business practices include inclusive decision-making, transparency and reporting, ethical practices and responsiveness and responsibility. The table explains these further:

Sustainable business practice	Description	Example
1. Inclusive decision-making	Companies are encouraged to involve a wide range of stakeholders in their decision-making processes. This inclusivity ensures that diverse perspectives are considered, leading to more balanced and sustainable business strategies.	Ben & Jerry's actively engages with local communities and social justice organisations to guide their business practices and ensure they align with broader societal goals. (**Source**: https://www.benjerry.com [Accessed 7 October 2024])
2. Responsiveness and Responsibility	Organisations that are responsive to stakeholder concerns demonstrate their commitment to accountability.	After receiving feedback from environmental groups, Coca-Cola pledged to reduce plastic waste by increasing the use of recycled materials in its packaging, showing responsiveness to stakeholder concerns. (**Source**: https://coca-cola.com/gb/en [Accessed 7 October 2024])

Sustainable business practice	Description	Example
3. Transparency and reporting	To be accountable, companies must transparently report their sustainability efforts and impacts. This includes disclosing information on environmental performance, social initiatives, and governance practices to stakeholders. Transparency in reporting and operations builds trust with stakeholders.	Nestlé applies Global Reporting Initiative (GRI) standards to provide comprehensive sustainability reports that cover various stakeholder concerns. (**Source**: https://nestle.co.uk/en-gb [Accessed 7 October 2024])
4. Ethical Practices	Businesses are expected to adopt ethical practices that respect stakeholder interests and promote sustainability. This includes reducing environmental footprints, ensuring fair labour practices, and contributing to community development.	Tony's Chocolonely has the mission statement '[t]o eliminate child labour and other illegal labour from the chocolate industry.' This is a disruptive mission statement which applies to the whole chocolate industry. The company are so committed to the cause that, in addition to demonstrating change through their own business practices they place pressure on the industry, lobby governments for mandatory legislation and help others, even their competitors, to change. (**Source**: https://tonyschocolonely.com/us/en/our-mission [Accessed 7 October 2024])

 Case Study

The following organisations demonstrate corporate accountability practices through their sustainability and corporate responsibility initiatives:

Ben & Jerry's (US)

Ben & Jerry's is a US-based ice cream manufacturer and retailer. The company has developed a reputation for strong social and environmental commitments, Ben & Jerry's engages with various stakeholders, including local communities, suppliers, and customers. The company uses fair trade ingredients and supports social justice causes, demonstrating a robust model of corporate accountability and stakeholder engagement.

Starbucks (US)

Starbucks engages with its stakeholders through its ethical sourcing practices, community involvement, and environmental initiatives. The company's 'Starbucks C.A.F.E. Practices' ensure that coffee is ethically sourced, benefiting farmers and promoting sustainable farming practices.

Unilever (Netherlands/UK)

Launched in 2010, Unilever's Sustainable Living Plan aimed to decouple strategic business growth from its environmental impact while increasing positive social impact. The company focuses on improving health and well-being, reducing its environmental footprint, and enhancing employee and supplier livelihoods. Unilever actively engages with various stakeholders, including customers, employees, suppliers, and communities, to realise their aims and to understand and address their concerns, and Unilever publishes detailed sustainability reports, providing transparent data on their environmental and social impact.

IKEA (Sweden)

IKEA commitment to sustainability and ethical practices is contained in its 'People & Planet Positive Strategy.' IKEA's sustainability strategy aims to use resources efficiently, promote renewable energy, and contribute to a circular economy by 2030. IKEA is also known for its efforts in ensuring ethical sourcing and working conditions throughout its supply chain and it audits suppliers regularly to ensure compliance with its code of conduct. Also, the IKEA Foundation supports numerous global initiatives to improve children's education and support refugee families.

Siemens (Germany)

Siemens has committed to becoming carbon-neutral by 2030. The company focuses on energy-efficient products and solutions, contributing significantly to reducing global emissions. Siemens actively promotes diversity and inclusion within its workforce, implementing policies to ensure equal opportunities for all employees and it has implemented a robust compliance framework to prevent corruption in its business practices, such as bribery and money-laundering, which ensures ethical conduct in all business activities.

Novo Nordisk (Norway)

Novo Nordisk aims to have zero environmental impact by 2030 through initiatives like recycling and reducing waste. The company follows GRI standards for sustainability reporting, ensuring transparency in their social and environmental impact and it runs several programs to make diabetes care affordable and accessible in low- and middle-income countries.

Each of these organisations exemplify corporate accountability through various initiatives, including rigorous sustainability practices, ethical supply chain management, transparent reporting, and proactive engagement with stakeholders. They set benchmarks in their respective industries, demonstrating that business success and corporate responsibility can go hand in hand.

4.3 Corporate accountability

Corporate accountability is the principle that companies should act ethically and be answerable to their stakeholders for their actions, decisions, policies and impacts on society and the environment.

Corporate accountability extends beyond financial performance to include social and environmental dimensions, ensuring that businesses contribute positively to sustainable development.

Pressure is increasing on companies to widen their scope of corporate public accountability. This pressure stems from **increasing expectations of stakeholders** and knowledge about the consequences of ignoring such pressures. There is an increasing expectation on companies to follow social policies of their business in addition to economic and environmental policies.

Grey and Adams (2014) define the three components which provide a comprehensive approach to sustainability accounting: environmental accountability, social accountability, and economic accountability.

4.4 Sustainability accounting

Sustainability accounting focuses on expanding traditional accounting practices to incorporate environmental and social impacts, requiring businesses to measure and report their impacts on the environment and society as well as their financial performance.

Sustainability accounting aims to provide a more comprehensive view of an organisation's performance by including the impacts of its activities on society and the environment, alongside the traditional financial metrics.

Gray and Adams (2014) define the three components which provide a comprehensive approach to sustainability accounting; environmental accountability, social accountability and economic accountability. Each of these is explained further below.

4.4.1 Environmental accountability

> **Key term**
>
> **Environmental accountability** is where organisations take responsibility for their environmental impacts by implementing sustainable practices and reducing their ecological footprint.

An example of environmental accountability is US company Tesla, which has been at the forefront of promoting electric vehicles to reduce carbon emissions over the past decade. Also, Apple, a US computer and smart device manufacturer, has committed to using 100% recycled aluminium in its products to reduce the environmental impact of its products.

4.4.2 Social accountability

> **Key term**
>
> **Social accountability** involves ensuring that business operations respect human rights, provide fair labour conditions, and contribute to the well-being of its employees and wider society.

An example of social accountability is US shoe manufacturer Nike's efforts to improve labour conditions in its supply chain after facing criticism for sweatshop practices. As a result, Nike regularly audits its factories and publishes detailed reports on labour conditions.

4.4.3 Economic accountability

> **Key term**
>
> **Economic accountability** is where companies are required, or voluntarily, demonstrate that their economic activities support sustainable development. This can include investing in local economies, supporting small businesses, and fostering inclusive growth.

An example of environmental accountability is Danone, a French multinational food-products corporation. Its operations fund the "Danone Communities" initiative which supports social businesses that address issues like malnutrition and access to clean water, creating economic opportunities in communities where access to food and clean water is challenging.

Environmental, Social and Economic accountability provide a comprehensive approach to sustainability accounting which provides transparency to stakeholders so they can fully understand the scope and impact of a company's operations and its commitment to meeting its sustainability objectives.

(**Source:** Gray, R., Adams, C. A., & Owen, D. (2014). *Accountability, Social Responsibility and Sustainability: Accounting for Society and the Environment*. Pearson Education Limited)

4.5 The triple bottom line

The concept of the triple bottom line emphasises that, although firms can be capable of socially and environmentally responsible action, many will only take such action if accounting conventions are changed to record and monitor the entire impact of business activities, and not just the financial (profit) benefits. There are also potentially a number of ways poor environmental behaviour can affect a firm: it could result in fines (for pollution or damages), increased liability to environmental taxes, loss in value of land, destruction of brand values, loss of sales, consumer boycotts, inability to secure finance, loss of insurance cover, contingent liabilities, lawsuits, and damage to corporate image.

4.5.1 People, Planet and Profit

The triple bottom line (TBL) is sometimes summarised as People, Planet, and Profit (**Elkington**, *Cannibals with forks: The triple bottom line of 21st century business,* 1998). It consists of:

- **Social justice**: fair and beneficial business practices towards labour and the community and the region in which a corporation conducts its business. A TBL company conceives a reciprocal social structure in which the wellbeing of corporate, labour and other stakeholder interests are interdependent.

- **Environmental quality**: a TBL company endeavours to benefit the natural order as much as possible, or at the least do no harm and curtail environmental impact. In this way, the company tries to reduce its ecological footprint by, among other things, carefully managing its consumption of energy and non-renewable resources, and by reducing manufacturing waste, as well as rendering waste less toxic before disposing of it in a safe and legal manner.

- **Economic prosperity**: the economic benefit enjoyed by the host society. It is the lasting economic impact the organisation has on its economic environment. Importantly, however, this is not as narrow as the internal profit made by a company or organisation.

For many years, sustainability has been seen from an environmental perspective, but now the social side of sustainability is gaining increasing importance. Issues such as the health and safety of workers, or paying workers a fair wage, are becoming increasingly important.

Case Study

Innocent Drinks is a company which advertises its ethical stance in its phrase:

'Little drinks, big dreams'

'We might be a company that makes little drinks and cracks some bad jokes, but we've got some big dreams bouncing around our heads. We had our first one back in 1999 when we decided to crush fruit into bottles to help people do themselves some good. Since then, our dreams have got bigger and bigger.

Now we have dreams to keep people healthy while making sure our communities and our planet are healthy too. It's the reason we became a B Corp, always give 10% of our profits to good causes and are working to halve our supply chain carbon footprint by 2030.'

(**Source**: https://www.innocentdrinks.co.uk [Accessed 7 October 2024])

Given that firms are more likely to embrace sustainability if it brings them a financial benefit, it is important to note that introducing better environmental management systems can create 'win – win' situations. For example, if introducing environmental management systems can allow a company to continue to produce the same amount of product by using less resources, and generating less waste, this is both economically efficient, and also beneficial from an environmental and ecological perspective.

5 Integrated reporting

FAST FORWARD
Integrated reporting combines financial and non-financial information into a single document which demonstrates how the organisation creates value.

An integrated report reports on both financial and non-financial information to demonstrates how the organisation creates value. The integrated report combines this information into a single document which is provided alongside the traditional financial statements.

This provides greater transparency to stakeholders, illustrates how a wide variety of stakeholder needs are met and demonstrates the commitment of the organisation to sustainable business practices.

Integrated reporting considers how value is created in terms of "six capitals"

5.1 Six capitals

FAST FORWARD
The concept of the 'six capitals' illustrates the various ways through which an organisation creates value.

The Integrated Reporting Framework for Sustainable Development introduces the concept of the "six capitals", which represent the various forms of resources and relationships that organisations utilise and affect through their activities.

The six capitals model provides a basis for understanding the long-term sustainability of a business. Organisations use six types of capital to deliver their products or services.

The six types of capital are as follows and are explained further below.

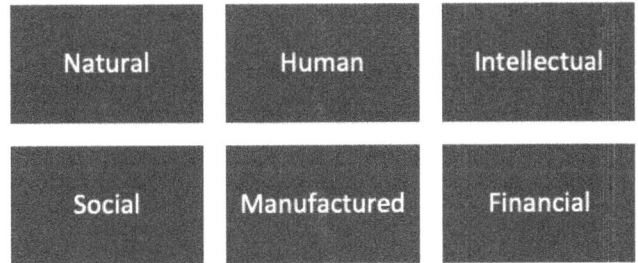

These six capitals are aligned to the triple bottom line reporting elements of profit, people and planet described in the section above.

5.1.1 Profit

1. **Financial capital**

   This includes the monetary resources available to an organisation, such as cash, investments, and income. Financial capital represents the financial value generated or consumed by the organisation's activities.

   For example, Apple, with its vast cash reserves, investments in various financial instruments, and steady income from product sales and services, possesses substantial financial capital resources that fuel its operations, investments in research and development, and strategic initiatives.

2. **Manufactured capital**

   Manufactured capital encompasses the physical infrastructure, equipment, and technology that organisations use to produce goods and services. Manufactured capital includes assets like buildings, machinery, and intellectual property.

For example, Toyota Motor Corporation exemplifies manufactured capital through its extensive physical infrastructure, advanced manufacturing facilities, and cutting-edge technology used in vehicle production. With state-of-the-art factories, machinery, and patented manufacturing processes, Toyota relies heavily on its manufactured capital to maintain its position as a leading global automobile manufacturer.

5.1.2 People

3. **Intellectual capital**

   Intellectual capital refers to the knowledge, expertise, and intellectual property owned or developed by an organisation. Intellectual capital includes patents, trademarks, copyrights, and the skills and capabilities of employees.

   For example, Microsoft Corporation showcases intellectual capital through its vast portfolio of patents, trademarks, and copyrights, along with the expertise and skills of its employees. As a technology giant, Microsoft owns valuable intellectual property rights to software products like Windows and Office, while also leveraging the knowledge and innovation of its workforce to develop new technologies and solutions.

4. **Human capital**

   Human capital represents the skills, experience, and capabilities of an organisation's workforce. Human capital encompasses factors such as employee education, training, health, and well-being.

   For example, Google demonstrates strong human capital through its highly skilled and diverse workforce, comprised of talented engineers, developers, and professionals across various fields. With a focus on employee education, training, and well-being, Google invests in nurturing its human capital to drive innovation, creativity, and productivity across its diverse range of products and services.

5. **Social capital**

   Social capital encompasses the relationships and networks that organisations have with stakeholders, including employees, customers, suppliers, communities, and society at large. It includes aspects such as trust, reputation, and social license to operate.

   For example, Starbucks Corporation exemplifies social capital through its extensive network of relationships with stakeholders, including employees, customers, suppliers, and communities. Through initiatives like ethical sourcing, community outreach programs, and employee welfare initiatives, Starbucks builds trust, fosters positive relationships, and earns social license to operate, enhancing its brand reputation and long-term sustainability.

5.1.3 Planet

6. **Natural capital**

   Natural capital refers to the environmental resources and ecosystems that provide essential services and benefits to organisations and society. Natural capital includes elements such as clean air and water, biodiversity, ecosystems, and natural resources like minerals and forests.

   For example, the Body Shop, a cosmetics company, emphasises natural capital through its commitment to sustainable sourcing, environmental conservation, and biodiversity preservation. By using natural ingredients, supporting fair trade practices, and advocating for environmental causes, The Body Shop relies on natural capital to create eco-friendly products and contribute to the preservation of natural resources and ecosystems.

6: SUSTAINABILITY, CSR AND ETHICS

Case Study

The Mitsubishi Corporation publishes an integrated report which contains a section dedicated to the six capitals. The report discusses each capital in turn, clearly explaining how the capital has been used by the corporation to generate value and improve sustainability.

The relevant section of the 2023 Integrated Report can be found here:

https://www.mitsubishicorp.com/jp/en/ir/library/ar/online2023/six-capitals/

Question — Integrated reporting

An organisation that has been in operation for several decades has built up a high degree of industry expertise and a sound understanding of the way in which it operates. To which of the following 'capitals' does this relate?

A   Human
B   Manufactured
C   Social
D   Intellectual

Answer

B   Industry expertise is an example of intellectual capital.

Intellectual capital refers to the knowledge, expertise, and intellectual property owned or developed by an organisation. Intellectual capital includes patents, trademarks, copyrights, and the skills and capabilities of employees.

Human capital is the skills and experience of the workforce; manufactured capital encompasses the physical infrastructure, equipment, and technology that organisations use to produce goods and services; and social capital encompasses the relationships and networks that organisations have with stakeholders, including employees, customers, suppliers, communities, and society at large.

5.2 Integrated reporting

Key term

> **Integrated reporting** is a reporting approach that aims to provide a holistic view of an organisation's performance, value creation, and impact across the six capitals.

Unlike traditional financial reporting, which focuses on financial capital, integrated reporting considers the organisation's broader value creation process and its interactions with various forms of capital.

Integrated reporting encourages organisations to communicate how they create value by utilising and affecting the six capitals. It emphasises the interdependencies between financial, environmental, social, and governance factors and their influence on organisational performance and sustainability.

Integrated reporting is highly relevant to sustainable development as it provides a comprehensive framework for organisations to assess and communicate their sustainability performance and impact.

By considering the interconnectedness of financial, environmental, social, and governance factors, integrated reporting enables organisations to:

Evaluate their contribution to sustainable development goals and objectives.

- Identify opportunities to enhance value creation while minimising negative impacts on society and the environment
- Engage stakeholders in meaningful dialogue about sustainability issues and performance
- Enhance transparency, accountability, and trust by providing a more complete picture of the organisation's activities and impacts
- Explanation of the IFRS International Integrated Reporting Framework

The International Integrated Reporting Framework (IFRS Framework) provides guidance and principles for organisations seeking to adopt integrated reporting practices. It outlines the fundamental concepts, content elements, and guiding principles of integrated reporting, helping organisations effectively communicate their value creation story.

The IFRS Framework emphasises the importance of connectivity, materiality, conciseness, and reliability in integrated reporting. It encourages organisations to tailor their reports to reflect the unique circumstances, strategies, and impacts relevant to their operations and stakeholders.

The diagram provided by the IFRS Framework illustrates the key components of integrated reporting, including the organisation's business model, governance structure, performance measures, and outcomes across the six capitals. It serves as a visual representation of how organisations can integrate financial and non-financial information to communicate their value creation process and impact on sustainable development.

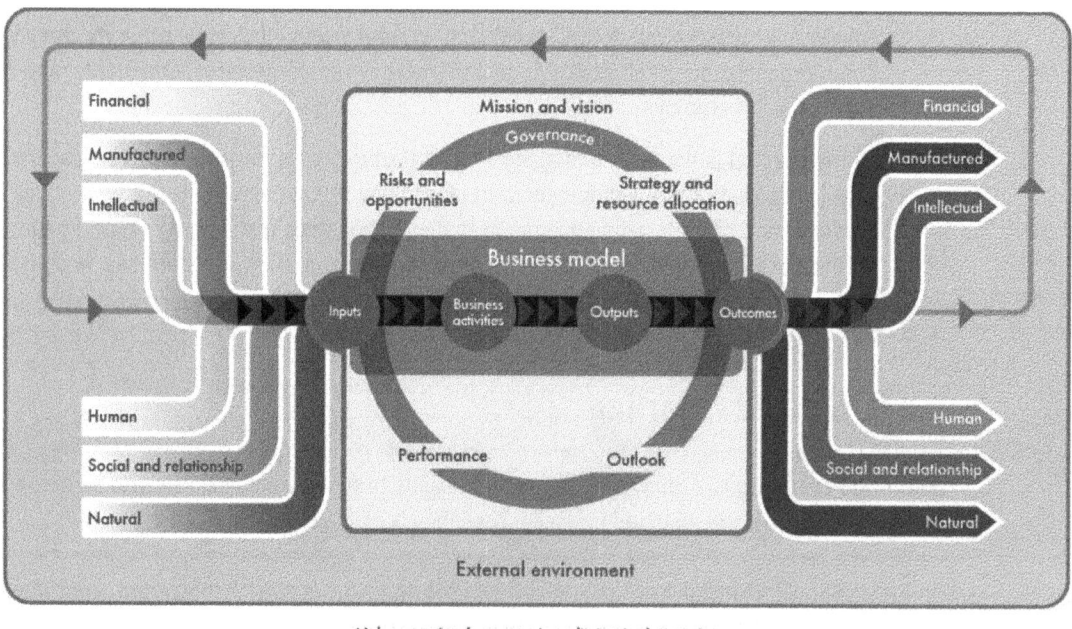

(**Source**: https://integratedreporting.ifrs.org/resource/internationa-ir-framework/ [Accessed 7 October 2024])

5.3 IR and the role of the management accountant

Traditional financial reports are based on historical results and are, generally, compiled by financial accountants.

Integrated reports, as we have seen, has a much broader focus and is forward looking in its approach.

Management accountants will, therefore, have a heavier involvement in compiling the information for inclusion in the integrated report. The roles carried out will be varied and might include:

- Forecasting and budgeting
- The provision of financial and non-financial information from a variety of sources
- Identification and appraisal of opportunities in the wider environment
- Risk assessments
- Ensuring compliance with regulation and legislation, for example environmental regulations such as emission levels, employment legislation to ensure equal opportunities, and so on
- Allocating resources in such a way that the creation of value is maximised
- Establishing KPIs in respect of each of the capitals and reporting on progress
- Environmental Management Accounting (EMA) is described in an earlier section

6 Sustainability strategy setting and management decision making

FAST FORWARD

In the pursuit of sustainability excellence, organisations must strategically set and effectively manage their sustainability initiatives.

6.1 Features of a sustainability strategy

Organisations are increasingly recognising the critical importance of integrating Environmental, Social, and Governance (ESG) aspects into their overall strategy and operations. This integration is driven by the need to attract and retain customers and providers of finance who are demanding improvements in corporate sustainability practices.

The following table includes examples of ESG strategies which organisations may adopt.

Category	Explanation	Examples ESG Strategies
Environmental (E) Neutralising the impact of economic activity on the environment	Promote resource and product sustainability by using renewable energy sources, using recycled materials and designing products which can be recycled. Innovate greener production technologies and minimise waste and pollution. Reduce CO_2 emissions levels, reduce energy consumption and improve air quality. Reduce waste, minimise use of natural resources and aim to use renewable sources, impacts of product use. Go beyond minimum compliance with environmental legislations.	Renewable energy investments, supply chain sustainability, climate risk assessment and management, water and waste management

Category	Explanation	Examples ESG Strategies
Social (S) Acting in a fair, just and honest way is a universal human expectation of each other and from organisations	Engage with local communities, for example, support local charities and social events, employ local people, invest in the local economy. Apply health and safety, workers' rights (in the business itself and its supply chain), pay and benefits, diversity and equal opportunities, responsible marketing, data protection and privacy, community impact and investment, supply chain impact, bribery/corruption principles. Also, consider economic stability and growth, provision of sustainable employment opportunities, local economic development, healthy competition, compliance with governance structures, transparency, long-term viability of businesses and investment in innovation/new product development.	Diversity and inclusion initiatives, community engagement and philanthropy, product innovation for sustainability
Governance (G) Complying with the law is a requirement in all societies, and this applies to organisations as well as individuals	Apply mandatory and best practice legal and regulatory governance frameworks. Set strategic objectives which aim to provide long term sustainable benefits to all stakeholders which includes environment, social and ethical objectives. Prevent short term profit motives overriding the exploitation of stakeholders and the environment. Adopt good governance and responsible business practices, for example, by eliminating self-interest, fraud, bribery, money laundering and other forms of corruption. Understand the benefits of diversity and shared decision making on the board and comply with employee health and safety regulations.	Ethical governance practises

6.2 Integration of sustainability objectives into the overall strategy

To achieve sustainable development, organisations must integrate ESG issues into their conventional strategic objective setting. This involves aligning strategic objectives with ESG and sustainability considerations to meet stakeholder expectations and promote responsible business practices.

A company's sustainability strategy typically encompasses many features aimed at addressing environmental, social, and governance (ESG) issues while promoting long-term value creation and responsible business practices. These include, but are not limited to, the following areas:

6.2.1 Vision and commitment

A sustainability strategy requires a clear vision statement and commitment to sustainability, outlining the company's goals and aspirations for environmental stewardship, social responsibility, and ethical governance.

For example, a global consumer goods corporation, has a clear vision and commitment to sustainability outlined in its corporate mission statement. The company pledges to minimise its environmental footprint, support community development initiatives, and uphold ethical business practices. This commitment is demonstrated through the integration of sustainability principles into the company's core values, strategic planning processes, and decision-making frameworks.

6.2.2 Materiality assessment

A sustainability strategy includes identification of material ESG issues that are most relevant to the company's operations, stakeholders, and long-term value creation, based on stakeholder engagement, risk assessments, and industry benchmarks.

For example, an organisation conducts a comprehensive materiality assessment to identify key environmental, social, and governance (ESG) issues that are most relevant to its business and stakeholders. Through stakeholder engagement sessions, industry research, and risk assessments, the company determines that reducing carbon emissions, ensuring responsible sourcing practices, and enhancing employee diversity and inclusion are the most critical material issues that could impact its long-term success and reputation.

6.2.3 Strategic goal setting and targets

A well-developed sustainability strategy includes the establishment of specific, measurable, and time-bound goals and targets to drive progress towards sustainability objectives, such as reducing greenhouse gas emissions, promoting diversity and inclusion, or enhancing supply chain transparency.

For example, a company sets strategic sustainability goals and targets to drive progress towards its environmental and social objectives. As part of its sustainability strategy, the company commits to achieving a 30% reduction in greenhouse gas emissions by 2030, sourcing 100% of its electricity from renewable energy sources by 2025 and increasing gender diversity in its leadership positions to 40% by 2023. These specific, measurable, and time-bound targets provide a roadmap for the company to align its actions with its sustainability aspirations and track progress over time.

6.2.4 Product development and innovation

Integrating ESG and sustainability objectives into product development involves designing products and services that minimise environmental impact, promote social responsibility, and meet stakeholder expectations.

For example, a clothing company may develop a line of sustainably sourced and ethically manufactured apparel made from organic cotton and recycled materials to reduce water usage and support fair labour practices.

6.2.5 Supply chain management

Incorporating ESG and sustainability considerations into supply chain management entails selecting suppliers and partners that adhere to responsible business practices, environmental standards, and labour rights.

For instance, a multinational corporation may implement supplier sustainability assessments and audits to ensure ethical sourcing practices, increased use of renewal or recycled materials, reducing the risks of child labour, reduced supply miles (lessening the distance to key suppliers) or reducing environmental degradation and damage in its supply chain.

6.2.6 Marketing strategy

Aligning marketing strategies with ESG and sustainability objectives involves communicating the organisation's commitment to responsible business practices, environmental stewardship, and social impact.

An example is a food company promoting its use of locally sourced, organic ingredients in its products through marketing campaigns that emphasise sustainability, health, and community support.

6.2.7 Financing strategy

Integrating ESG and sustainability considerations into financing strategies involves accessing capital markets that prioritise environmental, social, and governance criteria. An example is a renewable energy company issuing green bonds to finance solar or wind energy projects, attracting investors who prioritise investments with positive environmental impacts and sustainable returns.

6.2.8 Human resource strategy

Incorporating ESG and sustainability objectives into human resource strategies involves fostering a culture of sustainability within the organisation. Empowerment of employees through sustainability training, education, and awareness programs will build a culture of sustainability, foster employee engagement, and encourage innovation and continuous improvement.

For example, a technology company may offer sustainability training programs to employees, implement diversity and inclusion policies to promote equitable opportunities, and recognise employee contributions to environmental initiatives through rewards and incentives.

6.2.9 Managing stakeholder relationships

Integrating ESG considerations into stakeholder management involves engaging with stakeholders to understand their expectations and concerns regarding sustainability.

An example is a mining company consulting with local communities and indigenous groups to address concerns about environmental conservation, land rights, and community development in areas where it operates.

6.2.10 Measuring investment appraisal

Incorporating ESG factors into investment appraisal involves assessing the financial and non-financial impacts of investment decisions on environmental, social, and governance performance.

For instance, an infrastructure investment firm may evaluate the potential social and environmental risks and benefits of a new transportation project, considering factors such as community displacement, biodiversity impacts, and climate resilience.

6.2.11 ESG risk management

Integrating ESG considerations into risk management involves identifying, assessing, and mitigating environmental, social, and governance risks.

An example is a financial institution incorporating climate change risk assessments into its lending practices to evaluate the exposure of loan portfolios to physical risks (eg extreme weather events) and transition risks (eg policy changes, technological advancements) associated with climate change.

6.2.12 Integration with corporate governance:

Integration of sustainability principles into corporate governance structures, practices, and policies, including board oversight, executive compensation, and risk management frameworks, to ensure accountability, transparency, and ethical decision-making at all levels of the organisation. This will require the establishment of governance structures, policies, and practices that promote transparency, accountability, and responsible decision-making.

For example, a multinational corporation may appoint board members with expertise in sustainability to oversee ESG-related risks and opportunities, establish a sustainability committee to monitor performance, and integrate ESG criteria into executive compensation frameworks.

6.2.13 Codes of conduct and ethics

Embedding ESG and sustainability policies into codes of conduct involves setting ethical standards and guidelines for employee conduct, supplier relationships, and business operations.

An example is a pharmaceutical company implementing a code of conduct that prohibits bribery, corruption, and unethical marketing practices, and promotes compliance with environmental regulations and human rights standards in its global operations.

6.2.14 Continuous improvement

Implement a culture and commitment to continuous improvement and adaptation based on performance monitoring, feedback mechanisms, stakeholder engagement, and emerging trends and best practices in sustainability, to drive innovation, resilience, and long-term value creation.

6.2.15 ESG performance monitoring

Transparent reporting and disclosure of sustainability performance, initiatives, and progress against goals using standardised frameworks such as the Global Reporting Initiative (GRI) or the Sustainability Accounting Standards Board (SASB), to provide stakeholders with credible and comparable information.

Integrating ESG performance monitoring involves establishing metrics, KPIs, and reporting mechanisms to track progress towards sustainability goals.

For instance, a real estate investment trust may measure energy efficiency, water usage, waste management, and tenant satisfaction across its property portfolio to assess ESG performance and report on sustainability initiatives in annual reports and investor communications.

6.2.16 Community involvement

Integrating ESG considerations into community involvement involves engaging with local communities and other stakeholders to address social and environmental issues.

An example is a hospitality company partnering with local nonprofits to support education and healthcare initiatives in communities near its resorts, contributing to economic development and social well-being while promoting sustainable tourism practices.

Once a sustainability strategy has been development then integration of sustainability objectives and other considerations into the company's overall business strategy, decision-making processes, and operational practices to embed sustainability throughout the organisation and align with core business objectives.

Question — Embedding sustainability

How can an organisation build sustainability targets and KPIs into its performance management system?

(a) By aligning sustainability targets with the company's strategic objectives
(b) By incorporating sustainability considerations into policies, procedures and codes of conduct
(c) By using sustainability targets to set departmental goals
(d) By including sustainability targets in annual performance reviews

A   (a) only
B   (d) only
C   (a), (b) and (c)
D   (a), (b), (c) and (d)

Answer

D   (a), (b), (c) and (d)

All of these measures can help to build sustainability into an organisation's performance management system.

Incorporating sustainability into the organisations strategic objectives ensures the company as a whole is striving to achieve sustainability. It becomes part of the purpose for which the organisation operates and ensures it is given sufficient and focus at the highest level.

Embedding the principles into policies, procedures and codes of conduct communicates the expectation that responsible practices will be carried out as part of operations and provides an objective standard which must be met.

Building the targets into departmental goals ensures goal congruence with the overall strategy. This makes sure that the various functions and teams throughout the organisation have a responsibility to meet the sustainability targets required for the overall organisational strategy to be achieved.

Accountability is further ensured by building sustainability targets into individual performance reviews.

6.3 Sustainability management and decision making

Embedding sustainability within management decision-making processes is essential for organisations to effectively address environmental, social, and economic challenges while pursuing long-term success. By integrating sustainability considerations into decision-making frameworks, cultures, and support systems, organisations can make informed choices that align with their sustainability goals and create value for stakeholders.

This approach ensures that sustainability becomes an integral part of organisational strategy, operations, and culture, driving positive environmental and social impact while enhancing business resilience and competitiveness.

6.3.1 Sustainability-led decision-making culture

A culture that prioritises sustainability in decision-making fosters organisational values, norms, and behaviours that support environmental and social responsibility. Building a sustainable decision - making culture requires leadership, collaboration, and a commitment to continuous improvement.

- **Sustainability led leadership** – Organisations foster a culture of sustainability leadership, where senior executives champion sustainability initiatives and integrate sustainability into the organisation's values and vision.

    For example, a clothing retailer may appoint a chief sustainability officer (CSO) to oversee sustainability efforts and ensure alignment with business objectives.

- **Cross – functional collaboration** – Sustainability requires collaboration across departments and functions to address complex challenges.

    For example, a technology company may establish cross-functional sustainability task forces comprised of representatives from different departments, such as R&D, procurement, and marketing, to develop and implement sustainability initiatives.

- **Continuous improvement culture** – Organisations promote a culture of continuous improvement in sustainability performance, encouraging employees to identify opportunities for innovation and efficiency.

  For example, a hospitality company may implement employee suggestion programs to solicit ideas for reducing energy consumption, waste generation, and water usage, fostering a culture of sustainability innovation.

6.3.2 Sustainability-led decision-making frameworks

The application of sustainability focused decision-making frameworks provide the structure and guidance necessary for organisations to integrate sustainability considerations into their strategic planning and operational processes. These frameworks outline the principles, goals, and criteria that guide decision-making, ensuring alignment with sustainability objectives.

- **Sustainable strategy formulation** – This involves developing strategies that align with the organisation's sustainability goals and objectives.

  For example, an energy company may decide to invest in renewable energy projects as part of its strategy to reduce greenhouse gas emissions and transition to a low - carbon economy.

- **Sustainable operations planning** – Organisations need to consider sustainability principles when planning day-to-day operations.

  For example, a manufacturing facility may implement energy - efficient technologies and processes to minimise resource consumption and waste generation, aligning with sustainability objectives.

6.3.3 Sustainability-led decision-making processes

Effective decision-making processes enable organisations to assess the environmental, social, and economic impacts of their actions and make informed choices that support sustainability. These processes involve methodologies and tools that facilitate thorough analysis and stakeholder engagement to ensure holistic decision-making.

- **Life cycle assessment (LCA)** – Organisations conduct LCAs to evaluate the environmental impacts of products or services throughout their life cycle.

  For example, a food manufacturer may conduct an LCA to assess the carbon footprint of its products from sourcing raw materials to distribution and consumption, informing decisions to reduce emissions.

- **Triple bottom line analysis** – This approach considers environmental, social, and economic (ESG) impacts when evaluating alternatives. This is also known as the Three P's analysis – planet, people, profit

  For example, a construction company may use a triple bottom line analysis to assess the sustainability of different building materials, considering factors such as environmental impact, social equity, and long-term cost-effectiveness.

- **Stakeholder engagement** – Organisations are advised to engage stakeholders, including employees, customers, suppliers, and communities, to gather feedback and incorporate diverse perspectives and sustainability expectations into sustainability decision making processes.

  For example, a retail company may consult with local communities and environmental NGOs when selecting suppliers to ensure alignment with sustainability goals and address stakeholder concerns.

6.3.4 Sustainability-led decision support systems

Decision support systems provide sustainability related expertise and people resources and IT technologies necessary for organisations to collect, analyse, and visualise data related to sustainability performance and impacts. These systems enable organisations to make evidence-based decisions and monitor progress towards sustainability goals.

- **Environmental management systems (EMS)** – EMS help organisations manage and track their environmental performance, compliance obligations, and sustainability initiatives.

    For example, a manufacturing company may implement an EMS to monitor energy consumption, waste generation, and emissions, enabling data-driven decision-making to improve environmental performance.

- **Sustainability impact assessment tools** – Sustainability impact assessment tools evaluate the potential environmental and social impacts of decisions and projects.

    For example, before launching a new product line, a consumer goods company may use a sustainability impact assessment tool to identify potential risks and opportunities related to resource use, supply chain practices, and social equity.

- **Sustainability reporting platforms** – Organisations use sustainability reporting platforms to track and communicate their sustainability performance to stakeholders.

    For example, a financial institution may use a sustainability reporting platform to disclose its carbon footprint, social investments, and community engagement initiatives, demonstrating transparency and accountability in sustainability management.

Incorporating sustainability into management decision-making processes is vital for organisations to navigate environmental, social, and economic challenges while ensuring long-term success. By integrating sustainability considerations into decision-making frameworks, cultures, and support systems, organisations can make informed choices that align with their sustainability goals and create value for stakeholders.

This approach ensures that sustainability becomes ingrained in organisational strategy, operations, and culture, driving positive environmental and social impact while enhancing business resilience and competitiveness. Through the four components of sustainability-led decision-making explored in this discussion – cultures, frameworks, processes, and support systems – organisations can effectively navigate complex sustainability issues and contribute to a more sustainable future for all.

7 ESG risk management and metrics for sustainability performance monitoring and reporting

> **FAST FORWARD**
>
> Growing stakeholder expectations, regulatory pressures and market dynamics place organisations under increasing scrutiny to effectively identify, assess and mitigate ESG-related risks.

ESG risks encompass a wide range of issues that can significantly impact an organisation's long-term sustainability, reputation, and financial performance. These include climate change impacts, supply chain disruptions, human rights violations, regulatory non-compliance, ethical misconduct, and so on.

7.1 Benefits of ESG risk management

Implementing risk management processes within an organisation are beneficial for several reasons:

- **Enhanced resilience:** Proactively addressing ESG risks enables organisations to build resilience and adaptability. Early identification and mitigation of potential risks help organisations better anticipate and respond to disruptions, safeguarding their operations, supply chains, and stakeholder relationships.

- **Protection of reputation:** ESG risks have the potential to significantly impact an organisation's reputation and brand value. Proactive risk management helps organisations protect their reputation by addressing ESG issues before they escalate into crises. By demonstrating a commitment to responsible business practices and sustainability, organisations can enhance trust and credibility with stakeholders, safeguarding their brand reputation in the long term.

- **Regulatory compliance:** Many ESG risks are subject to regulatory requirements and reporting obligations. Proactive risk management ensures that organisations stay compliant with applicable laws, regulations, and industry standards related to environmental protection, labour practices, data privacy, and corporate governance. By staying ahead of regulatory developments, organisations can avoid costly fines, legal penalties, and reputational damage associated with non-compliance.

- **Investor confidence**: Investors and financial stakeholders are increasingly integrating ESG considerations into their investment decisions. Proactively managing ESG risks and disclosing sustainability performance can enhance investor confidence and attract capital from socially responsible investors. By demonstrating a commitment to ESG risk management and transparency, organisations can access new sources of financing and improve their access to capital markets.

- **Operational efficiency:** effective ESG risk management can drive operational efficiencies and cost savings by identifying opportunities for resource optimisation, waste reduction, and energy efficiency improvements. By implementing sustainable practices and reducing environmental impacts, organisations can lower operational costs, enhance resource efficiency, and improve overall profitability.

7.2 ESG risk management processes

An effective approach for organisations to manage sustainability and ESG risk involves:

- **ESG risk identification and assessment:** Begin by identifying and assessing sustainability and ESG risks relevant to your organisation's operations, supply chain, and stakeholders. This involves conducting comprehensive risk assessments to identify potential ESG risks that could impact the organisation's long-term viability, reputation, and performance.

- **ESG risk prioritisation:** Once risks are identified, prioritise them based on their likelihood and potential impact on the organisation's objectives and stakeholders. Focus on risks that pose the greatest threats to the organisation's sustainability goals, reputation, regulatory compliance, and financial stability.

- **Integration into existing risk management processes:** Integrate sustainability and ESG risk management into existing risk management processes and frameworks, such as enterprise risk management (ERM) systems. Ensure that sustainability and ESG risks are considered alongside traditional financial and operational risks, and that they are adequately addressed in risk mitigation strategies and action plans.

- **ESG metric measurement and monitoring:** Establish ESG metrics such as key performance indicators (KPIs) and other metrics to measure and monitor sustainability and ESG risks over time. Track progress against KPIs regularly and adjust risk management strategies as needed based on changes in risk exposure, stakeholder expectations, and regulatory requirements.

- **Stakeholder engagement:** Engage with stakeholders, including investors, customers, employees, suppliers, and communities, to understand their expectations and concerns regarding sustainability and ESG issues. Incorporate stakeholder feedback into risk management processes and decision-making to ensure alignment with stakeholder interests and values.

- **Transparency and reporting:** Communicate transparently with stakeholders about the organisation's sustainability and ESG risk management efforts, including the identification, assessment, and mitigation of risks. Provide regular updates and disclosures on sustainability performance, ESG initiatives, and progress towards risk management goals through internal reporting, sustainability reports, annual filings, and other communication channels.
- **Continuous Improvement:** Commit to continuous improvement in sustainability and ESG risk management practices by regularly reviewing and updating policies, procedures, and controls. Stay informed of emerging sustainability trends, regulatory developments, and best practices in ESG risk management, and adapt strategies accordingly.

By following this approach, organisations can manage sustainability and ESG risks, enhance resilience to environmental, social, and governance challenges, and create long-term value for stakeholders.

7.3 Sustainability performance monitoring

Environmental, Social, and Governance (ESG) metrics are instrumental in monitoring and reporting sustainability performance for organisations.

The purpose of ESG metrics for sustainability performance monitoring and reporting is to drive continuous improvement, mitigate risks, engage stakeholders, meet regulatory requirements, attract investment, and enhance long-term value creation for the organisation and society.

It is the role of the accountant to identify sustainability critical success factors (CSFs) and develop suitable key performance indicators (KPIs) through which they can be measured.

7.3.1 Sustainability critical success factors (CSFs)

It is important that sustainability critical success factors link directly to the mission and objectives of the organisation.

- Sustainability should be clearly embedded in the mission of the organisation
- Environmental objectives and targets should be developed that directly support the mission
- Specific critical success factors should then be developed in relation to those objectives and targets. CSFs are the specific processes in which the organisation will need to succeed if the sustainability targets are to be achieved.

7.3.2 Sustainability key performance indicators (KPIs)

Key performance indicators (KPIs) are the metrics that will be used to measure the progress towards achievement of the CSFs. They determine how well the sustainability objectives are being achieved and provide a metric for reporting.

Successful sustainability KPIs must:

- Effectively measure sustainability and recognise it's cross functional nature
- Focus on the organisation's most important sustainability issues
- Facilitate clear performance measurement and be measured on a regular basis so that performance can be tracked over time.

7.3.3 Example ESG metrics

In the next table are examples of ESG Metrics which organisations could implement to improve their sustainability performance and reporting.

Area	Suggested ESG metric	Measured by
Environment		
Greenhouse gas emissions (GHG)	• Absolute emissions	• CO_2e • CO_2e/unit of production
Energy consumption	• Absolute energy consumption • Energy consumption intensity	• Megawatt Hours (MWhs) • Megawatt Hours (MWhs)/unit of production
Water consumption	• Total water consumption • Water consumption intensity	• Metric litre or m^3 • Metric litre or m^3/unit of production
Waste generation	• Total waste generated	• Tonnes • Tonnes/time unit or unit of production
Social		
Gender diversity	• Current employees by gender • New hires and turnover by gender	• Percentage (%) or M:F ratio
Age-based diversity	• Current employees by age • New hires and turnover by age	• Percentage (%) or M:F ratio
Employment	• Total turnover • Total number of employees	• Number of employees with joiners and leavers • Percentage (%) or M:F ratio
Development & training	• Average training hours per employee • Average training hours per employee per gender	• Training Hours/numbers of employees
Occupational health & safety	• Fatalities • High-consequence injuries • Recordable injuries • Recordable work-related ill health cases	• Number of incidents • Percentage change (%)
Governance		
Board composition	• Board independence • Women on the board	• Percentage (%) • Percentage (%) or M:F ratio
Management diversity	• Women in the management team	• Percentage (%) or M:F ratio
Ethical behaviour	• Anti-corruption disclosures • Anti-corruption training for employees	• List • Number of days and • Percentage completed (%)
Certifications	• List all sustainability or ESG-related certification	• List
Alignment with frameworks	• The issuer needs to give priority to using globally recognised frameworks and disclosure practices to guide its sustainability reporting.	• Disclosure of frameworks • Exceptions • Non-compliance

Area	Suggested ESG metric	Measured by
Assurance	- Disclose whether sustainability report has undertaken: (a) External independent assurance (b) Internal assurance (c) No assurance - Provide scope of assurance if organisation has undertaken external or internal assurance.	- Case by case disclosure - Number of assurance engagements undertaken

Organisations can choose to support KPI disclosures with independent assurance to strengthen the credibility of ESG information disclosed, although currently, there are no mandatory audit of a company's sustainability reporting disclosures.

Case Study

(a) **Unilever**

Each year, Unilever publish the basis of preparation of each of its ESG performance metrics for transparency, so stakeholders can understand how each measure is determined.

See Sections 4.1 to 4.8 detail the basis of preparation for each sustainability performance measure

(**Source**: https://www.unilever.com/files/bd7239b8-a13b-483b-83a3-b9ea6e6148d8/unilever-basis-of-preparation-2023.pdf [Accessed 7 October 2024])

Unilever also publish its ESG performance metrics performance in the same report. For example, for climate, the following performance is disclosed for 2023.

Indicator	Performance measure	Reported performance result
Climate:		
Total greenhouse gas emissions	Total greenhouse gas (GHG) emissions, measured in metric tonnes of CO2-equivalent (tCO2e), between the period from 1 October 2020 to 30 September 2021.	121.12 million tonnes CO2e
100% renewable electricity by 2030	Percentage of electricity generated from renewable resources at operational sites in 2023 (covers the period 1 October 2022 to 30 September 2023).	92%
Replace fossil-fuel derived carbon with renewable or recycled carbon in all our cleaning and laundry product formulations by 2030	The total number of newly contracted partnerships to develop renewable or recycled carbon surfactants or renewable or recycled precursor feedstocks, between 1 January 2023 and 31 December 2023.	4

Other Unilever ESG performance metrics for 2023, can be viewed in the report.

(b) **Tesco**

Tesco is a UK based supermarket chain. It publishes its sustainability report each year. The Board at Tesco's has applied stakeholder feedback (employees, customers, suppliers, and shareholders) to identify it four most material sustainability areas: 1. Climate change, 2. Healthy sustainable diets 3. Diversity and Inclusion, and 4. Waste and packaging. These four areas provide a framework for its sustainability reporting.

Key headlines from Tesco's sustainability objectives are as follows:

- Tesco state they were the first business to set a zero-carbon goal back in 2009. Since 2015 Tesco claim to have reduced Group Scope 1 and 2 green-house gas emissions by 55%. Also, Tesco aim to be carbon neutral by 2035 and they are working with suppliers and partners to be net zero from farm to fork by 2050.
- In terms of community support, Tesco state that since 2015 they have supported tens of thousands of community projects with more than £100m in grants and through their partnerships with food banks they have donated over 52 million meals in unsold food from their stores.
- In terms of promoting healthy eating, Tesco state they have removed over 71 billion calories from the food they sell since 2018 through their product reformulation programme. Tesco is also encouraging their customers to try more plant-based diets that are kinder on the planet.
- In terms of diversity, Tesco say that 85% of Tesco colleagues agree that there is an inclusive culture at Tesco.

You can read more about Tesco's sustainability performance here which links to its sustainability reporting in its Annual Report here https://www.tescoplc.com/sustainability

Question — Importance of sustainability KPIs

Why are sustainability KPIs important for businesses?

(a) They help to improve the overall reputation of the business and increase stakeholder trust
(b) They can assist in the identification of cost-saving opportunities
(c) They can help to ensure compliance with regulations
(d) The provide a benchmark for technological innovation

A   (a) and (b) only
B   (a) and (c) only
C   (a), (b) and (c)
D   (a), (b), (c) and (d)

Answer

D   (a), (b) and (c)

Sustainability KPIs help to keep a business on track for achieving its sustainability goals and strategic objectives. Where these are communicated to stakeholders they can play a vital role in enhancing stakeholder trust and improving the reputation of the business.

They can also help to identify cost-saving opportunities, for example through ensuring the efficient use of resources and energy-conservation.

The KPIs are also likely to be linked to any sustainability-related regulations and legislation and as such can help ensure the targets are achieved.

Sustainability KPIs as a collective do not generally provide a benchmark for technological innovation.

8 The role of accountants and management in developing sustainability within organisations

FAST FORWARD

The role of accountants in implementing a credible sustainability strategy encompasses a diverse set of activities and responsibilities, from identifying and managing risks to providing reliable sustainability information.

8.1 Role of accountants in realising sustainable development goals

Key terms

Accountability, as defined by Gray, Owen, and Adams (1996), refers to the duty to provide an account or reckoning of actions for which one is responsible. This extends beyond merely financial reporting to encompass a broader spectrum of responsibilities and actions.

Stewardship entails the shared responsibility for maintaining the integrity of systems. In the context of sustainable development, stewardship involves overseeing the ecological resources (E), considering the impacts on people (S), and adhering to governance principles (G) that regulate behaviour and expectations.

To assist mitigation of the impact of human activities on the planet, accountants apply accountability and stewardship through the following.

- **Responsibility and accountability:** Accounting is a core function in ensuring responsibility and accountability for actions taken by individuals, organisations, and societies. Accountants provide transparent and accurate reporting to facilitate accountability to stakeholders and society at large.

- **Exercising control:** In the context of dynamic systems and the interaction of the six capitals (financial, manufactured, intellectual, human, social and relationship, and natural), accountants play a crucial role in exercising control. This includes implementing measures to manage resources sustainably, mitigate risks, and optimise performance across various dimensions.

- **Understanding dynamics:** Accountants need to have a comprehensive understanding of the dynamics of sustainable development, including planetary boundaries, limits, tipping points, and resilience to impacts. This knowledge enables them to assess risks, anticipate challenges, and develop strategies to address sustainability issues effectively.

- **Competencies for accountability and stewardship:** Developing suitable competencies is essential for citizens, managers, and accountants to demonstrate accountability and stewardship in response to risks facing the planet. These competencies encompass a range of skills, including ethical decision-making, environmental literacy, stakeholder engagement, and sustainability reporting expertise.

By fulfilling their responsibilities with integrity and diligence, accountants contribute to the collective effort to safeguard the planet's resources, mitigate environmental impacts, and create a more sustainable future for all.

8.2 Role of accountants and management in developing sustainability within organisations

Accountants shoulder key responsibilities in identifying and efficiently managing ESG risks and issues.

- **Compliance:** Ensure compliance with sustainability-related laws, regulations, and corporate governance codes.

- **Financial information and support**: Adeptly measure ESG-related liabilities, assess impaired assets and financial instruments, and navigate new forms of taxation, such as renewable energy incentives or carbon emission tariffs, while providing necessary assurance as required.

- **Risk management:** Design and operation of risk management and internal control systems to uphold sustainable practices within organisations.

  Advising on solutions to mitigate impacts and modelling how sustainability risks may influence an organisation's strategic direction or necessitate changes to its operations and reporting requirements.

- **Performance metrics:** Advising organisations on relevant sustainability metrics to monitor and report on all ESG-related activities

  Implementing methodologies, systems, and solutions to accurately measure these metrics and report progress against targets set by the board.

- **Reporting:** Transparency and credibility are key aspects of sustainability reporting, and accountants offer valuable assurance over both mandatory and voluntary sustainability information, enhancing stakeholders' trust.

  Beyond reporting responsibilities, accountants actively provide sustainability information that informs strategic and operational decision-making within organisations. Their advocacy for sustainable practices and ability to influence stakeholders contribute significantly to fostering positive change and promoting an organisation's sustainable performance.

9 Ethics and social responsibility

> **FAST FORWARD**
>
> **Ethical** and **social responsibility** are two key areas in which businesses have adopted non-financial objectives, partly in response to political and consumer pressure.

Key terms

> **Ethics** are the moral principles by which people act or do business.
>
> **Social responsibility** comprises those values and actions which the organisation is not obliged to adopt for business reasons, which it adopts for the good and well-being of stakeholders within and outside the organisation.

9.1 Why be socially responsible?

> **FAST FORWARD**
>
> There is pressure towards **corporate social responsibility (CSR)** from law and regulation, market forces and the stakeholder perspective.

Managers need to consider the effect of organisational outputs into the market and the wider **social community**, for several reasons.

(a) The modern **marketing concept** says that in order to survive and succeed, organisations must satisfy the needs, wants and values of customers and potential customers. Communication and education have made people much more aware of issues such as the environment, the exploitation of workers, product safety and consumer rights. Therefore an organisation may have to be seen to be responsible in these areas in order to retain public support for its products.

(b) There are skill shortages in the labour pool and employers must compete to attract and retain high quality employees. If the organisation gets a reputation as a socially responsible employer it will find it easier to do this, than if it has a poor '**employer brand**'.

(c) A business itself is a **social system**, not just an economic machine. Organisations **rely** on the society and local community of which they are a part, for access to facilities, business relationships, media coverage, labour, supplies, customers and so on. Organisations which acknowledge their responsibilities as part of the community may find that many areas of their operation are facilitated.

(d) Social responsibility recognises **externalities**: the costs imposed by businesses on other people. For example, it is recognised that industrial pollution is bad for health.

(e) Law, Regulation and Codes of Practice **impose** certain social responsibilities on organisations, in areas such as employment protection, equal opportunities, environmental care, health and safety, product labelling and consumer rights. There are financial and operational **penalties** for organisations which fail to comply.

Case Study

In September 2015, Volkswagen (VW) admitted that up to 11 million diesel-powered vehicles worldwide might be fitted with so-called 'defeat devices', which enabled them to meet emissions standards during laboratory tests, but did not reflect emissions during actual use.

VW's chief executive resigned after the company admitted the deception, and Volkswagen's share of the European car market was affected.

The stakeholder approach to organisations acknowledges that such parties have a **legitimate interest** – and may also have **influence** over the organisation. (Workers can withhold labour; customers can withhold business.) The objectives of the organisation should therefore take into account the needs and claims of influential stakeholder groups.

9.2 Areas of social responsibility

The perceived social responsibilities of a business, depending on the nature of its operations, may include the following matters.

(a) The impact of its operations on the **natural environment**

(b) Its **human resource management policies**: for example, the hiring and promotion of people from minority groups, policies on sexual harassment, refusal to exploit cheap labour in developing countries

(c) Non-reliance on contracts with **adverse political connotations**: sustainable business practices in developing countries, compliance with sanctions imposed by the international community and so on

(d) **Charitable support** and activity in the local community or in areas related to the organisation's field of activity

(e) **Above-minimum (legal) standards** of workplace health and safety, product safety and labelling, and so on

Question — Socially responsible activities

See if you can come up with examples of socially responsible activities, in line with (a) to (e) above.

Answer

Examples (our suggestions only) include:

(a) Cosmetic companies not using animal testing for ingredients; Shell (as a negative example) being held responsible for environmental devastation in Nigeria's river deltas; recyclable packaging

(b) The Body Shop building economic infrastructures in rural communities

(c) Sanctions or boycotts of countries such as (in the past) South Africa or Iraq

(d) Major supermarkets and retailers often sponsor community facilities, charities and sporting events.

(e) Some organisations have very stringent quality standards, and immediate no-strings product recall policies.

9.3 Limits of corporate social responsibility

There is a view that the only responsibility of a business organisation, as opposed to a public sector one, is to maximise wealth for its owners over the long term.

Socially responsible behaviour should only be pursued by an organisation in its own self-interest, to gain benefits in: employee recruitment, retention and commitment; customer retention; and public relations.

9.4 Business ethics

FAST FORWARD

Business ethics are the values underlying what an organisation understands by socially responsible behaviour.

An organisation may have values to do with non-discrimination, fairness and integrity. It is very important that managers understand:

- The importance of ethical behaviour
- The differences in what is considered ethical behaviour in different cultures

Writers have identified a number of key assumptions (in the form of questions) on which ethical stances are based.

Who is responsible for ethical conduct in business?	Is it the individual, or is control exercised socially, by governments?
Who is the key actor in business ethics?	Is it the corporation, or is it the Government or other collective bodies such as trade unions?
What are the key guidelines for ethical behaviour?	Again does it rest with the corporation in the form of corporate codes of ethics, or is the key guidance a legal framework negotiated with, or imposed on, business?
What are the key issues in business ethics?	Are they single-decision issues involving misconduct and immorality, or are they social issues surrounding the framework of business?

To whom are businesses responsible?	Should the focus be on enhancing shareholder value or on the interests of multiple stakeholder groups?
How should performance be measured?	Should it be measured by bottom line financial results or by pluralistic measures?
How should an ethical stance be incorporated into business activity?	Should an ethical stance be seen primarily in terms of compliance with law/corporate governance codes, or should it be actively incorporated into an organisation's mission and strategy?
How important is reputation?	Does it make any difference to financial results? Should organisations strive to have a good reputation even if doing so makes no demonstrable difference to their bottom line profits?

Theorist **Elaine Sternberg** (*Just Business: Business Ethics in Action*, 1995) suggests that two **ethical values** are particularly pertinent for business, because without them business could not operate at all. These are:

(a) **Ordinary decency**. This includes respect for property rights, honesty, fairness and legality.

(b) **Distributive justice**. This means that organisational rewards should be proportional to the contributions people make to organisational ends. The supply and demand for labour will influence how much a person is actually paid, but if that person is worth employing and the job worth doing, then the contribution will justify the expense.

Business ethics in a **global marketplace** are, however, far from clear cut.

(a) **Gifts** may be construed as bribes in some business circles, but may be considered common courtesy in others.

(b) Attitudes to **women** in business vary according to local traditions and religious practices.

(c) The use of **cheap labour** in very poor countries (eg through off-shoring) may be perceived as 'development' – or as 'exploitation'.

(d) The expression and nature of **agreements** vary according to cultural norms.

A business may operate on principles which strive to be:

- Ethical and legal (eg The Body Shop)
- Unethical but legal (eg arms sales to repressive regimes)
- Ethical but illegal (eg publishing stolen documents on government mismanagement)
- Unethical and illegal (eg the drugs trade, employing child labour)

9.4.1 Applying ethical principles

Assuming a firm wishes to act ethically, it can embed ethical values in its decision processes in the following ways.

(a) Include **value statements** in corporate culture, policy and codes of practice

(b) Ensure that **HR systems** (appraisal, training and rewards) are designed to support ethical behaviour

(c) Identify ethical objectives in the **mission statement**, as a public declaration of what the organisation stands for

6: SUSTAINABILITY, CSR AND ETHICS

Chapter roundup

- Sustainability is a multifaceted concept aimed at improving people's lives and safeguarding the planet for future generations
- The challenges of creating a sustainable world include addressing finite global resources, ensuring energy security, promoting water conservation, enhancing food production, and tackling poverty
- Sustainable development acknowledges the interconnectedness of economic, environmental, and social factors to address current challenges will safeguarding the well-being of future generations
- The United Nationals Global Compact is a non-binding United Nations pact of countries to persuade businesses and firms worldwide to adopt sustainable and socially responsible policies, and to report on their implementation. The Ten Principles of the United Nations Global Compact cover human rights, labour, the environment and anti-corruption.
- The United Nations Sustainable Development Goals (UN SDG's), also known as the Global Goals, are a universal call to action to end poverty, protect the planet, and ensure that all people enjoy peace and prosperity by 2030
- The Global Reporting Initiative (GRI) is an independent international organisation that provides guidelines for sustainability reporting, helping organisations communicate their impacts transparently.
- Environmental, Social and Governance (ESG) is also referred to as the three pillars of sustainability. ESG issues derive from increasing political and stakeholder concerns on the growing adverse effect of business operations on human sustainability
- **A sustainable organistion** is one that builds ESG factors into its decision making in such a way that it can ensure its own long-term survival without damaging the environment, communities or society as a whole.
- Integrated reporting combines financial and non-financial information into a single document which demonstrates how the organisation creates value.
- The concept of the "six capitals" illustrates the various ways through which an organisation creates value.
- In the pursuit of sustainability excellence, organisations must strategically set and effectively manage their sustainability initiatives.
- Growing stakeholder expectations, regulatory pressures and market dynamics place organisations under increasing scrutiny to effectively identify, assess and mitigate ESG-related risks.
- The role of accountants in implementing a credible sustainability strategy encompasses a diverse set of activities and responsibilities, from identifying and managing risks to providing reliable sustainability information.
- **Ethical** and **social responsibility** are two key areas in which businesses have adopted non-financial objectives, partly in response to political and consumer pressure.
- There is pressure towards **corporate social responsibility (CSR)** from law and regulation, market forces and the stakeholder perspective.
- **Business ethics** are the values underlying what an organisation understands by socially responsible behaviour.

PART B   MANAGEMENT PLANNING AND DECISION-MAKING

Quick quiz

1   Define sustainability.

2   The Paris Agreement was established to mitigate the impact of what major ESG issue?

3   What are the four areas covered by the Ten Principles of the United Nations Global Compact?

4   What does ESG stand for?

5   Environmental management accounting (EMA) involves generating and analysing only financial information to support environmental management and decision making. True or false?

6   What are the six capitals of integrated reporting?

7   Integrated reporting is highly relevant to sustainable development. True or false?

8   Organisations are increasingly recognising the critical importance of integrating Environmental, Social, and Governance (ESG) aspects into their overall strategy and operations. Give an example of an environmental strategy.

9   Lists the benefits of implementing ESG risk management processes in an organisation.

10 Socially responsible behaviour is a constraint on managerial decision-making, without significant business benefit. True or False?

Answers to quick quiz

1. **Sustainability** is defined as "development that meets the needs of the present without compromising the ability of future generations to meet their own needs".

2. The Paris Agreement is an international treaty on **climate change.**

3. The Ten Principles of the United Nations Global Compact cover human rights, labour, the environment and anti-corruption.

4. Environmental, Social, and Governance: ESG approaches the issue of sustainability through a corporate lens and considers only how these risks and opportunities affect a business and its enterprise value.

5. False. Environmental management accounting (EMA) involves generating and analysing financial **and non-financial** information to support environmental management and decision making.

6. Financial, manufactured, intellectual, human, social and environmental

7. True. Integrated reporting is highly relevant to sustainable development as it provides a comprehensive framework for organisations to assess and communicate their sustainability performance and impact.

8. Examples of environmental strategies include: Renewable Energy Investments, Supply Chain Sustainability, Climate Risk Assessment and Management, Water and Waste Management.

9. The benefits of implementing ESG risk management processes in an organisation are:
   - Helps organisations better anticipate and respond to risks
   - Protects the organisation's reputation and brand value
   - Helps to ensure regulatory compliance
   - Increases investor confidence
   - Improves operational efficiency
   - Lowers operational costs

10. False: Social responsibility allows businesses to retain and attract customers and employees and community support.

PART B MANAGEMENT PLANNING AND DECISION-MAKING

Organisational structures, cultures and systems

Organisation structure

Topic list	Syllabus reference
1 Organisation structure	D3
2 Tall and flat organisations	D3
3 Divisionalisation or departmentation	D3
4 Centralisation and decentralisation	D3
5 Stability or flexibility?	D3
6 Technology and structure	D3
7 Job design	D3

Introduction

Organisation structure and culture are also strategic issues. Structure describes how the organisation controls its work, and culture describes the mindset of managers and staff.

In **Section 1** we begin by looking at the characteristics of organisational structures and the mechanisms that co-ordinate them.

In **Sections 2 to 4**, we look at some of the key decisions that give organisations their distinctive 'shape'. We also consider how divisional performance can be measured within an organisation.

In **Section 5** we consider the impact that environmental circumstances have on structure and the need for more flexible organisations in conditions of uncertainty.

In **Section 6** we look at the influence and impact of technology on the way work is organised.

Lastly in **Section 7** we consider the design of individual jobs.

1 Organisation structure

> **FAST FORWARD**
>
> Organisations are characterised by formal division of labour, **hierarchies** of authority (scalar chains) and networks of **authority** and power. The organisation structure influences strategy, as it is one of the ways in which power is deployed and **information** communicated. Organisation structure determines how work is allocated, directed and controlled, in order to achieve the goals of the organisation.

A formal organisation structure has distinctive characteristics.

(a) A **division of labour**

(b) Planned **divisions of responsibility**

(c) **Power centres** which control its efforts

(d) **Substitution of personnel** (eg the position of financial controller does not disappear when the current occupant resigns)

(e) The ability to **group personnel** in different ways according to work

Organisation hierarchy outlines formal authority, but there are other sources of power within the organisation which influence what it can do.

The existing organisation structure is **worth reviewing regularly**.

(a) It can **help or hinder the mission** and effectiveness of the organisation.

(b) It might have to be **changed**, which takes time.

(c) It shapes the **deployment of value activities** and the management of the **linkages** between them.

(d) It **channels and filters information** from markets and personnel.

(e) It **is the arena for various political manoeuvrings** by management and other interest groups.

An organisation's structure must support its strategy. For instance, the classic division of large organisations into strategic business units (SBUs) arose because of the **diversity** of the products and markets concerned. Central control of detail became impracticable.

1.1 Components of organisational structure

Mintzberg (*The Structuring of Organizations*, 1979) believes there are two essential parts of every organisation:

- The five components of organisational structure
- The basic co-ordinating mechanisms that link them together

The five component parts introduced in Chapter 1 need to be connected to add value to the organisation.

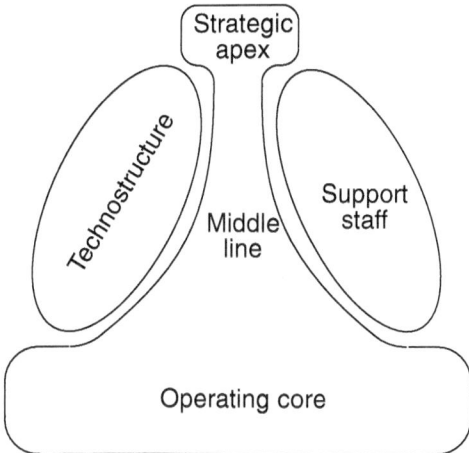

1.2 Co-ordinating tasks

Mintzberg suggests **five methods of co-ordination** which link the parts of the organisation together. The nature of co-ordination changes as the organisation increases in size and each component has its own **preferred co-ordination mechanism**.

(a) **Mutual adjustment**. People co-ordinate themselves.

(b) **Direct supervision**. One person is responsible for co-ordinating the work of others. This person issues instructions and monitors performance.

(c) **Standardisation of work processes**. The contents of work are 'specified or programmed' (eg standard procedures for carrying out an audit).

(d) **Standardisation of outputs**. Outputs in this instance can mean a set level of profits (or level of performance) but the work process itself is not designed or programmed.

(e) **Standardisation by skills and knowledge**. The kind of knowledge and training required to perform the work is specified. For example, doctors are trained in the necessary skills before being let loose on patients.

1.3 Significance of organisation structure for strategy

(a) **Different coalitions** in the organisation have their own agendas to promote and sources of power.

(b) Structure and **culture are closely related** and culture influences how managers interpret the world.

(c) **Implementing a strategy sometimes requires a change to the structure**.

(d) **Organisation structure** can influence managers' preferences for certain strategic choices. For example, an organisation which is very decentralised, and in which units actively compete with each other, may not take well to a strategy involving co-operation.

1.4 Communicating organisational structure

There are three main methods of communicating the organisational structure and employees' role within it.

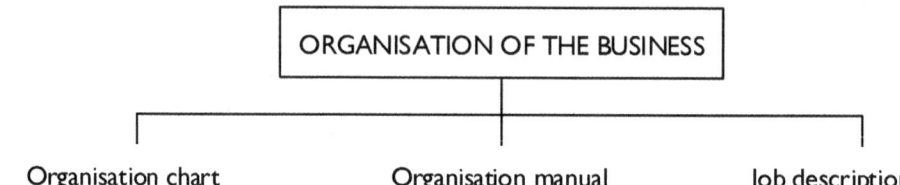

Organisation chart

Pictorial representation of the structure

Advantages
- Need to analyse organisation detail
- Provides at-a-glance information
- Highlights formal relationships

Disadvantages
- Frequent updating as people leave
- Informal relationships not shown
- May imply managers at the same level are equally important
- May encourage bureaucracy

Organisation manual

Includes
- Details about all positions in the organisation
- Standard principles and working practices

Job description

- A result of 'job analysis'
- Includes responsibilities, authority and work involved
- Typical descriptions
  - Job title
  - Department
  - Grade/level
  - Duties and responsibilities
  - Limits of authority
  - Superiors and subordinates

2 Tall and flat organisations

2.1 Span of control

FAST FORWARD

Span of control or 'span of management' refers to the number of subordinates responsible to a superior.

Key term

The **span of control** refers to the number of subordinates immediately reporting to a superior official.

In other words, if a manager has five subordinates, the span of control is five.

Classical theory of organisational structure suggests the following.

(a) There are physical and mental **limitations** to any given manager's ability to control people, relationships and activities.

(b) There needs to be **tight managerial control** from the top of an organisation downward.

(c) The span of control should therefore be **restricted**, to allow maximum control consistent with the manager's capabilities: usually between three and six. If the span of control is too wide, too much of the manager's time will be taken up with routine problems and supervision, leaving less time for planning.

(d) On the other hand, if the span is too **narrow**, the manager may fail to delegate, keeping too much routine work to himself and depriving subordinates of decision-making authority and responsibility. There may be a tendency to interfere in or over-supervise the work that is delegated to subordinates – and the relative costs of supervision will thus be unnecessarily high.

A number of factors influence the span of control.

(a) The **nature of the manager's workload**

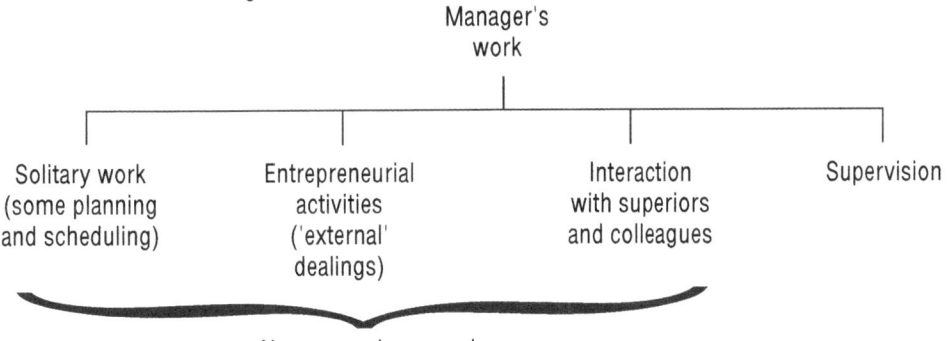

The more non-supervisory work in a manager's workload:

(i) The narrower the span of control
(ii) The greater the delegation of authority to subordinates

(b) The **geographical dispersion** of subordinates: dispersed teams require more effort to supervise.

(c) **Subordinates' work**: if all subordinates do similar tasks, a wide span is possible. If **close group cohesion** is desirable, a narrow span of control might be needed.

(d) The **nature of problems** that a supervisor might have to help subordinates with. Time consuming problems suggest a narrow span of control.

PART C ORGANISATIONAL STRUCTURES, CULTURES AND SYSTEMS

(e) The degree of **interaction between subordinates**. If subordinates can help each other, a wide span is possible.

(f) The amount of **support** that supervisors receive from other parts of the organisation or from technology (eg computerised work monitoring, or 'virtual meetings' with dispersed team members).

2.2 Tall and flat organisations

FAST FORWARD

Recent trends have been towards **delayering** organisations of levels of management. In other words, **tall organisations** (with many management levels, and narrow spans of control) are turning into **flat organisations** (with fewer management levels, wider spans of control) as a result of technological changes and the granting of more decision-making power to front line employees.

The span of control concept has implications for the length of the **scalar chain**.

Key terms

The **scalar chain** is the chain of command from the most senior to the most junior.

A **tall organisation** is one which, in relation to its size, has a large number of levels of management hierarchy. This implies a narrow span of control.

A **flat organisation** is one which, in relation to its size, has a small number of hierarchical levels. This implies a wide span of control.

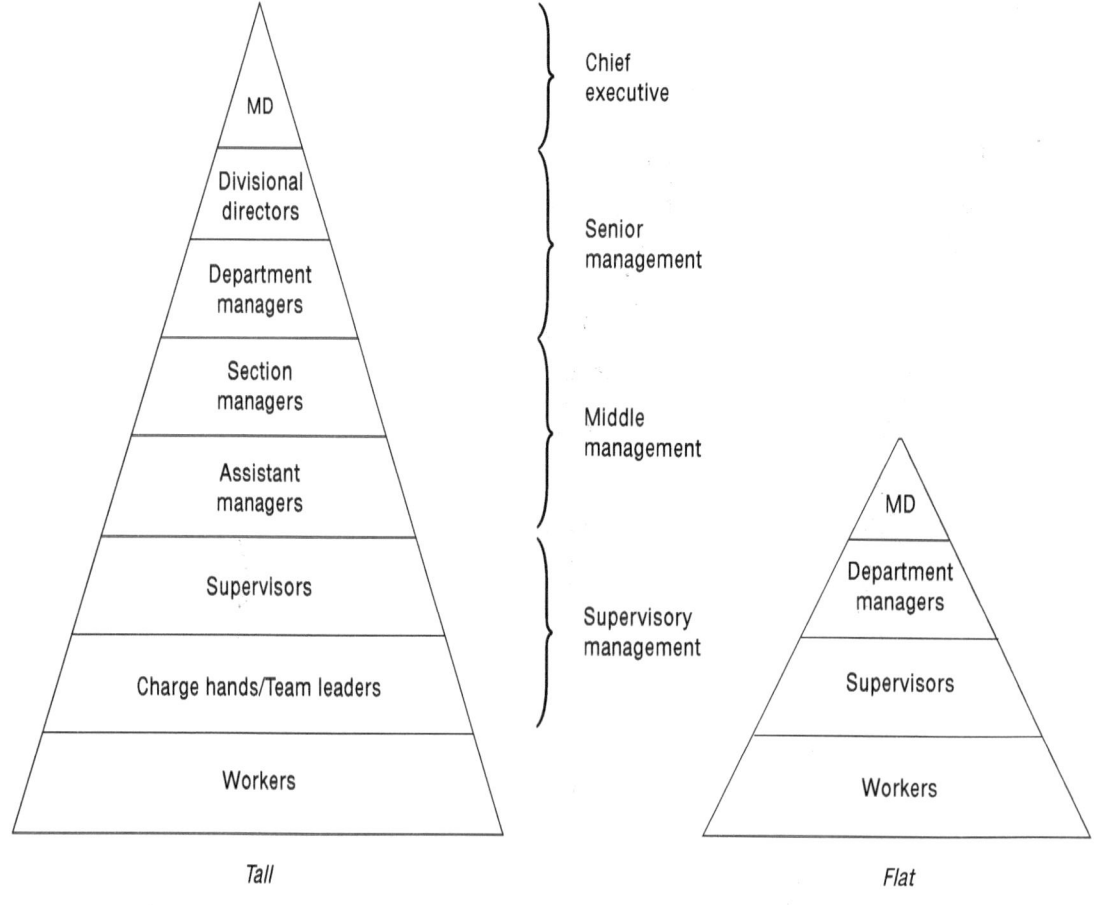

The advantages and disadvantages of these organisational forms can be summarised as follows.

Tall organisation

Advantages	Disadvantages
Narrow control spans	Inhibits delegation
Small groups enable team members to participate in decisions	Rigid supervision can be imposed, blocking initiative
A large number of steps on the promotional ladders – assists management training and career planning	The same work passes through too many hands Increases administration and overhead costs Slow decision-making and responses, as the strategic apex is further away

Flat organisation

Advantages	Disadvantages
More opportunity for delegation	Requires that jobs can be delegated. Managers may only get a superficial idea of what goes on. If they are overworked they are more likely to be involved in crisis management
Relatively cheap	Sacrifices control
In theory, speeds up communication between strategic apex and operating core	Middle managers are often necessary to convert the grand vision of the strategic apex into operational terms

2.3 Delayering

Key term

Delayering is the reduction of the number of management levels from bottom to top.

Many organisations are delayering. Organisations are increasing the average span of control, reducing management levels and becoming flatter.

(a) **Information technology** reduces the need for middle managers to process information.

(b) **Empowerment**. Many organisations, especially service businesses, are keen to delegate authority down the line to the lowest possible level. Front-line workers in the operating core are allowed to take decisions, in order to increase responsiveness to customer demands.

(c) **Economy**. Delayering reduces managerial/supervisory costs.

(d) **Fashion**. Delayering is fashionable: if senior managers believe that tall structures are inherently inflexible, they might cut the numbers of management levels.

3 Divisionalisation or departmentation

3.1 Divisionalisation

FAST FORWARD

In a **divisional structure** some activities are **decentralised** to business units or regions.

Key term

Divisionalisation is the division of a business into autonomous regions or product businesses, each with its own revenues, expenditures and capital asset purchase programmes, and therefore each with its own profit and loss responsibility.

Each division of the organisation might be:

- A subsidiary company under the holding company
- A profit centre or investment centre within a single company

Successful divisionalisation requires certain key conditions.

(a) Each division must have **properly delegated authority**, and must be held properly accountable to head office (eg for profits earned).

(b) Each unit must be **large enough** to support the quantity and quality of management it needs.

(c) The unit must not rely on head office for excessive **management support**.

(d) Each unit must have a **potential for growth** in its own area of operations.

(e) There should be scope and challenge in the job for the management of each unit.

(f) If units deal with each other, it should be as an 'arm's length' transaction. There should be no insistence on preferential treatment to be given to a 'fellow unit' by another unit of the overall organisation.

The advantages and disadvantages of divisionalisation may be summarised as follows.

Advantages	Disadvantages
Focuses the attention of management below 'top level' on business performance.	In some businesses, it is impossible to identify completely independent products or markets for which separate divisions can be set up.
Reduces the likelihood of unprofitable products and activities being continued.	Divisionalisation is only possible at a fairly senior management level, because there is a limit to how much discretion can be used in the division of work. For example, every product needs a manufacturing function and a selling function.
Encourages a greater attention to efficiency, lower costs and higher profits.	There may be more resource problems. Many divisions get their resources from head office in competition with other divisions.
Gives more authority to junior managers, and so grooms them for more senior positions in the future (planned managerial succession).	
Reduces the number of levels of management. The top executives in each division should be able to report directly to the chief executive of the holding company.	

3.2 Divisional performance measurement

FAST FORWARD

Return on capital employed and residual income are two methods of measuring divisional performance.

3.2.1 Return on capital employed (ROCE)

ROCE is also called return on investment (ROI) or return on net assets (RONA). This divisional performance target is calculated as:

$$\frac{\text{Profit for the period} \times 100\%}{\text{Capital employed}}$$

Where 'profit for the period' is usually based upon profit before interest and tax (PBIT). The figure for 'capital employed' in best calculated as the average during the period ((opening figure + closing figure)/2), but the closing figure is sometimes used.

The principle behind this measure is that the return derived should be in excess of the cost of capital of the firm in order to provide a suitable return to investors.

3.2.2 Residual income (RI)

This measure was developed to avoid a dysfunctional consequence of ROCE/ROI, namely that managers who are evaluated and rewarded against ROCE improvements may choose to forgo investments which are actually in the investor's interest. It is calculated as follows:

Residual income (RI) = A − (B × C)

Where
A = Net operating income
B = Minimum required return on assets
C = Average operating assets

Residual income is theoretically superior to ROI, but it is not widely used because:

- It is conceptually more complex than a simple percentage yield, and it might be difficult to determine what the required return is.
- It doesn't allow easy comparison of divisions of different sizes (because it is an absolute value rather a percentage).
- ROCE is still closely monitored by investment analysts who determine share prices with their buy/sell recommendations.

3.2.3 Problems of using ROCE/RI

Problems of both ROCE/ROI and RI in the evaluation and control of business divisions are:

- **Short-termist**: A focus upon annual profit figures will disregard the future earnings of the division.
- **Profit-based**: As they are both essentially profit-based measures (rather than looking at cash flows) they may not indicate how well a division is generating value.
- **Discourages investment in assets**: To boost ROI or RI, assets with low book values will be continue to be used in preference to replacing them with new assets.
- **Lack of strategic control**: Companies wish to co-ordinate and integrate operations of their divisions to gain group efficiencies. Financial control measures alone cannot do this.

3.2.4 Other considerations in divisional performance measurement

When assessing divisional performance, the following issues must also be considered:

- The division manager should only be held **accountable for factors within his/her control.** The divisional profit figure may be distorted by arbitrarily allocated Head office costs and thus performance measurement should focus on traceable profit.
- Where there is inter-divisional trade, careful consideration should be given to any **transfer pricing mechanism** in place, which may under or over-state the profits of a particular division.
- Divisions operating in different marketplaces and facing differing levels of competition **cannot be expected to produce similar returns**. Thus, in addition to comparing one division against another, external comparisons should be made via benchmarking, eg to an industry leader.

- Wider strategic issues need to be taken into account such as any **interdependence between divisions** eg shared distribution systems, shared customers, the impact that a division has on the portfolio of the business and its brand.
- In assessing the future strategic direction of the business, it is not just the historic performance of the division but also its **future potential** that is relevant.
- **Focus on a narrow set of financial measures** is unlikely to give a true picture of performance.

> **FAST FORWARD**
>
> Organisations can be **departmentalised** on a **functional** basis (with separate departments for production, marketing, finance etc), a **geographical** basis (by region, or country), a **product** basis (eg worldwide divisions for product X, Y etc), a **brand** basis, or a **matrix** basis (eg someone selling product X in country A would report to both a product X manager and a country A manager). Organisation structures often feature a variety of these types, as **hybrid** structures.

3.3 Geographic departmentation

Where the organisation is structured according to geographic area, some authority is retained at Head Office but day-to-day operations are handled on a **territorial** basis (eg southern region, western region). Many sales departments are organised territorially.

There are **advantages** to geographic departmentation.

(a) There is **local decision-making** at the point of contact between the organisation (eg a salesperson) and its customers, suppliers or other stakeholders.

(b) It may be **cheaper** to establish area factories/offices than to service markets from one location (eg costs of transportation and travelling may be reduced).

But there are **disadvantages** too.

(a) **Duplication** and possible loss of economies of scale might arise.
(b) **Inconsistency** in methods or standards may develop across different areas.

Geographic organisations

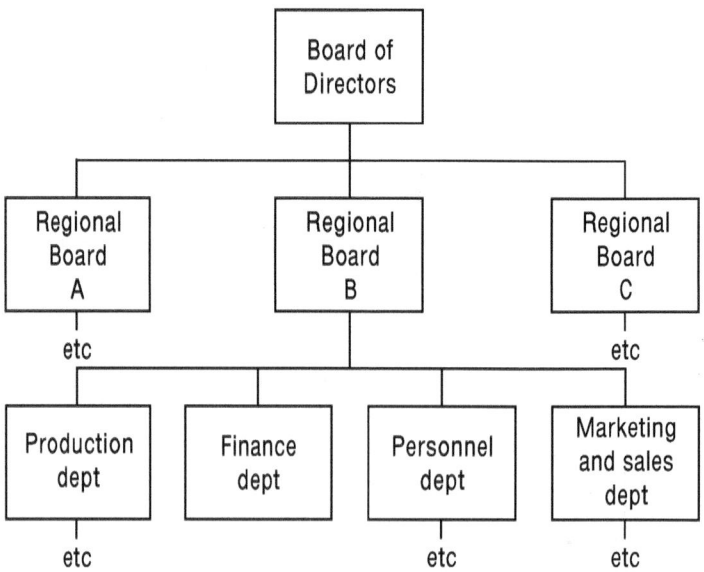

3.4 Functional departmentation

Functional organisation involves grouping together people who do similar tasks. Primary functions in a manufacturing company might be production, sales, finance, and general administration. Sub-departments of marketing might be market research, advertising, PR and so on.

Advantages include:

(a) **Expertise is pooled** thanks to the division of work into specialist areas.

(b) It **avoids duplication** (eg one management accounts department rather than several) and enables economies of scale.

(c) It **facilitates** the recruitment, management and development of functional specialists.

(d) It suits **centralised** businesses.

Disadvantages include:

(a) It focuses on internal **processes** and **inputs**, rather than the **customer** and **outputs**, which are what ultimately drive a business.

(b) **Communication problems** may arise between different functions, which each have their own jargon.

(c) **Poor co-ordination**, especially if rooted in a tall organisation structure. Decisions by one function/department involving another might have to be referred upwards.

(d) Functional structures create **vertical barriers** to information and work flow.

Functional orgranisation

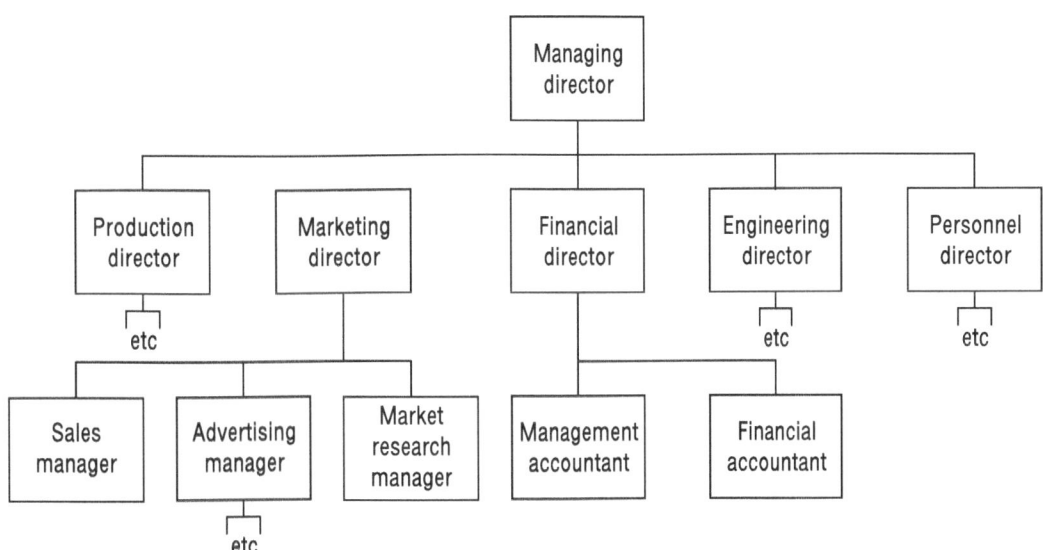

3.4.1 Product/brand departmentation

Some organisations group activities on the basis of **products** or product lines.

Advantages include:

(a) **Accountability**. Individual managers can be held accountable for the profitability of individual products.

(b) **Specialisation**. For example, some salespeople will be trained to sell a specific product in which they may develop technical expertise and thereby offer a better sales service to customers.

(c) **Co-ordination**. The different functional activities and efforts required to make and sell each product can be co-ordinated and integrated by the divisional/product manager.

Disadvantages include:

(a) It **increases the overhead costs** and managerial complexity of the organisation.
(b) Different product divisions may **fail to share resources** and customers.

A **brand** is the name or design which identifies the products or services of a manufacturer or provider and distinguishes them from those of competitors. Branding brings the product to the attention of buyers and creates brand **recognition**, **differentiation** and **loyalty**.

(a) Because each brand is packaged, promoted and sold in a distinctive way, the need for specialisation may make brand departmentation effective.
(b) Brand departmentation has similar advantages/disadvantages to product departmentation.

Product/brand organisation

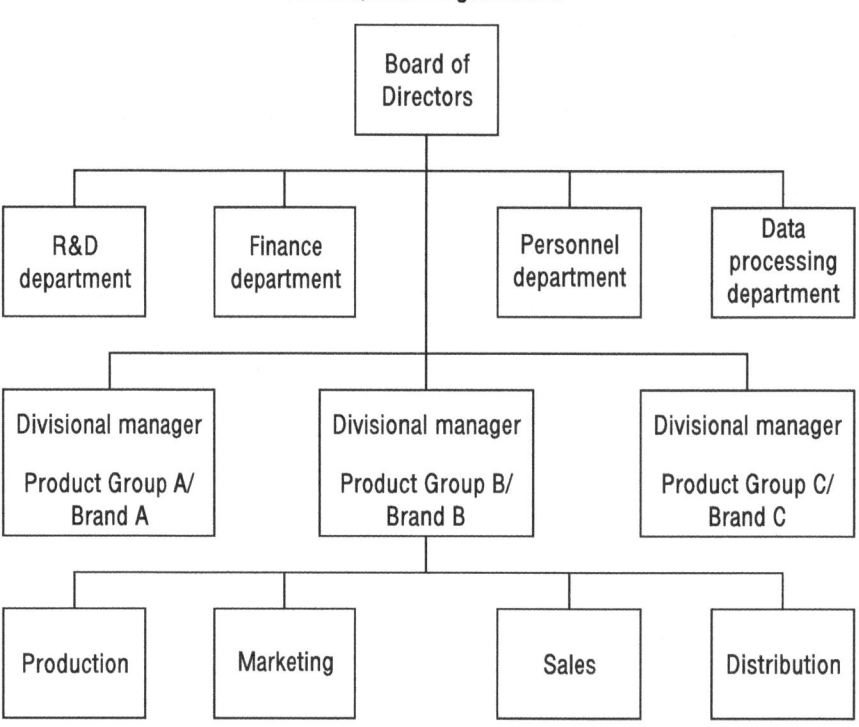

3.5 Customer departmentation

An organisation may organise its activities on the basis of types of customer, or market segment.

(a) Departmentation by customer is commonly associated with **sales departments** and selling effort, but it might also be used by a jobbing or contracting firm where a team of managers may be given the responsibility of liaising with major customers.
(b) Many businesses distinguish between **business** customers and **consumers**.

Question — Types of organisation

Looking at the 'Product/Brand Organisation' chart following Section 3.4.1 above, what types of organisation can you identify, and why are these appropriate for their purposes? What added type of organisation might this firm use, and in what circumstances?

Answer

- At the head office level, there is **functional** organisation. This enables standardisation of policy and activity in key 'staff' or support functions shared by the various divisions.

- At divisional level, there is **product/brand** organisation. This allows the distinctive culture and attributes of each product/brand to be addressed in production processes and marketing approach.
- For each product/brand, there is **functional** organisation, enabling specialist expertise to be directed at the different activities required to produce, market and distribute a product.
- This firm may further organise its marketing department by **customer,** if its customer base includes key (high-value, long-term) customer accounts with diverse service needs, for example.
- It may further organise its sales and distribution departments by **geographical area,** if the customer base is internationally or regionally dispersed: local market conditions and values, and logistical requirements of distribution, can then be taken more specifically into account.

3.6 Hybrid structures

'Hybrid' structures may involve a mix of functional departmentation, ensuring specialised attention to key functions, with elements of (for example):

(a) **Product organisation**, to suit the requirements of brand marketing or production technologies

(b) **Customer organisation**, particularly in marketing departments, to service key accounts

(c) **Territorial organisation,** particularly of sales and distribution departments, to service local requirements for marketing or distribution in dispersed regions or countries

3.7 Matrix and project organisation

Where hybrid organisation 'mixes' organisation types, **matrix** organisation actually crosses functional and product/customer/project organisation.

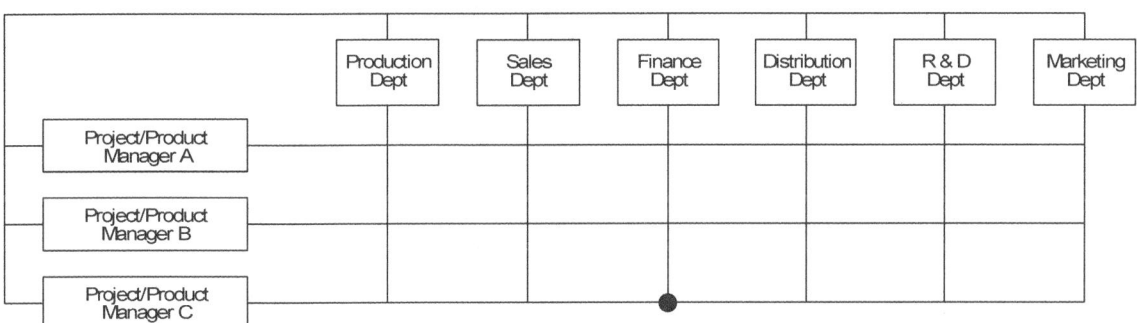

The employees represented by the dot in the above diagram, for example, are responsible to:

- The finance manager for their work in accounting and finance for their functional department; and
- To the project manager C for their work on the project team: budgeting, management reporting and payroll relevant to the project, say.

Advantages of matrix organisation include:

(a) Greater **flexibility** of:

  (i) **People**. Employees develop an attitude geared to accepting change, and departmental monopolies are broken down.

  (ii) **Workflow and decision-making**. Direct contact between staff encourages problem-solving and big picture thinking.

  (iii) **Tasks and structure**. The matrix structure may be readily amended, once projects are completed.

(b) **Inter-disciplinary co-operation** and a mixing of skills and expertise, along with **improved communication** and **co-ordination**.

(c) **Motivation and employee development**: providing employees with greater participation in planning and control decisions.

(d) **Market awareness**: the organisation tends to become more customer/quality focused.

(e) **Horizontal workflow**: bureaucratic obstacles are removed, and department specialisms become less powerful.

There are **disadvantages**, however.

(a) **Dual authority** threatens a **conflict** between functional managers and product/ project/area managers.

(b) An individual with two or more bosses may suffer stress from **conflicting demands** or **ambiguous roles**.

(c) **Cost**: product management posts are added, meetings have to be held, and so on.

(d) **Slower decision-making** due to the added complexity.

3.8 The new organisation

Some recent trends have emerged from the focus on **flexibility** as a key organisational value.

> **FAST FORWARD**
>
> Organisational **flexibility** means an ability to cope with unpredicatble changes in levels of demand for a product, changes in product specifications, or to cope with short term projects. This has led to the emergence of new forms of organisation, including **network organisations, venture team organisations, and modular organisations.**
>
> The shamrock organisation has a core of permanent managers and specialist staff supplied by a contingent workforce of contractors and part-time and temporary workers.

(a) **Flat structures**. The flattening of hierarchies does away with levels of organisation which lengthened lines of communication and decision-making and encouraged ever-increasing specialisation. Flat structures are more responsive, because there is a more direct relationship between the organisation's strategic centre and the operational units serving the customer.

(b) **Horizontal structures**. Functional versatility (through multi-functional project teams and multi-skilling, for example) is the key to flexibility.

(c) **'Chunked' and 'unglued' structures**. So far, this has meant team-working and decentralisation, or empowerment, creating smaller and more flexible units within the overall structure.

(d) **Output-focused structures**. The key to all the above trends is the focus on results, and on the customer, instead of internal processes and functions for their own sake.

(e) **'Jobless' structures**. This is an expression of the concept of **employability**, which says that a person needs to have a portfolio of skills which are valuable on the open labour market.

(f) **Virtual organisations**. The organisation may consist of individuals, teams, companies or stakeholders. Members are geographically dispersed and the organisation usually only exists electronically on the internet, without any physical premises. These organisations are entirely reliant on their technology and any problems could affect the operation of the organisation.

(g) In a **hollow organisation** people and activities are split between core and non-core competencies. All non-core processes and activities are outsourced. Such organisations can then focus on their core activities, but this structure depends on being able to find reliable subcontractors.

(h) In **modular organisations** different elements or components of the product or service the organisation produces are outsourced to different suppliers. The retained people within the organisation assemble or combine these elements to produce the final product or service. This structure enables the organisation to be more flexible and to respond to market needs more quickly, but also depends on reliable suppliers.

(i) **Boundaryless organisations** remove both the internal barriers that separate the hierarchy levels, different functions and different departments, and also remove the barriers between the organisation and its suppliers, customers and competitors.

3.8.1 The shamrock organisation

Key term

> **Handy** ('What's a business for?', *Harvard Business Review*, 2002) defines the **shamrock organisation** as a 'core of essential executives and workers supported by outside contractors and part-time help'. This structure permits the buying-in of services as needed, with consequent reductions in overhead costs.

The first leaf of the shamrock is the **professional core**. It consists of professionals, technicians and managers whose skills define the organisation's core competence. They are essential to the continuity and growth of the organisation. Their pay is tied to organisational performance.

The next leaf is made up of **self-employed professionals or technicians** or smaller specialised organisations who are hired on contract, on a project-by-project basis. They are paid in fees for results rather than in salary for time. They frequently **telecommute**. No benefits are paid by the core organisation, and the worker carries the risk of insecurity.

The third leaf comprises the **contingent work force**, whose employment derives from the external demand for the organisation's products. There is no career track for these people and they perform routine, temporary jobs.

A fourth leaf of the shamrock may exist, consisting of **consumers** who do the work of the organisation. Examples are shoppers who bag their own groceries and purchasers of assemble-it-yourself furniture.

This type of organisation provides three kinds of flexibility.

(a) **Personnel costs** can respond to market conditions of supply and demand for different types of labour and to the employer's financial position.

(b) Overall **personnel numbers** can be changed as required.

(c) The **skills** available can be modified fairly rapidly and multi-skilling can be encouraged.

There are other implications for employment patterns.

(a) All staff will have to be prepared to **widen their availability,** possibly moving from site to site as required.

(b) Staff must accept varying patterns of working hours, perhaps working on **annual hours** contracts which require extended shifts in busy times balanced with shorter ones in slack times.

(c) Contracts of employment will be **far less prescriptive of duties and responsibilities.**

3.9 Other flexible organisation structures

3.9.1 Network organisations

A network organisation is a collection of autonomous firms or business units that behave as a single larger entity. They rely on a combination of advanced IT systems (such as common databases of information, e-conferencing facilities, and email), and social networks between staff members to link these units together

There are four types of network organisations:

Internal network

Large company that sees its units as separate profit centres. It may encourage the units to sell its products outside the company as well. In these organisations, corporate headquarters acts like a ringmaster or broker between the units.

Stable network

The stable network consists of a central, permanent organisation that relies on outsourcing much of its operations to other companies. This central organisation may also have several joint ventures, alliances, long term contracts, etc. going with different companies.

Dynamic network

Dynamic networks are common in the fashion, toys, publishing, motion pictures, and biotech industries. A central firm, or brand, acts as an integrator to identify the market opportunity and then assemble the assets owned by other companies. Typically, the integrator is a downstream player whose core competence is understanding the market.

Market networks

These organisations don't have a lead player that coordinates the others. Instead, a collection of organisations trading in the same market and fall into a stable pattern of dealing with each other. These are common in banking and financial services.

3.9.2 Venture teams

The term **venture team** has its origins in the world of business finance and it referred to a team of managers assembled to run a new start-up business funded by venture capital.

More recently the term has been applied to specially formed internal management teams tasked with a new business venture such as new product development, opening a new office or factory, or entering a new geographical market.

3.9.3 Modular organisations

This concept of an organisational model has its origins in software engineering where parts of a given program are each designed to operate independently and are bolted together as suits the client needs. It describes an organisation made up of specialist independent units, each processing one sort of work.

For example a publisher may have separate modules for authoring, for typesetting, for print buying, for despatch, and for customer services. These are all specialised in what they do. Each may sell itself externally to clients as well as internally to other modules.

Financial control is exercised by each product 'buying time' or 'buying capacity' in the individual modules. There will be Service Level Agreements contracted between the buyers and the service-providing modules.

Question

Organisational structure

ABC Architects is a firm that specialises in working with individuals wanting to design and build their own homes. Currently located in London, one of the partners is about to relocate to a seaside town, whilst another partner is hoping to relocate to the countryside. Both partners want to continue working for ABC Architects whilst servicing their new local populations.

What is the most appropriate organisational structure for ABC Architects?

A   Functional
B   Geographic
C   Divisional
D   Matrix

Answer

B   Geographic

Geographic is most appropriate because clients are being served on the basis of their locations.

The business does not appear to have multiple functions and is not large enough for a divisional structure. A matrix structure involves serving more than one superior, which is not relevant for partners here.

4 Centralisation and decentralisation

4.1 What is centralisation?

FAST FORWARD

A **centralised** organisation is one in which authority is concentrated in one place.

We can look at centralisation in two ways.

(a)   **Geography**. Some functions may be centralised rather than 'scattered' in different offices, departments or locations. So, for example, secretarial support, IT support and information storage (filing) may be centralised in specialist departments rather than carried out by staff/equipment duplicated in each departmental office.

(b)   **Authority**. Centralisation also refers to the extent to which people have to refer decisions upwards to their superiors. Decentralisation therefore implies increased delegation, empowerment and autonomy at lower levels of the organisation.

4.2 Advantages and disadvantages of centralisation

FAST FORWARD

Centralisation offers greater control and co-ordination; **decentralisation** offers greater flexibility.

The table below summarises some of the arguments in favour of centralisation and decentralisation.

Pro centralisation	Pro decentralisation/delegation
Decisions are made at one point and so are easier to co-ordinate.	Avoids overburdening top managers, in terms of workload and stress.
Senior managers can take a wider view of problems and consequences.	Improves motivation of more junior managers who are given responsibility.

Pro centralisation	Pro decentralisation/delegation
Senior management can balance the interests of different functions – eg by deciding on the resources to allocate to each.	Greater awareness of local problems by decision-makers. (Geographically dispersed organisations are often decentralised on a regional/area basis for this reason.)
Quality of decisions is (theoretically) higher due to senior managers' skills and experience.	Greater speed of decision-making, and response to changing events, since no need to refer decisions upwards. This is particularly important in rapidly changing markets.
Possibly cheaper, by reducing number of managers needed and so lower costs of overheads.	Helps develop the skills of junior managers: supports managerial succession.
Crisis decisions are taken more quickly at the centre, without need to refer back.	Separate spheres of responsibility can be identified: controls, performance measurement and accountability are better.
Policies, procedures and documentation can be standardised organisation-wide.	Communication technology allows decisions to be made locally, with information and input from head office if required.

5 Stability or flexibility?

5.1 Burns and Stalker: Mechanistic and organic organisation

FAST FORWARD

Burns and Stalker noted that **mechanistic** (or **bureaucratic**) organisations are stable and efficient in conditions of slow change, but that **organic** organisation is required for adaptation and responsiveness in fast-change environments.

The terms 'mechanistic' and 'organic' were coined by **Burns and Stalker** (*The Management of Innovation*, 1961) to describe forms of organisation which are:

(a) Stable, efficient and suitable for slow-changing operating environments (mechanistic organisations, or 'bureaucracies'); and

(b) Flexible, adaptive and suitable for fast-changing or dynamic operating environments (organic organisations).

Factor	Mechanistic	Organic
The job	Tasks are **specialised** and broken down into sub-tasks.	Specialist knowledge and expertise is understood to contribute to the **common task** of the organisation.
How the job fits in	People are concerned with completing the task **efficiently**, rather than how the task can be made to improve organisational **effectiveness**.	Each task is seen and understood to be set by the **total situation** of the firm: focus is on the task's contribution to **organisational effectiveness**.
Co-ordination	**Managers** are responsible for co-ordinating tasks.	People adjust and redefine their tasks through interaction and **mutual adjustment** with others.
Job description	There are **precise** job descriptions and delineations of responsibility.	Job descriptions are **less precise**: people do what is necessary to complete the task.

Factor	Mechanistic	Organic
Commitment	**Doing the job** takes priority over serving the interests of the organisation.	**Commitment to the organisation** spreads beyond any technical definition of competence.
Legal contract vs common interest	**Hierarchical** structure of control. An individual's performance and conduct derive from a **contractual relationship** with an impersonal organisation.	**Network structure** of control. An individual's performance and conduct derive from a supposed **community of interest** between the individual and the organisation, and the individual's colleagues.
Decisions	Decisions are taken by **senior managers** who are assumed to know everything.	Relevant technical and commercial knowledge can be located **anywhere**.
Communication patterns	Communication is mainly **vertical** (up and down the scalar chain), and takes the form of **commands** and obedience.	Communication is **lateral** or networked, and communication between people of different rank represents **consultation**, rather than command.
Content of communications	Operations and working behaviour are governed by **instructions** issued by superiors.	Communication consists of **information and advice** rather than instructions and decisions.
Mission	Insistence on **loyalty** to the concern and **obedience** to superiors.	Commitment to the organisation's **mission** is more highly valued than loyalty as such.
Internal vs external expertise	**Internal knowledge** (eg of the organisation's specific activities) is more highly valued than general knowledge.	'Importance and prestige attach to affiliations and expertise valid in the industrial, technical and commercial milieus **external** to the firm.'

5.2 Mechanistic organisations: Bureaucracy

5.2.1 Legitimate authority (Weber)

The German writer **Max Weber** regarded an organisation as an **authority structure** in which people obey instructions because their superiors have authority that is legitimate and rational. He was interested in why individuals obeyed commands, and identified three grounds on which **legitimate authority** could exist.

(a) **Charismatic leadership**: the leader is regarded as having some special power or attribute.

(b) **Traditional, or patriarchal leadership**: authority is bestowed by tradition or hereditary entitlement, as in the family firm. Decisions and actions are bound by precedent.

(c) **Bureaucracy**: authority is bestowed by dividing an organisation into jurisdictional areas (production, marketing, sales and so on) each with specified duties. Authority to carry them out is given to the officials in charge, and rules and regulations are established in order to ensure their achievement.

5.2.2 What is bureaucracy?

Key term

> A **bureaucracy** is characterised by:
>
> - **Continuous organisation**. The organisation does not disappear if people leave: new people will fill their shoes.
> - **Official functions**. The organisation is divided into areas (eg production, marketing) with specified duties. Authority to carry them out is given to the officials in charge.
> - **Rules**. A rule defines and specifies a course of action that must be taken under given circumstances.

The characteristics of bureaucracy can be summarised as follows.

Characteristic	Description
Hierarchy of roles	An organisation exists even before it is filled with people. Each lower office is under the control and supervision of a higher one.
Specialisation and training	There is a high degree of specialisation of labour.
Professional nature of employment	Officials are full-time employees; promotion is according to seniority and achievement; pay scales are prescribed according to the position or office held in the organisation structure.
Impersonal nature	Employees work within impersonal rules and regulations and act according to formal, impersonal procedures.
Rationality	The jurisdictional areas of the organisation are determined rationally. The hierarchy of authority and office structure is clearly defined. Duties are established and measures of performance set.
Uniformity in the performance of tasks	Procedures ensure that, regardless of who carries out tasks, they should be executed in the same way.
Technical competence	All officials are technically competent. Their competence within the area of their expertise is rarely questioned.
Stability	The organisation rarely changes in response to environmental pressures.

5.2.3 Bureaucracy: good or bad?

It is common to think of bureaucracy as an old-fashioned and dysfunctional form of organisation, but it has some **advantages**.

(a) Bureaucracies are ideal for **standardised, routine tasks**. For example, processing driving licence applications is fairly routine, requiring systematic work.

(b) Bureaucracies can be very **efficient**.

(c) Rigid adherence to procedures may be necessary for **fairness**, adherence to the **law**, **safety** and **security** (eg procedures for data protection).

(d) Some people are **suited** to the structured, predictable environment. Bureaucracies tend to be long-lived because they select and retain bureaucratically-minded people.

In swiftly-changing environments, however, the **dysfunctions** of bureaucracy become apparent.

(a) It results in **slow decision-making**, because of the rigidity and length of authority networks.
(b) Uniformity creates **conformity**, inhibiting the personal development of staff.

(c) Bureaucracies suppress **innovation**: they can inhibit creativity, initiative and openness to new ideas and ways of doing things.

(d) Bureaucracies find it hard to **learn** from their mistakes, because of the lack of feedback (especially upwards).

(e) Bureaucracies are **slow to change**.

(f) **Communication** is restricted to established channels, ignoring opportunities for networking, upward feedback and suggestions that may contribute to customer service and innovation.

Question — Rules and procedures

Using Mintzberg's model, what component part of the organisation is responsible for designing rules and procedures?

Answer

The technostructure.

5.3 Organic organisations

FAST FORWARD

Organic organisations are controlled by mechanisms such as commitment and culture.

Organic organisations have their own structures and control mechanisms.

Control mechanism	Description
Status	Although organic systems are not hierarchical in the way that bureaucracies are, there are **differences of status**, determined by people's greater expertise, experience and so forth.
Commitment	The degree of **commitment** employees have to the goals of the firm and the team is more **extensive** in organic than in mechanistic systems.
Shared values and culture	Hierarchical control is replaced by the development of **shared beliefs and values**. In other words, corporate **culture** becomes a powerful guide to behaviour.

5.4 Beyond organic organisation?

Huczynski and **Buchanan** (*Organizational Behavior*, 2010) describe an even more fluid, flexible and adaptable organisation design called 'adhocracy'.

Adhocracy is associated with creative thinking, innovation and organisational learning. It would typically involve the use of a loose network of flexible, temporary, cross-functional project teams. While ideally suited to turbulent business environments, it also presents a challenge for managers and employees, since it means living with disorder, ambiguity and loss of security and identity.

5.5 Differentiation and integration

FAST FORWARD

Lawrence and Lorsch suggest that the degree of formality in an organisation's structure is related to the degree of environmental uncertainty and that different functions or departments within an organisation need different structures or systems according to their environment.

They believe organisations must balance **differentiation** (the need for differing structures and systems within an organisation) and **integration** (the process of co-ordinating the various parts of the organisation).

Organisations operating in stable predictable environments tend to be most efficient and productive with a traditional hierarchical structure. There is less need for innovation and for cross-department co-ordination.

Those exposed to rapidly changing environments or technologies succeed with more flexible structures and decentralised control, which facilitates faster adaptation and innovation. In such circumstances, more specialisation of departments is necessary and there is a greater need for communication and co-operation between the diverse parts of the organisation.

Within an organisation, production which performs simpler, more certain tasks is likely to have a more formal structure than R&D which focuses on more uncertain tasks, with a longer time horizon.

Question — Bureaucracy

Which of the following is NOT a benefit of using a bureaucratic form of organisation in a hospital?

A   Appointment based on technical competence
B   Clear rules and procedures
C   Lack of innovation
D   Decisions and action recorded

Answer

C   Lack of innovation

A lack of innovation is a problem because there may be newer, better treatments that could be used but are not because everyone is following standard procedures.

In a hospital it is important that staff are competent and that there are clear rules and procedures, because the risks of something going wrong are high and the consequences devastating. Decisions and actions must be recorded so that patients don't receive medication twice, for example.

6 Technology and structure

6.1 Joan Woodward: Type of production system

FAST FORWARD

Technology has a significant impact on the way work is organised.

Woodward (*Industrial Organization: Theory and Practice*, 1965), investigated specific features of organisation structure, such as span of control and the division of functions among specialists. She discovered considerable differences between firms, and suggested that the differences were related to the type of production technology in use.

(a) Production systems may be divided into three main categories, ranging from least to most **complex**.

    (i) **Unit production** eg production of simple units to customer orders, assembly of complex units in stages, or small batches

    (ii) **Mass production** eg production of components in large batches, assembly line type production

    (iii) **Process production** involving the monitoring of machinery and automated production processes

(b) The main point of difference was the **degree of control** possible over the output of the system. In the case of one-off production to customers' requirements, it is very difficult to predict the results of development work, while in continuous flow production, the equipment can be set for a given result.

Some aspects of the organisation vary directly as the technology varies. For instance, the length of the scalar chain increases as complexity increases. However, other variables, such as span of control, do not vary linearly.

6.2 Socio-technical systems: Trist

> **FAST FORWARD**
> The organisation may be seen as a **socio-technical system**.

Trist and Bamforth ('Some social and psychological consequences of the longwall method of coal getting', *Human Relations*, 1951) introduced the concept of the organisation as a socio-technical system, with at least two major sub-systems:

(a) **Technology**, including task organisation and methods (not just machinery and tools)
(b) **People** and their social arrangements: personal factors and interpersonal interactions

The socio-technical systems approach to organisation suggested that organisations should aim to find a 'fit' that will maximise efficiency (through use of technology) while at the same time ensuring member satisfaction and commitment (through meeting workers' social and psychological needs).

6.3 Information and communication technology (ICT)

> **FAST FORWARD**
> The global explosion of **ICT** has also had a major impact on work organisation.

ICT has created the concept of **virtual teams** and even **virtual organisations**. Virtual teams are interconnected groups of people who may not be present in the same office or organisation (and may even be in different areas of the world) but who:

- Share information and tasks (eg technical support provided by a supplier)
- Make joint decisions (eg on quality assurance or staff training)
- Fulfil the collaborative (working together) function of a team

ICT has facilitated this kind of collaboration, simulating team working via teleconferencing, video-conferencing, networked computers and the internet.

(a) Dispersed individuals and units can use such technology to access and share up-to-date research, product, customer, inventory and delivery information.

(b) Electronic meeting management systems allow virtual meeting participants to talk and listen to each other on teleconference lines, while sharing data and using electronic 'white boards' on their PCs.

This has enabled organisations to:

(a) **Outsource** areas of organisational activity to other organisations and freelance workers (even 'off-shore' in countries where skilled labour is cheaper), without losing control or co-ordination.

(b) **Organise 'territorially'** without the overhead costs of local offices, and without the difficulties of supervision, communication and control. Dispersed centres are linked to a 'virtual office' by communications technology and can share data freely.

(c) **Centralise** shared functions and services (such as data storage and retrieval, technical support or secretarial services) without the disadvantages of 'geographical' centralisation.

(d) **Adopt flexible cross-functional and multi-skilled working**, by making expertise available across the organisation. A 'virtual team' co-opts the best people for the task – regardless of location.

PART C ORGANISATIONAL STRUCTURES, CULTURES AND SYSTEMS

Question
Virtual teams

What areas of your own organisation's activities are currently 'outsourced' to other organisations, consultants or freelance workers?

Answer

Organisations often outsource activities such as recruitment and selection (for appropriate types of staff), sales (eg telemarketing) or research and development. You may have noted the use of external call centres for technical support, sales and customer service functions: these are often in overseas locations where labour is cost-effective (such as India) – but location is increasingly irrelevant to customers because of the technology available.

7 Job design

FAST FORWARD

Job design refers to how tasks are organised to create 'jobs' for individuals. **Fredrick Herzberg** identified two basic need systems: the need to avoid unpleasantness and the need for personal growth. He suggested factors which could be offered by organisations to satisfy both types of need: hygiene and motivator factors respectively. These should be reflected in job design.

7.1 Micro-design of jobs

One of the consequences of mass production and scientific management was what might be called a **micro-division** of labour, or **job simplification**. Micro-designed jobs have the following **advantages**.

(a) **Little training**. A job is divided up into the smallest number of sequential tasks possible. Each task is so simple and straightforward that it can be learned with very little training.

(b) **Replacement**. If labour turnover is high, this does not matter because unskilled replacements can be found and trained to do the work in a very short time.

(c) **Flexibility**. Since the skill required is low, workers can be shifted from one task to another very easily.

(d) **Control**. If tasks are closely defined and standard times set for their completion, production is easier to predict and control.

(e) **Quality**. Standardisation of work into simple tasks means that quality is easier to predict.

Disadvantages of micro-designed jobs, however, include the following.

(a) The work is **monotonous** and makes employees tired, bored and dissatisfied. The consequences will be high labour turnover, absenteeism, spoilage, unrest. People work better when their work is variable, unlike machines.

(b) An individual doing a simple task feels like a small cog in a large machine, and has no **sense of contributing** to the organisation's end product or service.

(c) Excessive specialisation **isolates** the individual in his or her work and inhibits not only social contacts with work mates, but knowledge generation.

(d) In practice, excessive job simplification leads to **lower quality**, through inattention and loss of morale.

7.2 Herzberg's two-factor theory

Herzberg's two-factor theory is based on two needs: the need to avoid unpleasantness, and the need for personal growth (*The Motivation to Work*, 1959).

(a) The need to avoid unpleasantness is satisfied through **hygiene factors**. Hygiene factors are to do with the environment and conditions of work, including:

- Company policy and administration
- Salary
- The quality of supervision
- Interpersonal relations
- Working conditions
- Job security

If inadequate, hygiene factors cause **dissatisfaction** with work (which is why they are also called 'dissatisfiers'). They work like sanitation, which minimises threats to health rather than actively promoting 'good health'.

(b) The need for personal growth is satisfied by **motivator factors**.

These actively create job satisfaction (they are also called 'satisfiers') and are effective in motivating an individual to superior performance and effort. These factors are connected to the work itself, including:

- Status (although this may be a hygiene factor too)
- Challenging work
- Advancement (or opportunities for it)
- A sense of achievement
- Recognition by colleagues and management
- Growth in the job
- Responsibility

A lack of motivator factors will encourage employees to concentrate on the hygiene factors, which will eventually dissatisfy.

Herzberg suggested that where there is evidence of poor motivation, such as low productivity, poor quality and strikes, management should not pay too much attention to hygiene factors such as pay and conditions. Despite the fact that these are the traditional target for the aspirations of organised labour, their potential for bringing improvements to work attitudes is limited. Instead, **Herzberg** suggested three types of **job design** which would offer job satisfaction through enhanced motivator factors.

7.3 Job design as a motivator

7.3.1 Job enrichment

Key term

> **Job enrichment** is planned, deliberate action to build greater responsibility, breadth and challenge of work into a job. Job enrichment is similar to **empowerment**.

Job enrichment represents a 'vertical' extension of the job into greater levels of responsibility, challenge and autonomy. A job may be enriched by:

- Giving the job-holder **decision-making tasks** of a higher order
- Giving the employee greater **freedom** to decide how the job should be done
- Encouraging employees to **participate** in the planning decisions of their superiors
- Giving the employee regular **feedback**

Job enrichment alone will not automatically make employees more productive.

7.3.2 Job enlargement

Key term

> **Job enlargement** is the attempt to widen jobs by increasing the number of operations in which a job-holder is involved.

Job enlargement is a 'horizontal' extension of the job by increasing task variety and reducing task repetition.

(a) Tasks which span a larger part of the total production work should reduce boredom and add to task meaning, significance and variety.

(b) Enlarged jobs might be regarded as having higher status within the department, perhaps as stepping stones towards promotion.

Job enlargement is, however, limited in its intrinsic rewards, as asking workers to complete three separate tedious, unchallenging tasks is unlikely to be more motivating than asking them to perform just one tedious, unchallenging task!

7.3.3 Job rotation

Key term

> **Job rotation** is the planned transfer of staff from one job to another to increase task variety.

Job rotation is a 'sequential' extension of the job. Job rotation is also sometimes seen as a form of training, where individuals gain wider experience by rotating as trainees in different positions.

It is generally admitted that the developmental value of job rotation is limited – but it can reduce the monotony of repetitive work.

7.3.4 Job optimisation

A well designed job should provide the individual with five **core dimensions** which contribute to job satisfaction.

(a) **Skill variety**: the opportunity to exercise different skills and perform different operations

(b) **Task identity**: the integration of operations into a 'whole' tasks (or meaningful segments)

(c) **Task significance**: the task is perceived to have a role, purpose, meaning and value

(d) **Autonomy**: the opportunity to exercise discretion or self-management (eg in areas such as target-setting and work methods)

(e) **Feedback**: the availability of performance feedback enabling the individual to assess his progress and the opportunity to give feedback, be heard and influence results

Chapter roundup

- Organisations are characterised by formal division of labour, **hierarchies** of authority (scalar chains) and networks of **authority** and power. The organisation structure influences strategy, as it is one of the ways in which power is deployed and **information** communicated. Organisation structure determines how work is allocated, directed and controlled, in order to achieve the goals of the organisation.

- **Span of control** or '**span of management**' refers to the number of subordinates responsible to a superior.

- Recent trends have been towards **delayering** organisations of levels of management. In other words, **tall organisations** (with many management levels, and narrow spans of control) are turning into **flat organisations** (with fewer management levels, wider spans of control) as a result of technological changes and the granting of more decision-making power to front line employees.

- In a **divisional structure** some activities are **decentralised** to business units or regions.

- Return on capital employed and residual income are two methods of measuring divisional performance.

- Organisations can be **departmentalised** on a **functional** basis (with separate departments for production, marketing, finance etc), a **geographical** basis (by region, or country), a **product** basis (eg world wide divisions for product X, Y etc), a **brand** basis, or a **matrix** basis (eg someone selling product X in country A would report to both a product X manager and a country A manager). Organisation structures often feature a variety of these types, as **hybrid** structures.

- Organisational **flexibility** means an ability to cope with unpredicatble changes in levels of demand for a product, changes in product specificsations, or to cope with short term projects. This has led to the emergence of new forms of organisation, including **network organisations**, **venture team organisations**, **and modular organisations**.

- The shamrock organisation has a core of permanent managers and specialist staff supported by a contingent workforce of contractors and part-time and temporary workers. This form is popular during recessions.

- A **centralised** organisation is one in which authority is concentrated in one place.

- **Centralisation** offers greater control and co-ordination; **decentralisation** offers greater flexibility.

- **Burns** and **Stalker** noted that **mechanistic** (or **bureaucratic**) organisations are stable and efficient in conditions of slow change, but that **organic** organisation is required for adaptation and responsiveness in fast-change environments.

- **Bureaucracy** is 'a continuous organisation of official functions bound by rules' (**Weber**). It is a form of mechanistic organisation.

- **Organic organisations** are controlled by mechanisms such as commitment and culture.

- **Lawrence** and **Lorsch** suggest that environmental uncertainty increases the need for **differentiation** (differing structures and systems within an organisation) and **integration** (the process of co-ordinating the various parts of the organisation).

- **Technology** has a significant impact on the way work is organised.

- The organisation may be seen as a **socio-technical system**.

- The global explosion of **ICT** has also had a major impact on work organisation.

- **Job design** refers to how tasks are organised to create 'jobs' for individuals. **Fredrick Herzberg** identified two basic need systems: the need to avoid unpleasantness and the need for personal growth. He suggested factors which could be offered by organisations to satisfy both types of need: hygiene and motivator factors respectively. These should be reflected in job design.

Quick quiz

1. Describe the five component parts of the organisation identified by **Mintzberg**.
2. What is meant by scalar chain?
3. 'Span of control' refers to the number of layers in the organisation hierarchy. True or False?
4. What is delayering?
5. What is functional organisation?
6. What is a matrix organisation?
7. Which of the following is not a type of legitimate authority identified by **Max Weber**?

    A   Charismatic
    B   Technostructure
    C   Traditional
    D   Bureaucratic

8. 'Horizontal' structures (**Peters**) would be an example of which type of organisation?

    A   Mechanistic
    B   Organic

Answers to quick quiz

1. Strategic apex; middle line; operating core; technostructure; support staff
2. The chain of command
3. False. It is the number of subordinates immediately reporting to a given official.
4. The reduction in the number of management levels
5. People are grouped together as they do similar work.
6. A matrix organisation crosses functional boundaries and involves overlapping chains of command.
7. B: 'Technostructure' is a term drawn from **Mintzberg's** model of organisational components.
8. B: Organic. Horizontal structures aim at flexibility.

PART C ORGANISATIONAL STRUCTURES, CULTURES AND SYSTEMS

Organisation culture

Topic list	Syllabus reference
1 What is culture?	D3
2 Organisation culture	D3
3 Culture and structure	D3
4 The impact of national culture	D3
5 The informal organisation	D3

Introduction

Organisation culture is, broadly, the distinctive way an organisation does things: its particular 'style'. We explore how this reveals itself in **Sections 1 and 2** of this chapter.

Like **structure**, which we discussed in Chapter 6, the concept of **culture** gives us a way of talking about how organisations 'work'. Particular structures suit particular cultures – as we see in **Section 3**: this is a useful model, which should be learned in detail.

The impact of national culture on organisational culture **(Section 4)** is not specifically mentioned in the syllabus, but you may want to bear it in mind when discussing management in multinational and cross-cultural contexts. With increasing globalisation and workforce diversity, this is useful awareness.

This chapter underpins much that follows in the Learning & Practice Workbook.

1 What is culture?

1.1 Spheres of culture

FAST FORWARD

Culture may be identified as ways of behaving, and ways of understanding, that are shared by a group of people.

Culture can be discussed on many different levels. The 'category' or 'group' of people whose shared behaviours and meanings may constitute a culture include:

- A nation, region or ethnic group
- Women versus men ('gender culture')
- A social class (eg 'working class culture')
- A profession or occupation
- A type of business (eg 'advertising culture')
- An organisation ('**organisational culture**')

1.2 Elements of culture

FAST FORWARD

Elements of culture include:

- Observable behaviour, artefacts, rituals and symbols
- Underlying values and beliefs which give meaning to the observable elements
- Hidden assumptions which unconsciously shape values and beliefs

Schein (*Organizational Culture and* Leadership, 1985) suggested that in fact there are different levels at which culture can be understood.

(a) The **observable**, expressed or 'explicit' elements of culture include:

- **Behaviour**: norms of personal and interpersonal behaviour; customs and rules about behaviours that are 'acceptable' or unacceptable

- **Artefacts**: concrete expressions such as art and literature, architecture and interior design (eg of office premises), dress codes, symbols and 'heroes' or role models

- **Rituals**: patterns of collective behaviour which have traditional or symbolic value, such as greeting styles, business formalities, social courtesies and ceremonies

Sometimes artefacts is used as a generic term to cover observable elements.

(b) Beneath these observable phenomena lie **values and beliefs** which give the behaviours, artefacts and rituals their special meaning and significance. For example, the design of office space (artefact) may imply status and honour, or reflect the importance of privacy, or reflect spiritual beliefs (as in feng shui) within a culture: it 'means' more than the observable features. Values and beliefs may be overtly expressed in sayings, mottos and slogans.

(c) Beneath values and beliefs lie **assumptions**: foundational ideas that are no longer consciously recognised or questioned by the culture, but which 'programme' its ways of thinking and behaving. Examples include the importance of the individual in many Western cultures: this is taken for granted in designing HR (human resources) policies, for example.

8: ORGANISATION CULTURE

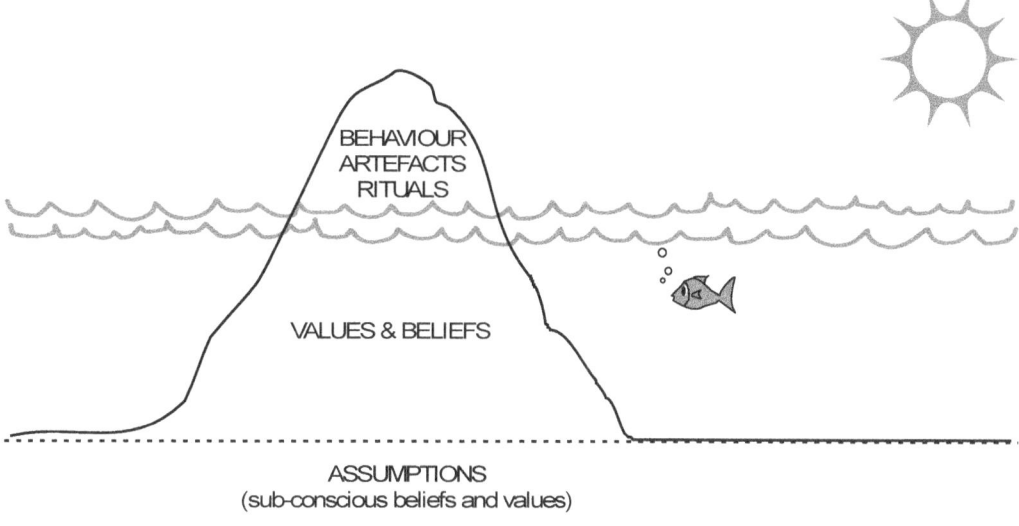

Cultural assumptions, values and beliefs influence the behaviour of individuals, groups and organisations. They create a shared 'style' of operating within a given culture – but also the potential for misunderstanding and conflict between different cultural groups.

Question — Values and beliefs

Which of the following would be values and beliefs in a culture?

- A Staff contentment
- B Quality product
- C Refunds cleared within three business days
- D Polite treatment of customers

Answer

A   Staff contentment

Values and beliefs are not observable but they have observable manifestations. Staff contentment is not visible in itself but will be manifested in staff attitudes towards their work and their customers.

A quality product, prompt refunds are observable and polite treatment of customers are all observable.

2 Organisation culture

FAST FORWARD

Organisation culture is '**the way we do things round here**' (Schein, *Organizational Culture and Leadership: A Dynamic View*, 1992).

2.1 Manifestations of culture in organisations

Examples of organisation culture include the following.

Item	Example
Beliefs and values, which are often unquestioned	'The customer is always right'

PART C ORGANISATIONAL STRUCTURES, CULTURES AND SYSTEMS

Item	Example
Behaviour	In many companies, standard business dress is still generally taken for granted.
Artefacts	Encouraging communication between employees by setting aside spaces for the purpose.
Rituals	In some firms, sales people compete with each other, and there is a reward, given at a ceremony, for the salesperson who does best in any period.
Symbols	Corporate logos are an example of symbols, but they are directed outwards. Within the organisation, symbols can represent power: dress, make and model of car, office size and equipment and access to facilities can all be important symbols.

Manifestations of culture in an organisation may thus include:

- How formal the organisation structure is
- Communication: are senior managers approachable?
- Office layout
- The type of people employed
- Symbols, legends, corporate myths
- Management style
- Freedom for subordinates to show initiative
- Attitudes to quality
- Attitudes to risk
- Attitudes to the customer
- Attitudes to technology

Question
Manifestations of culture

What do you think would differentiate the culture of a regiment in the army and an advertising agency?

Answer

Here are some hints. The Army is very disciplined. Decisions are made by officers; behaviour between ranks is sometimes very formal. The organisation values loyalty, courage and discipline and teamwork. Symbols and artefacts include uniforms, medals, regimental badges and so on. Rituals include corporate expressions such as parades and ceremonies.

An advertising agency, with a different mission, is more fluid. Individual flair and creativity, within the commercial needs of the firm, is expected. Artefacts may include the style of creative offices, awards or prizes, and the agency logo. Rituals may include various award ceremonies, team meetings and social gatherings.

2.2 What shapes organisation culture?

Influences on organisational culture include:

(a) The organisation's **founder**. A strong set of values and assumptions is set up by the organisation's founder, and even after he or she has retired, these values have their own momentum. An organisation might find it hard to shake off its original culture.

(b) The organisation's **history**:

   (i) Culture reflects the era when the organisation was founded.

   (ii) The effect of history can be determined by stories, rituals and symbolic behaviour. They legitimise behaviour and promote priorities.

(c) **Leadership and management style**. An organisation with a strong culture recruits and develops managers who naturally conform to it, who perpetuate the culture.

(d) The **organisation's environment**. As we have seen, nations, regions, occupations and business types have their own distinctive cultures, and these will affect the organisation's style.

2.3 The importance of culture

> **FAST FORWARD**
>
> **Cultural values** can be used to guide organisational processes without the need for tight control. They can also be used to motivate employees, by emphasising the heroic dimension of the task. Culture can also be used to drive change, although – since values are difficult to change – it can also be a powerful force for preserving the *status quo*.

Successful companies are good at two things:

- Producing commercially viable **new products**
- Responding to **changes in their environment**

A feature of these companies is their use of **cultural values** to guide business processes and motivate employees.

(a) Cultural norms can replace rules and guidelines, focusing on output values such as quality and customer service, and freeing employees to make more flexible decisions in pursuit of those values.

(b) Valued cultural symbols can be used as rewards and incentives, to help employees feel 'heroic' in pursuing organisational aims.

(c) Cultural values can be used to drive organisational change, on the basis that if values change, behaviour will follow.

3 Culture and structure

> **FAST FORWARD**
>
> **Harrison** classified four types of culture, to which **Handy** gave the names of Greek Gods.
>
> - **Power** culture (Zeus) is shaped by one individual.
> - **Role** culture (Apollo) is a bureaucratic culture shaped by rationality, rules and procedures.
> - **Task** culture (Athena) is shaped by a focus on outputs and results.
> - **Existential** or person culture (Dionysus) is shaped by the interests of individuals.

Harrison ('Understanding your organisation's character', *Harvard Business Review*, 1972) suggested that organisations could be classified into four types. His work was later popularised by **Charles Handy** (*Gods of Management*, 1976). The four types are differentiated by their structures, processes and management methods and the differences are so significant as to create **distinctive cultures**.

Zeus — Power culture	**Apollo** — Role culture
The organisation is controlled by a key central figure, owner or founder. Power is direct, personal, informal. Suits small organisations where people get on well.	Classical, rational organisation: bureaucracy. Stable, slow-changing, formalised, impersonal. Authority based on position and function.
Athena — Task culture	**Dionysus** — Person culture
Management is directed at outputs: problems solved, projects completed. Team-based, horizontally-structured, flexible, valuing expertise – to get the job done.	The purpose of the organisation is to serve the interests of the individuals who make it up: management is directed at facilitating, administering.

3.1 Power culture

Zeus is the god representing the **power culture** or **club culture**. Zeus is a dynamic entrepreneur who rules with snap decisions. Power and influence stem from a central source, perhaps the owner-directors or the founder of the business. The degree of formalisation is limited, and there are few rules and procedures. Such a firm is likely to be organised on a functional basis.

(a) The organisation is capable of adapting quickly to meet change.

(b) Personal influence decreases as the size of an organisation gets bigger. The power culture is therefore best suited to smaller entrepreneurial organisations, where the leaders have direct communication with all employees.

(c) Personnel have to get on well with each other for this culture to work.

3.2 Role culture

Apollo is the god of the **role culture** or **bureaucracy**. There is a presumption of logic and rationality.

(a) These organisations have a formal structure, and operate by well-established rules and procedures.

(b) Individuals are required to perform their job to the full, but not to overstep the boundaries of their authority. Individuals who work for such organisations tend to learn an expertise without experiencing risk; many do their job adequately, but are not over-ambitious.

(c) The bureaucratic style, as we have seen, can be very efficient in a stable environment, when the organisation is large and when the work is predictable.

3.3 Task culture

Athena is the goddess of the **task culture**. Management is seen as completing a succession of projects or solving problems.

(a) The task culture is reflected in project teams and task forces. In such organisations, there is no dominant or clear leader. The principal concern in a task culture is to get the job done. Therefore the individuals who are important are the experts with the ability to accomplish a particular aspect of the task.

(b) Performance is judged by results.

(c) Task cultures are expensive, as experts demand a market price.

(d) Task cultures also depend on variety, and to tap creativity requires a tolerance of perhaps costly mistakes.

3.4 Person culture

Dionysus is the god of the **existential** or **person culture**. In the three other cultures, the individual is subordinate to the organisation or task. An existential culture is found in an organisation whose purpose is to serve the interests of the individuals within it. These organisations are rare, although an example might be a partnership of a few individuals who do all the work of the organisation themselves (with perhaps a little secretarial or clerical assistance): for example, barristers (in the UK) work through chambers.

Management positions in these organisations are often lower in status than the professionals and are labelled secretaries, administrators, bursars, registrars or clerks.

The organisation depends on the talent of the individuals; management is derived from the consent of the managed, rather than the delegated authority of the owners.

Question — Task culture

Which of the following is NOT an advantage of a task culture?

- A Allows flexibility to solve problems
- B High creativity
- C Job satisfaction
- D Matrix structure that doesn't follow the traditional functional hierarchy

Answer

D Matrix structure that doesn't follow the traditional hierarchy

Using a matrix structure that doesn't follow a traditional functional hierarchy can be confusing for employees who now have more than one manager and may struggle to prioritise their workload effectively.

Flexibility, creativity and job satisfaction are all potential advantages.

3.5 A contingency approach

When thinking about these four types of culture, remember that they do not necessarily equate to specific organisation types, though some styles of organisation culture may accompany particular organisation structures. Also, it is quite possible for different cultures to prevail in different parts of the same organisation, especially large ones with many departments and sites. In other words, as the contingency approach says: 'it all depends'.

Case Study

Handy cites a pharmaceutical company which at one time had all its manufacturing subcontracted, until the turnover and cost considerations justified a factory of its own. The company hired nine talented individuals to design and run the factory. Result:

(a) The design team ran on a task culture, with a democratic/consultative leadership style, using project teams for certain problems. This was successful while the factory was being built.

(b) After its opening, the factory, staffed by 400, was run on similar lines. There were numerous problems. Every problem was treated as a project, and the workforce resented being asked to help sort out 'management' problems. In the end, the factory was run in a slightly more autocratic way. The task culture (setting something up) was superseded by a role culture (running it).

PART C ORGANISATIONAL STRUCTURES, CULTURES AND SYSTEMS

Handy also matched appropriate cultural models to Robert Anthony's 1965 classification of managerial activity.

(a) **Strategic management** (carried out by senior management) is concerned with direction-setting, policy-making and crisis handling. It therefore suits a **power culture**.

(b) **Tactical management** (carried out by middle management) is concerned with establishing means to the corporate ends, mobilising resources and innovating (finding new ways of achieving goals). It therefore suits a **task culture**.

(c) **Operational management** (carried out by supervisors and operatives) is concerned with routine activities to carry out tactical plans. It therefore suits a **role culture**.

Question — Classifications of culture

Review the following statements. Ascribe each of them to one of Handy's four corporate cultures.

People are controlled and influenced by:

(a) The personal exercise of rewards, punishments or charisma.

(b) Impersonal exercise of economic and political power to enforce procedures and standards of performance.

(c) Communication and discussion of task requirements leading to appropriate action motivated by personal commitment to goal achievement.

(d) Intrinsic interest and enjoyment in the activities to be done, and/or concern and caring for the needs of the other people involved.

Answer

(a) Zeus/power culture   (c) Athena/task culture
(b) Apollo/role culture   (d) Dionysus/person culture

4 The impact of national culture

FAST FORWARD

National culture influences organisation culture in various ways. One model of these effects is the 'Hofstede model' which describes four dimensions on which cultures differ:

- Power distance
- Uncertainty avoidance
- Individuality/collectivity
- Masculinity/femininity

Different countries have different ways of doing business, and different cultural values and assumptions which influence business and management styles.

4.1 The Hofstede model

A model was developed by **Geert Hofstede** (*Culture's Consequences: International Differences in Work Related Values*, 1980) in order to explain national differences by identifying 'key dimensions' which represent the essential 'programmes' forming a common culture in the value systems of all countries. Each country is represented on a scale for each dimension so as to explain and understand values,

attitudes and behaviour. In particular, Hofstede points out that countries differ on the following dimensions:

(a) **Power distance**. This dimension measures how far superiors are expected to exercise power. In a high power-distance culture, the boss decides and people do not question.

(b) **Uncertainty avoidance**. Some cultures prefer clarity and order, whereas others are prepared to accept novelty. This affects the willingness of people to **change** rules, rather than simply obey them.

(c) **Individualism**. In some countries individual achievement is what matters. A collectivist culture (eg people are supported – and controlled – by extended families) puts the interests of the group first.

(d) **'Masculinity'**. In 'masculine' cultures, gender roles are clearly differentiated. In 'feminine' ones they are not. 'Masculine' cultures place greater emphasis on possessions, status and display as opposed to quality of life and concern for others.

Hofstede groups countries into eight categories.

Group		Power distance	Uncertainty avoidance	Individualism	'Masculinity'
I	'More developed Latin' (eg Belgium, France, Argentina, Brazil, Spain)	High	High	Medium to high	Medium
II	'Less developed Latin' (eg Portugal, Mexico, Peru)	High	High	Low	Whole range
III	'More developed Asian' (eg Japan)	Medium	High	Medium	High
IV	'Less developed Asian' (eg India, Taiwan, Thailand)	High	Low to medium	Low	Medium
V	Near Eastern (eg Greece, Iran, Turkey)	High	High	Low	Medium
VI	'Germanic' (eg Germany)	Low	Medium to high	Medium	Medium to high
VII	Anglo (eg UK, US, Australia)	Low to medium	Low to medium	High	High
VIII	Nordic (eg Scandinavia, the Netherlands)	Low	Low to medium	Medium to high	Low

There are dangers in using these models. In the management of individual businesses, other factors may be more important.

(a) **Type of industry**: people working in information technology from two countries might have more in common with each other than they might with people working in a different industry.

(b) **Size of company**: some people may be accustomed to working in a **bureaucracy**.

5 The informal organisation

5.1 What is the informal organisation?

> **FAST FORWARD**
>
> An **informal organisation** always exists alongside the formal one. This consists of social relationships, informal communication networks, behavioural norms and power/influence structures, all of which may 'by-pass' formal organisational arrangements. This may be detrimental or beneficial to the organisation, depending how it is managed.

An **informal organisation** exists side by side with the formal one. When people work together, they establish social relationships and customary ways of doing things. Unlike the formal organisation, the **informal organisation** is loosely structured, flexible and spontaneous. It embraces such mechanisms as:

(a) Social relationships and groupings (eg cliques) within – or across – formal structures

(b) The 'grapevine', 'bush telegraph', or informal communication which by-passes the formal reporting channels and routes

(c) Behavioural norms and ways of doing things, both social and work-related, which may circumvent formal procedures and systems (for good or ill). New members must 'learn the ropes' and get used to 'the way we do things here'.

(d) Power/influence structures, irrespective of organisational authority: informal leaders are those who are trusted and looked to for advice.

5.2 Benefits of the informal organisation

Benefits of the informal organisation for managers include:

(a) **Employee commitment**. The meeting of employees' social needs may contribute to morale and job satisfaction, with benefits in reduced absenteeism and labour turnover.

(b) **Knowledge sharing**. The availability of information through informal networks can give employees a wider perspective on their role in the task and the organisation, potentially stimulating 'big picture' problem-solving, cross-boundary co-operation and innovation.

(c) **Speed**. Informal networks and methods may sometimes be more efficient in achieving organisational goals, where the formal organisation has rigid procedures or lengthy communication channels, enabling decisions to be taken and implemented more rapidly.

(d) **Responsiveness**. The directness, information-richness and flexibility of the informal organisation may be particularly helpful in conditions of rapid environmental change, facilitating both the mechanisms and culture of anti-bureaucratic responsiveness.

(e) **Co-operation**. The formation and strengthening of interpersonal networks can facilitate teamworking and co-ordination across organisational boundaries. It may reduce organisational politics – or utilise it positively by mobilising effective decision-making coalitions and by-passing communication blocks.

5.3 Managerial problems of informal organisation

Each of the positive attributes of informal organisation could as easily be detrimental if the power of the informal organisation is directed towards goals unrelated to, or at odds with, those of the formal organisation.

(a) **Social groupings may act collectively against organisational interests**, strengthened by collective power and information networks. Even if they are aligned with organisational goals, group/network maintenance may take a lot of time and energy away from tasks.

(b) The **grapevine is notoriously inaccurate** and can carry morale-damaging rumours.

(c) The informal organisation can become **too important in fulfilling employees' needs**: individuals can suffer acutely when excluded from cliques and networks.

(d) Informal work practices may **'cut corners'**, violating safety or quality assurance measures.

Managers can **minimise problems** by:

(a) Meeting employees' **needs** as far as possible via the formal organisation: providing information, encouragement, social interaction and so on.

(b) Harnessing the **dynamics** of the informal organisation – for example by using informal leaders to secure employee commitment to goals or changes.

(c) Involving **managers** themselves in the informal structure, so that they support information sharing, the breaking down of unhelpful rules and so on.

Question — Informal organisation structures

What 'informal organisation' structures are you involved in at work? How are they beneficial or detrimental to your work? What other satisfactions do they offer you?

Chapter roundup

- **Culture** may be identified as ways of behaving, and ways of understanding, that are shared by a group of people.

- **Elements of culture** include:
    - Observable behaviour, artefacts, rituals and symbols
    - Underlying values and beliefs which give meaning to the observable elements
    - Hidden assumptions which unconsciously shape values and beliefs

- Organisation culture is '**the way we do things round here**'.

- **Cultural values** can be used to guide organisational processes without the need for tight control. They can also be used to motivate employees, by emphasising the heroic dimension of the task. Culture can also be used to drive change, although – since values are difficult to change, it can also be a powerful force for preserving the *status quo*.

- **Harrison** classified four types of culture, to which **Handy** gave the names of Greek Gods.
    - **Power** culture (Zeus) is shaped by one individual
    - **Role** culture (Apollo) is a bureaucratic culture shaped by rationality, rules and procedures
    - **Task** culture (Athena) is shaped by a focus on outputs and results
    - **Existential** or person culture (Dionysus) is shaped by the interests of individuals

- **National culture** influences organisation culture in various ways. One model of these effects is the '**Hofstede** model' which describes four dimensions on which cultures differ:
    - Power distance
    - Uncertainty avoidance
    - Individuality/collectivity
    - Masculinity/femininity

- An **informal organisation** always exists alongside the formal one. This consists of social relationships, informal communication networks, behavioural norms and power/influence structures, all of which may 'by-pass' formal organisational arrangements. This may be detrimental or beneficial to the organisation, depending how it is managed.

Quick quiz

1. What are the elements of culture, according to **Trompenaars**?

2. 'Bureaucracy' is another name for a:

   A Power culture
   B Role culture
   C Task culture
   D Existential culture

3. A project team is most likely to be a role culture. True or False?

4. List the four dimensions of cultural difference according to the **Hofstede** model.

5. Quality circles are likely to be a manifestation of:

   A Low power distance
   B Low individuality
   C Neither A nor B
   D Both A and B

6. List the potential benefits of the informal organisation.

Answers to quick quiz

1. Observable phenomena (behaviour, artefacts, rituals), values and beliefs, assumptions
2. B: Such organisations have a formal structure, and operate by established rules and procedures.
3. False: It is most likely to be a task culture.
4. Power distance, uncertainty avoidance, individuality, masculinity
5. D: Quality circles suit employee responsibility and shared decision-making.
6. Meeting of employee needs offering morale and job satisfaction; knowledge sharing; speed of operation; responsiveness to change; support for teamworking and co-ordination

Managerial control: Managing information systems and tehcnology

Budget planning and control

Topic list	Syllabus reference
1 Controllability and responsibility reporting	D4
2 Budgetary planning and control systems	D4

Introduction

This chapter serves as an **introduction** to Part D of the Learning & Practice Workbook and examines the **overall planning and control system**.

The idea that different managers are held responsible for different costs and cost variances is introduced. This means that we must also identify which costs are **controllable** and which are not, so that managers are only answerable for costs and variances that they are able to influence.

PART D MANAGERIAL CONTROL: MANAGING INFORMATION SYSTEMS AND TECHNOLOGY

1 Controllability and responsibility reporting

FAST FORWARD

The selection of **budget centres** in an organisation is a key first step in setting up a control system. A system of **responsibility accounting** must be established.

Responsibility centres include **cost centres**, **profit centres** and **investment centres**.

In order to prepare a budget for an organisation as a whole, individual budgets have to be prepared for sub-sections of the organisation, such as individual subsidiaries within the group and individual departments, products or activities within each subsidiary.

Key term

Budget centre is a section of an organisation for which a budget is prepared.

Since budgets will be made for each of these budget centres, **control reporting** (the comparison of actual results against plan) will also be **based on budget centres**.

The **selection of budget centres** in an organisation is therefore a **key first step in setting up a control system**. What should the budget centres be? What income, expenditure and/or capital employment plans should each budget centre prepare? And how will measures of performance for each budget centre be made?

A well-organised system of control should have the following features.

Feature	Explanation
A hierarchy of budget centres	If the organisation is quite large a hierarchy is needed. Subsidiary companies, departments and work sections might be budget centres. Budgets of each section would then be consolidated into a departmental budget. Departmental budgets in turn would be consolidated into the subsidiary's budget, and the budgets of each subsidiary would be combined into a master budget for the group as a whole.
Clearly identified responsibilities for achieving budget targets	Individual managers should be made responsible for achieving the budget targets of a particular budget centre.
Responsibilities for revenues, costs and capital employed	Budget centres should be organised so that all the revenues earned by an organisation, all the costs it incurs, and all the capital it employs are made the responsibility of someone within the organisation, at an appropriate level of authority in the management hierarchy.

Budgetary control and budget centres are therefore part of the overall system of **responsibility accounting** within an organisation.

Key terms

Responsibility accounting is a system of accounting that segregates revenue and costs into areas of personal responsibility in order to monitor and assess the performance of each part of an organisation.

A **responsibility centre** is a unit of an organisation headed by a manager who has direct responsibility for its performance.

Responsibility centres might be a mixture of cost centres, profit centres and investment centres.

The following table highlights the differences between cost centres, profit centres and investment centres.

Type of responsibility centre	Manager has control over:	Principal performance measure
Cost centre	Controllable costs	Variance analysis
Profit centre	Controllable costs Sales volumes Sales prices	Profit
Investment centre	Controllable costs Sales prices Output volumes Investment in fixed and current assets	Return on investment and residual income

Question
Cost centres

Find out if your organisation has a system of cost, profit and investment centres. What is the scope of planning and control within each centre?

Question
Responsibility accounting

Why might responsibility accounting be difficult to implement in a not-for-profit organisation?

Answer

(a) Objectives are often unclear, so there is no obvious link between inputs and outputs. Responsibility is then hard to define.

(b) Budget-holders may have to monitor costs rather than control them. For example, budget-holders in a hospital are often not medical staff but medical decisions control the extent to which costs are incurred.

(c) The value-for-money objective of effectiveness is not measurable in money terms.

1.1 Controllable and non-controllable costs

FAST FORWARD

Controllable costs are items of expenditure which can be directly influenced by a given manager within a given time span.

A particular cost might be the responsibility of two or more managers (**dual responsibility**). A reporting system must allocate responsibility appropriately.

A cost which is not controllable by a junior manager might be controllable by a senior manager. For example, there may be high direct labour costs in a department caused by excessive overtime working. The junior manager may feel obliged to continue with the overtime to meet production schedules, but his senior may be able to reduce costs by hiring extra full-time staff, thereby reducing the requirements for overtime.

A cost which is not controllable by a manager in one department may be controllable by a manager in another department. For example, an increase in material costs may be caused by buying at higher

prices than expected (controllable by the purchasing department) or by excessive wastage (controllable by the production department) or by a faulty machine producing rejects (controllable by the maintenance department).

Some costs are **non-controllable**, such as increases in expenditure items due to inflation. Other costs are **controllable, but in the long-term rather than the short-term**. For example, production costs might be reduced by the introduction of new machinery and technology, but in the short-term, management must attempt to do the best they can with the resources and machinery at their disposal.

1.2 The controllability of fixed costs

It is often assumed that all fixed costs are non-controllable in the short-run. This is not so.

(a) **Committed fixed costs** are those costs arising from the possession of plant, equipment, buildings and an administration department to **support the long-term needs of the business**. These costs (depreciation, rent, administration salaries) are largely **non-controllable in the short-term** because they have been committed by longer-term decisions affecting longer-term needs.

(b) **Discretionary fixed costs**, such as advertising and research and development costs, are incurred as a result of a senior management decision, but could be **raised or lowered at fairly short notice** (irrespective of the actual volume of production and sales).

1.3 Controllability and apportioned costs

Managers should only be held accountable for costs over which they have some influence. This may seem quite straightforward in theory, but it is not always so easy in practice to distinguish controllable from uncontrollable costs. **Apportioned overhead costs provide a good example**.

Suppose that a manager of a production department in a manufacturing company is made responsible for the costs of his department. These costs include **directly attributable overhead items** such as the costs of indirect labour employed in the department and indirect materials consumed in the department. The department's overhead costs also include an apportionment of costs from other costs centres, such as rent and rates for the building it shares with other departments and a share of the costs of the maintenance department.

Should the production manager be held accountable for any of these apportioned costs?

(a) Managers should **not be held accountable** for costs over which they have **no control**. In this example, apportioned rent and rates costs would not be controllable by the production department manager.

(b) Managers should be held **accountable for** costs over which they have **some influence**. In this example, it is the responsibility of the maintenance department manager to keep maintenance costs within budget. But their costs will be partly variable and partly fixed. The variable cost element will depend on the volume of demand for their services. If the production department's staff treat their equipment badly we might expect higher repair costs. The production department manager should therefore be made accountable for the repair costs that the production department makes the maintenance department incur on its behalf.

Question
Fixed costs

Try to discover some of your organisation's committed fixed costs and discretionary fixed costs. You will then be able to use them as examples in the exam.

1.4 Controllability and dual responsibility

Quite often a particular cost might be the **responsibility of two or more managers**. For example, raw materials costs might be the responsibility of the purchasing manager (prices) and the production manager (usage). A **reporting system must allocate responsibility appropriately**. The purchasing manager must be responsible for any increase in raw materials prices, whereas the production manager should be responsible for any increase in raw materials usage.

1.5 Control reporting

Feedback periods ought to be planned, especially for routine control reporting.

(a) It is important to **avoid excessive reporting**. There is no point in producing control reports weekly if it takes several days to find out the cause of a variance and put it right. There has to be a reasonable interval between control reports so that managers can make a reasonable judgement about the effects of their past control actions.

(b) It is also important to **avoid unnecessary delays** in control reporting, by making the feedback period too long, or by taking too much time to put a feedback report together.

The most suitable frequency of routine control reporting will vary from operation to operation.

Control reports should be **clear** and **understandable** to the person receiving them. **Highlighting key results** and **exception reporting** are ways of improving clarity. Several reports will be prepared, all relating in some way to the same actual results. This is because reports will go to managers at different levels in the chain of command.

Question — Purpose of budgeting

Which of the following is NOT a purpose of budgeting?

A   Establish a basis of control of operations
B   Communicate targets to managers
C   Formulate strategic plans
D   Coordinate the organisation's activities

Answer

C   Formulate strategic plans

Budgeting is concerned with implementing plans at the operational level. The others are all purposes.

2 Budgetary planning and control systems

FAST FORWARD

Here are the **objectives of a budgetary planning and control system**:
- Ensure the achievement of the organisation's objectives
- Compel planning
- Communicate ideas and plans
- Co-ordinate activities
- Provide a framework for responsibility accounting
- Establish a system of control
- Motivate employees to improve their performance

PART D MANAGERIAL CONTROL: MANAGING INFORMATION SYSTEMS AND TECHNOLOGY

Objective	Comment
Ensure the achievement of the organisation's objectives	Objectives are set for the organisation as a whole, and for individual departments and operations within the organisation. Quantified expressions of these objectives are then drawn up as targets to be achieved within the timescale of the budget plan.
Compel planning	This is probably the most important feature of a budgetary planning and control system. Planning forces management to **look ahead**, to set out **detailed plans** for achieving the targets for each department, operation and (ideally) each manager and to anticipate problems. It thus prevents management from relying on ad hoc planning which may be detrimental to the performance of the organisation.
Communicate ideas and plans	A formal system is necessary to ensure that each person affected by the plans is aware of what he or she is **supposed to be doing.** Communication might be one-way, with managers giving **orders to subordinates**, or there might be a two-way dialogue and exchange of ideas.
Co-ordinate activities	The activities of different departments or sub-units of the organisation need to be co-ordinated to ensure **maximum integration** of effort towards common goals. This concept of co-ordination implies, for example, that the purchasing department should base its budget on production requirements and that the production budget should in turn be based on sales expectations. Co-ordination may be difficult to achieve. There is often '**sub-optimality**' and conflict between departmental plans in the budget so that the efforts of each department are not fully integrated into a combined plan to achieve the company's best targets.
Provide a framework for responsibility accounting	Budgetary planning and control systems require that managers of **budget centres** are made responsible for the achievement of budget targets for the operations under their personal control.
Establish a system of control	A budget is a **yardstick** against which actual performance is measured and assessed. Control over actual performance is provided by the comparisons of actual results against the budget plan. Departures from budget can then be investigated and the reasons for the departures can be divided into **controllable** and **uncontrollable** factors.
Motivate employees to improve their performance	The interest and commitment of employees can be retained via a system of **feedback of actual results**, which lets them know how well or badly they are performing. The identification of controllable reasons for departures from budget with managers responsible provides an incentive for improving future performance.

2.1 Fixed and flexible budgeting

FAST FORWARD

Fixed budgets remain unchanged regardless of the level of activity; **flexible budgets** are designed to flex with the level of activity.

Broad approaches to budgeting include **incremental**, **zero-based**, **rolling** and **activity-based**.

2.1.1 Fixed budgets

The master budget prepared before the beginning of the budget period is known as the **fixed** budget. By the term 'fixed', we do not mean that the budget is kept unchanged. Revisions to a fixed master budget will be made if the situation so demands. The term 'fixed' means the following.

(a) The budget is prepared on the basis of an estimated volume of production and an estimated volume of sales. No plans are made for the event that actual volumes of production and sales may differ from budgeted volumes.

(b) When actual volumes of production and sales during a control period (month or four weeks or quarter) are achieved, a fixed budget is not adjusted (in retrospect) to represent a new target for the new levels of activity.

The major purpose of a fixed budget lies in its use at the planning stage, when it seeks to define the broad objectives of the organisation.

Key term

A **fixed budget** is 'A budget which is normally set prior to the start of an accounting period, and which is not changed in response to subsequent changes in activity or costs/revenues. Fixed budgets are generally used for planning purposes.' (**CIMA**, *Official Terminology*, 2005)

Fixed budgets (in terms of a **pre-set expenditure limit**) are also useful for **controlling any fixed cost**, and **particularly non-production fixed costs** such as advertising, because such costs should be unaffected by changes in activity level (within a certain range).

2.1.2 Flexible budgets

Key term

A **flexible budget** is 'A budget which, by recognising different cost behaviour patterns, is designed to change as volume of activity changes' (**CIMA**, *Official Terminology*, 2005)

Uses of flexible budgets

(a) **At the planning stage**. For example, suppose that a company expects to sell 10,000 units of output during the next year. A master budget (the fixed budget) would be prepared on the basis of these expected volumes. However, if the company thinks that output and sales might be as low as 8,000 units or as high as 12,000 units, it may prepare **contingency** flexible budgets, at volumes of, say 8,000, 9,000, 11,000 and 12,000 units, and then assess the possible outcomes.

(b) **Retrospectively.** At the end of each control period, flexible budgets can be used to compare actual results achieved with what results should have been under the circumstances. Flexible budgets are an essential factor in budgetary control.

   (i) Management needs to know about how good or bad actual performance has been. To provide a measure of performance, there must be a yardstick (budget/ standard) against which actual performance can be measured.

   (ii) Every business is dynamic, and actual volumes of output cannot be expected to conform exactly to the fixed budget. Comparing actual costs directly with the fixed budget costs is meaningless.

   (iii) For useful control information, it is necessary to compare actual results at the actual level of activity achieved against the results that should have been expected at this level of activity, which are shown by the flexible budget.

2.2 Incremental budgeting

Key term

Incremental budgeting is 'A method of budgeting based on the previous budget or actual results, adjusting for known changes and inflation for example.'
(**CIMA**, *Official Terminology*, 2005)

The **traditional approach** to budgeting is to **base next year's budget on the current year's results plus an extra amount for estimated growth or inflation next year.** This approach is known as **incremental budgeting** since it is concerned mainly with the increments in costs and revenues which will occur in the coming period.

Incremental budgeting is a reasonable procedure if current operations are as effective, efficient and economical as they can be. It is also appropriate for budgeting for costs such as staff salaries, which may be estimated on the basis of current salaries plus an increment for inflation and are hence administratively fairly easy to prepare.

In general, however, it is an **inefficient form of budgeting** as it **encourages slack** and **wasteful spending** to creep into budgets. Past inefficiencies are perpetuated because cost levels are rarely subjected to close scrutiny.

2.3 Zero based budgeting (ZBB)

ZBB rejects the assumption inherent in incremental budgeting that this year's activities will continue at the same level or volume next year, and that next year's budget can be based on this year's costs plus an extra amount, perhaps for expansion and inflation.

Key term

> **Zero based budgeting** is 'A method of budgeting which requires each cost element to be specifically justified, as though the activities to which the budget relates were being undertaken for the first time. Without approval the budget allowance is zero.'
>
> (**CIMA**, *Official Terminology*, 2005)

In reality, however, managers do not have to budget from zero, but can **start from their current level of expenditure and work downwards**, asking what would happen if any particular aspect of current expenditure and current operations were removed from the budget. In this way, every aspect of the budget is examined in terms of its cost and the benefits it provides and the selection of better alternatives is encouraged.

2.3.1 Implementing ZBB

The implementation of ZBB involves a number of steps but of greater importance is the **development of a questioning attitude** by all those involved in the budgetary process. Existing practices and expenditures must be challenged and searching questions asked.

- Does the activity need to be carried out?
- What would be the consequences if the activity were not carried out?
- Is the current level of provision adequate?
- Are there alternative ways of providing the function?
- How much should the activity cost?
- Is the expenditure worth the benefits achieved?

The three steps of ZBB

Step 1　Define decision packages, comprehensive descriptions of specific organisational activities (decision units) which management can use to evaluate the activities and rank them in order of priority against other activities. There are two types.

　　(a) Mutually exclusive packages contain alternative methods of getting the same job done. The best option among the packages must be selected by comparing costs and benefits and the other packages are then discarded.

　　(b) Incremental packages divide one aspect of an activity into different levels of effort. The 'base' package will describe the minimum amount of work that must be done to carry out the activity and the other packages describe what additional work could be done, at what cost and for what benefits.

9: BUDGET PLANNING AND CONTROL

Step 2 **Evaluate and rank each activity (decision package)** on the basis of its benefit to the organisation. This can be a lengthy process. Minimum work requirements (those that are essential to get a job done) will be given high priority and so too will work which meets legal obligations.

Step 3 **Allocate resources** in the budget according to the funds available and the evaluation and ranking of the competing packages.

Advantages of ZBB

- It is possible to identify and **remove inefficient or obsolete operations**.
- It forces employees to **avoid wasteful expenditure**.
- It can **increase motivation**.
- It **responds to changes in the business environment.**
- ZBB **documentation provides** an in-depth **appraisal of an organisation's operations**.
- It **challenges the status quo**.
- In summary, ZBB should result in a **more efficient allocation of resources**.

Disadvantages of ZBB

The major **disadvantage** of ZBB is the **volume of extra paperwork** created. The assumptions about costs and benefits in each package must be continually updated and new packages developed as soon as new activities emerge. The following problems might also occur.

(a) **Short-term benefits** might be **emphasised** to the detriment of long-term benefits.

(b) It may give the impression **that all decisions have to be made in the budget**. Management must be able to meet unforeseen opportunities and threats at all times, however, and must not feel restricted from carrying out new ideas simply because they were not approved by a decision package, cost benefit analysis and the ranking process.

(c) It may be a **call for management skills** both in constructing decision packages and in the ranking process **which the organisation does not possess**. Managers may therefore have to be trained in ZBB techniques.

(d) The organisation's **information systems may not be capable of providing suitable information**.

(e) **The ranking process can be difficult**. Managers face three common problems.

   (i) A large number of packages may have to be ranked.

   (ii) It can be difficult to rank packages which appear to be equally vital, for legal or operational reasons.

   (iii) It is difficult to rank activities which have qualitative rather than quantitative benefits - such as spending on staff welfare and working conditions.

2.4 Rolling budgeting

Key term

A **rolling budget** is 'A budget continuously updated by adding a further accounting period (month or quarter) when the earliest accounting period has expired.'

(**CIMA**, *Official Terminology*, 2005)

Rolling budgets are also called **continuous budgets**. They are particularly **useful** when an organisation is facing a **period of uncertainty** so that it is difficult to prepare accurate forecasts. For example it may be difficult to estimate the level of inflation for the forthcoming period.

Rolling budgets are an attempt to prepare **targets and plans** which are **more realistic** and **certain**, particularly with a regard to price levels, by shortening the period between preparing budgets.

Instead of preparing a **periodic budget annually** for the full budget period, budgets would be prepared, say, every one, two or three months (four, six, or even twelve budgets each year). Each of these budgets would plan for the next twelve months so that the current budget is extended by an extra period as the current period ends: hence the name rolling budgets. **Cash budgets** are usually prepared on a rolling basis.

Advantages of rolling budgets

(a) They **reduce the element of uncertainty in budgeting**. If a high rate of inflation or major changes in market conditions or any other change is likely which cannot be quantified with accuracy, rolling budgets concentrate detailed planning and control on short-term prospects where the degree of uncertainty is much smaller.

(b) They **force managers to reassess the budget regularly**, and to produce budgets which are up to date in the light of current events and expectations.

(c) Planning and control will be based on a **recent plan** instead of an annual budget that might have been made many months ago and which is no longer realistic.

(d) There is always a budget which **extends for several months ahead**. For example, if rolling budgets are prepared quarterly there will always be a budget extending for the next 9 to 12 months. If rolling budgets are prepared monthly there will always be a budget for the next 11 to 12 months. This is not the case when annual budgets are used.

Disadvantages of rolling budgets.

(a) A system of rolling budgets calls for the routine preparation of a new budget at regular intervals during the course of the one financial year. This involves **more time, effort and money** in budget preparation.

(b) Frequent budgeting might have an **off-putting effect on managers** who doubt the value of preparing one budget after another at regular intervals, even when there are major differences between the figures in one budget and the next.

2.5 Activity-based budgeting

Key term

> **Activity based budgeting** is 'A method of budgeting based on an activity framework and utilising cost driver data in the budget-setting and variance feedback processes.' (**CIMA**, *Official Terminology*, 2005)

At its **simplest**, activity based budgeting (ABB) is merely the **use of costs determined using** activity-based costing **as a basis for preparing budgets**. A budget for an activity is therefore based on the **budgeted number of the activity's cost driver × the appropriate cost driver rate.**

Implementing ABB leads to the realisation that the **business as a whole** needs to be **managed** with far more reference to the behaviour of activities and cost drivers identified.

(a) **Traditional budgeting may make managers 'responsible' for activities which are driven by factors beyond their control**: the cost of setting-up new personnel records and of induction training would traditionally be the responsibility of the personnel manager even though such costs are driven by the number of new employees required by managers other than the personnel manager.

(b) The **budgets for costs not directly related to production** are often traditionally set using an **incremental approach** because of the difficulty of linking the activity driving the cost to production level. But this assumes that all of the cost is unaffected by any form of activity level, which is often not the case in reality. Some of the costs of the purchasing department, for example, will be fixed (such as premises costs) but some will relate to the number of orders placed or the volume of production, say. Surely the budget for the purchasing department should take some account of the expected number of orders?

ABB involves **defining the activities** that underlie the financial figures in each function and using the level of activity to decide **how much resource should be allocated,** how well it is being **managed** and to explain **variances** from budget.

2.6 Top-down and bottom-up budgeting

FAST FORWARD

There are basically two ways in which a budget can be set: from the **top-down (imposed** budget) or from the **bottom-up (participatory** budget).

2.6.1 Top-down budgeting

Key term

An **top-down/imposed budget** is 'A budget allowance which is set without permitting the ultimate budget holder to have the opportunity to participate in the budgeting process'.

(**CIMA**, *Official Terminology*, 2005)

In this approach to budgeting, **top management prepare a budget with little or no input from operating personnel** which is then imposed upon the employees who have to work to the budgeted figures.

The times when top-down budgets are effective

- In newly-formed organisations
- In very small businesses
- During periods of economic hardship
- When operational managers lack budgeting skills
- When the organisation's different units require precise coordination

Advantages of top-down budgeting

- **Strategic plans** are likely to be incorporated into planned activities.
- They **enhance the coordination** between the plans and objectives of divisions.
- They **use senior management's awareness of total resource availability**.
- They **decrease the input from inexperienced or uninformed lower-level employees**.
- They **decrease the period of time taken** to draw up the budgets.

Disadvantages of top-down budgeting

- **Dissatisfaction, defensiveness and low morale amongst employees.** It is hard for people to be motivated to achieve targets set by somebody else.
- The feeling of **team spirit may disappear**.
- The **acceptance of organisational goals** and objectives could be **limited.**
- The feeling of the budget as a **punitive device** could arise.
- Managers who are performing operations on a day to day basis are likely to have a **better understanding** of what is achievable.
- **Unachievable budgets** could result if consideration is not given to local operating and political environments. This applies particularly to overseas divisions.
- **Lower-level management initiative** may be **stifled.**

2.6.2 Bottom-up budgeting

Key term

Bottom-up/participative budgeting is 'A budgeting system in which all budget holders are given the opportunity to participate in setting their own budgets'. (**CIMA**, *Official Terminology*, 2005)

In this approach to budgeting, **budgets are developed by lower-level managers who then submit the budgets to their superiors**. The budgets are based on the lower-level managers' perceptions of what is achievable and the associated necessary resources.

Advantages of bottom-up budgets

- They are based on information from employees most **familiar with the department**.
- Knowledge spread among several levels of management is **pulled together**.
- **Morale and motivation** is improved.
- They **increase operational managers' commitment** to organisational objectives.
- In general they are **more realistic**.
- **Co-ordination** between units is improved.
- **Specific resource requirements** are included.
- Senior managers' **overview is mixed with operational level details**.
- Individual managers' **aspiration levels** are more likely to be taken into account.

Disadvantages of bottom-up budgets

- They **consume more time**.
- Budgets may be **unachievable if** managers are not qualified to participate.
- They may cause managers to introduce **budgetary slack** and budget bias.
- They can support **'empire building'** by subordinates.
- An **earlier start** to the budgeting process could be required.
- Managers may set **'easy' budgets** to ensure that they are achievable.

2.7 Budget slack and bias

Key term

Budget slack is 'The intentional overestimation of expenses and/or underestimation of revenues in the budgeting process'. (**CIMA**, *Official Terminology*, 2005)

In the process of preparing budgets, managers might **deliberately overestimate costs and underestimate sales**, so that they will not be blamed in the future for overspending and poor results.

In controlling actual operations, managers must then **ensure that their spending rises to meet their budget**, otherwise they will be 'blamed' for careless budgeting.

A typical situation is for a manager to **pad the budget** and waste money on non-essential expenses so that he uses all his budget allowances. The reason behind his action is the fear that unless the allowance is fully spent it will be reduced in future periods, thus making his job more difficult as the future reduced budgets will not be so easy to attain. Because inefficiency and slack are allowed for in budgets, achieving a budget target means only that costs have remained within the accepted levels of inefficient spending.

Budget bias can **work in the other direction** too. It has been noted that, after a run of mediocre results, some managers **deliberately overstate revenues and understate cost estimates**, no doubt feeling the need to make an immediate favourable impact by promising better performance in the future. They may merely delay problems, however, as the managers may well be censured when they fail to hit these optimistic targets.

Question — Budget bias

Which of the following is an example of budget bias?

A   A manager uses his best estimate of likely costs when setting the budget.

B   A manager consults with his team to try to establish an appropriate sales volume target.

C   A manager underestimates revenues when setting the budget to ensure that the budget target can be easily exceeded.

D   A manager's advertising budget is disproportionately large in comparison with the budgeted revenue to be generated.

Answer

C   A manager underestimates revenues when setting the budget to ensure that the budget target can be easily exceeded.

Budget bias involves setting low performance targets, so that they can easily be exceeded.

Using the best estimate of costs is part of normal budgeting and consultation with the team may well happen as part of the normal budgeting process. Mismatching expenditure and revenue is bad budgeting practice, but shows the manager in a poor light, whereas budget bias aims to show the manager in a good light.

Chapter roundup

- The selection of **budget centres** in an organisation is a key first step in setting up a control system. A system of **responsibility accounting** must be established.

- **Responsibility centres** include **cost centres**, **profit centres** and **investment centres**.

- **Controllable costs** are items of expenditure which can be directly influenced by a given manager within a given time span.

- A particular cost might be the responsibility of two or more managers (**dual responsibility**). A reporting system must allocate responsibility appropriately.

- Here are the **objectives of a budgetary planning and control system**:
    - Ensure the achievement of the organisation's objectives
    - Compel planning
    - Communicate ideas and plans
    - Co-ordinate activities
    - Provide a framework for responsibility accounting
    - Establish a system of control
    - Motivate employees to improve their performance

- **Fixed budgets** remain unchanged regardless of the level of activity; **flexible budgets** are designed to flex with the level of activity.

- Broad approaches to budgeting include **incremental**, **zero-based**, **rolling** and **activity-based**.

- There are basically two ways in which a budget can be set: from the **top-down** (**imposed** budget) or from the **bottom-up** (**participatory** budget).

Quick quiz

1 Fill in the blanks.

   A well-organised system of control should have the following features.

   (a) A hierarchy of ....

   (b) Clearly identified .... for achieving budget targets

   (c) Responsibilities for ...., ... and ....

2 Which of the following are not controllable by a production department manager?

   (a) Direct labour rate

   (b) Variable production overheads

   (c) Apportioned canteen costs

   (d) Increases in raw material costs due to inflation

   (e) Increases in overall material costs due to high levels of wastage caused by poor supervision of production workers

   (f) An increase in the level of idle time because of poorly-maintained machines

   (g) Depreciation

   (h) Advertising for production workers

3 Give two examples of a responsibility centre.

4 Which of the following is a discretionary fixed cost?

   A   Building depreciation
   B   Rent
   C   Advertising expenditure
   D   Rates

5 Match the description to the type of budget.

   Types of budget

   Incremental budget; rolling budget; zero base budget

   Description

   (a) Next year's budget is based on the current year's results plus an extra amount for estimated growth or inflation next year.

   (b) Each item in the budget is specifically justified, as though each activity were being undertaken for the first time.

   (c) The budget is continuously updated by adding a further accounting period when the earliest accounting period has expired.

6 Once a budget period has started, assuming a system of rolling budgets is **not** in operation, the original budget should never be adjusted. *True or false?*

7 *Fill in the blanks.*

   A flexible budget is a budget which, by recognising ...., is designed to .... as the level of activity changes.

Answers to quick quiz

1. (a) A hierarchy of budget centres
   (b) Clearly identified responsibilities for achieving budget targets
   (c) Responsibilities for revenues, costs and capital employed

2. (a), (c), (d), (f) if there is a maintenance department, (g) and (h)

3. Two of the following: cost centre; profit centre; investment centre

4. C: Discretionary costs are those that arise from shorter-term management decisions, and which can be increased or decreased relatively easily. Committed fixed costs are largely non-controllable in the short-term, because they have been committed to as a result of longer term decisions (such as the need for premises).

5. Incremental budget (a); rolling budget (c); zero base budget (b)

6. False. If the budget is found to be unrealistic or if actual conditions do not reflect those that could possibly have been anticipated, the remainder of the budget may be invalid and the budget committee may need to adjust it.

7. A flexible budget is a budget which, by recognising cost behaviour patterns, is designed to flex or change as the level of activity changes.

Managerial control

Topic list	Syllabus reference
1 The planning and control cycle	D4
2 The control process	D4
3 Feedback and feedforward control	D4
4 Performance evaluation – CSFs and KPIs	D4
5 The balanced scorecard	D4
6 Benchmarking	D4
7 The management of inventory	D4

Introduction

We look at the various stages in the planning process, and where the annual budget fits in to this. We also see how the budget is used in the control process.

Organisational performance needs to be evaluated to see how an organisation is progressing in the achievement of its objectives. Critical success factors and key performance indicators are discussed, along with the perspectives associated with the balanced scorecard and benchmarking performance.

This chapter also considers how inventory (stock) is managed.

1 The planning and control cycle

FAST FORWARD

Planning involves making choices between alternatives and is primarily a decision-making activity. **Control** refers to the steps to be taken after measuring the results against the plan, and the response required for any divergences.

The **planning and control cycle** has seven steps:

Step 1   Identify objectives
Step 2   Identify potential strategies
Step 3   Evaluate strategies
Step 4   Choose alternative courses of action
Step 5   Implement the long-term plan
Step 6   Measure actual results and compare with the plan
Step 7   Respond to divergences from the plan

The following diagram represents the planning and control cycle. The first five steps cover the planning process. **Planning** involves making choices between alternatives and is primarily a decision-making activity. The last two steps cover the **control** process, which involves measuring and correcting actual performance to ensure that the alternatives that are chosen and the plans for implementing them are carried out.

The planning and control cycle

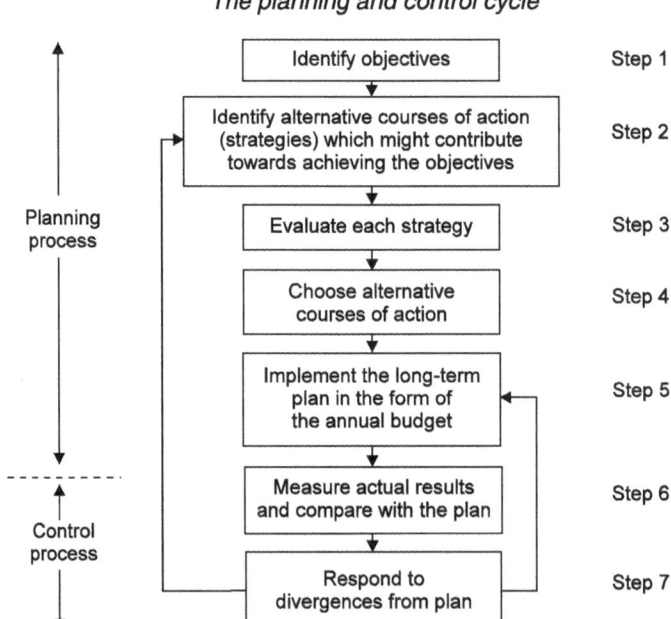

Step 1   Identify objectives

Objectives establish the direction in which the management of the organisation wish it to be heading. Typical objectives include:

- Maximise profits
- Increase market share
- Produce a better quality product than anyone else

Objectives answer the question: '**where do we want to be**?'

Step 2   Identify potential strategies

Once an organisation has decided 'where it wants to be', the next step is to identify a range of possible courses of action or **strategies that might enable the organisation to get there**. The organisation must therefore carry out an **information-gathering exercise** to ensure that it has a full **understanding of where it is now**. This is known as a '**position audit**' or '**strategic analysis**' and involves **looking** both **inwards** and **outwards**.

(a) The organisation must **gather information from all of its internal parts** to find out what resources it possesses: what its manufacturing capacity and capability is, what is the state of its technical know-how, how well it is able to market itself, how much cash it has in the bank and so on.

(b) It must also **gather information externally** so that it can assess its position in the environment. Just as it has assessed its **own strengths and weaknesses**, it must do likewise for its competitors (**threats**). Current and potential markets must be analysed to identify possible new **opportunities**. The 'state of the world' must be considered. Is it in recession or is it booming? What is likely to happen in the future?

Having carried out a strategic analysis, alternative strategies can be identified. An organisation might decide to be the lowest cost producer in the industry, perhaps by withdrawing from some markets or developing new products for sale in existing markets. This may involve internal development or a joint venture.

Step 3 Evaluate strategies

The strategies must then be evaluated **in terms of suitability, feasibility and acceptability**. Management should select those strategies that have the greatest potential for achieving the organisation's objectives.

Step 4 Choose alternative courses of action

The next step in the process is to collect the **chosen strategies** together and **co-ordinate them into a long-term financial plan**. Typically this would show:

- Projected cash flows
- Projected long-term profits
- A description of the long-term objectives and strategies in words
- Capital expenditure plans
- Balance sheet forecasts

Step 5 Implement the long-term plan

The **long-term plan** should then be **broken down into smaller parts**. It is unlikely that the different parts will fall conveniently into successive time periods. Strategy A may take two and a half years, while Strategy B may take five months, but not start until year three of the plan. It is usual, however, to break down the plan as a whole into equal time periods (usually one year). The resulting **short-term plan** is called a **budget**.

Question — Planning and control cycle

Is your organisation's planning and control cycle similar to the one described here? If it differs, how does it differ? Why does it differ? Try to find out your organisation's objectives and the strategies being adopted to attain these objectives.

Answers to this question could be usefully employed in the exam.

2 The control process

FAST FORWARD

Control is achieved through the **control cycle**. Actual performance is compared with planned performance and the appropriate action is taken for those items that are not proceeding according to plan.

Control is achieved through what is known as a control cycle. The elements in the control cycle (from the seven steps listed at the beginning of Section 1) are as follows.

Step 6 **Measure actual results and compare with the plan**

Information about actual results is fed back to the management concerned, often in the form of accounting reports. This reported information is **feedback**. **The feedback is used by management to compare** actual results with the plan or targets (what should be or should have been achieved).

Step 7 **Respond to divergences from the plan**

By comparing actual and planned results, management can then do one of three things, depending on how they see the situation.

(a) **They can take control action**. By identifying what has gone wrong, and then finding out why, corrective measures can be taken.

(b) **They can decide to do nothing**. This could be the decision when actual results are going better than planned, or when poor results were caused by something which is unlikely to happen again in the future.

(c) **They can alter the plan or target** if actual results are different from the plan or target, and there is nothing that management can do (or nothing, perhaps, that they want to do) to correct the situation.

It may be helpful at this stage to relate the control system to a **practical example**, **such as monthly sales**.

Steps 1–4 Based upon an organisation's objectives and its chosen strategies (having been through the planning process), a **sales budget** or plan is prepared for the year.

Step 5 Management implements the plan by **organising the business's resources** to achieve the budget targets.

Step 6 At the end of each month, **actual results** are **reported back to management**. Managers **compare actual results against the plan**.

Step 7 Where necessary, they **take corrective action to adjust the workings of the system**, probably by amending the inputs to the system.

- Salespeople might be asked to work longer hours.
- More money might be spent on advertising.
- Some new price discounts might be decided.
- Delivery periods to customers might be reduced by increasing output.

Where appropriate the sales plan may be revised, up or down.

In this example, however, we have **not allowed for several factors**.

(a) The **influence of the environment** (such as government legislation about safety standards, changing consumer demand, an unexpected rise in raw material prices, or a long strike in a supplier industry).

(b) **Whether control action is possible**. A sales manager might not be able to increase sales if the production department can't produce the desired output fast enough.

(c) **How much information should be measured and compared with planned results**. Not all output is measured, either because it would not have any useful value, or because the system does not provide for its measurement. The reasons why customers buy or don't buy from the company might be reported back, but they might not.

(d) The **plan might need to be changed** and a **comparison of actual results against the existing plan might be invalid**. Environmental influences could be responsible for the need to change the sales plan.

(e) **Not all inputs to the system are controllable**; a rise in raw material prices is outside the scope of management control. Other inputs might be controllable, but are **not controlled due to lax or inattentive management** (for example poor labour morale and a high labour turnover amongst sales staff).

3 Feedback and feedforward control

FAST FORWARD

Feedback is the process of reporting back control information to management and the control information itself.

Feedforward control is control based on comparing original targets or actual results with a forecast of future results.

3.1 Feedback

Key term

Feedback is both the process of reporting back control information to management and the control information itself. In a business organisation, it is information produced from within the organisation (management control reports) with the purpose of helping management and other employees with control decisions.

(a) **Single loop feedback**, normally expressed as feedback, is the feedback of relatively small variations between actual and plan in order that corrective action can bring performance in line with planned results. This implies that the existing plans will not change. This type of feedback is associated with budgetary control and standard costing.

(b) **Double loop feedback**, also known as **higher level feedback**, ensures that plans, budgets, organisational structures and the control systems themselves are revised to meet changes in conditions.

(c) Feedback will most often be **negative**: targets were missed and this was **not** what was required. It may, however, be **positive**: targets were missed, but other targets were hit which were better than those we were aiming at. Negative feedback would result in control action to get back onto target. Positive feedback means that the target should be moved.

The feedback loop in the control cycle is illustrated by the following diagram.

Feedback loop in the control cycle

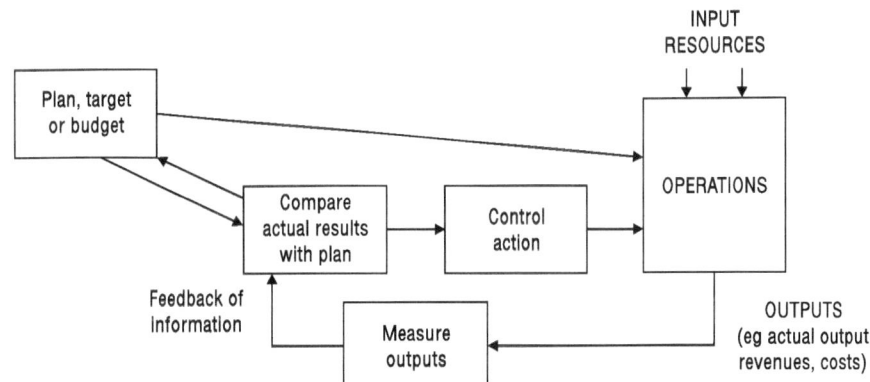

3.2 Feedforward control

Most control systems make use of a comparison between results of the current period (historical costs) and the planned results. Past events are therefore used as a means of controlling or adjusting future activity.

Consider, however, a **cash budget**. This is used to identify likely peaks and troughs in cash balances. If it seems probable that, say, a higher overdraft facility will be needed later in the year, control action will be taken in advance of the actual need, to make sure that the facility will be available. This is an example of **feedforward control**.

Key term

> **Feedforward control** is control based on comparing original targets or actual results with a forecast of future results.

The 'information revolution', which has arisen from computer technology, management information systems theory and the growing use of quantitative techniques has widened the scope for the use of this control technique. Forecasting models can be constructed which enable regular revised forecasts to be prepared about what is now likely to happen in view of changes in key variables (such as sales demand, wage rates and so on).

If regular forecasts are prepared, managers will have both the current forecast and the original plan to guide their action. The original plan may or may not be achievable in view of the changing circumstances. The current forecast indicates what is expected to happen in view of these circumstances.

3.2.1 Examples of control comparisons

Step 1   **Current forecast versus plan**. What action must be taken to get back to the plan, given the differences between the current forecast and the plan? Is any control action worthwhile?

Step 2   If **control action** is **planned**, the current forecast will need to be amended to take account of the effects of the control action and a **revised forecast** prepared.

Step 3   The next comparison should then be **revised forecast versus plan** to determine whether the plan is now expected to be achieved.

Step 4   A comparison between the **original current forecast** and the **revised forecast** will show what the expected effect of the control action will be.

Step 5   At the **end of a control period**, actual results will be analysed and two comparisons may be made.

- **Actual results versus the revised forecast**. Why did differences between the two occur?
- **Actual results so far in the year versus the plan**. How close are actual results to the plan?

Step 6   At the same time, a **new current forecast** should be prepared, and the cycle of comparisons and control action may begin again.

It is in this way that costs are constantly controlled and monitored.

4 Performance evaluation – CSFs and KPIs

FAST FORWARD

> **Critical success factors** are those elements which are central to future success of the organisation strategy.
>
> **A key performance indicator** is a measure used to assess whether the CSFs are being achieved.

4.1 Strategic, tactical and operational objectives

As we first saw in Chapter 3 in the context of strategic management, objectives can be classified as **strategic**, **tactical** or **operational**.

Strategic objectives: Set the overall long-term objectives for the organisation as a whole

Tactical objectives: The 'middle tier' of objectives, designed to plan and control individual functions or divisions within the organisation. Tactical objectives are then implemented by setting operational objectives

Operational objectives: Day to day performance targets to ensure that the organisation's operations are carried out efficiently or effectively

Strategic objectives concern the firm as **a whole.** For example, strategic objectives could relate to:

(a) Profitability
(b) Market share
(c) Growth
(d) Cash flow
(e) Return on capital employed
(f) Risk
(g) Customer satisfaction
(h) Quality
(i) Industrial relations
(j) Added value
(k) Earnings per share

Tactical objectives would concern the **efficient and effective use of** an organisation's **resources**; for example, target productivity.

Operational objectives would include guidelines for ensuring that **specific tasks are carried out**. For example, the manager of a sales territory may specify weekly sales targets for each sales representative.

Objectives are normally **quantified** statements of what the organisation actually intends to achieve over a period of time. They are often described using the 'SMART' mnemonic:

Specific	The objective is targeting a specific area.
Measurable	It is possible to quantify progress toward the objective.
Achievable	The objective is an achievable one.
Realistic	The objective is feasible, given available resources.
Time-bound	It is possible to specify when the objective can be achieved.

Objectives can also be used as standards **for measuring the performance** of the organisation and divisions within it. If an organisation has identified the components of its strategy where it needs to outperform the competition, it also needs some way of being able to measure its performance in those areas. How can progress towards these objectives be measured?

4.2 CSFs and KPIs

Mission statement	• The business's rationale for existing, and a statement of their aspirations
↓	
Strategic objectives	• Quantified embodiments of mission (timescales, profitability)
↓	
Critical success factors (CSFs)	• Elements which are central to future success
↓	
Key performance indicators	• Measures used to assess whether CSFs are being achieved

CSFs are measured using key performance indicators, or KPIs.

Key term

> A **key performance indicator (KPI)** is a quantifiable measure that a company or industry uses to evaluate or compare performance in terms of meeting strategic and operational goals. KPIs vary between companies and industries, depending on their priorities or performance criteria.

CSFs focus management attention on what is important. The advantages of building a control system based around CSFs are:

(a) The process of identifying CSFs will help alert management to the things that need controlling (and show up the things that are less important).

(b) The CSFs can be turned into key performance indicators (KPIs) for periodic reporting in the same way as budgetary control reports on costs. CSFs represent 'what' an organisation needs to do in order to be successful. KPIs are the actual measures that are then used to assess whether or not the CSFs are being achieved. For example, 'ensuring high quality' is a CSF because it is what a company wants to achieve. By contrast, 'the number of complaints' or 'the number of defects' would be KPIs, because they are measurable.

(c) CSFs can guide the development of information systems, by ensuring that managers receive regular information about the factors that are critical to their business.

(d) They can be used for benchmarking organisational performance internally and against rivals).

Case Study

CSFs, core competences, KPIs and targets:

An internet retailer identifies that its critical success factor (CSF) is delivering goods to mainland UK consumers within 24 hours of an order being placed over the internet. One of the core competences associated with that CSF is having sufficient capacity and reliability in its IT systems. A key performance indicator (KPI) to be measured for this is the level of downtime in its IT systems per month. If the business can achieve its target downtime of only, say, 2% per month then it may be satisfied that it is on the way to achieving its CSF.

In order to be successful, organisations have to perform well across a range of key processes. Therefore CSFs and KPIs should focus on key operational processes, and should avoid focusing on financial performance alone.

For example, if next-day delivery were an objective, an employee attitude survey that revealed indifference towards customer complaints about late deliveries would be an indication of failure. If quality is important, a business first needs to ascertain the quality expected by customers, and then set appropriate targets which might include the percentage of products returned or the amount spent on warranties.

CSFs differ from one business to another, and even between business divisions; in some areas of a business, keeping the right price level for the consumer may be key, whereas in others the more important areas to focus on may be quality targets or delivery schedules.

4.3 Examples of KPIs

Some examples of KPIs which can be used to measure the effectiveness of different areas of the organisation, and which cover both financial and non-financial criteria, are outlined below.

Activity	KPIs
Marketing	Sales volume
	Market share
	Return on marketing investment
Production	Capacity utilisation
	Quality standards
Logistics	Capacity utilisation
	Level of service
New product development	Trial rate
	Repurchase rate
Sales programmes	Contribution by region, salesperson
	Controllable margin as percentage of sales
	Number of new accounts
	Salesmen travel costs
Advertising programmes	Awareness levels
	Attribute ratings
	Cost levels
Pricing programmes	Price relative to industry average
	Price elasticity of demand
Management information	Timeliness of reports
	Accuracy of information

Case Study

TDM is a private educational institution. It offers a variety of courses aimed at professional qualifications. TDM has always concentrated on the quality of its courses and learning materials. It has never seen the need for market and customer research, as it has always achieved its sales targets and maintained a large market share. Its students consistently achieve good pass rates.

In recent years, TDM has experienced an increasing rate of employee turnover. Some competitors have started to develop their own courses and products.

In the light of these developments, the CEO is keen to improve performance measurement at TDM, and accordingly wants to identify some appropriate CSFs and KPIs.

(a) Four critical success factors which may be appropriate for TDM are:

    i   Customer satisfaction with courses and learning materials
    ii   Employee satisfaction
    iii The quality of its teaching and materials
    iv Reputation and brand image

(b) KPIs for each of the CSFs could be:

Customer satisfaction

Student satisfaction rating – At the end of a course students could be asked to complete a questionnaire rating their satisfaction with various aspects of the course (for example, the knowledge levels of the staff, the quality of the supporting materials and the approachability/availability of staff to ask them questions).

Client retention – A number of the students attending the courses aimed at professional qualifications are likely to have been funded by their employers. If employers continue to send their students to TDM rather than one of its rivals in the market, this suggests they are happy with the level of tuition and service their students are receiving. The pass rates that students achieve are likely to be a significant influence on client satisfaction in this respect.

Employee satisfaction

Staff turnover – The quality of TDM's teaching staff is crucial in maintaining customer satisfaction, so it is important for TDM to retain its best staff.

Staff absenteeism – High levels of absence are likely to also indicate dissatisfaction among the staff. If absenteeism is rising in conjunction with employee turnover, then there is a danger that the quality of service provided for students will suffer.

Quality of teaching and materials

Market share – It will be important to monitor TDM's market share, because the share of the market TDM can capture will have a direct impact on its revenues.

Accreditations – TDM's courses will be accredited by academic and professional bodies. TDM has always concentrated on the quality of its courses and learning materials, so external accreditations will provide an independent corroboration of this quality. The quality of course tuition and learning materials, in turn, is likely to feed back into the level of customer satisfaction with TDM's courses.

Reputation and brand image

Brand reputation – Given a possible entrance of new competitors into the market, TDM needs to ensure that its brand reputation is maintained. One way of evaluating its reputation could be by measuring the levels of awareness of the brand in the market.

Pass rates – If students, or their employers, think that selecting one tuition provider in preference to another can affect their chances of passing their exam, they are likely to select the tuition provider with the highest pass rate.

5 The balanced scorecard

> **FAST FORWARD**
>
> The **balanced scorecard** approach to controlling and measuring performance focuses on four different perspectives and uses financial and non-financial indicators.

Although segments of a business may be measured by a single performance indicator such as ROI, profit, or cost variances, it might be more suitable to use multiple measures of performance where each measure reflects a **different aspect of achievement**. Where multiple measures are used, several may be **non-financial**.

The most popular approach in current management thinking is the use of a **'balanced scorecard'** consisting of a variety of indicators both financial and non-financial. It was devised by **Kaplan and Norton** ('The balanced scorecard: measures that drive performance', *Harvard Business Review*, 1992).

Key term

> The **balanced scorecard** approach emphasises the need to provide management with a set of information which covers all relevant areas of performance in an objective and unbiased fashion. The information provided may be both financial and non-financial and cover areas such as profitability, customer satisfaction, internal efficiency and innovation.

5.1 Perspectives

The balanced scorecard focuses on **four different perspectives**, as follows.

Perspective	Question	Explanation
Customer	What do existing and new customers value from us?	Gives rise to targets that matter to customers: cost, quality, delivery, inspection, handling and so on
Internal	What processes must we excel at to achieve our financial and customer objectives?	Aims to improve internal processes and decision-making
Innovation and learning	Can we continue to improve and create future value?	Considers the business's capacity to maintain its competitive position through the acquisition of new skills and the development of new products
Financial	How do we create value for our shareholders?	Covers traditional measures such as growth, profitability and shareholder value but set through talking to the shareholder or shareholders direct

Performance targets are set once the key areas for improvement have been identified, and the balanced scorecard is the main monthly report.

The scorecard is '**balanced**' as managers are required to think in terms of **all four** perspectives, to prevent improvements being made in one area at the expense of another.

5.2 Advantages and disadvantages

Important features of this approach are:

(a) It looks at both **internal and external** matters concerning the organisation.
(b) It is related to the key elements of a company's **strategy**.
(c) **Financial and non-financial** measures are linked together.

However, as with all techniques, problems can arise when it is applied.

Problem	Explanation
Conflicting measures	Some measures in the scorecard such as research funding and cost reduction may naturally conflict. It is often difficult to determine the balance which will achieve the best results.
Selecting measures	Not only do appropriate measures have to be devised but the number of measures used must be agreed. Care must be taken that the impact of the results is not lost in a sea of information.
Expertise	Measurement is only useful if it initiates appropriate action. Non-financial managers may have difficulty with the usual profit measures. With more measures to consider this problem will be compounded.
Interpretation	Even a financially-trained manager may have difficulty in putting the figures into an overall perspective.

The scorecard should be used **flexibly**. The process of deciding **what to measure** forces a business to clarify its strategy. For example, a manufacturing company may find that 50% – 60% of costs are represented by bought-in components, so measurements relating to suppliers could usefully be added to the scorecard. These could include payment terms, lead times, or quality considerations.

5.3 Example: Balanced scorecard

An example of how a balanced scorecard might appear is offered below.

Balanced scorecard

Financial perspective	
Goals	**Measures**
Survive	Cash flow
Succeed	Monthly sales growth and operating income by division
Prosper	Increase market share and ROI

Customer perspective	
Goals	**Measures**
New products	Percentage of sales from new products
Responsive supply	On-time delivery (defined by customer)
Preferred supplier	Share of key accounts' purchases
Customer partnership	Ranking by key accounts
	Number of co-operative engineering efforts

Internal business perspective	
Goals	**Measures**
Technology capability	Manufacturing configuration vs competition
Manufacturing excellence	Cycle time Unit cost Yield
New product introduction	Silicon efficiency Engineering efficiency
Design productivity	Actual introduction schedule vs plan

Innovation and learning perspective	
Goals	**Measures**
Technology leadership	Time to develop next generation of products
Manufacturing learning	Process time to maturity
Product focus	Percentage of products that equal 80% sales
Time to market	New product introduction vs competition

Question — Balanced scorecard

Growth in which of the following areas is most likely to be found as part of the internal perspective of the balanced scorecard?

A Professional development days
B Economies of scale
C Service excellence
D Market share of current products

Answer

B Economies of scale

These will increase as a result of changes in internal processes resulting from increased volume.

Professional development days will be part of the innovation and learning perspective. Service excellence is most likely to be found in the customer perspective. Market share of existing products will be part of the financial perspective.

6 Benchmarking

FAST FORWARD

> Operational effectiveness is vital in the delivery of customer satisfaction and maintaining profitability. This is why firms **benchmark** others in the same industry – although this may lead to imitation where differentiation would be more appropriate.

Key term

Benchmarking

Benchmarking is 'the establishment, through data gathering, of targets and comparators, through whose use relative levels of performance (and particularly areas of underperformance) can be identified. By the adoption of identified best practices it is hoped that performance will improve. Types of benchmarking include:

- **Internal benchmarking** A method of comparing one operating unit or function with another within the same industry.

- **Functional benchmarking** Internal functions are compared with those of the best external practitioners of those functions, regardless of the industry they are in (also known as operational benchmarking or generic benchmarking).

- **Competitive benchmarking** Information is gathered about direct competitors, through techniques such as reverse engineering.

- **Strategic benchmarking** A type of competitive benchmarking aimed at strategic action and organisational change.' (**CIMA** *Official Terminology*, 2005)

6.1 Advantages of benchmarking

(a) **Position audit**. Benchmarking can **assess a firm's existing position**.

(b) The comparisons are carried out by **the managers who have to live with any changes** implemented as a result of the exercise.

(c) Benchmarking **focuses on improvement in key areas** and sets targets which are challenging but **achievable**. What is really achievable can be discovered by examining what others have achieved: managers are thus able to accept that they are not being asked to perform miracles.

6.2 Dangers of benchmarking

(a) It **implies there is one best way** of doing business – arguably this boils down to the difference between efficiency and effectiveness. A process can be efficient but its output may not be useful. Other measures such as developing the value chain may be a better way of securing competitive advantage.

(b) The benchmark may be **yesterday's solution to tomorrow's problem**.

(c) It is a **catching-up exercise** rather than the development of anything distinctive. After the benchmarking exercise, the competitor might improve performance in a different way.

(d) It **depends on accurate information** about competitors, in the case of competitor benchmarking, or an **appropriate analogies** in other industries, in the case of process benchmarking.

(e) If **all firms provide the same standard of quality**, it **ceases to be a source of competitive advantage**.

(f) It is **not cost-free** and **diverts management attention**.

(g) It can become a **hindrance** and even a **threat**: sharing information can compromise **commercial security**.

To make benchmarking work, it is important to **compare like with like**.

6.3 Steps in a benchmarking process

Benchmarking can be divided into stages.

Stage 1

The first stage is to **ensure senior management commitment** to the benchmarking process. This will only be genuinely available when the senior managers have a full appreciation of what is involved.

Stage 2

The areas to be benchmarked should be determined and objectives should be set.

Stage 3

Key performance measures must be established. This will require an understanding of the systems involved, which, in turn, will require discussion with key stakeholders and observation of the way work is carried out.

Stage 4

Select organisations to benchmark against. Internal benchmarking may be possible where, for example, there are local shops. Where internal departments have little in common, comparisons must be made against equivalent parts of other organisations. The aim will be to find an organisation that does similar things but which is not in competition with the organisation.

Stage 5

Measure own and others' performance.

Stage 6

Compare performance. Raw data must be carefully analysed if appropriate conclusions are to be drawn.

Stage 7

Design and implement improvement programmes. It may be possible to import complete systems; alternatively, it may be appropriate to move towards a synthesis that combines various elements of best practice. Sometimes, improvements require extensive **reorganisation** and **restructuring**. In any event, there is likely to be a requirement for **training**. Improvements in administrative systems often call for investment in new equipment, particularly in IT systems.

Stage 8

Monitor improvements. The continuing effectiveness of improvements must be monitored. At the same time, it must be understood that **improvements are not once and for all** and that further adjustments may be beneficial.

When selecting an appropriate **benchmark basis**, companies should ask themselves the following questions.

(a) Is it possible and easy to obtain reliable competitor information?

(b) Is there any wide discrepancy between different internal divisions?

(c) Can similar processes be identified in non-competing environments and are these non-competing companies willing to co-operate?

(d) Is best practice operating in a similar environmental setting?

(e) What is our timescale?

(f) Do the chosen companies have similar objectives and strategies?

7 The management of inventory

FAST FORWARD

An **economic order quantity** can be calculated as a guide to minimising costs in managing **inventory** (or stock) levels. **Bulk discounts** can however mean that a different order quantity minimises inventory costs.

Almost every company carries inventory or stock of some sort, even if it is only consumables such as stationery. For a manufacturing business, inventory in the form of **raw materials**, **work in progress** and **finished goods** may amount to a substantial proportion of the total assets of the business.

Some businesses attempt to control inventory on a scientific basis by balancing the costs of inventory shortages against those of inventory holding. The 'scientific' control of inventory may be analysed into three parts:

(a) The **economic order quantity (EOQ) model** can be used to decide the optimum order size for inventory which will minimise the costs of ordering inventory plus holding costs.

(b) If **discounts for bulk purchases** are available, it may be cheaper to buy in large order sizes so as to obtain the discounts.

(c) Uncertainty in the demand for inventory and/or the supply lead time may lead a company to decide to hold **buffer inventory** in order to reduce or eliminate the risk of 'stock-outs'.

Stock costs	
Holding costs	The cost of capital Warehousing and handling costs Deterioration Obsolescence Insurance Pilferage
Procuring costs	Ordering costs Delivery costs
Shortage costs	Contribution from lost sales Extra cost of emergency stock Cost of lost production and sales in a stock-out
Cost of stock	Relevant particularly when calculating discounts

7.1 The basic EOQ formula

Key term

The **economic order quantity (EOQ)** is the optimal ordering quantity for an item of inventory which will minimise costs.

Let D = usage in units for one period (the demand)

P = purchase price per item
Co = cost of placing one order   } relevant costs only
C_H = holding cost per unit of inventory for one period
Q = reorder quantity

Assume that demand is constant, the lead time is constant or zero and purchase costs per unit are constant (ie no bulk discounts).

The total annual cost of having inventory is:

(a) Holding costs + ordering costs

$$\frac{Q \times C_H}{2} + \frac{Co \times D}{Q}$$

The more orders are made each year the higher the ordering costs, but the lower the holding costs (as less inventory is held).

(b) The objective is to minimise $T = \frac{Q \times C_H}{2} + \frac{Co \times D}{Q}$

The order quantity, EOQ, which will minimise these total costs is:

$$EOQ = \sqrt{\frac{2CoD}{C_H}}$$

7.2 Example: Economic order quantity

The demand for a commodity is 40,000 units a year, at a steady rate. It costs $20 to place an order, and 40c to hold a unit for a year. Find the order size to minimise inventory costs, the number of orders placed each year, and the length of the inventory cycle.

Solution

$$Q = \sqrt{\frac{2CoD}{C_H}} = \sqrt{\frac{2 \times 20 \times 40{,}000}{0.4}} = 2{,}000 \text{ units.}$$

This means that there will be:

$$\frac{40{,}000}{2{,}000} = 20 \text{ orders placed each year}$$

The inventory cycle is therefore:

$$\frac{52 \text{ weeks}}{20 \text{ orders}} = 2.6 \text{ weeks}$$

Total costs will be (20 × $20) + ((2,000/2) × 40c) = $800 a year

10: MANAGERIAL CONTROL

Question
Order quantity

Quarterly demand for Product Yx is 60,000 units. The monthly cost of holding a unit of Yx in stock is $4. Ordering costs of Product Yx are $25 per order.

What is the economic order quantity for product Yx?

- A 250 units
- B 500 units
- C 866 units
- D 1,732 units

Answer

B 500 units

EOQ = $\sqrt{(2 \times 25 \times 60,000 \times 4/(4 \times 12))}$ = 500 units

250 units is the answer if quarterly demand is not grossed up to annual demand. 866 units is the answer if quarterly demand is not grossed up to annual demand and monthly ordering costs are not grossed up to annual ordering costs. 1,732 units is the answer if monthly ordering costs are not grossed up to annual ordering costs.

7.3 Uncertainties in demand and lead times: A re-order level system

Uncertainties in demand and lead times taken to fulfil orders mean that inventory will be ordered once it reaches a reorder level (maximum usage × maximum lead time).

Key term

Reorder level is maximum usage × maximum lead time.

The reorder level is the measure of inventory at which a replenishment order should be made.

(a) If an order is placed **too late**, the organisation may run out of stock, resulting in a loss of sales and/or a loss of production.

(b) If an order is placed **too soon**, the organisation will hold too much inventory, and holding costs will be excessive.

Use of a reorder level builds in a measure of safety and minimises the risk of the organisation running out. This is particularly important when the volume of demand or the supply lead time are uncertain.

The **average annual** cost of such a safety inventory would be:

$$\frac{\text{Quantity of safety inventory}}{\text{(in units)}} \times \frac{\text{Inventory holding cost}}{\text{per unit per annum}}$$

7.4 Maximum and minimum inventory levels

Key term

Maximum inventory level is reorder level + reorder quantity − (minimum usage × minimum lead time).

The maximum level acts as a warning signal to management that inventories are reaching a potentially wasteful level.

PART D MANAGERIAL CONTROL: MANAGING INFORMATION SYSTEMS AND TECHNOLOGY

Key term

Minimum inventory level or **buffer safety inventory** is reorder level − (average usage × average lead time).

The minimum level acts as a warning to management that inventories are approaching a dangerously low level and that stock-outs are possible (ie the business could run out of inventory).

Key term

Average inventory = Minimum level + $\dfrac{\text{reorder level}}{2}$

This formula assumes that inventory levels fluctuate evenly between the minimum (or safety) inventory level and the highest possible inventory level (the amount of inventory immediately after an order is received, safety inventory and reorder quantity).

This approach assumes that a business wants to minimise the risk of stock-outs at all costs, as in the modern manufacturing environment stock-outs can have a disastrous effect on the production process.

If, however, you are given a question where the risk of stock-outs is assumed to be worth taking, and the costs of stock-outs are quantified, the reorder level may not be calculated in the way described above. For **each possible reorder level**, and therefore each **possible level** of buffer inventory, **calculate**:

- The **costs of holding buffer inventory** per annum
- The **costs of stock-outs** (cost of one stock-out × expected number of stock-outs per order × number of orders per year)

The expected number of stock-outs per order reflects the various levels by which demand during the lead time could exceed the reorder level.

7.5 Example: Possibility of stock-outs (1)

If reorder level is four units, but there was a probability of 0.2 that demand during the lead time would be five units, and 0.05 that demand during the lead time would be six units, then expected number of stock-outs = ((5 − 4) × 0.2) + ((6 − 4) × 0.05) = 0.3.

7.5.1 Demand normally distributed

Alternatively, you may be told that demand is normally distributed. If this is the case you need to know:

- Average weekly demand
- Standard deviation of demand
- Lead time
- Acceptable risk levels

Reorder level = (average weekly demand × lead time) + $x\sigma$

Where x = number of standard deviations that correspond to the chance business wishes to have of avoiding stock-outs

σ = standard deviation of demand

7.6 Example: Possibility of stock-outs (2)

Average weekly demand is 200 units, the standard deviation of demand (σ) is 40 units and demand is normally distributed. Lead time for orders is one week. What reorder levels should the business set if it wishes to have:

(a) A 90% chance
(b) A 95% chance
(c) A 99% chance

of avoiding running out of stock. The relevant values from normal distribution tables are respectively:

(a) 1.28
(b) 1.65
(c) 2.33

Solution

Reorder level = (average weekly demand × lead time) + xσ

(a) Reorder level = (200 × 1) + (1.28 × 40)
= 251.2 units

(b) Reorder level = 200 + (1.65 × 40)
= 266 units

(c) Reorder level = 200 + (2.33 × 40)
= 293.2 units

7.7 The effect of discounts

The solution obtained from using the simple EOQ formula may need to be modified if bulk discounts (also called quantity discounts) are available. To decide mathematically whether it would be worthwhile taking a discount and ordering larger quantities, it is necessary to minimise:

Total purchasing costs + ordering costs + stockholding costs

The total cost will be minimised:

- At the pre-discount EOQ level, so that a discount is not worthwhile; or
- At the minimum order size necessary to earn the discount.

7.8 Example: Bulk discounts

The annual demand for an item of inventory is 45 units. The item costs $200 a unit to purchase, the holding cost for one unit for one year is 15% of the unit cost and ordering costs are $300 an order. The supplier offers a 3% discount for orders of 60 units or more, and a discount of 5% for orders of 90 units or more. What is the cost-minimising order size?

Solution

(a) The EOQ ignoring discounts is:

$$\sqrt{\frac{2 \times 300 \times 45}{15\% \text{ of } 200}} = 30 \text{ units}$$

	$
Purchases (no discount) 45 × $200	9,000
Holding costs ($^{30}/_2$) 15 units × $30	450
Ordering costs 1.5 orders × $300	450
Total annual costs	9,900

(b) With a discount of 3% and an order quantity of 60 units costs are:

	$
Purchases $9,000 × 97%	8,730
Holding costs 30 units × 15% of 97% of $200	873
Ordering costs 0.75 orders × $300	225
Total annual costs	9,828

(c) With a discount of 5% and an order quantity of 90 units costs are:

	$
Purchases $9,000 × 95%	8,550.0

Holding costs 45 units × 15% of 95% of $200   1,282.5
Ordering costs 0.5 orders × $300   150.0
Total annual costs   9,982.5

The cheapest option is to order 60 units at a time.

Question   Bulk orders

A company uses an item of inventory as follows.

Purchase price:	$96 per unit
Annual demand:	4,000 units
Ordering cost:	$300
Annual holding cost:	10% of purchase price
Economic order quantity:	500 units

Should the company order 1,000 units at a time in order to secure an 8% discount?

Answer

The total annual cost at the economic order quantity of 500 units is:

	$
Purchases 4,000 × $96	384,000
Ordering costs $300 × (4,000/500)	2,400
Holding costs $96 × 10% × (500/2)	2,400
	388,800

The total annual cost at an order quantity of 1,000 units would be:

	$
Purchases $384,000 × 92%	353,280
Ordering costs $300 × (4,000/1,000)	1,200
Holding costs $96 × 92% × 10% × (1,000/2)	4,416
	358,896

The company should order 1,000 units at a time, saving $(388,800 − 358,896) = $29,904 a year.

7.9 Just-in-time (JIT) procurement

Some manufacturing companies have sought to reduce their inventories of raw materials and components to as low a level as possible. **Just-in-time procurement** describes a policy of obtaining goods from suppliers at the latest possible time (ie when they are needed) and so avoiding the need to carry any materials or components inventory. Introducing JIT might bring the following potential benefits.

- Reduction in inventory holding costs
- Reduced manufacturing lead times
- Improved labour productivity
- Reduced scrap/rework/warranty cost

Reduced inventory levels mean that a lower level of investment in working capital will be required.

JIT will not be appropriate in some cases. For example, a restaurant might find it preferable to use the traditional economic order quantity approach for staple non-perishable food inventory but adopt JIT for perishable and 'exotic' items. In a hospital, a stock-out could quite literally be fatal and so JIT would be quite unsuitable.

7.10 Inventory ratios

Key terms

$$\text{Inventory days} = \frac{\text{Average stock}}{\text{Cost of sales}} \times 365 \text{ days}$$

$$\text{Inventory turnover} = \frac{\text{Cost of sales}}{\text{Average stock}}$$

The optimum period of **inventory days** will vary industry by industry, and may vary for different lines held by the same firm.

A high inventory days or low inventory turnover figure may arise for various reasons. It may be that the firm is being excessively **prudent** in its stockholding policies, or it may be due to **obsolete** or **slow-moving** inventory.

An excessively low figure for **inventory days** or **high turnover** figure may also give cause for concern. It may indicate **supply difficulties**, and that there is a significant chance that the company will run out of inventory and hence lose sales.

Chapter roundup

- **Planning** involves making choices between alternatives and is primarily a decision-making activity. **Control** refers to the steps to be taken after measuring the results against the plan, and the response required for any divergences.

- The **planning and control cycle** has seven steps:

    Step 1 Identify **objectives**

    Step 2 Identify potential **strategies**

    Step 3 Evaluate strategies

    Step 4 Choose alternative courses of action

    Step 5 Implement the long-term plan

    Step 6 Measure actual results and compare with the plan

    Step 7 Respond to divergences from the plan

- **Control** is achieved through the **control cycle**. Actual performance is compared with planned performance and the appropriate action is taken for those items that are not proceeding according to plan.

- **Feedback** is the process of reporting back control information to management and the control information itself.

- **Feedforward** control is control based on comparing original targets or actual results with a forecast of future results.

- **Critical success factors** are those elements which are central to future success of the organisation strategy.

- A **key performance indicator** is a measure used to assess whether the CSFs are being achieved

- The **balanced scorecard** approach to performance measurement focuses on four different perspectives and uses financial and non-financial indicators.

- Operational effectiveness is vital in the delivery of customer satisfaction and maintaining profitability. This is why firms **benchmark** others in the same industry – although this may lead to imitation where differentiation would be more appropriate.

- An **economic order quantity** can be calculated as a guide to minimising costs in managing **inventory** levels. **Bulk discounts** can however mean that a different order quantity minimises inventory costs.

- **Uncertainties** in demand and lead times taken to fulfil orders mean that inventory will be ordered once it reaches a reorder level (maximum usage × maximum lead time).

Quick quiz

1 Put the following steps in the planning cycle in the correct order.

- Evaluate strategies
- Implement the long-term plan
- Identify objectives
- Choose alternative courses of action
- Identify potential strategies

2 A 'strategic audit' or 'position analysis' is an information gathering exercise carried out by an organisation to ensure that it has a full understanding of where it is now. True or False?

3 What question does an objective answer?

4 Complete the following steps in the control cycle.

Step 1..

Step 2..

Step 3..

Step 4..

Step 5..

Step 6..

    (a) ....

    (b) ....

    (c) ....

5 Match the following terms to the correct description.

Terms
- Programming
- Operating and measurement
- Reporting and analysis
- Feedback
- Budgets

Descriptions

(a) The cornerstone of management control and the management control system

(b) Collection of actual costs and outcomes identified to both programmes and responsibility centres

(c) Identification of the products a company intends to develop and projects which management intend to pursue to meet the organisation's overall goals

(d) Used to compare actual results with targets

(e) Used as a basis for control, for the coordination of activities and as a basis for future decisions perhaps to change the original plan

PART D MANAGERIAL CONTROL: MANAGING INFORMATION SYSTEMS AND TECHNOLOGY

6   Which of the following is a KPI?

    A   Producing quality products
    B   Achieving 15% market share in the coming year
    C   Improving staff retention
    D   Recruiting and training a new salesforce

7   Which of the following are the four perspectives of the balanced scorecard?

    A   Innovation and learning, customer, financial, competitive
    B   Financial, quality, innovation, internal business
    C   Internal business, financial, innovation and learning, customer
    D   Customer, quality, competitive, flexibility

8   The basic EOQ formula for inventory indicates whether bulk discounts should be taken advantage of. True or False?

9   Identify the potential benefits of JIT manufacturing.

10 PB Ltd uses 2,500 units of component X per year. The company has calculated that the cost of placing and processing a purchase order for component X is $185, and the cost of holding one unit of component X for a year is $25.

    What is the economic order quantity (EOQ) for component X, and assuming a 52-week year, what is the average frequency at which purchase orders should be placed?

11 The economic order quantity model can be used to determine:

Order quantity?	Buffer inventory?	Reorder level?
Yes/No	Yes/No	Yes/No

Answers to quick quiz

1. Identify objectives
   Identify potential strategies
   Evaluate strategies
   Choose alternative courses of action
   Implement the long-term plan

2. False. A 'position audit' or 'strategic analysis' is being described.

3. 'Where do we want to be?'

4. Step 1   Plans and targets are set for the future.
   Step 2   Plans are put into operation.
   Step 3   Actual results are recorded and analysed.
   Step 4   Information about actual results is fed back to management.
   Step 5   Management uses the feedback to compare actual results and targets.
   Step 6   The comparison leads management to do one of three things.

       (a) Take control action
       (b) Decide to do nothing
       (c) Alter the plan or target

5. Programming   (c)
   Operating and measurement   (b)
   Reporting and analysis   (e)
   Feedback   (d)
   Budgets   (a)

6. B: All of the other options are CSFs. Option B is the only one that is quantified

7. C: Internal business, financial, innovation and learning, customer

8. False. It may be necessary to modify the formula to take account of bulk discounts.

9. (a) Reduction in inventory holding costs
   (b) Reduced manufacturing lead times
   (c) Improved labour productivity
   (d) Reduced scrap/warranty/rework/costs
   (e) Price reductions on purchased materials
   (f) Reduction in the number of accounting transactions

10. C $EOQ = \sqrt{\dfrac{2C_o D}{C_h}}$

    $$\text{Economic order quantity} = \sqrt{\dfrac{2 \times 185 \times 2{,}500}{25}}$$

    $$= 192 \text{ units}$$

    $$\text{Frequency of ordering} = \dfrac{192}{2{,}500} \times 52 \text{ weeks}$$

    $$= 4 \text{ weeks}$$

11. The EOQ model finds order quantity only, not buffer inventory and reorder level.

PART D MANAGERIAL CONTROL: MANAGING INFORMATION SYSTEMS AND TECHNOLOGY

Organisational information requirements

Topic list	Syllabus reference
1 Information requirements	D4
2 The value of information	D4
3 Information management	D4
4 Information sources and capture	D4
5 Types of information system	D4
6 Information system security	D4
7 Systems development	D4

Introduction

We start by looking at what information an organisation requires to **operate** and **plan efficiently** and **effectively**; and how information can be used to **improve competitive advantage**.

Sections 2 to 4 look at the value and sources of information and the fact that, as a valuable resource, it needs to be managed.

A variety of information systems exist to help provide the different information organisations require and these are discussed in **Section 5**.

Section 6 considers the need for security controls to protect data and information.

Section 7 looks at the need for a structured approach to developing computer systems.

1 Information requirements

Key terms

> **Data** are simple facts that can be organised in a way that creates **information**.
>
> **Information** is data that has been processed in such a way as to be meaningful to the person who receives it.

FAST FORWARD

> All organisations require information for a range of **purposes** including **planning, controlling, recording transactions, performance measurement** and **decision-making**.

1.1 Planning

Planning requires a knowledge of the available resources, possible time-scales and the likely outcome under alternative scenarios. Information is required that helps **decision-making**, and how to implement decisions taken.

1.2 Controlling

Once a plan is implemented, its actual performance must be controlled. Information is required to assess **whether it is proceeding as planned** or whether there is some unexpected deviation from plan. It may consequently be necessary to take some form of corrective action.

1.3 Recording transactions

Information **about each transaction or event** is required. Reasons include:

(a) Documentation of transactions can be used as **evidence** in a case of dispute.

(b) There may be a **legal requirement** to record transactions, for example for accounting and audit purposes.

(c) **Operational information** can be built-up, allowing control action to be taken.

1.4 Performance measurement

Just as individual operations need to be controlled, so overall performance must be measured. **Comparisons against budget or plan** can be made. This may involve the collection of information on, for example, costs, revenues, volumes, time-scale and profitability.

1.5 Decision-making

FAST FORWARD

> **Strategic planning, management control** and **operational control** may be seen as a **hierarchy** of planning and control decisions.

As we have already seen earlier in this text, strategic planning, management control and operational control may be seen as a hierarchy of planning and control decisions.

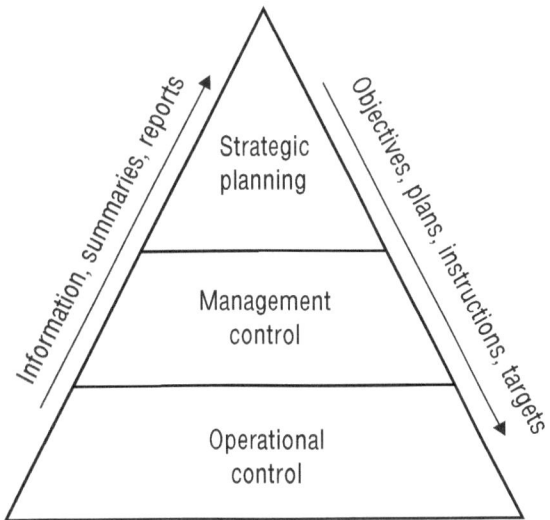

1.5.1 Strategic information

Strategic information is used to **plan** the **objectives** of the organisation, and to assess whether the objectives are being met in practice. Such information includes overall profitability, the profitability of different segments of the business, future market prospects, the availability and cost of raising new funds, total cash needs, total manning levels and capital equipment needs.

Strategic information is:

- Derived from both **internal and external** sources
- **Summarised** at a high level
- Relevant to the **long-term**
- Concerned with the **whole organisation**
- Often prepared on an ad hoc basis
- Both **quantitative and qualitative**
- **Uncertain**, as the future cannot be accurately predicted

1.5.2 Tactical information

Tactical information is used to decide **how the resources of the business should be employed**, and to **monitor** how they are being and have been employed. Such information includes productivity measurements (output per hour) budgetary control or variance analysis reports, and cash flow forecasts, staffing levels and profit results within a particular department of the organisation, labour turnover statistics within a department and short-term purchasing requirements.

Tactical information is:

- Primarily generated internally (but may have a limited external component)
- **Summarised at a lower level**
- Relevant to the **short- and medium-term**
- Concerned with **activities or departments**
- Prepared **routinely and regularly**
- Based on **quantitative** measures

1.5.3 Operational information

Operational information is used to ensure that **specific operational tasks** are planned and carried out as intended.

In the payroll office, for example, operational information relating to day-rate labour will include the hours worked each week by each employee, the rate of pay per hour, details of deductions, and for the purpose of wages analysis, details of the time each employee spent on individual jobs during the week. In this example, the information is required weekly, but more urgent operational information, such as the amount of raw materials being input to a production process, may be required daily, hourly, or in the case of automated production, second by second.

Operational information is:

- Derived from **internal** sources
- **Detailed**, being the processing of raw data
- Relevant to the **immediate term**
- **Task-specific**
- Prepared very **frequently**
- Largely **quantitative**

It may help to clarify the above to consider it in terms of how well **structured** the problem situation is. Examples of unstructured and structured decisions at the different levels of management are given in the following table.

	Example of a structured decision	Example of a semi-structured decision	Example of an unstructured decision
Operational level	Devising inventory control procedures	Selecting a new supplier	Employing a supervisor
Tactical level	Selecting products to discount	Budget calculation and allocation	Expanding into a new design
Strategic level	Major investment decisions	Entering a new market; producing a new product line	Restructuring the organisation

1.5.4 Bounded rationality

The concept of bounded rationality suggests that at whatever level managers are taking decisions, they will try to do so rationally, but may be limited by not being able to analyse all possible information or all possible decision options. This will mean that they opt for solutions that are acceptable (known as satisficing) rather than the best possible solution (maximising).

Question

Information systems

Which of the following is an example of an operational level information system?

- A Order tracking
- B Production scheduling
- C Quarterly budgeting
- D Human resource planning

Answer

A Order tracking

Order tracking relates to day-to-day transactions.

Production scheduling and quarterly budgeting relate to activity over a time period, so are managerial level systems. Human resource planning takes place over the longer-term, so is a strategic system.

1.6 The qualities of good information

> **FAST FORWARD**
>
> 'Good' information aids **understanding**. ACCURATE is a handy mnemonic for the qualities of good information.

'Good' information is information that adds to the understanding of a situation. The qualities of good information are outlined in the following table.

Quality	Example
Accurate	Figures should add up, the degree of rounding should be appropriate, there should be no typos, items should be allocated to the correct category, assumptions should be stated for uncertain information.
Complete	Information should includes everything that it needs to include, for example external data if relevant, or comparative information.
Cost-beneficial	It should not cost more to obtain the information than the benefit derived from having it. Providers or information should be given efficient means of collecting and analysing it. Presentation should be such that users do not waste time working out what it means.
User-targeted	The needs of the user should be borne in mind, for instance senior managers need summaries, junior ones need detail.
Relevant	Information that is not needed for a decision should be omitted, no matter how 'interesting' it may be.
Authoritative	The source of the information should be a reliable one (not, for instance, 'Joe Bloggs Predictions Page' on the internet, unless Joe Bloggs is known to be a reliable source for that type of information).
Timely	The information should be available when it is needed.
Easy to use	Information should be clearly presented, not excessively long, and sent using the right medium and communication channel (email, telephone, hard-copy report etc).

1.7 Improvements to information

The following table contains suggestions as to how poor information can be improved.

Feature	Example of possible improvements
Accurate	Use computerised systems with automatic input checks rather than manual systems.
	Allow sufficient time for collation and analysis of data if pinpoint accuracy is crucial.
	Incorporate elements of probability within projections so that the required response to different future scenarios can be assessed.
Complete	Include past data as a reference point for future projections.
	Include any planned developments, such as new products.
	Information about future demand would be more useful than information about past demand.
	Include external data.
Cost-beneficial	Always bear in mind whether the benefit of having the information is greater than the cost of obtaining it.

Feature	Example of possible improvements
User-targeted	Information should be summarised and presented together with relevant ratios or percentages.
Relevant	The purpose of the report should be defined. It may be trying to fulfil too many purposes at once. Perhaps several shorter reports would be more effective. Information should include exception reporting, where only those items that are worthy of note – and the control actions taken by more junior managers to deal with them – are reported.
Authoritative	Use reliable sources and experienced personnel. If some figures are derived from other figures the method of derivation should be explained.
Timely	Information collection and analysis by production managers needs to be speeded up considerably, probably by the introduction of better information systems
Easy-to-use	Graphical presentation, allowing trends to be quickly assimilated and relevant action decided upon. Alternative methods of presentation should be considered, such as graphs or charts, to make it easier to review the information at a glance. Numerical information is sometimes best summarised in narrative form or vice versa. A 'house style' for reports should be devised and adhered to by all. This would cover such matters as number of decimal places to use, table headings and labels, paragraph numbering and so on.

1.8 Information requirements in different sectors

The following table provides examples of the typical information requirements of organisations operating in different sectors.

Sector	Information type	Example(s)	General comment
Manufacturing	Strategic	Future demand estimates New product development plans Competitor analysis	The information requirements of commercial organisations are influenced by the need to make and monitor profit. Information that contributes to the following measures is important: • Changeover times • Number of common parts • Level of product diversity • Product and process quality
	Tactical	Variance analysis Departmental accounts Inventory turnover	
	Operational	Production reject rate Materials and labour used Inventory levels	

Sector	Information type	Example(s)	General comment
Service	Strategic	Forecast sales growth and market share Profitability, capital structure	Organisations have become more customer and results-orientated over the last decade. As a consequence, the difference between service and other organisation's information requirements has decreased. Businesses have realised that most of their activities can be measured, and many can be measured in similar ways regardless of the business sector.
	Tactical	Resource utilisation such as average staff time charged out, number of customers per hairdresser, number of staff per account Customer satisfaction rating	
	Operational	Staff timesheets Customer waiting time Individual customer feedback	
Public	Strategic	Population demographics Expected government policy	Public sector (and non-profit-making) organisations often don't have one overriding objective. Their information requirements depend on the objectives chosen. The information provided often requires interpretation (eg student exam results are not affected by the quality of teaching alone). Information may compare actual performance with: Standards Targets Similar activities Indices Activities over time as trends
	Tactical	Hospital occupancy rates Average class sizes Per cent of reported crimes solved	
	Operational	Staff timesheets Vehicles available Student daily attendance records	

Sector	Information type	Example(s)	General comment
Non-profit/charities	Strategic	Activities of other charities Government (and in some cases overseas government) policy Public attitudes	Many of the comments regarding Public Sector organisations can be applied to not-for-profit organisations. Information to judge performance usually aims to assess economy, efficiency and effectiveness. A key measure of efficiency for charities is the percentage of revenue that is spent on the publicised cause (eg rather than on advertising or administration).
	Tactical	Per cent of revenue spent on administration Average donation 'Customer' satisfaction statistics	
	Operational	Households collected from / approached Banking documentation Donations	

1.9 Strategic value of information

Information and information systems can be used as a source of competitive advantage.

- Capturing data about customers from web sites and loyalty schemes may help **understand purchasing patterns and allow better tailoring of products/services** to customer needs, hence improving revenue streams.

- IT can be used to **reduce costs** across the company eg improved supply chain management, more efficient production scheduling and control, online ordering.

- Improved communication increases the ability to co-**ordinate and control** geographically widespread activities and facilitates activities such as outsourcing and the use of strategic alliances.

- Technology can be used to **improve response times and increase customer service levels.**

- The widespread availability of accurate and up-to-date information provides benefits in terms of **managerial decision-making** – better information about trends in the external environment, analysis of competitors

2 The value of information

FAST FORWARD

> The **cost and value** of information are often not easy to quantify – but attempts should be made to do so.

Information is now recognised as a valuable resource, and a **key tool in the quest for a competitive advantage**. Easy **access** to information, the quality of that information and **speedy methods of exchanging** the information have become essential elements of business success.

Organisations that make **good use of information** in decision-making, and which use new technologies to access, process and exchange information are likely to be **best placed to survive** in increasingly competitive world markets.

Unlike certain commodities the value of **information in general** is **not** based on **scarcity**: indeed the most frequent complaint of many modern managers is that there is **far too much of it about**.

Moreover, the value of information is **in the eyes of the beholder** to some extent: information about a new type of plastic may be of keen interest and value to a car manufacturer, but of no value whatsoever to a software house.

2.1 Factors that make information a valuable commodity

The **factors which make information valuable** are:

(a) The **source** of the information

If the information comes from a source that is widely known and respected for quality, thoroughness and accuracy it will be more valuable to users than information from an unknown or untested source, because it can be relied upon with confidence.

(b) The **ease of assimilation**

Modern methods of presentation can use not only words and figures but also **colour**, **graphics**, **sound and movement**. This makes the receipt of information a richer (and so more valuable) experience, and it means that information can be more easily, and therefore more quickly, understood: again a feature that people will be willing to pay for.

(c) **Accessibility**

If information can be made available in an easily accessible place (such as the **internet**) users do not have to commit too much time and effort to retrieve it. If just a few sentences of information is required, and they can find these (for instance using an internet search engine) without having to buy a whole book or newspaper, then they should be willing to pay for this convenience. With the rise of data analytics and developments in software, companies can now monitor the most popular items or issues that are trending online, which could provide valuable information for marketing strategies or other stakeholder communications.

2.2 The value of obtaining information

In spite of its value in a general sense, information which is **obtained but not used** has no actual value to the person that obtains it. It is only the **action taken** as a result of a decision which realises actual value for a company. An item of information which leads to an actual increase in profit of $90 is not worth having if it costs $100 to collect.

Question — Assessing information value

The value of information lies in the action taken as a result of receiving it. What questions might you ask in order to make an assessment of the value of information?

Answer

(a) What information is provided?
(b) What is it used for?
(c) Who uses it?
(d) How often is it used?
(e) Does the frequency with which it is used coincide with the frequency of provision?
(f) What is achieved by using it?
(g) What other relevant information is available which could be used instead?

An assessment of the value of information can be derived in this way, and the cost of obtaining it should then be compared against this value. On the basis of this comparison, it can be decided whether certain items of information are worth having. It should be remembered that there may also be intangible benefits which may be harder to quantify.

Deciding whether it is worthwhile having more information should depend on the **marginal benefits** expected from getting it and the **extra costs** of obtaining it. The benefits of more information should be measured in terms of the difference it would make to management decisions if the information were made available.

2.3 Assessing cost and value

The information system is used to produce a wide variety of information. The cost of an individual item of information is **not always easy to quantify**. For example, if a manager uses an ESS (executive support system) to enquire into the company's database, what is the cost of this enquiry?

(a) The information is **already existent anyway**, as it is used for a number of different purposes. It might be impossible to predict how often it will be used, and hence the economic benefits to be derived from it.

(b) The information system which is used to process these requests has also been purchased. Its **cost is largely fixed**.

Just as the costs of an item of information are harder to assess than might appear superficially, so too the **benefits are often hard to quantify**. While nobody doubts that information is vital, it is not always easy to construct an economic assessment of the value of information.

(a) A monthly variance analysis will only generate economically consequential decisions if there is some **control failure** leading to variances, and control failures are not easy to predict.

(b) The economic consequences of a decision are **not always easy to predict**.

2.3.1 Traditional investment appraisal methods

Traditional **investment appraisal methods** can be applied with varying degrees of success to problems of this kind. The principal methods of evaluating a capital project are:

- Payback method (time taken for incremental cash flows to repay the initial investment)
- Accounting rate of return (accounting profit as a percentage of initial investment)
- Net present value (is a project profitable in today's terms?)
- Internal rate of return (the discount rate required to achieve a zero net present value on the initial investment)

Exam focus point

Application of these investment appraisal techniques is outside the syllabus.

2.4 The benefits of a proposed information system

The benefits from a proposed information system should be evaluated against the costs. To quantify the benefits several factors need to be considered.

(a) **Increased turnover**

Improved data collection, storage and analysis tools may indicate previously unknown opportunities for sales. Such tools may include **data-mining** software, which allows relationships to be discovered between previously unrelated data.

(b) **Cost reduction**

New technology can be used to automate previously manually intensive work. This saves staff time and may result in a smaller workforce being required.

Systems such as inventory control can benefit as losses from obsolescence and deterioration are reduced.

(c) **Enhanced service**

Computerised systems that create a more prompt and reliable service will increase customer satisfaction. In some cases it may be a source of **competitive advantage**.

(d) **Improved decision-making**

Providing decision-makers with the most accurate and up-to-date information that is possible can have substantial benefits such as:

(i) **Forecasting**

Models can be created to forecast sales trends and the likely affect on costs. Organisations that can make accurate forecasts are in a better position to plan their structure and finances to ensure long-term success.

(ii) **Developing scenarios**

Organisations facing uncertain times, or those which operate in dynamic, evolving environments, need to make complex decisions (often quickly) to take advantage of opportunities or to avoid threats. Scenario-planning models enable a wide range of variables to be changed (such as inflation rates or sales numbers), the overall effect on the business to be identified and a business plan to be constructed.

(iii) **Market analysis**

Modelling can be extended into the market that the organisation operates in. Trends such as sales volumes, prices and demand can be analysed. Relationships between price and sales volume can be identified. These can be used by an organisation when deciding on a pricing strategy. Setting the best price for a product can help drive up sales and profitability.

(iv) **Project evaluation**

Organisations will benefit from improved decision-making where systems can accurately evaluate a wide range of projects. Investment decisions often involve large capital outlays and if the system prevents bad decisions it can prevent the organisation wasting large sums of money.

Systems can also prevent an organisation agreeing 'bad' deals. Tenders for suppliers or other long-term contracts can prove costly if the wrong choice is made.

3 Information management

FAST FORWARD

Information is a **valuable resource** that requires efficient **management**.

Information should be managed just like any other valuable organisational resource.

Key term

Information management (IM) refers to the basic approach an organisation has to the management of its information systems, including:

- Planning IS/IT developments
- Organisational environment of IS
- Control
- Technology

3.1 Information management tasks

Information management entails the following tasks:

(a) Identifying current and future **information needs**

(b) Identifying information **sources**

(c) **Collecting** the information

(d) **Storing** the information

(e) **Facilitating** existing methods of using information and identifying new ways of using it

(f) Ensuring that information is **communicated** to those who need it, and is **not communicated** to those who are not entitled to see it

Technology has provided new sources of information, new ways of collecting it, storing it and processing it, and new methods of communicating and sharing it. This in turn has meant that information needs have changed and will continue to change as new technologies become available.

3.1.1 Responsibility for information management

In a small company or organisation information systems may be the responsibility of the finance director or the company secretary or simply an office manager. In larger organisations there may be a dedicated information director.

Whatever the case, the manager in charge of information systems needs the following skills:

- General management ability
- An understanding of organisational activities and functions
- Technical expertise in developing and running information systems

The information systems manager is responsible for ensuring that the organisation's acquisition and use of information technology and computer systems fits the goals and objectives of the organisation as a whole. The **information systems strategy** should tie in with the overall organisation strategy.

Question

The use of information

Drawing on personal experience (if possible), give examples of the inefficient production or use of information.

Answer

Some examples are:

(a) Information which is collected but not needed
(b) Information stored long after it is needed
(c) Useful information which is inaccessible to potential users
(d) Information disseminated more widely than is necessary
(e) Inefficient methods used to collect, analyse, store and retrieve information
(f) Collection of the same information by more than one group of people
(g) Duplication of the same information

3.2 Users of information

The information generated by an organisation may be used internally or externally.

Internal users of information include (by status) the following.

- The board (or equivalent)
- Directors with functional responsibilities
- Divisional general managers
- Divisional heads
- Departmental heads
- Section leaders, supervisors
- Employees

Question — External information users

Information is often required by people outside the organisation for making judgements and decisions relating to an organisation. Give four examples of decisions which may be taken by outsiders.

Answer

There are many possible suggestions, including those given below.

(a) The organisation's **bankers** take decisions affecting how much they are prepared to lend.
(b) The **public** might be interested in information about an organisation's products or services.
(c) The **media** (press, television etc) use information generated by organisations in news stories, and such information can adversely or favourably affect an organisation's relationship with its environment.
(d) The **government** (for example the Department for Business, Energy and Industrial Strategy in the UK) regularly requires organisational information.
(e) **HM Revenue and Customs** in the UK requires information for taxation and VAT assessments.
(f) An organisation's **suppliers** and customers take decisions whether or not to trade with the organisation.

3.3 Information infrastructure

The information systems manager may be responsible for the overall design of an organisation's information systems. This responsibility is likely to be delegated on a day-to-day basis. Furthermore, the information systems manager should ensure that IT systems activities undertaken by users should first, satisfy **user demands** and second, **not be sub-optimal** to the overall system goals and organisational objectives.

This activity will include overall responsibility for the construction of an **information infrastructure** comprising:

- **Technical** standards
- **Software** standards
- Establishment of **corporate databases**
- Providing an information systems **service function**

3.4 Liaison

Liaison between information systems professionals and the **rest of the organisation** is a key role. Such functions include:

(a) Provision of **technical assistance**

(b) Informal discussions with **users as to their needs** before detailed feasibility studies are carried out, which can also include discussions as to the payoffs of a particular IS investment

(c) Advice on the impact of information systems on **organisational structure**, **working environment** and so forth

3.5 The environment

Interaction with the environment is important. This is essential for a strategic perspective. An organisation's information systems can affect the way it trades, as there are a growing number of **information systems connections between different organisations** (eg Electronic Data Interchange). The information systems manager will seek to dovetail these types of facility into the organisation's overall commercial strategy.

Links with external organisations can also be important if the organisation takes over another. **Incompatible information systems** between merged organisations can add significantly to the cost of the merger. Information system **flexibility** is therefore a desirable aim. A suitable approach to public relations is desirable to convince customers and suppliers of the benefits to them of new information systems.

The information systems manager will gather information relating to the **legal environment of information systems**. This includes handling the impact of data protection legislation, rules governing cross-border dataflows, and ensuring that other areas of legislation are accounted for in information systems development.

3.6 Constraints on strategy development

There are a variety of problems facing senior information systems managers, and their job may require them to implement the organisation's information systems strategy within the framework of certain inevitable constraints.

- Shortage of skilled staff
- Backlogs in application development due to previous time over-runs
- The pressure for continued expansion

3.7 Two worlds

To summarise, the information systems manager needs to be able to travel between two worlds: the **organisation as a whole**, its culture, internal politics and strategic objectives, and the specialised world of **information technology**.

(a) The information systems manager, and his or her subordinates, should therefore be able to devise relevant **technical solutions** to identified problems.

(b) The information systems manager must also be a **propagandist**. The information systems manager should make sure that IT is an important issue for senior management involvement and understanding.

4 Information sources and capture

> **FAST FORWARD**
>
> Data and **information** come from **sources** both **inside** and **outside** an organisation. An organisation's information systems should be designed so as to obtain – or **capture** – all the relevant data and information required.

4.1 Internal information

Capturing data and information from inside the organisation involves designing a system for collecting or measuring data and information which sets out procedures for:

- What data and information is collected
- How frequently
- By whom
- By what methods
- How data and information is processed, filed and communicated

4.1.1 The accounting records

The accounting ledgers provide an excellent source of information regarding what has happened in the past. This information may be used as a basis for predicting future events eg budgeting.

4.1.2 Other internal sources

Much information that is not strictly part of the accounting records nevertheless is closely tied in to the accounting system.

(a) Information about **personnel** will be linked to the **payroll** system. Additional information may be obtained from this source if, say, a project is being costed and it is necessary to ascertain the availability and rate of pay of different levels of staff, or the need for and cost of recruiting staff from outside the organisation.

(b) Much information will be produced by a **production** department about machine capacity, fuel consumption, movement of people, materials, and work in progress, set-up times, maintenance requirements and so on. A large part of the traditional work of cost accounting involves ascribing costs to the **physical information** produced by this source.

(c) Many **service** businesses, notably accountants and solicitors, need to keep detailed records of the **time spent** on various activities, both to justify fees to clients and to assess the efficiency and profitability of operations.

Staff themselves are one of the primary sources of internal information. Information may be obtained either informally in the course of day-to-day business or through meetings, interviews or questionnaires.

4.1.3 External information

Formal collection of data from outside sources includes the following.

(a) A company's **tax specialists** will be expected to gather information about changes in tax law and how this will affect the company.

(b) Obtaining information about any new legislation on health and safety at work, or employment regulations, must be the responsibility of a particular person – eg the company's **legal expert** or **company secretary** – who must then pass on the information to other managers affected by it.

(c) Research and development (R&D) work often relies on information about other R&D work being done by another company or by government institutions. An **R & D official** might be made responsible for finding out about R&D work in the company.

(d) **Marketing managers** need to know about the opinions and buying attitudes of potential customers. To obtain this information, they might carry out market research exercises.

External information is available from a wide range of sources:

(a) The Government.
(b) Advice or information bureaux, eg Reuters.
(c) Consultants.
(d) Newspaper and magazine publishers.
(e) There may be specific reference works which are used in a particular line of work.
(f) Libraries and information services.
(g) Increasingly businesses can use each other's systems as sources of information, for instance via extranets or electronic data interchange (EDI).
(h) **Electronic sources** of information are becoming increasingly important.
   (i) Companies such as **Reuters** operate primarily in the field of provision of information.
   (ii) The **internet** is a vast source of information. We look at big data in Chapter 11.

Key terms

> The phrase **environmental scanning** is often used to describe the process of gathering external information.
>
> **Data mining** refers specifically to analysing databases to discover patterns and new information.

4.2 Efficient data collection

To produce meaningful information it is first necessary to capture the underlying data. The method of **data collection** chosen will depend on the nature of the **organisation**, **cost** and **efficiency**.

4.3 Data warehouses

Key term

> A **data warehouse** consists of a database containing data from various systems and reporting and query tools.

A data warehouse is a large-scale data collection and storage area containing data from various operational systems, plus reporting and query tools which allow the data to be analysed. The key feature of a data warehouse is that it provides a single point for storing information, which can then be used across an entire organisation for management analysis and decision-making.

For example, if a supermarket introduces a customer credit card, the history of customers' transactions on their cards could be stored in a data warehouse so that management could analyse spending patterns.

5 Types of information system

FAST FORWARD

Organisations require **different types of information system** to provide **different levels of information** in a **range of functional areas**.

A modern organisation requires a **wide range of systems** to hold, process and analyse information. We will now examine the various information systems used to serve organisational information requirements.

Organisations require different types of information system to provide different **levels of information** in a range of functional areas. One way of portraying this concept is shown in the following diagram (**Laudon and Laudon**, *Management Information Systems*, 2013).

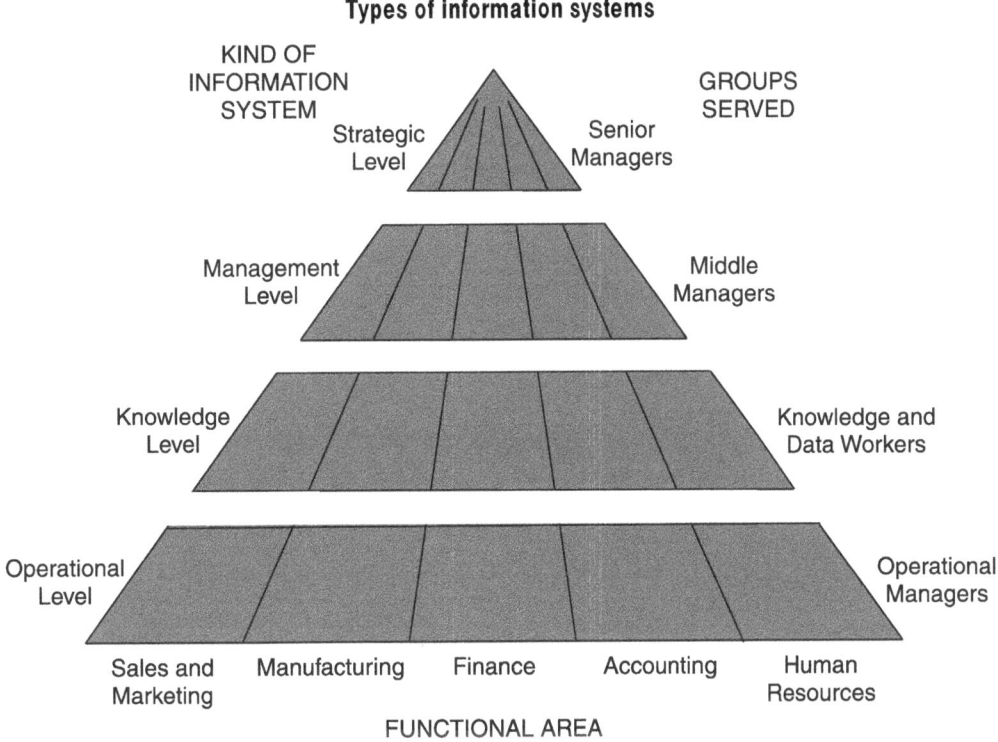

Types of information systems

System level	System purpose
Strategic	To help senior managers with long-term planning. Their main function is to ensure changes in the external environment are matched by the organisation's capabilities.
Management	To help middle managers monitor and control. These systems check if things are working well or not. Some management-level systems support non-routine decision making such as 'what if?' analyses.
Knowledge	To help knowledge and data workers design products, distribute information and perform administrative tasks. These systems help the organisation integrate new and existing knowledge into the business and to reduce the reliance on paper documents.
Operational	To help operational managers track the organisation's day-to-day operational activities. These systems enable routine queries to be answered, and transactions to be processed and tracked.

Systems can be classified under these systems as follows:

TYPES OF SYSTEMS	Strategic-level systems				
Executive support systems (ESS)	5-year sales trend forecasting	5-year operating plan	5-year budget forecasting	Profit planning	Human resource planning

	Management-level systems				
Management information systems (MIS)	Sales management	Inventory control	Annual budgeting	Capital investment analysis	Relocation analysis
decision support systems (DSS)	Sales region analysis	Production scheduling	Cost analysis	Pricing/ profitability analysis	Contract cost analysis

	Knowledge-level systems		
Knowledge work systems (KWS)	Engineering workstations	Graphics workstations	Managerial workstations
Office automation systems (OAS)	Word processing	Document imaging	Electronic calendars

	Operational-level systems				
Transaction processing systems (TPS)		Machine control	Securities trading	Payroll	Compensation
	Order tracking	Plant scheduling		Accounts payable	Training & development
	Order processing	Material movement control	Cash management	Accounts receivable	Employee record-keeping
	Sales and marketing	Manufacturing	Finance	Accounting	Human resources

5.1 Executive support systems (ESS)

Key term

An **executive support system (ESS)** pools data from internal and external sources and makes information available to senior managers in an easy-to-use form. ESS help senior managers make strategic, unstructured decisions.

An ESS should provide senior managers with easy access to key **internal and external** information. The system summarises and tracks strategically critical information, possibly drawn from internal MIS and DSS, but also including data from external sources, eg competitors, legislation, external databases such as Reuters.

An ESS is likely to have the following features.

- Flexibility
- Quick response time
- Sophisticated data analysis and modelling tools

A model of a typical ESS is shown below.

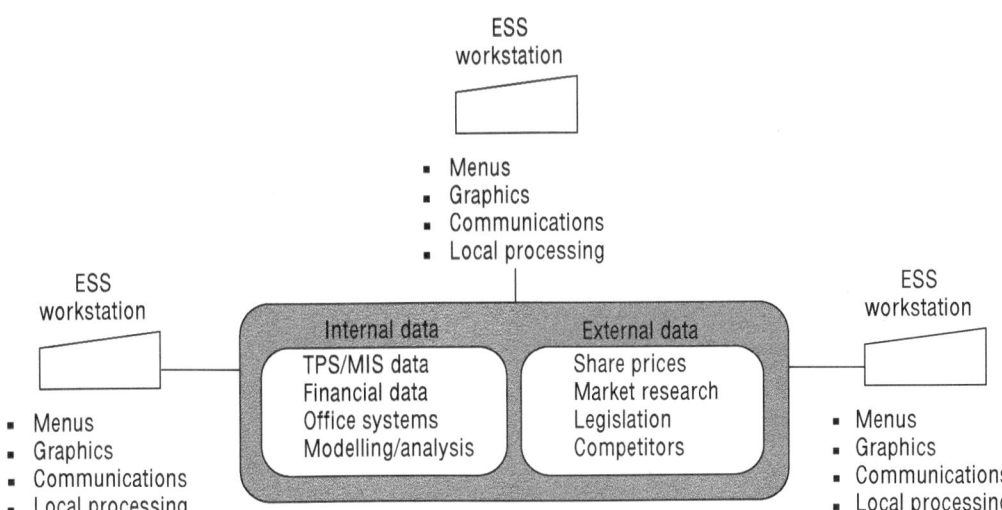

An Executive Support System (ESS)

5.2 Management information systems (MIS)

Key term

Management information systems (MIS) convert data from mainly internal sources into information (eg summary reports, exception reports). This information enables managers to make timely and effective decisions for planning, directing and controlling the activities for which they are responsible.

An MIS provides regular reports and (usually) online access to the organisation's current and historical performance.

MIS usually transform data from underlying transaction processing systems into summarised files that are used as the basis for management reports.

MIS have the following characteristics:

- Support **structured** decisions at operational and management control levels
- Designed to report on existing operations
- Have little analytical capability
- Relatively **inflexible**
- Have an internal focus

Exam focus point

You may see the term **MIS** as an umbrella term for **all information systems** within an organisation.

5.3 Decision support systems (DSS)

Key term

Decision support systems (DSS) combine data and analytical models or data analysis tools to support semi-structured and unstructured decision-making.

DSS are used by management to assist in making decisions on issues which are subject to high levels of uncertainty about the problem, the various **responses** which management could undertake or the likely **impact** of those actions.

Decision support systems are intended to provide a wide range of alternative information gathering and analytical tools with a major emphasis upon **flexibility** and **user-friendliness**.

DSS have more analytical power than other systems enabling them to analyse and condense large volumes of data into a form that aids managers make decisions. The objective is to allow the manager to consider a number of **alternatives** and evaluate them under a variety of potential conditions.

5.3.1 Expert systems

Key term

> **Expert systems** are a form of DSS that allow users to benefit from expert knowledge and information. Such systems consist of a **database** holding specialised data and **rules** about what to do in, or how to interpret, a given set of circumstances.

For example, many financial institutions now use expert systems to process straightforward **loan applications**. The user enters certain key facts into the system such as the loan applicant's name, their most recent addresses, their income, monthly outgoings and details of other loans. The system will then:

(a) **Check the facts** given against its database to see whether the applicant has a good credit record.

(b) **Perform calculations** to see whether the applicant can afford to repay the loan.

(c) **Match up other criteria** such as whether the security offered for the loan or the purpose for which the loan is wanted is acceptable and the applicant's is risk profile. The system makes these judgements based on previous experience (as represented within the system).

A decision is then suggested, based on the results of this processing. This is why it is possible to get a loan or arrange insurance **over the telephone**.

There are many other **business applications** of expert systems:

(a) **Legal** advice

(b) **Tax** advice

(c) **Forecasting** of economic or financial developments, or of market and customer behaviour

(d) **Surveillance**, eg of the number of customers entering a supermarket to decide when more checkouts need to be opened – or of machines in a factory, to determine when they need maintenance

(e) **Diagnostic systems** to identify causes of problems, for example in production control in a factory, or in healthcare

(f) **Project management**. Knowledge-based expert systems can be used in project monitoring and control. Such systems use computer programs that can undertake intelligent tasks usually performed by highly skilled people

(g) **Education** and **training**, diagnosing a student's or worker's weaknesses and providing or recommending extra instruction as appropriate

An organisation can use an expert system when a number of **conditions** are met:

(a) The problem is reasonably **well-defined**.

(b) The expert can **define some rules** by which the problem can be solved.

(c) The problem **cannot be solved by conventional transaction processing or data handling**.

(d) The expert could be **released to more difficult problems**. Experts are often highly paid, meaning the value of even small time savings is likely to be significant.

(e) The investment in an expert system is **cost-justified**.

5.4 Knowledge work systems (KWS)

Key terms

Knowledge work systems (KWS) are information systems that facilitate the creation and integration of new knowledge into an organisation.

Knowledge workers are people whose jobs consist of primarily creating new information and knowledge. They are often members of a profession such as doctors, engineers, lawyers and scientists.

KWS help knowledge workers create new knowledge and expertise.

Examples include:

- Computer-aided design (CAD)
- Computer-aided manufacturing (CAM)
- Specialised financial software that analyses trading situations

5.5 Office automation systems (OAS)

Key term

Office automation systems (OAS) are computer systems designed to increase the productivity of data and information workers.

OAS support the major activities performed in a typical office such as document management, facilitating communication and managing data.

Examples include:

- Word processing, desktop publishing, and digital filing systems
- Email, voice mail, videoconferencing, groupware, intranets, schedulers
- Spreadsheets, desktop databases

5.6 Transaction processing systems (TPS)

Key term

A transaction processing system (TPS) performs and records routine transactions.

TPS are used for routine tasks in which data items or transactions must be processed so that operations can continue. TPS support most business functions in most types of organisations. The following table shows a range of TPS applications.

5.6.1 Batch processing and online processing

A TPS will process transactions using either **batch** processing or online processing.

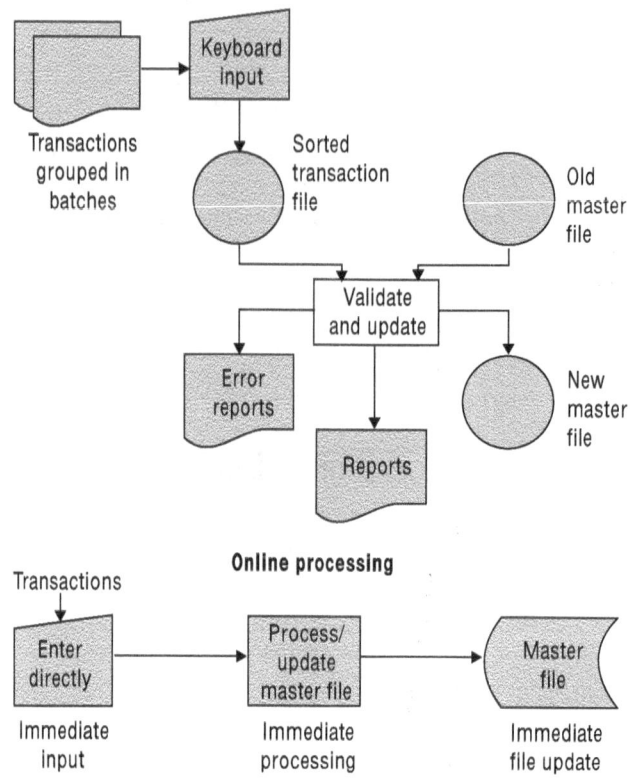

5.7 System dependencies and integration

FAST FORWARD

The ease of which data flows from one system to another depends on the **extent of integration** between them.

The types of system we have identified exchange data with each other. The ease with which data flows from one system to another depends on the extent of **integration** between them. The level of integration will depend on the nature of the organisation and the systems involved.

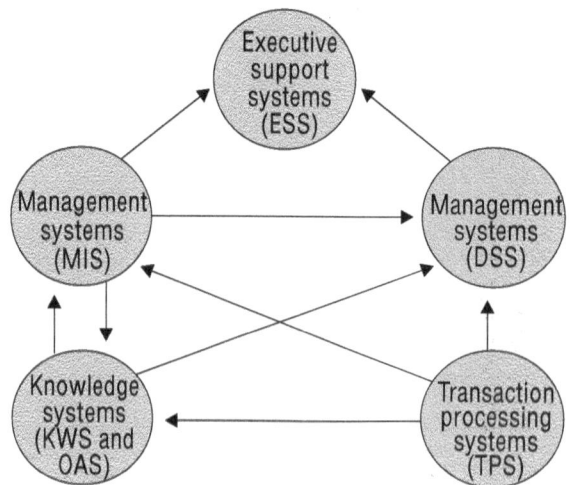

5.8 Information systems: Holding knowledge

There are other types of system that you need to know, relating to how knowledge is held.

5.9 Database systems

The way in which data is held on a system affects the ease with which the data is able to be accessed and manipulated.

Key term

> A **database** is a collection of data organised to service many applications. The database provides convenient access to data for a wide variety of users and user needs.

A database system has the following characteristics.

(a) **Shared**. Different users are able to access the same data for their own processing applications. This removes the need for duplicating data on different files.

(b) **Controls** to preserve the **integrity** of the database. Users should not be able to alter the data on file so as to **spoil** the database records for other users. However, users must be able to make **valid** alterations to the data.

(c) **Flexibility**. The database system should provide for the **needs of different users**, who each have their own processing requirements and data access methods. The database should be capable of **evolving** to meet **future** needs.

5.10 The advantages and disadvantages of database systems

The **advantages** of a database system are as follows.

(a) **Avoidance of unnecessary duplication of data**. It recognises that data can be used for many purposes but only needs to be input and stored once.

(b) **Multi-purpose data**. From (a), it follows that although data is input once, it can be used for several purposes.

(c) **Data for the organisation as a whole, not just for individual departments**. The database concept encourages management to regard data as a resource that must be **properly managed** just as any other resource. Database systems encourage management to analyse data, relationships between data items, and how data is used in different applications.

(d) **Consistency**. Because data is only held once, it is easier to ensure that it is up-to-date and consistent across departments.

(e) **New uses for data**. Data is held independently of the programs that access the data. This allows greater flexibility in the ways that data can be used. New programs can be easily introduced to make use of existing data in a different way.

(f) **New applications**. Developing new application programs with a database system is easier as a central pool of data is already available to be drawn upon.

(g) **Flexibility**. Relational systems are extremely flexible, allowing information from several different sources to be combined and providing answers to ad hoc queries.

PART D MANAGERIAL CONTROL: MANAGING INFORMATION SYSTEMS AND TECHNOLOGY

The **disadvantages** of a database systems relate mainly to security and control.

(a) There are potential problems of **data security** and **data privacy**. Administrative procedures for data security should supplement software controls.

(b) Since there is only one set of data, it is essential that the data should be **accurate** and free from corruption. A back-up routine is essential.

(c) Initial **development costs** may be high.

(d) For hierarchical and network structures, the access paths through the data must be **specified in advance**.

(e) Both hierarchical and network systems require intensive **programming** and are **inflexible**.

5.11 Database management systems

Key term

> A **database management system (DBMS)** is the software that centralises data and manages access to the database. It is a system which allows numerous applications to extract the data they need without the need for separate files.

A database management system is software that controls all access to the database and provides an interface between the database and users and user applications. There is (usually) one person, the database administrator, responsible for all the data and the database structure.

The major features of a database management system are as follows:

(a) It **handles all access by users** and application programs.

(b) It provides the user with a **logical view of data** within the database that is relevant to the user's requirements.

(c) It ensures **data consistency** for all users of the database.

(d) It can allow **access** to some restricted parts of the database only to authorised users.

A database management system also includes various utility programs, such as:

(a) **Report generators**. These are pieces of software to assist users with the production of reports from the database.

(b) **Automatic back-up of data and recovery in case of loss of data.**

(c) **Control over concurrent usage.** Concurrent usage happens when two database users are trying to access and amend the same data on the database at the same time. This DBMS utility software prevents more than one modification to a data item at the same time.

(d) **Data dictionaries**. A database dictionary is utility software that defines the types of data held on the database (for example by means of characteristics such as record type, and field type).

5.12 Knowledge management systems (KMS)

Information held on a KMS is easily accessed and shared by employees. Examples of information held in a KMS include facts, solutions to problems, relevant legislation and intellectual property.

A KMS is primarily of benefit to **knowledge based organisations**, such as those involved in research and development or providing services such as legal advice. This is because their information is best suited to storing and sharing by a database.

11: ORGANISATIONAL INFORMATION REQUIREMENTS

Benefits of a KMS include:

(a) **Valuable data is preserved** for the future and not lost, for example, where an employee leaves.

(b) The data is **easily shared**.

(c) **Data duplication** (or data redundancy) is **avoided**.

(d) It allows employees to 'get up to speed' on knowledge quickly and easily and this may **reduce the time they need to spend training**.

5.13 Enterprise-wide systems

Under an enterprise-wide system, each business area (such as accounts, HR, production and sales) is provided with a system that fulfils its needs, however each module shares a **common database** that is the basis of all the information within the organisation.

The central database allows each business area to **access** and **update information** in **real-time** and this means that information is **easy to share**, **available** to all business areas, and above all, **reliable**.

6 Information system security

> **FAST FORWARD**
>
> Computer systems, particularly those with links to other systems such as the Internet, are exposed to privacy and security risks. Security controls, integrity controls and contingency controls are used to protect data and information.
>
> **Security risks** include **hackers** and **eavesdroppers, viruses, hoaxes** and **denial of service attacks**. Organisations can take various **measures** against privacy and security risks, including **anti-virus software, firewalls, encryption, authentication** and **dial-back security**.

We have established that information is a valuable resource and a key tool in the quest for a competitive advantage.

As such, measures need to be taken to ensure data and information entering an organisation's information systems is **reliable** and **accurate**. Once captured by the system, the information must be kept secure and any processing must preserve accuracy.

Key term

> **Security** means the protection of data from unauthorised modification, disclosure or destruction, and the protection of the information system from the degradation or non-availability of services.

The measures an organisation can take to protect information and information systems can be classified into:

- Security controls
- Integrity controls
- Contingency controls

6.1 Security controls

Computer systems are exposed to security risks that threaten the security and integrity of both the system and the data held in it. Some of the main risks are explained below.

Privacy and security risks	
Risk	**Explanation**
Hackers and eavesdroppers	Hackers attempt to gain unauthorised access to computer systems. They may attempt to damage a system or steal information. Hackers use tools like electronic password generators which enable rapid multiple password attempts.
	Data that is transmitted across telecommunications links is exposed to the risk of being intercepted or examined during transmission (eavesdropping).
Viruses	A virus is a small piece of software which performs unauthorised actions and which replicates itself. Viruses may cause damage to files or attempt to destroy files and damage hard disks. When transmitted over a network such as the Internet, into a 'clean' system, the virus reproduces and infects that system.
	Types of virus:
	• Email viruses spread using email messages and replicate by mailing themselves to addresses held in the user's contacts book.
	• Worms copy themselves from machine to machine on a network.
	• Trojans or Trojan horses are hidden inside a 'valid' program but perform an unexpected act. Trojans therefore act like a virus, but aren't classified as a virus as they don't replicate themselves.
	• Trap doors are undocumented access points to a system allowing controls to be bypassed.
	• Logic bombs are triggered by the occurrence of a certain event.
	• Time bombs are triggered by a certain date.
Hoaxes	An associated problem is that of hoax virus warnings. There are a vast number of common hoaxes, most of which circulate via email.
Denial of service attack	Another threat to websites is the 'denial of service attack'. This involves an organised campaign to bombard a site with excessive volumes of traffic at a given time, with the aim of overloading the site.
Natural disasters	Fires, floods and other natural events may damage the place where the system is stored. It is important for the organisation to protect the system by selecting a suitable location and environment to house it. Backups should be taken regularly and be stored in a separate location so that the system can be restored if necessary. Steps should be taken to prevent risks as far as possible, for example by installing sprinkler systems and locating the system on a high floor to avoid flooding.
Hardware and software failure	Systems may malfunction for a number of reasons. This risk can be minimised by designing them to cope with extreme volumes of demand. Backups will enable the system to be restored if it does fail.
Human error	Operators may accidently damage or delete information held on the system. This risk can be minimised by staff training and in-built protections, such as only allowing certain individuals to alter or amend information.

Security controls can be subdivided into a number of aspects.

(a) **Prevention**. It is in practice impossible to prevent all threats cost-effectively.

(b) **Detection**. Detection techniques are often combined with prevention techniques: a log can be maintained of unauthorised attempts to gain access to a computer system.

(c) **Deterrence**. As an example, computer misuse by personnel can be grounds for dismissal.

(d) **Recovery procedures**. If the threat occurs, its consequences can be contained.

(e) **Correction procedures**. These ensure the vulnerability is dealt with (for example, by instituting stricter controls).

(f) **Threat avoidance**. This might mean changing the design of the system.

6.1.1 Physical security

A system needs to be protected against **natural and man-made disasters**. Protective measures include the following.

- Site preparation, eg fireproof materials
- Detection equipment, eg smoke detectors
- Extinguishing equipment, eg sprinklers
- Use of uninterruptable power supplies (UPS)

Physical access controls are designed to prevent intruders getting near to computer equipment.

(a) Personnel, including receptionists and, outside working hours, security guards, can help control human access.

(b) Door locks can be used where frequency of use is low.

(c) Locks can be combined with:

　(i) A keypad system, requiring a code to be entered
　(ii) A card entry system, requiring a card to be 'swiped'

(d) Intruder alarms

Much computer equipment is easily portable and therefore susceptible to theft. Laptops and small printers are designed for portability; even desktops and laser printers can be easily carried by one person. Several protective measures can be taken:

- An equipment log, including booking-out procedures
- Postcoding of equipment
- Bolts and/or locks to secure equipment to desks
- Secure storage of mobile storage items (memory sticks)

6.2 Integrity controls

Key terms

Data integrity in the context of security is preserved when data is the same as in source documents and has not been accidentally or intentionally altered, destroyed or disclosed.

Systems integrity refers to system operation conforming to the design specification despite attempts (deliberate or accidental) to make it behave otherwise.

Data will maintain its **integrity** if it is **complete** and **not corrupted**. This means that:

(a) The original input of the data must be controlled in such a way as to ensure that the results are complete and correct.

(b) Any processing and storage of data must maintain the completeness and correctness of the data captured.

(c) That reports or other output should be set up so that they, too, are complete and correct.

6.2.1 Anti-virus software and firewalls

The main protection against viruses is **anti-virus software**, which searches systems for viruses and removes them. Anti-virus programs include an auto-update feature that downloads profiles of new viruses, enabling the software to check for all known or existing viruses. Very new viruses may go undetected by anti-virus software (until the anti-virus software vendor updates their package – and the organisation installs the update).

Additional precautions include disabling external media to prevent viruses entering an organisation via external storage devices. However, this can disrupt work processes. At the very least, organisations should ensure all files received via external media and email are virus checked.

External email links can be protected by way of a **firewall** that may be configured to virus check all messages, and may also prevent files of a certain type being sent via email (eg .exe files, as these are the most common means of transporting a virus). Firewalls can be implemented in both hardware and software, or a combination of both. A firewall disables part of the telecoms technology to prevent **unauthorised intrusions**. However, a determined hacker may well be able to bypass this.

6.2.2 Input controls

Input controls should ensure the accuracy, **completeness and validity** of input. Examples of such controls include ensuring data entered matches source documents and is complete and reasonable.

Data may be **valid** (for example in the correct format) but still not match source documents.

6.2.3 Processing controls

Processing controls should ensure the accuracy and completeness of processing. Programs should be subject to development controls and to rigorous testing. Periodic running of test data is also recommended.

6.2.4 Output controls

Output controls should ensure the accuracy, completeness and security of output. The following measures are possible.
- Investigation and follow-up of error reports and exception reports
- Batch controls to ensure all items processed and returned
- Controls over distribution/copying of output
- Labelling of disks/tapes

6.2.5 Backup controls

Backup controls aim to maintain system and data integrity. Backup means to make a copy in anticipation of future failure or corruption. A backup copy of a file is a duplicate copy kept separately from the main system and only used if the original fails.

Data stored for a long time should be tested periodically to ensure it is still restorable – it may be subject to **damage** from environmental conditions or mishandling.

11: ORGANISATIONAL INFORMATION REQUIREMENTS

In a well-planned data backup scheme, a copy of backed-up data is delivered (preferably daily) to a secure off-site storage facility, or, increasingly, to storage facilities in 'the cloud'. **Cloud computing** involves a network of servers and at its simplest means the storing and accessing of data and programs over the internet, instead of on a computer's hard drive.

A well-planned backup and **archive strategy** should include:

(a) A plan and schedule for the regular backup of **critical data**
(b) Archive plans
(c) A disaster recovery plan that includes off-site storage

6.2.6 Passwords and logical access systems

Unauthorised persons may circumvent physical access controls. A **logical access system** that allocates each user a user-name and requires a password enables:

- Identification of the user
- Authentication of user identity
- Checks on user authority

6.2.7 Encryption and authentication

Data that is transmitted across telecommunications links is exposed to the risk of being **intercepted or read during transmission** (known as 'eavesdropping'). **Encryption** is used to reduce this risk and involves scrambling the data at one end of the line, transmitting the scrambled data, and unscrambling it at the receiver's end of the line. A person intercepting the scrambled data is unable to make sense of it.

Authentication is a technique of making sure that a message has come from an **authorised sender**. Authentication involves adding extra data in a form previously agreed between sender and recipient.

Dial-back security operates by requiring the person wanting access to dial into the network and identify themselves first. The system then dials the person back on their authorised number before allowing access

6.2.8 Administrative controls

Measures to control personnel include the following.

- Careful recruitment
- Job rotation and enforced vacations
- Systems logs
- Review and supervision

Segregation of duties remains a core security requirement. This involves division of responsibilities into separate roles.

- Data capture and data entry
- Computer operations
- Systems analysis and programming

6.2.9 Audit trail

Key term

> An **audit trail** is a record showing who has accessed a computer system and what operations he or she has performed. Audit trails are useful both for maintaining security and for recovering lost transactions.

An audit trail should be provided so that every transaction on a file contains a **unique reference** (eg a sales ledger transaction record should hold a reference to the customer order, delivery note and invoice).

Question — Data confidentiality

Which of the following controls would NOT help ensure the security of confidential information?

- A Use of data encryption software
- B A formal company policy on regularly changing passwords
- C Access tests during system development
- D Storage of back-up copies of data in another location

Answer

D Storage of back-up copies of data in another location

Storage elsewhere would be a safeguard against loss or corruption of data, but would not enhance security.

Encryption means that the data could not be understood without the key. Regular password changes should make the system less vulnerable to unauthorised users accessing the system using valid passwords. System development tests can establish whether controls preventing unauthorised access are working as intended.

6.3 Contingency controls

Key term

A **contingency** is an unscheduled interruption of computing services that requires measures outside the day-to-day routine operating procedures.

The preparation of a contingency plan (also known as a disaster recovery plan) is one of the stages in the development of an organisation-wide security policy. A contingency plan is necessary in case of a major disaster, or if some of the **security measures** discussed elsewhere **fail**.

Any disaster recovery plan must therefore provide for:

(a) **Standby procedures** so that some operations can be performed while normal services are disrupted.

(b) **Recovery procedures** once the cause of the breakdown has been discovered or corrected.

(c) **Personnel management** policies to ensure that (a) and (b) above are implemented properly.

6.3.1 Disaster recovery plan

The contents of a disaster recovery (or contingency plan) will include the following.

Section	Comment
Definition of responsibilities	It is important that somebody (a manager or co-ordinator) is designated to take control in a crisis. This individual can then delegate specific tasks or responsibilities to other designated personnel.
Priorities	Limited resources may be available for processing. Some tasks are more important than others. These must be established in advance. Similarly, the recovery programme may indicate that certain areas must be tackled first.
Backup and standby arrangements	These may be with other installations, with a company that provides such services (eg maybe the hardware vendor); or reverting to manual procedures.

Section	Comment
Communication with staff	The problems of a disaster can be compounded by poor communication between members of staff.
Public relations	If the disaster has a public impact, the recovery team may come under pressure from the public or from the media.
Risk assessment	Some way must be found of assessing the requirements of the problem, if it is contained, with the continued operation of the organisation as a whole.

7 Systems development

FAST FORWARD

Key stages of the **systems development lifecycle** are **feasibility study, systems investigation, systems analysis, systems design and programming, systems testing, systems conversion, systems implementation**.

New information systems often fail to bring the benefits expected. Most research seems to indicate that the major cause of information systems failure is **inadequate user involvement**. Users need to be involved in the development process at all stages – including system design.

7.1 Dissatisfaction with information systems

Other common causes of dissatisfaction with information systems include:

(a) IS project managers are often **technicians**, not managers. Technical ability for IS staff is no guarantee of management skill – an individual might be a highly proficient analyst or programmer, but **not a good manager**.

(b) The project manager may accept **an unrealistic deadline** – the timescale is fixed early in the planning process. User demands may be accepted as deadlines before sufficient consideration is given to the realism of this.

(c) **Poor or non-existent planning** is a recipe for disaster. Unrealistic deadlines would be identified much earlier if a proper planning process was undertaken.

(d) A lack of **monitoring** and **control**

(e) Users **change their requirements**, resulting in costly changes to the system as it is being developed.

(f) **Poor timetabling and resourcing**. The development and implementation of a computer project may take a considerable length of time (perhaps 18 months for a medium-sized installation). A proper plan and time schedule for the various activities must be drawn up.

7.2 Information systems projects

The project manager has a number of **conflicting requirements**:

(a) The **systems manager**, usually the project manager's boss, wants the project **delivered on time**, to specification and within budget.

(b) **User** expectations may be misunderstood, ignored or unrealistic.

(c) The project manager has to plan and supervise the work of **analysts** and **programmers** and these are rather different roles.

The project manager needs to develop an **appropriate management style**. What he or she should realise is the extent to which the project will fail if users are not consulted, or if the project team is unhappy. As the project manager needs to encourage participation from users, an excessively authoritarian style is not suitable.

7.3 Systems development lifecycle

The systems development lifecycle is a phased way of developing and introducing a new system, designed to prevent operational problems and user dissatisfaction. There are a number of possible systems development lifecycle models. This is one version of it:

SYSTEMS DEVELOPMENT LIFE CYCLE	
Feasibility study	Briefly review the existing system
	Identify possible alternative solutions
Systems investigation	Obtain details of current requirements and user needs such as data volumes, processing cycles and timescales
	Identify current problems and restrictions
Systems analysis	Consider why current methods are used and identify better alternatives
Systems design and programming	Determine what inputs, processing and storage facilities are necessary to produce the outputs required
	Consider matters such as program design, file design and security
	Prepare a detailed specification of the new system
	Write or acquire software
Systems testing	Testing should include: • System testing (input, capacity, flexibility) • System logic testing (logic devised by system analyst) • Program testing (use of test data) • User acceptance testing (test whether system meets users' needs)
Systems conversion	Convert files
Systems implementation	Install hardware
	Start running the new system

A **formal post-implementation review** should establish whether the objectives and targeted performance criteria have been met, and if not, why not, and what should be done about it.

There should also be ongoing review that the system continues to meet users' needs and that its performance is satisfactory.

7.3.1 Problems with systems development

Problems that occur when implementing a new information system can usually be traced to deficiencies in the development process.

Stage/activity	Problems
Systems analysis	The problem the system is intended to solve is not fully understood.
	Investigation of the situation is hindered by insufficient resources.
	User input is inadequate through either lack of consultation or lack of user interest.
	The project team is unable to dedicate the time required.
	Insufficient time spent planning the project.
Systems design and programming	Insufficient user input.
	Lack of flexibility. The organisation's future needs are neglected.
	The system requires unforeseen changes in working patterns.
	Failure to perform organisation impact analysis. An organisational impact analysis studies the way a proposed system will affect organisation structure, attitudes, decision-making and operations.
	Organisational factors sometimes overlooked include: • Ergonomics (equipment, work environment and user interfaces) • Health and safety • Compliance with legislation • Job design • Employee involvement
	Insufficient time and money allocated to programming.
	Programmers supplied with incomplete or inaccurate specifications.
	Logic of the program is misunderstood.
	Poor programming technique results in programs that are hard to modify.
	Programs are not adequately documented.
Systems testing	Insufficient time and money allocated to testing.
	Failure to develop an organised testing plan.
	Insufficient user involvement.
	User management do not review and sign-off the results of testing.
Systems conversion	Insufficient time and money allocated to data conversion.
	Insufficient checking between old and new files.
	The process is rushed to compensate for time overruns elsewhere.
Systems implementation	Insufficient time, money and/or appropriate staff mean the process has to be rushed.
	Lack of user training increases the risk of system under-utilisation and rejection.
	Poor system and user documentation.
	Lack of performance standards to assess system performance against.
	System maintenance provisions are inadequate.

7.3.2 Overcoming user resistance

A recurring theme when examining the reasons for information system failure is user resistance.

The three types of theories to explain user resistance are explained in the following table.

Theory	Description	Overcoming the resistance
People-orientated	User-resistance is caused by factors internal to users as individuals or as a group. For example, users may not wish to disrupt their current work practices and social groupings.	User training Organisation policies Persuasion User involvement in system development
System-orientated	User-resistance is caused by factors inherent in the new system design relating to ease of use and functionality.	User training and education Improve user-interface Ensure users contribute to the system design process Ensure the system 'fits' with the organisation
Interaction	User-resistance is caused by the interaction of people and the system. For example, the system may be well-designed but its implementation will cause organisational changes that users resist eg reduced chance of bonuses, redundancies, monotonous work.	Re-organise the organisation before implementing the system Redesign any affected incentive schemes to incorporate the new system Promote user participation and encourage organisation-wide teamwork Emphasise the benefits the system brings

Chapter roundup

- All organisations require information for a range of **purposes** including **planning, controlling, recording transactions, performance measurement** and **decision-making**.
- **Strategic planning, management control** and **operational control** may be seen as a **hierarchy** of planning and control decisions.
- 'Good' information aids **understanding**. ACCURATE is a handy mnemonic for the qualities of good information.
- The **cost and value** of information are often not easy to quantify – but attempts should be made to do so.
- **Information** is a **valuable resource** that requires efficient **management**.
- Data and **information** come from **sources** both **inside** and **outside** an organisation. An organisation's information systems should be designed so as to obtain – or **capture** – all the relevant data and information required.
- Organisations require **different types of information system** to provide **different levels of information** in a **range of functional areas**.
- The ease of which data flows from one system to another depends on the extent of **integration** between systems.
- Computer systems, particularly those with links to other systems such as the Internet are exposed to privacy and security risks. Security controls, integrity controls and contingency controls are used to protect data and information.
- **Security risks** include **hackers** and **eavesdroppers, viruses, hoaxes** and **denial of service attacks**. Organisations can take various **measures** against privacy and security risks, including **anti-virus software, firewalls, encryption, authentication** and **dial-back security**.
- Key stages of the **systems development lifecycle** are **feasibility study, systems investigation, systems analysis, systems design and programming, systems testing, systems conversion, systems implementation**.

PART D MANAGERIAL CONTROL: MANAGING INFORMATION SYSTEMS AND TECHNOLOGY

Quick quiz

1. List five uses of information.
2. List five characteristics of strategic information.
3. What is data integrity?
4. List five characteristics of operational information.
5. Match the following abbreviations with the appropriate description.

    TPS, OAS, KWS, MIS, DSS, ESS

    (a) Information systems that facilitate the creation and integration of new knowledge into an organisation

    (b) A system that pools data from internal and external sources and makes information available to senior managers in an easy-to-use form

    (c) Computer systems designed to increase the productivity of data and information workers

    (d) A system that converts data, mainly from internal sources into information (eg summary reports, exception reports)

    (e) A system that combines data and analytical models or data analysis tools to support semi-structured and unstructured decision-making

    (f) A system to perform and record routine transactions

6. 'Full integration across all organisational information systems is vital.' Do you agree with this statement? Justify your answer (very briefly).

Answers to quick quiz

1. Planning, controlling, recording transactions, measuring performance and making decisions.

2. [Five of]

    Derived from both internal and external sources

    Summarised at a high level

    Relevant to the long-term

    Concerned with the whole organisation

    Often prepared on an ad hoc basis

    Both quantitative and qualitative

    Uncertain, as the future cannot be predicted accurately

3. Data integrity is the assurance that data is the same as it is in the source documents, and has not been accidentally or intentionally altered, destroyed or disclosed.

4. [Five of]

    Derived from internal sources

    Detailed, being the processing of raw data

    Relevant to the immediate term

    Task-specific

    Prepared very frequently

    Largely quantitative

5.
    (a) KWS
    (b) ESS
    (c) OAS
    (d) MIS
    (e) DSS
    (f) TPS

6. Disagree. A high degree of integration is usually desirable, but in all cases the costs of integration should be considered against the value of the expected benefits integration would bring.

PART D: MANAGERIAL CONTROL: MANAGING INFORMATION SYSTEMS AND TECHNOLOGY

The impact of IT on work practices

Topic list	Syllabus reference
1 The impact of IT on organisations	D4
2 IT and the employee/employer relationship	D4
3 Individual information requirements	D4
4 Social, political and ethical issues	D4
5 Developments in information and communications technology (ICT)	D4
6 Automation in business	D4
7 Big data	D4
8 Costs, benefits, risks and implementing new information systems	D4
9 Cybersecurity	D4

Introduction

The **impact of technology** on organisations in recent years has been dramatic. This chapter explores some of the issues arising from this change, and some of the key developments in the context of the management of important business information.

The chapter includes a discussion of the **wider ethical issues** raised by the increasingly significant role of information technology and the power of information systems in today's society.

1 The impact of IT on organisations

1.1 Organisation structure

FAST FORWARD

> Information systems and information technology have played a significant role in the development of the modern business environment including encouraging the **flattening** of **organisation hierarchies** and widening **spans of control**.

Information systems and information technology have played a significant role in the development of the modern business environment. For example, modern communications technology makes decentralised organisations possible, allowing decision-making to be passed down to 'empowered' workers or outsourced to external companies.

There is a trend towards smaller, more **agile companies**. **Flexibility** and speed are increasingly seen as the key to competitive advantage. Advances in IT have allowed complex operating processes to be accelerated and made feedback information available almost immediately.

1.1.1 Span of control

Span of control, or 'span of management', refers to the number of subordinates responsible to a superior. If a manager has five subordinates, the span of control is five. This was covered in detail in Chapter 6.

Business automation and rationalisation, and improved management information systems, have often resulted in reduced staffing levels. In particular, layers of middle management have been removed in many organisations. Managers or staff 'lower down' the hierarchy have been empowered to make decisions previously made by middle managers. Information technology has therefore had the effect of flattening organisation hierarchies and **widening spans of control**.

An **information system**, such as an intranet, can help provide organisation unity and coherency in flat, decentralised organisations.

The trend towards flatter structures is evidenced by talk of an 'e-lance economy', characterised by shifting **coalitions** of small firms collaborating on particular **projects**.

1.1.2 Organisation structure and information systems

The structure of an organisation and the way in which the organisation's information system is arranged are **related** issues.

Centralised systems means holding and processing data in a central place, such as a computer centre at head office. Data will be collected at 'remote' (ie geographically separate) offices and other locations and sent in to the central location.

Decentralised systems have the data/information processing carried out at several different locations, away from the 'centre' or 'head office'.

As we have emphasised elsewhere in this Text, information systems strategy **should support the overall business strategy**.

1.2 Other effects of IT on organisations

FAST FORWARD

Other **effects of IT on organisations** include:

- Routine processing (bigger volumes, greater speed, greater accuracy)
- Digital information and record-keeping
- New skills required and new ways of working
- Reliance on IT
- New methods of communication and of providing customer service
- Interoperability (encourages collaboration across organisation boundaries) and open systems
- The view of information as a valuable resource
- The view of information as a commodity which can be bought, sold or exchanged ('information market')

1.2.1 Routine processing

Information technology enables the processing of data to be performed in bigger volumes, at greater speed and with greater accuracy.

1.2.2 Digital information and record-keeping

Information storage and transmission is now largely digital rather than paper-based. However, many people like 'hard copies' and print out information as required.

The nature and quality of management information has also changed.

(a) Managers have access to more information – eg from an ESS. Information is also likely to be more timely, accurate, reliable and up-to-date.

(b) More detailed planning is possible through the use of models (eg spreadsheets).

(c) Information for control should be more readily available.

(d) Decision-making should improve as a consequence of better quality information.

1.2.3 Employment issues

The infiltration of IT into almost every area of business means that the vast majority of employees are now expected to utilise information technology. IT skills are required and new ways of working have emerged.

1.2.4 Technological change

A reliance on information technology commits an organisation to **continual change**. Systems are likely to be superseded after a few years.

1.2.5 Customer service

Information technology has enabled organisations to provide better customer service. Customer databases, EDI, extranets, websites, data-mining and other systems discussed throughout this book can all be applied to improving service levels.

1.2.6 Interoperability and open systems

Interoperability means that any party can **share** and **exchange** information and facilities with other parties without having to use the same service provider or technology platform. Interoperability facilitates the formation of strategic alliances and encourages collaboration across organisation boundaries.

The term 'open systems' is a similar concept to interoperability although it is usually (but not always) used in the context of different systems within the same organisation. An open systems infrastructure supports **organisation-wide functions** and allows for the transfer of information between networks and systems.

1.2.7 Backward compatibility

Technology is said to be backward compatible if it can use files and data created with an older similar technology. Backward compatibility makes the adoption of new technologies less risky and less time-consuming – it eliminates the need to start afresh.

1.2.8 Legacy system

A legacy system is a computer system or application program which continues to be used because of the prohibitive cost of replacing or redesigning it. The implication is that the system is large, monolithic and difficult to modify.

Legacy software may only run on antiquated hardware, and the cost of maintaining this may eventually outweigh the cost of replacing both the software and hardware. Recent developments in software have been towards systems that can interact with legacy systems – often through an ability to import data from such a system.

1.2.9 Information markets

The term '**information market**' reflects the growing view that information is a **commodity** which can be bought, sold or exchanged.

There has been a growing realisation that information is a resource and that it has many of the characteristics of any other resource. A key theme of this syllabus is the benefits which information, properly managed and used, can bring to an organisation.

1.2.10 Developments in communications

Communications technology is probably having a greater impact on organisational life than computers are at present. **Email** provides a quick and **efficient** means of communicating worldwide. Computer telephony integration (CTI) systems can **route** incoming calls, whether to landline or mobile handsets. CTI also enables information about callers to be gathered and stored allowing **personalised** communication.

Computer conferencing systems and organisation-wide **bulletin boards** encourage **communication** – both formal and **informal**.

Video conferencing (eg using Skype) allows face-to-face contact between people who are spread widely across the world. If a video conference is deemed sufficient, **travel costs** can be reduced.

2 IT and the employee/employer relationship

FAST FORWARD

The widespread use of information technology in the workplace has affected the relationship between **employers and employees**:

- Reduced need to follow the chain-of-command
- Nature of work
- Close business relationships regardless of geographical location
- More flexible working arrangements
- Greater monitoring and control
- Information overload

As already stated, the widespread use of information technology in the workplace has affected the relationship between employers and employees. Some of the effects are explained in the following table.

Effect of IT	Comment
Reduced need to follow the chain-of-command	Information technology allows quick and easy communication between staff at all levels. For example, an employee may be willing to email the managing director, but would be unwilling or unable to telephone him or her.
	Efficient channels of communication that operate independently of the organisation hierarchy reduce the need to pass communications up the chain of command.
Nature of work	Technology has enabled the automation of many unskilled and semi-skilled tasks. This has resulted in the degrading of old skills and the requirement for employees to learn new skills.
	Some employees have found the change to well-established working patterns extremely stressful. Others have preferred to take redundancy or early retirement.
	Employers may need to provide training and re-training programs for staff.
	As technology becomes more user-friendly there could be opportunities for greater flexibility and job rotation.
Close business relationships regardless of geographical location	Information technology enables people located all over the world to enjoy close working relationships.
	Technology enables operations to be sited anywhere in the world.
More flexible working arrangements	Advances in technology mean many tasks are able to be performed off-site. The need for flexibility in employee and employer attitudes has resulted in trends away from 'a job for life', towards shorter terms of service, freelance workers and contracting. Part-time positions are increasing.
	We look at homeworking later in this chapter.
Greater monitoring and control	Improved information systems should help managers to plan and control work more effectively.
	Technology also enables untrusting employers to monitor employee behaviour.
	Closed-circuit cameras are now relatively cheap and easy to operate.
	Personal email sent using the organisation's server can be monitored.
	Computer telephony integration (CTI) systems record phone numbers called and the call length.
	Privacy laws regarding such activities differ from country to country. In many countries relevant law is still developing.

Effect of IT	Comment
Information overload	Computing and communications developments have led to the capture, analysis and transmission of ever-increasing amounts of information.
	However, only relevant information is useful. An excess of irrelevant information is harmful. A person is more likely to miss or mis-interpret vital information if they are swamped with irrelevant material. We cover approaches to avoiding information overload later in this chapter.

2.1 Remote working or homeworking

Some employers have encouraged **remote working** or **home working**, sometimes in conjunction with a move towards a pool of **freelance workers**. Developments in information technology (eg email, remote access network) allow these workers to be based off-site, often at home. Homeworking is sometimes known as **telecommuting**.

2.1.1 Advantages and disadvantages of homeworking

The **advantages to the employer** of homeworking include:

- **Cost savings on office accommodation**

    Fewer staff in the offices reduces the amount of desk space required and other expensive facilities that offices contain.

- **A larger potential pool of employees**

    The employer can source employees from a wider geographical area as well as those who would not otherwise be able to work for them due to their circumstances, eg those with small children.

- **Flexibility**

    The employer can make use of freelance staff so it can accurately match staffing levels with demand, cutting the cost of unproductive staff during quiet periods.

- **Improved productivity**

    Employees are often more relaxed working at home as they can work without distractions and avoid having to travel in to work.

The **advantages to the employee** include:

- **Better use of time**

    Employees can arrange their **working hours** around their other commitments and save time on commuting.

- **Money saving**

    Less commuting may mean **cost savings** to the employee in terms of travel (petrol and parking) and other costs such as food (cheaper to eat at home than at the office).

- In some situations there may be **fewer distractions** out of the office.

The **disadvantages for employers** are chiefly problems of **control**. Managers who like to practise close supervision and who lack trust in their employees may view homeworking as an opportunity for laziness.

If needed the **problems of control** depend to a large extent on the individual involved. Other issues could include:

- **Co-ordination of homeworkers**

    Where employees are **geographically dispersed**, communication will be reduced which may cause management problems in co-ordinating staff.

- **Training**

    Training staff in their homes will prove too **expensive** so they will need to return to the office. Where and when will training be performed?

- **Culture**

    Away from direct **contact** with the organisation, employees may lose their sense of belonging to the company, this may reduce their loyalty.

Possible problems for homeworkers include:

- **Isolation**

    Working at home reduces contact with others.

- **Domestic intrusions**

    Children and partners may require attention during working hours. Less monitoring of their time by managers may increase time spent on **unproductive activities**.

- **Adequate space**

    Not all employees will have a **room available** to dedicate as an office or to store work materials.

- If contracting or freelance, **fewer employment rights**

    Self-employed staff have fewer rights in terms of **job protection**, **pay**, **holidays** and **redundancy pay**. They also have less protection in other legal areas such as **discrimination** and **working hours**.

2.2 Sociotechnical design

> **FAST FORWARD**
>
> **Sociotechnical design** attempts to produce information systems that are technically efficient but also take into account organisational and staff needs.

The way in which information systems are designed can impact on the employer-employee relationship. While modern system building approaches attempt to ensure end-user input into system design this input tends to focus on operational aspects of the system.

Sociotechnical design looks at the wider picture. It recognises that an organisation is a **sociotechnical** system, consisting of **three sub-systems:**

(a) A formal structure

(b) A technological system consisting of the work to be done, and the machines, tools and other facilities available to do it

(c) A social system consisting of the people within the organisation, the ways they think and the ways they interact with each other

Key term

> **Sociotechnical design** attempts to produce information systems that are technically efficient but also take into account organisational and staff needs

Sociotechnical design gives users a say in the design of the information system and a say in the **role of information systems** in their workplace. A sociotechnical design plan would include human factors such as work group structures and job satisfaction. Technical and social factors are considered together and the alternative that best meets technical **and social** objectives is selected.

By ensuring organisational and social objectives are considered, employers are **reducing the risk** of a new system causing unforeseen disruption. In particular, employee acceptance of the system should be increased.

Before adopting a sociotechnical approach employers must be sure that they do wish to take employees' views into account. To solicit employee views, and then **ignore** them, is likely to cause **resentment** and increase the risk of employee rejection of the system.

'Human issues' a sociotechnical approach could consider include:

- The skills required to operate the system and the skills of employees
- Task variety – ensuring monotonous tasks are spread around
- Autonomy – ensuring supervision and monitoring levels are not oppressive
- Ergonomics and employee health and safety issues (eg breaks from VDU work)
- User interface design

3 Individual information requirements

3.1 Critical success factors

Key term

> **Critical success factors** (CSFs) 'are those product features that are particularly valued by a group of customers, and, therefore, where the organisation must excel to outperform the competition'.
> (Johnson, Scholes & Whittington, *Exploring Corporate Strategy*, 2005)

FAST FORWARD

> **Critical success factors** (CSFs) can be used to establish the **information needs** of individual managers.

The organisational CSFs that an individual manager is responsible for should be the driving force behind the manager's information needs.

The process is summarised as follows:

Step 1	Interview managers to obtain their CSFs.
Step 2	Aggregate individual CSFs to establish organisational CSFs.
Step 3	Determine the performance indicators used to monitor each CSF.
Step 4	Determine what information is required to track each performance indicator.
Step 5	Review information and information systems to establish if this information is available.
Step 6	Take action to provide any missing information (eg system amendments, new systems).
Step 7	Provide each individual manager with a summary of the information that will be provided to support the CSFs they are responsible for.

3.2 Information overload and intelligent agents

FAST FORWARD

To avoid **information overload**, only good quality information should be communicated (ACCURATE mnemonic). The number of information sources feeding an individual can be managed.

- Delegate to colleagues
- Review reports received for duplication
- Re-route incoming telephone calls
- Voice-mail
- Filter incoming email
- Use an internet news-clipping service
- Use intelligent agents

Many managers complain that they receive too much irrelevant information. There are two main approaches to avoiding information overload. First, the **characteristics of the information** need to be considered. Second, the **number of information sources** feeding an individual can be managed.

3.2.1 Limiting the number of information sources

The approach taken to limiting the sources of information will depend on the situation. In some instances it may be sufficient to implement temporary measures to **delay** non-urgent information reaching a person at a particularly busy time. Other situations may require a **permanent change** to information flows. Some examples are shown in the following table.

Limiting tool	Comment
Delegate to colleagues	Communications regarding certain issues may be dealt with by others within the organisation. For example, routine client contact could be delegated to junior staff, and only strategic issues referred 'up the chain'.
Review reports received for duplication	Regular reviews of information received should be made. If information is duplicated one source should be deleted. The review should also consider what information would best be received together to aid interpretation.
Re-route incoming telephone calls	A secretary could be allocated to take telephone messages, putting through only calls of significance that require immediate attention. To be effective, the instructions concerning calls that should be put through, and how messages should be relayed must be specific.
Voice-mail	While voice-mail can be frustrating when trying to reach someone, it may be useful to temporarily divert calls to voice-mail when work pressures require no interruptions – and no other staff are available to divert calls to.
Filter incoming email	Email programs have the ability to review and re-direct messages based on the message content, priority, sender and/or intended recipients. Non-selected messages may be copied to a selected person, or redirected to a non-urgent inbox to be dealt with later.
Use an internet news-clipping service	A person may face a constant stream of industry-related journals. These should be reviewed for relevant information – a time-consuming process. However, a news-clipping service could review relevant journals and newspapers on the internet, and forward via email copies of articles that meet user-defined criteria.
Use intelligent agents	These are discussed in the following section.

3.3 Intelligent agents

Intelligent agents are programs that perform tasks such as retrieving and delivering information and automating repetitive tasks. **Intelligent agent** software can be applied to monitor an individual's use of a computerised system and 'learn' what the user wants, and does not want, by monitoring what he does day-by-day.

The term **intelligent agent** is used to denote a computer system that has the following properties:

(a) **Autonomy**: agents operate without direct intervention.

(b) **Social ability**: agents interact with other agents and people.

(c) **Reactivity**: agents perceive their environment and respond to changes that occur in it.

(d) **Proactiveness**: agents do not only act in response to their environment, they are able to exhibit goal-directed behaviour by **taking the initiative**.

Agents are an example of '**push**' **technology**. Instead of searching through large quantities of information to find what is relevant, selected information is 'pushed' to the user.

3.3.1 Interface agents

Interface agents are computer programs that employ artificial intelligence techniques in order to provide assistance to a user dealing with a particular application. A fairly crude example is the Office Assistant within Microsoft Office.

Interface agents are used to decrease the complexity of information systems. They may add speech and natural language understanding to otherwise dumb interfaces, or add presentation ability to systems.

3.3.2 Information agents

An **information agent** is able to collate and manipulate information obtained from various sources to meet parameters set by users and other agents. The information sources may include traditional databases or internet searches.

Case Study

Intelligent software agents – an attempt at classification

The following are examples of developed, ready-to-run, agent software that may be used on a company intranet to enhance information retrieval and knowledge management. Agents may be categorised as:

System agents run as integrated parts of operating systems or network protocol devices. They help managing complex distributed computing environments by doing hardware inventory, interpreting network events, managing backup and storage devices, and performing virus detection. These agents do not primarily work with end-user information.

Advisory agents are used in (complex) help or diagnostics systems.

Filtering agents are used to reduce information overload by removing unwanted data, ie data that does not match the user's profile, from the input stream. Simple versions are built-in to many email clients and Agentware and InfoMagnet provide a more general kind of server-based filtering capability.

Retrieval agents search and retrieve information and serve as information brokers or document managers.

Navigation agents are used to navigate through external and internal networks, remembering short-cuts, pre-load caching information, automatically bookmarking interesting sites. IBM's Web Browser Intelligence (WBI – pronounced Webby) is an example.

Monitoring agents provide the user with information when particular events occur, such as information being updated, moved, or erased. Enterprise Minder does this but is no agent. WBI from IBM has this as a feature, as do BullsEye and SmartBookmarks.

Recommender agents are usually collaborative; they need many profiles to be available before an accurate recommendation can be made. Examples are Agentware, Firefly, and GroupLens, which are all server-based. Learn Sesame is user-orientated and bases its conclusion on the user's previous behaviour.

Profiling agents are used to build dynamic sites with information and recommendations tailored to match each visitor's individual taste and need. The main purpose is to build customer loyalty and profitable one-to-one relationships. Available examples are Agentware, Firefly, and GroupLens on the server side. Learn Sesame and IBM's Knowledge Utility also do this but on a user-orientated level.

4 Social, political and ethical issues

> **FAST FORWARD**
>
> Many commentators refer to our period in history as the **information age**.

4.1 The age of information

Many commentators refer to our period in history as the **age of information**, or the **information age**. In the short time since humans took over the world, there have been rapid changes in the nature of society and the role of information.

What we are living through now is the change from the industrial age to the **communications** age or **information society**. As this shift occurs we can expect the pace of life to increase.

The average life cycle of a business is now only seven years. Technologies are being superseded before they have been fully implemented eg, WAP. The world is changing so fast that businesses must attempt to predict the future.

Wealth in the information society is linked to **knowledge**. The rich and powerful of our era will be those who find ways to turn raw data into usable knowledge. This generation needs creative, inventive, imaginative people. The structure of '**jobs**' is reducing as the industrial age fades.

4.2 The moral dimensions of the information age

Laudon and Laudon (*Management Information Systems,* 2013) identified **five moral dimensions of the information age**, arising from ethical, social and political issues surrounding information systems:

- Information rights and obligations
- Property rights
- Accountability and control
- System quality
- Quality of life

4.2.1 Information rights and obligations

Individuals and organisations expect to have certain rights regarding the information that others hold about them. Those who hold information about others should expect certain obligations placed upon them to protect that information.

Information issues focus on **privacy** and include:

(a) The storage of **credit histories** about individuals that are used to make decisions about future credit applications

(b) Internet '**cookies**' that store information about individuals on their computer

(c) Computer controlled circuit television (**CCTV**) systems that may monitor an individual's movements

The following table summarises some ethical, social and political issues raised.

Ethical	How can individuals and organisations justify an invasion of privacy? Do we have a right to notification every time information is stored about us?
Social	Where do we draw the line between private and public information? Is it reasonable to expect personal emails sent from work to be monitored?
Political	Governments have taken some steps to protect the privacy of individuals by requiring data gatherers to register, awarding individuals certain legal rights and having data users adhere to data protection principles.

4.2.2 Property rights

Developments in technology have made duplication of software, knowledge and other intellectual property reasonably easy to duplicate. The internet and email allows information to be transferred around the world in seconds.

Information issues focus on the **copying and distribution** of **copyrighted material** such as:

- Downloaded music and video
- Software (games and applications)
- Web site designs

The following table summarises the main ethical, social and political issues raised.

Ethical	If individuals can get perfect copies of copyrighted material for free, why should they pay for a legitimate version? The chances of being caught are low.
Social	**Filesharing** and the **internet** mean that more people are obtaining copyrighted material for free. This may damage future investment in technology and its development.
Political	There is pressure to internationalise the laws on copyright protection and enforcement. Organisations such as **FAST** (Federation Against Software Theft) seek to encourage prosecution against law-breakers.

4.2.3 Accountability and control

Technological advances are challenging established practices regarding who or what is **accountable** for their actions. Many **processes are automated** with decisions being taken by computers, for example 'expert' systems authorising **loan advances** or making **medical diagnoses**. In the event of damage being done, who should be liable?

The following table summarises the main ethical, social and political issues.

Ethical	Should developers of systems be **liable** for the consequences of their use?
	Do **users** share or **accept responsibility** for the outputs of a system following their inputs?
Social	What expectations should society have regarding the **availability**, **accuracy** and **safety** of information systems?
	Should **individuals** be **responsible** for protecting data they enter into systems by taking backups?
	Should society take action against **libellous** or **offensive** websites?
Political	The government needs to **balance** the need of developers to be absolved from liability if their system fails, or harms others, with the need to protect the interests of the individual.

4.2.4 System quality

This ties in with the ideas around **accountability** and **control**.

At some stage in the development of software or a system, a decision is made that no more work will be done and that the product is ready for distribution.

Obviously nothing is perfect but users should expect a system to meet a certain level of quality. Developers need to weigh up the **costs of continued development** with those incurred when the **product fails** (fixing bugs and payment of damages to those harmed).

The following table summarises the main ethical, social and political issues.

Ethical	What level of quality should be achieved before a product is released?
	When should a developer offer improvements at no cost to the user?
Social	Awareness of problems surrounding the reliability should be raised. A **balance** should be struck between **expectations** of **infallible technology** and informing users of the **risk of its failure**.
Political	Issues of **legal accountability** for failures should be addressed.
	Should the government intervene to set **minimum standards of quality**, or should it allow the industry to regulate itself?

4.2.5 Quality of life

Advances in technology have improved quality of life in many ways but also has negative aspects that should be addressed. **Laudon and Laudon** (2013) identified the following issues.

(a) **The work/life balance.** Improvements in communications with **mobile phones** and **devices**, the **internet** and the **availability of technology** in people's homes blur the boundary between work life and home life.

(b) **Dependence and vulnerability.** More and more organisations such as schools, charities, private associations and businesses are **increasingly dependent** on technology to function. Failure of systems is **highly damaging** to them.

(c) **Computer crime.** Technology has **increased** opportunities for crime. Individuals and organisations are at risk from hackers, viruses and theft.

(d) **Re-engineering job losses.** Advances in technology filter down through organisations and employees are required to keep their skills **up-to-date** or face losing their jobs. Technology may make certain roles **obsolete**. Employees should be retrained where possible.

(e) **Class divide**. Technology can be expensive. Individuals on **low incomes** may not be able to afford it and as a result are **disadvantaged** as they are not party to the availability of information that those on a higher income enjoy.

(f) **Health issues**. **Repetitive stress injury** (RSI), **carpal tunnel syndrome** (CTS) and **computer vision syndrome** (CVS) are examples of physical problems caused by technology. **Technostress**, which manifests itself as aggravation, impatience and fatigue, has also been identified due to the cold, emotionless interaction that technology provides humans – especially when things go wrong.

4.3 Ethical issues

FAST FORWARD

The power and potential of information systems, and the general tend towards businesses being expected to act ethically, has led to discussion regarding the ethical use of information systems.

Key term

Ethics is concerned with judgements about whether human behaviour is morally right or wrong.

We have already seen some ethical issues raised by the information age that we live in.

4.3.1 Ethical analysis

We will look at **three examples** of ethical issues relating to the use of information systems.

(a) Suppose a university's computer is used for sending an email message to a friend or for conducting a private business (billing, payroll, inventory, etc). An observer could say that both activities are unethical (while recognising a difference in the amount of wrong being done). Another might say that the latter activities were wrong because they tied up too much memory and slowed down the machine, but the email message wasn't wrong because it had no significant effect on operations.

(b) A university lecturer uses her account to acquire the current grade average of a student from a class which she instructs. She obtained the password for this restricted information from someone in the Records Office who erroneously thought that she was the student. An observer could say that the instructor acted wrongly, since the only person who is entitled to this information is the student. Another may ask why the instructor wanted the information. If she replied that she wanted it to be sure that her grading of the student was consistent with the student's overall academic performance record, some may agree that such use was acceptable.

(c) At a particular university, if a professor wants an email account, all she or he need do is request one but a student must obtain faculty sponsorship in order to receive an account. Some observers may think this policy perfectly acceptable. Someone else may, on the other hand, question what makes the two situations essentially different (eg are professors assumed to have more need for email than students? Are students more likely to cause problems?).

There are no right or wrong answers to such questions, as in 'grey areas' moral and ethical judgements depend on who is making them.

Question   **Ethics and IT**

Here are questions covering a variety of issues that may arise in connection with the use of IT.

- Is personal email private?
- Is it necessary to encrypt email files?
- Is it appropriate to read someone else's computer files without permission?
- Is it acceptable to copy computer programs or data files?

Think about the relevant issues from the points of view of: the organisation that owns the system; the individual accessing the system or information; and the individual whose privacy could be invaded.

5 Developments in information and communications technology (ICT)

FAST FORWARD

Important developments in ICT include:

- The growth of Web 2.0 and social media
- The growth and development of e-commerce
- Customer relationship management
- Cloud computing
- Mobile technology
- Process automation
- Artificial intelligence (AI)
- Distributed ledger technology and blockchain
- Cryptocurrencies
- The internet of things (IoT)
- Big data

Exam focus point

Information and communications technology (ICT) is an area that develops constantly, and you need to have an awareness of it.

5.1 The impact of technological developments

The development of technology over time has allowed the accountant's role to be elevated beyond the mechanical recording of transactions to ensure the accounts balance and are accurate. Technology has allowed much of this historically administrative work to be automated, freeing the accountant's role up for more value adding work.

There are many studies which demonstrate that technology can increase in the value of workers, including accountants, in the following three main ways:

- It enables them to work faster.
- It enables them to work more efficiently.
- It makes them more productive at new tasks.

These attributes of technology can be seen as an opportunity for accountants to elevate their role to a more strategic level, where they can add more commercial value to the business than ever before. It could also be a threat to certain finance roles, such as those that historically have processed transactions, as technology is increasingly making this type of role redundant.

Whether an opportunity or a threat, technology continues to advance so the finance function needs to adapt its skill sets to keep up and make the best use of technology in the workplace.

5.2 The growth of Web 2.0 and social media

Web 2.0 applications are 'second generation' internet-based services. These sites usually include tools that let people collaborate and share information online.

Social media is defined by **Kaplan and Haenlein** ('Users of the world, unite! The challenges and opportunities of Social Media', *Business Horizons*, 2010) as 'internet applications that build on the foundations of Web 2.0 and that allow the creation and exchange of user-generated content'.

Examples of social media include:

- Blogs (short for 'web log')
- Micro-blogging (X, previously known as Twitter)

- Social-networking sites (Facebook, LinkedIn)
- Virtual social worlds (Second Life)
- Collaborative projects (Wikipedia)
- Content communities (YouTube)
- Virtual game worlds (World of Warcraft)

As well as being used by employees as alternatives to the telephone or email, social networking sites give businesses a fantastic opportunity to widen their circle of contacts and enhance their customer relationship management programmes. Using Facebook, for example, a small business can target an audience of hundreds of thousands relatively easily. Organisations may use social media to communicate directly with customers, such as through Facebook posts. Sales promotions and new products can be advertised quickly and at a low-cost.

There is also the opportunity for the customer to communicate directly with the company, for example by providing feedback on the service they received. This feedback is often able to be viewed by a wider audience (eg feedback provided using X).

A potential downside for organisations is the employee hours lost if employees waste time on social media sites.

Question
Web 2.0

Which of the following is the primary function of Web 2.0 technology?

A Increase sales
B Increase customer satisfaction
C Increase customer interaction
D Reduce delays in order processing

Answer

C Increase customer interaction

Web 2.0 is usually focused on collaborating and sharing information.

The other choices may follow from the sharing of information, but they are not the primary purpose of the technology.

5.3 The growth and development of e-commerce

E-commerce (the selling of goods or services over the internet) has grown rapidly over the past few years.

The trend is towards providing the customer with a unique shopping experience that is tailored to their needs. The view and products presented to a customer is geared to their individual tastes, based on their profile and past behaviour on the site.

Most organisations have e-commerce capability on their website. Many have gone further. For example, Amazon suggests potential purchases for customers when they log-on. These suggestions are driven by the customer's previous orders and their history of viewing products. The following points should be considered when building a website with e-commerce capability:

(a) Ensure transactions are **secure**, and tell customers they are. Customer trust is essential.
(b) Comply with all applicable consumer, privacy and data protection legislation.
(c) Have clear **terms of use** for the site.
(d) Don't require customers to provide excessive amounts of information as this may deter them.
(e) Maintain **ongoing communication** with willing customers, for example by email.

The term **e-business** refers to conducting business on the internet. It has a wider meaning than e-commerce, because it covers not only buying and selling but also servicing customers and collaborating with suppliers.

Benefits to a business of using e-commerce include; improved marketing and decision making though the collection of sales and customer data, increased sales as customers increasingly look to the internet to purchase goods, and reduced costs as it is cheaper to operate a website than a physical shop.

Despite the benefits of e-commerce, some organisations face a number of challenges when adopting it. For example, they may lack the necessary in-house skills to develop the website, it may be expensive to set up and maintain the trading platform, it may be difficult to integrate back-office and fulfilment systems and there are security issues that require addressing.

5.3.1 Digital markets and digital goods

The development of e-commerce has led to digital markets and goods. A **digital market** is a segment of a business' overall market that is found online rather than in the real world. It may include, for example, an internet shop that supplies physical products and services, or digital only content known as digital goods.

Digital goods have no physical presence and can be transferred from the seller to buyer almost instantaneously over the internet. Examples of digital goods include music, movies, books and magazines.

The main issue for a seller of digital goods is to ensure that it has a suitable online presence to attract customers and deliver the product effectively. Apple's iTunes software is a good example of how digital goods (music, movies and apps) can be advertised and sold.

5.4 Customer relationship management systems

Key term

> **Customer relationship management (CRM)** systems are software applications which specialise in providing information concerning an organisation's products, services and customers, the use of which can contribute towards the development of valuable customer relationships. Social media sites are often used by companies as part of their CRM strategy.

Most CRM systems are based on a **database** which stores data about customers such as their **order history** and **personal information** such as address, age and any marketing feedback they have provided. These systems allow a personalised service to be provided to the customer as well as a swift reply to their queries.

CRM systems are often used by customer facing staff who handle **customer enquiries**, **orders** or **complaints** and who need to understand the customer's immediate needs and provide an appropriate response.

The **benefits of CRM systems** are in regards to **customer retention** and **targeted marketing**. Better understanding of the customer, and being able to deal with them as an individual, should help generate customer loyalty. Since the needs of the customer are appreciated, marketing material can be better targeted.

5.4 The growth of cloud computing

Key term

> **Cloud computing** is a model for enabling ubiquitous, convenient, on-demand network access to a shared pool of configurable computing resources (eg networks, servers, storage, applications and services) that can be rapidly provisioned and released with minimal management effort or service provider interaction
>
> (**Source**: https://nvlpubs.nist.gov/nistpubs/legacy/sp/nistspecialpublication800-145.pdf [Accessed 7 October 2024])

Cloud computing involves sharing resources, software and information over a network (typically the internet).

The following diagram shows how the cloud works.

Cloud computing

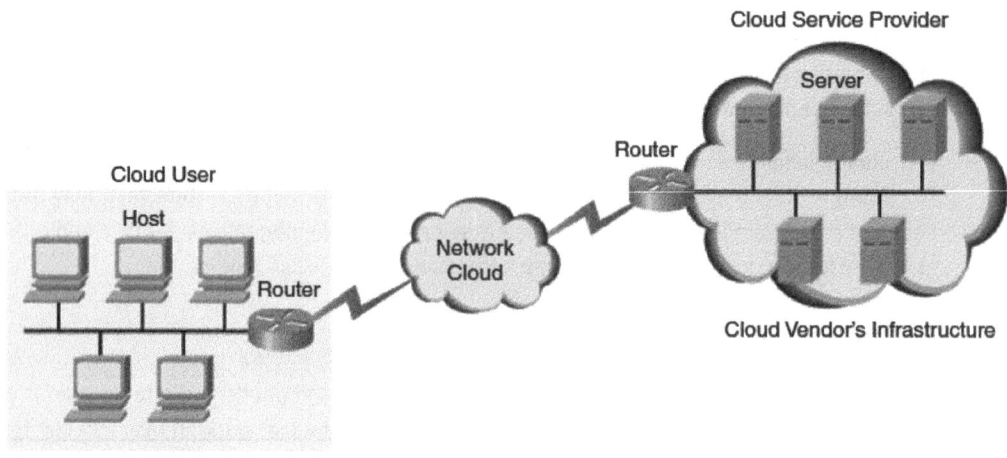

A cloud can be public or private:

- A public cloud service provider provides cloud services to anybody through the internet.
- A private cloud in limited in terms of who is able to access those services. An entirely private cloud will be hosted within one organisation.
- A hybrid of the two is a 'virtual private cloud' which is in fact hosted using public cloud resources but looks, feels and works like a private cloud.

The goal of cloud computing is to provide easy, scalable access to computing resources and IT services.

5.4.1 Popular examples of cloud computing

Web-based email services such as Hotmail, Yahoo! Mail and Gmail are simple examples of cloud computing, as the software and storage for the account exists in the service's computer, accessed via 'the cloud'.

Google, the internet giant, hosts a set of online productivity tools and applications in the cloud including email, word processing, calendars, photo sharing, and website creation tools. Apple also offers cloud computing that allows synchronisation of a user's various Apple devices so that the same information is automatically available on all of them.

DropBox is another popular service used to transfer files between users and devices, and to facilitate collaborative working.

5.4.2 Characteristics of cloud computing

A cloud computing service has distinct characteristics that differentiate it from traditional hosting:

Characteristic	Explanation
Sold on demand	Users pay for cloud services only when they use them (for example by the day, month or year).
Elastic	Cloud computing shifts the bulk of IT costs from capital expenditures (or buying and installing servers, storage, networking and related infrastructure) to an operating expense model, where users pay for the usage of these types of resources.
Fully managed	Users do not have to set up any machines, manage their systems, update them, or back them up as these aspects are mostly taken care of for the users by the service provider.
Scalable and self-service	Cloud computing allows for the expansion and reduction of resources according to specific service requirements.

5.4.3 Benefits and risks of cloud computing

Cloud computing may provide an organisation with a number of benefits; however, these need to be considered against the risks:

Benefits	Risks
Using cloud computing services may be more cost effective than operating in-house technology.	The organisation has to give up control of its data to an external party being the cloud-based service provider. Such providers may be in remote locations and as a result this increases the risk should the provider suffer some form of disaster event.
Cloud computing offers greater flexibility to organisations as there are lots of service providers around to choose from.	Data held by the service provider may be stolen, lost or corrupted.
Establishing a cloud-based approach to data storage and management can be done more quickly than establishing the technology in-house.	Increased danger that the service provider's own staff may interfere with data stored on its servers.
Storing organisational data on the cloud means that it is accessible anywhere around the world where there is internet connectivity.	Failure to keep up payments to the service provider to store data on the organisation's behalf may lead to a loss of access or even the deletion of data.
Cloud computing is available to both very large organisations and smaller entities.	

5.4.4 Impact on the finance function

Cloud computing is changing the structure and working of the finance function by:

- Allowing flexible working as staff can work in different locations at different times
- Allowing collaboration as files can be shared and updated by multiple staff in real-time
- Keeping software continuously up to date and improving compliance with data protection regulations
- Improving the integration of software as, eg, customer relationship management software can be linked to accounting software
- Improving data security as cloud providers better understand how to protect data

Finance functions use cloud computing in a similar way to other parts of the business. Files and software can be stored in cloud servers so that they can be easily shared by all users and accessed by employees whether they are located in the organisation's offices or not.

One application of cloud computing that is specific to finance functions is cloud accounting. Cloud accounting is the provision of accountancy software through the cloud. Users log in to the accountancy software to process financial transactions and produce management reports through a web browser or app. The software is hosted through the cloud but essentially behaves in the same way as if the software was installed on their own machine.

Examples of providers of cloud accounting software include QuickBooks, Xero and Sage.

This means accounting processing can be conducted from anywhere, at any time. All that is required is internet access (and a computing device). The output can also be easily shared around without having to email what is quite possibly commercially sensitive information.

5.5 Mobile technology

Mobile technology is concerned with technology that is portable. Mobile technology devices include laptops, tablet computers, smartphones, GPS technologies. Such devices enable users to communicate with one another in different ways, some of which may make use of the internet. Communicative features of mobile technologies include Wi-Fi connectivity, Bluetooth and 4G technologies.

Mobile technology has two types of impact on organisations:

- **New products and services**: For example, organisations can develop apps for smart devices that allow users to control home technology when away from the property (eg smart thermostats).
- **Freedom of location**: Employees can connect to their workplace wherever they are, providing they have internet access.

Mobile technology also contributes to efficiencies due to:

- Its scalability
- Facilitates flexible working
- Less paper – logging and recording information is done online
- Real time availability of information meaning business decisions are improved

It should be noted that laptops, netbooks and smartphones have security issues – they are easy to steal or lose. When using mobile devices it is important to ensure that employees are aware of their responsibilities and the need to keep both mobile devices and business information secure. If using public WiFi to access the internet, it may not always be possible to find a secure and available network. This may prevent access to business information when required.

There are costs involved in setting up the equipment and training required to make use of mobile devices. Mobile IT devices can expose valuable data to unauthorised people if the proper precautions are not taken to ensure that the devices, and the data they can access, are kept safe.

5.6 Process automation

Key term

> **Process automation** refers to the ability of systems to perform routine activities (such as the processing of data and assembling electronic components) without the input of a human. It is important to note this is not limited to physical automation (for example of production lines), but online automation, for example processing and responding to customer queries.

Robotic process automation (RPA) is the term given to the use of technology to facilitate the automation of previously manual and often routine processes. This increases speed, reliability and efficiency of processes and reduced staff costs.

We shall look at automation again later in this chapter when we shall see how it has transformed the finance function.

5.7 Artificial intelligence (AI)

Key term

> **Artificial intelligence (AI)** refers to the ability of a machine to perform cognitive functions we associate with human minds, such as perceiving, reasoning, learning and problem solving' and acting in a way that we would consider to be 'smart' (McKinsey and Co, no date).
>
> **Machine learning** is an application of AI in which systems or machines can learn from very large data sets, identify patterns and make decisions with minimal human intervention.

AI is a field of computer science that can mimic human intelligence. It is a technology that we can use to create systems that simulate human intelligence – for example, Apple's Siri or Amazon's Alexa.

AI is driven by machine learning.

A machine's learning algorithm empowers it to recognise patterns within observed data, constructing models that elucidate these patterns or make predictions. A fundamental characteristic of machine learning is its iterative nature: as models encounter new data, they autonomously adapt, modifying the underlying algorithm based on insights gained from the data.

AI enables computers to learn from data, enabling accurate execution of novel tasks and the generation of dependable decisions and outcomes. Consequently, AI, founded on machine learning, empowers organisations to make decisions without direct human involvement.

Machine learning manifests in various forms:

- **Supervised learning:** In this approach, training data and human feedback are used to demonstrate relationships between inputs and outputs. This entails human labelling of input data and output data. The algorithm learns to correlate inputs and outputs, and upon completion, is applied to new data.

- **Unsupervised learning:** Here, an algorithm explores input data without explicit output variables. The algorithm receives unlabelled data, deduces data structures, and identifies groups of behaviour with similar patterns.

- **Reinforcement learning:** This type involves an algorithm learning to perform a task, aiming to maximise rewards for its actions. The process includes the algorithm taking an action, receiving a reward if the action aligns with the objective, and optimising its actions over time by self-correction.

Machine learning algorithms do not require explicit programming but instead learn by doing. They adapt to new data and experiences, progressively enhancing their effectiveness in performing tasks and generating dependable decisions. An illustrative example is the predictive text feature on smartphones and internet search engines, where the algorithm becomes more accurate in predicting user inputs based on their past texts or searches.

Machine learning decisions are based on three important aspects of analytics:

- **Description** ('descriptive analytics'): shows correlations between historic and current variables, and attempts to explain the correlation

- **Prediction** ('predictive analytics'): anticipating what will happen, based on the data and patterns in the data

- **Prescription** ('prescriptive analytics'): providing recommendations for what to do in order to achieve goals or objectives

Applications of AI

The following are some examples of the ways AI and machine learning can be applied:

- Transportation – autonomous vehicles (self-driving cars) could potentially transform the way people move around.

- Route optimisation – analysing real-time information to identify potential problems and traffic jams, and to suggest alternative routes, can be very important for transport and delivery companies.

- Personalised recommendations – websites recommend items a customer might want to buy based on buying history (eg Amazon), or Netflix recommends programmes to watch based on previous viewing.

- Healthcare – machines can record and process vast amounts of patient data and can analyse it using sophisticated AI algorithms. As such, technology can be used to diagnose illnesses and create personalised medicines based on a deep knowledge of a person's genetics to help clinicians do their jobs more effectively. AI can also help to predict people who are at risk from certain diseases and target them for early intervention, thereby reducing the cost of future treatments which would otherwise be required.

- Portfolio management – 'robo-advisors' (eg Betterment or Wealthfront) use algorithms to tailor investment portfolios to the goals and risk appetite of the investor, and to adjust these for real-time changes in the market.
- Fraud detection – detecting anomalies in patterns of payments or receipts.
- Cybersecurity – AI makes decisions very quickly. One of the problems that cyber defence teams face is that they get so many alerts it is difficult to know how to prioritise them. AI can detect anomalies, and so can alert defence teams to the specific data they need to look at.

Note. In many of these cases, the volume of data available enables algorithms to find patterns and trends. In effect, AI is being used to analyse 'big data' – so it is important to note the links between AI and big data in this context.

Benefits and limitations of AI

AI offers many benefits to organisations but does not come without problems and limitations.

Benefits of AI	Limitations of AI
AI is able to quickly process large amounts of structured and unstructured data, providing fast, accurate and reliable outputs.	Although machine learning enables machines to adapt algorithms, the technology is only as good as the data it receives. (Maintaining high-quality data is crucial to a successful AI platform.)
AI can identify complex patterns in data, to enable better decision making and strategic planning.	Machines 'learn' from the data they are given, but if there are gaps or biases in the initial 'training' data, then the models the machines learn could be incomplete or inaccurate.
Machine learning can provide consistency with regard to decision making. Machines do not suffer tiredness like humans do. If the data that it is trained on is biased the algorithm will be biased. Also, crucially, machines' capacity for learning means they are able to process data and identify patterns without the need for human monitoring. (This is an important feature that distinguishes AI from big data analytics. Patterns and trends in data are also identified in big data analytics, but in AI the machines identify the trends and issues themselves without being prompted to do so by people.)	Machine learning models can lack flexibility; they can learn to carry out specific tasks but cannot reproduce the level of multifaceted analysis carried out by the human brain. (Eg, the technology in an autonomous vehicle enables it to drive a car, but it can only perform tasks related to driving the car.)

Some examples of how AI can support the finance function include:

- Simple processes can be automated, such as highlighting significant variances for further investigation.
- Predictive analytics can help forecast costs and revenues.
- AI enables improved analysis of unstructured data in contacts and emails, for example sifting through an email database for discussion around certain topics.

Question

Can you think of how AI might support an accountant who is working in an organisation's management accounting team?

Answer

AI might support an accountant working in a management accounting team by assisting them to prepare a commentary relating to a draft set of management accounts. AI could highlight key elements for discussion, and even contribute towards the narrative by identifying possible factors that have influenced the key elements.

5.8 Distributed ledger technology and blockchain

Key term

Distributed ledger technology is a technology that allows organisations and individuals who are unconnected to share an agreed record of events, such as ownership of an asset.

Blockchain is a public form of bookkeeping that uses a digital ledger to allow individuals to share a record of transactions.

Distributed ledger technology eliminates the need for data and information to be stored and managed centrally. Furthermore, it allows an accurate, up-to-date, single, trusted and transparent record to be shared between numerous parties.

Blockchain is a type of incorruptible distributed ledger that allows information to be recorded and shared with a network of individuals. In essence, blockchain is a public form of bookkeeping which makes use of internet technologies to instantly verify and record the transactions that take place between individuals. The public nature of blockchain means that every individual can view the transactions made by participants in that network. This means that participants can view the date, time, value of transactions, and the individuals involved, thereby creating a shared record of events.

It is anticipated that blockchain will have a disruptive impact on a wide range of industries as it increases the levels of transparency over transactions. Greater use of blockchain should allow organisations including firms of accountants and auditors to more easily verify the transactions undertaken by clients when preparing (and auditing) financial statements. The use of blockchain should also make it easier for accountants to verify the background and transactional history of prospective new clients, especially when undertaking money laundering procedures. Blockchain will also be beneficial to providers of finance as they will be able to make more informed decisions about which prospective clients they should lend to.

Participants of a blockchain record transactions on an online network that is publicly available and distributed to everyone.

Details of transactions are recorded by all participants. Transactions are only accepted once all participants have updated their ledgers to reflect them.

Network computers verify the transaction to make sure the records have all been updated correctly. Once the validation work is complete, the transaction is authorised and added to the blockchain. This means that a single system cannot itself add new blocks to the chain.

Blocks are connected to a blockchain using a cryptographic hash that is generated from the previous block. This means the chain cannot be broken and each block is preserved permanently. It is only possible to amend previous blocks if the subsequent blocks are altered first.

Stages in a blockchain transaction	Description
Stage 1	A transaction is requested
Stage 2	A digital representation of the transaction is requested (a block)
Stage 3	The block is sent to all nodes in the network (distributed ledger)
Stage 4	The authenticity of the transaction is verified by each node
Stage 5	A reward for the verification is sent to each node (such as a bitcoin)
Stage 6	The completed and authorised block is added to the chain

The ICAEW's report Blockchain and the Future of Accountancy (ICAEW, 2018) identifies three key features of blockchain, known as the Three Ps.

Feature	Description
Propagation	There are many copies of a blockchain ledger, but no master copy. All versions are identical. When new transactions occur, they propagate to all copies of the blockchain.
Permanence	Every user has their own copy of the blockchain, and past transactions cannot be edited. Therefore, the blockchain is a permanent record. Each copy can be inspected and verified.
Programmability	Blockchains may allow program code to be stored as well as transaction information. Such code may create ledger entries when triggered, allowing so-called smart contracts, which carry out actions automatically when certain conditions are met.

Question

Which of the following describes a way in which blockchain technology can assist with the prevention of fraud within accountancy?

- A By creating a tamper-proof and transparent record of all transactions
- B By ensuring only accountants have the ability to modify transaction records
- C By reducing the extent to which an external audit is required
- D By offering a digital currency through which transactions will be made

Answer

The correct answer is A: By creating a tamper-proof and transparent record of all transactions.

Blockchain does not allow accountants to modify transactions; this would facilitate fraud.

The need for an external audit is not reduced where blockchain is used.

Although blockchains have allowed for the development of digital currencies, this is not their only application. The currency in which the distributed ledger was held would have no bearing on the effectiveness of the technology to prevent fraud.

Distributed ledger technology and blockchain can increase the clarity and transparency in the recording of business transactions.

Key uses are in regard to measuring the value of assets and verifying asset ownership and accounting transactions, which are of interest to financial reporting and internal audit. Accurate and transparent records can be created of asset ownership and associated transactions. This helps to reduce the need for internal auditors and financial accountants to check transactions and verify the ownership of assets because they have a source of information about the assets that they can trust.

Blockchain may have the following impacts on the finance function:

- Cryptocurrency (see below) allows money to cross borders easily and seamlessly by avoiding traditional intermediaries such as banks.
- The security and traceability of transactions may impact how businesses record their dealings with third parties.
- Smart contracts can be created which are self-executing agreements that utilise cryptography, digital signatures and secure completion. If certain obligations are met, they can be automatically executed on a particular date and time.

5.9 Cryptocurrencies

Cryptocurrencies such as bitcoin are digital tokens that allow users to trade with each other online. They are an alternative to traditional currencies.

Many of the cryptocurrencies use distributed ledgers and blockchain technology to maintain records of transactions, and owner's currencies are kept in 'digital wallets'. Unlike traditional currencies, no third parties (such as banks or online payment agencies) are required to record transactions. This can save transaction costs and provide greater privacy to the traders.

There is still scepticism amongst individuals, and regulatory institutions concerning cryptocurrencies. Companies would be mindful of the following concerns:

- As cryptocurrencies are unregulated by a central bank, their values are often exceptionally volatile.
- Cryptocurrencies provide anonymity to traders, meaning that they can be used to finance illicit activities (eg cybercriminals often demand payment in cryptocurrency).
- A number of governments have banned the use of cryptocurrencies which may limit their acceptability as a means of payment.

5.10 Internet of things ('IoT')

Key term

The internet of things (IoT) include physical devices with internet connectivity enabling them to interact with many other devices via the internet, as well as enabling the user to control them remotely. For example, the Amazon Echo can play music, make calls, set alarms/timers, answer user questions, manage shopping lists, control Bluetooth enabled lights and so on.

The internet of things includes smart devices, sensors and security devices which are connected over the internet to perform a range of tasks. They can record and store data as well as transferring the data over the internet to other devices. They can also be controlled remotely by other connected devices, such as apps on a smart phone.

By combining connected devices with automated systems, it is possible to gather information, analyse it and create an action to perform a task or learn from a process.

The internet of things provides businesses with more data about the products or services, thereby improving their ability to make changes.

The following are some of the potential applications of the internet of things:

- Sensors on products (or components) transmit data about how that product is performing. This can help a company identify if a product, or component, is likely to fail, meaning it can carry out preventative maintenance before the failure causes any damage.

- Real-time data generated by sensors on products can be used to make supply chains more efficient, for example by being able to track the location of freight which is being delivered. (RFID – radio frequency identification – can also be useful in inventory and supply chain management, allowing organisations to keep track of assets by tagging them.) Sensors monitoring traffic flows can provide information about the best routes for delivery drivers to take.

- Sensors in smart buildings can adjust temperature automatically – for example, turning on air conditioning if sensors detect a conference room is occupied, or turning the heating in a building down once everyone has gone home.

Question

In what way can the internet of things (IoT) impact on business management?

A   Improving decision making through the provision of real-time data from interconnected devices
B   It automates repetitive and time-consuming tasks
C   It provides real-time access to financial information from anywhere in the world
D   It eliminates the need to access the internet via more traditional routes

Answer

The correct answer is A: Improving decision making through the provision of real-time data from interconnected devices.

The internet of things (IoT) facilitates the provision of real-time data from connected devices. The availability of data, and the speed with which is it delivered can benefit managers as it improves the decision making process, for example decisions are likely to be better informed and can be taken quickly allowing for competitive advantage to be achieved.

The automation of repetitive and time consuming tasks is achieved through process automation.

The provision of real-time access to financial information from anywhere in the world is an advantage of mobile technology and cloud computing.

The IoT is unlikely to have much bearing on the extent to which managers would need to access the internet.

6 Automation in business

Process automation refers to the ability of systems to perform routine activities (such as the processing of data and assembling electronic components) without the input of a human. It is important to note this is not limited to physical automation (for example production lines), but online automation, eg processing and responding to customer queries.

Three types of activities will continue to evolve in business

6.1 Machine-only activities

These are activities where machines will always outperform humans. They typically involve routine processing of transactions, making rational predictions and generating answers to questions. However, some degree of human involvement is currently needed to put the output into context and resolve errors that might arise, however AI will increasingly take on this more complex role.

6.2 Human-only activities

These are activities where humans will always outperform machines. They typically involve the application of knowledge across a range of different tasks and finding patterns of interest. They may also involve making predictions based on a higher level of judgement than making a rational prediction. That said, AI can increasingly take on what have historically been seen as human-only roles.

6.3 Human and machine hybrid activities

These are activities where technology can augment human intelligence to make finance professionals faster, more efficient and more productive. Such activities can be significantly enhanced because of the value humans bring to machines by training, programming and maintaining the machines and because machines can amplify the work humans can do.

6.4 The automation paradox

The automation paradox occurs as technology takes tasks out of human control, resulting in loss of skills in these areas. However, atypical events might occur that systems are not designed to cope with or do not have the capacity to deal with. In such circumstances, the deskilling of humans means that the tasks cannot be quickly or easily performed. The paradox can be overcome by ensuring staff have a full understanding of how the systems work so that they can either assist the system to overcome the problem or to perform the task manually themselves.

6.5 Impact of automation on business management

Automation has had a significant impact on business management, resulting in many benefits such as increased efficiency and cost savings. However, it also presents managers with the challenges associated with job displacement such as a need to upskill and retrain staff, re-deploy resources and manage redundancy processes.

Impacts on business management include the following.

Increased productivity and efficiency	The automation of repetitive tasks allow work to be carried out quickly, efficiently and accurately.
	This also frees up the time of human staff, allowing them to focus on the more challenging, creative or strategic aspects of their roles.
Improved data accuracy	Automation of repetitive tasks remove or reduce the potential for human error.
	This can result in the provision of more reliable data which improves management decision making.

Cost savings	Operational costs, such as wages and salaries, will be reduced due to the lower requirement for human staff.
	The reduction of time spent correcting errors, and the reduced risk of the consequences associated with poor decision making, should also lead to cost savings.
	Lower operational costs can either be passed on to consumers to potentially undercut the competition, or the savings retained for investment elsewhere. Either way could lead to higher profitability.
Workplace safety	Automation could either increase or decrease the risks related to work place safety.
	On one hand, the increased requirement to work alongside machinery or technology might bring new health and safety risks.
	On the other hand, there will be fewer employees and the increased time available and cost savings should allow for investment in safety measures and improved staff training.
Improved customer service	Newly freed up staff time can be redeployed into customer facing roles allowing for customer service to be improved, for example through faster response times and a more personalised service.
	Further, customer needs can be better addressed due to the increased availability and reliably of data obtained through automation, again improving customer service and satisfaction levels.
Improved flexibility and scalability	Where an organisation uses automation, growth can be easier accommodated, for example additional services can easily be added or more data capacity purchased. This is quicker, simpler and cheaper than the time and costs involved in recruiting more labour to meet the increased demand.
Security	There are both positive and negative considerations in relation to security.
	The opportunities for error and fraud are likely to be lower with process automation, and the ability of the system to detect cyber threats may reduce the risk of them occurring or increase the speed to which they can be responded to.
	On the other hand, the introduction of technology to the business increases cybersecurity risks such as hacking and malware (viruses).
Systems downtime and connectivity issues	If an automated system cannot be accessed due to internet connectivity issues or systems downtime this can cause several issues. For example, work could grind to a halt if automated processes cannot be carried out. Additionally customer service might be affected, for example if a customer is unable to access customer support resources, which can have a direct impact on customer satisfaction, particularly if unavailability becomes a regular occurance.
Job displacement	Automation will inevitably create changes in the workforce. This will present specific problems for managers in terms of managing redundancies, identifying roles for staff elsewhere in the organisation and identifying and providing training and upskilling needs to re-deployed staff.

Change management	Automation is likely to involve a significant degree of change. Managers will need to carefully manage this process. For example they will need to transparently communicate the change, respond to the concerns and needs of staff, manage staff resistance to the change, develop new processes, ensure the co-ordination of the new processes with the rest of the organisation, identify training needs and so on.
New skills	Managers are likely to need training and new skills to be able to carry out the role required of them in terms of implementing the new processes, managing the change, and overseeing the new process.

6.6 Impact of automation on the components of the finance function

The table below summarises some examples of how automation impacts the work of the finance function. Most of the impacts are to remove roles which a computer can be programmed to do and to create roles that add value to the information generated by technology.

Component of the finance function	Examples of automation
Financial reporting	Downloads of bank transactions into the accounting system
	Posting of bank transactions to nominal accounts
	Reconciliations of bank, supplier and customer accounts
	Creation of statutory accounts
	Exception reports to identify possible errors or areas requiring professional attention
Management accounting	Generation of management accounts
	Calculation of variances and finance ratios
	In-depth analysis of results and data analytics to support theories of why performance was as it was
	Budgeting based on current actuals
	Forecasting based on assumptions set by the finance team
Treasury	Investment appraisal calculations
	Analysis of financial markets to predict costs of capital
	'What if' scenario planning to analyse potential outcomes for investments
	Monitoring of currency markets to identify the best opportunities to buy and sell different currencies
	Cash flow forecasting to identify future requirements for cash to reduce shortfalls
Internal audit	Routine monitoring of transactions to identify only suspicious transactions that need investigation
	Routine testing of controls and procedures (such as tracing invoices through the system)
	Simulations of cyberattacks to test the strength of IT systems and risk of attack
	Real-time feedback of system controls and monitoring via a dashboard
	Vulnerability testing to identify potential weaknesses and impacts on the business if they occur

McKinsey (2017) identified five functions that can be automated by technology. (**Source**: https://www.mckinsey.com/featured-insights/digital-disruption/harnessing-automation-for-a-future-that-works/de-DE [Accessed 7 October 2024]). The following table sets out the percentage of the functions that could be automated and the level of the finance function that they can be found.

PART D MANAGERIAL CONTROL: MANAGING INFORMATION SYSTEMS AND TECHNOLOGY

Function	Percentage that can be automated	Level in the finance function
Managing others	9%	Leading the finance team
Stakeholder interactions	20%	Partnering for value and shaping how the organisation creates and preserves value
Applying expertise	18%	
Data processing	69%	Generating insights in specialist areas
Data collection	64%	Assembling and extracting data, providing limited insight

However, in general, automation is changing the work of the accountant from recording and verifying low-level transactions to higher-level activities such as producing and analysing reports.

Automation is increasing the effectiveness of accountants because they can spend less time on simple, routine tasks and more time on value-adding services, making better use of the professional knowledge and skills that they have.

There are a number of advantages and disadvantages to finance functions of investing in process automation.

Advantages	Disadvantages
Frees up staff time to focus on value-adding activities	Systems are only as effective as the person who creates them. Therefore, the programmer must be competent and understand the existing process completely.
Headcount can be reduced as work is automated, this helps to reduce costs	Introducing the system involves change which must be managed carefully and thoughtfully.
Removal of human error will improve accuracy of information	Systems may create uncertainty over job security and future prospects in staff.
Can be used as a catalyst to help the organisation adapt and improve in response to change	Training costs can be significant.

Question

Which of the following statements about business automation are true?

(a) Process automation removes all need for human judgment in the financial decision making process.

(b) Process automation can significantly reduce the number of accounting errors in the financial recording system.

A   Both statements are true
B   Only statement (a) is true
C   Only statement (b) is true
D   Both statements are false

Answer

The correct answer is C: Only Statement (b) is true.

It is not true that process automation removes all need for human judgment in the financial decision making process. While much of the repetitive and time-consuming tasks can be automated, human judgment will still be needed to interpret data and information and make sound decisions.

7 Big data

FAST FORWARD

Big data analytics is a term used to describe the extraction of meaning from vast quantities of data. Organisations are particularly interested in identifying trends and correlations in the data that they collect and store with the aim of putting this to commercial use.

Big data has been said to be comprised of four Vs (volume, velocity, variety and veracity).

7.1 What is big data?

Key term

Big data is used to describe the vast volumes of data which is captured from various sources, both internally and externally, and includes structured data, as well as unstructured data such as social media posts, news stories, video and audio clips. This is often analysed to reveal patterns or trends, especially relating to human behaviour or interactions.

Big data is an emerging technology that has implications across all business departments. It involves the collection and analysis of large amounts of data to find trends, understand customer needs and help organisations to focus resources more effectively.

The term 'big data' is used to describe the exponential growth and availability of data, both structured and unstructured.

In a commercial setting 'big data' is being used to identify trends that may exist in vast quantities of data in the pursuit of value creation. These trends can then be 'commercialised' – in other words, fed into business decision that help further the organisations objectives. For example, an understanding of customer tastes can inform design decisions for the next generation of products.

Sources of big data include:

- Human interactions with social networks, search engines, online retailers, and so on
- Machines, such as smart devices with sensors (the IoT)
- Open data sources, such as statistics published by the government and public services
- Closed data sources, such as marketing databases, where data has been processed by research organisations and is available for a fee

Historically, organisations have been restricted as to the amount of data that they can process due to the storage limitations of existing computer systems.

Due to the emergence of 'cloud based' data storage providers and improved computer technologies, these problems are gradually being overcome.

7.2 Characteristics of big data

'Big data has four characteristics

Volume	The volume of data generated is a key feature of 'big data'. The quantity of data now being produced is being driven by social media and transactional-based data sets recorded by large organisations, for example data captured from in-store loyalty cards and till receipts.
Velocity	Velocity refers to the speed at which 'real time' data can be accessed by the organisation. Big data is often available to an organisation in real time rather than at intervals such as on a weekly or monthly basis. To make data valuable it needs to be processed in a reasonable time frame.

Variety	Variety concerns the forms that big data can take. Structured data may take the form of numerical data whereas un-structured data may be in the format of email or video. Big data is often un-structured. This presents challenges for organisations as it is more complex, takes up more storage space, and processing varied forms of data requires significant investment in people and IT infrastructure.
Veracity	Veracity concerns the trustworthiness, or accuracy, of big data. Despite an organisation's best efforts, data sets will contain inaccuracies, bias, anomalies and irrelevant 'noise'. Therefore, as much as possible needs to be done to verify the data before it can be trusted as accurate.
	Data cleansing aims to ensure the veracity of information. It seeks to identify inaccurate, incomplete or irrelevant information. Once this is done, action can be taken to rectify problems or discard the information if problems with it make it worthless.

7.2.1 Characteristics and components of big data and the finance function

Finance functions use data analytics to provide insights that can add value to decision makers in the organisation. The table below considers how the characteristics and components of big data can be managed by the finance function.

Characteristic	Components of big data and management by the finance function
Volume (the quantity of data that is available)	Because big data is readily available and in vast quantities, a key component of big data is the infrastructure used to store it.
	The role of finance here is to assist management in determining the storage needs of the organisation. Volumes of data stored should be closely monitored and predictions run on future demand for storage.
	A key risk for the business will be running out of data storage and therefore internal audit should be involved in ensuring the ever-increasing need for data storage is met. Cloud storage would be a good solution because it can be scaled up or down as needed.
Velocity (the speed at which big data can be streamed)	Because big data can be streamed in real time, another component is the network and communications system used to distribute and view it.
	A key role for finance is to provide benchmarking insights (for example, on system speeds and downtime) to the IT function. If data cannot be streamed as fast as the business requires, then the infrastructure should be upgraded or replaced.
Variety (the different forms that big data can take)	Because big data comes from many sources and can take many forms (such as structured and unstructured), another component is the data connection and visualisation tools that can make sense of it.
	A key role for finance is to ensure that these data connection and visualisation tools enable the function to meet the organisation's need for insight.
Veracity (the trustworthiness or accuracy of big data)	Due to the volume of data held, a certain percentage of data sets will contain inaccuracies, bias, anomalies and 'noise'.
	The finance function has a key role to play in cleansing the data before it can be trusted as accurate.

7.3 Big data, digitisation and decision making

Key term

> **Data analytics** is the collection, management and analysis of large data sets with the objective of discovering useful information that an organisation can use for decision making.

There are numerous uses of big data in the business context. At this stage will shall consider how it is relevant to businesses decision making.

Businesses make all kinds of decisions every day, for example should it enter a new market, redesign its packaging, re-organise the sales team or keep the organisation the same. Such decisions are often more complicated than they first appear because many factors will come into play to determine whether or not the decision will be successful. In very complex decisions, some factors are beyond the knowledge of those taking them. The key role of big data is to analyse all relevant information and to generate a predictive model of what the outcome of the decision will be. Only data that has been digitised, or in a digital form, can be analysed.

7.3.1 Big data and business value

Business value is measured in many ways, such as profit, shareholder value, brand value and intellectual value. Big data can be used to analyse opportunities to increase revenue and reduce costs, thereby increasing profit. For example, a holiday company can use big data to analyse trends in where tourists are visiting in order to improve the range of holiday locations that it offers.

7.3.2 Big data and the customer

Understanding the customer is a key benefit of big data analytics. By understanding the customer, the business can respond to their needs and tailor the customer experience to be more personal and therefore improve customer loyalty.

7.3.3 Big data and corporate strategy

To be successful, big data must fit into the organisation's overall corporate strategy and be used to help drive what the strategy is. After identifying how business value can be improved, and the requirements of the customer, business priorities can be determined – eg which markets or customers are the most important in terms of increasing business value. Once the priorities are established, the organisation should analyse its current capability to meet the priorities. Decisions can be taken, based on data, that are most appropriate and have the best predicted chance of success.

7.4 Effect of big data on decisions

The key effects of big data on decisions can be summarised as follows:

- Decisions can be made quickly.
- Businesses can respond earlier to environmental changes and be more flexible in their response.
- Decisions can be based on current situation but also have an element of taking potential future situations into account.
- Decisions are made on hard data evidence that can be quantified.
- Decisions can be made on a collaborative basis because data is easily shared and converted from one form into another.
- 'Outside the box' decisions are more likely because all factors are taken into account, not just the ones managers think of.

7.5 Benefits of 'big data' analytics

There are a number of potential benefits to organisations undertaking big data analytics.

Benefits	Comment
Examine vast quantities of data relatively quickly	Big data analytics allows for large quantities of data to be examined to identify trends and correlations eg shopper buying habits.
Fresh insight and understanding	Intelligent use of data can reveal patterns and insight into how a business operates and identify previously unknown issues
Improved performance	The processing of data and the creation of relevant management information in real-time can result in improvements to operations, decision making and resource utilisation.
Improves organisational decision making	Better data analysis help management to take advantage of current social trends by introducing new products to meet customers' needs. Decisions can also be made faster due to the real-time processing of data, offering the organisation advantage over the competition.
Innovation	Existing products can be improved through the organisation better understanding the aspects of the product that customers value the most. New products can also be developed.
Segmentation and customisation of markets	The needs and wants of customer groups can be increasingly refined, leading to better personalisation and customisation of products and services.
Greater focus on the individual customer	Organisations can target special offers or discounts directly to individual customers to entice repeat business.
Cost reduction	Improved data about customers and internal operations may help to reduce costs. This is illustrated in the following case study.
Risk management	Data analytics can support all aspects of the risk management process.

7.6 Criticisms of 'big data'

Some doubt the ability of 'big data' to deliver the anticipated benefits. Critics argue:

- 'Big data' is simply a buzzword, a vague term that has turned into an obsession in large organisations and the media. Relatively few examples exist where analysing vast amounts of data have resulted in significant new discoveries.

- The benefits of big data for an organisation depend very much upon having both the IT systems capability, and people with sufficient skills, to be able to analyse it

- There is a focus on finding correlations between data sets, and less of an emphasis on causation. Critics suggest that it is easier to identify correlations between two variables than to determine what is actually causing the correlation.

12: THE IMPACT OF IT ON WORK PRACTICES

Question — Big data

Which of the following is NOT an advantage of using big data?

- A Making faster, better decisions
- B Creating brand-new revenue streams
- C Increased volume of data within the organisation
- D Generating insights to tackle important challenges

Answer

C Increased volume of data within the organisation

More volume doesn't necessarily mean that volume will be used well.

However big data should result in better insights and decisions providing the data is analysed quickly. It can then be used to generate new revenue streams.

8 Costs, benefits, risks and implementing new information systems

FAST FORWARD

The costs of an information system include equipment costs, installation costs, development costs, personnel costs and operating costs.

The benefits of an information system include increases in efficiency, capacity, accuracy, decision making, collaboration and customer service, and decreases in costs and errors.

There are a number of risks involved in implementing a new information system. Risks can occur at a number of stages, in particular at the design and development stages.

8.1 Cost benefit analysis and reviews

Cost-benefit analysis and cost-benefit reviews can be used to determine whether or not it is worthwhile developing a new information system and to determine whether, after a new system has been implemented, it achieves the benefits that it set out to.

Cost-benefit analysis is performed before or during the development of an information system. Its performance is complicated by the fact that many of the system cost elements are estimates or are unknown and that benefits can often be highly qualitative and subjective in nature.

A cost-benefit review is similar to a cost-benefit analysis, except that it is performed after the system has been implemented. Therefore, actual data can be used in the review.

The main analysis and review techniques are:

- The payback method
- Discounted cashflow
- Accounting rate of return/Return on investment

8.2 Costs of information systems

The costs of an information system can be categorised as development, implementation and running costs.

- Development costs are incurred before the system has been implemented.
- Implementation costs are incurred to get the developed system ready for use.
- Running costs are incurred on a day-to-day basis as the system is operated and maintained.

System costs can also be analysed under the following headings.

Cost type	Examples
Equipment costs	Computer and peripherals
	Ancillary equipment
Installation costs	New buildings (if necessary)
	The computer room (wiring, air-conditioning if necessary)
Development costs	Measuring and analysing the existing system
	Software/consultancy work
	Systems analysis and programming
	Changeover costs such as file conversion
Personnel costs	Staff training
	Staff recruitment/relocation
	Staff salaries and pensions
Operating costs	Consumable materials
	Maintenance
	Accommodation costs
	Heating/power/insurance/telephone
	Standby arrangements, in case the system breaks down

8.3 Benefits of information systems

The benefits of an information system can be categorised as direct and indirect.

- Direct benefits include reduced operating costs, for example lower staff overtime payments. These are often financial and easy to quantify.

- Indirect benefits might include better decision making and the freeing of human 'brainpower' from routine tasks so that it can be used for more creative work. These are often non-financial and hard to quantify.

General benefits from a proposed new system may include:

- Savings because an inefficient old system will no longer be operated

- Extra savings or revenue benefits because of the improvements or enhancements that the new system should bring

- Greater customer satisfaction, arising from a prompter service

- Improved staff morale from working with a 'better' system
- Better decision making is hard to quantify, but may result from better systems
- Faster processing speed of routine tasks and outputs
- Reduced scope for human error improves accuracy of input
- Increased volumes of data that can be processed
- Ability to handle more complexity in terms of the number of data streams
- Improved collaboration across all business functions due to real-time sharing of data
- Improved methods of presenting data in a user-friendly way that is easier to understand (data visualisations)

8.4 Risks of new information systems

There are a number of risks involved in implementing a new information system. Risks can occur at a number of stages, in particular at the design and development stages.

8.4.1 Risks in the design stage

A key risk is that the system is not designed appropriately so that it does not meet the needs of end-users. A common cause of dissatisfaction with new information systems is insufficient user involvement when establishing requirements for the new system.

Other risks that can cause dissatisfaction with information systems at this stage, include the following:

(a) Project managers are often technicians, not managers. However, technical ability of IT staff is also no guarantee of project management skill. An individual might be a highly proficient analyst or programmer, but not a good manager.

(b) The project manager may accept an unrealistic deadline where the timescale is fixed early in the planning process. User demands may be accepted as deadlines before sufficient consideration is given to the realism of this.

(c) Poor or non-existent planning is a recipe for disaster. Unrealistic deadlines would be identified much earlier if a proper planning process was undertaken.

(d) There is a lack of monitoring and control.

(e) Users change their requirements, resulting in changes to the system as it is being developed.

(f) Poor timetabling and resourcing. It is no use being presented on Day 1 with a team of programmers when there is still systems analysis and design work to do. The development and implementation of a computer project may take a considerable length of time (perhaps two years for a relatively large installation). Major projects require formal planning and scheduling.

8.4.2 Risks in the development process

Issues that occur when implementing a new system can usually be traced to deficiencies in the development process.

The table that follows outlines some common risks and mistakes that adversely affect the implementation process, and the systems development stage or activity they relate to.

Stage/activity	Problems
Analysis	The problem the system is intended to solve is not fully understood.
	Investigation of the situation is hindered by insufficient resources.
	User input is inadequate through either lack of consultation or lack of user interest.
	The project team is unable to dedicate the time required or insufficient time spent planning the project.
Design	Insufficient user input
	Lack of flexibility – the organisation's future needs are neglected.
	The system requires unforeseen changes in working patterns.
	Failure to perform organisation impact analysis. An organisational impact analysis studies the way a proposed system will affect organisation structure, attitudes, decision making and operations. The analysis aims to ensure the system is designed to best ensure integration with the organisation.
	Organisational factors sometimes overlooked include: • Ergonomics (including equipment, work environment and user interfaces) • Health and safety • Compliance with legislation • Job design • Employee involvement
Programming	Insufficient time and money allocated to programming
	Programmers supplied with incomplete or inaccurate specifications
	The logic of the program is misunderstood
	Poor programming technique results in programs that are hard to modify
	Programs are not adequately documented.
Testing	Insufficient time and money allocated to testing
	Failure to develop an organised testing plan
	Insufficient user involvement
	User management do not review and sign off the results of testing.
Conversion	Insufficient time and money allocated to data conversion
	Insufficient checking between old and new files
	The process is rushed to compensate for time overruns elsewhere.
Final implementation	Insufficient time, money and/or appropriate staff mean the process has to be rushed.
	Lack of user training increases the risk of system underutilisation and rejection.
	Poor system and user documentation
	Lack of performance standards to assess system performance against
	System maintenance provisions inadequate

8.5 Implementing new information systems

FAST FORWARD

The main steps in the implementaton of an information system are installation, testing, training, file conversion, change over and post-implementation review.

Once a new system has been through a cost benefit analysis, and has been designed and developed, it is ready to be implemented. The main steps in the implementation of an information system are as follows:

8.5.1 Installation

Installing involves setting up the computer hardware and loading the software onto it. It also involves setting up local networks and internet connections. Historically the software would have been loaded onto a central mainframe computer, although more recently, client server networks are used, whereby programmes are loaded onto servers and accessed from 'client' PCs for shared programmes (eg the accounting system). Many programmes are loaded directly onto the users' PCs.

The growth of cloud computing means that much of the hardware and software may be located remotely on the cloud service provider's hardware, accessed via the internet. If that is the case, the installation stage will involve giving users access to the cloud-based systems.

8.5.2 Testing

A system must be thoroughly tested before implementation, to prevent the system 'going live' with faults that might prove costly. The scope of tests and trials will vary with the size and complexity of the system. To ensure a coherent, effective approach to testing, a testing strategy should be developed.

A testing strategy should cover the following areas.

Testing strategy area	Comment
Strategy	A testing strategy should be formulated that details the approach that will be taken to testing, including the tests to be conducted and the testing tools/techniques that will be used.
Test plan	A test plan should be developed that states what will be tested, when it will be tested (sequence), and the test environment.
Test design	The logic and reasoning behind the design of the tests should be explained.
Test procedures	Detailed procedures should be provided for all tests. This explanation should ensure tests are carried out consistently, even if different people carry out the tests.
Documentation	It must be clear how the results of tests are to be documented. This provides a record of errors, and a starting point for error correction procedures.
Retesting	The retest procedure should be explained. In many cases, after correction all aspects of the software should be retested to ensure the corrections have not affected other aspects of the software.

Four stages of testing can be identified as:

Stage	Comment
Testing system logic	Before any programs are written, the logic devised by the systems analyst should be checked. This process often involves the use of flowcharts or data flow diagrams. Both tools involve the manual plotting of different types of data and transactions through the system. The object is to ensure that all possibilities have been catered for and that the processing logic is correct. When all results are as expected, programs can be written.

Stage	Comment
Program testing	Program testing involves processing test data through all system programs. Test data should be of the type that the program will be required to process and should include invalid/exceptional items to test whether the program reacts as it should. The testing process should be fully documented – recording data used, expected results, actual results and action taken. This documentation may be referred to at a later date, for example if program modifications are required. Two types of program testing are unit testing and unit integration testing.
System integration testing	System integration testing has a wider focus than program testing. It will involve testing both before installation (known as off-line testing) and after implementation (on-line testing). As many problems as possible should be identified before implementation, but it is likely that some problems will only become apparent when the system goes live.
User acceptance testing	The purpose of user acceptance testing is to establish whether users are satisfied that the system meets the system specification when used in the actual operating environment. Users process test data; system performance is closely monitored, and users report whether they feel the system meets their needs. Test data may include some historical data, because it is then possible to check results against the 'actual' output from the old system.

8.5.3 Types of tests

To ensure as many scenarios as possible are tested, testing should include the following types of tests:

(a) **Realistic tests.** These involve using the system in the way it will be used in reality – ie the actual environment, users and types of data.

(b) **Contrived tests.** These are designed to present the system with unusual events to ensure these are handled correctly, for example that invalid data is rejected.

(c) **Volume tests.** These present the system with large numbers of transactions to see how the system copes.

(d) **Acceptance tests.** These are undertaken by users to ensure the system meets user needs.

8.5.4 Training

Staff training in the use of a new system is essential if the system is to meet its full potential. Training should be provided to all staff who will use the system. Training should focus on the specific tasks the user is required to perform, such as entering an invoice or answering a query. There are a range of options available to deliver training, as shown below.

Training method	Comment
Individual tuition 'at desk'	A trainer could work with an employee observing how they use a system and suggesting possible alternatives.
Classroom course	The software could be used in a classroom environment, using 'dummy' data.
Computer-based training	Online training can be provided over an intranet or via an interactive website.
Case studies and exercises	Regardless of how training is delivered, it is likely that material will be based around a realistic case study relevant to the user.
Software reference material	Users may find online help, built-in tutorials and reference manuals useful.

8.5.5 File conversion

File conversion means converting existing files into a format suitable for the new system.

Most computer systems are based around files containing data. When a new system is introduced, files must be created that conform to the requirements of that system. The various scenarios that file conversion could involve are outlined in the following table.

Existing data	Comment
Held in manual (ie paper) files	Data will be keyed into the new system – probably via input forms, so that data entry operators have all the data they require in one document. This is likely to be a time-consuming process. Such situations are very rare, as most new systems replace existing computerised systems rather than manual systems.
Held in existing computer files	How complex the process is in converting the files to a format compatible with the new system will depend on technical issues and the coding systems used. It may be possible to automate much of the conversion process.
Held in both manual and computer files	Two separate conversion procedures are required.
Existing data is incomplete	If the missing data is crucial, it must be researched and made available in a format suitable for the new system – or suitable for the file conversion process.

8.5.6 Changeover

Once the new system has been fully and satisfactorily tested, the final stage of implementation, changeover, can begin. There are four approaches to system changeover; each varies in terms of time required, cost and risk.

- Direct ('Big Bang') changeover – the old system is completely replaced by the new system in one move.
- Parallel running – the old and new systems are run in parallel for a period of time.
- Pilot operation – a part or parts of an organisation are selected to operate the new system in parallel with the existing system.
- Phased or modular implementation – a complete section of the system is selected for a direct changeover.

The advantages and disadvantages of the various changeover methods are outlined below.

Method	Advantages	Disadvantages
Direct ('Big Bang') changeover	Quick Minimal cost Minimal workload	Risky Could disrupt operations If fails, will be costly
Parallel running	Safe Provides a way of verifying results of the new system	Costly, two systems need to be operated Time consuming Additional workload
Pilot operation	Less risky than direct changeover Less costly than complete parallel running	Can take a long time to achieve total changeover Not as safe as complete parallel running
Phased or modular changeover	Less risky than a single direct changeover Any problems should be in one area – other operations unaffected	Can take a long time to achieve total changeover Interfaces between parts of the system may make this impractical

Question

A hospital has identified a need for a new computer system to administer patients that it is looking after in its accident and emergency department (A&E). The current system consists of a database that records and store basic patient information, such as name, age and date of birth. However, the new system will also be used to record the patient's diagnosis, medicines to be given and other information that is critical to the treatment of the patient. This information is currently being recorded in a paper-based system kept by each patient's bed. The new system will store all of this information in a new central database that doctors and nurses will access via a tablet or other smart device.

In this situation, which method of system changeover would present the least risks and most benefits to the hospital?

A   Direct changeover
B   Parallel running
C   Pilot operation
D   Phased/modular changeover

Answer

B: Parallel running

In this situation the hospital is moving from two systems (one to record basic information in a database and a paper-based one to record treatment information) to a single system that stores both. Because the system will be used to store critical information, there is a high risk to the patients if the system does not work correctly. Therefore, the least risky option should be selected – parallel running. This method of changeover has the additional benefit of verifying the new system works correctly as compared to the existing system.

A direct changeover is not suitable due to the high risk to the patients if it does not work correctly.

A pilot operation is not applicable because the system is only being installed in one area of the organisation (the A&E department).

A phased, or modular, changeover might be an alternative solution. In this case the hospital would bring in one part of the system (either the basic patient information part, or the critical information part). However, this method of changeover doesn't have the additional benefit of verifying the performance of the new system. As it presents less benefits to the hospital it would not be the best choice for this situation and is therefore not the correct answer.

8.6 Post-implementation review

Once the system is up and running, it is good practice to perform a post-implementation review ('postmortem'). The objective of this is to ensure that the benefits that were identified when the new system was first planned have been met, and to compare the costs of the system with what was expected. The expected benefits and costs would have been documented in the cost benefit analysis, if one was performed, before the decision to go ahead with the systems implementation was made.

A post-implementation review usually takes place a few months after the system has been implemented when the system is up and running. By this time, the staff will have become used to the system and will be able to give a better-informed view of how the system is working.

9 Cybersecurity

FAST FORWARD

As technology continues to develop, so too does the need to protect the systems and data from cybersecurity issues such as unauthorised access, hacking, file corruption and so on.

9.1 Cybersecurity issues

The table below contains examples of the common types of cybersecurity issues.

Type of cyberattack	Description
Phishing	The cyberattacker sends emails to the victim which appear to be from a trusted source, for example a bank. The emails request the victim sends back security information (such as usernames and passwords) and personal details and the cyberattacker uses this information to steal funds from the victim.
Pharming	Cyberattackers target an organisation's website by automatically redirecting visitors from the organisation's website to a bogus website. The intention is to collect data in order to commit fraud and is similar to phishing.
Hacking	The cyberattacker uses specialist software and other tools to gain unauthorised access to an organisation's computer system and take administrative control. Such control allows them to view and copy system records, as well as amend or delete information that they find. Some hackers may try to stop the system working altogether.
Distributed Denial of Service (DDoS) attack	The cyberattacker attempts to disrupt an organisation's online activities by preventing people from accessing the organisation's website. Botnets (large numbers of individual computers which have been taken over without the user knowing) are instructed to overwhelm the organisation's website with a wave of internet traffic so that the system is unable to handle it and may crash.
Webcam manager	The cyberattacker uses software to take control of the user's webcam.
File hijacker/ransomware	Cyber attackers gain access to the user's system to hijack their files and hold them to ransom.
Keylogging	The cyber attacker plants software onto the user's computer to record what the user types onto their keyboard. The objective is to learn passwords and user details to gain access to confidential information.
Screenshot manager	The cyber attacker obtains information from the victim by installing software onto the user's computer to enable screenshots of the user's computer screen to be taken. Like other cyberattacks, the purpose can be to steal information, funds, or may even be to perform corporate espionage.
Ad clicker	The cyber attacker directs the victim's computer to a bogus website by encouraging them to click on a specific link contained in online advertising.

9.2 Cybersecurity methods

The table below contains some common cybersecurity methods used by organisations.

Cybersecurity method	Description
Access control	These are physical and network procedures to restrict access to a system.
Firewalls	Firewalls intercept data being transmitted in and out of a system.
Malware protection and virus protection	Malware protection software prevents installation and removes suspicious programs (such as Trojans) and viruses from a system.

Cybersecurity method	Description
Ensure software is regularly updated	This is a system procedure rather than a hardware or software solution. The organisation should ensure that the latest software updates are installed on the system when available.
Secure configuration	The organisation should have a policy which states that systems should be set up with cybersecurity as a priority.

Other threats to information systems include the following.

Threat	Description
Natural disasters	Examples include floods and fire. Risk can be mitigated by establishing policies and procedures, insurance, locating systems in less vulnerable areas and controlling the physical environment around the system.
Malfunctions	For example, breakdowns due to inability to cope with high volumes of data. Backup procedures can protect data and good network design that can deal with higher volumes than expected can mitigate the risk.
Unauthorised access, theft and damage	Physical security can be used to prevent unauthorised access to systems and controls can be put in place to ensure work-related devices are not left unattended in vulnerable areas.
Unintentional human errors	For example, accidental deletions of data. Proper training and input/output controls can be used to validate changes to data or new inputs.
Personnel injury or health problems	For example, eye strain and repetitive strain injury. The use of ergonomic workstations and other devices (such as anti-glare screens) can minimise the risk of injury.

Chapter roundup

- Information systems and information technology have played a significant role in the development of the modern business environment including encouraging the **flattening** of **organisation hierarchies** and widening **spans of control**.

- Other **effects of IT on organisations** include:
    - Routine processing (bigger volumes, greater speed, greater accuracy)
    - Digital information and record-keeping
    - New skills required and new ways of working
    - Reliance on IT
    - New methods of communication and of providing customer service
    - Interoperability (encourages collaboration across organisation boundaries) and open systems
    - The view of information as a valuable resource
    - The view of information as a commodity which can be bought, sold or exchanged ('information market')

- The widespread use of information technology in the workplace has affected the relationship between **employers and employees**:
    - Reduced need to follow the chain-of-command
    - Nature of work
    - Close business relationships regardless of geographical location
    - More flexible working arrangements
    - Greater monitoring and control
    - Information overload

- **Sociotechnical design** attempts to produce information systems that are technically efficient but also take into account organisational and staff needs.

- **Critical success factors** (CSFs) can be used to establish the **information needs** of individual managers.

- To avoid **information overload**, only good quality information should be communicated (ACCURATE mnemonic). The number of information sources feeding an individual can be managed in a number of ways such as
    - Delegate to colleagues
    - Review reports received for duplication
    - Re-route incoming telephone calls
    - Voice-mail
    - Filter incoming email
    - Use an internet news-clipping service
    - Use intelligent agents

- Many commentators refer to our period in history as the **information age**.

- The power and potential of information systems, and the general tend towards businesses being expected to act ethically, has led to discussion regarding the ethical use of information systems.

Chapter roundup continued

- Important developments in ICT include:
  - The growth of Web 2.0 and social media
  - The growth and development of e-commerce
  - Customer relationship management
  - Cloud computing
  - ''Mobile technology
  - Process automation
  - Artificial intelligence (AI)
  - Distributed ledger technology and blockchain
  - Cryptocurrencies
  - The internet of things (IoT)
  - Big data

- **Process automation** refers to the ability of systems to perform routine activities (such as the processing of data and assembling electronic components) without the input of a human. It is important to note this is not limited to physical automation (for example production lines), but online automation, for example processing and responding to customer queries.

- Big data analytics is a term used to describe the extraction of meaning from vast quantities of data. Organisations are particularly interested in identifying trends and correlations in the data that they collect and store with the aim of putting this to commercial use.

- Big data has been said to be comprised of 4 Vs (volume, velocity, variety and veracity).

- The costs of an information system include equipment costs, installation costs, development costs, personnel costs and operating costs.

- The benefits of an information system include increases in efficiency, capacity, accuracy, decision making, collaboration and customer service, and decreases in costs and errors.

- There are a number of risks involved in implementing a new information system. Risks can occur at a number of stages, in particular at the design and development stages.

- The main steps in the implementation of an information system are installation, testing, training, file conversion, change over and post-implementation review.

- As technology continues to develop, so too does the need to protect the systems and data from cybersecurity issues such as unauthorised access, hacking, file corruption and so on.

Quick quiz

1. List five factors that should be considered when considering an appropriate span of control.
2. Define interoperability.
3. 'Information overload is not a serious problem. More information is better than less.' Do you agree? Briefly justify your answer.
4. A sociotechnical system consists of three sub-systems. Name them.
5. Distinguish between consumer privacy and employee privacy.
6. What is the key feature of Web 2.0 applications?
7. AI and machine learning are the same thing. True or false?
8. What are the 'four Vs' used when describing the features of big data?
9. The main role of a firewall is to prevent installation of malware and removes suspicious programs (such as Trojans) and viruses from a system. True or false?

Answers to quick quiz

1. Ability of the manager

    Ability of the subordinates

    Nature of the task

    The geographical dispersal of the subordinates

    The availability of good quality information

2. Interoperability refers to the ability of entities to share and exchange information and facilities with other parties without having to use the same service provider or technology platform. Interoperability facilitates the formation of strategic alliances and encourages collaboration across organisation boundaries.

3. An excess of irrelevant information is harmful – a person is more likely to miss or misinterpret vital information if they are swamped with irrelevant material.

4. A formal structure

    A technological system consisting of the work to be done, and the machines, tools and other facilities available to do it.

    A social system consisting of the people within the organisation, the ways they think and the ways they interact with each other.

5. Consumer privacy considers the information complied by data collectors such as marketing firms, insurance companies and retailers, the use of credit information collected by credit agencies and the rights of the consumers to control information about themselves and their commercial transactions.

    Employee privacy deals with the use of electronic monitoring and other mechanisms to analyse work habits and measure employee productivity.

6. People are able to collaborate and share information online.

7. False. Machine learning is a subset of AI. Machine learning is the ability of systems or machines learn from a very large data set, identify patterns and make decisions with minimal human input. Artificial Intelligence (AI) refers to the ability of machines to perform cognitive functions we associate with human minds. This intelligence has been developed via machine learning.

8. Volume, velocity, variety and veracity

9. False. The main role of a firewall is to intercept data being transmitted in and out of a system.

    Anti-malware software prevents installation and removes suspicious programs (such as Trojans) and viruses from a system

Exam question bank

Chapter 1 The organisation of work and the work of management

1   In Mintzberg's managerial roles model, which of the following is NOT an informational role of a manager?

   A   Monitor
   B   Spokesperson
   C   Disturbance handler
   D   Disseminator

2   Which of the following is a definition of the cognitive skills required by management?

   A   Ability to use complex techniques
   B   Ability to perceive complex decisions
   C   Ability to perceive what motivates other employees
   D   Ability to promote change

3   The classical approach to management emphasised:

   A   The organisation as an open system interacting with its environment
   B   Application of techniques to plan, measure and control work for maximum productivity
   C   Industrial relations characterised by trust, co-operation and mutual adjustment
   D   Importance of motivation, group and individual behaviour

4   The situational or contingency approach to management emphasised:

   A   There is no universally best organisation structure
   B   Authority being exercised down a clear chain of command
   C   The need for workers to have challenge and responsibility in their jobs
   D   Concern for employee welfare inside and outside the organisation

5   The ……. studies is the name given to experimental social research which identified the influence exercised by social needs and informal groups in the workplace, and gave rise to the human relations school of management.

   Which word correctly completes the sentence?

   A   Fayol
   B   Hawthorne
   C   Taylor
   D   Mintzberg

6   Which of the following is NOT one of Fayol's functions of management?

   A   Planning
   B   Organising
   C   Commanding
   D   Motivating

7   Peter Drucker grouped management activities or operations into a number of categories.

   Which of the following is NOT one of those categories?

   A   Setting objectives
   B   The job of measurement
   C   Motivating employees
   D   Planning and control

8   Which of Mintzberg's managerial roles is being exercised by a manager who gathers information from contacts within and outside the organisation?

   A   Monitor
   B   Leader
   C   Spokesperson
   D   Disseminator

9   .... is the managerial function concerned with establishing a structure of tasks; grouping and assigning them to appropriate departments and establishing lines of information and communication.

   Which managerial function is referred to in this definition?

   A   Planning
   B   Organising
   C   Controlling
   D   Leading

10 Which job design technique was advocated by the scientific management school?

   A   Micro-division of labour
   B   Job enlargement
   C   Empowerment
   D   Synergising

11 According to Drucker, which is the main function of management?

   A   Providing information to stakeholders
   B   Developing people
   C   Coordinating activities
   D   Managing economic performance

12 Which of the following writers is NOT a member of the school of management thought to which the others belong?

   A   F W Taylor
   B   Elton Mayo
   C   Douglas Mcgregor
   D   William Ouchi

13 What is the key contribution of the contingency approach to management?

   A   Awareness that workers are affected not just by financial rewards but by the social environment at work
   B   Awareness of the importance of job specialisation, clear statements of responsibilities and promotion on merit
   C   Awareness of the many different factors that affect the way that a manager acts in each situation
   D   Awareness that organisational success can only be achieved through both satisfying individual needs and meeting organisational goals

14 In Mintzberg's classification of managerial roles, which of the following is an 'interpersonal' role of management?

   A   Spokesperson
   B   Figurehead
   C   Negotiator
   D   Resource allocator

15 According to Drucker, which of the following is a management task?

   A   Informational
   B   Developmental
   C   Interpersonal
   D   Decisional

16 Which management writer(s) saw employees motivated by the Japanese values consensus decision-making and mutual loyalty in the employment relationship?

   A   Ouchi
   B   Fayol
   C   Peters and Waterman
   D   Taylor

17 The management of Guenguiss Company runs a relaxed system, with flexi-time, few rules and encouragement for employees to use their initiative. 'Ok,' says the general manager, 'if you allow people freedom at work, they will be happy, their productivity will improve and their work will be of a higher standard.'

   Which of Douglas McGregor's 'theories' does this management team subscribe to?

   A   Theory W
   B   Theory X
   C   Theory Y
   D   Theory Z

18 Which of the following best describes the most important role of an organisation's most senior managers when an organisation is planning and implementing change?

   A   Challenge things that are taken for granted
   B   Manage the day to day change implementation process
   C   Select the best theory of change to follow
   D   Get others to follow the change willingly

19 Which of Mintzberg's managerial roles is being exercised by a manager who is communicating with other staff outside her chain of command?

- A Disseminator
- B Liaison
- C Negotiator
- D Figurehead

20 Which of the following would NOT be characteristic of the work of the supervisor (the lowest level of management)?

- A Front-line management dealing with day-to-day operational matters
- B Spending the great majority of time on managerial activities
- C Filter for communication between more senior management and non-managerial staff
- D Use of frequent and detailed information

Chapter 2 Effective leadership

21 What type of power is best used to describe the behaviour of a manager who is refusing a request for one of his team members to help with the workload of another department?

   A   Expert
   B   Negative
   C   Coercive
   D   Personal

22 According to Fiedler, which of the following are true of psychologically distant managers?

   (i)   They judge their staff on the basis of performance
   (ii)   They are primarily task-oriented
   (iii) They prefer formal consultation methods rather than seeking staff opinions
   (iv)   They are closer to their staff

   A   (i) and (ii)
   B   (ii) and (iii)
   C   (i), (ii) and (iii)
   D   (i), (iii) and (iv)

23 According to the Ashridge model which of the following statements is true of a 'consults' style of management compared to other styles?

   A   It is most popular amongst subordinates.
   B   It is most popular amongst leaders.
   C   It encourages the highest productivity.
   D   It is always the best style.

24 What is delegated by a superior to a subordinate?

   A   Authority
   B   Power
   C   Responsibility
   D   Accountability

25 Which of the following leadership styles gives the most discretion or decision-making power to subordinates?

   A   Consultative
   B   Democratic
   C   Autocratic
   D   Persuasive

26 John Adair's action-centred leadership model is part of which school of thought?

   A   Trait theories
   B   Style theories
   C   Contingency theories
   D   Behavioural theories

27 Which leadership approach sees the leadership process in a context made up of three interrelated variables: task needs, the individual needs of group members and the needs of the group as a whole?

A   Action-centred leadership
B   Contingency theory
C   The managerial grid
D   The Ashridge model

28 Which of the following activities is associated with leadership rather than management?

A   Co-ordination
B   Focus on systems and controls
C   Innovation
D   Focus on immediate results

29 Which of the following terms is used to describe the duty to perform an action or task in an organisation?

A   Responsibility
B   Authority
C   Power
D   Influence

30 Leaders may be distinguished from managers by the fact that they do not depend on.. in the organisation.

Which of the following types of power correctly completes this statement?

A   Person
B   Position
C   Expert
D   Physical

31 Renesis Likert identified four management or leadership styles. What are they?

A   Benevolent autocratic, participative, democratic, exploitative autocratic
B   Exploitative autocratic, participative, laissez faire, benevolent autocratic
C   Benevolent autocratic, consultative participative, laissez faire, exploitative
D   Benevolent authoritative, participative, democratic, exploitative authoritative

32 Who was responsible for developing the situational leadership model?

A   Blake and Mouton
B   Katz and Kahn
C   Hersey and Blanchard
D   Tannenbaum and Schmidt

33 Leadership involves activities that are generally people-centred.

Which of the following activities is NOT people-centred?

A   Creating the culture
B   Inspiring and motivating others
C   Reconciling individual needs with the needs of the organisation
D   Allocating scarce resources

34 Which of the following describes the impoverished style of leadership identified by Blake and Mouton's managerial grid?

- A High concern for people and high concern for the task
- B High concern for people and low concern for the task
- C Low concern for people and high concern for the task
- D Low concern for people and low concern for the task

35 According to the Ashridge studies on leadership style, what is most important to subordinates about the style of their leader?

- A Consultation
- B Direction
- C Consistency
- D Speed

36 Which leadership style from the Ashridge model least acknowledges the contribution that subordinates make?

- A Authoritarian
- B Autocratic
- C Authoritative
- D Assertive

37 Which of the following is a feature of ineffective delegation by a manager or leader?

- A Specifying performance levels and the results expected of a subordinate
- B Obtaining the subordinate's agreement with the task and expected results
- C Ensuring that all the subordinate's decisions are confirmed or authorised by the superior
- D Ensuring that the subordinate reports the results of their decisions to the superior

38 Which of the following is NOT a style of leadership identified by Lewin, Lippitt and White?

- A Autocratic
- B Authoritative
- C Laissez-faire
- D Democratic

39 Which of the Is of leadership identified by Bass and Avolio would a leader who is showing strong business ethics be demonstrating?

- A Idealised influence
- B Inspirational motivation
- C Intellectual stimulation
- D Individualised consideration

40 Andrea and Kim are interviewing Nigel for a role managing a team of subordinates. They believe that Nigel is very concerned with keeping staff happy and developing good working relations, but may not be strict enough in enforcing deadlines or high standards of work.

Which management style do Andrea and Kim think that Nigel will exhibit if he is appointed as a manager?

A   Impoverished
B   Country club
C   Dampened pendulum
D   Team

Chapter 3 Strategic planning and management by objectives

41 Which of the following is the objective of efficient business processes?

  A Creating the maximum output
  B Creating the best quality output from available input
  C Creating the maximum output from minimum input
  D Creating a given level of output from minimum input

42 Whether an organisation should be classified as a business or not will be indicated by its:

  A Secondary objective
  B Primary objective
  C Unit objective
  D Mission

43 Which of the following measures will NOT help an organisation limit its environmental impact?

  A Recycling waste
  B Turning lights off at night
  C Disclosing environmental impacts in its annual report
  D Buying raw materials locally

44 Which of the following stakeholders will be most concerned about a company improving its return on investment?

  A Customers
  B Bankers
  C Employees
  D The government

45 Which of the following is an example of an internal stakeholder?

  A An employee
  B The government
  C The local community
  D A customer

46 Which of the following is an example of an external stakeholder?

  A A supplier
  B A director
  C A shareholder
  D A pressure group

47 'An organisation is a social arrangement which pursues collective......................, which controls its own performance and which has a boundary separating it from its environment.'

Which of the following words best completes this sentence?

  A Profits
  B Stakeholders
  C Goals
  D Tactics

48 Which of the following groups may be considered to be stakeholders in the activities of a major power station?

(i) The government
(ii) Environmental pressure groups
(iii) Employees
(iv) Local residents

A (i), (iii) and (iv)
B (i), (ii) and (iv)
C (ii) and (iii)
D (i), (ii), (iii) and (iv)

49 The term 'internal stakeholders' describes which group of stakeholders?

A Stakeholders who have a direct interest in the organisation but do not work for it
B Stakeholders who work for the organisation
C Stakeholders who conduct transactions with the organisation
D Stakeholders who are not connected with the organisation

50 Which of the following organisations would be more concerned with efficiency than profitability?

A A private accountancy college
B A local authority
C A small retailer
D A bank

51 Which two of the following stakeholders will be most directly affected if a business overstates its financial position?

(i) Staff
(ii) Customers
(iii) Investors
(iv) Suppliers

A (i) and (ii)
B (ii) and (iii)
C (iii) and (iv)
D (ii) and (iv)

52 What is the main financial objective of a commercial organisation?

A Profit maximisation
B Efficient use of resources
C Avoidance of loss
D Stakeholder satisfaction

53 Daniel carries out routine processing of invoices in the purchasing department of L Company. Peter works processing sales invoices. Daniel and Peter report to Lisha, their supervisor. Trina is considering new markets that L Company may enter in the future.

Which member of L Company carries out activities concerned with business-level strategy?

A Daniel
B Peter
C Lisha
D Trina

54 The question 'what business should we be in' is associated with which level of strategy?

    A   Corporate
    B   Functional
    C   Business
    D   Mission

55 Which of the following statements best defines an organisation's mission statement?

    A   The organisation's overriding purpose
    B   The future state desired by the organisation's strategists
    C   A statement of a general aim
    D   A statement of a specific aim

56 For what function of an organisation would information about social class be most relevant?

    A   Human resources
    B   Marketing
    C   Finance
    D   Research and development

57 Which of the following is NOT characteristic of a strategic decision?

    A   Matches the organisation's activities to its environment
    B   Sets the organisation's overall long-term direction
    C   Determines which marketing agency to use for a marketing campaign
    D   Has important implications for organisational change

Chapter 4 Internal analysis

58 Which of the following is a primary activity in value chain management?

  A Procurement
  B After-sales service
  C Technology development
  D Human resources management

59 Which of the following is NOT a primary activity in value chain management?

  A Operations
  B Outbound logistics
  C Marketing and sales
  D Firm infrastructure

60 In Porter's value chain, procurement is:

  A A primary activity involving warehousing and inventory control
  B A secondary activity involving warehousing and inventory control
  C A secondary activity involving purchasing materials and equipment
  D A primary activity involving packaging and distribution to customers

61 According to the BCG model, which of the following are businesses that operate in high-growth markets, but have a low relative market share?

  A Star
  B Cash cow
  C Question mark
  D Dog

62 Which of the following is a secondary or support activity in Porter's value chain model?

  A Procurement
  B Operations
  C Marketing and sales
  D Inbound logistics

63 BCD Co is a large trading company. Steve is the administration manager and is responsible for legal and compliance functions. Sheila is responsible for preparing marketing literature and reviewing the results of marketing campaigns. Sunny deals with suppliers and negotiates on the price and quantity of inventory. He is also responsible for identifying the most appropriate suppliers of plant and machinery for the factory. Sam is the information technology manager and is responsible for all information systems within the company.

According to Porter's value chain, which of the managers is involved in a primary activity?

  A Steve
  B Sheila
  C Sunny
  D Sam

64 Which of the following would be included in the resource audit of a business?

(i) Suppliers
(ii) Utilisation rate of fixed assets
(iii) Brands
(iv) Culture

A (i) and (ii)
B (ii) and (iii)
C (i),(iii) and (iv)
D (i), (ii),(iii) and (iv)

65 Which of the following looks at the relationships between the goods and services produced and the resources used to produce them?

A Efficiency
B Economy
C Effectiveness
D Energy

66 Which of the following is NOT a feature of a core competence, according to Hamel and Prahalad?

A Competitively unique
B Disproportionate contribution to value
C Necessary for the firm to stay in business
D Extendable

67 Which of the following statements about critical success factors is NOT true?

A They can be seen as product features particularly valued by customers.
B Organisations must excel in them to outperform the competition.
C They are unique to each business.
D The business needs to carry out key tasks to fulfil critical success factors.

68 Which of the following is NOT an advantage of outsourcing?

A It can save on costs.
B It can increase effectiveness.
C It allows focus on core competencies.
D It allows the organisation to exercise greater control over quality.

69 Cheese and onion crisps are an example of what classification of product?

A Product class
B Product form
C Generic product
D Brand

70 Which of the following is NOT a problem of the product life cycle model?

A The model is predictive not descriptive.
B Some products have no maturity phase.
C A product may be at different stages of its lifecycle in different markets.
D The model does not consider links with other products in the product portfolio.

71 Which of the following is NOT a hard element in the McKinsey model, dealing with facts and rules?

   A   Structure
   B   Strategy
   C   Skills
   D   Systems

72 The General Electric Business Screen model weighs up which of the following elements?

   A   Market growth vs Relative market share
   B   Revenue/Profit vs Time
   C   Business strength vs Market attractiveness
   D   Bargaining power of customers vs Bargaining power of suppliers

73 Which part of a marketing audit is likely to consider market segmentation, basis of competitive advantage and product portfolio?

   A   Marketing mix effectiveness
   B   Marketing strategy
   C   Marketing structure
   D   Marketing systems

Chapter 5 Environmental analysis

74 Which of the following is a quantitative forecasting technique?

    A   Delphi technique
    B   Regression analysis
    C   Industry scenario building
    D   Porter's five forces analysis

75 ABC Co sells a product with a number of important accessories that can only be used with that product. To which of Porter's five forces is that strategy intended to respond?

    A   Bargaining power of customers
    B   Bargaining power of suppliers
    C   Intensity of competitive rivalry
    D   Threat of new entrants

76 Which of the following is an acronym used to describe the key elements of an organisation's external environment?

    A   ICT
    B   PEST
    C   SWOT
    D   HRM

77 Which of the following is likely to be identified as a political factor in the macro-economic environment of a business?

    A   The entry of new competitors into the market
    B   Increasing concern about green issues amongst consumers
    C   A general election
    D   Rising inflation

78 A SWOT analysis includes an internal appraisal and an external appraisal. Which component or components of a SWOT analysis are part of the external appraisal?

    A   Strengths
    B   Opportunities and threats
    C   Threats
    D   Strengths and weaknesses

79 Commercial organisations are now expected to act as 'responsible corporate citizens'. Which of the following environmental factors has contributed most directly to this development?

    A   Social
    B   Economic
    C   Political
    D   Technological

80 What is an acronym used to describe a corporate appraisal?

    A   SWOT
    B   SMART
    C   CRM
    D   PEST

81   When analysing the current situation in a business, a consultant will review the general environment surrounding it.

Which of the following would NOT be included in this analysis?

A   New legislation coming into effect
B   Activities of overseas competitors
C   Interest rates
D   External experience of non-executive directors

82   Porter's five forces model identifies factors which determine the nature and strength of competition in an industry.

Which of the following is NOT one of the five forces identified in Porter's model?

A   Substitute products or services
B   New entrants to the industry
C   Bargaining power of customers
D   Government regulation of the industry

83   In Porter's five forces model, which of the following would NOT constitute a barrier to entry?

A   Scale economies available to existing competitors
B   High capital investment requirements
C   Low switching costs in the market
D   High degree of brand loyalty

84   Systems are sometimes described as open or closed.

Which of the following is true of a closed system?

A   It is incapable of further technical enhancement.
B   It is protected from unauthorised access.
C   It relates to the external environment in a prescribed manner.
D   It is isolated from the external environment.

85   Which set of environmental factors is most directly influenced by birth and mortality rates?

A   Political
B   Economic
C   Social
D   Technological

86   Which of the following would be classified as a political factor in the PEST model?

A   Rise in inflation rates
B   An ageing population
C   Increase in internet coverage by providers
D   Consumer protection policy

87   Which of the following combinations contribute to low environmental uncertainty?

A   Stability and dynamism
B   Dynamism and complexity
C   Stability and simplicity
D   Stability and complexity

88   In the context of characteristics of society's culture, what does cumulative mean?

    A   Transferred in institutions and through ongoing social interaction
    B   Offers order, direction and guidance
    C   Handed down to each new generation
    D   Adapts to changes in society

89   Which of the following is a disadvantage of the use of expected values?

    A   Expected values use probabilities that may be inaccurate estimates.
    B   Expected values are influenced by the time value of money.
    C   Expected values can only be used for one-off decisions.
    D   Expected values are not influenced by extreme results.

Chapter 6 Sustainability, CSR and ethics

90 Which of the following best defines sustainability?

 A The adoption of 'green' practices in the management, procedures and operations of an organisation

 B Sacrificing the needs of today to be able to meet the needs of the future

 C The ability of an organisation to overcome challenges which allow it continue, or sustain, for a long period of time

 D Meeting the needs of the present without compromising the ability of future generations to meet their own needs

91 What is the primary goal of the United Nations Sustainable Development Goals (SDGs)?

 A To maximise profits for businesses

 B To address various challenges and guide efforts towards sustainable development worldwide

 C To ignore environmental, social, and governance factors in decision-making

 D To promote excessive consumption practices

92 The Paris Agreement aims to achieve which of the following goals regarding climate change?

 A Limit global warming to well below 1 degree Celsius above pre-industrial levels
 B Limit global warming to well below 2 degrees Celsius above pre-industrial levels
 C Achieve net zero emissions globally by 2030
 D Reduce greenhouse gas emissions by 50% by 2050.

93 The 17 U.N. Sustainable Development Goals are aimed at which of the following?

 (i) Individuals
 (ii) Businesses and organisations
 (iii) Governments

 A (ii) only
 B (i) and (ii) only
 C (ii) and (iii) only
 D (i), (ii) and (iii)

94 Which of the following is NOT one of the four categories of environmental cost as defined by the US Environmental Protection Agency?

 A Conventional costs
 B Image and relationship costs
 C Social costs
 D Potentially hidden costs

95 Grey and Adams (2014) define the three components which provide a comprehensive approach to sustainability accounting

Which of the below describe the three components?

- A   Environmental accountability, social accountability, and economic accountability
- B   Environmental accountability, social accountability, and corporate governance
- C   Corporate accountability, internal accountability, and external accountability
- D   Corporate accountability, local accountability, and global accountability

96 Which of the below statements about integrated reporting are true?

- (i)   An integrated report reports on both financial and non-financial information to demonstrates how the organisation creates value
- (ii)   The information in the integrated report is combined and provided in place of the traditional financial statements
- (iii) Integrated reporting considers how value is created in terms of "six capitals"

- A   (i) and (ii) only
- B   (i) and (iii) only
- C   (ii) and (iii) only
- D   (i), (ii) and (iii)

97 Sustainability KPIs for organisations may be categorised as environmental, social or governance (ESG)

Which of the following KPIs is a social KPI?

- A   Percentage of women on the board (percentage)
- B   Average training hours per employee (hours)
- C   Total waste generated (tonnes)
- D   Total water consumption (metric litres)

98 Which of the following is a benefit of managing environmental risks?

- A   Reduction of operational costs
- B   Mitigation of the need to comply with environmental regulations
- C   Avoids the reputational damage associated with poor labour practices
- D   Ensures a transparent and ethical decision making process

99 Which of the following measures best integrates sustainability into strategic business planning?

- A   Considering sustainability as a core-component alongside financial and market analysis
- B   Improving compliance levels by outsourcing production to companies with less stringent environmental regulations
- C   Generating cost savings by outsourcing production to companies with a lower cost of living
- D   Donating a percentage of the profits to unrelated international charities

100 Which of the main sources of rules, that regulate the behaviour of business, sets minimum levels of acceptable behaviour?

- A Non-legal rules and regulations
- B Ethics
- C The law
- D Society

101 Which of the following statements about social responsibility is true?

- A CSR guarantees increased profit levels.
- B CSR adds costs to organisational activities and reduces profit levels.
- C Social responsibility is a concern confined to business organisations.
- D Social responsibility may have commercial benefits.

102 Which of the following is NOT one of the three Ps of triple bottom line accounting for the environment?

- A People
- B Processes
- C Planet
- D Profit

Chapter 7 Organisation structure

103 Mintzberg's design of an effective organisation does NOT include which of the following elements?

- A Support staff
- B Network
- C Middle line
- D Technostructure

104 Which of the following is a benefit of a matrix organisation structure?

- A An individual has a single boss.
- B Decisions are made quicker.
- C Inter-departmental co-operation is improved.
- D It encourages staff specialisation.

105 What can be defined as the number of subordinates responsible to a superior?

- A Span of control
- B Scalar chain
- C Line of command
- D Strategic apex

106 Which of the following is characteristic of a tall organisation?

- A Short scalar chain, wide span of control
- B Short scalar chain, narrow span of control
- C Long scalar chain, wide span of control
- D Long scalar chain, narrow span of control

107 Which of the following is NOT a benefit of a functional structure?

- A Facilitation of the recruitment of specialists
- B Good level of communication between different functions
- C Expertise being pooled
- D Clear segregation of duties between different functions

108 Which of the following would NOT be considered as part of the design of organisation structure?

- A Span of control
- B Scalar chain
- C Enrichment
- D Degree of centralisation

109 What term or phrase is given to the idea that individuals and departments in an organisation should focus on one area or work or expertise?

- A Synergy
- B Specialisation
- C Efficiency
- D Team work

110 Which of the following principles of classical or traditional management is challenged by matrix management?

- A Structuring the organisation on functional lines
- B Structuring the organisation on divisional lines
- C Unity of command
- D Decentralisation of decision-making

111 Y Co is a growing organisation which has recently diversified into a number of significant new product markets. It has also recently acquired another company in one of its overseas markets.

What would be the most appropriate form of organisation for Y Co?

- A Geographical departmentation
- B Divisionalisation
- C Network
- D Functional departmentation

112 Which of the following is a benefit of decentralisation?

- A Decisions made at one place in the organisation
- B Reduction in bureaucracy
- C Better crisis management
- D Improvement in motivation of junior managers

113 Empowering workers, reducing management control and removing levels in the organisational hierarchy reflect an approach consistent with the theories of which management writer?

- A Herzberg
- B Fayol
- C Taylor
- D Weber

114 An employer, Red Company, offers its employees:

- (i) Sensible company policies
- (ii) Good salaries and bonuses
- (iii) Considerate supervision
- (iv) Training programmes

According to Herzberg's two-factor theory, which of these things will satisfy employees in such a way as to motivate them to superior effort in the long-term?

- A (ii) only
- B (iv) only
- C (i) and (iii)
- D (i), (ii), (iii) and (iv)

115 Management theories such as McGregor's Theory Y encourage managers to empower employees and to allow employees to take 'ownership' of the tasks they perform. However, others have argued that 'empowerment' is a fashionable buzzword that is unworkable in reality.

In which of the following circumstances is employee empowerment most likely to be inappropriate?

    A   Customer-service call centre
    B   Fast food restaurant
    C   Supermarket
    D   Army

116 Which of the following best describes job rotation?

    A   The redesign of an individual's job based upon job analysis
    B   The movement of an individual to several other roles to gain experience
    C   The expansion and enrichment of an individual's job content
    D   The termination of an individual's employment

117 All of the following, except one, are alternative terms for the same concept. Which of the following is the exception?

    A   Motivator factor
    B   Maintenance factor
    C   Hygiene factor
    D   Environmental factor

118 The following, except one, are claimed as advantages for job enrichment as a form of job re-design. Which of the following is the exception?

    A   It increases job satisfaction.
    B   It enhances quality of output.
    C   It replaces monetary rewards.
    D   It reduces supervisory costs.

119 Which of the following statements about an organisation chart is NOT true?

    A   An organisation chart can provide a summary of the structure of a business.
    B   An organisation chart can improve communications within a business.
    C   An organisation chart can improve employees' understanding of their responsibilities.
    D   An organisation chart can indicate functional authority but not line authority within a business.

120 Which of the following terms is NOT used by Mintzberg in his description of organisational structure?

    A   Strategic apex
    B   Support base
    C   Technostructure
    D   Operating core

121 Which of the following is a benefit of centralisation?

- A It helps to develop the skills of junior managers.
- B It avoids overburdening top managers in terms of workload and stress.
- C It is responsive to local conditions.
- D Senior managers can take a wider view of problems and consequences.

122 Of which of Mintzberg's organisational components would a canteen worker be part?

- A Operating core
- B Support staff
- C Strategic apex
- D Middle line

Chapter 8 Organisation culture

123 Which of the following is classed as an artefact of organisational culture in Schein's model?

- A Code of employee conduct
- B Design of office premises
- C Ways of addressing work superiors
- D Company slogan

124 Which of the following is classed as a ritual of organisational culture in Schein's model?

- A Dress code
- B Office mentoring
- C Lunch to welcome new staff
- D Managers being given their own office

125 Which of the following statements is/are true?

(i) An informal organisation exists within every formal organisation.

(ii) The objectives of the informal organisation are broadly the same as those of the formal organisation.

(iii) A strong, close-knit informal organisation is desirable within the formal organisation.

- A (i) only
- B (i) and (iii) only
- C (ii) and (iii) only
- D (iii) only

126 Which of the following statements is most likely to be true?

- A Strong values improve corporate financial performance.
- B Strong values can replace rules and controls in an organisation.
- C Strong values minimise conflict within an organisation.
- D Strong values are dangerous if they filter out uncomfortable environmental information.

127 Which is the deepest set of underlying factors which determine culture and the hardest to manage?

- A Values
- B Artefacts
- C Rituals
- D Assumptions

128 Which of the following statements about the informal organisation is NOT true?

- A In the informal organisation, group norms and dynamics can have a significant impact on productivity.
- B The informal organisation can pose a threat to employee health and safety.
- C The informal organisation can stimulate innovation.
- D Managers in positions of authority cannot generally be part of the informal organisation.

129 BM Company is run by its founder, Burton Modi, who is chair and chief executive. All the other directors on the board have been personally appointed by Burton. All expenditure above a certain limit has to be approved by Burton and Burton has the final say on all recruitment decisions.

BM Company is an example of what type of culture?

A Role
B Task
C Power
D Person

130 Which of the following is NOT used by Hofstede to describe a key dimension of culture?

A Power distance
B Acquisitive
C Individualism
D Uncertainty avoidance

131 Culture is the collective programming of the mind which distinguishes the members of one …….. from another?

Which of the following words or phrases most accurately completes the definition?

A Nation
B Category of people
C Social class
D Organisation

132 Mr Q is manager of a division that is undergoing a business downturn. He tries to shelter the workforce from the effects of downsizing: taking time for consultation, organising counselling and refusing to institute compulsory redundancies.

Which of the following cultural types identified in the Hofstede model is the manager most likely to represent?

A Low power-distance
B Low masculinity
C Low uncertainty avoidance
D High individuality

133 Company W focuses on autonomy of its employees. Task achievement is seen as more important than working relationships. The company is impersonal and defends its business interests.

Which of Hofstede's four main dimensions of cultural difference is Company W displaying?

A Power distance
B Uncertainty avoidance
C Individualism
D Masculinity

134 Company X has a strict task structure with written rules and regulations that are adhered to by all employees. Dissent is not tolerated.

Which of Hofstede's four main dimensions of cultural difference is Company X displaying?

- A Power distance
- B Uncertainty avoidance
- C Individualism
- D Masculinity

135 Which of the following factors help shape an organisation's culture?

- (i) The person who founded the organisation
- (ii) The failures and successes experienced by the organisation
- (iii) Recruitment and selection
- (iv) The industry the organisation is in
- (v) Labour turnover

- A (ii) and (iv)
- B (i),(ii) and (iv)
- C (i),(iii) and (v)
- D (i),(ii),(iii),(iv) and (v)

136 A large, well-established, construction company organises itself on a project basis, using temporary project team structures.

What cultural type is most likely to fit this organisation?

- A Role
- B Task
- C Power
- D Person

137 Which of the following is NOT a benefit of an informal organisation?

- A Faster communication
- B Better morale through meeting employees' social needs
- C Cutting corners
- D Greater co-operation between teams

138 According to Handy, what type of culture best suits tactical management?

- A Role
- B Task
- C Power
- D Person

139 A meeting space where employees can converse informally is an example of what manifestation of culture?

- A Artefact
- B Symbol
- C Ritual
- D Behaviour

140 Which of the following would NOT generally be a feature of a power culture, as identified by Handy?

- A Quick decision-making
- B Functional structure
- C Adaptability to change
- D Project teams

141 What can be defined as culturally acceptable ways of behaving in given situations?

- A Values
- B Rituals
- C Artefacts
- D Customs

Chapter 9 Budget planning and control

142 Which of the following definitions describe zero-based budgeting?

A   A method of budgeting where an attempt is made to make the expenditure under each heading as close to zero as possible

B   A method of budgeting where the budget remains the same in real terms

C   A method of budgeting where all activities are re-evaluated each time a budget is formatted

D   A method of budgeting where the sum of revenues and expenditures in each budget centre must equal zero

143 Which of the following is NOT a common criticism of incremental budgeting?

A   It assumes that all current activities and costs are still needed.
B   There is no requirement for management to justify existing costs.
C   There is no incentive for managers to reduce costs.
D   There are no performance targets for managers.

144 Which of the following would be the first stage in activity-based budgeting?

A   Take action to adjust the capacity of resources to match the projected supply
B   Determine the resources that are required to perform organisational activities
C   Estimate the production and sales volume by individual products and customers
D   Estimate the demand for organisational activities

145 Are the following statements about rolling budgeting true or false?

(i)   Rolling budgets may be used to alter plans instead of encouraging managers to focus on improving performance.

(ii)   Rolling budgets are not worth preparing unless there is a persistent and large amount of uncertainty about the future.

A   Both statements are true.
B   Statement (i) is true. Statement (ii) is false.
C   Statement (i) is false. Statement (ii) is true.
D   Both statements are false.

146 Which of the following weaknesses in a budgeting system is most likely to be found in a top-down system of budgeting?

A   Management budgets may include excessive amounts of slack (unnecessary budget spending allowances).

B   Management budgets may be too ambitious and beyond the realistic resource capabilities of the organisation.

C   Management budgets may not be realistic in practice.

D   Management budgets may be inconsistent with the long-term strategy of the organisation.

147 Which of the following is NOT a reason why budgeting is more difficult in public sector organisations (such as government and the police force) than in private sector companies?

- A Difficulty in quantifying objectives
- B Spending limits imposed by government
- C Changing political pressures
- D Difficulty in quantifying outputs

148 What is a budget cost allowance?

- A A budget of expenditure applicable to a particular function
- B A budget that is set without permitting the ultimate budget manager the opportunity to participate in setting the budget
- C The budgeted cost expected for the actual level of activity achieved during the period
- D A fixed budget allowance for expenditure which is expected every period regardless of the level of activity

149 What is a flexible budget?

- A A budget, which by recognising different cost behaviour patterns, is designed to change as volume of activity changes
- B A budget for a twelve month period that includes planned revenues, expenses, assets and liabilities
- C A budget which is prepared for a rolling period, which is reviewed monthly, and updated accordingly
- D A budget for semi-variable overhead costs only

150 Are the following statements about setting budget targets true or false?

(i) Setting ideal standards as targets for achievement should motivate employees to perform to the best of their ability.

(ii) Setting low standards as targets for achievement should motivate employees because they should usually achieve or exceed the target.

- A Both statements are true.
- B Statement (i) is true. Statement (ii) is false.
- C Statement (i) is false. Statement (ii) is true.
- D Both statements are false.

151 What is a budget that has been prepared by updating the current budget to reflect a change in economic conditions?

- A Incremental budget
- B Flexible budget
- C Rolling budget
- D Zero-based budget

152 Which of the following are possible responsibility centres in a system of budgeting?

- (i) Cost centre
- (ii) Revenue centre
- (iii) Investment centre

A (i) and (ii)
B (i) and (iii)
C (ii) and (iii)
D (i), (ii) and (iii)

153 Residual income is a possible financial measure for what type of budgetary centre?

A Investment centre
B Profit centre
C Cost centre
D Revenue centre

154 Which of the following statements about controllable and non-controllable costs is NOT true?

A Costs may be under the control of two or more managers.

B Committed fixed costs may be non-controllable in the short-term.

C Discretionary fixed costs are non-controllable in the long-term.

D Managers should be held responsible for apportioned costs from another department if they have some influence over them.

155 Deliberate over-estimation of costs in a budget is known as:

A Flexible budgeting
B Incremental budgeting
C Budgetary slack
D Participative budgeting

156 Which of the following is an advantage of zero-based budgeting?

A It focuses on what went wrong in the past.
B It requires budgeted costs to be justified by expected benefits.
C It is an easy system to use to rank budgeting priorities.
D It requires significant management time.

157 Which of the following is the most likely problem with bottom-up budgeting?

A Managers setting budgets in line with wider organisational objectives and not local conditions

B Managers being given too much resource due to budgetary slack

C Managers being demotivated by being forced to meet unrealistic targets

D Senior managers at the centre having to spend more time on budgeting

Chapter 10 Managerial control

158 Which KPI for the production function measures the proportion of time that a process was actually running compared with the time for which it could have run?

    A   Capacity utilisation
    B   Downtime
    C   Rejection rate
    D   Level of service

159 Which of the following KPIs measures employee participation in the company's affairs?

    A   Employee turnover
    B   Employee engagement level
    C   Employee satisfaction index
    D   Employee utilisation rate

160 Which of the following is a definition of feedforward control?

    A   Comparing original targets or actual results with future forecasts

    B   Reporting control information to management

    C   Measuring whether critical success factors are being achieved

    D   Revising plans, budgets, organisational structures and control systems to meet changes in conditions

161 Which of the following would be a feedback control in the context of dealing with fraud in a company?

    A   Fraud policy statement
    B   Obtaining references for new staff
    C   Bringing the police in to investigate fraud
    D   Staff training about fraud

162 Which of the following is NOT part of the planning process?

    A   Identifying objectives
    B   Comparing results with the plan
    C   Choosing alternative courses of action
    D   Evaluating strategies

163 The economic order quantity for inventory is defined as:

    A   The optimal quantity of material usage
    B   The quantity of inventory held at which inventory has to be re-ordered
    C   The minimum level of inventory
    D   The optimal quantity of inventory to be ordered at regular intervals

164 Which of the following performance objectives would be included in the customer perspective of the balanced scorecard for a hairdresser?

    A   Rating in on-line local guide
    B   Contribution per haircut
    C   Qualifications staff have achieved
    D   Average waiting time per customer

165 Which of the following performance objectives would be included in the learning and growth (innovation and learning) perspective of the balanced scorecard for a new car sales outlet?

   A   Number of new models introduced in year
   B   Customers buying their second or subsequent car from the outlet
   C   Time spent dealing with after-sale service queries from customers
   D   Sales growth of existing models

166 Which of the following statements best describes functional benchmarking?

   A   Comparison of the processes of one division with a competitor to identify superior performance
   B   Comparison of the processes of two divisions within a company
   C   Comparison of the processes of one division with another company in the same industry, but not a competitor
   D   Comparison of the processes of one division with the best external practitioners of those processes

167 Are the following statements relating to the balanced scorecard true or false?

   (i)   The balanced scorecard approach is only applicable to organisations aiming to make profits.
   (ii) The financial perspective's prime role is to consider whether the business will be able to create future value.

   A   Both statements are true.
   B   Statement (i) is true. Statement (ii) is false.
   C   Statement (i) is false. Statement (ii) is true.
   D   Both statements are false.

168 If a business's results diverge from what is planned, which of the following is/are courses of action that a business could consider taking?

   (i)   Carry out control actions to correct the difference
   (ii)   Change the plan
   (iii) Do nothing

   A   (i) only
   B   (ii) only
   C   (i) and (ii)
   D   (i),(ii) and (iii)

169 What does the mnemonic SMART stand for?

   A   Specific, Measurable, Achievable, Realistic, Time-bound
   B   Specific, Motivational, Authoritative, Realistic, Time-bound
   C   Specific, Motivational, Achievable, Relevant, Timely
   D   Specific, Measurable, Authoritative, Relevant, Time-bound

170 Which of the following is least likely to be a strategic objective of a business?

   A   Increasing market share
   B   Decreasing risk
   C   Decreasing amounts owed by customers
   D   Increasing quality

171 Which of the following is NOT a holding cost of stock?

    A   Obsolescence
    B   Emergency stock
    C   Pilferage
    D   Insurance

172 Monthly demand for Product Xy is 3,000 units. The annual cost of holding a unit of Xy in stock is $8. Ordering costs of Product Xy are $40 per order.

What is the economic order quantity for product Xy?

    A   122 units
    B   173 units
    C   424 units
    D   600 units

173 The following information is available for stock.

Maximum weekly usage	800 units
Maximum lead time	5 weeks
Minimum weekly usage	550 units
Minimum lead time	3 weeks

What is the stock re-order level?

    A   4,000 units
    B   2,750 units
    C   2,400 units
    D   1,650 units

174 The following information is available for stock.

Maximum weekly usage	800 units
Maximum lead time	6 weeks
Average weekly usage	640 units
Average lead time	5 weeks
Minimum weekly usage	500 units
Minimum lead time	4 weeks
Re-order level	4,800 units
Re-order quantity	5,600 units

What is the minimum inventory level or buffer safety inventory?

    A   0 units
    B   1,600 units
    C   2,400 units
    D   2,800 units

175 The following information is available for stock.

Maximum inventory level	4,500 units
Minimum inventory level	1,000 units
Re-order level	2,700 units
Re-order quantity	3,200 units

What is the average inventory level?

A   2,350 units
B   2,600 units
C   3,700 units
D   4,200 units

176 The following information is available for stock.

Maximum weekly demand	800 units
Average weekly demand	500 units
Standard deviation of demand	80 units
Order lead time	2 weeks
95% normal distribution value	1.65

What reorder level should the business set if it wishes to have a 95% chance of avoiding running out of stock?

A   632 units
B   932 units
C   1,132 units
D   1,732 units

177 Annual demand for Product Zy is 40,000 units. The purchase price of one unit is $8. The annual cost of holding a unit of Zy in stock is $25. Ordering costs of Product Zy are $50 per order. The supplier of Zy has offered a 5% discount for orders of 2,000 units or more.

Which of the following statements is true?

A   Ordering the economic order quantity each order will have a lower total cost.

B   Ordering 2,000 units each order will have a lower total cost.

C   There is no difference in total cost between the two alternatives.

D   It is impossible to tell which has the lower total cost from the information provided.

Chapter 11 Organisational information requirements

178 What process is used to gather external data from a range of sources?

    A   Environmental scanning
    B   Market research
    C   Informal data collection
    D   Data warehousing

179 Which of the following statements about information costs is true?

    A   The value of information should be less than the cost of obtaining it.
    B   The value of information should be greater than the cost of obtaining it.
    C   The cost of information does not include the cost of data analysis.
    D   The value of information is measured purely in financial terms.

180 What is the strategic objective of collecting customer data and increasing understanding about their requirements?

    A   Enhancing distribution arrangements
    B   Reducing product quality problems
    C   Enhancing value
    D   Reducing customer complaints

181 Which of the following is a direct source of customer data?

    A   Website clicks
    B   Office automation system
    C   Data warehouse
    D   Logical access system

182 What does an expert system provide for management?

    A   Combination of models to aid unstructured decision-making
    B   Specialised information and specialist problem solving techniques
    C   Integration of new knowledge into an organisation
    D   Internal and external information available in an easy-to-use form for strategic decision-making

183 Which of the following is an example of a knowledge work system?

    A   Diagnostic system
    B   Computer aided design
    C   Intranet
    D   Digital filing system

184 An information system making knowledge available to managers in easy-to-use forms to enable them to make unstructured decisions is known as:

    A   An enterprise wide system
    B   An expert system
    C   An executive support system
    D   A knowledge work system

185 In strategic planning, what is the purpose of environmental scanning?

- A Monitor PEST factors
- B Appraise SWOT factors
- C Analyse competitors
- D Monitor economic factors

186 A small company's computer system comprises five desktop personal computers located in separate offices linked together in an intranet in the same building. The computers are not connected to the internet and employees are not allowed to take storage media in and out of the building. Information which the business owner wishes to keep confidential to herself is stored on one of the computers.

Which of the following statements can be concluded from this information?

- A The company's computer system does not need a back-up storage system.
- B The company's computer system does not need a password protection system.
- C This company's computer system does not need virus protection software.
- D This company's computer system does not need rules about email usage.

187 Which of the following statements about data security is NOT true?

- A Loss or corruption of data is always non-deliberate.
- B New staff in particular pose a threat.
- C It is impossible to prevent all threats cost-effectively.
- D Smoke detectors are a form of data protection.

188 Which of the following is what office automation systems are mainly designed to increase?

- A Productivity
- B Flexibility
- C Decision-making capability
- D Long-term planning capability

189 The use of uninterruptible (protected) power supplies is a method of protecting data and IT systems from what sort of security threat?

- A Accidental damage
- B Weather
- C Hacking
- D Denial of service attack

190 Which of the following would be classified as a disaster recovery control?

- A Passwords
- B Off-site storage
- C Job rotation
- D Anti-virus software

191 Which of the following is an advantage of computerised accounting systems over manual systems?

- A The risk of errors is eradicated.
- B Information cannot be stolen.
- C Information is less accessible.
- D Processing is faster.

192 Which of the following is an example of a physical access control?

A   System backups
B   Intruder alarms
C   Segregation of duties
D   Encryption

193 Which of the following represents data or information captured from outside the organisation?

A   Information about personnel from the payroll system
B   Value of sales from the accounting records
C   Market information on buying habits of potential customers from the marketing manager
D   Information on decisions taken from the minutes of a meeting

194 In the context of data security systems, which of the following are examples of physical access controls to protect computer equipment or data storage media?

(i)   Card entry systems
(ii) Personal identification numbers
(iii) Logical access controls

A   (i) and (ii)
B   (i) and (iii)
C   (ii) and (iii)
D   (i), (ii) and (iii)

195 Which of the following is an example of a system used by a company to record sales orders and wages?

A   Transaction processing system
B   Management information system
C   Office automation system
D   Decision support system

196 When an organisation carries out an environmental scan, it analyses which of the following?

A   Strengths, weaknesses, opportunities and threats
B   Political, economic, social and technological factors
C   Strategic options and choice
D   Inbound and outbound logistics

197 Which of the following is NOT part of the system testing process in systems development?

A   Systems logic testing
B   User acceptance testing
C   Program testing
D   Feasibility testing

198 Which of the following is NOT a characteristic of good information?

A   Relevant
B   Communicated
C   Authoritative
D   Timely

Chapter 12 The impact of IT on work practices

199 Which of the following statements about big data analytics is correct?

- A Big data analytics relies on digital information.
- B Big data analytics relies on internal information.
- C Big data analytics relies on financial information.
- D Big data analytics relies on written information.

200 Which of the following statements about big data analytics is NOT correct?

- A Big data analytics can include analysis of informal sources such as social media posts.
- B Big data analytics allows large volumes of data to be analysed quickly.
- C Big data analytics needs to include assessment of the reliability of data.
- D Big data analytics ensures companies respond quickly to information becoming available.

201 What technology allows identification of patterns or trends in data or information?

- A Mobile apps
- B Data analytics
- C Big data
- D Interoperability

202 To which characteristic of big data is data cleansing relevant?

- A Volume
- B Variety
- C Velocity
- D Veracity

203 A Co uses a variety of computer models in its budgetary and control process.

Which of the following models are a feedforward control model?

- (i) A model used to prepare a forecast of sales volumes each month. If these forecasts indicate that budgeted sales levels will not be achieved, the marketing department is required to take appropriate control action.

- (ii) An inventory control model used to determine minimum and maximum levels for each inventory item. The model produces an exception report whenever the actual inventory level reaches minimum level or maximum level, so that control action by the inventory control department can be taken if necessary.

- (iii) A target is set for month-end cash balances. A spreadsheet model is used to forecast the net cash flow and the resulting cash balance for each month. Control action is taken if necessary by the finance department to achieve the desired cash balance.

- A (i) and (ii)
- B (i) and (iii)
- C (ii) and (iii)
- D (i),(ii) and (iii)

204 Which of the following is NOT a physical problem caused by technology?

- A Repetitive strain injury
- B Carpal tunnel syndrome
- C Worm virus
- D Computer vision syndrome

205 Which of the following is NOT an advantage of increased homeworking by employees?

- A Cost savings for the employee
- B Larger pool of employees
- C Cost savings for the employer
- D Increased contact with other employees

206 Which of the following are characteristics of a legacy system?

- (i) Backward compatibility
- (ii) Difficult to modify
- (iii) Requiring antiquated hardware

- A (i) and (ii)
- B (i) and (iii)
- C (ii) and (iii)
- D (i),(ii) and (iii)

207 Which of the following is a characteristic of an intelligent agent ?

- A Retrieval of information and automation of repetitive tasks
- B Information application that takes into account organisation and staff needs
- C Provision of information about organisation's products and services to consumers
- D Supplier of remote working services

208 Which of the following statements about the use of information technology is/are true?

- (i) Increased use of information technology lengthens organisational hierarchy.
- (ii) Increased use of information technology widens spans of control

- A Both statements are true.
- B Statement (i) is true. Statement (ii) is false.
- C Statement (i) is false. Statement (ii) is true.
- D Both statements are false.

209 Concerns over the copying and distribution of copyrighted material are primarily to do with which moral dimension of the information age, identified by Laudon and Laudon?

- A Property rights
- B Accountability and control
- C System quality
- D Quality of life

210 Which of the following would NOT be a method of dealing with information overload?

- A Delegating
- B Filtering incoming email
- C Using advisory agent
- D Deleting duplicate information

211 Which of the following is NOT a method for storing information that is relevant to an organisation?

- A Cloud computing
- B Big data analytics
- C Knowledge management system
- D Customer relationship management system

212 What can be defined as 'internet applications that build on the foundations of Web 2.0 and that allow the creation and exchange of user-generated content'?

- A Cloud applications
- B Social media applications
- C Big data applications
- D FAST applications

213 Which of the following is a drawback of cloud computing?

- A Cloud computing is only available to large organisations
- B Access to the cloud may be lost if payments are missed or delayed
- C Cloud computing offers less flexibility than in-house technology
- D Cloud computing is usually more expensive than establishing in-house technology

214 In the context of blockchain technology, what is a smart contract?

- A Self-executing agreements that use cryptography, digital signatures and secure completion
- B Documents that legally evidence the purchase and ownership of cryptocurrencies
- C Legal documents produced in PDF format that can be shared over a secure network and signed remotely by the parties using digital signatures
- D Contracts that are produced using AI in response to spoken requests made by the parties that will be bound by the contract

Exam answer bank

EXAM ANSWER BANK

Chapter 1 The organisation of work and the work of management

1   C   Disturbance handler

Monitor (A) spokesperson (B) and disseminator (D) are informational roles, but disturbance handler (C) is a decisional role.

2   B   Ability to perceive complex decisions

Ability to use complex techniques (A) is a technical skill, ability to perceive what motivates other employees (C) is a personal skill, ability to promote change (D) is a managerial skill.

3   B   Application of techniques to plan, measure and control work for maximum productivity

The organization as an open system (A) is a system-based approach. Trust, co-operation and mutual adjustment (C) are emphasised in Theory Z. Motivation, group and individual behaviour (D) are emphasised in the human relations approach.

4   A   There is no universally best organisational structure.

Authority being exercised down a clear chain of command (B) is characteristic of the classical approach. The need for workers to have challenge and responsibility in their jobs (C) is characteristic of a (neo) human relations approach. Concern for employee welfare inside and outside the organisation (D) is characteristic of a Theory Z approach.

5   B   Hawthorne

The studies were initiated by Elton Mayo and carried out at the Hawthorne Plant of Western Electric.

Fayol (A) was concerned with universal, rational principles of management. Taylor (C) was a pioneer of scientific management. Mintzberg (D) was concerned with how managers actually spent their time.

6   D   Motivating

It is assumed that subordinates will carry out a command whether motivated or not.

Planning (A), organising (B) and commanding (C) are all functions of management.

7   D   Planning and control

Planning and control are included within setting objectives and measurement.

Setting objectives (A), the job of measurement (B) and motivating employees (C) are all categories used by Drucker.

8   A   Monitor

The monitor role involves scanning the environment and gathering information from a network of contacts.

Leadership (B) is a wider concept. As a spokesperson (C), the manager can then provide information on behalf of the department or organisation to interested parties. As a disseminator (D), a manager can spread relevant information to team members.

EXAM ANSWER BANK

9	B	Organising

Planning (A) is about determining objectives and how to reach them. Controlling (C) involves measuring and adjusting activities in line with plans. Leadership (D) focuses on interpersonal tasks and creating directions rather than detailed work like this.

10	A	Micro-division of labour

Micro-division of labour (or job simplification) is breaking down jobs into their smallest possible components, and having one person carry out one component.

Job enlargement (B) implies greater task variety, and empowerment (C), greater task significance and responsibility. Synergising (D) is to do with business combinations, ensuring the whole is greater than the sum of the parts.

11	D	Managing economic performance

Providing information to stakeholders (A), developing people (B) and coordinating activities (C) are not main functions.

12	A	F W Taylor

F W Taylor is associated with scientific management.

Mayo (B), Mcgregor (C) and Ouchi (D) are associated with the human relations school.

13	C	Awareness of the many different factors that affect the way that a manager acts in each situation

The contingency school is based on the idea that there is no universally best way of managing, and that the most appropriate way will depend on the factors in the circumstances.

Concern with the social environment at work (A) is characteristic of the human relations school of management. Job specialisation, clear statements of responsibilities and promotion on merit (B) relate to a bureaucratic structure. Concern with both satisfying individual needs and meeting organisational goals (D) describes the rationale behind the systems approach.

14	B	Figurehead

Spokesperson (A) is an informational role. Negotiator (C) and resource allocator (D) are decisional roles.

15	B	Developmental

Informational (A), interpersonal (C) and decisional (D) are all Mintzberg's managerial role types.

16	A	Ouchi

Ouchi was concerned with the application of Japanese values in a Western context.

Fayol (B) was concerned with the importance of hierarchy. Peters and Waterman (C) were concerned with the values of high-performing companies. Taylor (D) thought that reward was the main motivator.

EXAM ANSWER BANK

17 C Theory Y

Theory Y is the managerial assumption that people can be motivated to accept challenge and responsibility and contribute willingly to the firm.

Theory X (B) frowns on the idea of freedom at work and does not give priority to employees being happy.

Theory W (A) and Theory Z (D) are not theories of Douglas McGregor.

18 D Get others to follow the change willingly

The most important role of senior management in a change initiative is to ensure widespread support for the change across the organisation. Senior management are able to do this through communicating the importance of the change and demonstrating their commitment to it.

Challenging things that are taken for granted (A), managing change implementation process (B) and selecting the best theory of change (C) are other things management might do but are not the most important ones.

19 B Liaison

The role of disseminator (A) involves distributing information to subordinates. Liaison may involve negotiation (C) but may also have other purposes. Figurehead (D) is a representational rather than a communication role.

20 B Spending the great majority of time on managerial activities

The supervisor is likely to have operational responsibilities that take up a significant amount of time as well as managerial responsibilities.

Dealing with day-to-day matters (A), being a filter for communication (C) and using frequent and detailed information (D) are all characteristics of a supervisor's role.

Chapter 2 Effective leadership

21 B Negative

Negative power is the use of disruptive behaviour to stop things from happening.

Expert power (A) is based on experience, qualifications or expertise. Coercive power (C) is based on the threat of physical force or punishment. Personal power (D) is based on the force of personality.

22 C (i), (ii) and (iii)

Psychologically distant managers (PDMs) maintain distance from their subordinates, so (iv) is wrong.

(A) misses out (iii), B misses out (i), D incorrectly includes (iv) and misses out (ii).

23 A It is most popular amongst subordinates.

Tells or sells appears to be most popular amongst leaders (B). A tells style is more likely to encourage high productivity (C). The Ashridge model does not identify any style as being universally best (D).

24 A Authority

The essence of delegation is that the superior gives the subordinate part of his or her own authority.

Power (B) is not conferred by the organisation, so it cannot be delegated: it must be possessed. Responsibility (C) is not delegated: the superior makes the subordinate responsible to him for the authority he has delegated, but he remains responsible for it to his own boss and will be accountable (D) to his own boss.

25 B Democratic

Consultative (A) means that the leader takes subordinate views into account, but still makes the decision. Autocratic (C) is a 'tells' style and persuasive (D) is a 'sells' style.

26 C Contingency theories

Contingency theories are based on the belief that there is no 'one best way' of leading but that effective leaders adapt their behaviour to changing variables. Adair's model sees the leadership process in a context made up of the task needs, individuals' needs and group needs.

Trait theories (A) relate to personality characteristics that leaders supposedly have. Style theories (B) broadly relate to whether the leader is focused on the task or on people. Behavioural theories (D) relate to motivation rather than leadership.

27 A Action-centred leadership

Contingency theory (B) considers other elements as well as these variables. The managerial grid (C) balances concern for the task against concern for people. The Ashridge model (D) considers four management styles.

EXAM ANSWER BANK

28	C	Innovation

According to Zaleznik, leaders direct their energies towards introducing new approaches and ideas.

Co-ordination (A), focus on systems and controls (B) and focus on immediate results (D) are associated with management.

29	A	Responsibility

Authority (B) provides the right to perform an action. Power (C) is the ability to perform an action (and in particular, to influence others). Influence (D) is a process by which a person can direct or modify the behaviour of another person.

30	B	Position

Position power is legitimate organisational authority, by virtue of a position in the organisation hierarchy: managers depend largely on it for their influence.

Leaders are often required to exercise informal, interpersonal forms of influence, such as person power (A) (charisma, inspiration) and expert power (C) (valued knowledge). Physical power (D) (intimidation) should not be used by managers and leaders.

31	D	Benevolent authoritative, participative, democratic, exploitative authoritative

Benevolent autocratic and exploitative autocratic are incorrect in (A) and (B), along with laissez faire in (B). All elements in (C) are incorrect.

32	C	Hersey and Blanchard

Blake and Mouton (A) looked at the importance of task and people. Katz and Kahn (B) focused on the influential increment over and above mechanical compliance that effective leadership produced. Tannenbaum and Schmidt (D) looked at use of authority by the leader versus area of subordinate freedom.

33	D	Allocating scarce resources

This could be concerned with people as a resource, but is not people-centred.

Creating the culture (A), inspiring and motivating others (B) and reconciling individual needs with the needs of the organisation (C) are all people-centred activities.

34	D	Low concern for people and low concern for the task

This is the worst of all worlds.

(A), (B) and (C) are all incorrect as they have high concern for either or both elements.

35	C	Consistency

The studies showed that consistency was more important to subordinates than any style.

Ideally subordinates preferred to be consulted (A) and felt in practice leaders tried to direct them (B). Speed of decision-making (D) was not a highlighted factor.

36   B   Autocratic

Autocratic is the term for the least participative of the styles in the Ashridge model.

Authoritarian (A), authoritative (C) and assertive (D) are all terms that could be used for strong leadership, but are not correct here.

37   C   Ensuring that all the subordinate's decisions are confirmed or authorised by the superior

There is a fine distinction between making the subordinate accountable and interfering. If the superior doesn't trust the subordinate to make decisions, they shouldn't have delegated at all.

Specifying performance levels and results (A), obtaining the subordinate's agreement (B) and ensuring that the subordinate reports results (D) are all examples of effective delegation practice.

38   B   Authoritative

Exploitative authoritative and benevolent authoritative are two leadership styles described by Likert.

Autocratic (A), laissez-faire (C) and democratic (D) are the three styles identified by Lewin, Lippitt and White.

39   A   Idealised influence

This involves the leader acting as a role model, here in acting ethically.

Inspirational motivation (B) is about encouraging team behaviour and commitment. Intellectual stimulation (C) is about encouraging questioning, creativity and problem-solving. Individual consideration (D) is about treating followers on their own merits, accepting individual differences and promoting development opportunities.

40   B   Country club

Country club implies high concern with relationships with the team, but possibly at the expense of the task.

Impoverished (A) implies little concern with task or team. Dampened pendulum (C) and team (D) imply higher concern with the task as well as the team.

Chapter 3 Strategic planning and management by objectives

41 D Creating a given level of output from minimum input

Creating maximum output (A) is incorrect as it takes no account of input. Creating the best quality output from available input (B) is a quality objective, creating the maximum output from minimum input (C) is a definition of effectiveness.

42 B Primary objective

Secondary objectives (A) and unit objectives (C) (objectives for parts of the organisation) are derived from primary objectives. Mission (D) focuses on the general purpose of the organisation and the main objective to seek profit may not be apparent from its mission.

43 C Disclosing environmental impacts in its annual report

Disclosure of impacts may lead to pressure on the company to reduce impacts, but it will not itself be a reduction in impacts.

Recycling waste (A), turning off lights (B) and buying raw materials locally (D) (by minimising resources needed to transport supplies) will all reduce environmental impacts.

44 B Bankers

Bankers have a level of financial interest in the company that the other stakeholders lack, and will be concerned if low returns threaten interest payments.

Customers (A) will be concerned about threats to supply, employees (C) threats to their jobs and the government (D) threats to tax revenues.

45 A An employee

The government (B) and the local community (C) are external stakeholders. A customer (D) is a connected stakeholder.

46 D A pressure group

A director (B) is an internal stakeholder, a supplier (A) and a shareholder (C) are connected stakeholders.

47 C Goals

Profits (A) are not the objectives of all organisations. Stakeholders (B) doesn't fit pursues. Tactics (D) are at a lower level than goals.

48 D (i),(ii), (iii) and (iv)

All these groups have a legitimate stake in the enterprise: the government (i), as a regulator; employees (iii), as participants in the business; and the environmental pressure group (ii) and local residents (iv), due to the potential impact that the power station may have on their interests.

(A) misses out environmental pressure groups. (B) misses out employees. (C) misses out the government and local residents.

49	B	Stakeholders who work for the organisation

Stakeholders who have a direct interest in the organisation but do not work for it (A) and stakeholders who conduct transactions with the organisation (C) are connected stakeholders. Stakeholders who are not connected to the organisation (D) are external stakeholders.

50	B	A local authority

A local authority is a non-profit making organisation.

A private accountancy college (A), a small retailer (C) and a bank (D) all primarily aim to make profits.

51	C	(iii) and (iv)

Investors (iii) will be making decisions (and taking risks) on inaccurate information. Suppliers (iv) will extend credit without knowing the true financial position of the company. Staff (i) and customers (ii) may eventually be affected, for example if shortfalls in working capital threaten the business, but the immediate impact on them is less.

(A) states staff and customers and not suppliers and investors. (B) states customers and not suppliers. (D) states customers and not investors.

52	A	Profit maximisation

Efficient use of resources (B) and stakeholder satisfaction (D) are non-financial objectives. Avoidance of loss (C) is a financial objective, but businesses have to make profits to warrant their owners investing in them.

53	D	Trina

Business-level strategy involves making decisions about how to compete in the organisation's markets. These strategies involve making decisions about the products that the business should make, the new products it should develop, and the new markets in which to sell its products. (This is sometimes called product-market strategy.)

Daniel (A), Peter (B) and Lisha (C) work at operational level as they are concerned with routine activities.

54	A	Corporate

The question 'what business should we be in' is a fundamental, high level question associated with corporate level strategy.

Functional (B) and Business (C) are lower level strategies. Mission (D) is concerned with overall purpose, Why rather than What.

55	A	The organisation's overriding purpose

Although there is no one single format for mission statements, the best option from those available is that the mission statement describes the organisation's overriding or overall purpose.

The future desirable state (B) would be the vision, aims (C) and (D) are what the organisation intends to achieve rather than the organisation's purpose.

56 B Marketing

Socio-economic groupings are often the basis on which markets are segmented, so that products/services and marketing messages can be targeted appropriately (to people with the right levels of income, aspiration, education and so on).

Human resources (A) is incorrect as social class includes education factors, but the data cannot be used to predict skill availability. The data is not relevant to finance (C) or research and development (D).

57 C Determines which marketing agency to use for a marketing campaign

This is a lower-level decision than strategy, as it will derive from the strategy chosen and the approach to marketing it.

Matching activities to environment (A), setting overall long-term direction (B) and having important implications for strategic change (D) are all characteristic of strategic decisions.

EXAM ANSWER BANK

Chapter 4 Internal analysis

58   B   After-sales service

Procurement (A), technology development (C) and human resources management (D) are all support activities.

59   D   Firm infrastructure

Operations (A), outbound logistics (B) and marketing and sales (C) are all primary activities.

60   C   A secondary activity involving purchasing materials and equipment

Inbound logistics is a primary activity involving warehousing and inventory control (A/B), outbound logistics is a primary activity involving packaging and distribution to customers (D).

61   C   Question mark

Star (A) is high growth and high market share. Cash cow (B) is low growth and high market share. Dog (D) is low growth and low market share.

62   A   Procurement

Operations (B), marketing and sales (C) and inbound logistics (D) are all primary activities in Porter's value chain model.

63   B   Sheila

Marketing is a primary activity in the value chain model.

Administration (Steve (A)) is part of the firm's infrastructure, a support activity. Dealing with suppliers and finding sources of supply (Sunny (C)) is part of procurement, a support activity. Sam's work (D) relates to technology development, which is a support activity.

64   D   (i),(ii),(iii) and (iv)

These are all aspects of a resource audit.

(A), (B) and (C) are wrong as they miss out one or more aspects.

65   A   Efficiency

Economy (B) is about minimising inputs for given outputs or maximising outputs for given inputs. Effectiveness (C) looks at what has been achieved. Energy (D) is a resource used by a business.

66   C   Necessary for the firm to stay in business

Surprisingly maybe. A threshold competence is what is necessary for a firm to stay in business.

Being competitively unique (A), making a disproportionate contribution to value (B) and being extendable (D) are the qualities of core competences.

67   C   They are unique to each business.

Some critical factors will be industry-wide.

Product features particularly valued by customers (A) is a definition of core competences and organisations need to excel in them (B) by carrying out key tasks (D).

EXAM ANSWER BANK

68	D	It allows the organisation to exercise greater control over quality.

It is likely to be more difficult to exercise quality if a third party carries out the outsourced service rather than if it is carried out internally.

The outsourced supplier may be able to supply the service more cheaply (A) than if it is carried out in-house, it can increase effectiveness (B) if the outsourced supplier has greater expertise in the service than is available in-house. By outsourcing non-core competencies, the business can focus more on core competencies (C).

69	B	Product form

Product form is a sub-group within the product class (A) or generic product group (C) of crisps. Brand (D) would be cheese and onion crisps manufactured by a particular producer.

70	A	The model is predictive, not descriptive.

The model primarily describes what happens to a product during its life, and making precise predictions from it about future sales is very difficult.

Products not having a maturity phase (B), being at different stages in different markets (C) and not being linked to other products in the portfolio (D) are all problems of the model.

71	C	Skills

Skills are a soft element in the model.

Structure (A), strategy (B) and systems (D) are the three hard elements of the model.

72	C	Business strength v Market attractiveness

Market growth and relative market share (A) are elements of the BCG model. Revenue/profit and time (B) are considered in the product lifecycle. Bargaining power of customers and Bargaining power of suppliers (D) are part of Porter's five forces model.

73	B	Marketing strategy

Segmentation, basis of competitive advantage and product portfolio are higher level strategic issues.

Audit of marketing mix effectiveness (A) would consider the combination of product, price, promotion and distribution. Marketing structure audit (C) would consider organisational issues such as training and communication. Marketing systems audit (D) would cover information, planning and control systems.

Chapter 5 Environmental analysis

74 B Regression analysis

Delphi technique (A) is a qualitative method of forecasting involving the use of experts. Industry scenario building (C) and Porter's five forces analysis (D) are not forecasting techniques.

75 D Threat of new entrants

Having to invest in the accessories as well as the primary product will mean high capital costs and deter new entrants.

The tactic does not alter the bargaining power of suppliers (A), the bargaining power of customers (B) or the intensity of competitive rivalry (C).

76 B PEST

These are the political, economic, socio-cultural and technological aspects of the environment.

ICT (information and communication technologies) (A) relates to use of technology. SWOT (Strengths, Weaknesses, Opportunities, Threats) (C) relates to the internal environment as well as the external environment. HRM (human resources management) (D) relates to human resources.

77 C A general election

A general election brings political uncertainty as there may (or may not) be a new government and new government policies.

Entry of new competitors (A) and rising inflation (D) would be economic factors. Increased consumer concern about green issues (B) would be a social factor.

78 B Opportunities and threats

The external appraisal identifies opportunities that can be exploited by the organisation and also identifies threats against which the company must protect itself.

Strengths (A) and weaknesses (D) are internal factors. The appraisal looks at opportunities, not just threats (C).

79 A Social

The expectation that commercial organisations will act as 'responsible corporate citizens' reflects a change in the expectations of society as a whole – a social change.

Expectations of society may influence politicians (C), but this influence is indirect. Economic (B) and technological (D) are not correct.

80 A SWOT

SWOT (Strengths, Weaknesses, Opportunities, Threats) analysis looks at internal and external factors that affect a corporate body.

SMART (B) (Specific, Measurable, Attainable, Relevant, Time-bounded) refers to objective-setting.

CRM (C) is customer relationship management.

PEST (D) (Political, Economic, Socio-cultural and Technological) is a related exercise, as PEST data is fed into the opportunities/threats part of the business appraisal.

EXAM ANSWER BANK

81   D   External experience of non-executive directors

Directors are an internal factor.

New legislation (A), competitor activity (B) and interest rates (C) are all external factors.

82   D   Government regulation of the industry

Substitute products or services (A), new entrants to the industry (B) and bargaining power of customers (C) are all Porter forces.

83   C   Low switching costs in the market

Low switching costs mean that it will be easy for customers to change from existing suppliers to a new supplier, facilitating entry into the market.

New entrants may not be big enough to benefit from economies of scale (A). The funds required for high capital investment (B) may be a deterrent. It may be difficult to overcome brand loyalty to existing firms (D).

84   D   It is isolated from the external environment.

Being incapable of further technical enhancement (A) is a stage in system development. Protection from unauthorised access (B) refers to security arrangements. Relation to external environment in a prescribed manner (C) refers to a semi-closed system.

85   C   Social

In the PEST model, social factors include demographics – the study of population and characteristics, which are affected, amongst other things, by birth and death rates.

Birth and death rates are not significant factors in the political (A), economic (B) and technological (D) elements of the model.

86   D   Consumer protection policy

This represents government action to safeguard consumer interests.

Increasing inflation rates (A) is an economic factor. An ageing population (B) is a social factor (B). An increase in internet coverage by providers (C) is a technological factor.

87   C   Stability and Simplicity

A stable environment with a lack of complexity (that is, simplicity) will have low environmental uncertainty.

Stability and complexity (D) is therefore wrong.

Stability and dynamism (A) have opposite meanings. Dynamism and complexity (B) are symptomatic of high environmental uncertainty.

88   C   Handed down to each new generation

Learned culture is transferred in institutions and through ongoing social interaction (A). Purposeful culture offers order, direction and guidance (B). Dynamic culture adapts to changes in society (D).

89   A   Expected values use probabilities that may be inaccurate estimates.

Expected values do not take the time value of money into account (B). Expected values are long-term averages and may be of limited use for one-off decisions (C). Expected value calculation takes all values into consideration, including extreme values (D), although it is impossible to tell from the result of the calculation the range of values considered.

Chapter 6 Sustainability, CSR and ethics

90	D	Sustainability is defined as 'development that meets the needs of the present without compromising the ability of future generations to meet their own needs'.

'Green' practices and environmental concerns is only one aspect of sustainability. Sustainability is a broader concept which also considers the social and economic impact of an organisation (A)

It is important that the present needs are met. While the ability of future generations must be ensured, this should not be at the expense of meeting current needs (B).

Sustainability is about the practices employed by the organisation, not its ability to survive (C).

91	B	To address various challenges and guide efforts towards sustainable development worldwide.

The primary goal of the United Nations Sustainable Development Goals (SDGs) is to address various challenges and guide efforts towards sustainable development worldwide. This is correct because SDGs aim to promote economic growth, social inclusion, and environmental sustainability.

Maximising profits for businesses is not the primary goal of SDGs, which focus on broader sustainable development objectives (A).

Ignoring environmental, social, and governance factors in decision-making goes against the goals of SDGs, which emphasise considering these factors for sustainable development (C).

Promoting excessive consumption practices contradicts the goals of SDGs, which include promoting responsible consumption and production patterns (D).

92	B	Limit global warming to well below 2 degrees Celsius above pre-industrial levels

The Paris Agreement aims to limit global warming to well below 2 degrees Celsius above pre-industrial levels, with efforts to limit it to 1.5 degrees Celsius. This is correct because the agreement sets ambitious targets to mitigate climate change and its impacts.

Option A is incorrect because the Paris Agreement aims to limit global warming to well below 2 degrees Celsius, not 1 degree Celsius.

Achieving net zero emissions globally by 2030 is not a specific goal of the Paris Agreement (C).

While reducing greenhouse gas emissions is a goal of the Paris Agreement, there is no specific target mentioned in the agreement to reduce emissions by 50% by 2050 (D).

93	D	(i), (ii) and (iii)

The 17 Sustainable Development Goals provide a shared framework and roadmap for governments, businesses, civil society organisations, and individuals to work together towards a more equitable, resilient, and sustainable future.

EXAM ANSWER BANK

94 C Social costs is not a recognised category of environmental cost.

The four categories of environmental cost are defined by the US Environmental Protection Agency (1998) as

Conventional costs: These are the environmental costs of materials and energy which can be captured within cost systems

Potentially hidden costs: These costs are difficult to identify, for example they may be captured in the costing system but lost within 'general overheads'.

Contingent costs: These are environmental costs the organisation may face in the future, for example clean-up cost

Image and relationship costs: These environmental costs are intangible by nature and relate to the costs associated with developing and promoting an environmental image for the company. This category also includes the costs of poor environmental activities, for example the revenue that is lost following an environmental disaster such as an oil spill.

95 A Environmental accountability, social accountability, and economic accountability

Grey and Adams (2014) define the three components which provide a comprehensive approach to sustainability accounting: environmental accountability, social accountability, and economic accountability.

96 B (i) and (iii) only.

It is true that an integrated report reports on both financial and non-financial information to demonstrates how the organisation creates value. It is also true that integrated reporting considers how value is created in terms of 'six capitals'.

However, the information in the integrated report is combined and provided **alongside**, not in place of the traditional financial statements.

97 B Average training hours per employee (B)

This KPI relates to the training and development of staff, which is a social factor.

The percentage of women on the board relates to board composition, which is a governance factor.

The amount of waste generated and the amount of water consumed relate to usage of natural resources and the planetary impact of business, which are both environmental factors.

98 A Reduction of operational costs.

Managing environmental risks can create operational cost savings through the minimisation of the use of resources.

Environment regulations must still be complied with even if environmental risks are managed. However, by managing the risks the regulations should be complied with as standard (B).

Avoiding the reputational risk associated with poor labour practices is a benefit of managing social risks (C).

Ensuring a transparent and ethical decision making process is a benefit of managing governance risks (D).

99 A Considering sustainability as a core-component alongside financial and market analysis

By considering sustainability as a core-component alongside financial and market analysis the organisation builds sustainable goals into its overall objectives and corporate strategies. This ensures sufficient consideration and prioritisation is given to sustainability matters and that they considered in all aspects of the management and decision making process.

Outsourcing to countries with lower environmental regulations (B) or lower labour standards (C) both represent practices that go against the concept of sustainability.

Donation of a percentage of profits (D) might be a kind act, however the charities are described as 'unrelated' and as such have no bearing on the strategy, operations or actions of the organisation and as such cannot be viewed as measure which integrates sustainability into an organisation's strategic business planning.

100 C The law

The saying is: 'the law is a floor'.

By meeting non-legal regulations (A) (including the rules of your workplace) you should meet a higher standard of behaviour than the legal requirements. Ethical behaviour (B) is a higher moral standard, based on society's expectations and principles (D).

101 D Social responsibility may have commercial benefits.

There is no guarantee of increased profit levels (A) and some CSR activities may not have any costs (B). Other organisations are often more concerned with social responsibility than businesses (C), for example charities and government bodies.

102 B Processes

The three Ps are people (A), planet (C) and profit (D).

Chapter 7 Organisation structure

103 B Network

Support staff (A), middle line (C) and technostructure (D) are all elements of Mintzberg's framework.

104 C Inter-departmental co-operation is improved.

An individual has more than one boss in a matrix organisation (A) and decision-making may be slower because more individuals are involved (B). These are both disadvantages of a matrix organisation. Greater specialisation (D) is a characteristic of a bureaucracy.

105 A Span of control

The scalar chain (B) and line of command (C) both refer to the chain of command from the most senior to the most junior. The strategic apex (D) is the top component of Mintzberg's model.

106 D Long scalar chain, narrow span of control

A tall organisation has many levels of management (long scalar chain), with each manager having few direct subordinates (narrow span of control).

Short scalar chain and wide span of control (A) are characteristic of a flat organisation. (B) and (C) each have one correct, one incorrect element for a tall organisation.

107 B Good level of communication between different functions

There may be communication problems between functions that have their own ways of doing things.

Facilitation of specialist recruitment (A), pooling of expertise (C) and clear segregation of duties (D) are all benefits of a functional structure.

108 C Enrichment

Enrichment is part of job design.

Span of control (A), scalar chain (B) and degree of centralisation (D) are all elements of organisation structure.

109 B Specialisation

Specialisation involves people and/or departments focusing on a limited area of tasks or expertise.

Synergy (A) is the idea that people working together achieve more than would be possible working apart, sometimes referred to as 'the 2 + 2 = 5 factor'. Efficiency (C) is concerned with maximising the level of outputs relative to inputs. Team work (D) involves people co-operating to work together.

110 C Unity of command

The matrix organisation is based on dual command. The classical or traditional principle of unity of command is 'one person, one boss'.

Functional structuring (A), divisional structuring (B) and decentralisation of decision-making (D) are not classical management principles.

111　B　Divisionalisation

Y Co's situation suits divisionalisation: more or less autonomous product and regional businesses, with co-ordination from head office. 'Diversification' and 'acquisition' are good pointers to divisionalisation.

There are elements of geographical departmentation (A) and functional departmentation (D) but these structures would involve less autonomy. A network (C) is a more complex structure and the elements within it behave as a single entity.

112　D　Improvement in motivation of junior managers

Decisions being made in one place in the organisation (A) is more likely to be a benefit of centralisation. Reduction in bureaucracy (B) and better crisis management (C) are not necessarily features of decentralisation.

113　A　Herzberg

Herzberg believed that the workplace should be designed in a way that enabled workers to use their initiative and that the content of the work itself had an effect on motivation and performance.

Fayol (B) proposed universal principles of organisation, Taylor (C) was concerned with the most efficient methods, Weber (D) was concerned with authority structures.

114　B　(iv) only

In Herzberg's theory, only training (iv) is a 'motivator factor'. Sensible company policies (i), good salary and bonuses (ii) and considerate supervision (iii) are all 'hygiene' factors: if they are inadequate, employees will be dissatisfied, but even if they are got right, they will not provide lasting satisfaction or motivation. Herzberg argued that satisfaction comes only from the job.

(A) is incorrect because it lists (ii) as a factor and not (iv). (C) is incorrect because it lists (i) and (iii) as factors and not (iv). (D) is incorrect because it lists (i),(ii) and (iii) as factors.

115　D　Army

In the army, strict control and rigid lines of command are most likely to be appropriate.

Empowerment is usually appropriate in roles that interact with customers, to enable those dealing with customers to implement a solution. Roles could include customer service call centre (A), fast-food restaurant (B) and supermarket (C).

116　B　The movement of an individual to several other roles to gain experience

Job rotation involves an employee moving between several roles or jobs in succession to gain experience of a wide range of activities.

Redesign (A) is a fundamental change to the same role. Expansion and enrichment of job content (C) is job enrichment. Terminating an individual's employment (D) is redundancy.

117 A Motivator factor

Herzberg used the other three terms to describe the same set of factors: the ones that maintain morale but do not positively motivate (maintenance) (B); prevent dissatisfaction but do not promote satisfaction, in the same way that hygiene prevents ill-health but does not promote well-being (hygiene) (C); and that relate to the environment of work rather than to the work itself (environmental) (D).

118 C It replaces monetary rewards.

Job enrichment cannot offer management a cheap way of motivating employees. Even those who want enriched jobs will expect to be rewarded with more than job satisfaction.

Increased job satisfaction (A), enhanced output quality (B) and reduction in supervisory costs (D) have been found in practice to be benefits of job enrichment.

119 D An organisation chart can indicate functional authority but not line authority within a business.

Line authority can easily be shown on an organisation chart.

An organisation chart provides an easy-to-read summary of business structure (A). By showing internal positions and links it can help staff understand with whom to communicate (B) and their own responsibilities in the business (C).

120 B Support base

Strategic apex (A), technostructure (C) and operating core (D) are all elements of Mintzberg's organisational structure.

121 D Senior managers can take a wider view of problems and consequences.

Development of junior managers' skills (A), avoiding overburdening top managers (B) and responsiveness to local conditions (C) are advantages of decentralisation.

122 B Support staff

The canteen worker provides ancillary services and therefore is part of support staff.

The operating core (A) would include those responsible for producing goods and services. The strategic apex (C) would be the board and senior management. The middle line (D) would be operational management.

Chapter 8 Organisation culture

123   B   Design of office premises

The code of employee conduct (A) would be classified as behaviour, ways of addressing work superiors (C) would be classified as rituals, the company slogan (D) would be part of values and beliefs.

124   C   Lunch to welcome new staff

Dress code (A) and office mentoring (B) are artefacts. Managers being given their own offices (D) is an element of status, part of values and beliefs.

125   A   (i) only

Statement (ii) is not true, because an informal organisation can have its own agenda that is different from that of the main organisation. Statement (iii) is not true, because a strong informal organisation with its own agenda can undermine the formal organisation: create damaging rumours, safety/quality shortcuts, distractions from task goals etc.

(B) is wrong because it includes statement (iii), C is wrong because it includes statements (ii) and (iii) and omits (i), D is wrong because it includes statement (iii) and omits (i).

126   D   Strong values are dangerous if they filter out uncomfortable environmental information.

Filtering out information that doesn't fit the existing consensus can be a problem with strong cultures (and ultra-cohesive groups).

Some strong values (A) may not improve corporate financial performance (ethical/social responsibility). Values will need to be supplemented by rules and controls (B) in some areas (for example, health and safety). Strong values may lead to conflict (C) if not everybody likes them and tries to find ways of not following them.

127   D   Assumptions

Assumptions are foundational ideas that are no longer even consciously recognised or questioned by the culture, but which 'programme' its ways of thinking and behaving.

Values (A) are the next level up. They are consciously held concepts which give meaning to the next level up again – observable factors such as artefacts (B) and rituals (C).

128   D   Managers in positions of authority cannot generally be part of the informal organisation.

Managers can feed information into the grapevine and be part of their own informal networks.

Group norms and dynamics (A) can have a significant impact on productivity. The informal organisation can pose a threat to health and safety (B), because of informal 'short cuts' which are often developed and shared, by-passing health and safety rules and procedures. Informal organisations can stimulate innovation (C), because the 'grapevine' encourages knowledge sharing and multi-directional communication.

EXAM ANSWER BANK

129 C Power

Power culture is leader-focused.

Role culture (A) is a bureaucratic or mechanistic culture. Task culture (B) is project-focused. Person culture (D) is employee-focused.

130 B Acquisitive

Masculinity is missing from the list.

Power-distance (A), individualism (C) and uncertainty avoidance (D) are all used by Hofstede.

131 B Category of people

Culture applies broadly to categories of people.

Nation (A), social class (C) and organisation (D) are narrower terms.

132 B Low masculinity

Low masculinity or femininity is about high regard for values such as focus on relationships and quality of working life, and the acceptability of such values for both men and women. Mr Q's nurturing style would score in this dimension.

His approach does not really say anything about power-distance (A). There are elements of **high** uncertainty avoidance, not low (C), in his attempt to minimise staff insecurity. Individualism (D) is not really relevant.

133 C Individualism

The concern with the task and the lack of concern with working relationships is symptomatic of high individualism.

Power distance (A) is incorrect as there is nothing about how power is exercised. Uncertainty avoidance (B) is incorrect as certainty is not raised as an issue. Masculinity (D) is incorrect as the scenario is about the achievement of work tasks specifically, not what is considered rewarding.

134 B Uncertainty avoidance

The concern with structure and rules shows a high level of uncertainty avoidance.

Power distance (A) is incorrect as there is nothing about how power is exercised. Individualism (C) is incorrect as the focus is on rule compliance rather than work achievement. Masculinity (D) is incorrect as the scenario is not about what is considered rewarding.

135 D (i), (ii), (iii), (iv) and (v)

The founder (i) influences culture through creating founding values. History/experience (ii) influence culture through creating expectations and stories. Recruitment and selection (iii) influence culture by choosing people who will fit or change the culture. Industries (iv) have their own culture. Labour turnover (v) allows people who don't fit the culture to get out.

(A), (B) and (C) are all wrong as they don't include one of the elements listed.

136 B Task

A task culture suits project management structures, with their focus on deliverables (project completion) rather than processes.

A role culture (A) would suit longer-term bureaucratic structures. A power culture (C) would be more suitable for entrepreneurial structures. A person culture (D) would focus on those involved rather than project completion.

137 C Cutting corners

Cutting corners when rules are there for a good reason (health and safety, for example) may be a problem of informal organisations.

Faster communication (A), better morale (B) and greater co-operation (D) are all possible benefits of the informal organisation.

138 B Task

Tactical management has several tasks to carry out, including resource and production planning.

Handy thought that a role culture (A) was best suited to operational management and a power culture (C) was best suited to strategic management. A people culture (D) was not linked to any specific level of management.

139 A Artefact

An artefact here is an concrete item here serving a specific practical purpose (facilitate communication).

The meeting space's primary purpose is not to signify anything outside the organisation, so it is not a symbol (B). Ritual (C) is a part of organisational and social behaviour (D) and thus is about what is done rather than where it is done.

140 D Project teams

Project teams are more likely to be found in a task culture and are signs of a more complex structure and devolved decision-making, which is not generally true of a power culture (simple structure with one person making the main decisions).

Quick decision-making (A), functional structure (B) and adaptability (C) to change are typical features of a power culture.

141 D Customs

Values (A) relate to what people feel should be done rather than do. Rituals (B) are fixed, symbolic methods of haviour that are repeated over time. Artefacts (C) are physical objects that are part of the culture.

Chapter 9 Budget planning and control

142 C A method of budgeting where all activities are re-evaluated each time a budget is formatted

Making expenditure as close to zero as possible (A) and summing revenues and expenditures to zero (D) are not valid ways of budgeting. The budget remaining the same in real terms (B) is an approach to incremental budgeting.

143 D There are no performance targets for managers.

There will be performance targets, but they may well not be very challenging.

Incremental budgeting assumes all current activities and costs are still needed (A), managers are not required to justify existing costs (B) and there is no incentive for managers to reduce costs (C) (in fact there is an incentive for managers to spend up to their budgetary limit to make sure they receive the same spending in next year's budget).

144 C Estimate the production and sales volume by individual products and customers

The next stages would be estimating the demand for organisational activities (D); determining the resources required (B); adjusting resource capacity to match projected supply (A).

145 A Both statements are true.

By producing new plans at regular intervals, such as every three months, there may be a tendency for managers to focus on changes in the plan rather than aspects of performance that should be controlled. They are time-consuming and are only worthwhile when there is continual and substantial uncertainty about the future.

(B), (C) and (D) are incorrect because they say that either or both statements are false.

146 C Management budgets may not be realistic in practice.

When senior managers impose budgets on managers below them in the organisation hierarchy, there is a risk that the imposed budgets may be unrealistic, as senior managers may not have a full understanding of operational realities.

Management budgets including slack (A), being too ambitious (B) and being inconsistent with long-term strategy (D) can all be characteristics of bottom-up budgeting.

147 B Spending limits imposed by government

Budgeting within a spending limit should not necessarily make the budgeting process a difficult task.

In private sector companies, objectives and outputs are fairly easy to identify, at least in the short-term, as sales and profits. In the public sector there are multiple non-financial objectives (A), which may change as the political climate changes (C), and many different ways of measuring output (D), which creates complexity in the process.

148 C The budgeted cost expected for the actual level of activity achieved during the period

A budget cost allowance is the expected expenditure in a budget which has been flexed to the actual level of activity. It includes a basic, unchanged, allowance for fixed costs and an amount for variable costs according to the level of activity.

A budget of expenditure applicable to a particular function (A) is a functional budget. A budget set without permitting the ultimate budget manager the opportunity to participate in budget setting (B) is an imposed or top-down budget. A fixed budget allowance for expenditure which is expected every period regardless of the level of activity (D) is incorrect, as a budget cost allowance includes an amount for variable overhead.

149 A A budget, which by recognising different cost behaviour patterns, is designed to change as volume of activity changes

Flexible budgets are designed to flex with the level of activity.

A budget for a twelve month period (B) is a fixed budget, used for planning. A rolling budget (C) is updated in response to changes in the environment, not in the level of activity. A flexible budget includes all cost types, not just semi-variable costs (D).

150 D Both statements are false.

There is likely to be a demotivating effect when ideal standard of performance are set (i), as staff's efficiency will always be lower. A low standard of efficiency (ii) is also demotivating, because there is no sense of achievement in attaining the required standards. Managers and employees will often outperform the standard or target when in fact they could have performed better if they had been sufficiently motivated.

(A), (B) and (C) are all incorrect, as they state that either or both statements are true.

151 C Rolling budget

An incremental budget (A) involves adding an allowance to last year's budget. A flexible budget (B) means adjusting the budget for the level of activity. A zero-based budget (D) involves fresh justification of each figure in the budget each period.

152 D (i), (ii) and (iii)

Cost, profit and investment centres are all possible budgetary centres.

(A), (B) and (C) are all incorrect, as they miss out one of the centres.

153 A Investment centre

The level of investment helps determine the residual income figure.

Profit (B), cost (C) and revenue (D) are all incorrect as the managers do not have control over investment levels.

154 C Discretionary fixed costs are non-controllable in the long-term.

Discretionary fixed costs should be controllable in the short-term and certainly the long-term.

EXAM ANSWER BANK

Some costs may be under the control of two or managers (A), committed fixed costs may be non-controllable in the short-term (B). Managers should be held responsible for costs incurred by a service department that have been apportioned to their department (D) if they have influenced the level of activity undertaken or costs incurred by the service department by their demands on it.

155   C   Budgetary slack

Flexible budgets (A) adjust budgets to the level of activity. Incremental budgets (B) use last year's budget plus an allowance for inflation or a general uplift. Participative budgeting (D) involves local managers setting their own budgets. This can lead to budgetary slack but is not certain to do so.

156   B   It requires budgeted costs to be justified by expected benefits.

The focus of zero-based budgeting is on the future, not the past (A). It can be difficult to rank competing priorities from different departments (C). Zero-based budgeting can require significant management time (D), but this is a disadvantage, not an advantage.

157   B   Managers being given too much resource due to budgetary slack.

Managers failing to take into account local conditions (A) and being demotivated by unrealistic targets (C) are problems with top-down budgeting. Bottom-up budgeting should require less senior central management time (D), as senior managers should only be overseeing the budgets rather than preparing them in detail.

Chapter 10 Managerial control

158 A Capacity utilisation

Downtime (B) involves comparing actual production with what was planned. Rejection rate (C) is a quality control measure. Level of service (D) relates to dealings with customers or suppliers.

159 B Employee engagement level

Employee turnover (A) measures the rate of change of staff. Employee satisfaction (C) relates to how happy staff are (they may be unhappy even though they are participating). Employee utilisation rate (D) is a measure of how much time is spent on value-adding activities.

160 A Comparing original targets or actual results with future forecasts

Reporting control information to management (B) is simple feedback control. Measuring whether critical success factors have been achieved is done by use of key performance indicators (C). Revising plans, budgets, organisational structures and control systems to meet changes in conditions (D) is double loop feedback.

161 C Bringing the police in to investigate fraud

The purpose of using the police is to obtain information about what actually happened.

A fraud policy statement (A), obtaining references for new staff (B) and staff training about fraud (D) are all measures taken in advance to stop fraud happening and so are feedforward controls.

162 B Comparing results with the plan

Comparing results with the plan is part of the control process.

Identifying objectives (A), choosing alternative courses of action (C) and evaluating strategies (D) are all part of the planning process.

163 D The optimal quantity to be re-ordered at regular intervals

The optimal quantity of material usage (A) relates to material input. The quantity of inventory at which inventory has to be re-ordered (B) is the reorder level, not the reorder quantity. The minimum level of inventory held (C) is known as the safety or buffer inventory.

164 A Rating in on-line local guide

This will relate to quality of customer experience.

Contribution per haircut (B) is a financial perspective measure. Qualifications staff have achieved (C) is a learning and growth perspective measure. Average waiting time per customer (D) is an internal business process perspective measure.

165 A Number of new models introduced in year

Repeat customers (B) is a customer perspective measure, time spent on after-sales queries (C) is an internal business process measure. Sales growth of existing models (D) is a financial measure.

EXAM ANSWER BANK

166 D Comparison of the processes of one division with the best external practitioners of those processes

Comparison with a competitor (A) is competitive benchmarking, comparison within a company (B) or with another company in the same industry (C) are both internal benchmarking.

167 D Both statements are false.

The balanced scorecard can be adopted for non profit-making organisations (i). The financial perspective looks at the value that has been created, but it is the innovation and learning perspective that looks at what the organisation needs to create future value (ii).

(A), (B) and (C) are incorrect because they say that either or both statements are true.

168 D (i), (ii) and (iii)

Taking corrective action (i) seems obvious, but the plan may be altered (ii) if there is nothing management can do to correct things, Management may decide to do nothing at all (iii) if actual results are better than planned.

(A), (B) and (C) are wrong as they all miss out one or more of the possible choices.

169 A Specific, Measurable, Achievable, Realistic, Time-bound

In (B) motivational and authoritative are incorrect, in (C) motivational, relevant and timely are incorrect, and in (D) authoritative and relevant are incorrect.

170 C Decreasing amounts owed by customers

This relates to operational working capital management.

Improving market share (A), decreasing risk (B) and improving quality (D) are all possible strategic objectives.

171 B Emergency stock

Emergency stock is a cost of stock shortage.

Obsolescence (A) is a cost of writing off stock that has been held for too long. Pilferage (C) is a cost of theft of stock held. Stock held is also generally insured (D) against theft or natural disaster.

172 D 600 units

$$EOQ = \sqrt{\frac{2C_o D}{C_h}}$$

EOQ = √ (2 × 40 × 3,000 × 12/8) = 600 units

If you chose 122 units (A), you forgot the 2 in the calculation and used the monthly demand rather grossing up to the annual demand.

If you chose 173 units (B), you used the monthly demand rather grossing up to the annual demand.

If you chose 424 units (C), you forgot the 2 in the calculation.

173 A 4,000 units

Re-order level = Maximum usage × Maximum lead time = 800 units × 5 = 4,000 units

If you chose 2,750 units (B), you calculated re-order level using minimum usage and maximum lead time.

If you chose 2,400 units (C), you calculated re-order level using maximum usage and minimum lead time.

If you chose 1,650 units (D), you calculated re-order level using minimum usage and minimum lead time.

174 B 1,600 units

Minimum inventory level = Re-order level − (Average usage × Average lead time)
= 4,800 − (640 × 5) = 1,600 units

If you chose 0 units (B), you calculated minimum inventory level using maximum usage and maximum lead time.

If you chose 2,400 units (C), you calculated minimum inventory level using re-order quantity.

If you chose 2,800 units (D), you calculated minimum inventory level using minimum usage and minimum lead time.

175 A 2,350 units

Average inventory level = Minimum inventory + (Re-order level/2) = 1,000 + (2,700/2) = 2,350 units

If you chose 2,600 units (B), you used re-order quantity, not re-order level.

If you chose 3,700 units (C), you did not divide re-order level by 2

If you chose 4,200 units (D), you used re-order quantity, not re-order level, and you did not divide it by 2.

176 C 1,132 units

Reorder level = (Average weekly demand × Lead time) + (Standard deviation × Normal distribution factor) = (500 × 2) + (80 × 1.65) = 1,132 units

If you chose 632 units (A), you failed to multiply by the order lead time.

If you chose 932 units (B), you failed to multiply by the order lead time and you used the maximum weekly demand.

If you chose 1,732 units (D), you used the maximum weekly demand.

177 C There is no difference in total cost between the two alternatives.

$$EOQ = \sqrt{\frac{2C_oD}{C_h}}$$

EOQ = √(2 × 50 × 40,000/25) = 400 units

Total annual cost = $50 × (40,000/400) + $25 × (400/2) + 40,000 × $8 = $330,000

Using 2,000 units

Total annual cost = $50 × (40,000/2,000) + $25 × (2,000/2) + 40,000 × $8 × 0.95 = $330,000

Using the EOQ (A) and taking the bulk discount (B) are not cheaper. Enough information is provided (D) to make an assessment.

Chapter 11 Organisational information requirements

178   A   Environmental scanning

Environmental scanning is wide analysis of the environment where the business is located.

It includes, but is not limited to, market research (B) and informal data collection (C). Data warehousing (D) relates to how the information collected is stored.

179   B   The value of information should be greater than the cost of obtaining it.

Value/benefit exceeding cost is an important general rule for whether to undertake any business activity.

The opposite statement (A) of value being less than cost is therefore wrong. Data analysis costs (C) are often a significant part of information costs. Data may have non-financial benefits (D), for example improved efficiency of managerial decision-making.

180   C   Enhancing value

Enhancing value is the main strategic objective.

Enhancing distribution arrangements (A), reducing product quality problems (B) and reducing customer complaints (D) can all be classified as operational objectives.

181   A   Website clicks

Website clicks indicate customers' interest in different areas of the website.

Office automation systems (B) are designed to increase the productivity of data workers. Data warehouses (C) store information from across the organization – this may include customer information, but the information in the warehouse comes directly from internal sources. A logical access system (D) is a form of security control.

182   B   Specialised information and specialist problem solving techniques

The combination of models to aid unstructured decision-making (A) is a decision support system. The integration of new knowledge into an organisation (C) is supplied by a knowledge work system. Internal and external information being made available in an easy-to-use form for strategic decision-making (D) is an executive support system.

183   B   Computer aided design

A diagnostic system (A) is an example of an expert system. Intranet (C) and digital filing system (D) are examples of office automation systems.

184   C   Executive support system

An enterprise wide system (A) is designed primarily to integrate and coordinate all organisational functions, resources and information. An expert system (B) involves more narrow decision-making than wide strategic decisions, with decisions based on specialist knowledge. A knowledge work system (D) primarily facilitates the creation and integration of new knowledge.

EXAM ANSWER BANK

185 A Monitor PEST factors

Environmental scanning involves looking outside the organisation to analyse the external environment. This involves considering the PEST factors.

SWOT factors (B) are internal as well as external factors. Environmental scanning looks at wider issues than just competitors (C). Economic factors (D) are only a part of environmental analysis (the E in PEST).

186 D This company's computer system does not need rules about email usage.

Because the system is not connected to the internet, users cannot receive email.

Back-up storage (A), password protection (B) and virus detection software (C) are basic requirements of any computer system, regardless of whether it is connected to the internet.

187 A Loss or corruption of data is always non-deliberate.

Data can be lost or corrupted as a result of deliberate actions such as fraud, sabotage, commercial espionage or malicious damage, as well as human error.

New staff (B) pose a data security risk because of the risk of human error, if they are inexperienced or untrained. It is impossible to prevent all threats (C). Smoke detectors (D) protect data from the physical risk of fire.

188 A Productivity

Office Automation Systems with functions such as word processing, digital filing, email, schedulers and spreadsheets are primarily designed to streamline administrative tasks.

Higher-level executive systems are designed to aid flexibility (B), decision-making capability (C) and long-term planning capability (D).

189 B Weather

Lightning strikes or electrical storms are a key course of power supply failures and surges which may affect computer functions.

Accidental damage (A) can take place even if the power supply is guaranteed. Hacking (C) is a non-physical threat not connected with the power supply. Denial of service attack (D) is not to do with the power supply, but involves overloading a site by flooding it with excessive volumes of traffic.

190 B Off-site storage

Off-site storage means that if a disaster strikes the main site and data there is destroyed, it is available elsewhere.

Passwords (A) are an access control. Job rotation (C) is a personnel control, designed to limit the opportunity for fraud. Anti-virus software (D) is designed to prevent problems occurring to data.

191 D Processing is faster.

The risk of errors (A) is reduced, not eliminated, information can be stolen by hackers (B) and information is more, not less, accessible (C).

192 B Intruder alarms

System backups (A) are a disaster recovery control if data has been lost or corrupted. Segregation of duties (C) refers to division of duties, not physical separation. Encryption (D) denies hackers the chance to intercept data by scrambling it.

EXAM ANSWER BANK

193 C Market information on buying habits of potential customers from the marketing manager

Market information is captured from outside the organisation, although it is circulated from within the organisation.

Internal information comes from transaction systems (A), the accounting records (B) or is communicated formally or informally (D).

194 A (i) and (ii)

Physical access controls are lock and key systems. Card entry (i) and PIN (ii) systems are ways of identifying yourself (by swipe card and keypad entry respectively) in order to gain authorised entry to an area or storage device. Logical access systems (iii) are non-physical access controls, involving password-protected access to data in the system.

(B), (C) and (D) incorrectly include logical access controls, (B) also misses out PINs, (C) misses out card entry.

195 A Transaction processing systems

A management information system (B) converts the detailed records of sales, purchases, wages and other transactions into information for management. An office automation system (C) provides facilities to improve the efficiency of data workers. Decision support systems (D) contain analytical models and tools to support semi-structured and unstructured decision-making.

196 B Political, economic, social and technological factors

These are the external environmental factors that impact the business.

A SWOT analysis (A) considers internal and external factors. There are various models that consider strategic options and choice (C), including the suitability, acceptability, feasibility model. Analysis of inbound and outbound logistics (D) is part of Porter's value chain analysis.

197 D Feasibility testing

A feasibility study should be undertaken before going ahead with the systems development.

Systems logic testing (A), user acceptance testing (B) and program testing (C) should all be part of system testing.

198 B Communicated

Relevant(A), authoritative (C) and timely (D) are all qualities of good information.

Chapter 12 The impact of IT on work practices

199 A Big data analytics relies on digital information.

Internal information (B), financial information (C) and written information (D) can all be part of big data, but must be held in digital form for big data analytics to be used.

200 D Big data analytics ensures companies respond quickly to information becoming available.

Rapid analysis does not imply that companies will take action quickly based on the analysis.

The other options relate to the characteristics of big data. Analysis of informal sources (A) relates to its variety, rapid analysis of large data volumes (B) relates to volume and velocity, analysis of data's reliability (C) relates to its veracity.

201 B Data analytics

Mobile apps (A) and big data (C) are sources of data, but may well not provide the data in the form required. Interoperability (D) relates to sharing and exchange of information, not analysis.

202 D Veracity

Data cleansing improves the trustworthiness of data, not its amount (volume (A)), the different sources used (variety (B)) or the speed at which it is obtained (velocity(C)).

203 B (i) and (iii)

A feedforward control system involves forecasting future outcomes and comparing them with desired outcomes. Control action, here by the marketing (i) and finance (iii) departments, is taken to minimise any differences. These two models are therefore feedforward control models.

(A), (C) and (D) are incorrect, as they include the action taken by the inventory control department (ii), which is a feedback control, because it provides information on what has already happened, for comparison with a standard or plan (the maximum and minimum inventory level). (A) also misses out the action taken by the finance department. (C) misses out the action taken by the marketing department.

204 C Worm virus

A worm virus attacks computer systems.

Repetitive strain injury (A), carpal tunnel syndrome (B) and computer vision syndrome (D) are all physical problems that can affect computer users.

205 D Increased contact with other employees

Reduced contact with other employees and feelings of isolation can be a problem with homeworking.

The employee can make a potentially big cost saving (A) on travel costs and the employer can save on the costs (C) of accommodating the employee in the office. The employer can draw on a wider pool of employees (B), employees who are unable or unwilling to travel to the office each day.

EXAM ANSWER BANK

206 C (ii) and (iii)

Being difficult (and costly) to modify (ii) and requiring antiquated software to run it (iii) are characteristics of many legacy systems. Backwards compatibility (i) is a characteristic of a newer system that can use files or data created with an older, similar technology.

(A), (B) and (D) all incorrectly include (i) as correct, (A) also omitting (iii) and B omitting (ii).

207 A Retrieval of information and automation of repetitive tasks

Taking into account organisation and staff needs (B) as well as being technically efficient is characteristic of sociotechnical systems. Provision of information to consumers (C) is likely to be part of a customer relationship management system. A supplier of remote working services (D) is likely to be a tele-commuter.

208 C Statement (i) is false. Statement (ii) is true.

Increased use of information technology allows increased delegation, removing layers of management and flattening organisational hierarchy.

(A) incorrectly says that statement (i) is true. (B) incorrectly says that statement (i) is true and statement (ii) is false. (D) incorrectly says that statement (ii) is false.

209 A Property rights

The concern is users getting for free material that producers have rights over and for which they believe they deserve payment.

Accountability and control (B) is to do with who is responsible for output and accuracy. System quality (C) is about what level of quality should be expected of what has been developed. Quality of life concerns (D) relate to wider social issues, including dependence on technology.

210 C Using advisory agent

Advisory agents are used for help in complex diagnostic situations, not primarily to filter information.

Delegating (A), filtering incoming email (B) and deleting duplicate information (D) would all be means of dealing with excessive information being received.

211 B Big data analytics

Big data analytics involves examining the data rather than storing it.

Cloud computing (A), knowledge management systems (C) and customer relationship management systems (D) are all means of storing data.

212 B Social media applications

Exchange is a key element of this definition, which doesn't necessarily apply to cloud applications (A) and big data applications (C). FAST (D) stands for Federation Against Software Theft, which aims to discourage illicit exchange of software.

213 B Access to the cloud may be lost if payments are missed or delayed.

Cloud computing is available to all organisations, both large and small (A). It is usually also more cost effective as the solutions offered are scalable and organisation pay only for the amount of storage, features and/or applications they need (D). This scalability, and the many providers from which organisations can choose, means that cloud computing also offers more, not less, flexibility than in-house technology (C).

214 A Smart contracts are self-executing agreements that use cryptography, digital signatures and secure completion.

Smart contracts can be used for a wide variety of purposes, for example house purchases, non-disclosure agreements, employment contracts and so on. They are not specific to cryptocurrency transactions (B).

Smart contracts are electronic documents, they are not produced in PDF formats. The ability to sign a PDF digitally does not make it a smart contract, it simply a traditional paper contract which has been digitally signed (C).

Smart contracts are not produced with AI using voice commands (D).

Exam question bank

Past Exams: November 2021

1. In Mintzberg's managerial roles model, which ONE of the following is NOT an informational role of management?

    A Monitor
    B Resource allocator
    C Spokesperson
    D Disseminator

2. Which ONE of the following is not a form of legitimate authority according to Weber?

    A Charismatic leadership
    B Traditional leadership
    C Bureaucracy
    D Coercive leadership

3. Which of the following is a definition of the cognitive skills required by managers?

    A The ability to work well with other people and in a group
    B Job-specific knowledge and techniques needed to proficiently perform tasks
    C The ability to think about abstract and complex situations
    D The ability to inspire commitment

4. Modern approaches to management emphasise:

    A Efficiency
    B Mathematical and statistical solutions to management problems
    C Flexibility
    D Controlling resources

5. Which of the following is an approach to leadership that argues that the effectiveness of a work group depends on the interrelation of task needs, trust between the leader and group, and the power of the leader?

    A The Ashridge Model
    B Autocracy
    C Contingency theory
    D Blake and Moulton's Managerial Grid

6. According to Mendelow's stakeholder mapping, which category of stakeholders should be kept satisfied?

    A Low power, low level of interest
    B Low power, high level of interest
    C High power, low level of interest
    D High power, high level of interest

7. Which of the following items are included as one of the four purposes of planning?

    (i) Minimising waste.
    (ii) Providing direction.
    (iii) Variance analysis.
    (iv) Accurate record keeping.

    A (i) and (ii) only
    B (iii) and (iv) only
    C All of the above
    D (i), (ii) and (iii)

8   Gathering information about target customers or markets is known as:

    A   Market research
    B   Data mining
    C   Corporate espionage
    D   Competitor intelligence

9   Which of the following are potential obstacles to successful value chain management?

    (i)   Organisational barriers
    (ii)   People
    (iii) Capabilities
    (iv)   Inbound logistics

    A   (i) only
    B   (i) and (ii)
    C   (i), (ii) and (iii)
    D   All of the above

10 Which of the following is a quantitative forecasting technique?

    A   Customer evaluation
    B   Delphi technique
    C   Regression analysis
    D   Industry scenario building

11 According to the Boston Consulting Group (BCG) model, which of the following are businesses or SBUs that operate in low-growth markets with a low relative market share?

    A   Star
    B   Cash cow
    C   Dog
    D   Question mark

12 Which of the following are included in Mintzberg's five components organisational structure?

    (i)   Strategic apex
    (ii)   Technostructure
    (iii) Standardisation of work processes
    (iv)   Middle line

    A   (i) only
    B   All of the above
    C   (i), (ii) and (iv)
    D   (iii) and (iv)

13 Which of the following is a definition of job enlargement as an element of job design?

    A   The attempt to widen jobs by increasing the number of operations in which a jobholder is involved

    B   Planned, deliberate action to build greater responsibility, breadth and challenge of work into a job

    C   Focusing on how jobs are increasingly based on social relationships

    D   Increasing job complexity

14 Which of the following is NOT a characteristic advantage of a flat organisational structure?

    A   More opportunity for delegation
    B   Faster decision-making
    C   Sacrifice of control
    D   Relative cost reduction

15 Which of Harrison's four types of organisational culture best describes a bureaucratic organisation?

    A   Power culture
    B   Role culture
    C   Task culture
    D   Person culture

16 Competing on the basis of having the lowest costs in the industry is known as:

    A   Retrenchment
    B   Cost leadership
    C   Differentiation
    D   Focus

17 Which of the following is an example of a key performance indicator (KPI)?

    A   Ensuring quality products are produced
    B   Increasing market share by 10% in the next year
    C   Improving customer satisfaction
    D   Low production costs

18 Which ONE of the following is NOT an element of the control process?

    A   Measuring actual performance
    B   Identifying objectives
    C   Comparing actual performance against planned performance
    D   Responding to divergences from plan

19 The following statements relate to the process of budgetary control:

    (i)   A cash budget is an example of a feedback mechanism of control.

    (ii) When employees are encouraged to participate in the setting of budgets, they are more likely to have a positive view of the budgeting process.

    Which of the above statements is/are true?

    A   (i) only
    B   (ii) only
    C   Neither (i) nor (ii)
    D   Both (i) and (ii)

20 Which of the following is categorised as a holding cost in the Economic Order Quantity model?

    A   Delivery costs
    B   Obsolescence
    C   Extra cost of emergency inventory
    D   Contribution from lost sales

21 Within which of the four perspectives of a balanced scorecard would 'sales growth by division' appear?

- A   Financial
- B   Customer
- C   Internal processes
- D   Innovation and learning

22 Which of the following statements best describes the process of competitive benchmarking?

- A   Comparison of internal functions with those of the best external practitioners of those functions
- B   Comparison of one operating unit or function with another within the same industry
- C   Comparison of internal functions with direct competitors' functions using reverse engineering
- D   Comparison of the practices of one operation or business with another aimed at strategic action and organizational change

23 An expert system is one which:

- A   Perform and records routine transactions
- B   Converts data, mainly from internal sources, into information
- C   Holds specialised data and rules about what to do in, or how to interpret, a given set of circumstances
- D   Is designed to increase the productivity of data and information workers

24 Which of the following involves the collection and analysis of large amounts of data to find trends, understand customer needs and help organisations to focus resources more effectively:

- A   Sociotechnical design
- B   Enterprise wide system
- C   Big data
- D   Cloud computing

25 Which of the following are advantages of benchmarking?

- (i)   Provides a position audit for the firm.
- (ii)   Focuses on improvement in key areas.
- (iii) Identifies the single best way to organise operations.

- A   (i) and (ii) only
- B   All of the above
- C   (ii) and (iii) only
- D   (i) and (iii) only

Past Exams: May 2022

26 Which of Fayol's principles of management suggests that harmony and teamwork are essential in order for an organisation to function efficiently and effectively?

- A Stability
- B Unity of direction
- C Subordination
- D Espirit de corps

27 Which ONE of the following is not an advantage of a bureaucratic form of organisation?

- A Rigid authority networks
- B Suitability for standardized, routine tasks
- C Adherence to laws, regulations and procedures
- D Tendency to facilitate long-lived organisations

28 Which of the following is a definition of the leadership qualities required by managers?

- A The ability to work well with other people and in a group
- B Job-specific knowledge and techniques needed to proficiently perform tasks
- C The ability to think about abstract and complex situations
- D The ability to inspire commitment

29 Which type of power is based on on force of personality, or 'charisma', which can attract, influence or inspire other people?

- A Coercive
- B Reward
- C Referent
- D Expert

30 Which of the following is an approach to leadership that was designed as an appraisal and management development tool recognising that a balance is required between concern for task and concern for people?

- A The Ashridge Model
- B Autocracy
- C Contingency theory
- D Blake and Moulton's Managerial Grid

31 According to Mendelow's stakeholder mapping, which category of stakeholders require minimal effort?

- A Low power, low level of interest
- B Low power, high level of interest
- C High power, low level of interest
- D High power, high level of interest

32 Which ONE of the following would be best described as a connected stakeholder for a manufacturing company?

- A Employees
- B Government
- C Customers
- D Local communities

33 The attempt to analyse databases to discover patterns and new information is known as:

    A   Market research
    B   Data mining
    C   Corporate espionage
    D   Competitor intelligence

34 Which of the following are support activities in Porter's value chain?

    (i)   Human resource management
    (ii) Procurement
    (iii) Operations
    (iv) Inbound Logistics

    A   (i) only
    B   (i) and (ii)
    C   (i), (ii) and (iii)
    D   All of the above

35 Delphi is a forecasting technique developed to:

    A   Mathematically analyze economic variables and their interrelationships
    B   Measure and model underlying correlations between two variables
    C   Facilitate the use of judgement in forecasting
    D   Calculate the expected value of a range of possible outcomes

36 According to the Boston Consulting Group (BCG) model, which of the following are businesses or SBUs that operate in high-growth markets with a low relative market share?

    A   Star
    B   Cash cow
    C   Dog
    D   Question mark

37 Which of the following are observable elements of culture?

    (i)   Assumptions
    (ii) Values and beliefs
    (iii) Artefacts
    (iv) Rituals.

    A   (i) only
    B   All of the above
    C   (i), (ii) and (iv)
    D   (iii) and (iv)

38 Which of the following is a definition of job enrichment as an element of job design?

    A   The attempt to widen jobs by increasing the number of operations in which a jobholder is involved

    B   Planned, deliberate action to build greater responsibility, breadth and challenge of work into a job

    C   Focusing on how jobs are increasingly based on social relationships

    D   The transfer of staff from one job to another to increase task variety

39   A company consisting of a core of essential executives and workers supported by outside contractors and part-time help is which type of organisation?

　　A   Shamrock
　　B   Network
　　C   Modular
　　D   Virtual

40   Which of the following is NOT a benefit of the informal organisation for managers?

　　A   Responsiveness in decision making
　　B   The development of exclusive social cliques
　　C   Knowledge sharing
　　D   Employee commitment

41   The process of gathering external information is known as:

　　A   Data mining
　　B   Environmental scanning
　　C   Scenario building
　　D   Forecasting

42   Which of the following is an example of a key performance indicator (KPI) that might be used to measure performance in a production department?

　　A   Market share
　　B   Transportation costs
　　C   Timeliness of reports
　　D   Capacity utilisation

43   Which ONE of the following is NOT an element of the strategic planning process?

　　A   Identifying objectives
　　B   Respond to divergences from the plan
　　C   Evaluating strategies
　　D   Implementing the long-term plan

44   Which of the following is a common criticism of incremental budgeting?

　　A   It is time-consuming.
　　B   There is no requirement for management to justify existing costs.
　　C   There is an incentive for managers to reduce costs.
　　D   There are no performance targets for managers.

45   Monthly demand for Product X is 4,000 units. The annual cost of holding a unit of X in stock is $16. Ordering costs of Product X are $40 per order.

What is the Economic Order Quantity for Product X to the nearest unit?

　　A   141 units
　　B   346 units
　　C   490 units
　　D   566 units

46   Unit cost of production is primarily a measure in which of the balanced scorecard's perspectives?

　　A   Financial
　　B   Customer
　　C   Internal business
　　D   Innovation and learning

47   Which of the following is NOT an advantage of homeworking from an employer perspective?

   A   Flexibility
   B   A larger pool of potential employees
   C   Cost savings on office accommodation
   D   Control and supervision

48   A decision support system is one which:

   A   Perform and records routine transactions
   B   Converts data, mainly from internal sources, into information
   C   Holds specialised data and rules about what to do in, or how to interpret, a given set of circumstances
   D   Combines data and analytical models to support semi-structured and unstructured decision-making

49   Office automation systems are mainly designed to improve:

   A   Decision-making
   B   Strategic planning
   C   Productivity
   D   Recording of routine transactions

50   Which of the following is an example of an operational level information system?

   A   Employee record keeping
   B   Production scheduling
   C   Human resource planning
   D   Inventory control system

Past Exams: November 2022

51 Which ONE of the following is not included in Fayol's five functions of management?

   A   Planning
   B   Organising
   C   Motivating
   D   Controlling

52 Which ONE of the following is not a key feature of a supervisor's role?

   A   Dealing with front-line management tasks
   B   Devoting most of their time to strategic management
   C   Being a gatekeeper between managerial and non-managerial staff
   D   Controlling work by means of day-to-day, frequent and detailed information

53 Which of the following is a definition of the trait theory of leadership?

   A   There are certain personality characteristics common to successful leaders.
   B   Leadership is an interpersonal process in which different leader behaviours influence people in different ways.
   C   Effective leaders adapt their behaviour to specific and changing organisational variables.
   D   The ability to spot business opportunities and mobilise resources to capitalise on them.

54 According to the Ashridge College Management Model, which of the following describes a 'Sell' management style?

   A   The leader makes all the decisions and issues instructions which must be obeyed without question.
   B   The leader confers with subordinates and takes their views into account, but retains the final say.
   C   The leader still makes all the decisions, but believes that subordinates have to be motivated to accept them.
   D   Leader and followers make the decision on the basis of consensus.

55 Which of the following is intended to be an appraisal and management development tool?

   A   Contingency theory
   B   Autocracy
   C   Empowerment
   D   Blake and Mouton's Managerial Grid

56 According to Mendelow's stakeholder mapping, which category of stakeholders should be kept informed?

   A   Low power, low level of interest
   B   Low power, high level of interest
   C   High power, low level of interest
   D   High power, high level of interest

57 What type of power is based on being given authority within an organisation?

- A Legitimate
- B Coercive
- C Reward
- D Expert

58 Which of the following best describes critical success factors?

- A Product features that are particularly valued by a group of customers and, therefore, where the organisation must excel to outperform the competition
- B What an organisation has or is able to do
- C Means by which a firm creates value in its products
- D Shared assumptions, ways of working and attitudes of management

59 Which of the following is one of Porter's five competitive forces?

- A Government intervention
- B Technological change
- C The threat of new entrants
- D Sustainability

60 Which of the following is NOT a quantitative forecasting technique?

- A Time series analysis
- B Delphi technique
- C Regression Analysis
- D Econometrics model

61 According to the Boston Consulting Group (BCG) model, which of the following are businesses that operate in high-growth markets with a low market share?

- A Star
- B Cash cow
- C Dog
- D Question mark

62 Which of the following is NOT included in Mintzberg's five components organisational structure?

- A Strategic apex
- B Operating core
- C Standardisation by skills and knowledge
- D Technostructure

63 Which of the following is a definition of job enrichment as an element of job design?

- A The attempt to widen jobs by increasing the number of operations in which a jobholder is involved
- B Planned, deliberate action to build greater responsibility, breadth and challenge of work. into a job
- C The planned transfer of staff from one job to another to increase task variety
- D Increasing job complexity

64 In a flat organisation structure with no employee participation in decision-making, which of Hofstede's four main dimensions of cultural difference is the organisation exhibiting?

A Power distance
B Uncertainty avoidance
C Individualism
D Masculinity

65 Which of Harrison's four types of organisational culture best describes an organisation shaped by a focus on output and results?

A Power culture
B Role culture
C Task culture
D Person culture

66 Competition on the basis of having unique products that are widely valued by customers is known as:

A Retrenchment
B Cost leadership
C Differentiation
D Focus

67 Which of the following is a definition of a flexible budget?

A A budget which recognises different cost behaviour patterns, and is designed to change as volume of activity changes

B A budget set prior to the start of an accounting period which is not changed in response to subsequent changes in activity or costs/revenues

C A budget based on previous budget or actual results, adjusting for known changes and inflation

D A budget which requires each cost element to be specifically justified, as though the activities to which the budget relates were being undertaken for the first time

68 Which ONE of the following is an element of the control process?

A Identify objectives
B Measure actual results and compare with the plan
C Choose alternative courses of action
D Evaluate strategies

69 A procurement policy of obtaining goods from suppliers only when required is known as:

A First-in, first-out
B Just-in-time
C Bulk discounting
D Transaction processing

70 Which of the following is categorised as a procurement cost in the Economic Order Quantity model?

A Delivery costs
B Obsolescence
C Extra cost of emergency inventory
D Cost of capital

71 In which of the four perspectives of a balanced scorecard would 'production efficiency' appear?

  A Financial
  B Customer
  C Internal business
  D Innovation and learning

72 Which of the following statements best describes the process of internal benchmarking?

  A Comparison of internal functions with those of the best external practitioners of those functions
  B Comparison of one operating unit with another within the same industry
  C Comparison of internal functions with direct competitors' functions using reverse engineering
  D Comparison of the practices of one operation or business with another aimed at strategic action and organisational change

73 An executive support system is one which:

  A Perform and records routine transactions
  B Converts data, mainly from internal sources, into information
  C Pools data from internal and external sources and makes information available to senior managers in an easy-to-use form
  D Is designed to increase the productivity of data and information workers

74 Which of the following involves using a network of servers to store and access data and programs over the internet, instead of on a computer's hard drive?

  A Sociotechnical design
  B Enterprise wide system
  C Big data
  D Cloud computing

75 What does variety mean in relation to the concept of big data?

  A The speed at which 'real time' data is being received
  B The quantity of data received
  C The truthfulness of the data
  D Structured and unstructured forms of data

Past Exams: May 2023

76 Which ONE of the following is not included in Taylor's principles of scientific management?

- A The science of work
- B The progressive development of workers
- C The closeness to customers
- D The constant co-operation between management and workers

77 Which ONE of the following is a definition of Fayol's guiding principle of management known as unity of command?

- A There should be one head and one plan for each activity.
- B For any action, a subordinate should receive orders from one manager only.
- C Authority should flow vertically down a clear chain of command from highest to lowest rank.
- D There should be continuity of employment where possible.

78 Which of the following is a system of management identified by Likert?

- A Exploitative authoritative in which the leader has no confidence in subordinates
- B A country club approach in which the manager is attentive to staff needs and has developed satisfying relationships
- C An action-centred leadership model
- D Situational leadership

79 Power based on force of personality, or 'charisma', is known as?

- A Referent power
- B Reward power
- C Expert power
- D Negative power

80 Which of the following defines synergy in the context of organisations?

- A A flow of new business possibilities within the organisation
- B The interface between the operational core workers and management
- C Encouraging employees to take initiative, spot and seize opportunities
- D A combination of businesses, internal services and organisation structure which enables the whole to be worth more than the sum of the parts

81 Within business ethics, distributive justice is defined as:

- A Organisational rewards being proportional to the contributions people make to organisational ends
- B Respect for property rights, honesty, and fairness
- C A process of adapting our behaviour so that our goals may be more effectively met in the future
- D A process whereby individual goals are integrated with the corporate plan

82 Which ONE of the following is NOT a feature of performance management according to Armstrong?

   A   An agreed framework of goals, standards, and competence requirements
   B   Shared understanding
   C   Achievement
   D   An examination of the current status of the organisation's products and markets

83 Which ONE of the following is an advantage of an organisation chart?

   A   It highlights formal relationships within the organisation.
   B   It may encourage bureaucracy.
   C   It implies managers at the same level are of equal importance.
   D   It needs frequent updating as employees join and leave the organisation.

84 Which of the following is one of Porter's five competitive forces?

   A   Government policy
   B   Market development
   C   The bargaining power of customers
   D   Social justice

85 Which of the following forecasting techniques would be more appropriate for dynamic or complex conditions?

   A   Time series analysis
   B   Extrapolation
   C   Regression Analysis
   D   Scenario building

86 How does the Boston Consulting Group (BCG) model classify businesses that operate in low-growth markets with a high relative market share?

   A   Star
   B   Cash cow
   C   Dog
   D   Question mark

87 Which of the following would be categorised as a connected stakeholder of a firm?

   A   Local communities
   B   Customers
   C   Pressure groups
   D   Government

88 Which of the following is an advantage of a tall organisational structure?

   A   More opportunity for delegation
   B   Narrow control spans
   C   Faster communication between strategic apex and operating core
   D   Relatively inexpensive

89 Which ONE of the following is a disadvantage of divisionalisation?

   A   May be more resource problems
   B   Promotes a greater attention to efficiency, cost reduction and higher profits
   C   Reduces the number of levels of management
   D   Reduces the likelihood of unprofitable products and activities being continued

90 A modular organisation is one in which:

A People and activities split between core and non-core competencies

B Internal barriers that separate the hierarchy levels, different functions and different departments removed

C Different components of a product or service are outsourced to different suppliers

D A core of essential executives and workers are supported by outside contractors

91 An organisation is extending the scope of its jobs by increasing the number of operations in which a jobholder is involved. This is an example of:

A Job enrichment
B Job rotation
C Job enlargement
D Job empowerment

92 The approach that suggests that organisations should aim to find a 'fit' that will maximise efficiency while at the same time ensuring member satisfaction and commitment is:

A The socio-technical systems approach
B The organic organisation approach
C The bureaucratic approach
D The adhocracy approach

93 Which ONE of the following is NOT an objective of a budgetary planning and control system?

A Ensuring the achievement of an organisation's objectives
B Providing a framework for responsibility accounting
C Motivating employees to improve their performance
D Formulating strategies

94 Which one of the following describes zero-based budgeting?

A A method of budgeting based on the previous budget or actual results, adjusting for known changes

B A budget which, by recognising different cost behaviour patterns, is designed to change as volume of activity changes

C A method of budgeting which requires each cost element to be specifically justified, as though the activities to which the budget relates were being undertaken for the first time

D A budget which is normally set prior to the start of an accounting period, and which is not changed in response to subsequent changes in activity

95 Which of the following is a holding cost in the Economic Order Quantity model?

A Delivery costs
B Insurance
C Extra cost of emergency inventory
D Cost of capital

96 Which one of the following is an advantage of undertaking benchmarking?

- A It enables a position audit for an organisation.
- B It implies there is a single best way of operating a business.
- C It diverts management attention from other tasks.
- D It is a catching-up exercise rather than the development of distinctive capabilities.

97 Which of the following is a disadvantage of bottom-up budgets?

- A They improve operational managers' commitment to organisational objectives.
- B Specific resource requirements are included.
- C Employee motivation is improved.
- D They can support 'empire building' by subordinates.

98 Which of the following is an example of a semi-structured decision at the operational level?

- A Devising inventory control procedures
- B Budget calculation and allocation
- C Selecting a new supplier
- D Entering a new market

99 Which ONE of the following is a disadvantage of database systems?

- A Data is held independently of the programs that access the data.
- B Data can be used for many purposes but only needs to be input and stored once.
- C Data can be updated easily.
- D Both hierarchical and network systems require intensive programming.

100 What does velocity mean in relation to big data?

- A The speed at which 'real time' data is being received
- B The quantity of data received
- C The extent to which data is free from bias
- D The use of data analytics

Past Exams: November 2023

101 Which one of the following is not included in Fayol's five functions of management?

- A Planning
- B Co-ordinating
- C Controlling
- D Communicating

102 Which one of the following is a definition of Peters and Watermans' designation of excellence in a firm?

- A Demonstrating autonomy and entrepreneurship
- B Generating an above average return on investment and having a reputation for innovation
- C Achieving productivity through people
- D Avoiding complicated organisational structures

103 Which of the following roles is assigned to the decisional role category within Mintzberg's framework?

- A Leader
- B Disseminator
- C Spokesperson
- D Disturbance handler

104 The view that leadership is an interpersonal process whereby different leader behaviours influence people in different ways is known as?

- A A trait theory of leadership
- B Reward power
- C A style theory of leadership
- D A contingency theory of leadership

105 According to Fiedler, psychologically distant managers prefer which ONE of the following?

- A Formal consultation methods rather than seeking the opinions of their staff informally
- B Maintaining good human relationships with staff
- C Informal contact rather than formal meetings
- D To not formalise roles and relationships with superiors and subordinates

106 The analysis of databases to discover patterns and new information is known as:

- A Market research
- B Data mining
- C Corporate espionage
- D Competitor intelligence

107 Which one of the following is **NOT** an advantage of management by objectives?

- A Focusing organisational attention on key tasks and problem areas
- B The potential for significant change in attitudes and style of leadership
- C Systematic information for managerial planning and control
- D Securing the commitment of individuals to defined targets and areas of accountability

108 Which one of the following is defined as a primary activity in Porter's Value Chain?

- A Outbound logistics
- B Firm infrastructure
- C Procurement
- D Human resource management

109 Which of the following is **NOT** one of Porter's five competitive forces?

- A The threat of new entrants to the industry
- B The rivalry amongst current competitors in the industry
- C The bargaining power of customers
- D The impact of government policy on the industry

110 Which of the following would be classified as a non-financial objective?

- A Cash generation
- B Restrictions on gearing
- C Profit retention
- D Maintaining competitive position and market share

111 In Mendelow's stakeholder mapping model, which category of stakeholders should be kept informed?

- A Low power, low level of interest
- B Low power, high level of interest
- C High power, low level of interest
- D High power, high level of interest

112 Which of the following describes a critical success factor?

- A What an organisation is able to do
- B A type or standard of performance that allows objectives to be achieved
- C A quantifiable measure that a company or industry uses to evaluate or compare performance to goals
- D A group or individuals having a legitimate interest in the activities of an organisation

113 Which of the following is an advantage of a flat organisational structure?

- A More opportunity for delegation
- B Narrow control spans
- C Small groups enable team members to participate in decisions
- D A large number of steps on the promotional ladders

114 Which one of the following is a disadvantage of functional departmentation?

- A The creation of vertical barriers to information flow
- B Facilitates the recruitment, management, and development, of specialists
- C The pooling of expertise
- D Aligned with the needs of centralised organisations

115 A shamrock organisation is one in which:

- A A collection of autonomous firms or business units behave as a single larger entity
- B The internal barriers that separate different functions and different departments have been removed
- C Different elements of a product or service are outsourced to different suppliers
- D A core of essential executives and workers are supported by outside contractors

116 An organisation is bureaucratic, stable, formalised in structure with well-established rules and procedures. Authority is based on position and function within the organisation. Using Harrison's typology, this is an example of which of the following?

- A Power culture
- B Task culture
- C Role culture
- D Person culture

117 If authority in organisation is bestowed by tradition or hereditary entitlement, and decisions and actions are bound by precedent, this is best described as an instance of:

- A Democratic leadership
- B Bureaucratic leadership
- C Charismatic leadership
- D Patriarchal leadership

118 A management information system consists of a database holding specialised data and rules about what to do in, or how to interpret, a given set of circumstances. How would such a system be classified?

- A A knowledge works system
- B An office automation system
- C A transaction processing system
- D An expert system

119 Which one of the following describes top-down budgeting:

- A A method of budgeting based on the previous budget or actual results, adjusting for known changes
- B A budgeting system in which all budget holders are given the opportunity to participate in setting their own budgets
- C A method of budgeting in which a budget allowance is set without permitting the ultimate budget holder to have the opportunity to participate in the budgeting process
- D A method of budgeting based on an activity framework, utilizing cost driver data in the budget-setting and variance feedback processes

120 Which of the following is a shortage cost in the Economic Order Quantity model?

- A Cost of capital
- B Obsolescence
- C Extra cost of emergency inventory
- D Delivery cost

121 Which one of the following is a disadvantage of undertaking benchmarking?

- A It enables a position audit for an organisation.
- B The comparisons are carried out by the managers who are accountable for changes made because of benchmarking.
- C It sets targets which are challenging but achievable.
- D It is a catching-up exercise rather than the development of distinctive capabilities.

122 Which of the following is **NOT** an advantage of database systems?

- A Hierarchical and network systems require intensive programming.
- B Data is held independently of the programs that access the data.
- C There is avoidance of unnecessary duplication of data.
- D Developing new application programs is easier as a central pool of data is already available to be drawn upon.

123 A small piece of software which performs unauthorised actions and which replicates itself is known as which type of security risk?

- A A denial-of-service attack
- B Hacking
- C Eavesdropping
- D A virus

124 Which one of the following is a potential advantage to employers of staff working from home?

- A Employees possibly losing their sense of belonging to the company
- B The need to trust employees to work effectively at home
- C Co-ordination of homeworkers
- D A larger pool of potential employees is available

125 What does veracity mean in relation to big data?

- A The rate at which 'real time' data is being received
- B The quantity of data generated
- C The extent to which data is free from bias and consistent
- D The structured and unstructured forms of data

Exam answer bank

Past Exams: November 2021

1   B   The distractors are as follows:

Resource allocator is part of the decisional role of management.

2   D   The distractors are as follows:

Answers (A), (B) and (C) are all forms of legitimate authority according to Weber; answer (D) is not a form of legitimate authority but rather an exercise of illegitimate power.

3   C   The distractors are as follows:

Answer (A) refers to communication skills; answer (B) to technical skills; and answer (D) refers to leadership qualities.

4   C   The distractors are as follows:

Answer (A) is a feature of classical theories of management; answer (B) developed within the quantitative approach to management; and answer (D) is a feature of classical theories of management.

5   C   The distractors are as follows:

Answer (A) distinguished four styles of management; answer (B) is a style of management that involves issuing orders and overseeing activities; and answer (D) is a means of analysing managerial styles.

6   C   The distractors are as follows:

Answer (A) these stakeholders require minimal effort; answer (B) should be kept informed, and (D) are key players for whom strategy must be acceptable.

7   A   The distractors are as follows:

Items (1) and (2) are specifically identified as an element of the purpose of planning.

8   A   The distractors are as follows:

Answer (B) describes the attempt to analyse databases to discover patterns and new information; (C) refers to the use of espionage techniques to obtain commercial and corporate data; and part (D) is gathering information about competitors that allows managers to anticipate competitor actions.

9   C   The distractors are as follows:

Items (1) to (3) are identified by Robbins and Coulter (*Management* (2017) p. 607) as potential obstacles to successful value chain management. Item (4) is an element of Porter's Value Chain.

10   C   The distractors are as follows:

Answers (A) and (B) are examples of qualitative forecasting techniques. Answer (D) is not a forecasting technique.

11   C   The distractors are as follows:

Answer (A) describes high growth and high relative market share; answer (B) describes low-growth markets with a high relative market share; and answer (D) low relative market share and a high growth rate.

EXAM ANSWER BANK

12   C   The distractors are as follows: Items (1), (2) and (4) are included in Mintzberg's five components of organisational structure, but the standardisation of work processes is categorised as one of the five methods of co-ordination which link parts of the organisation together.

13   A   The distractors are as follows:

Answer (B) is increasing job enrichment; answer (C) relates to the relational perspective of work design; and answer (D) is about technical requirements.

14   C   The distractors are as follows:

Only answer (C) is not a characteristic advantage of a flat organisational structure.

15   B   The distractors are as follows:

Answer (A) describes control by a key figure in an organisation; answer (C) is management by outputs; and answer (D) describes management directed towards serving the interests of the individuals within the organisation.

16   B   The distractors are as follows:

Answer (A) refers to a short-run renewal strategy to deal with minor performance problems; answer (C) refers to competing on the basis of having unique products that are widely valued by customers; and answer (D) refers to adopting a cost or differentiation focus in a narrow segment of the market.

17   B   The distractors are as follows:

(A), (C) and (D) are all examples of CSFs. Answer (B) is a KPI as it is a measure used to assess whether a CSF is being achieved.

18   B   The distractors are as follows:

Answer (B) is part of the strategic planning process; the other items are identified as part of the control process.

19   B   The distractors are as follows:

Statement (i) is false – the cash budget is an example of a feedforward control.

20   B   The distractors are as follows:

Answer (A) is categorised with procurement costs; answers (C) and (D) are examples of shortage costs.

21   A   The distractors are as follows:

Answers (B–D) are focused on non-financial aspects of the business.

22   C   The distractors are as follows:

Answer (A) describes functional benchmarking; answer (B) describes internal benchmarking; answer (D) describes strategic benchmarking.

23   C   The distractors are as follows:

Answers (A) describes a transaction processing system; answer (B) describes a management information system; and answer (D) describes office automation systems.

24	C	The distractors are as follows:

Answer (A) attempts to produce information systems that are technically efficient but also take into account organisational and staff needs; answer (B) designed primarily to integrate and coordinate all organisational functions, resources and information (D) involves sharing resources, software and information over a network (typically the internet).

25	A	The distractors are as follows:

Item (3) is a danger of benchmarking as it can imply that there is one best way to doing business, but this is not generally the case as the final strategy has to balance efficiency with effectiveness.

Past Exams: May 2022

26	D	The distractors are as follows:	
		(A)	Suggests that here should be continuity of employment where possible; answer
		(B)	Suggest that here should be one head and one plan for each activity; and answer
		(C)	Argues that the interest of one employee or group of employees should not prevail over that of the general interest of the organisation
27	A	The distractors are as follows:	
		(B), (C) and (D) are all potential advantages of a bureaucracy.	
28	D	The distractors are as follows:	
		(A)	Refers to communication skills
		(B)	Refers to technical skills
		(C)	Refers to cognitive skills
29	C	The distractors are as follows:	
		(A)	Is the power of physical force or punishment
		(B)	Is based on access to or control over valued resources
		(D)	Is based on experience, qualifications or expertise
30	D	The distractors are as follows:	
		(A)	Distinguished four styles of management
		(B)	Is a style of management that involves issuing orders and overseeing activities
		(C)	Sees effective leadership as being dependent on a number of variable or contingent factors
31	A	The distractors are as follows:	
		(B)	Should be kept satisfied
		(C)	Must be kept informed
		(D)	Are key players for whom strategy must be acceptable
32	C	The distractors are as follows:	
		(A)	Would be categorised as an internal stakeholder
		(B) and (D) are examples of external stakeholders.	
33	B	The distractors are as follows:	
		(A)	Describes the gathering information about target customers or markets
		(C)	The use of espionage techniques to obtain commercial and corporate data
		(D)	Is gathering information competitors that allows managers to anticipate competitor actions

EXAM ANSWER BANK

34	B	The distractors are as follows:

Items (i) and (ii) are support activities. Items (iii) and (iv) are primary activities in Porter's value chain.

35	C	The distractors are as follows:

- (A) Describes econometrics
- (B) Describes regression analysis
- (D) Describes expected value analysis

36	D	The distractors are as follows:

- (A) Describes high growth and high relative market share
- (B) Describes low-growth markets with a high relative market share
- (C) Low relative market share and a low growth rate

37	D	The distractors are as follows:

Items (iii) and (iv) are classified as observable elements of culture by Schein, but items (i) and (ii) lie below observation and act as the foundational ideas and meaning-giving elements of culture.

38	B	The distractors are as follows:

- (A) Is increasing job enlargement
- (C) Relates to the relational perspective of work design
- (D) Is job rotation

39	A	The distractors are as follows:

- (B) Is a collection of autonomous firms or business units that behave as a single larger entity
- (C) Describes an organisation made up of specialist independent units, each processing one sort of work; and answer
- (D) Are organisations whose members are geographically dispersed, and the organization usually only exists electronically on the internet, without any physical premises

40	B	The distractors are as follows:

Answers (A), (C) and (D) are all potential benefits of the informal organisation. (B) is a disadvantage.

41	B	The distractors are as follows:

- (A) Refers specifically to analysing databases to discover patterns and new information
- (C) Is used to model the future by building potential scenarios which represent internally consistent views of what the future might hold
- (D) Refers to a range of methods that seek to model future outcomes and allow for an assessment of changes in key variables

42	D	The distractors are as follows:

- (A) Is used to measure performance in marketing
- (B) Is used to measure logistics performance
- (C) Is a KPI relating to management information

EXAM ANSWER BANK

43	B	The distractors are as follows:

(A), (C) and (D) are elements of the strategic planning process which involves identifying key strategic objectives; evaluating potential strategies for meeting strategic objectives; and the implementation of the long term strategic plan.

44	B	The distractors are as follows:

- (A) Is a criticism of more complex forms of budgeting, but not incremental budgeting
- (C) Is not a significant feature of incremental budgeting
- (D) Is not the case as incremental budgeting can include performance targets

45	C	EOQ = $\sqrt{[2C_oD/C_h]}$

EOQ = $\sqrt{(2 \times 40 \times 4,000 \times 12/16)}$ = 490 units

The distractors are as follows:

- (A) 141 is given if the wrong EOQ formula is computed, ie $\sqrt{(2 \times 40 \times 4,000/16)}$ = 141 units
- (B) 346 is given if the wrong EOQ formula is computed, ie $\sqrt{(40 \times 4,000 \times 12/16)}$ = 490 units
- (D) 566 is given if the wrong EOQ formula is computed, ie $\sqrt{(2 \times 40 \times 4,000)}$ = 566 units

46	C	The distractors are as follows:

The internal business perspective may focus on unit cost to achieve the goal of manufacturing excellence; answers (A), (B) and (D) relate to other types of measure.

47	D	The distractors are as follows:

(A), (B) and (C) are all advantages of homeworking from an employer's perspective.

48	D	The distractors are as follows:

- (A) Describes a transaction processing system
- (B) Describes a management information system
- (C) Describes an expert system

49	C	The distractors are as follows:

- (A) Decision making is supported by decision support or expert systems
- (B) Strategic planning is supported by executive information systems
- (D) Recording of routine transactions is provided by a transaction processing system

50	A	The distractors are as follows:

- (B) Production scheduling relates to activity over a time period, and hence is a managerial level system
- (C) Takes place over the longer-term, so is a strategic system
- (D) Relates to activity over a time period, and hence is a managerial level system

Past Exams: November 2022

51	C	As the classical view of management assumed that subordinates will carry out tasks when 'commanded' or instructed to do so, regardless of whether or how far they may 'want' to
		The distractors are as follows:
		(A), (B) and (D) are included in Fayol's five functions of management.
52	B	The distractors are as follows:
		Answers (A), (C) and (D) are all key features of the low-level management role of supervisors; answer (B) is normally associated with senior management teams.
53	A	The distractors are as follows:
		Answer (B) describes a style theory of leadership; answer (C) to contingency theories of leadership; and answer (D) refers to entrepreneurship rather than a theory of leadership.
54	C	The distractors are as follows:
		Answer (A) describes a 'tell' style of management; answer (B) describes a 'consult' style of management; and answer (D) describes a 'joins' style of management.
55	D	The distractors are as follows:
		Answer (A) is an approach to leadership that argues that the effectiveness of a work group depends on the interrelation of task needs, trust between the leader and group and the power of the leader; answer (B) is a style of management that involves issuing orders and overseeing activities; and answer (C) is a term for making workers (and particularly work teams) responsible for achieving, and even setting, work targets.
56	B	The distractors are as follows:
		Answer (A) these stakeholders require minimal effort; answer (C) should be kept satisfied and (D) are key players for whom strategy must be acceptable.
57	A	The distractors are as follows:
		Answer (B) coercive power is based on the threat of physical force or punishment; answer (C) reward power is based on control over valued resources; and answer (D) expert power is based on experience, qualifications or expertise.
58	A	The distractors are as follows:
		Answer (B) describes the competences of an organisation; (C) describes value activities; and part (D) describes corporate culture.
59	C	The distractors are as follows:
		Answer (A) refers to external regulatory action; answer (B) describes a contextual element of business operations; and answer (D) involves developing strategies so that companies only use resources at a rate that allows them to be replenished.
60	B	The distractors are as follows:
		Answers (A), (B) and (D) are all examples of quantitative forecasting techniques.

| 61 | D | The distractors are as follows: |

Answer (A) describes high growth and high market share; answer (B) describes low-growth markets with a high relative market share; and answer (C) describes low-growth markets with low-market share.

| 62 | C | The distractors are as follows: |

Answers (A), (B) and (D) are included in Mintzberg's five components of organisational structure, but standardisation by skills and knowledge is categorised as one of the five methods of co-ordination which link parts of the organisation together.

| 63 | B | The distractors are as follows: |

Answer (A) is job enlargement; answer (C) is job rotation; and answer (D) is about technical requirements.

| 64 | A | The distractors are as follows: |

Answer (B) uncertainty avoidance is incorrect as uncertainty is not raised as an issue; answer (C) individualism is incorrect as the focus is on decision-making rather than work achievement; answer (D) masculinity is incorrect as the scenario is not about the types of rewards that are valued.

| 65 | C | The distractors are as follows: |

Answer (A) describes control by a key figure in an organisation; answer (B) is management by rules and procedures; and answer (D) describes management directed towards serving the interests of the individuals within the organisation.

| 66 | C | The distractors are as follows: |

Answer (A) refers to a short-run renewal strategy to deal with minor performance problems; answer (C) refers to competing on the basis of having the lowest costs in the industry; and answer (D) refers to adopting a cost or differentiation focus in a narrow segment of the market.

| 67 | A | The distractors are as follows: |

Answer (B) defines a fixed budget; answer (C) defines an incremental budget and answer (D) defines a zero-based budget

| 68 | B | The distractors are as follows: |

Answer (A), (C) and (D) are elements of the strategic planning process.

| 69 | B | The distractors are as follows: |

Answer (A) refers to a method for valuing inventories; answer (C) refers to discounts obtained on large-order purchases; and answer (D) refers to a type of information system.

| 70 | A | The distractors are as follows: |

Answer (B) is a holding cost; answer (C) is a shortage cost; and (D) is a holding cost.

| 71 | C | The distractors are as follows: |

Answer (A) focuses on how value for shareholders is created; answer (B) focuses on how customers value the business; and answer (D) focuses on how the business improves.

EXAM ANSWER BANK

72 B   The distractors are as follows:

Answer (A) describes functional benchmarking; answer (C) describes competitive benchmarking; answer (D) describes strategic benchmarking.

73 C   Directors

Answer (A) describes a transaction processing system; answer (B) describes a management information system; and answer (D) describes office automation systems.

74 D   The distractors are as follows:

Answer (A) attempts to produce information systems that are technically efficient but also take into account organisational and staff needs; answer (B) designed primarily to integrate and coordinate all organisational functions, resources and information; and answer (C) involves the collection and analysis of large amounts of data to find trends, understand customer needs and help organisations to focus resources more effectively.

75 D   The distractors are as follows:

Answer (A) refers to the velocity of data; answer (B) refers to the volume of data; and answer (C) refers to the veracity of big data.

Past Exams: May 2023

76	C	As closeness to customers is one of the attributes of successful firms identified by Peters and Waterman.
		The distractors are as follows:
		(A), (B) and (D) are included in Taylor's principles of scientific management.
77	B	The distractors are as follows:
		Answer (A) denotes unity of direction; answer (C) denotes the scalar chain; and answer (D) denotes stability of personnel.
78	A	The distractors are as follows:
		Answer (B) describes an approach to management included in Blake and Mouton's Managerial Grid; answer (C) is connected to contingency theories of leadership; and answer (D) connected to contingency theories of leadership.
79	A	The distractors are as follows:
		Answer (B) describes power based on access to or control over valued resources; answer (C) describes power based on experience, qualifications, or expertise; and answer (D) describes the power to disrupt operations.
80	D	The distractors are as follows:
		Answer (A) describes a news stream within Kanter's managers and innovation framework; answer (B) describes the concept of supervision; and answer (C) is a way of defining autonomy and entrepreneurship.
81	A	The distractors are as follows:
		Answer (B) describes ordinary decency; answer (C) describes the process of learning; and (D) describes management by objectives.
82	D	The distractors are as follows:
		Answers (A), (B) and (C) are all features of performance management. Answer (D) denotes a position audit.
83	A	The distractors are as follows:
		Answers (B), (C) and (D) are all disadvantages of organisation charts.
84	C	The distractors are as follows:
		Answer (A) refers to external regulatory action; answer (B) denotes a strategy for growth; and answer (D) is an element of the triple bottom line framework.
85	D	The distractors are as follows:
		Answers (A), (B) and (C) are all examples of forecasting techniques that are suited to simple, static conditions.
86	B	The distractors are as follows:
		Answer (A) describes high growth and high relative market share; answer (C) describes low-growth markets with low relative market share; and answer (D) describes high-growth markets with low relative market share.
87	B	The distractors are as follows:
		Answers (A), (C) and (D) are all categorised as external stakeholders.

EXAM ANSWER BANK

88	B	The distractors are as follows:
		Narrow control spans (B) is an advantage of a tall organisation structure. Answers (A), (C) and (D) all describe advantages of a flat organisational structure.
89	A	The distractors are as follows:
		Answers (B), (C) and (D) are all advantages of divisionalisation.
90	C	The distractors are as follows:
		Answer (A) describes a hollow organisation; answer (B) describes a boundaryless organisation; and answer (D) describes a shamrock organisation.
91	C	The distractors are as follows:
		Answer (A) refers to planned, deliberate action to build greater responsibility, breadth and challenge of work into a job; (B) refers to the planned transfer of staff from one job to another to increase task variety; (D) refers to a form of job enrichment.
92	A	The distractors are as follows:
		Answer (B) the organic approach is suitable for fast-changing or dynamic operating environments; answer (C) is an approach in which authority is bestowed by dividing an organisation into jurisdictional areas each with specified duties and answer (D) adhocracy is associated with creative thinking, innovation and organisational learning.
93	D	The distractors are as follows:
		Answer (A), (B) and (C) are all objectives of a budgetary planning and control system.
94	C	The distractors are as follows:
		Answer (A) describes incremental budgeting; answer (B) describes flexible budgets; and answer (D) describes fixed budgets.
95	D	The distractors are as follows:
		Answers (A) and (B) are procurement costs; answer (C) is a shortage cost.
96	A	The distractors are as follows:
		Answers (B), (C) and (D) are all disadvantages of benchmarking.
97	D	The distractors are as follows:
		Answers (A), (B) and (C) are all advantages of bottom-up budgets.
98	C	The distractors are as follows:
		Answer (A) is a structured decision at the operational level; answer (B) describes a semi-structured decision at the tactical level; and answer (D) describes a semi-structured decision at the strategic level.
99	D	The distractors are as follows:
		Answers (A), (B) and (C) are advantages of database systems.
100	A	The distractors are as follows:
		Answer (B) refers to the volume of data; answer (C) refers to the veracity of big data; and answer (D)

Past Exams: November 2023

101	D	As communicating is not included in Fayol's classification even though it is implied in co-ordinating and controlling.
		The distractors are as follows:
		(A), (B) and (C) are included in Fayol's five functions of management.
102	B	The distractors are as follows:
		Answers (A), (C) and (D) denote attributes of an excellent firm but are not the more general designation of excellence.
103	D	The distractors are as follows:
		Answer (A) the role of leader is included in the interpersonal role category; Answer (B) the role of disseminator is included in the informational role category; answer (C) the role of spokesperson is included in the informational role category.
104	C	The distractors are as follows:
		Answer (A) is based on analysing the personality characteristics or preferences of successful leaders; answer (B) describes power based on access to or control over valued resources; and answer (D) describes the belief that there is no 'one best way' of leading, but that effective leaders adapt their behaviour to the specific and changing variables in the leadership context.
105	D	The distractors are as follows:
		Within Fielder's framework, answers (A), (B) and (C) are all characteristics of psychologically close managers.
106	B	The distractors are as follows:
		Answer (A) describes collecting information about target customers or markets; answer (C) the use of espionage techniques to obtain commercial and corporate data; and answer (D) is obtaining information about competitors to anticipate competitor actions.
107	B	The distractors are as follows:
		Answers (A), (C) and (D) are all potential advantages of management by objectives.
108	A	The distractors are as follows:
		Answers (B), (C) and (D) are all designated support activities within Porter's Value Chain.
109	D	The distractors are as follows:
		Answers (A), (B) and (C) are all included within the five competitive forces, whereas answer (D) refers to external regulatory action taken by a non-competitor.
110	D	The distractors are as follows:
		Answers (A), (B) and (C) are all examples of financial objectives.

EXAM ANSWER BANK

111	B	The distractors are as follows:

Answer (A) these stakeholders require minimal effort; answer (C) these stakeholders should be kept satisfied; and (D) are key players for whom strategy must be acceptable.

112	B	The distractors are as follows:

Answers (A) describes a competence of an organisation; answer (C) describes a key performance indicator; and answer (D) describes stakeholders in an organisation.

113	A	The distractors are as follows:

An advantage of a flat structure is that is offers more opportunity for delegation. Answers (B), (C) and (D) all describe advantages of a tall organisational structure.

114	A	The distractors are as follows:

Answers (B), (C) and (D) are all advantages of functional departmentation.

115	D	The distractors are as follows:

Answer (A) describes a network organisation; answer (B) describes a boundaryless organisation; and answer (C) describes a modular organisation.

116	C	The distractors are as follows:

Answer (A) refers to an organisation controlled by a key central figure, owner or founder; answer (B) refers to management directed at outputs, ie problems solved, projects completed; and answer (D) refers to organisations for which the purpose of the organisation is to serve the interests of its constituent individuals.

117	D	The distractors are as follows:

Answer (A) occurs when leaders and followers make decisions on the basis of consensus; answer (B) occurs when authority is bestowed by dividing an organisation into jurisdictional areas, each with specified duties; and answer (C) occurs when the leader is regarded as having some special power or attribute.

118	D	The distractors are as follows:

Answer (A) refers to information systems that facilitate the creation and integration of new knowledge into an organisation; answer (B) refers to computer systems designed to increase the productivity of data and information workers; and answer (C) refers to systems that perform and record routine transactions.

119	C	The distractors are as follows:

Answer (A) describes incremental budgeting; answer (B) describes bottom-up budgeting; and answer (D) describes activity-based budgeting.

120	C	The distractors are as follows:

Answers (A) and (B) are holding costs; answer (D) is a procurement cost.

121	D	The distractors are as follows:

Answers (A), (B) and (C) are all advantages of benchmarking.

122	A	The distractors are as follows:

Answers (B), (C) and (D) are all advantages of database systems.

123 D The distractors are as follows:

Answer (A) is an organised campaign to bombard a site with excessive volumes of traffic at a given time, with the aim of overloading the site; answer (B) describes an attempt to gain unauthorised access to computer systems; and answer (C) describes data that is transmitted across telecommunications links is exposed to the risk of being intercepted or examined during transmission.

124 D The distractors are as follows:

Answers (A), (B) and (C) are potential disadvantages of homeworking from the employer perspective.

125 C The distractors are as follows:

Answer (A) refers to the velocity of data received; answer (B) refers to the volume of data; and answer (D) refers to variety in data received.

Mock exam 1
questions and answers

MOCK EXAM 1 QUESTIONS

1   In Mintzberg's managerial roles model, which of the following is an interpersonal role of a manager?

    A   Monitor
    B   Entrepreneur
    C   Negotiator
    D   Leader

2   What is the key contribution of the human relations approach to management?

    A   Proof of a clear link between job satisfaction, worker motivation and business success
    B   Concern for productivity and efficiency
    C   Awareness that the best way of managing will depend on the specific and changing variables in the situation
    D   Awareness of the importance of group dynamics and worker attitudes as an influence on productivity

3   Which of the following is NOT a contingency variable as described in situational approaches to organisation?

    A   Age of organisation
    B   Size of organisation
    C   Structure of organisation
    D   Use of technology by organisation

4   Monica is a manager in the finance department of P Co and she has several staff working under her. She has become quite friendly with most of her staff and they like her and appreciate that she does everything she can to attend to their needs. Which type of managerial style does Monica practice or adopt?

    A   Impoverished
    B   Task management
    C   Dampened pendulum
    D   Country club

5   Which of the following terms is used to describe the right to perform an action in an organisation?

    A   Responsibility
    B   Authority
    C   Power
    D   Influence

6   The problem of the separation of ownership and control principally affects which pair of stakeholders?

    A   Shareholders and employees
    B   Directors and employees
    C   Shareholders and directors
    D   Directors and auditors

7   The question of 'what new computer systems should we buy' is associated with which level of strategy?

    A   Corporate
    B   Functional
    C   Business
    D   Mission

8 Which of the following would NOT be an objective of stakeholder management in relation to suppliers?

- A Continuity of supply
- B Flexibility of supply
- C Information sharing
- D Mutual dependency

9 NB Co is a large business. Ruth oversees staff appraisals. Esther is supervisor of the after-sales services department. Joel arranges delivery of raw materials with suppliers. Amos is responsible for e-marketing campaigns.

According to Porter's value chain, which of the employees is involved in a secondary or support activity?

- A Ruth
- B Esther
- C Joel
- D Amos

10 Which of the following would be characteristic of the growth stage of the product life cycle?

- A High unit costs due to low output and promotions
- B Marketing expenditure to differentiate the firm's product from its competitors
- C Launch of spin-off products
- D More purchases by existing customers than by new customers

11 Which of the following is potentially a weakness of an organisation that would be included in a SWOT analysis?

- A Loss of support from its bank
- B Takeover by a competitor
- C High level of debts from customers
- D Exhaustion of supply source

12 Which of the following factors indicates that suppliers have high bargaining power in an industry?

- A There are a large number of suppliers.
- B Switching costs for customers are low.
- C The product supplied is highly differentiated.
- D Product quality is not important to customers

13 Which of the following is a benefit of a centralised organisation structure?

- A It is cheaper as it reduces the number of managers needed over the whole organisation.
- B It avoids overburdening managers.
- C It leads to greater awareness of local problems.
- D It encourages development of junior managers.

14 Which of the following statements describes job design?

- A Planned, deliberate action to build greater responsibility, breadth and challenge of work into a job
- B How tasks are organised to create jobs or roles for individuals
- C A horizontal extension of the job by increasing task variety and reducing task repetition
- D The planned transfer of staff from one job to another to increase task variety

15 BZ Ness Company is an organisation with a strongly traditional outlook. It is structured and managed according to classical principles: specialisation, the scalar chain of command, unity of command and direction. Personnel tend to focus on their own distinct tasks, which are strictly defined and directed. Communication is vertical, rather than lateral. Discipline is much prized and enshrined in the rule book of the company.

What sort of culture does BZ Ness Company have, using Harrison's classifications?

- A   Role
- B   Task
- C   Person
- D   Power

16 Company Y has a flat organisation structure and a high level of employee participation in decision-making.

Which of Hofstede's four main dimensions of cultural difference is Company Y displaying?

- A   Power distance
- B   Uncertainty avoidance
- C   Individualism
- D   Masculinity

17 Which of the following is an advantage of non-participative budgeting compared with participative budgeting?

- A   It increases motivation.
- B   It decreases budgetary slack.
- C   It increases acceptance.
- D   It increases the likelihood of the budgets produced being achieved.

18 Which of the following statements about a system of responsibility accounting is NOT true?

- A   It cannot be used if it is impossible to separate controllable and uncontrollable costs.
- B   It can be used with feedback and feedforward control.
- C   It requires responsibilities for capital employed to be determined.
- D   It requires each cost to be the sole responsibility of one manager.

19 What does the KPI for the human resources function of staff turnover measure?

- A   How content employees are
- B   How productive employees are
- C   How frequently employees leave the business
- D   How much employee time is not spent on productive activity

20 Which of the following statements apply to feedforward control?

(i)   It is the measurement of differences between planned outputs and actual outputs.

(ii) It is the measurement of differences between planned outputs and forecast outputs.

(iii) It is a proactive technique.

- A   (i) only
- B   (ii) only
- C   (i) and (iii)
- D   (ii) and (iii)

21 Annual demand for Product Yx is 30,000 units. The monthly cost of holding a unit of Yx in stock is $1. Ordering costs of Product Yx are $20 per order.

What is the economic order quantity for product Yx?

- A 190 units
- B 224 units
- C 316 units
- D 1,095 units

22 Which of the following is an example of decision-based software?

- A Transaction processing system
- B Knowledge work system
- C Office information system
- D Expert system

23 Which of the following is NOT an access control in a computer–based system?

- A Firewall
- B Password
- C Encryption
- D Back-up

24 Which of the following is a key feature of big data?

- A Simplicity
- B Variety
- C Accessibility
- D Structure

25 Which of the following types of intelligent agent is least likely to address the problem of information overload?

- A Filtering agent
- B Navigation agent
- C Profiling agent
- D Systems agent

MOCK EXAM 1 ANSWERS

1   D   Leader

Monitor (A) is an informational role, entrepreneur (B) and negotiator (D) are decisional roles.

2   D   Awareness of the importance of group dynamics and worker attitudes as an influence on productivity

Proving the link between job satisfaction, worker motivation and business success (A) would be very difficult. Concern for productivity and efficiency (B) is more associated with the scientific school. The specific and changing variables (C) are highlighted by the contingency school.

3   C   Structure of organisation

Contingency variables are determinants of what the best organisational structure is.

Age (A), size (B) and use of technology (D) are all contingency variables.

4   D   Country club

Country club is low task, high people focus on Blake and Mouton's managerial grid.

Impoverished (A) is low task, low people focus, task management (B) is high task, low people focus and dampened pendulum (C) is a middle position.

5   B   Authority

Responsibility (A) is the duty to perform an action. Power (C) is the ability to perform an action (and in particular, to influence others). Influence (D) is a process by which a person can direct or modify the behaviour of another person.

6   C   Shareholders and directors

Shareholders have ownership, directors exercise control.

Employees do not have ownership nor exercise control so (A) and (B) are incorrect, likewise auditors so (D) is incorrect.

7   B   Functional

The purchase decision of a specific computer system relates to functional operations.

Corporate (A) and business (C) would be higher-level decisions, Mission (D) is purpose rather than a specific decision.

8   D   Mutual dependency

Dependency increases stakeholder power and creates risks and constraints. A buyer would not necessarily want a supplier to be dependent on its business (for ethical reasons), any more than it would want to be dependent on a supplier (for bargaining and supply risk reasons).

Continuity of supply (A), flexibility of supply (B) and information sharing (C) are all objectives of supplier stakeholder management.

9   A   Ruth

Overseeing appraisals is one of the functions of the human resources department, which is a support activity.

Service (Esther (B)), inbound logistics (Joel (C)) and marketing (Amos (D)) are all primary activities in Porter's value chain.

MOCK EXAM 1 ANSWERS

10   B   Marketing expenditure to differentiate the firm's product from its competitors

The growth stage is when competitors are particularly likely to enter the market and the firm has to take action to counter this.

High unit costs due to low output and promotions (A) are characteristic of the introduction stage when few units are sold and the product is being marketed intensively. A greater number of repeat purchases (D) is characteristic of the maturity stage and the firm will try to extend the product's life during the maturity stage by launching spin-off products (C).

11   C   High level of debts from customers

High level of debts from customers suggests poor credit control by the business, which is a weakness.

Loss of bank support (A), takeover (B) and supply source exhaustion (D) are all external threats.

12   C   The product supplied is highly differentiated.

This will mean that only a small number of suppliers (perhaps only one) will supply it.

A large number of suppliers (A), low switching costs (B) and a lack of concern with quality (D) all make it easy for the customer to switch suppliers.

13   A   It is cheaper as it reduces the number of managers needed over the whole organisation.

Avoiding overburdening managers (B), greater awareness of local problems (C) and encouraging the development of junior managers (D) are all advantages of a decentralized structure.

14   B   How tasks are organised to create jobs or roles for individuals

Action to build greater responsibility, depth and challenge of work (A) is job enrichment. Increasing task variety and reducing task repetition (C) is job enlargement. Transferring staff from one job to another to increase task variety (D) is job rotation.

15   A   Role

The role culture is a bureaucratic or mechanistic culture, as described in the scenario.

Task culture (B) is project-focused; person culture (C) is employee-focused; and power culture (D) is leader-focused.

16   A   Power distance

The focus on decision-making and the amount of employee participation suggests low power distance.

Uncertainty avoidance (B) is incorrect as uncertainty is not raised as an issue. Individualism (C) is incorrect as the focus is on decision-making rather than work achievement. Masculinity (D) is incorrect as the scenario is not about what is considered rewarding.

17   B   It decreases budgetary slack.

Employees who participate in the budget-setting process are more likely to incorporate budgetary slack than those that have budgets imposed on them.

Increased motivation (A), acceptance (C) and achievement of the budgets being produced (D) are all advantages of participative budgeting.

18   D   It requires each cost to be the sole responsibility of one manager.

More than one manager may be responsible for a particular cost (dual responsibility).

Responsibility accounting requires costs that are controllable by managers to be determined (A). The system can be used with feedback and feedforward control (B). A full system requires responsibility for capital investment and employed to be allocated (C), as well as revenue and costs.

19   C   How frequently employees leave the business

Employee contentment is measured by a satisfaction ratio (A), employee productivity (B) is measured by a measure of production per employee (revenue per employee or number of goods produced per employee), time not spent on productive activity can be measured by idle time (D).

20   D   (ii) and (iii)

The difference is between planned and forecast (ii), not planned and actual (i). It is a proactive technique (iii), as it anticipates problems before they actually occur.

(A) says (i) is correct, not (ii) and (iii). (B) misses out (iii). (C) includes (i) and misses out (ii).

21   C   316 units

$$EOQ = \sqrt{\frac{2C_oD}{C_h}}$$

EOQ = √ (2 × 20 × 30,000/12) = 316 units

If you chose 190 units (A), you mixed up ordering and holding costs.

If you chose 224 units (B), you forgot the 2 in the calculation

If you chose 1,095 units (D), you didn't gross up the monthly holding costs to an annual amount.

22   D   Expert system

A transaction processing system (A) provides detailed information about transactions. A knowledge work system (B) allows the integration of new knowledge. An office automation system (C) improves productivity of data workers.

23   D   Back-up

Back-up is a data integrity and disaster recovery control.

Firewall (A), password (B) and encryption (C) are all access controls.

24   B   Variety

Variety is one of the key features of big data.

Big data may be simple or complex (A), easy or difficult to access (C), structured or unstructured (D).

MOCK EXAM 1 ANSWERS

25   D   Systems agent

Systems agents help manage complex computer environment and are not primarily concerned with information supplied to users.

A filtering agent (A) reduces information overload by stopping the user receiving unwanted data. A navigation agent (B) helps the user find what is of interest to them. A profiling agent (C) builds websites that have information tailored to users' wants and needs.

Mock exam 2
questions and answers

MOCK EXAM 2 QUESTIONS

1 Which of the following is NOT a technique of scientific management?

   A Micro-design of jobs
   B Work study techniques to establish efficient methods
   C Multi-skilled teamworking
   D Financial incentives

2 The management of Top Cans runs a 'tight ship', with clocking-on timekeeping systems, close supervision and rules for everything. 'Well,' says the general manager, 'if you allow people to have any freedom at work, they will take advantage and their work rate will deteriorate'.

   Which of Douglas McGregor's 'theories' does this management team subscribe to?

   A Theory X
   B Theory Y
   C Situational theory
   D Theory of needs

3 The following two statements relate to leadership.

   (i) Adair's leadership model focuses on what leaders do and not what they are.
   (ii) The Ashridge leadership model proposes that a democratic approach to leadership is best.

   Which one of the following is correct?

   A Both statements are true.
   B Statement (i) is true. Statement (ii) is false.
   C Statement (i) is false. Statement (ii) is true.
   D Both statements are false.

4 Which of the following is a disadvantage of the Joins approach to leadership?

   A Employees are not aware of the reasons for decisions.
   B Communications are one-way.
   C It does not encourage initiative and commitment from subordinates.
   D Decision-making may take a long time.

5 Bruce has just been in charge of a team to work on a specific project. The team members appear to be keen for the project to succeed, but, unlike Bruce have little experience of work on projects of this type. Bruce regards his team as a low-moderate readiness team in line with the classifications developed by Hersey and Blanchard.

   What type of leadership style is likely to be most appropriate for Bruce's project team?

   A Joining
   B Participating
   C Selling
   D Telling

6 Abena works for a toy company called K Co. She telephones Binta at P Co on a daily basis to order parts. Abena has no contact with customers but does deal with complaint letters from D Group, an organisation against slave labour. D Group believes that K Co uses slave labour in the toy manufacturing factories.

   Which of the following are internal stakeholders of K Co?

   A Abena only
   B Abena and Binta at P Co
   C Abena and D Group
   D Abena, Binta and D Group

7 Which of the following is an example of stakeholder interests being aligned?

   A   Shareholders wanting a takeover to take place but directors wishing to maintain control
   B   Shareholders wanting the company to maximise profits, but the local community being concerned about emissions from the company's factory
   C   Giving employees the chance to become shareholders through a share scheme
   D   Suppliers wishing to be paid on time, customers wishing for credit to be lengthened

8 Wader Co manufactures womenswear. Demand for a new range of formal wear has initially been slow, but the fashion media has suggested that formal fashions are going to become more popular.

   In terms of the BCG matrix, which of the following strategies would be recommended?

   A   Hold
   B   Build
   C   Harvest
   D   Divest

9 In order to exercise strategic control, what needs to be identified for each core competence?

   A   Critical success factor
   B   Key task
   C   Priority
   D   Key performance indicator

10 A recent trend in organisation and management is the rise in 'virtual organisation' and 'virtual teamworking'. To which of the following environmental (PEST) factors is this most directly attributed?

   A   Political
   B   Economic
   C   Socio-cultural
   D   Technological

11 Which of the following is NOT a business concern that will be influenced by the physical environment?

   A   Resource inputs
   B   Exchange rates
   C   Disaster planning
   D   Logistics

12 Which of the following would NOT be considered a desirable feature of a centralised organisation with a very formal structure?

   A   Empowered individuals enabled to use their own initiative and make decisions
   B   The promotion of individuals within the organisation based on their achievement
   C   Division of labour and specialisation of work
   D   A clear hierarchy of authority

13 What is the function of the middle line in Mintzberg's organisation framework?

   A   Provides ancillary services such as HR
   B   Analyses the best way of doing a job
   C   Ensures that the organisation follows its strategic mission
   D   Converts what the strategic apex wants into what the operating core does

14 Which of the following forms of organisation is least likely to encourage employee flexibility?

    A   Matrix
    B   Shamrock
    C   Bureaucracy
    D   Flat structure

15 Research has indicated that workers in Country A display characteristics such as toughness and the desire for material wealth and possessions, whereas workers in country B value personal relationships, belonging and the quality of life.

    According to Hofstede's theory, these distinctions relate to which of the following dimensions?

    A   Masculinity
    B   Power distance
    C   Individualism
    D   Uncertainty avoidance

16 Which type of culture according to Handy's cultural model would best fit with a matrix structure?

    A   Person
    B   Role
    C   Power
    D   Task

17 What can be described as a system of accounting that segregates revenue and costs into areas of personal accountability to monitor and assess performance?

    A   Management accounting
    B   Budgetary accounting
    C   Responsibility accounting
    D   Financial accounting

18 Which of the following would NOT be used to describe activity-based budgeting?

    A   A method of budgeting based on an activity framework and utilising cost driver data in the budget-setting and variance feedback process
    B   The use of costs determined using activity-based costing as the basis for preparing budgets
    C   The definition of the activities that underlie the financial figures in each function, and the use of the level of activity to decide how much resource should be allocated, how well it is being managed and to explain variances from budget
    D   A method of budgeting using base and incremental packages as a basis for determining budget allowances

19 Which of the following is a criticism of the balanced scorecard approach?

    A   It ignores non-financial measures.
    B   It sees financial factors as driving the business.
    C   The measures it provides may not give a clear overall picture of performance.
    D   It focuses on the short-term.

20 The following information is available for stock.

Maximum weekly usage	600 units
Maximum lead time	4 weeks
Minimum weekly usage	450 units
Minimum lead time	2 weeks
Re-order level	2,400 units
Re-order quantity	3,000 units

What is the maximum inventory level?

- A 3,000 units
- B 3,600 units
- C 4,200 units
- D 4,500 units

21 Which type of security risk is software that replicates itself and performs unauthorised actions?
- A Virus
- B Trojan horse
- C Denial of service attack
- D Electronic password generator

22 Which of the following would be a direct benefit of introducing an office automation system within a company?

- A Automated strategic decision-making
- B Better document management
- C Provision of a single point for storing information
- D Automated recording of routine transactions

23 The following are examples of business information:

(i)   Annual forecasts of revenues and costs for a department
(ii) Product development plans for the next 5 years
(iii) Labour turnover statistics

Which of the above would be classified as tactical information?

- A (i) and (ii)
- B (i) and (iii)
- C (ii) and (iii)
- D (i), (ii) and (iii)

24 Which of the following is a definition of interoperability?

- A Users being able to use files or data created with an older, similar technology
- B A system for routing incoming calls to landlines or mobile handsets
- C Users sharing and exchanging information with other users without having to use the same technology platform
- D Users being enabled by information technology to work off-site

25 To remain competitive, businesses are dependent upon increasing the use of data. Which of the following is a particular problem relating to this dependence?

- A The organisation is vulnerable to having its data hacked.
- B The organisation is increasingly dependent on real-time data.
- C The organisation must use external data storage providers.
- D The organisation may be depending on poor quality or untrue data.

MOCK EXAM 2 ANSWERS

1   C   Multi-skilled team-working

Multi-skilling is the opposite of key aspects of scientific management. The approach of scientific management is to break jobs down into single, simple, repetitive tasks which are allocated to an individual as a whole job.

Micro-design of jobs (A), work study techniques to establish efficient methods (B) and financial incentives (D) are all aspects of scientific management.

2   A   Theory X

Theory X is the managerial assumption that most people dislike work and responsibility and will avoid them if possible. They have to be coerced and controlled to work adequately – hence the kinds of management measures described.

Theory Y (B) is the managerial assumption that people can be motivated to accept a challenge and responsibility and contribute willingly to the firm – resulting in a quite different management style.

Hersey and Blanchard are associated with situational theory (C). Maslow devised the theory of needs (D).

3   B   Statement (i) is true. Statement (ii) is false.

The statement 'The Ashridge leadership model proposes a democratic approach to leadership is best' is false – the model is not intended to recommend one style for all situations.

(A) is incorrect because it says Statement (ii) is true. (C) is wrong about both statements. (D) is incorrect because it says that Statement (i) is false.

4   D   Decision-making may take a long time.

Using the Joins style means everybody contributing and eventually reaching a consensus, which may be time-consuming and difficult to achieve.

Employees not being aware of the reasons for decisions (A) is likely to be a problem with the tells style of leadership. Communication being one-way (B) and not encouraging initiative and commitment from subordinates (C) can be problems with the tells or sells styles.

5   C   Selling

The team is inexperienced, so requires some direction but is likely to respond well to the encouragement that a sells style will give them.

The team is enthusiastic, so does not need the coercive approach of a telling style (D). The team's lack of experience may mean that joining (A) or participating (B) styles are ineffective.

6   A   Abena only

Internal stakeholders include employees and management and so Abena is the only internal stakeholder. Customers and suppliers (like Binta at P Co) are connected stakeholders. Pressure groups such as D Group are external stakeholders.

B incorrectly includes Binta. C incorrectly includes D Group. D incorrectly includes Binta and D Group.

MOCK EXAM 2 ANSWERS

7 C Giving employees the chance to become shareholders through a share scheme.

This will align employee and shareholder interests.

The directors may lose control of the company if there is a takeover (A) so will not want it to go ahead. Dealing with emissions (B) will incur costs, reducing profits. If customer credit is lengthened (D), liquidity will be reduced, reducing the ability of the company to pay suppliers on time.

8 B Build

The product can be classified as a question mark, with low current market, but which seems likely to grow, therefore the strategy is to build.

The product has growth potential, so the company should do more than hold it (A) and should not consider harvesting it (C) or divesting it (D).

9 D Key performance indicator

Control is exercised by feedback and measurement, which a key performance indicator provides.

Core competences are needed to fulfil critical success factors (A) by carrying out key tasks (B), with priorities (C) indicating the order in which tasks are completed.

10 D Technological

Virtual organisation is the collaboration of geographically dispersed individuals and teams, specifically using the latest information and communication technology (ICT) enablers: the Internet, web-conferencing and so on.

Political (A), economic (B) and, socio-cultural (C) are valid PEST factors, but not primarily related to the virtual organisation.

11 B Exchange rates

Exchange rates will be influenced by the financial markets and financial indicators, not physical factors.

Resource inputs (A) will include physical raw materials, the availability of which will be determined by the physical environment. Disaster planning (C) will be influenced by the risk of extreme events such as flooding in the physical environment. Aspects of logistics (D), the movement of goods, may be affected by the physical environment.

12 A Empowered individuals enabled to use their own initiative and make decisions

The idea of empowered employees acting on their own initiative (rather than following orders and the hierarchy) does not fit with this type of organisation.

Promotion based on achievement (B), division of labour and specialisation (C) and a clear hierarchy of authority (D) could all be seen as advantages.

13 D Converts what the strategic apex wants into what the operating core does.

Providing ancillary services (A) relates to the support services element, the technostructure is responsible for analysing the best way of doing a job (B) and the strategic apex is responsible for ensuring that the organisation follows its strategic mission (C).

MOCK EXAM 2 ANSWERS

14   C   Bureaucracy

A bureaucracy involves specified duties, and rules and regulations, limiting flexibility.

Matrix (A) and shamrock (B) are particular forms of a flexible organisation, while a flat organisation (D) allows employees significant decision-making powers.

15   A   Masculinity

Power distance (B) is about the exercise of power, individualism (C) is about individual achievements v contribution, uncertainty avoidance (D) is about preference for order v novelty.

16   D   Task

The matrix structure requires a culture that reacts quickly to change and focuses on particular projects or tasks as dictated by the needs of the business. A task culture will suit this best as it focuses on achievement of the task above all else, and is flexible and reactive to changes in the environment.

A person culture (A) will focus on the individuals involved, not the task. A role culture (B) focuses on clearly-defined responsibilities, so is unlikely to be flexible enough. A power culture (C) focuses on one individual, and is not suited to the more complicated authority arrangements in a matrix structure.

17   C   Responsibility accounting

Responsibility or accountability is the key element.

Management accounting (A) is a wider term for all internal activities. It is possible to have a system of budgetary accounting (B) without personal responsibility, although it may not be very effective. Financial accounting (D) relates to the activities necessary to prepare the annual accounts.

18   D   A method of budgeting using base and incremental packages as a basis for determining budget allowances

Base and incremental packages are characteristic of zero-based budgeting.

Activity-based budgeting is based on an activity framework and utilises cost driver data (A). It uses costs determined using activity-based costing (B). It is concerned with the activities that underlie the financial figures and uses the level of activity as a basis for decisions (C).

19   C   The measures it provides may not give a clear picture of performance.

Short and long-term measures may conflict for example.

The balanced scorecard pays significant attention to non-financial measures (A) and sees non-financial factors (B) driving the business in the longer-term (D).

20   D   4,500 units

Maximum inventory level = Reorder level + Reorder quantity − (Minimum usage × Minimum lead time) = 2,400 + 3,000 − (450 × 2) = 4,500 units

If you chose 4,200 units (C), you calculated maximum inventory level using maximum usage and minimum lead time.

If you chose 3,600 units (B), you calculated maximum inventory level using minimum usage and maximum lead time.

If you chose 3,000 units (A), you calculated maximum inventory level using maximum usage and maximum lead time.

21 A Virus

A Trojan horse (B) performs unauthorised actions but doesn't replicate itself. A denial of service attack (C) overloads an internet site with traffic. An electronic password generator (D) is an aid to hacking.

22 B Better document management

One benefit of an office automation system is improved information processes.

Strategic decision-making is unlikely to be automated in most companies (A), provision of a single point for storing information is the function of a data warehouse (C), automated recording of routine transactions (D) is provided by a transaction processing system.

23 B (i) and (iii)

Tactical information is medium-term in nature and does not include longer-term product development plans. It does include annual forecasts and labour turnover statistics, which would generally not be meaningful over a short period.

(A), (C) and (D) all incorrectly include product development plans, (A) also missing out labour turnover statistics, (C) also missing out annual forecasts of revenues and costs.

24 C Users sharing and exchanging information with other users without having to use the same technology platform

Users being able to use files or data created with an older, similar technology (A) is a definition of backwards compatibility. A system for routing incoming calls to landlines or mobile handsets (B) is a computer telephony integration system. Users being enabled by information technology to work off-site (D) is a definition of tele-commuting.

25 D The organisation may be depending on poor quality or untrue data.

Increased use may mean that there is insufficient time to consider the reliability and veracity of data.

Vulnerability to hacking (A) is not dependent upon usage of data. Depending on what it does, the organisation may not necessarily need more real-time information (B). It may be convenient to use an external storage provider (C), but many organisations retain data storage in-house.

Bibliography

Bibliography

Books

Adair, J. (1979) *Action-Centred Leadership*. Farnham, Gower Publishing Ltd.

Ansoff, H. I. (1987) *Corporate Strategy*. 2nd edition. London, Penguin.

Anthony, R. N. (1965) *Planning and Control Systems: A Framework for Analysis*. Boston, Harvard Business School Press.

Argyris, C. (1960) *Understanding Organizational Behavior*. Homewood, IL, Dorsey Press.

Armstrong, M. (2012) Armstrong's Handbook of Human Resource Management Practice. London, Kogan Page.

Armstrong, M. (2003) *A Handbook of Human Resource Management Practice*. 9th edition. London, Kogan Page.

Blake, R. and Mouton, J. (1964) *The Managerial Grid*. Houston, TX, Gulf Publishing.

Buchanan, D. and Huczynski, A. (2010) *Organisational Behaviour*. 7th edition. Harlow, Financial Times Prentice Hall.

Burns, T. and Stalker, G. (1961) *The Management of Innovation*. London, Tavistock

CIMA (2005). *CIMA Official Terminology*. Oxford, CIMA.

Cyert, M. and March, J. (1992) *A Behavioral Theory of the Firm*. 2nd edition. New Jersey, Prentice Hall.

Daft, R. (2001) *Organisation Theory and Design*. 7th edition. London, Pearson.

Drucker, P. (1990) The New Realities: in Government and Politics, in Economics and Business, in Society and World View. New York, Harper Collins.

Drucker, P. (1993) *Management: Tasks, Responsibilities, Practices*. New York, Harper Business.

Elkington, J. (1998) Cannibals with Forks: Triple Bottom Line of 21st Century Business. Michigan, New Society Publishers.

Fayol, H. (1916) *General and Industrial Management*. London, Pitman.

Fiedler, F. E. (1967) *A Theory of Leadership Effectiveness*. New York, McGraw Hill.

French, J. R. P. and Raven, B. (1959) The bases of social power. In D. Cartwright (Ed.), *Studies in social power* (p. 150–167). Michigan, Institute for Social Research

Haynes, M. (1997) *Project Management (Fifty-Minute)*. Menlo Park, CA, Crisp Publications.

Herzberg, F. et al. (1959) *The Motivation to Work*. New York, John Wiley & Sons Inc.

Hofstede, G. (1980) *Culture's Consequences*. California, Sage.

Johnson, G., Scholes, K. and Whittington, R. (2007) *Exploring Corporate Strategy*. 8th edition. Harlow, Pearson Education Limited.

Kaplan, R. S. and Norton, D. P. (1996) *The Balanced Scorecard: Translating Strategy into Action*. Boston, Harvard Business School Press.

Katz, D. and Kahn, R. (1978) *The Social Psychology of Organisations*. New York, John Wiley & Sons

Kotter, J. (1990) A force for change: How leadership differs from management. New York, Free Press.

Laudon, J. P. and Laudon, K. C. (2012) *Management Information Systems: Managing the Digital Firm*. 12th edition. Harlow, Pearson.

Likert, K. (1961) *New Patterns of Management*. New York, McGraw Hill.

Lynch, R. (2006) *Corporate Strategy.* 4th edition. Harlow, Pearson Education Limited.

Mayo, E. (1933) The Human Problems of an Industrial Civilisation. London, Routledge.

McGregor, D. (1987) *The Human Side of Enterprise.* New York, McGraw Hill.

Mendelow, A. (1991) Proceedings of the 2nd International Conference on Information Systems. Cambridge, MA, IEEE Computer Society.

Mintzberg, H. (1999) *The Strategy Process.* Harlow, Prentice Hall.

Mintzberg, H. (1994) *The Rise and Fall of Strategic Planning.* Hemel Hempstead, Financial Times Prentice Hall.

Mintzberg, H. (1980) *The Nature of Managerial Work.* New Jersey, Prentice Hall.

Mintzberg, H. (1979) *The Structuring of Organisations.* New Jersey, Prentice Hall.

Mintzberg, H. (1989) *Mintzberg on Management.* New Jersey, Prentice Hall.

Mintzberg, H. (1983) *Power In and Around Organizations.* New Jersey, Prentice Hall.

Ouchi, W. (1982) *Theory Z.* Boston, Addison Wesley.

Peters, T. and Waterman, R. (1982) *In Search of Excellence.* New York, Harper and Row.

Porter, M. (1985) *Competitive Advantage.* New York, Free Press.

Porter, M. (1980) *Competitive Strategy.* New York, Free Press.

Robbins, S. and Coulter, M. (2017) *Management.* 14th edition. Harlow, Pearson.

Schein, E. (1985) *Organisational Culture and Leadership*:A Dynamic View. San Francisco, Jossey-Bass.

Sternberg, E. (1995) *Just Business: Business Ethics in Action.*Oxford, Oxford University Press

Stewart, R.(1963) *The Reality of Management.* London, Heinemann.

Taylor, F. (1911) *The Principles of Scientific Management.* New York, Harper and Row.

Urwick, L.F. (1944) *The elements of administration.* California Harper & brothers, 1944

Weber, M. (1947) *The Theory of Social and Economic Organisation.* Translated by A. Henderson and T. Parsons. New York, Free Press.

Woodward, J. (1965) *Industrial Organisation: Theory and Practice.*Oxford, Oxford University Press.

Yukl, G. A. (2009) *Leadership in Organizations.* 7th edition. New York, Pearson Education.

eBooks

Taylor, F. (1911) *Shop Management.* [eBook]. New York, Harper and Row. Available from: http://www.gutenberg.org/ebooks/6464 [Accessed 7 October 2024].

Journals

Bamforth, K. and Trist, E. (1951) Some logical and psychological consequences of the longwall method of goal getting. *Human Relations,* 4, 6-27 and 37-38.

Donaldson and Preston (1995) The Stakeholder Theory of the Corporation: Concepts, Evidence, and Implications. *The Academy of Management Review,* 20 (1) 65–91.

Hamel, G. (1996) Strategy as revolution. *Harvard Business Review,* 74 (4), 69–82.

Hamel, G. and Prahalad, C. K. (1990) The core competence of the corporation. *Harvard Business Review,* 68 (2), 79–91.

Handy, C. (2002) What's a business for. *Harvard Business Review,* 80(12),49–55.

Harrison, R. (1972) Understanding your organisation's character. *Harvard Business Review* 50(3), 119–128.

Hersey, P. and Blanchard, K.H. (1969) Life cycle theory of leadership. *Training and Development Journal*,23(5), 26–34.

Kaplan, R. (1992) The balanced scorecard: measures that drive performance. *Harvard Business Review,* 70 (1), 71–79.

Kaplan, A. and Haenlein, M. (2010) Users of the world, unite! The challenges and opportunities of Social Media', *Business Horizons,* 53(1),59–68.

Kaplan, R. S. and Norton, D. P. (2000) Having trouble with your strategy? Then map it. *Harvard Business Review,* 78 (5), 167–176.

Kaplan, R. and Norton, D. (1996) Using the balanced scorecard as a strategic management system. *Harvard Business Review,* 74 (1), 75–85.

Lawrence, P. and Lorsch, J. (1967) Differentiation and Integration in Complex Organisations. *Administrative Science Quarterly,* 12 (1), 1–47.

Lewin, K., Lippitt, R. and White R.K. (1939) Patterns of aggressive behaviour in experimentally created social climates.' *Journal of Social Psychology,* 10, 271–301.

Mercer, D. (1995) Simpler scenarios. *Management Decision,* 33 (4), 32–40.

Mintzberg, H. (1987) Crafting strategy. *Harvard Business Review,* 65 (4), 66–75.

Mintzberg, H. and Waters, J. A. (1985) Of strategies, deliberate and emergent. *Strategic Management Journal,* 6 (3), 257–272.

Ouchi, W. G. (1979) A conceptual framework for the design of organizational control mechanisms. *Management Science,* 25 (9), 833–848.

Tannenbaum and Schmidt (1973) How to Choose a Leadership Pattern. *Harvard Business Review,* 51, 162–180.

Zaleznik, A. (1977) Managers and Leaders: are they different? *Harvard Business Review,* 55 (3),67–76.

Newspapers/magazines (online and print)

The Economist (2009) Triple bottom line. *Economist.* [Online] Available from: https://www.economist.com/node/14301663 [Accessed 7 October 2024]

Harford, T. (2014) Big data: are we making a big mistake? *Financial Times.* [Online]. Available from: https://www.ft.com/content/21a6e7d8-b479-11e3-a09a-00144feabdc0 [Accessed 7 October 2024].

Web pages

Henderson, B. (1970) *The product portfolio*. [Online]. Available from: https://www.bcg.com/en-gb/publications/1970/strategy-the-product-portfolio [Accessed 7 October 2024].

Index

> Note. **Key Terms** and their page references are given in **bold**.

7S, 117

Acceptance tests, 362
Accountability, 47, 49, **186**
Accountability and control, 333
Accounting records, 299
Accounting-led, 59
Action-centred leadership, 41
Activity based budgeting, **252**
Adhocracy, 217
Annual hours, 211
Anthony hierarchy, 64
Apollo, 232
Apps, 342
Artefacts, 230
Artificial intelligence (AI), **342**
Ashridge studies, 33
Athena, 232
Audit trail, **313**
Authentication, 313
Authority, **45**
Average inventory, **276**

Back-up, 312
Backward compatibility, 326
Balanced scorecard, **269**
Bargaining power of customers, 135
Bargaining power of suppliers, 135
Barriers to entry, 134
Batch processing, 305
Beliefs and values, 229
Benchmarking, **271**
  Competitive benchmarking, **271**
  Functional benchmarking, **271**
  Internal benchmarking, **271**
  Strategic benchmarking, **271**
Big data, **353**
Blake and Mouton, 35
Blockchain, **345**
Boston classification, 111
Boston Consulting Group (BCG), 111
Boston Matrix, 111
Bottom-up/participative budgeting, **254**
Boundaries, 105
Boundaryless organisations, 211
Brand departmentation, 208
Budget, 261
Budget bias, 254
Budget centre, **244**
Budget slack, **254**

Budgetary planning and control systems, 247
Budgetary slack, 254
Buffer safety inventory, **276**
Bulk discounts, 277
Bureaucracy, **216**, 232
Burns and Stalker, 214
Business ethics, 129, 189, 191
Business plan, 93
Business strategy, 64
BYOD, 342

Cash cows, 112
Centralisation, 213
Centralised processing, 324
Chain-of-command, 327
Changeover, 363
Climate change, **151**
Closed system, 122
Cloud computing, **339**
Club culture, 232
Coalition for Environmentally Responsible Economics, 131
Competitive advantage, 62
Competitive forces, 134, 138
Competitive rivalry, 136
Competitive strategies, 62
Complexity, 138
Computer conferencing, 326
Computer games, 137
Computer Telephony Integration (CTI), 326
Consensus theory of company objectives, 78
Consultancies, 300
Consumer groups, 76
Consumerism, **76**
Contingency, **314**
Contingency plans, 21
Contingency theory, 10, 38
Continuous organisation, **216**
Contrived tests, 362
Control, 201, 260
Control cycle, 262
Control process, 262
Control reporting, 247
Controllability, 244, 246
Controllable costs, 245
Controlling, 286
Controls, 21
Co-ordination, 213
Core competences, **101**
Core employees, 127
Corporate culture, 190

Corporate governance, 78
Corporate objectives, 83, 265
Corporate social responsibility (CSR), 72, 187, 191
Corporate strategy, 63
Cost centre, 245
Cost-benefit, 357
Critical success factors, 102, 264, 266, **330**
Culture, 50, 229
Customer care, 102
Customer departmentation, 208
Customer relationship management (CRM), 339
Customer service, 325
Customers, 71, 135

Data, 286
Data analytics, 355
Data capture, 299
Data cleansing, 354
Data integrity, 311
Data mining, 300
Data warehouse, 300
Database, 307, 308
Database management system (DBMS), 308
Database system, 307
Decentralisation, 213
Decentralised processing, 324
Decision making, 286
Decision packages, 250
Decision support systems (DSS), 303
Decision tree, 143
Decision units, 250
Decisional role, 19
Decline, 108
Delayering, 51, 203
Delegation, 48
Delphi, 143
Demography, 127
Denial of service attack, 310
Developing people, 16
Developmental goals, 90
Developments in communications, 326
Dial-back security, 313
Digital goods, 339, 340, 341
Digital markets, 339, 340, 341
Dionysus, 233
Directly attributable overhead, 246
Disaster recovery plan, 314
Discipline, 9
Discounts, 277
Discretionary fixed costs, 246
Disseminator, 19

Distributed ledger, 345
Disturbance handler, 19
Divisional performance measurement, 204
Divisionalisation, 203
Double loop feedback, 263
Douglas MacGregor, 20
Drucker, 15
Dual responsibility, 247

Eavesdroppers, 310
E-business, 339
Ecology, 133
E-commerce, 338
Economic accountability, 167
Economic growth, 130
Economic objectives, 68
Economic order quantity (EOQ), 274
Economic performance, 15
Economy, 87
Effect of IT, 327
Effectiveness, 87
Efficiency, 87
Electronic Data Interchange (EDI), 300
Email viruses, 310
Employee/employer relationship, 327
Employees, 71
Empowerment, 10, **51**, 203, 221, 324
Encryption, 313
Enterprise-wide systems, 309
Entrepreneur, 19
Environment, 124, 298
Environmental, 161
Environmental accountability, 167
Environmental costs, 132
Environmental influences, 68
Environmental management accounting (EMA), 162
Environmental performance, 132
Environmental risk screening, 131
Environmental scanning, 300
Environmental taxes, 132
Environment-related management accounting, 132
Ethical analysis, 336
Ethical safeguards, 74
Ethics, 129, **187, 336**
Excellence, 17, 231
Executive Share Options Plans (ESOPs), 82
Executive support system (ESS), 302
Existential culture, 233
Exit barriers, 136
Expected value, 143
Expert power, 44

INDEX

Expert systems, 304
Experts, 232
External information, 300

Fayol, 13
Feasibility study, 316
Feedback, 262, **263**
   Negative, 263
   Positive, 263
Feedforward control, **264**
Figurehead, 19
Financial accounts, 69
Financial management, 69
Firewall, 312
Five competitive forces, 134
Five moral dimensions of the information age, 333
Fixed budget, 248, 249
Flat organisation, **202**
Flat structures, 210
Flexibility, 10, 51
Flexible budget, **249**
Forecasts, 141
Formal organisation structures, 7
Founder, 231
Freelancers, 324
French and Raven, 44
Functional authority, **46**
Functional organisation, 207

GE Business Screen, 113
General Electric Business Screen, 113
Generic strategies, 62, 137
Governance, **161**
Government, **76**
Green concerns, 88

Hackers, 310
Handy, 39, 231
Hardware and software failure, 310
Harrison, 231
Hawthorne studies, 15
Hersey and Blanchard, 40
Herzberg, 220, 223
Hierarchy, 216
Hierarchy of objectives, 90, 95
Higher level feedback, 263
Hoaxes, 310
Hollow organisation, 211
Homeworking, 328
Horizontal structures, 210

Human error, 310
Human Resource Management (HRM), 104
Hybrid structures, 209
Hygiene factors, 221

Imposed/top-down budget, **253**
Inbound logistics, 103
Incremental budgeting (ZBB), **249**
Incremental packages, 250
Individualism/collectivism, 235
Industry life cycle, 110
Information and Communication Technology (ICT), 219
Information, **286**
Information as a commodity, 293
Information benefits, 294
Information bureaux, 300
Information director, 296
Information infrastructure, 298
Information management (IM), **296**
Information market, 326
Information overload, 328, 331
Information rights and obligations, 333
Information services, 300
Information society, 292, 309
Information system security, 309
Information systems manager, 296
Information systems strategy, 296, 298
Information value, 292
Informational role, 19
Innovation, 17, 18, 110
Installation, 361
Institutional shareholders, 75
Institutional strategies, 62
Integrated reporting, **171**
Integration, 306
Intelligent agents, 332
Interaction theory, 318
Internal data sources, 299
Internet, 136, 300
Interoperability, 326
Interpersonal role, 19
Inventory days, **279**
Inventory turnover, **279**
Investment centre, 245
IT impact on organisations, 324

Job description, 200
Job enlargement, **222**
Job enrichment, **221**
Job optimisation, 222
Job rotation, **222**

Job simplification, 220
Jobless structures, 210
Johnson, Scholes and Whittington, 102, 330, 58

Kanter, 17
Katz and Kahn, 28
Key customer analysis, 116
Key performance indicator, 264, **266**
Key tasks, 102
Knowledge Management Systems, 308
Knowledge work systems (KWS), 305
Knowledge workers, 51, **305**
Kotter, 28

Leader, 19
Leadership, 28, 215, 231
Leadership style, 32
Leading indicators, 141
Legacy system, 326
Legitimate authority, 215
Legitimate or position power, 44
Lewin, Lippitt and White, 35
Liaison, 19, 298
Libraries, 300
Likert, 34
Line authority, 46
Linkages, 104, 198
Logic bomb, 310
Long-term creditors, 81
Long-term plan, 261

Machine learning, **342**
Management, 11, 28
Management accounts, 69
Management by objectives, 90
Management information systems (MIS), 301, **303**
Management principles, 13
Managerial grid, 36
Managerial role, 18
Managerial skills, 29
Managing a business, 15
Managing life cycle costs, 132
Managing managers, 15
Managing worker and work, 16
Marketing and sales, 103
Marketing audit, 114, 118
Masculinity, 235
Matrix organisation, 10, 209
Maturity, 108
Maximum inventory level, 275
Mayo, 14

McGregor, 20
McKinsey 7S, 117
Mechanistic organisations, 214
Mendelow's matrix, 77
Middle line, 7
Minimum inventory level, 276
Mintzberg, 18
Mission statement, 190
Mission, 65, 83
Modular organisations, 211
Monitor, 19
Multi-skilling, 10
Mutual adjustment, 199
Mutually exclusive packages, 250

Natural disasters, 310
Negotiator, 19
Neo-human relations school, 15
New technology, 51
Non-controllable costs, 246
Non-financial objectives, 88

Objective setting, 67, 95
Objectives of organisations, 83
Objectives, 11, 16, 65, **67**, 90, 260
Office automation systems (OAS), 304, **305**
Official functions, 216
Online processing, 305
Open system, 122
Operating core, 7
Operational and functional strategies, 64
Operational information, 287, 288
Operational management, 64
Operations, 103
Organic organisations, 214
Organisation, 4, 130
Organisation chart, 200
Organisation impact analysis, 317, 360
Organisation manual, 200
Organisation structure, 7, 24, 62, 324
Organisational components, 7
Outbound logistics, 103
Output or improvement targets, 90
Output-focused structures, 210
Outsourcing, 104

Packaged holidays, 129
People-orientated theory, 318
Perception, 89
Performance agreement, 93
Performance and development plan, 93
Performance evaluation, 264
Performance management, 93

Performance measurement, 286
Periodic budget, 252
Peripheral employees, 127
Peters and Waterman, 17
Physical security, 311
Physical, coercive power, 44
Planning and control cycle, 260
Planning, 260, 286
Political issues, 333
Porter, M, 103, 134
Portfolio planning, 110
Position audit, **100**, 261
Positioning-based strategies, 139
Power, **43**
Power culture, 232
Power-distance, 235
Primary activities, 103
Primary objective, 84
Principles of organisation, 8
Priorities, **102**
Prioritisation, 21
Priority, 22
Private sector, 12
Process automation, **342**
Product class, 107
Product differentiation, 135
Product form, 107
Product innovation, 110
Product life cycle, 106, 110
Product portfolio, 106
Product/brand departmentation, 207
Production possibility curve, 130
Productivity through people, 17
Product-market strategies, 62
Profit centre, 245
Profit vs non-profit orientation, 6
Profitability, 85
Profit-making organisations, 75
Profit-related pay, 82
Project, **22**
Property rights, 333
Psychologically close managers (PCMs), 38
Psychologically distant managers (PDMs), 38
Public sector, 12
Push technology, 332

Quality of life, 333
Quantity discounts, 277
Question marks, 112

Random outcome points, 143
Rational model of strategic planning, 60
Rationality, 216

Realistic tests, 362
Reference works, 300
Regression analysis, 141
Remote working, 328
Remuneration, 9
Renewable and non-renewable resources, 132
Reorder level, **275**
Residual income (RI), 205
Resource audit, 100
Resource planning, 62
Resource plans, 102
Resource power, 44
Resource-based approach, 59
Resource-based strategies, 139
Resources, 22
Responsibility, **47**
Responsibility accounting, **244**
Responsibility centre, **244**
Responsibility reporting, 244
Responsibility without authority, 47
Return on capital employed (ROCE), 204
Rituals, 128, 230
Rivalry, 137
Role culture, 232
Rollback technique, 145
Rolling budget, **251**
Rules, **216**

Scalar chain, 8, 202
Scale economies, 134
Scenario, **141**
Scheduling, 21
Scientific management, 13
Secondary objectives, 84
Security, 81, **309**
Self regulation, 82, 83
Semi-closed system, 122
Service industries, 6
Shamrock organisation, **211**
Share option scheme, 82
Shareholders, 71, 75
Single loop feedback, 263
Situational Leadership, 40
Smartphone, 342
Social accountability, **167**
Social issues, 333
Social media, 337
Social responsibility, **187**, 191
Social, **161**
Sociotechnical design, 329, **330**
Socio-technical systems, 219
Span of control, **201**, 324
Specialisation, 216

INDEX

Spokesperson, 19
Staff authority, 46
Stakeholder bargaining strength, 72, 74
Stakeholder engagement, 79
Stakeholder mapping, 77, 78
Stakeholder risks, 72
Stakeholder view of company objectives, 78
Stakeholders, 69
Standing aims and objectives, 90
Sternberg, 190
Stewardship, 186
Stocks, 273
Strategic alliances, 18
Strategic analysis, 60, 261
Strategic apex, 7
Strategic choice, 62
Strategic financial management, 69
Strategic group analysis, 138
Strategic information, 287
Strategic level information system, 301
Strategic management, 58, 64
Strategic objectives, 265
Strategic planning, 58
Strategic planning model, 60
Strategic position, 60
Strategies, 260
Strategy, 58
Strategy implementation, 62
Strategy selection, 62
Subcultures, 129
Subordination of individual interests, 8
Substitute products, 135
Sunrise replacements, 132
Sunsetting of products, 132
Supervision, 20
Suppliers, 71, 76
Support activities, 104
Support staff, 8
Sustainability, 132
Sustainability, 132, 133, **150**
Sustainable Development Goals, 156
Sustainable organistion, 164, 191
Switching costs, 135
SWOT analysis, 138
Symbols, 230
Synergy, 17
System, 122
System quality, 333
System-orientated theory, 318
Systems analysis, 316
Systems approach, 11, 122
Systems conversion, 316
Systems design, 316

Systems development, 315
Systems development lifecycle, 316
Systems implementation, 316
Systems integrity, 311
Systems investigation, 316
Systems testing, 316

Tablets, 342
Tactical information, 287
Tactical management, 64
Tactical objectives, 265
Tall organisation, 202
Tannenbaum and Schmidt, 32
Targets, 87
Task culture, 232
Taylor, 13
Technological change, 325
Technology and structure, 218, 220
Technology development, 104
Technostructure, 8
Telecommuting, 328
Testing, 361, 364
The internet of things (IoT), 347
Theory X, 20, 24
Theory Y, 20, 24
Theory Z, 16
Third wave, 333
Threat of new entrants, 134
Time bomb, 310
Time series analysis, 141
Top-down budget, 253
Trade-off between objectives, 84
Training, 362
Trait theory, 31
Transaction processing system (TPS), 305
Transactional leaders, 28
Transactions, 286
Transformational leaders, 28
Trap door, 310
Triple bottom line, 168
Trist and Bamforth, 219
Trojan horses, 310
Trompenaars, 228
Trust-control dilemma, 50
Types and differences, 4
Types of power, 44

Uncertainty-avoidance, 235
Unglued structures, 210
Unique resource, 100
Unit objectives, 84

United Nations Global Compact, 154
Unity of direction, 8
Universality of management principles, 13
Upward delegation, 49
Urwick, 9
Users of information, 297

Valdez, 131
Value activities, 103
Value activities, 198
Value chain, 103
Value system, 105
Video conferencing, 326
Virtual organisations, 210
Virtual teams, 219
Viruses, 310

Volatility, 138
Volume tests, 362
Voluntary code of conduct, 83

Waste minimisation schemes, 132
Web 2.0, 337
Woodward, 218
Work planning, 21
Worms, 310

Yukl, 28

Zaleznik, 28
Zero base budgeting (ZBB), 250
Zeus, 232

INDEX